Homeowner's Complete

OUTDOOR BUILDING BOOK

wood and masonry construction

Homeowner's Complete OUTDOOR BUILDING BOOK

wood and masonry construction

by John Burton Brimer

Drawings by the author

Published by

NEW YORK

Published by
Popular Science Books
Times Mirror Magazines, Inc.
380 Madison Avenue
New York, NY 10017

Distributed to the trade by
Rodale Press Inc.
33 East Minor Street
Emmaus, PA 18049

Produced by Soderstrom Publishing Group Inc.
Book design by Jeff Fitschen

Library of Congress Cataloging in Publication Data
Brimer, John Burton.
Homeowner's complete outdoor building book.

Includes index.
1. Garden structures. 2. Building, Wooden.
3. Masonry. I. Title.
TH4961.B76 1985 690'.89 85-3448
ISBN: 0–943822–47–5

Manufactured in the United States of America

my wife Katherine, who has suffered me
through all three editions

CONTENTS

PREFACE TO THE THIRD EDITION

WHAT WILL THIS BOOK DO FOR ME? That was the question posed in the Preface of both previous editions of this work. By now that question seems to have been answered by the over 400,000 do-it-yourselfers who bought the original and the second editions. This book must offer something worthwhile.

At my publisher's request, I have thoroughly updated and revised the text, added many new photographs, and drawn new designs and plans. The amendments to the text present the latest materials and the newer and better building methods. I have also added tools that will keep you up to date.

My publisher has called this book the most durable of its kind. That may be true, for it has been in print a long time, and three separate book clubs have helped swell the publication totals. I hope this edition will continue to be useful for years to come.

In each edition I have tried to make the text clear and to the point so that, combined with the plans and drawings or photos, the book will seem rather like teaching without a teacher, as all good self-help books should.

The several basic small projects are aimed at the novice—man, woman, or youngster—and are useful in themselves but also may serve as learning devices. By building some of the less formidable projects, you can develop your manual skills, honing them to a finer edge for later, more-demanding projects. Also, if a small project does not turn out well, you can discard it with little loss of time or materials. Should this happen, assay the cause of the failure and try again. Then, with experience racked up and new confidence engendered, you can launch into more complex projects.

Do not be alarmed or discouraged if you make mistakes. I can testify that some of the best pieces of scrap wood in my stock box were picked up on construction sites. They were discarded because of mistakes by professionals who presumably had experience enough to know better. I use these scraps for small projects, and they cost me nothing. Go slow and use your head. A little time spent thinking your way through a project before doing it will show that intelligence is a means of acquiring experience without making many mistakes along the way.

Many readers of the previous editions have reported finding satisfactions beyond their expectation in creating useful and beautiful outdoor projects. In most of us lurks the spirit of those pioneer forebears who either did it themselves or did without. Also, there are great rewards and satisfactions to be gained through the "therapy" of using the hands. Last, but by no means least, this book provides a means of having a fuller life, using the money saved by doing it yourself.

GIMMICKS OR GOOD TASTE?

With the cost of materials ever escalating, it is more than ever important to choose wisely. So many plans and photographs of projects offered today are of such dubious design that they seem to adorn the yard without improving the landscape. They do not seem to suit any known style of house. That is why in this edition I have added many new designs especially suited to today's houses.

On the other hand, many of the designs are particularly applicable to older houses, yet they may also lend character to some newer ones. This should be of interest to the purchasers of older homes as the trend of flight from cities is reversed, with near-suburb homes and even inner-city buildings being rehabilitated.

ESPECIALLY FOR MODERN HOUSES

While the word "modern" has become a catchall for many vastly different styles, it probably best describes the no-nonsense house of simple and unadorned lines. For such houses, some of the simpler and more serene designs for fences, garden houses, and so on would be a logical choice. Here ornamentation, if any, should be sparingly applied.

On the other hand, on the West Coast and in scatterings elsewhere across the country, the simple and sparingly adorned houses that are adaptations of the oriental styles or the severely plain, boxlike older modern houses may benefit from use of the designs with an oriental flavor, warming the austerity of boxlike modern and contributing the human quality that has come to be associated with the newer aspects of home architecture.

BUT CAN YOU DO IT?

Even if you have never sawed a board, laid a brick, driven a nail, or built a birdhouse, you can learn how to do these projects and more, and in the process become a competent do-it-yourselfer. Millions of people have become do-it-yourselfers and enjoyed the process of learning by doing. Anyone of ordinary intelligence who has the desire to learn can develop the skills of building and thereby enrich his life. Start small and work up to bigger things, keeping track of your progress. You will be amazed how it all falls into place.

WHAT THIS BOOK IS NOT

This book is not intended to be the book to end all books on outdoor projects. Although I have aimed it primarily at beginners, this book is also useful to experienced builders, who may be inspired to adapt, to change, or to create whatever seems to fit their needs and tastes.

Note that there are certain repetitions in the text and the directions. This is deliberate because I have always found it highly frustrating—in other books—to encounter in the middle of a project a cross reference to some other page or direction. Therefore, in most cases I have provided full directions, rather than asking you to consult other pages. In cases when a full explanation would have taken excessive space to repeat, I do refer you to the page with the full explanation.

Before launching into building a project here, read thoroughly all the text involved to get the general picture in mind. If you find a cross reference or if you wish further instruction, put page markers in the book for quick cross reference. I have found that a little forethought of this kind can reduce the number of swear words drastically.

A FINAL WORD

For those who might like to build but find that time or physical limitations make it impossible to pursue a project to the conclusion, this book can be a source with which to guide a professional builder, a carpenter, or a mason to achieve what you want and not the banal run-of-the-mill designs these pros usually offer. You can also use this book to check on what pros do for you—seeing that the construction details are followed rather than ignored or skimped.

However you use this book, I hope it will give you as much enjoyment as its preparation has given me, both during the years of research and earlier work as well as during the months of revision for this, the third edition.

J.B.B.

ACKNOWLEDGMENTS

Of the over 190 photos in this book, more than 100 are new in this third edition. Photo contributors are listed below, alphabetically. I am particularly indebted to Richard Day for 80 new photos. Rich also served as technical editor, helping update the woodworking section and expanding the masonry construction section.

—J.B.B.

American Plywood Association: pages 48, 88, 154 left, 161, 206, 423
BondX Inc.: page 280
Brick Association of North Carolina: pages 417 top, 452 top
California Redwood Association: pages 49 (top & bot. left), 64, 86, 90, 150, 153, 195 top, 196, 197 bot., 200, 208 top & bot.
Robert C. Cleveland: page 459
Richard Day: pages 264–267, 270, 272 top & bot. right, 273, 274, 275 top left, 276, 277 top & bot. left, 287, 296, 301, 303, 305–310, 319 bot., 320, 321 top & bot. left, 327, 328, 329, 330, 354–356, 363, 399, 402, 403, 407
Earth Resource Technology: page 352
Filon Corporation: pages 89, 154, 155
Masonite Corporation: page 158 right
National Concrete Masonry Association: pages 417 bot., 418 bot.
Portland Cement Association: pages 271, 272 bot. left, 275 top right & bot., 277 bot. right, 319 top, 321 bot. right, 325, 326, 333, 337, 359, 413, 418, 421, 429, 431, 432, 434, 449, 450, 451, 452 bot., 453–458
Stanley Works: pages 49 (bot. right), 208 middle, 209 bot.
George Taloumis: pages 65, 87, 91, 93, 94, 95, 284, 346, 379, 385
Western Wood Products Association: pages 156, 157, 193, 194, 195 bot., 197 top, 205, 350

PART I

WOODWORKING

CHAPTER 1

HAND TOOLS

The most essential tools for the amateur woodworker are few in number, but they are indispensable. You will want to add others as the need arises and as your budget will permit, but these minimum requirements will be a good base on which to build. Since we, as human beings, are inclined to lose our senses a bit when confronted by the tempting displays of the hardware stores, a word of caution may be in order before launching this discussion.

That word is: Go slowly in buying tools; be sure you know what you need; and make certain you get your money's worth when buying.

By that I do not mean to have you seek only bargains—although no one is averse to taking advantage of a true bargain when it is offered. Instead, what I mean is that *good* tools of honest value—because they

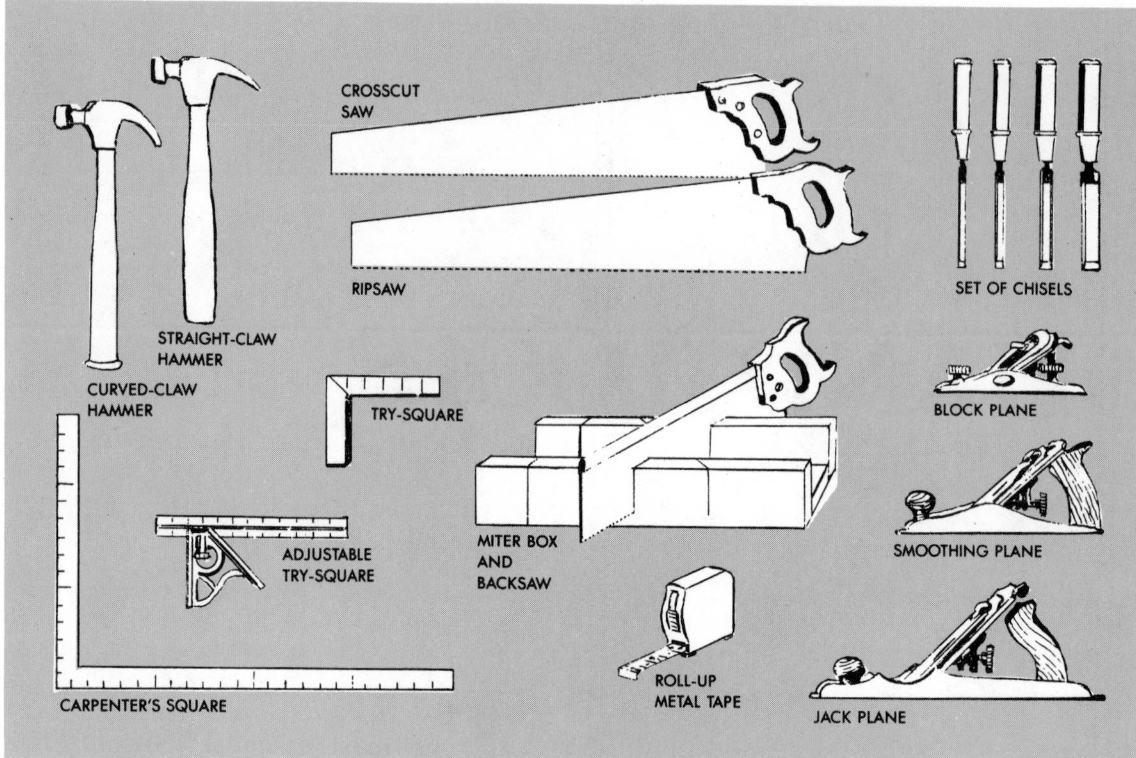

are made of good materials, superior quality hardwood and other high quality materials—*good* tools cost a bit more than tools whose makers have skimped on quality in order to produce them at a low price. But in the long view, tools of good quality will outlast any others because they *are* made of fine materials, so that in the end they become the most economical. Good tools also work more easily and better, and are less likely to injure you. Certainly the basic or minimum list of tools should include the very best tools you can afford—or a little better.

HAMMER AND SAW

First, acquire a hammer and a saw, for many of the projects outlined and detailed in this book can be done with only these two indispensable tools. A good hammer is to be prized—one that is well balanced, has a good steel head neither too heavy nor too light, one with a handle you can easily grasp. Try out several in the store, if it has a sufficiently large stock from which to choose, selecting the one which fits *your* hand and is right for your purpose. Test the all-steel hammers which have a molded rubber or plastic grip to see if that type pleases you more than the conventional wooden-handled types. If you are going to do a good bit of hammering, however, be warned that they lack the spring of the wooden-handled kinds and are more tiring to use. On the other hand, there is no danger of break-

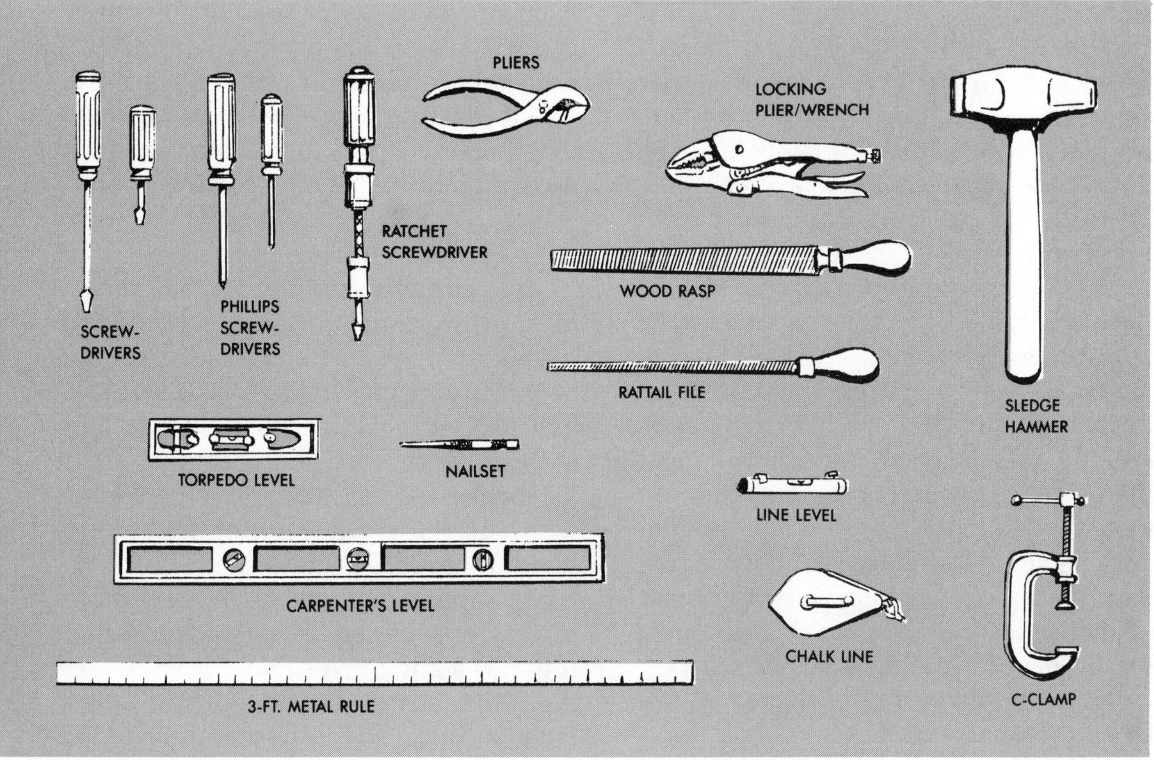

ing the handle or of throwing off the head, which sometimes happens with wooden-handled hammers. Also try out the plastic-handled hammers with heads that stay tight, yet have the balance and feel of a wooden-handled hammer.

You'll probably find the 10- to 16-ounce curved claw hammer the most useful, the curving claws being well adapted to extracting bent nails. (It is also known as a nailing hammer.) If you need a second hammer, consider the straight-claw type, also called a ripping hammer. This is particularly useful for tearing apart woodwork and boards fastened together. Don't buy a heavy hammer. It will tire you and you'll regret it. On the other hand, one which is too light will use more of your energy in performing the tasks for which you use it, and it, too, will be fatiguing. A good medium-weight hammer is the best answer.

When it comes to saws, the choice may be bewildering if you don't know which saw is used for what operation. Each saw is designed to do a specific job. The crosscut saw (the first to buy) is made to cut across the grain of wood for small projects and where fine work is desired. The teeth of a good crosscut saw—and it is by the teeth you will distinguish a crosscut from a ripsaw—are bent alternately outward from the blade, each sharpened on one side only, but with alternates sharpened on opposite sides. Crosscut teeth are smaller than those of a ripsaw and are pointed, while those of a ripsaw are squared on the ends like tiny chisels. Crosscut teeth are usually set at a wider angle (i.e., extending outward more from the body of the blade). Probably the most useful size of crosscut saw will be in the 24- to 28-inch range, having 8 to 10 teeth to the inch.

A good saw is ground to taper toward the back from the widest thickness, in which the teeth are cut, making it easier to saw as the blade pushes back and forth in the saw cut. The stainless steel saws are said to be tougher, stay sharp longer than those of ordinary steel, and because they are nonrusting are easier to maintain. Laminated wooden handles are preferred to regular wooden handles because of their additional strength. The newer plastic handles seem to be satisfactory. Handles should be firmly riveted or fastened to the saw blade.

Try out the handle of the saw you have selected to make sure that it is comfortable in your hand. If the grasp is too small for the hand, you will find that you'll acquire blisters very quickly. A good saw with a comfortable handle will speed your work and be worth whatever you pay for it. A cheap one will not stay sharp very long and will therefore cost more for upkeep, and it probably won't have a properly designed handle or be well balanced. Consider well before purchasing.

SCREWDRIVERS

Now that the hammer and saw are taken care of, let me suggest that the minimum tool chest will also contain several screwdrivers, a try square, a smoothing plane, a chisel (several sizes if you can manage it), a 3-foot metal rule, a steel tape, a pair of pliers, as well as a locking plier/wrench. A brace and bit set of good quality might be added if you do not yet have an electric drill, and a full set of wood-boring bits. You'll also need a level 24 to 28 inches in length, and a ripsaw if you plan to do any great amount of sawing *with* the grain of boards. A chalk line is handy to have for large outdoor building projects.

Screwdrivers come in a great variety of sizes, from about 3 inches long to 18 inches or more, with the width of the blade varying considerably, too. For general use, one about 8 to 10 inches long is best, along with a stubby one about 3 inches long having a medium-width blade, which is useful where long-handled regular screwdrivers will not have room to operate. Where many screws must be set, a spiral ratchet screwdriver is a good investment. It will speed the work tremendously. Most of these have a chuck which permits the use of interchangeable blades of various sizes to fit different kinds of screws preventing injury to the slots and avoiding marring the surrounding wood. Also, it is possible to buy replacements should a blade be damaged or lost. A reversible ratchet makes it possible to remove screws quickly, too, when this is necessary. With this type of screwdriver, once the screw is started, only one hand is needed for setting it. Also include a No. 2 Phillips for those ubiquitous Phillips-head screws.

With the standard type of screwdriver either wooden or plastic handles are satisfactory, so long as one doesn't use a hammer to pound them. Handles thus treated will splinter or shatter.

SQUARES

The try square has a thin steel blade set into a wooden or metal handle, the blade being marked off in fractions of an inch and usually 6 inches or more in length. Handle and blade are set at right angles (90° exactly) so that the try square may be used for marking either across lumber or on the edge for true cuts. It may also be used to test and true up cuts and for trueness when boards are planed smooth. An adjustable try square, although more expensive than the fixed-blade types, will prove a useful tool, for it has a 45° angle as well as a right angle. It has a movable blade which may be adjusted at various lengths for use as a marking gauge, for measuring the depth of a hole, for scaling an odd-shaped piece of wood, and for many other uses in addition to the conventional one. Some varieties of adjustable try squares have spirit bubbles placed in the stock, making them usable as levels in small quarters.

A carpenter's square is all metal and much larger than a try square. It is most useful for larger projects such as building gazebos and decks. It also can be used to mark angled cuts and joints in framing members.

PLANES

A smoothing plane or a jack plane is also a necessity where any finishing work is to be done. Except in the top-quality woods, most boards will need considerable finishing work to smooth them and true them up so that they will take paint well and not harbor moisture, which will foster decay in the little roughnesses, destroying the wood. Smoothing planes are small, about 6 to 10 inches long, with blades from 1¼ to about 2⅜ inches wide. I recommend the 9-inch size as the most useful. If a larger one is needed for preliminary smoothing, a jack plane—11½ to 14 inches—or a fore plane 18 inches long will be desirable. Some planes come with the bottom corrugated, rather than smooth as conventional planes are, the theory being that this causes less friction and allows the planes to operate with less effort.

A block plane is the smallest kind of plane, being only about 4 inches in length, with a blade 1 to 1⅝ inches wide. It is used for smoothing the grain across the ends of boards and for minor smoothing on small pieces of wood, or for small work in general.

All planes should be made of the finest quality of steel, and should have easily adjusted screws and good blades. Handles should be made of hardwood and well finished.

CHISELS

If you can afford only one chisel, buy a ¾-inch size, which is of medium width and adapts to a number of jobs. Other chisels come in a variety of widths, from ⅛ inch to about 2 inches depending upon their type. Tang chisels (the tang, or top end of the chisel, is driven into the handle) are made for hand use and light tapping with mallets. Socket chisels are of heavier construction, the blade ending in a socket fitted with a replaceable wooden handle which may be hammered with a heavy mallet. A butt chisel has a one-piece blade and shank which extends through the plastic or wooden handle and may be tapped with a steel hammer. Other chisels are made entirely of steel.

Gouges are used for cutting grooves and for finishing edges or paring them down. The blades have a curved cutting edge.

For all chisels, forged, heat-treated

steel is recommended, vanadium steel being the best and most expensive.

RULES

Because you'll need to make accurate measurements to do good work, you'll need a roll-up steel tape 6 feet in length or longer (tapes up to 30 feet are available). The square-bottomed types allow for measurements inside nooks by adding the measure of the case or by looking in a top window in the case. Long steel tapes or white-finished steel tapes of 50 or 100 feet are also useful if fences or other large projects are to be laid out which, unless measured in a straight line, may contain discrepancies. Fabric tapes are also found in these long tapes but are much less desirable, the fabric sometimes stretching a little and also wearing out in time. Steel tapes are lasting.

For both measuring and drawing straight lines, the metal yardstick is one of the handiest helpers you can have. While you cannot rule a straight line against a retracting metal tape measure, you can use the metal yardstick for all kinds of ruling jobs—laying out cuts, trimming panels, and such.

PLIERS

A pair of pliers of a size between 5 and 10 inches plus two or three other kinds will always be useful. Those made of forged alloy or carbon steel with a cutter between the adjustable jaws are most versatile, adding wire cutting to their virtues.

The toggle-locking plier/wrench is a good tool, used for tough loosening, tightening, and holding tasks. The 6- or 8-inch size is perhaps most useful around the house. Adjustable to size required, it clamps onto the work; to release, you simply lift the locking lever and the jaws pop open. The common name for this tool is Vise-Grip, which is a brand name.

BRACE AND BIT

If you are going to make any of a number of projects requiring largish round holes, such as a dowel fence, a dowel trellis, a birdhouse, and so on, a good brace and bit will be needed. The brace should have a good center grip of wood or plastic and a hardwood or plastic head, both of which turn freely and with ease. The chuck should open or loosen easily, too, a ball-bearing chuck being preferred. The brace should have a ratchet to permit easy and quick reversal of direction, for the removal of the bit from the hole and also for quarter turns in close, constricted areas. This ratchet probably will be more or less enclosed to protect it from fouling with dirt and rust. The chuck should take all sizes of square-shank bits; good ones will also accept ⅛- to ½-inch round-shank bits, although this is not an absolute necessity for most projects. If you have or plan to buy an electric drill, however, it costs much less to purchase a set of wood-boring bits in these sizes. They're easier to use, too.

LEVELS

Carpenters' levels are made either of wood or of aluminum alloy. Both are good in whatever size you choose. They come in 18- to about 48-inch sizes but the 24- to 28-inch sizes are best for most carpentry work. If you can squeeze out of your budget a 9- to 12-inch torpedo level, you will find it handy for leveling shelves and other narrow or constricted bits of work. The larger sizes made for professionals have as many as six spirit bubbles in glasses set into the body of the level, although the standard ones usually have but three. Sometimes you will find levels with the spirit bubbles adjustable to a 45° angle, which you may find an advantage in some projects. The main advantage in having the maximum number of bubbles is that, whichever way you may pick up the level, it is ready for use without having to be turned over as will be the case with those having only one to three bubbles.

RIPSAW

A ripsaw may be placed very near the top of your priority list instead of at the end if you are planning a good deal of sawing *with* the grain of the wood. It is, as its name implies, a saw which rips quickly through wood. It is not recommended for sawing plywood, plasterboard, or hardboard because its chisel-like teeth will tear or splinter them rather than make the good smooth cut possible with a crosscut saw. But for quickly ripping the length of other boards it is unexcelled. Keep it sharp for best results.

CHALK LINE

For getting parts lined up and for getting edges cut off straight there is no better tool than the chalk line. It consists of an enclosed cavity containing a reel, similar to a fishing reel, with a stout stringline wound up on it. When carpenter's chalk powder—available in many colors—is poured into the cavity and the cap replaced, chalk coats the stringline evenly as it is unwound. With the line tautly stretched between two points, the line can be snapped like a bowstring to transfer a straight line of chalk to the work surface. As the stringline is rewound and unwound again, it gets recoated with chalk for the next use. The chalk line can also be weighted and suspended until it comes to rest. Once the lower end is secured to the work, a perfectly vertical line can be snapped onto the work surface.

A line level is useful in conjunction with a chalk line or stringline. It makes a level out of a line by clipping a bubble level onto the center of the span. One end of the line is raised or lowered until the bubble centers, then you know that the entire line is level.

Chalk and stringlines have a practical working limit up to about 30 feet. If you pull the line as taut as you dare, sight down it, and see a slump, you're trying for too much distance. Nails or other intermediate supports may be placed by sighting to keep the line from sagging on long pulls.

OTHER TOOLS FOR ENTHUSIASTS

The right tool at hand when needed will shorten and make any job easier. Some of the following suggested tools may become necessities, depending upon the kind of work planned.

A good miter box of metal with a saw carriage or guide rigid enough to guarantee accurate cutting is a good investment. For those not so loaded with ambition—or money—a hardwood or hard-plastic miter box slotted with 45°- and 90°-angle cuts will suffice. A good miter box saw (frequently sold as a "back saw") will be necessary for use with either kind of miter box. Keep its fine crosscut teeth sharp for accurate cutting.

A spokeshave is helpful for planing down convex or concave surfaces of wood edges, while a drawknife will rough out and quickly cut to approximate shape all manner of curved and uneven shapes. It is operated by grasping both handles and drawing it toward you across the wood, which should be firmly clamped in the vise. The more modern wood-forming tool, such as the Stanley Surform, is a lower-cost substitute for a spokeshave. A keyhole saw or a compass saw will cut wood on a curved line, too, the point of the saw being inserted in a hole bored alongside the line of the cut. Hacksaws for cutting metal and coping saws for jigsaw work are also useful appurtenances in the home workshop. A #2 or #1 half-hatchet is good for certain chopping work. (Hatchets have a nail-driving head, while axes do not.)

A 5- or 10-pound sledgehammer is good to have for driving stakes into the ground, a job often encountered in many outdoor building projects. It can also be used for chipping or breaking up stones where these are a problem, or for breaking up old concrete when it must be replaced.

A set of files of various sizes and shapes and a wood rasp will prove of value in the home workshop. Files for woodworking are used to smooth and shape wood, while rat-tail files are used in round holes and on curving cuts. The heavy wood rasp file is needed for quick and rough reduction of wood to nearly its final shape. Files are used on metal to remove burrs resulting from cutting and to smooth surfaces, also to shape metal and to smooth out rough cuts and curving cuts.

Certain tools are best sharpened by filing, for power tools used for grinding may heat steel so much in some cases as to destroy its true temper. Filing will prevent such damage to steel.

A hand drill, a push drill, or both, will lend themselves to many projects, often performing in ways not possible with an electric drill. The first has a small-toothed wheel turned by a handle and a chuck which accepts small bits and twist drills. The push drill also has a chuck which admits small drills of a type specially made for it, usually coming with the drill and being stored in the handle. It will be useful for making starting holes for screws or for large bits. A countersink bit, which may be used in either a hand drill or a large brace, permits the countersinking of screws to the level of the wood surface or just below it without marring the wood around them.

A good many outdoor projects involve working with the soil. For this you'll need a shovel, an earth tamper (homebuilt is fine), perhaps a posthole digger, and certainly a wheelbarrow. It may be well to have both a long-handled shovel and a narrow square-bottomed spade.

FINAL WORDS OF ADVICE

In general, I would advise against the purchase of multi-purpose tools, such as most saws with many demountable blades, screwdrivers with hammer head and other fittings which can be stored in the handle, and so on. The *best* tool is the one which is designed specifically for its job. Multi-purpose tools, however interesting they may be as curiosities, can never do *any one* of the jobs as well as one *made* for the purpose. The best home workshop has no room for gadgets unless they earn their keep.

CHAPTER 2

POWER TOOLS

The power tools you may need will depend upon three factors: *What kind of work* you expect to do, both now and later on; *how much work* is to be done; and the final, governing consideration, what *your budget* will permit.

Certainly power tools will provide you with the means of doing with ease a great many jobs which, if hand-done, would require many man-hours and much back-breaking labor. On the other hand, if you are building only a short run of fence, a small trellis, or a few oddments here and there, and have no plans for future wood-working projects outdoors or indoors, it would be false economy to invest in much power equipment.

Whatever your final decision may be, give the most careful consideration to the matter. If you decide to buy power tools, don't rush into their purchase, but do a

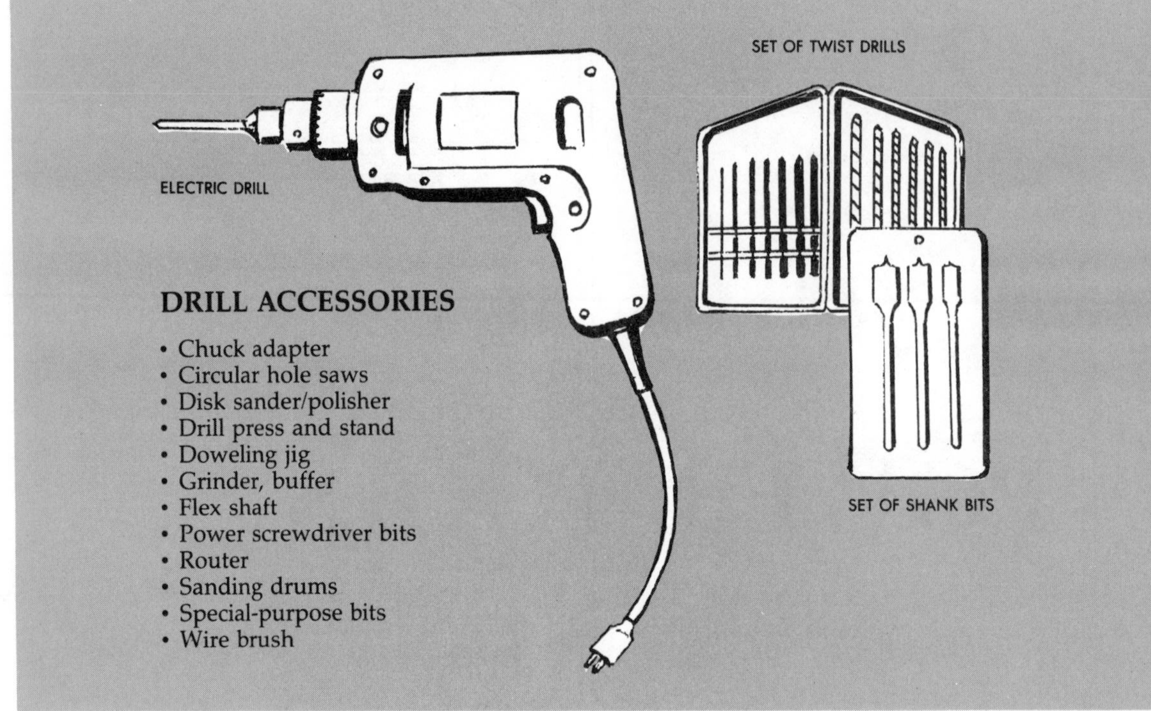

bit of shopping and looking to be sure that you buy the right kind of tool which will serve you well for years to come. Don't end up with a shopful of gadgets with very little use and no real wear in them, merely because you leaped before you looked. *Good* power tools will do many different tasks: sawing, planing, drilling, jointing, making mortises, dovetailing, and other kinds of fitted joints, and in general provide the opportunity of turning out work of professional quality, if they are operated efficiently and properly to take full advantage of their many mechanical attributes.

PORTABLE POWER TOOLS

While most power tools are more or less portable in that they may be moved on occasion, the truly portable tools for home use are the small ones which are operated by holding them in the hand, tools which may be carried easily to the location of the job to be done. Precisely because of their light weight, however, it must be remembered that there is a limit to their capacity. They must not be overloaded or overtaxed by your trying to make them do more than they were intended to do. Improper use means *trouble*—burned-out motors or other expensive and annoying inconveniences resulting from lack of consideration for the machine's limitations.

Electric drill. Because of its versatility, an electric hand drill is probably the first tool you'll want to consider. Drills range

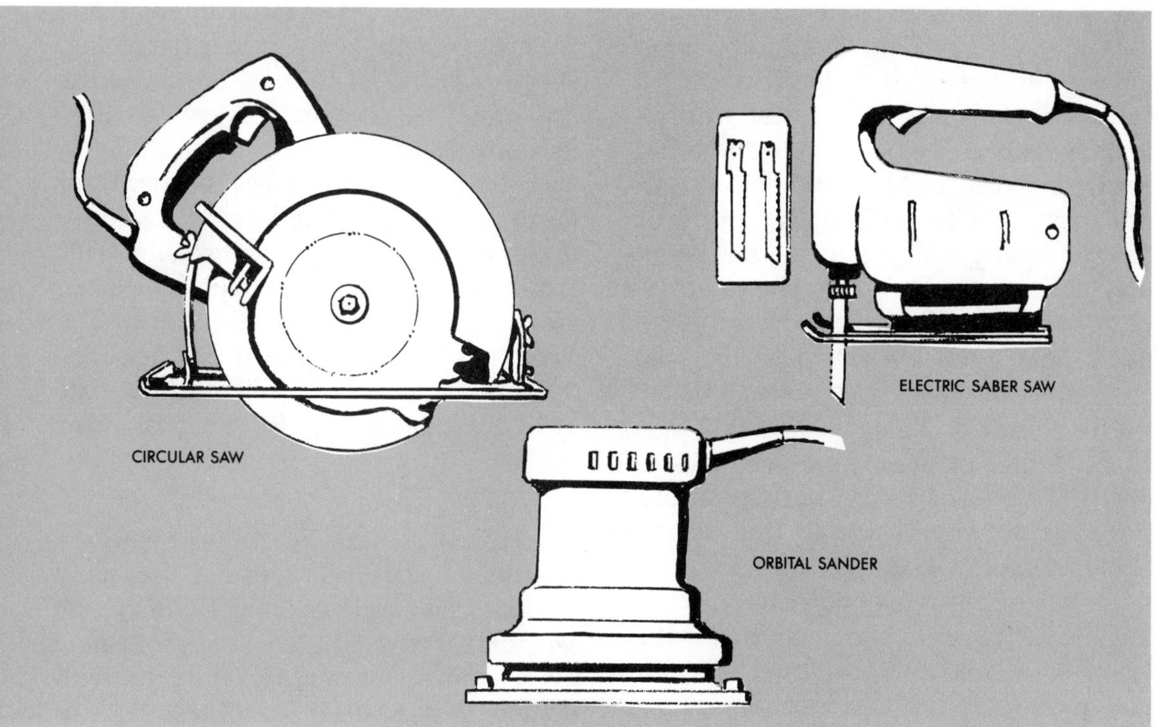

in price from about $20 to $100 or more, coming in various sizes with different types of handles, and many accessories and auxiliary fittings to extend their usefulness. These latter may be purchased separately.

When shopping for a drill, the amateur may be confused at first by some of the terminology and by the profusion of choices offered. Speed, power output, and type of chuck are the three major considerations, but to simplify things let me state that any of the medium- or lower-priced drills made expressly for the do-it-yourselfer will perform *well* any of their assigned tasks. The speeds and power outpouts which are found in the average ¼-inch drill will be sufficient for any legitimate accessory or auxiliary equipment used with such a drill. There are, however, variable-speed drills which are geared for both heavy and light work. This may be a factor to consider if you think you may need a drill for heavy work later on.

As to chucks—the clamping jaws holding the drills—the geared chuck is the best and most trustworthy type, as well as the easiest to use. Other types which require hand tightening or the use of small L-shaped hexagonal steel wrenches to tighten the chuck are satisfactory, but the geared chuck which uses a geared key to tighten the chuck, or to open it to remove or admit drills and other equipment, is the easiest and most efficient kind to use.

Choose your drill by hefting several

kinds to see how they fit your hand—how they balance when held in position for use. Be sure that the drill is *not too heavy* for you to operate easily without unduly fatiguing yourself. On the other hand the very small, very lightweight drills may not be sufficiently sturdy or heavy to perform some of the tasks you may have in mind for them later on. Medium-weight drills, which are comparatively light, would seem to be the best answer for the majority of users.

An electric drill may be your first purchase. Either of two chuck sizes is suitable: ¼- or ⅜-inch. The size of chuck indicates the largest size of drill bit the chuck can hold. It's also a rough indication of the drill's power potential. The ¼-inch drill is easier to handle and costs the least, equal quality considered. But for heavy wood-boring jobs involving wood bits up to 2 inches in diameter—designed to be chucked into a ¼-inch or larger drill—undue strain may be put on the drill which is better suited to light duty. For heavier work consider a ⅜-inch drill with a rechargeable battery pack. It is somewhat heavier and more cumbersome to work with than smaller units, and costs more, too, but does a bigger job. The price may be upwards of $100 with the charger and equipment that goes with it, but it can be used anywhere in your yard without rigging extension cords for power.

For people with modest budgets it is fortunate that a very good ¼-inch electric drill may be purchased in the $20 range.

Electric drills—both ¼-inch and ⅜-inch—can double as power screwdrivers when screwdriver bits are chucked into them. The best ones for this purpose are variable-speed units. How far you pull the trigger controls the drilling (screwing) speed. Of course, to remove screws the drill must be reversible. Most variable-speed drills are.

Electric drills may also be used for boring small holes in masonry when a masonry bit is installed in the chuck. This is a heavy-duty use, however, which can shorten the life of a light-duty drill. The ⅜-inch is much preferred for masonry boring, or, better yet, a ½-inch electric drill; but that's too big for most backyard uses.

Drill attachments. When you are shopping for a drill, consider the many auxiliary kits and appliances which may be purchased separately, or which may even be included in a package price with certain makes of drills. These attachments allow the drill to be used as a sander, polisher, buffer, grinder, circular saw, hedge clipper, jigsaw or saber saw, planer, drill press, and for performing many other tasks. In general, these extra uses will work out satisfactorily if, as noted above, they do not overtax the motor. While it will enable the do-it-yourselfer to do these jobs, if the various attachments are acquired, the power hand drill is in no sense a complete substitute for the proper equipment specifically designed to do a *particular* job and no other, nor will it stand up to prolonged strains during extensive use. Power tools do best the job for which they are designed. In this instance, power drills are made primarily for drilling holes of sizes up to the limit which the chuck will admit (¼ or ⅜ inch). Any other work done by attachments must be considered *extra* functions to be performed as well as the drill's capacities and your skill will permit, and nothing should be demanded beyond the capabilities of such a tool.

Portable sander. Another great boon to the woodworker is the powered portable sander. Two major types are offered. One is a belt sander having a continuous belt of sandpaper driven horizontally, the upper part of the belt riding within the housing of the tool; the lower just below the bottom of the housing. The other type operates by means of short strokes of a flat piece of sandpaper clamped on a padded bottom plate of the machine. Both have their advantages. The continuous belt type is excellent for quick, rough sanding and for most finishing if an extremely fine grade of sandpaper is used, but some people find this a more tiring tool to use than the flat-bed type. This latter may also be used with good effect for either heavy-duty or fine finishing, depending upon the grade of sandpaper used, the weight of the machine, and also the efficiency of the particular model.

Heavyweight stationary sanders which are attachable to benches or power tool stands are also available, but since they are not needed for the work shown in this book they will not be discussed here.

Circular saw. For cutting plywood and other large sheets of board, sawing lumber up to 2-inch stock for rafters and joists, as well as for many other uses, a ½- to 1½ hp portable circular saw is most convenient. It can be used to build fences or for other outdoor work right on the spot, avoiding the laborious toting back and forth necessary if a stationary bench saw is used, and saving endless muscle strain and man-hours over manually operated handsaws. The circular blades are similar to those used on bench saws (see descriptions of all types of blades under "Bench saws" on upcoming pages). In the better type of portable saw, the blade is adjustable to various depths and angles of cutting. A good saw of this kind has a sizable base plate, a built-in adjustable ripping gauge, a sawdust blower, and a blade guard. Both motor and saw arbor are mounted with ball bearings for easy operation. The saw blade should be set on the right-hand side of the handle, *away* from a right-handed operator, with all the adjustments and buttons on the rear of the saw housing so that the operator can see them easily and adjust them quickly. Handles are usually the D-type with a trigger switch enclosed in the handle where a finger can operate it with ease. A portable circular saw can be converted into a bench saw by the purchase of a steel table made for the purpose, enabling it to do many of the things a bench saw will accomplish. In my opinion, however, it can never supplant the stationary bench saw, although it might be useful.

STATIONARY POWER TOOLS

Most of these tools are large and heavy, coming either with their own tables or ready to be mounted on a bench or support. Although more expensive in general than the portable hand tools, they are capable of astonishing feats, for they are versatile in their accomplishments, as well as precise. For the do-it-yourselfer who intends to make woodworking a hobby for many years, a selection of good-quality stationary power tools is a good investment. The amount and type of work intended to be done and the amount of money available for buying the equipment desired will influence the choice here, too.

Bench or table saw. A bench saw (sometimes known as a "table saw" or a "circular bench saw") will cost about $80 and up, some of the more elaborate professional models costing in the hundreds. The least expensive kinds are, naturally, less versatile, less durable, and sometimes less accurate than the medium-priced and expensive saws. Also, the cost does not always include the price of motors, belts, stands, and other fittings required to make them ready to perform their tasks.

The higher-priced saws frequently feature built-in motors, and their stands or benches may be a part of the machine. You can get a good one for $300 to $400. Carefully milled fittings which adjust to a fraction of an inch will assure complete accuracy in the work they do. Many stands are fitted with casters which lock in place when not being used to move the machine into a more convenient position, so that they are stationary in one sense and mobile in another.

Good medium-priced saws have tabletops of heavy steel and include a "fence" (a steel bar which can be clamped to the tabletop parallel to the saw blade and adjusted to the proper width, becoming a guide for wood as it passes through the saw, so that accurate widths may be cut).

All saws should include a blade guard. Most saws now include a tilting mechanism which enables the saw to cut at any angle up to 45°. Some remain fixed, with only the tabletop tilting, but this is less convenient and may even be dangerous in my opinion. The alternative kind has a tilting arbor to angle the saw, with the tabletop remaining level.

The blades run from about 6 inches in diameter up to 12 inches or more, the most usual sizes in saws for home use being found in the 7- to 10-inch range. The depth of cut depends upon the size of the blade and, to a certain degree, upon the make of saw, which will govern the angle of the cut with the tilting arbor. All good bench saws can be adjusted for depth of cut, being set for the various thicknesses of wood to be cut, or for the depth of cut when dadoes or other special cuts are being made. The straight depth of cut will vary with individual makes from 2 to about 3½ inches, depending upon the design of the saw, the size of blade, and the power of the motor.

One thing to check on before purchasing is the method of removing blades when replacement or changing to another type of tooth is necessary. This is very important because you may find that you'll change the blade a half-dozen times or more in the course of some projects in order to take advantage of your saw for ripping, crosscutting, dadoing, or whatever cuts are indicated. If the nut holding the blade is located in an open position, enabling you to use a wrench easily and quickly, you will be able to change blades fast. If, however, the housing restricts the wrench movement or does not permit insertion of the hand to use the wrench, it will take more time and many curses to complete the change.

Check also on the bore of the saw

blade. I recommend a ⅝-inch bore, because replacement blades (unless made by the manufacturer of your saw) frequently come with ⅝-inch bores and have small bushings which adapt them to a ½-inch shaft. You will find that the bushing pushes out during installation, gets lost in sawdust on the floor, and is generally a nuisance. By purchasing a ⅝-inch bore in the beginning you can avoid all this. If you already have a ½-inch type, wire or Scotch tape the bushing to the blade each time you remove it to prevent its being lost.

Radial saw. A radial saw does the same work that a table saw does. Its chief advantage is in crosscutting when the saw is moved through the wood rather than the wood through the saw. And the cut is always topside where you can see whether it's on the mark. Because the motor and blade are above the table, the radial saw makes blade changes super-easy. A disadvantage is that it's easy to cut off a finger if you are not careful. A radial saw excels at trimming large planks to length, cutting angles in wood, and cutting masonry by using an abrasive masonry-cutting blade. For ripping it is no better than a table saw of similar quality. And for handling of large sheets, it is less suitable than a good table saw with table extensions. Some people prefer a table saw; some prefer a radial. Study both types before you buy and judge which seems better for your purpose. In general, a radial saw wins at crosscutting, square and angled, while a table saw wins at everything else except ripping, which is a draw. Both radial and table saws use the same kinds of blades.

Kinds of blades. There are different blades for different kinds of work just as there are in handsaws. Each is useful for its particular job. The crosscut blade is used for cutting *across the grain* of the wood, for mitering, and for finished work. Ripsaw blades are used for quick cutting *with the grain* of the wood. Combination blades which join the good qualities of both rip and crosscut teeth are good all-around blades for general work, although they will not cut as quickly as a ripsaw nor as finely as a crosscut blade. Flat-ground blades, usually found in saw blades of lower prices, are perfectly useful and desirable; but hollow-ground blades will give a much finer, smoother cut, although sawing may take a trifle longer.

A special plywood blade is made for cutting plywood with a minimum of splintering. Nail-cutting blades which rip through old lumber and slice through nails and other metal where encountered are distinctly useful special-purpose blades when used lumber or old construction must be cut.

Carbide-tipped saw blades are long-lasting and extremely tough, although much more expensive than other blades. Usually, however, they more than pay for themselves by lasting better than several ordinary blades. Each tooth is faced with carbide which is set to extend a tiny fraction of an inch above the noncutting steel part of the blade. These blades will cut through almost anything except masonry, stone, concrete, steel, or other hard metals. They are splendid for cutting plastics, Formica, laminates, plywood, wallboard, asphalt roofing or siding, hardboard, aluminum, and insulating boards. In addition, they will make any kind of cut on wood—crosscut, rip, bevel, or miter.

One function of the bench saw, which it performs very well indeed, is the groove cut called "dado." (A groove cut, when the term is used properly, describes a furrow cut *with the grain* of the wood; a dado cut on the other hand is a furrow cut *across the grain* of the wood.) A special cutter, called a "dado head," a "dado assembly," or sometimes just a "dado," is mounted on the saw shaft to replace the usual blade. It can be adjusted to the width of furrow desired, and either a groove cut or a dado cut can be made with it.

There are two types of dado heads. One is a single blade of heavy steel with an adjustable hub which can be set to tilt the blade and make it waggle as it spins. According to the tilt of the blade, the dado will be wider or narrower in the final cut. The other head—better but costlier—is an assembly of several chipper blades set between two saw blades, the cut being made wider or narrower by inserting or taking out chippers. Some chippers are 1⁄16 inch in width; others are heavier, varying with the individual make of dado head. In addition to making dado cuts across the grain, dado blades also may be used for making rabbet cuts, for grooving, and for certain kinds of joints, such as tenons.

By using a molding-cutter head, a bench saw can be made to extend its services still further. An auxiliary head holds variously shaped sets of steel cutter bits which may be changed to produce moldings, cut tongues and grooves, beadings, flutings, coves, glue joints, and many other shapes. If you are interested in this feature, be sure to check whether or not the bench saw you are buying will permit the use of this head. It will be most useful in cabinet work and for fine trimming of all sorts, as well as for making the cuts listed above.

Saber saw. A saber saw is a portable version of the shop jigsaw. It is almost as good as a portable circular saw for cutting pieces of plywood and generally straight and curved sawing in materials of less than an inch thick. But as the material thickness reaches the capacity of the saw, its sawing speed greatly decreases and the squareness of the cut disappears. It features a tilting adjustment for making angled cuts as well as square ones. A number of different blade types are available, including blades for metal cutting.

Jigsaw. A powered jigsaw is most useful where fretwork, scroll work, and circular cutting are to be done. It may be used as well for making straight cuts, for bevel cutting, for shaping the legs of furniture, and more. It is also useful for cutting tabletops, medallions for decoration, and arcs or double curves.

A good jigsaw has a "throat" size of 18 inches or more (the throat is the distance between the blade and the arm at the rear which supports the saw), although other sizes ranging from 12 to 24 or even 30 inches are made. However, the 18-inch size will permit circles of 36-inch diameter to be cut, which is usually large enough for most purposes.

Good jigsaws usually have a tilting tabletop or a tilting arm to permit bevel cutting, the tabletop being fitted with a clamp to hold the wood firmly against the top while it is being cut. The saw head as-

BLADES FOR SABER AND CIRCULAR SAWS

Blades are designed for efficient cutting of specific materials. For quick rough work, fewer and larger teeth speed the job. For finer and finish work, for sawing across the grain (especially true for splintery woods), finer teeth are required.

Saber saws: Coarse-toothed blades cut quickly but may splinter wood on the under side. Fine-toothed blades cut slower but do a smoother job. Don't push the saw to speed the work; otherwise you'll put undue strain on saw and blade and may also have less satisfactory cuts. Narrow blades make curving cuts and intricate "jigsaw" work possible and are useful for rough shaping, too.

Circular saw blades: Various toothed blades in diameters to fit standard sizes of stationary or portable saws are made, each aimed at specific tasks.

Crosscut: for cutting across the grain.

Ripping: for quick cutting with the grain.

Combination (portable saws): for both ripping and cross cutting

Combination (stationary saws): for general ripping and cross cutting.

Plywood combination: for various smooth cuts; fine teeth, taper-ground.

Carbide tipped: long-lasting blade for hardboard or where much plywood must be cut.

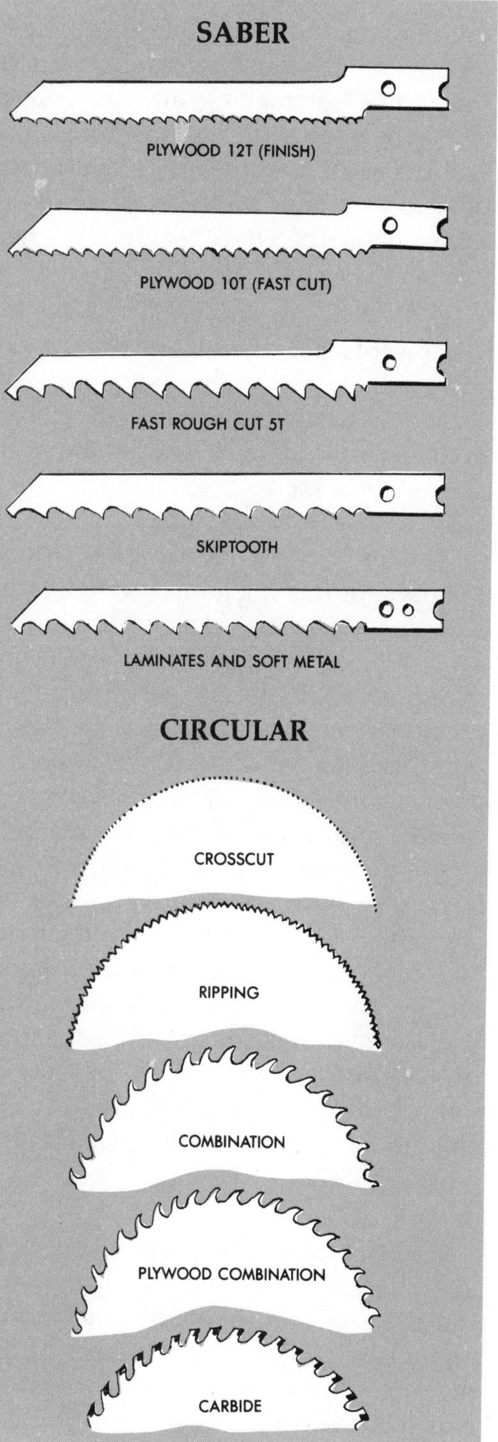

sembly may also be designed to accept saber saw blades and saber files. The latter are used for finishing interior cuts and the former for making intricate internal or pierced cuts. Such a powered jigsaw will do work as intricate as that accomplished by a hand coping saw, with only a fraction of the effort required for hand sawing.

Power lathes. Useful for turning work such as balusters, table legs, and spindles, power lathes are not needed for any of the projects in this book; therefore they are not discussed.

Jointer. Despite its name, a jointer is not used for making joints but for planing and smoothing the edges of lumber and for cutting rabbets. Beveling is also done by adjusting the jointer according to the maker's directions, shaping table legs, tapering round wood stock (or squared-off pieces), and doing may other things. It is called a jointer because it smooths wood so precisely that perfectly fitting joints can be made, with roughness of saw cuts smoothed off as well as or better than a jack plane or block plane would do the job by hand. Cabinetwork and indoor projects require such uses more than the projects shown in this book, but use of a jointer on anything which requires smoothing and beautiful, quick finishing will definitely cut down on labor.

Drill press. A drill press, too, is not absolutely essential for use with any of the projects in this book, but it would materially cut down on the labor of drilling holes in those projects which use many dowels, such as fences, trellises, and so on. By setting up a jig, or frame, to hold the wood, holes can be drilled at any angle. The depth of drilling can be controlled, too, which will save much time and effort and mental stress. With the proper attachments a drill press is valuable also for sanding, shaping, mortising, and routing. It is very handy for use in metal work.

A portable hand drill may be converted into a drill press by purchasing a frame made for this purpose. It will then serve for performing the lighter tasks of a drill press, but it must be remembered that it should not be expected to do everything that a heavyweight, stationary drill press can achieve.

Bench grinder. One of the first power tools to consider is the bench grinder. Having one is the only way you can keep your hand tools sharp. You don't need a large expensive one. A light-duty ¼-hp model with two ½″ × 6″ grinding wheels will do the job nicely. Such grinders come with one medium-grit wheel and one fine-grit. The former is for heavy metal removal, the latter for finer finish grinding.

A WORD OF CAUTION: BE CAREFUL!

Now that power tools have come into general use, the safety factor tends to be ignored. *Familiarity breeds carelessness*, as the annual statistics of accidents prove. Most accidents would be definitely preventable if only a little *forethought* and *care* were used. All the jokes about the do-it-yourselfer's mishaps are funny enough until they happen to YOU. Then the tragic side sinks in—but too late to save the finger, the thumb, the eye, the limb—

perhaps even the life of the unfortunate but careless victim.

Any machine is a splendid assistant as long as the person operating it uses vigilance and intelligence in guiding it through its appointed task. No machine is safer than the limit of the care exercised by its operator.

POINTS FOR ACCIDENT PREVENTION

- Always wear eye protection matched to the job. In some cases you need face protection as well. It's a good idea to wear an eye protector even when hammering nails, because a chip can fly off and hit you in the eye. Always wear it when working with power tools where anything could fly off from the materials.
- When power-sanding or doing other dusty jobs, it pays to wear a respirator to keep the particles out of your nasal passages, mouth, and lungs. Always wear a respirator when spray painting.
- Do not run any kind of power tools in an explosive atmosphere where, for example, gas has been escaping or gasoline has been spilled on the floor. The sparks can set off an explosion even in an enclosed space where spray painting has just been done.
- Wear clothing which fits tightly so that it will not be snagged by moving parts.
- Roll up shirt sleeves or wear short-sleeve shirts. Sleeves of coveralls or smocks should securely fasten at the wrists.
- Don't wear dangling clothing or jewelry, which may come into contact with shafts and moving machinery parts. It's a good idea to tuck in shirttails so they don't get snagged.
- Use 3-prong extension cords with grounding plugs placed in grounding outlets when operating portable power tools. It is dangerous to use ordinary extension cords or to plug into lamp sockets or some outlets in walls, if wiring is not of sufficient strength to withstand amount of current demanded by the tool. Fires can result from overheated wires in walls or you may become part of the circuit yourself if the tool short-circuits, since you will be the grounding agent.
- Do not use power tools while standing on damp ground, in water, or in contact with grounded metal (such as pipes).
- Never turn on the power or put a plug into a socket without first checking the tool to be sure it is turned off, and make sure that the operating parts are clear, so that nothing will be snagged from the table and thrown, injuring you or fouling the machine. Always *turn off the power* before pulling out the plug when work is finished.
- Unplug tools before changing bits, blades, sandpaper, and the like.
- Never reach across a *running* power tool. Train yourself to make this a good habit so that you'll avoid trouble before it occurs.
- Always use the safety guards on machines which have them. They are put on the tool to protect you, if you will only let them. (Example: saw guards on bench saws.)
- Never, *never* try to force wood into a bench saw which is taking it with difficulty. When it is necessary to guide wood close to a saw or cutting edge, use as long a scrap of wood as possible; *never use your fingers.*
- Keep your tools clean. Remove pitch

from saw blades with turpentine or other solvent; keep sawdust off moving parts and sweep it from the tabletops and from crevices. *Caution*: Sawdust causes wear when it gets into working parts of the motor and machinery. Using a vacuum cleaner once in a while and keeping the motor covered when not in use will help to prevent this.

- Keep your tools oiled so that they will remain in good working order. Periodically go over all parts to make sure that bolts, clamps, and so on, are tightened and secure.
- Sweep the floor at the end of each day's work, or more frequently if the job is creating a good deal of debris. You won't track around so much sawdust in other parts of the house, and family relations will remain peaceful.
- A box, keg, or barrel kept near the power tool makes a good repository for scraps of lumber and will also hold sawdust sweepings. Keep scraps out from underfoot—a stumble can cause serious injury.
- Don't try to remove or pick up by hand any wood scraps from a bench saw table *while the saw is running*. Use a long, sturdy pusher stick to shove scraps off the table, or turn off the motor and wait until the saw ceases to turn before removing the scraps.
- Keep children, particularly small ones, out of the shop while you are working. They may get caught in moving machinery while they are exploring, or they may get underfoot and be injured when heavy pieces of material are being moved. Also, even very small children have an amazing adeptness at imitating adults and are quite likely to turn on switches, damaging your work or causing bad accidents to themselves and you. Better to exclude them from the shop than to face this possibility.
- Even in a home with no small children it is a good plan to install a locking switch box which also contains a circuit breaker. Feed all electricity through this to the power tools. The circuit breaker prevents overloading of the lines and short circuiting, with its attendant dangers. It also prevents the need for fuse replacement because as soon as the overloading cause is removed, the flip of a switch will restore the circuit. Throw the switch and lock the box after each use to prevent others from using the tools when you are not present. Another expedient for those who have no such switch box is to pull the plugs, remove extension cords, and put into place an inexpensive plug lock which fits into the wall plugs.

Or, install a new switch box with circuit breakers on all circuits. Old houses with obsolete fuse or switch boxes may be dangerous if power tools overload a circuit or two.

In conclusion, let me sum up the basis for caution in a few words: Your tools need your brain to guide them and to take necessary precautions to make them safe. Tools alone will never be safer than the operator's intelligence—not until someone invents a good $5.98 Electronic Brain to guide them safely. Until then it is up to you.

CHAPTER 3

CHOOSING LUMBER

Lumber is not cheap—in fact, it can be very expensive if the wrong sort is chosen for the job you will be doing. Read carefully the suggestions and the listings given here, come to know the various kinds and sizes of lumber and their grades, and your job's requirements, so that you may save yourself a good bit of money and in addition have a more satisfactory project. Look into the facts *before* you buy lumber; consider them as carefully as if you were buying a car. Well chosen, carefully cut, and properly installed, lumber will outlast several dozen cars, yet many people (often the same ones who try out every car in the field and buy a car with great care and consideration) will rush out and buy some lumber, *any* lumber, for a woodworking project.

Like a car, lumber has certain definite

characteristics. It will perform more or less well in a general way, but usually there is one particular job for which each grade is outstandingly well fitted.

Several methods are used in grading lumber by the various suppliers, but all of them are similar to or approximate the pine grading listed on upcoming pages. The thing to remember in ordering lumber is that you need *not* use the *highest* quality or the best grades for *everything* that you build. If you are in doubt as to what kind or grade of lumber to use, talk over your project with your home center or lumber dealer. Tell him what your plans are, how the lumber is to be used, and ask for his advice. Most dealers are reputable and are sympathetic with the do-it-yourselfer. If you have not come to him on a busy Saturday morning when all the other local amateurs are besieging the yard for materials to use over the weekend, your dealer will be able to advise you and will do so. If you find yourself in doubt about what he advises, it is always possible to thank him for his advice and say that you will consider the matter. Then go to another dealer to see how the advice checks out, using your common sense to decide which is the better of the two suggestions. It is probable that they will be similar.

After a few projects you will probably be able to choose your own lumber. You will have evaluated the advice given so that you will know which lumber yard to use and which was attempting (possibly) to make a "fast buck" at your expense. The project and where you plan to build it will always govern the type of lumber you must choose. For most outdoor projects you will probably choose one of the common grades of softwood lumber. Properly painted and with the right preservatives applied they will last a long time. They are the cheapest grades of lumber and offer a reasonably wide choice of woods, among which you will surely find one which will fit your needs and give you good service.

SOFTWOODS

Those most frequently available in wide distribution are cedar, cypress, fir (Douglas fir is especially good), hemlock, larch, redwood, spruce, and pine (both white and yellow pine are available in most places).

Softwoods least likely to shrink, swell, warp, or otherwise prove unsatisfactory are white pine, cedar, cypress, redwood, and spruce. For structures needing strength in their frames, use larch, yellow pine, or Douglas fir. All woods, of course, should be properly seasoned or kiln dried.

The kinds most easily worked with in sawing, planing, and general shaping are cedar, spruce, white pine, and redwood. Those most decay-resistant are cedar, cypress, redwood, and white pine. If the lumber is cut from the heart of the log where the cellular makeup is particularly dense, cedar, cypress, and redwood will be especially rot-resistant. Contrary to popular belief, not *all* redwood, cedar, or cypress lumber is resistant to decay; boards cut from just under the bark of these trees will decay nearly as soon as some of the woods more usually thought to be susceptible to rot. Therefore, for decay-resistant redwood, select the heartwood grades. However, redwood may not always be widely available east of the Mississippi River.

TREES AND THEIR WOODY PARTS

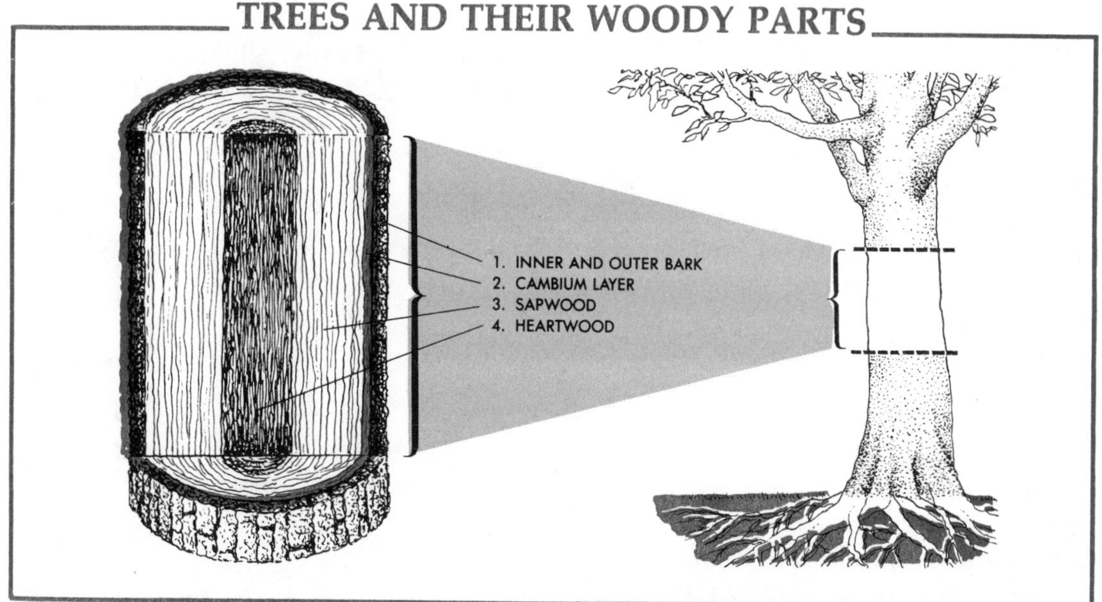

It is the trunk of the tree, from close above the roots to the lower limbs or sometimes above them, that is of greatest interest to woodworkers. But not all portions of this section are useful.

1. *Outer bark* is rougher and drier, the part that shields the tree from many insects and diseases and protects it from injury from casual blows. *Inner bark* is finer, the area all around the tree that conveys plant foods back down from the top parts after it has risen from the roots to the leaves and twigs, feeding the trunk of the tree.

2. *Cambium layer*, occurring between the bark and the woody inner portions of the trunk, forms new woody structure. The outer portion forms new bark while the inner side creates new sapwood.

3. *Sapwood* is the outer area of the part of the tree of use to the builder. It carries sap upward from roots to leaves and twigs.

4. *Heartwood* is the darker, innermost and most close-grained part of the tree, formed as sapwood matures and becomes inactive.

PRESERVING WOOD

Modern science has stepped in, coming to the rescue of the do-it-yourselfer as well as the professional builder. There are now a number of effective wood preservatives which can be painted on lumber, or in which the cut ends of posts and other lumber may be soaked for full absorption. Decay-killing elements which are present in these fluids kill or hold at bay the bacteria and moisture organisms which may enter pores and cause the wood to rot. Posts which might otherwise last only five or six years now have their lives doubled and even tripled. Some preservatives have added ingredients which will nearly always make them completely resistant to water and moisture penetration. Since these preservative materials and methods of application are taken up more thoroughly in the following chapter, suffice it to say that they merit your consideration.

Now widely available for outdoor use in contact with the ground or near it is pressure-treated lumber. It is processed to force preservatives deep into the board's wood fibers. It has a greenish or yellowish color when you buy it, but soon turns to a silver-gray color outdoors. It can also be stained or painted without special treatments. It should be allowed to season for several weeks before using in a project. Any wood in contact with concrete should be either pressure-treated or a decay-resistant wood such as redwood, cedar, or cypress. *Caution*: Wear a dust mask when cutting or sanding treated wood.

LUMBER GOOD SENSE

The smart lumber buyer needs an understanding of the differences between hardwood and softwood, along with knowing that the stated or nominal sizes of lumber are not the same as the actual finished dimensions (unless, of course, the lumber is unfinished).

Nominal vs. actual. Lumber measures less than the size it goes by, which is its nominal size. For example, the nominal-sized 2″×4″ is really a half-inch smaller in thickness and width, thus actually measuring 1½″×3½″. This is because some of the original wood is planed off in finishing it. A 1″×4″ actually measures ¾″×3½″, and a 1″×12″ is really only ¾″×11¼″ in size. Shrinkage is also responsible for some of the loss. And modern kiln-drying, which practically all lumber goes through today, increases the amount of shrinkage over former air-drying. Surprisingly, only the thickness and width are affected by shrinkage; length stays the same. Milling on all four sides takes off a little more material to leave the lumber at its actual size. The table, above right, shows both the actual and nominal sizes of lumber you are likely to use. Incidentally, lumber that is surfaced on all four sides is termed S4S.

QUICK AND EASY REFERENCE TABLE OF NOMINAL AND ACTUAL SIZES OF LUMBER

Lumber	*Nominal size*	*Common actual size*
Furring strips	1″×2″	¾″×1½″
Boards	1″×3″	¾″×2½″
	1″×4″	¾″×3½″
	1″×6″	¾″×5½″
	1″×8″	¾″×7¼″
	1″×10″	¾″×9¼″
	1″×12″	¾″×11¼″
Dimension lumber	2″×2″	1½″×1½″
	2″×3″	1½″×2½″
	2″×4″	1½″×3½″
	2″×6″	1½″×5½″
	2″×8″	1½″×7½″
	2″×10″	1½″×9¼″
	2″×12″	1½″×11¼″
Posts	4″×4″	3½″×3½″
	4″×6″	3½″×5½″
	6″×6″	5½″×5½″

NOTE: Plywood, hardboard, and particle board (also known as chip board or flake board) are actual size in width, length, and thickness. Furniture-grade hardwoods that are also used for interior woodwork are usually found in actual size or in some places may be nominal size. Be sure to check on which is offered and be sure you specify what you need.

Lumber grading. All lumber is graded according to quality of wood. Hardwood is graded 1st and 2nd (FAS), Select, or No. 1 Common. Softwood, the kind you'll most likely use for outdoor building, is graded: Select (B and Better, C, and D), which has two good faces that make it ideal for showy projects; and Common (#1, #2, #3, and #4, in descending order of quality). Common grades are good enough for most other projects. Ask your dealer for advice if you are not sure which grade to buy for a project. If you want lumber that is free from knots, which is called "clear," your dealer will usually let you go out to the pile of Select lumber and pick out the pieces you like—for a slight extra charge, of course. For outdoor use, D Select lumber is probably best for projects where a good finish is required. And No. 1 Common is best for all-around use where defects are not a factor but strength is.

Lineal foot vs. board foot. Lumber may be sold by the *lineal foot* or the *board foot*. Figuring up lineal feet of lumber is easy, because you just add up the lengths of the boards you need. However, the prices per lineal foot of 2″×4″s and 2″×12″s will be quite different, because there is a lot more wood in a lineal foot of 2″×12″ than 2″×4″; three times as much. While a lineal foot is a 1-foot length of the particular size board you are considering, a board foot equals a piece 1 inch thick, 12 inches long, and 12 inches wide (nominal size: 1″×12″×12″). So a lineal foot of 2″×4″ is two-thirds of a board foot, while a lineal foot of 2″×12″ is 2 board feet. You don't need to know how a car's brakes work to stop one; likewise, you don't need to know board feet to buy lumber. Most dealers sell to do-it-yourselfers by the lineal foot, anyway.

Redwood. The grade of wood, as well as the type of wood, affects its price. Pine and fir are low-cost softwoods, good for most projects. So is spruce. Because of its decay-resistance, redwood is excellent for many outdoor building uses, but at higher cost than for some other softwoods. Redwood grades are different from those of other softwoods, but there is one for every job. Use heartwood on or near the ground where decay and insects are a problem; use sapwood (it's cheaper) where moisture is less prevalent.

There are two grades of redwood: garden grades and architectural grades. The garden grades are recommended for outdoor projects around the house, as they are much less costly and much more available. These grades are: Construction Heart, Construction Common, Merchantable Heart, and Merchantable. Construction Heart is all heartwood and contains knots. Use it for posts, beams, and framing on or near the ground and for deckboards around hot tubs and spas. Construction Common is similar but contains sapwood. It is ideal for deckboards. Merchantable Heart contains heartwood, larger knots, and some holes. It is ideal for many garden structures such as fences. Merchantable is similar but contains sapwood. It can be used for trellises and other deck furnishings above ground. For load-bearing situations, remember that merchantable grades are not as strong as construction grades.

Other grades are sometimes specified as Select Heart and Select, having knots smaller than Construction Heart. The architectural grades are Clear All Heart, Clear, and B Grade. These would be used for luxury projects where cost is less a factor than being knot-free.

Lumber lengths. Although the nominal and actual lengths are the same, you cannot always count on a mill's having squared up the ends, particularly when lower-priced grades of wood are being ordered. You therefore will have to square-cut them yourself, losing a half-inch or more in length. Therefore it is well to examine and measure the wood first, plan how best to utilize it before rushing into the project under construction. If upon examining the wood at the lumber yard you find slanted ends, perhaps it would be best to order longer lengths and waste some, or use the scrap wood for small projects. Or if the project admits the possibility of shorter lengths, such as in fencing, the length desired may be ordered and then incorporated with due attention paid to the ultimate lengths of the entire project.

HOW TO SAVE MONEY ON LUMBER

Don't feel that you must always use the best grades of wood. Instead, save money and buy one of the lower grades which will be adequate for your project. This is particularly true where wood is to be painted with an opaque color, for paint covers many imperfections and if the knots are properly shellacked and pretreated they will not bleed through the paint. As suggested earlier, if you are inexperienced, ask your local lumber dealer to recommend the cheapest grade of wood which you can use satisfactorily on this project, showing him the plans and telling him the exposure of the project.

Another way of saving money is to buy a low grade of lumber and, by using your utmost ingenuity, utilize it to good advantage. By careful planning you can often use clear lumber on either side of a major knot. Cut your pieces so the knot can be discarded. Big knots may severely weaken wood, causing it to break under stress. Also it is possible to make minor repairs to the wood itself, filling small imperfections with putty or with waterproof outdoor glue and sawdust mixed. Often, warped or bowed boards can be straightened by weighting them on the central parts, where the bowing or warping usually occurs. The method is this: Build up under the ends with cinder blocks, one or two set on top of each other, or use sawhorses for support. Place the board to be straightened on the support and weight the ends in place with a cinder block. In the middle or where the warping occurs, place a heavy stone, a 2- or 4-inch cinder block, a pile of bricks, or any other manageable weight. Don't *over*weight the board, or it may crack. Don't try to rush things: straightening will take time and it will be a mistake to try to speed it up. Permanent results take time and patience. If you have a number of boards the same size as the warped one, you may pile them on top of the warped one, add a bit of weight, and allow them to do the straightening.

Knots which are a little loose may loosen further and fall out as the wood seasons and shrinks after it has been built into place outdoors. To prevent this, examine all knots and press out any which are a little loose, taking care to do it so that the wood is not injured. Coat both the inside of the knothole and the edge of the knot with waterproof outdoor glue; then push it back into place, removing any excess glue from the surface of the board before it hardens into place. When the board has been painted, this knot should remain in place as long as the wood itself.

Checking—a narrow crack occurring usually at the ends of boards due to shrinkage of the wood or excess exposure to sun and heat—can be a very serious matter, especially on outdoor projects where water may seep in. Exposure to hot sunlight may cause further shrinkage and extend the checking so that it eventually splits the board. If the checking is severe, it is best to cut off the board as far as is necessary to eliminate the checking. Then treat the ends with wood preservative before building it into your project. If checking is minor, filling the cracks with waterproof glue mixed with sawdust will usually suffice to prevent further damage. Work the mixture well into the cracks with a putty knife. Fence post checks should be thoroughly brushed with a wood preservative and, in addition, the below-ground parts should be well tarred to fill all cracks and prevent decay organisms from entering the wood. On the top of the posts, cap blocks an inch or more larger in all directions will cover the ends and prevent further damage.

PLYWOOD

One of the most versatile and useful of the modern developments in the woodworking field is plywood. Recent years have seen many innovations in this material so that now plywood can be purchased to do practically any job for which you may wish to use wood. Almost invariably when plywood is specified for projects in this book *exterior* grades are required. Several manufacturers make the claim that their products are so waterproof that they may be boiled without the various layers of wood separating, so they are safe to use outdoors.

Plywood is available in many grades. The best grade should be good on both sides, with no knotholes or other mars in the surface, should be sanded smooth, and should have good, square, unmarred corners. The other grades, in descending order, permit some knots and minor splits in the plies; some are perfect on one side only, the other side having imperfections and being unusable for finished work but reducing the cost over both-sides-perfect types; still other grades may have circular or diamond-shaped plugs set into the ply to repair knotholes or other blemishes, but are well sanded so that they may be used for painted work, concrete forms, and other jobs requiring good smooth surfaces where perfection of grain is not important. This grade may also possess small, tight knots. Properly shellacked and finished with paint, these will be no problem, either.

For an outdoor project, choose an exterior type of plywood. When finished properly with a stain or paint, it will withstand the most severe weather conditions. The 100 percent waterproof glueline in exterior panels will keep the plies from separating when they get wet. If both sides of an exterior panel will be visible, choose A–B Exterior so both will be smooth and paintable. For a more natural look, a water-repellent wood preservative will leave the grain exposed. If only one side of the project will show, as is often the case, A–C Exterior panels are all that's necessary. These are widely available at lumber and building materials dealers.

Utility grades of plywood appropriate for outdoor projects, such as a storage shed, include B–B and B–C Exterior. C–C Plugged panels make an excellent base for tile. (C–C Plugged, which is sanded, should not be confused with unsanded C–C Exterior.)

The most paintable surface is found on MDO (Medium Density Overlay) plywood. Because the face is heat-fused to a smooth or textured resin-treated fiber surface, MDO rarely develops the surface checking that often appears on other plywood after exposure to weathering. MDO is particularly good for furniture and cabinets.

Whatever project is planned, designing with economy in mind is important, so select the best thickness for the job. Plywood thicknesses from ½ to ¾ inch are the most common. Often ¾ inch is a good choice. Half-inch panels will take spans of 24 inches and less with most uses, but for heavy tools, building materials, stacks of flower pots, or other weighty materials, make them of ⅝- or ¾-inch plywood.

In some uses orientation of the face grain is important, as in making shelves. For greatest stiffness and strength, always run the face grain across the supports.

Sometimes available in addition to the usual 4′ × 8′ stock size is a 4′ × 4′ or 2′ × 4′ panel. If these are adaptable to your project, the already-cut sizes will save labor. Note, too, that the nominal and actual sizes of plywood panels are the same.

Some of the higher-grade interior plywood, in addition to the master panel size of 4′ × 8′, may be ordered in widths of 30, 36, and 42 inches, and in lengths of from 5 to 12 feet in even-foot sizes. Special panels made for outdoor use on porches or decks come in lengths of 10 to 24 feet. It must be pointed out, though, that not all of these may be stocked by your local dealer, and he may be well within his rights in refusing to special-order them for you, unless you use at least two-thirds of the minimum "package" his wholesaler may force him to buy. However, if you have some special project in mind, check with your dealer what sizes he regularly stocks and the possibility of special orders. If your project is large enough to make it worth his while, he may be able to obtain what you wish, provided that you can wait for the length of time it will take to have the special order filled and delivered. You may find that it will be to your advantage to use the more readily available sizes and adapt them to your project.

USED LUMBER OR SALVAGED WOOD

House-wrecker's storage yards may be profitable places for you to explore, for they can save you money at times. Many fences, garden houses, shelters, and so on, can be built at a considerable reduction in cost by using salvaged wood. Old studs, joists, planks, and boards *which are in good condition* may be found in the wrecker's yards "filed" according to size. The thing to remember here is that key phrase "in good condition," for it is important to you. You must carefully look over the lumber where the dealer has stored it, usually arranged by its size and length. Most often, dealers will permit you to examine and select what you want. You may either take it away yourself, if you have a pickup truck or station wagon or if the pieces are small enough to be accommodated in your car. Or you can have the dealer send them to you in his truck and pay for delivery. You will have to pull out remaining nails and be careful when sawing to avoid any which may have been broken off and left in the wood. It would be well to use the wood in its rough condition rather than to try planing it, because of the hazard of nails damaging the plane blade. If time is less of a factor than money, you can certainly save money this way.

Another way to save would be to purchase the wood from some building that is to be razed and pull it down yourself, doing your own house-wrecking and nail-pulling. This is a strenuous occupation but it need not be dangerous if intelligent care is exercised; climbing, prying, and pulling down structures always demand the caution which common sense dictates. I once pulled down a large shed with the help of my wife, and some assistance from two other men when large beams and other pieces had to be brought down. It was a large task to remove all the nails, but the wood was so well seasoned and in such good condition that it was easily re-used to make a fine, sturdy structure. Examine old buildings and wood to be sure that neither dry rot, termites, nor other insects are present, or the lumber will be a poor investment.

Another source of lumber usually overlooked is wood crates and boxes. These can be utilized in numerous ways, depending upon the quality of the wood and its size. Retailers usually will give away the crates or sell them for a nominal sum. If they are carefully pulled apart the wood can be used in many different projects. When the wood is rough it can be planed or sanded smooth with a power sander, but sometimes the very roughness will be an asset, adding an attractive texture to a fence, even though it will not add to the ease of painting.

These foregoing facts about lumber do not exhaust the subject, but they will give the amateur a good groundwork on which to build further knowledge about woods.

CHAPTER 4

WOOD PRESERVATIVES

The U.S. Environmental Protection Agency (EPA) has restricted over-the-counter sale to the public of many wood preservatives that contain any of the three types of highly toxic wood preservatives—creosote, inorganic arsenical compounds, and pentachlorophenols. All have been linked with cancers, birth defects, and other physical problems in laboratory animals or humans. These preservatives may now be applied only by state-certified people trained in proper application methods and protected by specified clothing and, in some cases, respiratory masks.

Pressure-treated wood containing preservatives is used for garden timbers, fence posts, railroad ties, utility poles, deck lumber, and elsewhere around the home. (Railroad ties and used utility poles are often resold for garden use.) Toxic preservatives are also brushed or sprayed on fence rails and posts, lawn furniture, particle board, and some plywoods, and they have been used in millwork. Creosote may not be used indoors, even for window or door frames. Pentachlorophenols may be if covered with two coats of sealant. Arsenicals may be used indoors without sealants.

Be cautious in handling and using pressure-treated or other treated woods in building. Use dust masks whenever cutting or sanding these woods. After building, use sealants wherever treated wood will come in frequent contact with flesh, as on garden seats, decks on which people may walk barefoot, and so on. Use two coats of sealant. The EPA suggests sealing creosote-treated wood with urethane, shellac, or epoxy. For pentachlorophenol-treated wood, use urethane, shellac, latex epoxy enamel, or varnish. Do not use treated woods where they may come in contact with food for animals or humans. And I would not use them for plant boxes or where they may contaminate irrigation or drinking water. If using treated wood under cover, as in a garden shelter, seal wood there, too. The EPA says that eating, drinking, or smoking while using preservatives is taboo. Certified workers must also wear discardable rubber gloves when handling treated wood and wear long-sleeved and long-legged garments to be really safe.

This picture of possible hazards is ultra-cautious, but it's better in this case to be very cautious. There is one preservative I have always favored because it was less lethal to plants, and is still approved and available. It may be used by the amateur for preserving wood in plant boxes, in greenhouse structures, and elsewhere.

A WOOD PRESERVATIVE YOU CAN USE

The EPA does not require that you be certified to apply Cuprinol wood preservatives. These products are available in two varieties, Cuprinol No. 10 Green Wood Preservative and Cuprinol No. 20 Clear Wood Preservative. The green preservative is based on copper naphthenate, a fungicide that has been used safely for many decades. This heavy-duty preservative is designed to protect wood that will be in contact with soil or water. It can be applied by brushing, dipping or spraying. Typical uses are for docks, fence post bottoms, and porches. It can also be used in greenhouses and around shrubbery since it is nontoxic to most plants. The clear Cuprinol preservative is based on zinc naphthenate. Like the green preservative it has been used with safety for many years. It is designed to protect wood above ground or water from rot and mildew while allowing it to weather naturally. It can also be applied by brushing, dipping or spraying. The clear preservative is used on decks, fences, outdoor furniture and home wood siding. In addition to their wood preservative action, Cuprinol preservatives contain water repellents that help prevent wood warping or cracking.

These preservatives should be applied to unpainted wood since they must penetrate in order to provide effective protection. Wood treated with the green preservative will fade in color on exposure to sunlight and weathering but the preservative action will continue for many years. Clear Cuprinol can be painted 24 to 48 hours after being applied. Green

Cuprinol should be allowed to weather until the color fades before it is painted.

Cuprinol preservatives should be applied out of doors in a well-ventilated place. Avoid breathing the vapor or spray mist. Because some people find these preservatives to be mild skin irritants, wear rubber gloves and long-sleeved and long-legged garments during application. Also, wear eye protection to ward off possible splashes. Again, do not eat, drink or smoke while using Cuprinol. Since these preservatives contain mineral spirits, a flammable solvent, it is good practice to keep them away from open flame, pilot lights or sources of sparks.

Cuprinol wood preservatives are manufactured by the Darworth Company, Avon, CT 06001.

A FEW EXTRA CAUTIONS

If you are buying wood preservatives, beware of purchasing old stock containing compounds now restricted for use. In any case, as with buying paints, read the labels carefully, paying attention to the list of ingredients. If you find any of the three restricted ingredients listed, obtain certification before using them. When you buy pressure-treated woods, try to find out what preservatives were used. Under the new EPA rulings, information on treated wood should be available from the dealer. Act accordingly. Do not burn treated wood scraps in fireplaces or stoves. Dispose of them via the regular trash collections or bury them deeply in the soil but not where ground water might carry contaminants into drinking or irrigating water.

Lawn furniture over six months old and having been exposed to weathering is probably not harmful. New outdoor wood furniture that has not been sealed should receive two coats. Besides the safety factor, the sealers will help prolong the life of the wood.

At this writing, industry chemists are working overtime to produce new and safer wood preservatives. Meantime, read the labels.

WHY SHOULD WE USE PRESERVATIVES?

Added to the chore of building, application of preservatives to wood may sound arduous and possibly unnecessary. Yet preservatives are effective especially in damp climates or wherever wood is likely to be exposed to moisture. With all woods constantly escalating in price, even for inferior grades, you can prolong wood life by this extra work, not to mention saving repetition of the entire task of rebuilding in a period of years when the wood has deteriorated and rotted. A little forethought and care *now* will pay off by saving expense and tiresome labor *later*.

CHAPTER 5

LITTLE PROJECTS

Presented here are a number of small projects which will not take much time to build, or very much in the way of material, either. Some may utilize leftover scrap wood from big projects or recycled wood gleaned from suitable sources. They will serve, I hope, as a good introduction to woodworking. Even if you are a proficient woodworker, you may still be interested in them because they are all useful and beautiful in their way—objects which you can make for your own yard or build as gifts for friends.

The simplest of these projects are the bird feeders, birdhouses, and shelters. They may be built of scrap lumber if you wish, requiring only a little initial skill in construction in order to complete them. But if you persevere and do the work carefully, step by step, many of the principles and practices used will help to train and hone your skills for more ambitious projects.

The plant-stands and outdoor shelves for summering houseplants outdoors are practical solutions to an ever-present problem of the indoor gardener. Whether they are simple demountable ones or more permanent types, they will assist the gardener to keep houseplants in good order during their summer vacation outdoors.

The plant shield project can probably be adapted to many more uses than those shown here. Every gardener recognizes the need for shielding tender plants from the winter sun and cold blasts of wind. By using a decorative shield (something more pleasant to look at out the window than the torn and ragged strips of sagging burlap sacking one usually sees), the sad winter landscape can be made more appealing. The frames can be painted any color you wish, making them distinct assets rather than bitter necessities when they are installed in your garden.

The cold frame is another project which may be built with very little tool experience. An old window or two may be utilized to top the frame. Measure it, then proceed to construct the cold frame to fit the sash. Advanced workers may go a step further and build the sash. There are many changes which can be made on the construction of the frame. Permanent sides of brick, concrete, or other masonry may be used, with a wooden frame made to fit over the top to hold the sash. If such a frame is used as a hot bed, permanent masonry sides are recommended because of high temperatures and humidity which may rot the sides of the type shown.

The plant boxes can be adapted to whatever sizes of pots you wish to use in them. Containers with flowering plants make a bright spot of color beside your front door, on the patio, or wherever you finally decide to use them. By fitting with wheels, you'll be able to move a plant box from spot to spot, changing about each day or each week, or whenever you give a party.

The "Ugly Duckling Doors" also require little skill and only a bit of patience for their rebirth and refurbishment. Old cracked panels and odd, mismatched doors can be made into nice, fresh ones and will last many years when they are covered and brought up to date this way.

These, then, are the Little Projects, which I hope will inspire you to find fun in building and will give you many years of pleasure and profit from their use when completed.

May all your Little Projects become big ones as your skill and confidence grow.

BIRDHOUSES AND FEEDERS

With the encroachment of building developments around cities, more and more wooded areas are being eliminated, sometimes being destroyed altogether, sometimes merely cut severely. Birds are having a rather thin time of it these days when it comes to finding suitable quarters for building nests and rearing families. Every person who has the faintest interest in outdoor life and in conservation will want to help remedy this deplorable situation, not only for the amusement afforded by watching the birds as they go about the business of rearing their young, but for the very sound, practical reason that they do so much good in ridding gardens and trees of insects.

What can you do? Build birdhouses and shelters and make feeding stations, so that during the winter you can supplement their natural rations, particularly during the severe days when native foods may be iced over and unavailable.

A great many birds adapt to dwelling in man-made houses and also are tolerant of living near human habitations. If you wish to lure birds into your backyard, the main consideration will be to construct a house which will fit the requirements of the kinds of birds you wish to attract. For instance, robins, phoebes, wrens, and bluebirds, all fairly common in a good many areas, are amenable to living in man-made shelters. Purple martins and flickers, song sparrows, titmice, nuthatches, barn swallows, house finches, woodpeckers, and even some of the owls are known to be open-minded about setting up housekeeping in civilized houses. But each kind of bird prefers a certain kind of house, usually liking it placed at a certain convenient level and in an environment suited to its needs or attractive to the species. The size of access hole, the depth of the enclosed space, and other factors are also to be considered.

Anyone who can hold a saw, hammer a nail, use a screwdriver, or bore holes can make birdhouses and feeders which will not only be suitable, but will be "received with open wings" by the feathered populace. It needn't cost much, either, to do your part in relieving the housing shortage in the bird world. You can either buy the materials or use remnants of boards left over from other projects, packing-case boards, plywood scraps, or seasoned wood from old pieces of furniture which have been discarded. The only limit is the ingenuity of the builder, who may well be someone embarking upon the hobby of becoming a do-it-yourselfer.

Materials chosen particularly for the purpose may look better to the human eye, but the birds won't mind if you use oddments. Cedar, cypress, redwood, and hardwoods will last longer; but poplar, white pine, and practically any kind of wood which is easily worked will do if it is of suitable size and thickness. Wet and green lumber should be avoided. When the house is finished, it should be stained or painted. It should then be taken down each autumn, cleaned, and occasionally given another coat of stain or paint to make it last as long as possible. Make any necessary repairs at that time, too.

You can build a birdhouse as good as or better than the best offered commercially. Some professionally made birdhouses (and many of the homemade kind, too, regrettably) are "cute little numbers" painted in garish colors and made to simulate human dwellings. They look as if they belonged in the plastic department of the local chain store. The birds don't like them very much, usually, so you may be wasting your time if you go off on this tack.

The most successful birdhouses are engineered for the birds' use, not to tickle the eyes of humankind. They strive to emulate as far as possible what is known about the natural preferences of the birds. While some may nest in brightly painted houses, most birds seem to prefer a nesthouse which is less conspicuous. This doesn't mean that you have to go to the length of making everything brown and green, as some bird lovers advocate. Neutral gray, soft blue-green like that of spruce needles, medium blue, terra cotta, or any of the pleasant colors which are not too brilliant will not offend the birds, and will charm the human eye, too.

An exception might be made of the phoebe shelter, which is best placed under the eaves of the house or in a protected spot around human habitations. It can be painted to conform with the walls or trim color of the house so that it assumes protective coloration by *not* standing out against its background. Don't paint birdhouses too often, for birds seem to like houses which have weathered a bit.

Feeders may also be painted, unless you happen to subscribe to the nature school, which insists that everything out of doors must be stained a dingy brown. Actually, I believe that it is the paint odor which birds dislike and not the color. I have always painted feeders and houses the same soft but not dull blue-spruce color we used on the shutters of our home, and have never lacked either tenants or free-lunchers. However, I always try to get the houses and feeders painted several weeks ahead of the need for them outdoors. If the structure is built early in winter and painted by late winter, any paint odor will have dissipated by house-hunting and nesting time. Put out the house somewhat earlier than you think it may be needed. This will allow it to weather a bit and it will also be ready for early arrivals to stake out their claim and start building. You can check with your local Audubon Society group as to the approximate times of arrival and nesting in your climate and region, if you want to be really certain. Don't be alarmed if birds don't nest the first year; you may have missed their arrival time, or they may have a new-season's lease where they were last year. Next year you may be their landlord.

WHERE TO PLACE THE BIRDHOUSE

A suitable site for the house is of primary importance, naturally, for if the location is not to the liking and needs of its potential tenants it will remain vacant. There should be safety from marauding squirrels and cats; there must be sun (or shade, according to species); and the house must be placed at a suitable height for the kind of bird.

Be sure to face the house away from prevailing winds, so that rain will not be driven into the entrance hole. Never tilt the front of the house upward if you are affixing it to a tree trunk, or rain will enter. Either place it vertically or slant it downwards. Some houses may be hung from two wires below a horizontal limb, the wires preventing it from spinning in the breezes. Select a large enough limb so that the house is not constantly jouncing about.

Except in isolated cases, the minimum height at which to set birdhouses is 4 to 5 feet, or even at the height of a fence post. Although in nature bluebirds nest much higher, they will sometimes adapt themselves to the low placement. Most birds seem to prefer a height of 8 to 12 feet or more from the ground for their houses. The table at the end of this section will give you recommendations for placement, as well as other information on building houses for specific species. If you are troubled with squirrels—they often steal eggs and rip up the nests—or with neighborhood cats, the answer may be to place the house on a pipe post in the open where it will be beyond leaping distance from trees or buildings. Neither cats nor squirrels can climb a pipe, and their jumping capacities are limited, too.

BUILDING THE HOUSE

If you are buying new wood, the best and lasting kinds are cypress, cedar, and redwood. White pine and poplar may also be used. Purchase the 1-inch thickness (note that the *finished* size is less than that, when you are making your measurements and preparing to cut the wood) except if plywood is to be used, when ½-inch or ¾-inch may be bought. (Thickness measurements in plywood are reasonably exact.) Aluminum or brass screws and nonrusting nails are recommended and, if hinges are required, purchase nonrusting types. Countersinking screws and puttying all holes will also make a better-looking and longer-lasting birdhouse or shelter.

Two coats of stain or paint should be given initially, and refinishing the houses should be done every three or four years, to keep the structures in good condition. Yearly cleaning of the houses to remove nesting materials will help keep them attractive to birds. Although many bird lovers take their houses down and store them indoors in winter, it is recommended that they be left out as winter shelters, particularly in cold regions. On cold nights many birds are known to enter houses, often piling up on top of each other to keep warm, even if the house is not the type they would use for nesting.

Several types of cleanouts are shown in the upcoming drawings. They may be adapted to any of the houses shown in the design pages. When you have cleaned the house, it may be well to take it down and refinish it so that it will withstand winter moisture better, and also to be certain that the paint smell will have dissipated long before spring nesting time.

Don't fail to drill holes for drainage in the floors and the vent holes around the tops where recommended. The bottom holes will permit any moisture to drain out should a hurricane force it into the house in quantity, and both floor and top holes will help to ventilate the house on hot days. The thickness of the wood in the box-type houses will help somewhat to insulate the houses.

Observe the sizes given for the entrance holes and *use them*. While birds may nest in houses with larger holes, competitors or enemies may also be able to enter. For example, if you enlarge the hole in a bluebird house to 1¾ to 2 inches in diameter, starlings will enter and displace or fight with the bluebirds, even usurp the nest. If it is only the correct 1½ inches, these slum-children on the bird-world will be excluded. Similar considerations have brought about the choice of sizes for the entrance holes for all birds.

Some species have more than one nesting each season, and each nesting requires a new nest. If all the old material is cleaned out after the fledglings of the first brood have departed, it is quite possible that the house will be used for the second nesting. If you have woodpeckers, they will appreciate 2 inches of sawdust placed loosely in the bottom of their box houses. They seem to require it for their nest, probably because they are used to having wood chips or rotting wood in natural nesting cavities in dead trees in the woods.

As indicated in the plans, entrance holes are placed high so that the mother bird is concealed when she is sitting on the nest. Holes must not be placed lower or higher (this latter will make it difficult for the bird to enter), but at the position indicated. A natural twig or a dowel set in a hole bored in the front of the house will give birds an alighting place from which they can hop up into the entrance hole. Some bird observers claim that robins need a good-sized branch extending out and below the shelter, stating that robins like to alight and walk up to the nest. This theory would seem to be borne out by the fact that robins like to nest on flat limbs in orchards.

Much more might be written about attracting birds and building homes for them (much more has been, in fact), but that is not the function of this book. This section serves as an introduction, so I have given as much space as can be spared to material which will help you to get houses built properly and birds coming around regularly each year to nest and to be fed. For further information on birdhouses and attracting birds, most good bookstores can

SAME HOUSE, DIFFERENT SIZES FOR WRENS OR BLUEBIRDS

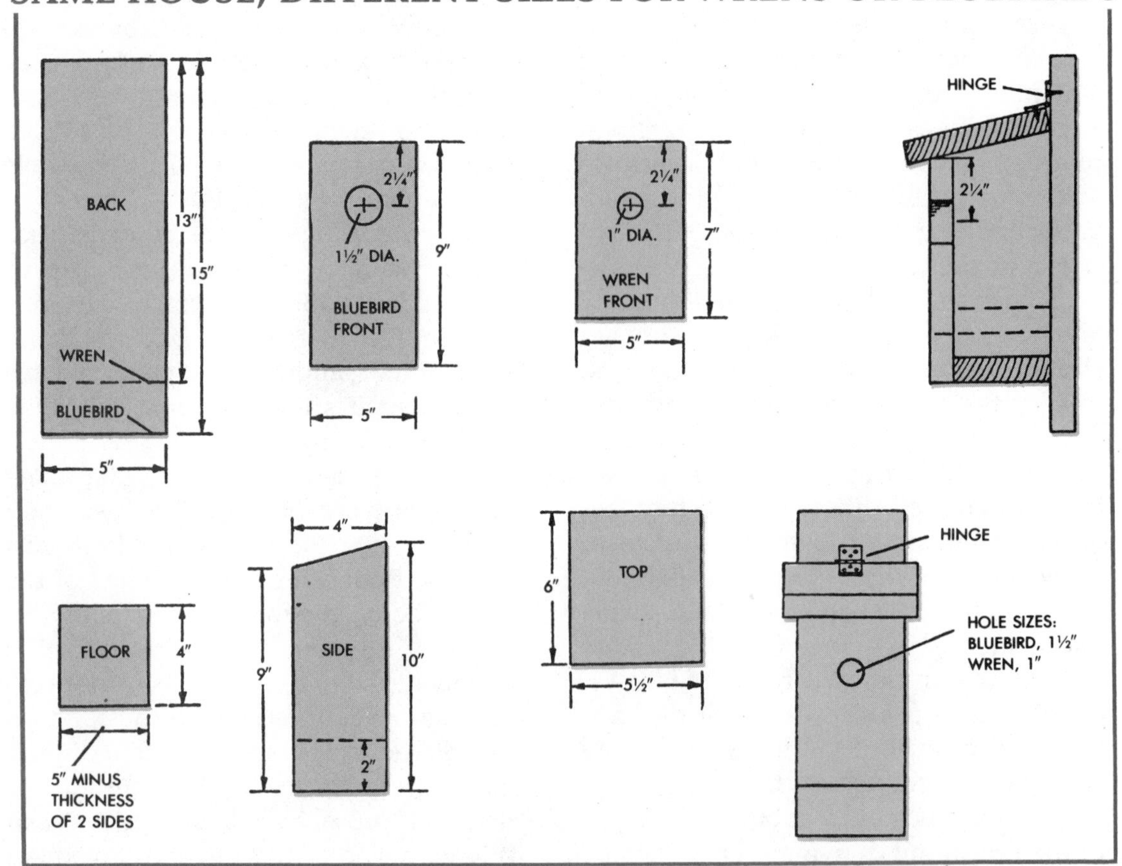

provide a worthy selection. Also, the U.S. departments of Agriculture and Interior have issued many national and regional pamphlets on these subjects. You would also be well advised to check on bird publications of your state environmental conservation agency or agencies of nearby states because those publications would focus on the needs of birds in your region. In addition, the Boy Scouts of America have a pamphlet in their merit badge series called *Bird Study*; younger builders will be interested in this publication and adults will find enlightenment here too. You might also consult a local chapter of the National Audubon Society. For information on local birding organizations, write National Audubon Society, 950 Third Avenue, New York, NY 10022.

BIRDHOUSE CLEANOUTS

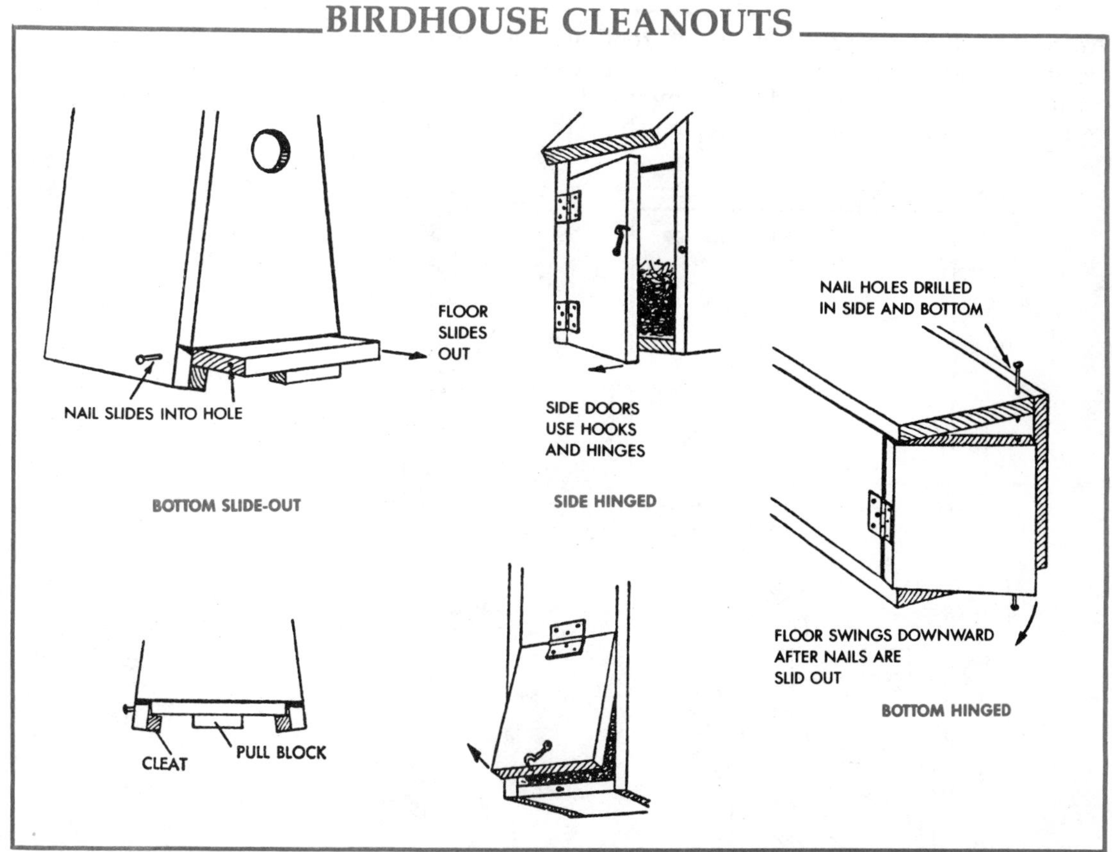

After the brood has flown, the house should be cleaned out to allow it to be used again for a second nesting if the species of bird desires to do so. Birds don't use the same nest twice and are more likely to renest in a clean house than in one they must clean themselves. The house needn't be taken down for cleaning if easy cleanouts such as those shown here are constructed— slide bottom, hinged sides, and hinged bottom. Note that all of them provide for securing the cleanout during the nesting periods.

ALL YEAR BIRD SHELTER-FEEDER

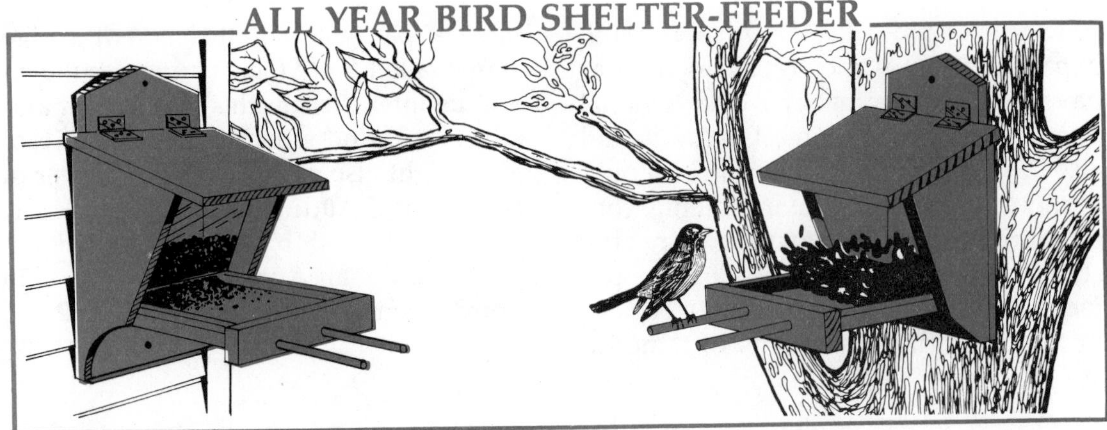

An open shelter, comprised of a shelf, roof, and half sides is preferred by phoebes, barn swallows, and robins. But this shelter can also be used as a feeder when it is not being used for nesting. Its roof is hinged, allowing it to lift so that the glass which holds the seed can be removed or inserted, and for replenishing the seed when necessary.

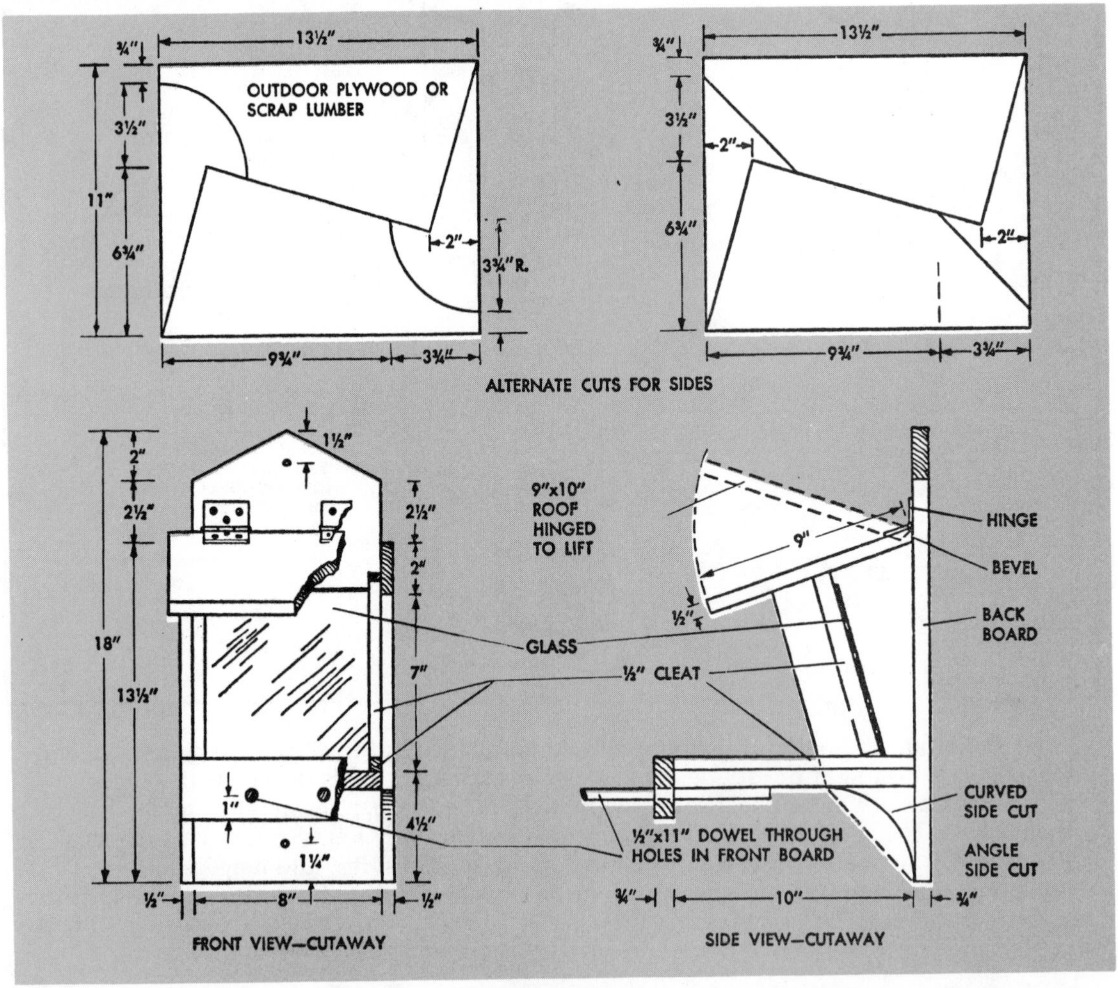
13½"
¾"
11"
3½"
6¾"
OUTDOOR PLYWOOD OR SCRAP LUMBER
2"
3¾" R.
9¾"
3¾"
13½"
¾"
3½"
2"
6¾"
2"
9¾"
3¾"
ALTERNATE CUTS FOR SIDES
1½"
2"
2½"
18"
13½"
2½"
2"
7"
4½"
1"
1¼"
½"
8"
½"
9"x10" ROOF HINGED TO LIFT
9"
½"
HINGE
BEVEL
BACK BOARD
GLASS
½" CLEAT
CURVED SIDE CUT
ANGLE SIDE CUT
½"x11" DOWEL THROUGH HOLES IN FRONT BOARD
¾"
10"
¾"
FRONT VIEW—CUTAWAY
SIDE VIEW—CUTAWAY

OPEN HOUSE FOR "FRESH-AIR BIRDS"

Certain birds will nest only in shelters with open fronts. By placing the shelter under the eaves of a building with the open front protected from prevailing winds, you will attract phoebes and barn swallows to nest in it. Robins sometimes nest near houses, but more frequently prefer the shelter to be placed fairly high in a tree on the trunk or on a major limb. Here, too, wind protection is essential for attracting the birds.

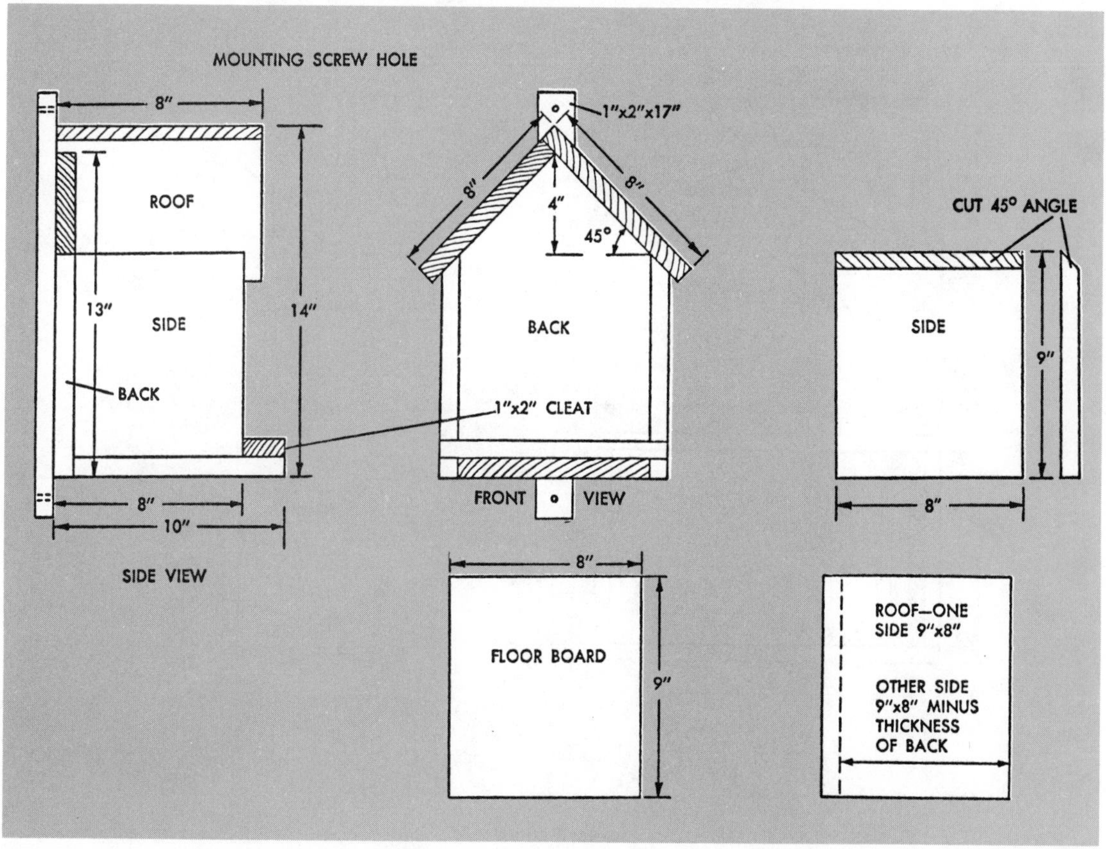

MOUNTING SCREW HOLE
8″
ROOF
13″
SIDE
14″
BACK
8″
10″
SIDE VIEW

1″x2″x17″
8″
8″
4″
45°
BACK
1″x2″ CLEAT
FRONT VIEW

CUT 45° ANGLE
SIDE
9″
8″

8″
FLOOR BOARD
9″

ROOF—ONE SIDE 9″x8″
OTHER SIDE 9″x8″ MINUS THICKNESS OF BACK

WINDOWSILL FEEDER

Conveniently placed below a window so you can see the birds from inside, this feeder features a hinged roof, allowing the glass-fronted seed hopper to be easily refilled on inclement days without your leaving the house. Brackets may be used to attach it to the wall, or merely to stabilize it if long hooks screwed firmly into the windowsill are used.

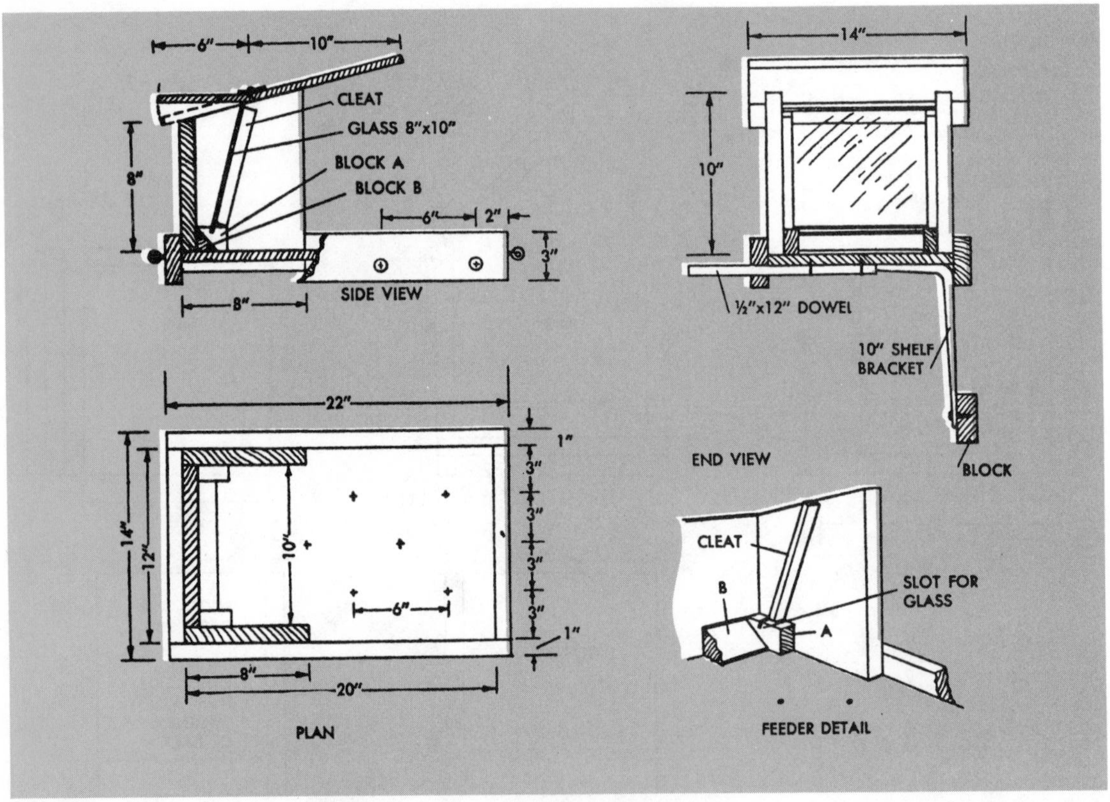

6" 10"
CLEAT
GLASS 8"x10"
BLOCK A
BLOCK B
8"
6" 2"
3"
8"
SIDE VIEW

14"
10"
½"x12" DOWEL
10" SHELF BRACKET
END VIEW
BLOCK

22"
1"
3"
3"
3"
3"
1"
14"
12"
10"
6"
8"
20"
PLAN

CLEAT
B
SLOT FOR GLASS
A
FEEDER DETAIL

TREE-LIMB FEEDER

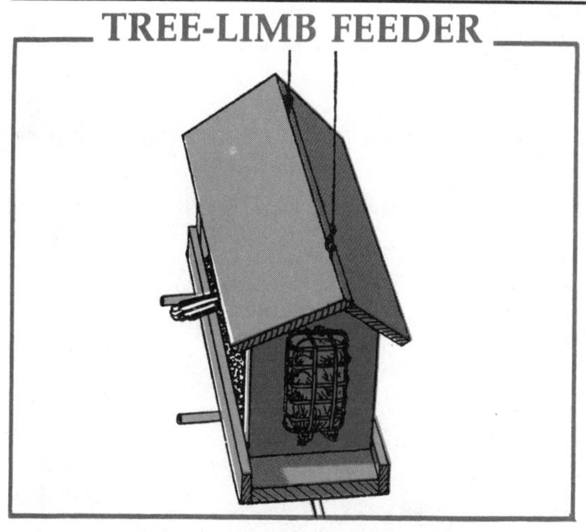

This feeder can be swung below a tree limb on copper wires, the hopper letting down more food as it is needed. The wire soap dish holds suet and is kept in place by three cup hooks. The angle hooks inside will hold paper cups of peanut butter or other food. Note the short dowels run through screw eyes and nailed in place to provide safe, comfortable landing perches.

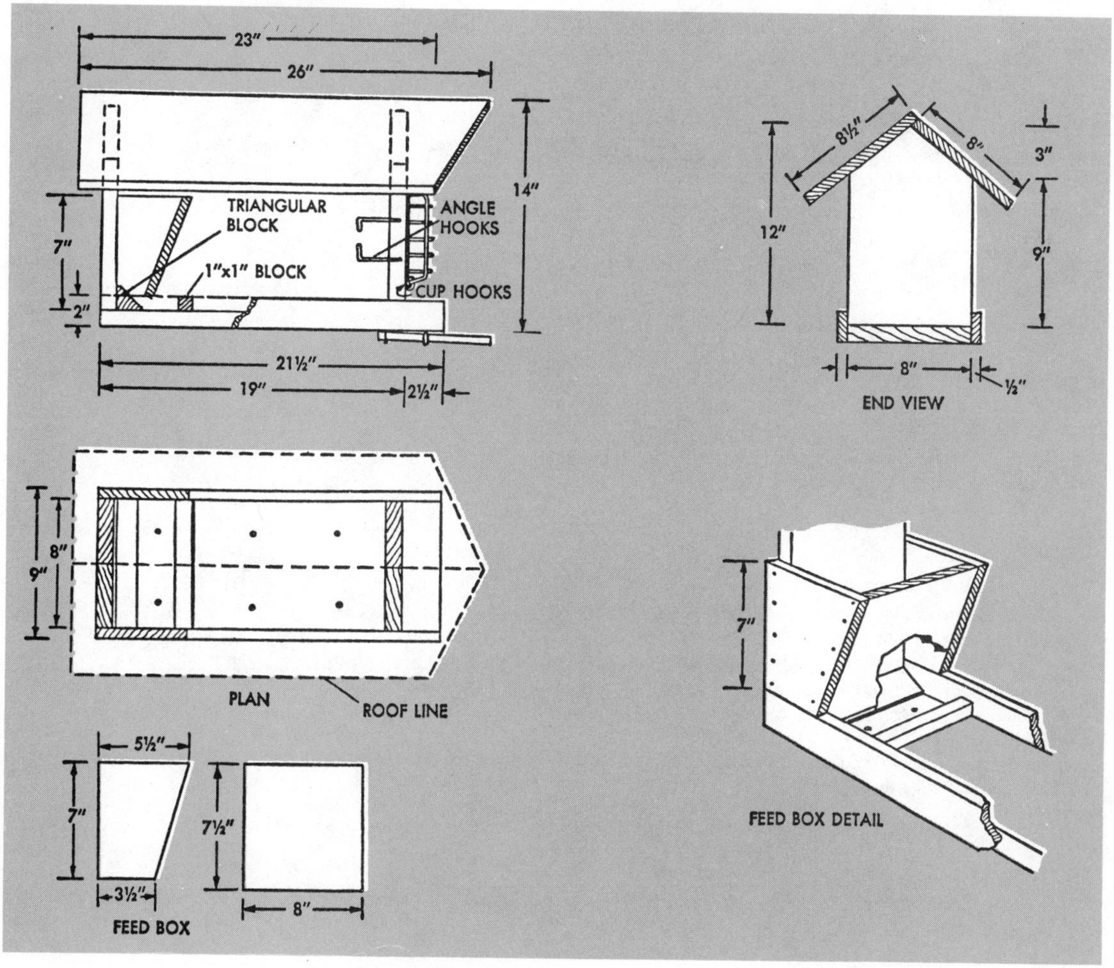

23"
26"
14"
7"
2"
TRIANGULAR BLOCK
1"x1" BLOCK
ANGLE HOOKS
CUP HOOKS
21½"
19"
2½"

8½"
8"
3"
12"
9"
8"
½"
END VIEW

8"
9"
PLAN
ROOF LINE

7"
FEED BOX DETAIL

5½"
7"
3½"
7½"
8"
FEED BOX

NESTING BOXES

Bird species	Floor of cavity	Depth of cavity	Entrance above floor	Diameter of entrance	Height above ground	Preferred habitat codes[b]
Enclosed	*Inches*	*Inches*	*Inches*	*Inches*	*Feet*	
House wren	4×4	6–8	4–6	1–1¼	4–10	2,7
Chickadees	4×4	9	7	1⅛	4–15	2
Bewick's wren	4×4	6–8	4–6	1¼	5–10	2,7
Titmouse	4×4	9	7	1¼	5–15	2
Downy woodpecker	4×4	9	7	1¼	5–15	2
Prothonotary warbler	4×4	6	4	1⅜	4–12,3Water	3,5
Nuthatches[a]	4×4	9	7	1⅜	5–15	2
Carolina wren	4×4	6–8	4–6	*1½	5–10	2,7
Bluebirds	4×4	8–12	6–10	*1½	3–6	1
Tree swallow	5×5	6–8	4–6	*1½	4–15	1
Violet-green swallow	5×5	6–8	4–6	*1½	4–15	1
Ash-throated flycatcher	6×6	8–10	6–8	*1½	8–20	1,6
Hairy woodpecker	6×6	12–15	9–12	1⅝	12–20	2
Great crested flycatcher	6×6	8–10	6–8	1¾	8–20	1,2
Golden-fronted woodpecker	6×6	12	9	2	10–20	2
Red-headed woodpecker	6×6	12	9	2	10–20	2
Purple martin	6×6	6	1	2¼	10–20	1
Saw-whet owl	6×6	10–12	8–10	2½	12–20	2
Flicker	7×7	16–18	14–16	2½	6–30	1,2
Screech owl	8×8	12–15	9–12	3	10–30	2
American kestrel	8×8	12–15	9–12	3	10–30	1,4
Barn owl	10×18	15–18	0–4	6	12–18	4
Wood duck	12×12	22	17	4	10–20,6Water	3,5
One or More Open Sides						
Phoebe	6×6	6	—	(2)	8–12	7,8
Barn swallow	6×6	6	—	(2)	8–12	7,8
Robin	6×8	8	—	(2)	6–15	7

*Precise measurement required. If diameter over 1½ inches, then starlings may usurp cavity.

[a]Brown-headed and pygmy nuthatches (1⅛), red-breasted nuthatch (1¼), and white-breasted nuthatch (1⅜) will all use the same box. However, the smaller opening sizes where appropriate may discourage use by house sparrows.

[b]Preferred habitat codes. The numbers in the last column refer to the habitat types listed here:

1. Open areas in the sun (not shaded permanently by trees), pastures, fields, or golf courses.
2. Woodland clearings or the edge of woods.
3. Above water, or if on land, the entrance should face water.
4. On trunks of large trees, or high in little-frequented parts of barns, silos, water towers or church steeples.
5. Moist forest bottomlands, flooded river valleys, swamps.
6. Semi-arid country, deserts, dry open woods and wood edge.
7. Backyards, near buildings.
8. Near water; under bridges, barns.

(Reprinted from *Homes for Birds*, Conservation Bulletin #14, U.S. Dept. of the Interior, Fish and Wildlife Service. For sale by Superintendent of Documents, U.S. Government Printing Office, Washington, DC 20402.)

LOG FEEDER

There are, of course, many other ways of feeding birds which are approved by bird lovers. One very simple and inexpensive method is shown here: A short length of tree limb with a few shortened twigs has had some holes 1″ to 2″ in diameter bored an inch or so deep. These are filled periodically with peanut butter, with suet, or with wild bird seed mixed with peanut butter. Where there are no twigs, use short dowel sticks to provide alighting spots for the birds, inserting them in holes bored just below the food holes. Hang by a copper wire through a screw eye in the top. Using paint may be frowned on by some purists, but the birds do not seem to mind—they'll nest in houses and eat from feeders long before the paint smell dissipates. Also, do not feel that you must stick to stains of woodsy brown or leaf green for all your birdhouses and feeders.

PREDATOR GUARD

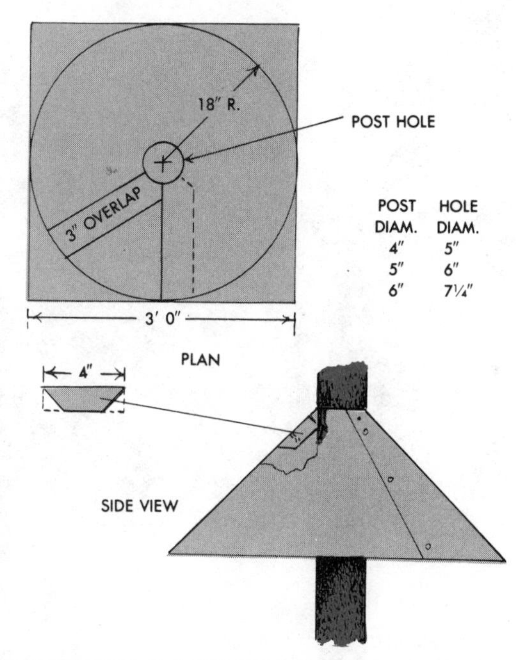

POST DIAM.	HOLE DIAM.
4″	5″
5″	6″
6″	7¼″

When a bird feeder or house is set on a post a conical sheet-metal guard will thwart climbing predators as well as thieving rats, mice, and squirrels.

Use a 3′-square piece of 26-gauge galvanized metal for a circle with an 18-in. radius. With tin shears, cut a center hole to fit the post diameter (see drawing). A pie-shaped piece is cut with a generous overlap for securing the two edges with ¼″ stove bolts, lock washers, and nuts. Mount three wooden blocks on the post, the guard secured to them with a nail inserted through a previously drilled pilot hole and a ¾″ wood screw below. Guards should be set a minimum of 3′ above water, 5′ above ground.

OTHER LITTLE PROJECTS

Every wood worker sooner or later finds there is an accumulation of wood left-overs—too good to throw away, too small for most major projects. And in these days of recycling, you can always keep an eye out for wood discards left out for trash collection by the unimaginative or the too-rich-to-care. Many a fine "little" project has made use of discards that were picked up at streetside. On upcoming pages are a few of many kinds of small, easy-to-make projects that could use scrapwood or recycled woods from other sources. Use these ideas as springboards from which to vault into creations of your own.

Gardens go portable with planters of ¾" grooved exterior plywood. The square box here is easiest to build—slant-sided types must have beveled top so mitered 1" × 2" finish frame can lie flat. All joints are nailed, waterproof glued; set box on a 2" × 4" drainage frame.

An interesting plant box, well-scaled to make a weighty accent at the corner of the patio, provides plants with the necessary soil and also gives drainage through the pierced bottom into oversized pebbles around the handsome elevated base. Redwood is used throughout.

Clear, All-Heart redwood 2″ × 6″s were used to build this hexagonal planter. To avoid exposed nails, all joints were mitered and glued with waterproof glue. While the glue set, pressure was held by hand-clamping.

This handsome redwood planter has 4″ × 4″ vertical corners. Decorative side boards are nailed to backer strips inset from post edges.

Dress up potted plants with an easily made bottomless box made of 14″-long picket-shaped 1″ × 4″s spaced ½″ apart. The 1″ × 2″ top and bottom frames are corner-braced with angle irons to hold the pickets rigidly. Note how corner pickets overlap in rotation.

A GARDEN SHRINE

Light enough to be hung on a fence, yet of sturdy enough construction to stand by itself, this little shrine will add interest to the garden. Shown here is a reproduction of a plaque of St. Fiacre, the patron saint of gardeners; the box at his feet will hold either flowers or green vines. At left below and at right are shown two versions of the shrine. At left is a pot pocket with holes bored in the bottom for drainage. At right is the version shown in the top illustration with a hole cut in the bottom to admit a pot of flowers. Version at left has pocket fastened to back and has short side pieces screwed to pocket. Plaque hangs on hook.

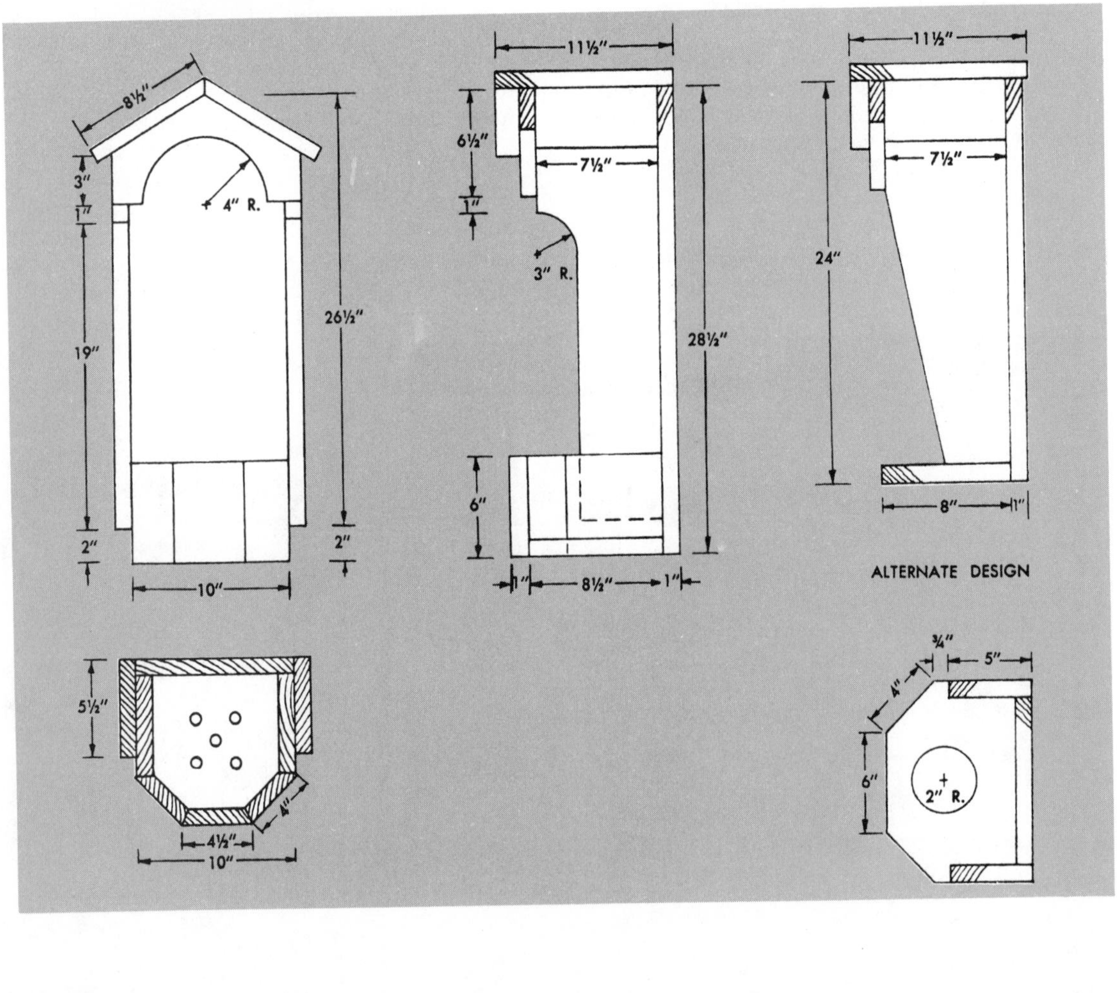

ALTERNATE DESIGN

SHOW-OFF FOR POTTED PLANTS ON THE PATIO

Either houseplants or potted plants prepared for patio use outdoors will find graduated shelves like these the best possible way to make their contribution. Note the alternate methods (below left) of making the shelves, with wooden gratings to allow circulation of air and good drainage. Use either bolts or dowels to hold shelves in place, decorate with trellis slats.

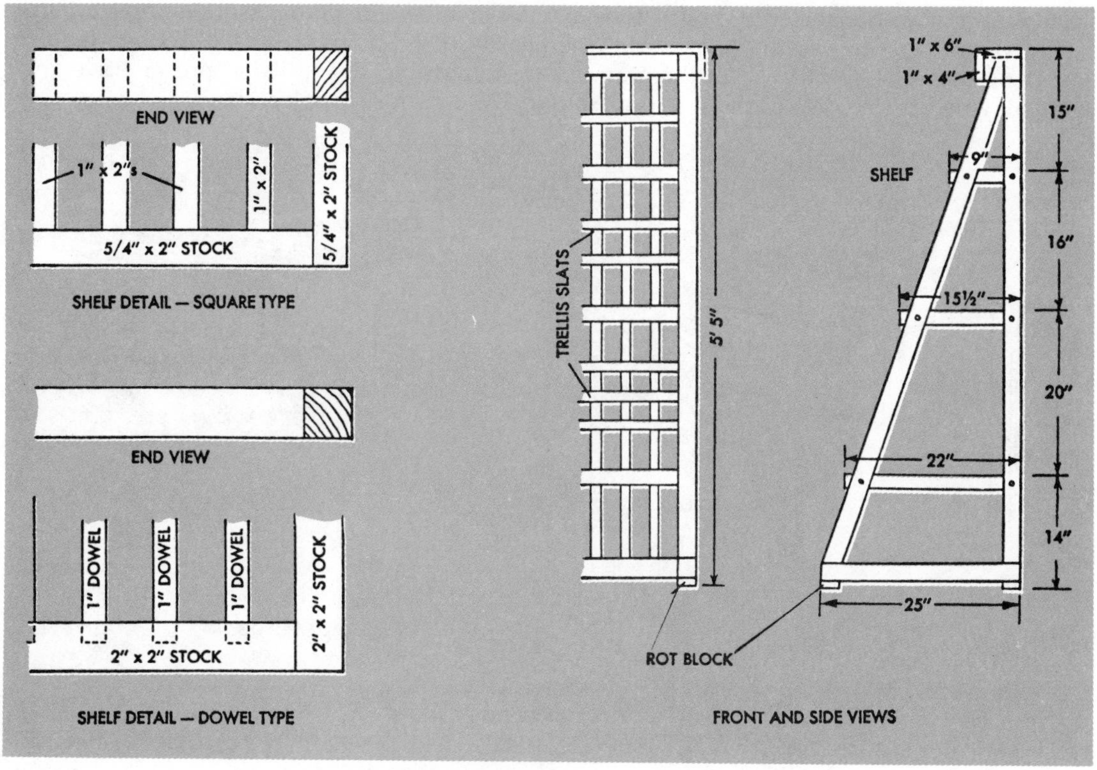

END VIEW
1" x 2"s
1" x 2"
5/4" x 2" STOCK
5/4" x 2" STOCK

SHELF DETAIL — SQUARE TYPE

END VIEW
1" DOWEL
1" DOWEL
1" DOWEL
2" x 2" STOCK
2" x 2" STOCK

SHELF DETAIL — DOWEL TYPE

TRELLIS SLATS
5' 5"
ROT BLOCK
1" x 6"
1" x 4"
15"
9"
SHELF
16"
15½"
20"
22"
14"
25"

FRONT AND SIDE VIEWS

VACATION SPOT FOR HOUSEPLANTS

If you have a few steps down from a north door of your house, you have an ideal spot for summering your houseplants. Build steps of exterior plywood to match stairs, topping them with wooden gratings so that plants can drain easily. Plant steps are easily transportable for winter storage because all of the gratings are removable. Use a wood preservative and give all wood three coats of paint. Note "rot blocks" which are replaceable.

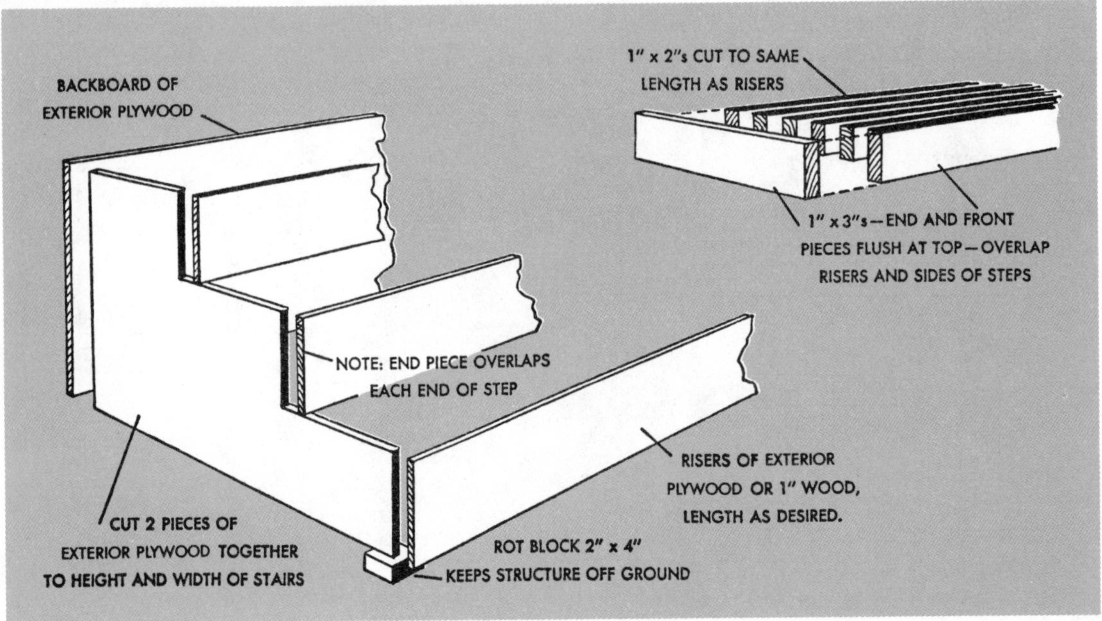

BLOCK AND TRESTLE

For renters and homeowners who don't want a permanent plant stand on the patio, this block and trestle idea is close to the ideal. It can be demounted in the fall and stored, or if you want to make it permanent, mortar the blocks together. Two versions of shelves to choose from give further adaptability, the crossbars fitting into the cores of the blocks. Shelves are staggered to make room for higher-growing plants on the shelves below.

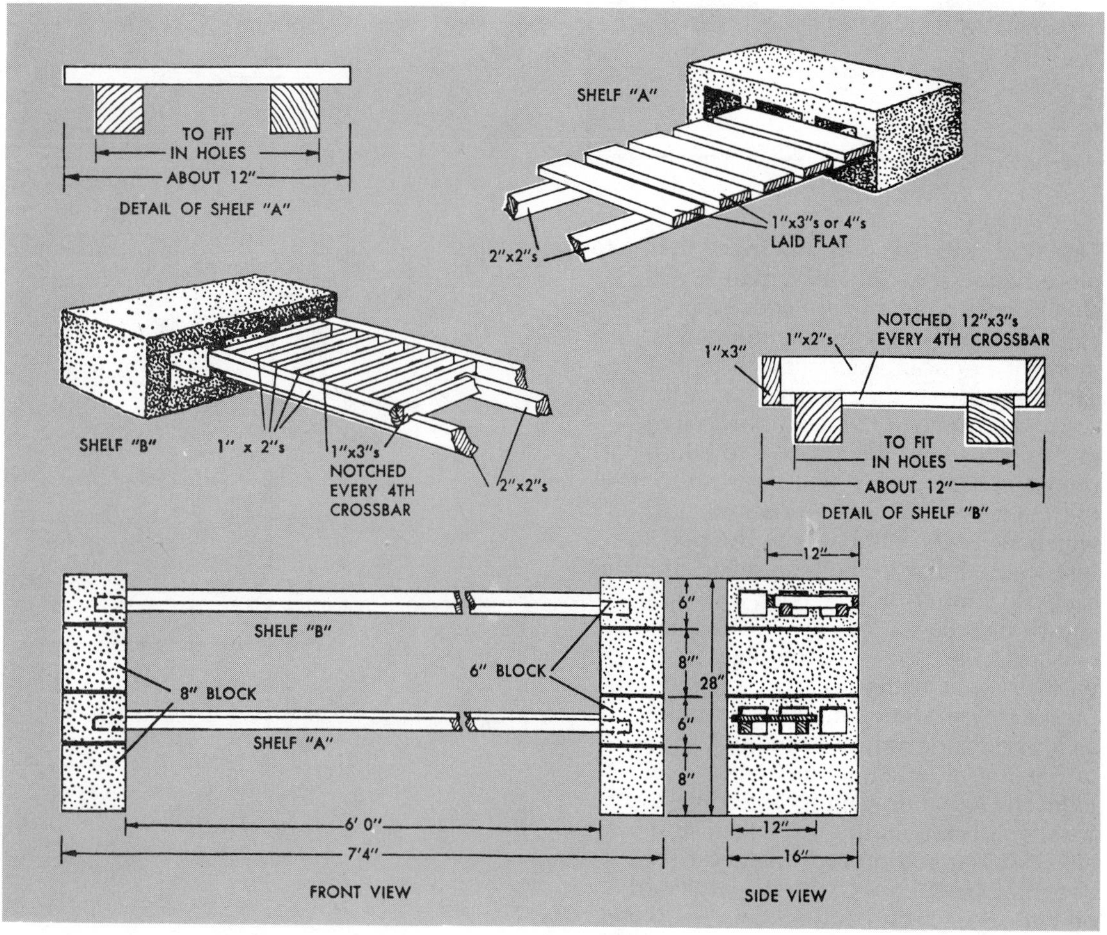

EVER-BLOOMING PLANT BOX

One way of dressing up the front door is to place beside it a plant box, which will always greet your visitors with a burst of blossom. The plants are "demountable" at a moment's notice, taken out and replaced easily as soon as they begin to fade, thus assuring yourself of all-summer beauty at your doorstep. Inexpensive to build—scrap lumber may be used for most of it—the plant box features a series of tiers which allow the shoulders of the pots to rest on the box edges, giving good drainage and also support for the pots. The trellis shown may be used or not, made a bit taller or shorter, according to the plants you wish to use. Geraniums can be trained up on the trellis, and vining houseplants such as ivy or philodendron (if there is shade) or a pot of morning glories can be used. Paint the wood or stain it, according to what you prefer in the way of finish, but always use wood preservative over the entire surface of the box first, particularly on cut edges, then paint or stain the wood.

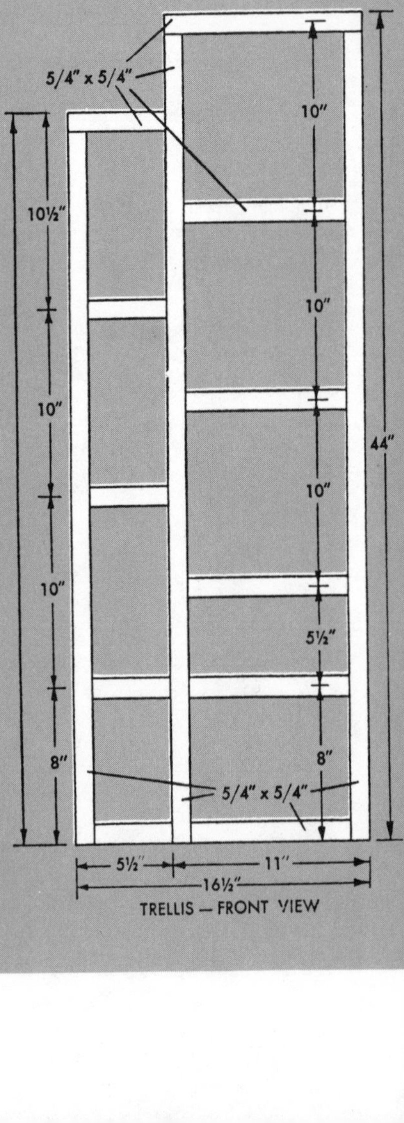

5/4" x 5/4"
10"
10½"
10"
10"
10"
10"
44"
5½"
8"
8"
5/4" x 5/4"
5½"
11"
16½"

TRELLIS — FRONT VIEW

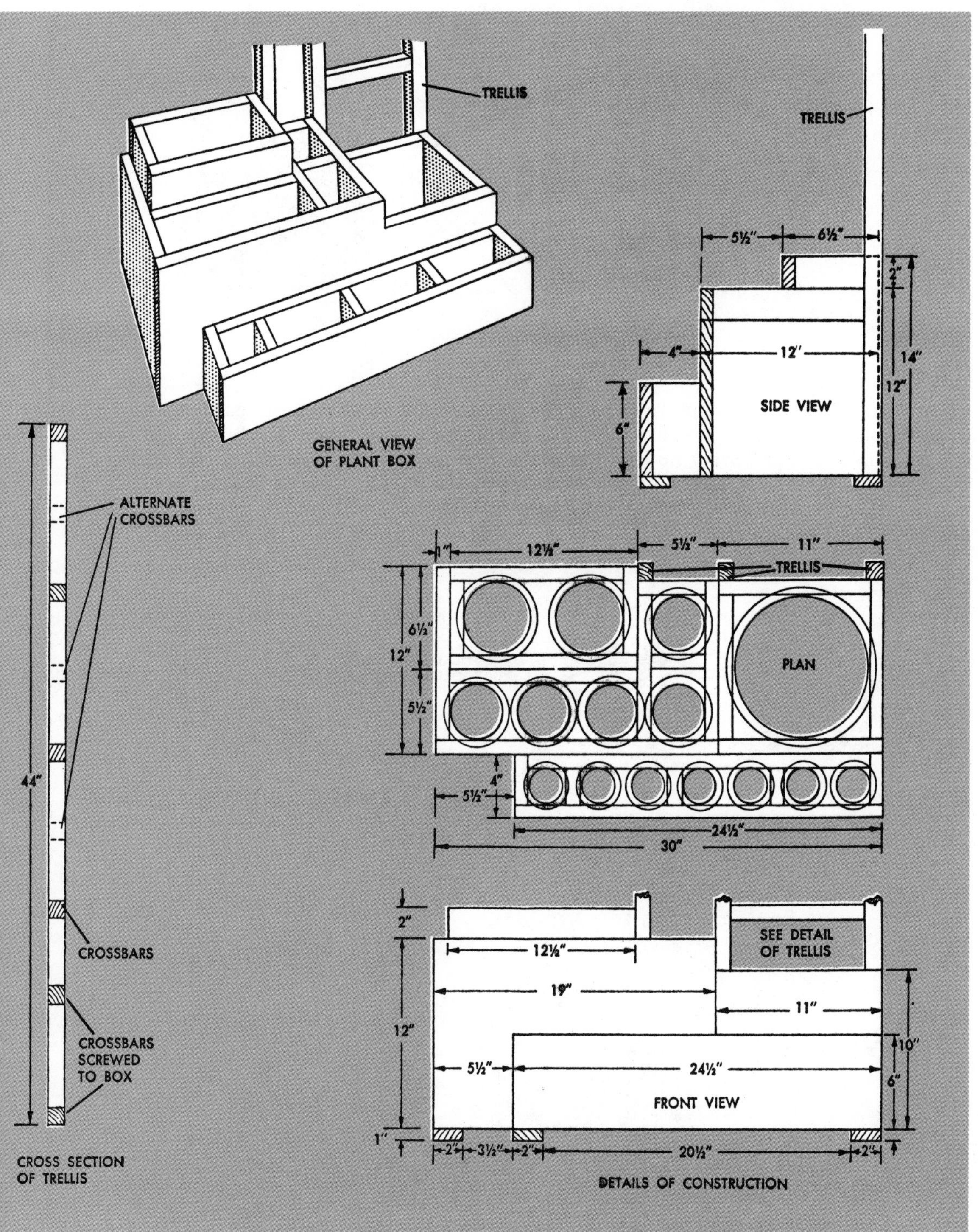
TRELLIS
GENERAL VIEW
OF PLANT BOX
TRELLIS
5½"
6½"
2"
4"
12"
14"
12"
6"
SIDE VIEW
ALTERNATE
CROSSBARS
44"
CROSSBARS
CROSSBARS
SCREWED
TO BOX
CROSS SECTION
OF TRELLIS
1"
12½"
5½"
11"
TRELLIS
6½"
12"
5½"
PLAN
4"
5½"
24½"
30"
2"
SEE DETAIL
OF TRELLIS
12½"
19"
11"
12"
10"
5½"
24½"
6"
FRONT VIEW
1"
2"
3½"
2"
20½"
2"
DETAILS OF CONSTRUCTION

VERSATILE PLANT SHIELD

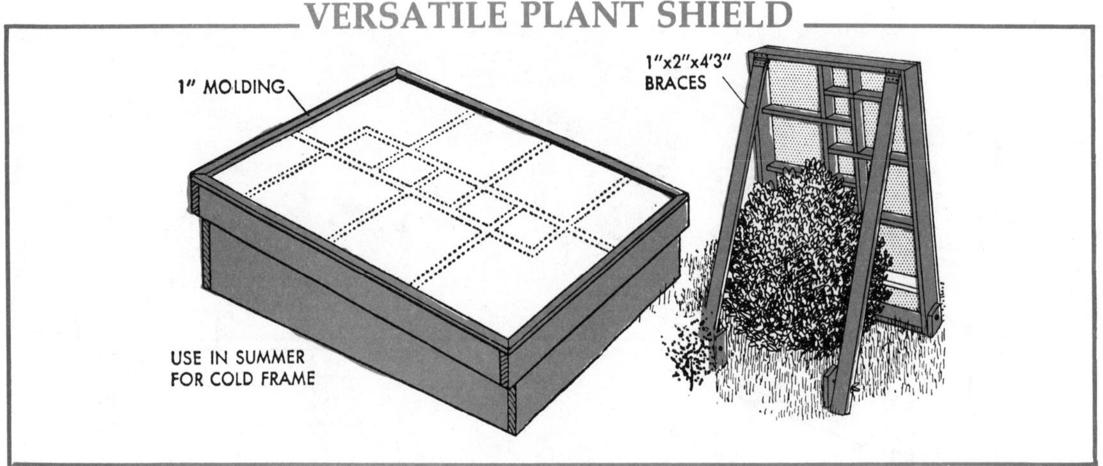

Wrapping plants with burlap or setting up a screen of old sacks makes a garden very unsightly. Make a wind-and-sun screen like this and anchor it with back braces and four stakes, using bolts and wing nuts to secure it, or hinge two frames together and anchor. Boxwood or evergreens will be protected and your garden will look neat all winter. In summer, use the shield as a cold frame cover, making the cold frame to fit inside the shield, and use the same hinges to attach to frame. Cover with plastic wire-screen cloth.

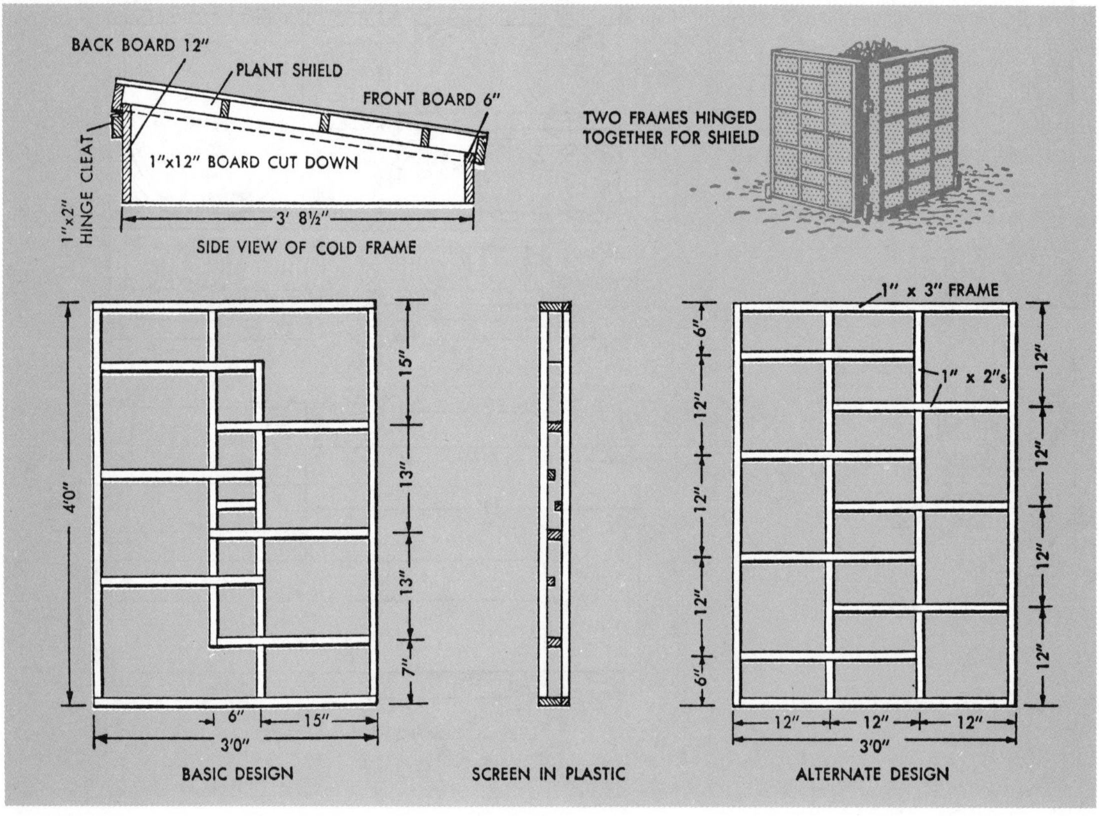

BACK BOARD 12"
PLANT SHIELD
FRONT BOARD 6"
1"x2" HINGE CLEAT
1"x12" BOARD CUT DOWN
3' 8½"
SIDE VIEW OF COLD FRAME

TWO FRAMES HINGED TOGETHER FOR SHIELD

4'0"
15"
13"
13"
7"
6"
15"
3'0"
BASIC DESIGN

SCREEN IN PLASTIC

1" x 3" FRAME
1" x 2"s
6"
12"
12"
12"
6"
12"
12"
12"
12"
12" 12" 12"
3'0"
ALTERNATE DESIGN

EVERY GARDEN CAN USE A COLD FRAME

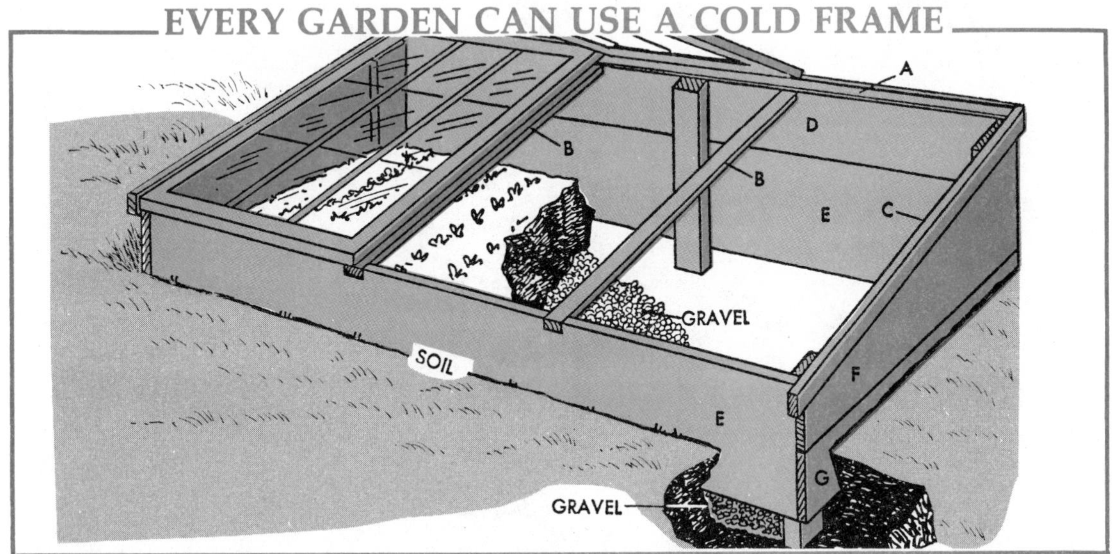

For starting seeds early, for wintering-over tender plants, and for starting perennials in late summer, nothing can replace a cold frame. Cypress sash already made up is convenient, if available, or make your own frames of durable wood topped with clear acrylic or Plexiglas. Sizes are usually: 2′×4′, 3′×4′, and 3′×6′, and come glazed or unglazed. For walls, cypress is preferred because it is long lasting; but other woods may be used if treated with wood preservative, replacing in a few years if necessary; or walls may be built of concrete or brick with wood frame around the top for hinging frame and a tight fit. Make a set of sash to fit frame, covering them with laths, to use when the weather warms enough to make shade desirable and glazed sash unnecessary. Propping block holds sash up at various levels.

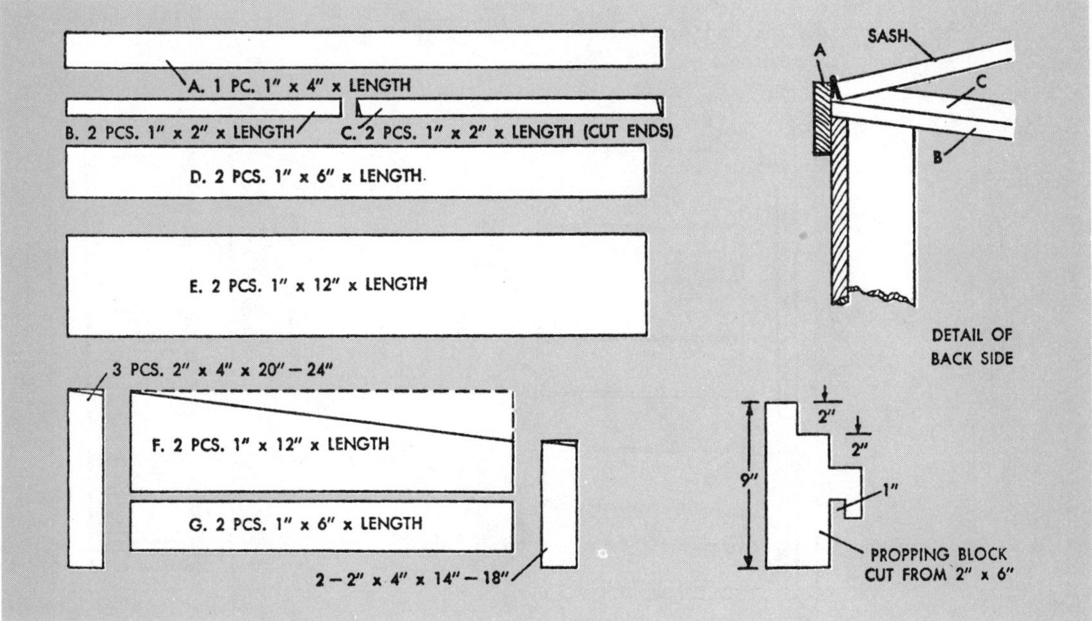

MAKE OVER UGLY DUCKLING DOORS

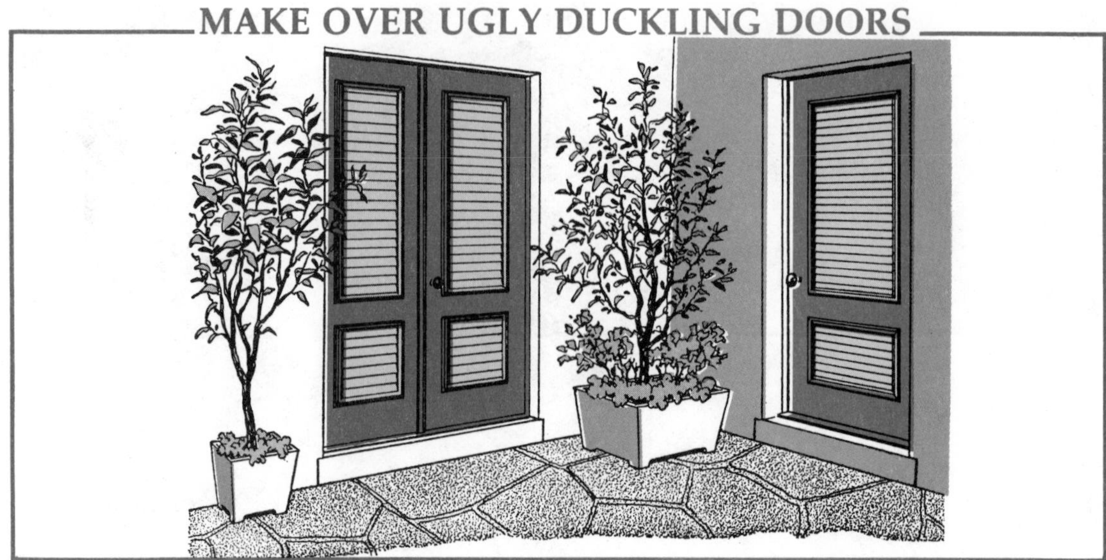

Old doors in bad condition or those which have panels of an ugly shape can be brought beautifully up to date. Cover them with a sheet of ½″ exterior plywood with moldings framing shutter-effect panels made from overlapping trellis slats. Use a base of 1½″ doorstop molding, secured to plywood with waterproof glue and brads, a second molding on top overlaps slats ½″. Either high-crowned or flatter moldings may be used for the second one, depending on the effect desired. Bore holes of lock, knob, and cut slots for hinges if necessary. Use wood preservative before painting, fasten plywood to door with waterproof glue or screws and nails of rustproof metal.

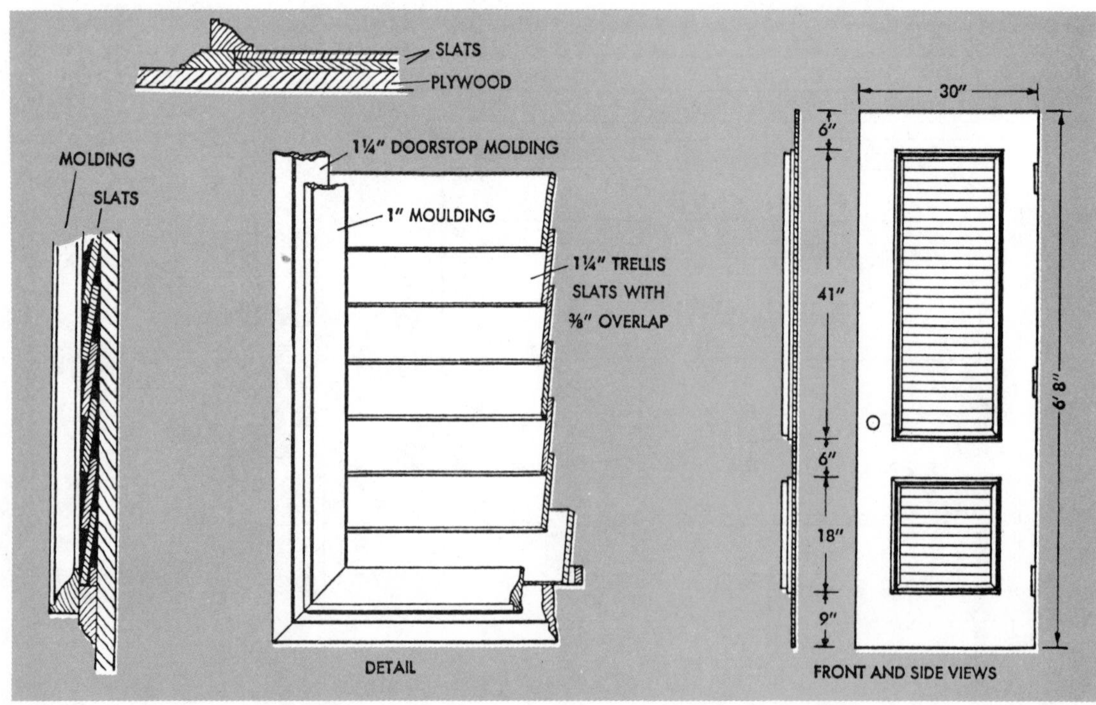

PROJECTS FOR SCRAP WOOD

Don't throw away scraps of good wood. Keep useful sizes in a box or bin in the workshop and use them for useful small projects. Because oddments seldom match, painting rather than staining is usually better for bringing harmony to the finished piece. Among many possible small projects are birdhouses and feeders, small pot plant boxes, plant trays, and tool racks. You can probably think of many others, maybe suggested by scraps themselves.

TRAY FOR SERVING OR FOR PLANTS

Make sides of clear scrap wood; glue the dowels in holes bored in the side pieces and support them with a central slat. Dowels will ensure good drainage for potted plants, yet make the tray light enough to carry glasses and plates from house to patio and serve as a tray, too. If good enamel is used, it can serve as a draining tray for washed glasses. Finish side bases with bits of matching moldings and use handsome brass drawer pulls for handles.

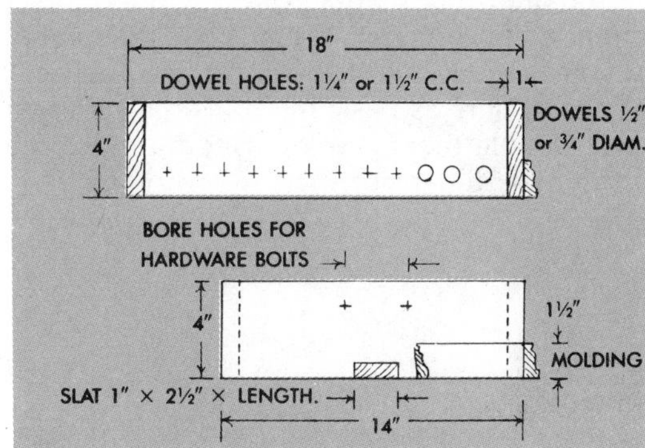

OPPORTUNISTIC STORAGE

Bare studs in a garage or shed let you build racks and shelves. To make tool racks, round wooden clothespins can serve as pegs. Squeeze the shanks to admit them into holes bored at intervals in 3" or 4" scrap boards. Pound lightly to set them; then amputate the excess on the back of the board. Fasten rack to studs.

Cut shelves to fit snugly between the studs. Support them on short cleats or by nails through studs. A cleat projecting slightly above the front of the shelf will help hold items inside.

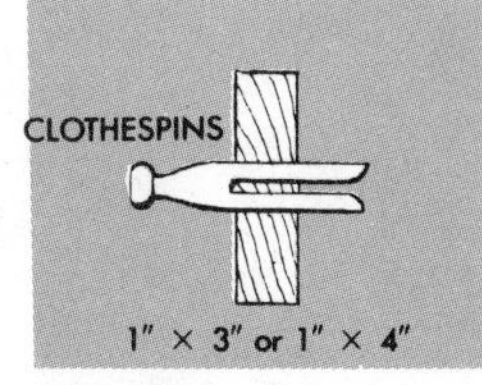

ENHANCE YOUR PLANT COLLECTION

All too often pot plants grouped indoors or put outdoors for the summer look junglish, untended and messy. A plant box adequate to house several pots or one for a single large pot enhances the looks of the plant and focuses interest on the foliage and flowers. Consider the boxes here as basic modules, but alter or extend them to fit the requirements of your own pots. Double them, triple, or add a half measure and adapt the applied exterior decoration to the new dimensions.

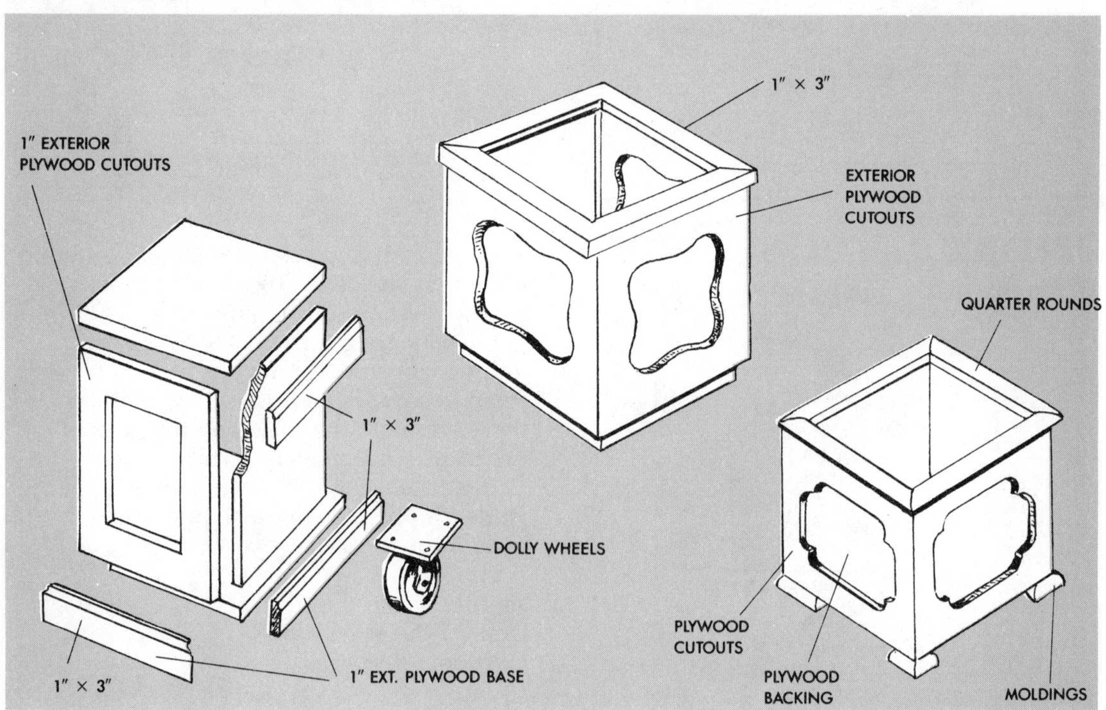

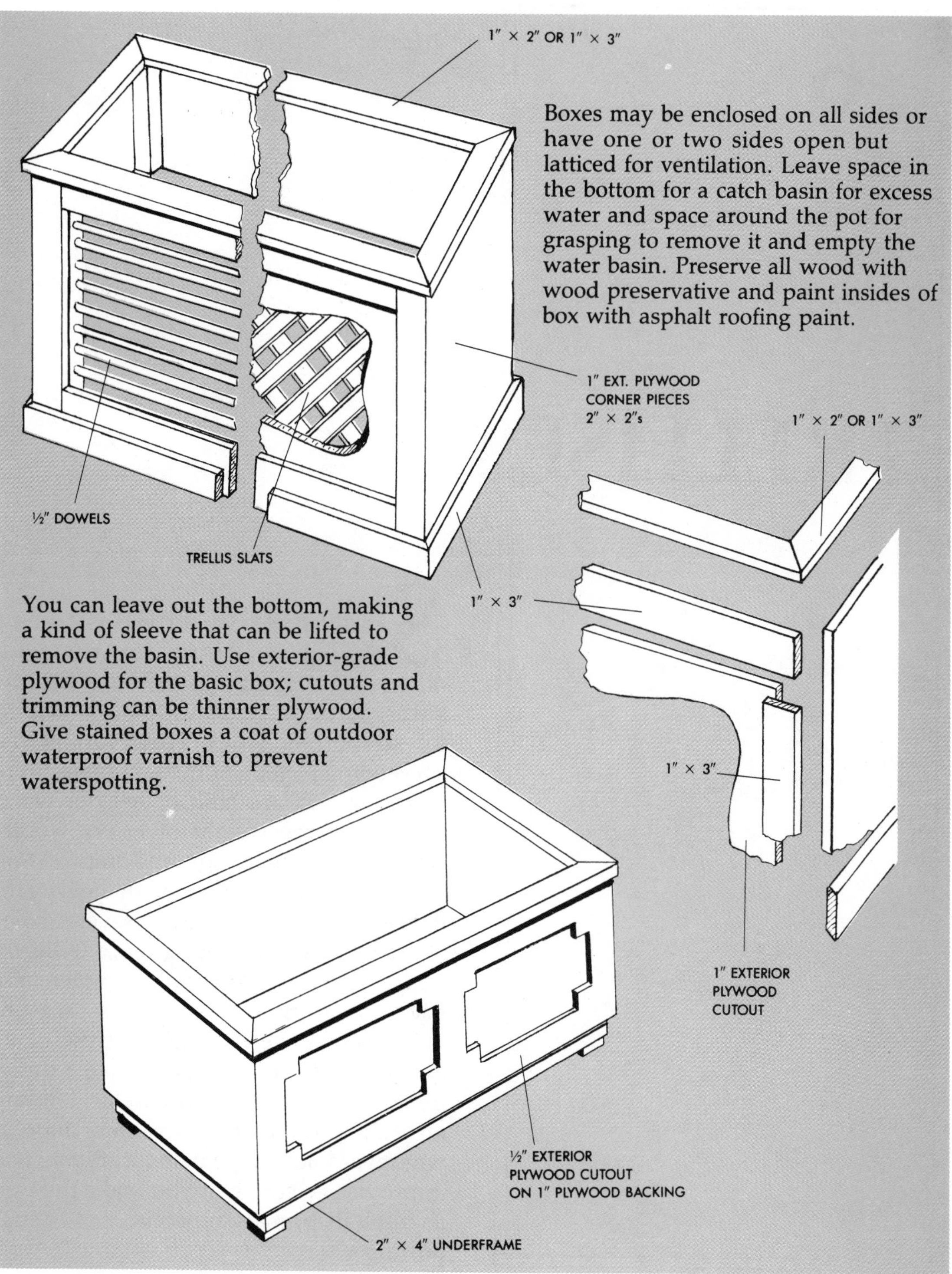

Boxes may be enclosed on all sides or have one or two sides open but latticed for ventilation. Leave space in the bottom for a catch basin for excess water and space around the pot for grasping to remove it and empty the water basin. Preserve all wood with wood preservative and paint insides of box with asphalt roofing paint.

You can leave out the bottom, making a kind of sleeve that can be lifted to remove the basin. Use exterior-grade plywood for the basic box; cutouts and trimming can be thinner plywood. Give stained boxes a coat of outdoor waterproof varnish to prevent waterspotting.

CHAPTER 6

TRELLISES

Strictly speaking, a trellis is a frame of light wood strips crossing each other, with open spaces between the strips, particularly such a frame as is used for supporting vines. However, in the succeeding pages a number of trellises are shown which are built of heavier wood to support the weight of heavy woody vines. Take any design and improve on it as you will, building it of heavier or lighter wood, or repeating it several times to make a wide screening-fence trellis on which growing vines will complete the cover-up during the outdoor season. Perhaps you will want to make two units and set them at an angle to give a three-dimensional quality to the trellis, lending an individual air to your front door or wherever you will be using it. But as you improvise be sure that you make the trellis fulfill its primary function, that of supporting vines.

CHOOSING A TRELLIS

In choosing a trellis, you will naturally start with the site where it is to be placed. This will govern the size, the design, and what you will plant to grow on it. In turn, what you are going to plant will influence the choice, because heavy vines require a heavy trellis, twining vines or vines with tendrils need a different kind of support, and so on. All these factors are tied in together, and all must be considered and worked out before the trellis is built.

Annual vines, as anyone who has grown morning glories can attest, may become quite heavy with the quick rush of growth in a single season. They often break the fragile strings which hopeful gardeners use as support, up which the vines twine so gaily when they are slender young plants. Perennial and woody vines also tend to become quite heavy with age and exert great pressures on any structure they climb, sometimes pulling roofs apart and even causing weak structures to collapse. You can see, therefore, that there is much more to choosing, planning, and building a trellis than would appear at first sight. On the other hand, there is nothing more calculated to give any house that final look of "home" than a bit of greenery twining around the door on a trellis which is as good to look at in winter as it was in summer.

Does your front door satisfy you? Is your back door merely a way of getting out of the kitchen to go to the trash can? Is there a starkness about the front of your garage which a trellis filled with roses would relieve? Perhaps the answer in all cases is a trellis and a vine. Your front door can be made different from its neighbors, your kitchen door a charming entrance which is a pleasure to use each day.

Is your home modern, traditional, French provincial, of Spanish or Mediterranean inspiration; built of brick or frame; one or two stories in height? All of these factors will be pertinent in your planning.

If your home is modern, perhaps it could stand a little restrained design: something slightly oriental in feeling, or perhaps just geometric without being dull and rigid. That is the trend in the newest modern homes today. If your house is traditional—Cape Cod or Georgian—you can give it a lift by using a trellis which is somewhat modern, but is restrained enough not to clash with the pure lines of the traditional house.

Possibly you will want to follow the 18th century precedent of using one of the modified Chinese patterns such as were employed for balustrades or porch railings, arbors, and fences in those early homes. Because they were simple in design, they somehow fitted very well with that classic inspiration from Italy which brought forth the English Palladian houses in the 18th century from which our own colonial architecture descended. Therefore, if you feel you need a precedent, you have an excellent one for choosing a Chinese fretwork design for your trellis.

If you are fencing the backyard or building a privacy fence around your patio, as so many of us are doing today, use a trellis as a gateway or as a fence topper, or to tie the fence in with the house. This will add a friendly touch and keep it from looking too coldly architectural by softening it with living greenery all through the growing season. And when the leaves have fallen, it will give the fence more interest during the bleakness of winter.

If you don't find exactly the trellis you have in mind in these pages, look through the other sections of this book and see if you find a design among the fences or other structures which you like. Adapt it. Be creative and use the design you like, but make it of the weight of material needed for your purpose and adapt its proportions as best you can to the space your trellis must occupy. Only one caution must be observed: Keep the design open and simple, making sure that it will integrate well with the lines of your house. And, of course, never forget that a trellis is primarily a vehicle for the support of vining plants, and only secondarily is it an entertainment for the eye.

THE VINE FOR YOUR TRELLIS

Most vines, like most children, are charming and inoffensive when they are small and youthful, but within a few years they may become veritable Frankensteins of monster proportions. But also like children, most vines, even rampant ones like wisteria or the trumpet vine, can be kept within bounds and relatively civilized by exercising care and discipline. Pruning shears in a firm hand will keep them at bay, and will even benefit wisteria, forcing it to bloom well. Trumpet vines may grow sulky and push up more shoots from the roots, making you think the "Frankenstein" story has changed into the

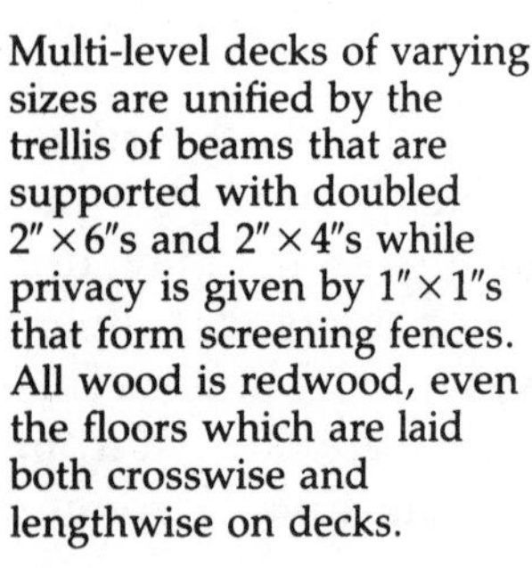

Multi-level decks of varying sizes are unified by the trellis of beams that are supported with doubled 2″ × 6″s and 2″ × 4″s while privacy is given by 1″ × 1″s that form screening fences. All wood is redwood, even the floors which are laid both crosswise and lengthwise on decks.

"Legend of the Dragon's Teeth." In any case, pruning is a chore under which you will chafe in years to come, so it is well to outwit it right at the beginning by choosing some lightweight, less rampant, and less demanding vine, possibly an annual one.

Roses, of course, leap to mind when a trellis is mentioned. It is a delight to see the wayward curves of a climbing rose threading its way through the crisp architectural lines of a good-looking trellis. If a pillar rose is planted, rather than one of the rampant climbers which may go up as high as 20 feet or more, the rose will not get out of bounds but will beautifully clothe your trellis with its blossoms, with a minimum of pruning on your part. Everblooming roses, such as 'Dream Girl,' 'American Pillar,' 'Summer Snow,' or any of the other excellent modern roses, are obtainable from all good nurseries. Yearly pruning, as recommended by your nursery when you buy them, will keep the roses strong and blossoming as you want them to do.

Clematis is another lovely vine, airy, light in weight, and with a wealth of fine flowers once it is established. It offers a good choice of color, time of bloom, and size of blossom. It blooms best when its roots are shaded, so a planting of low shrubs or perennial flowers to perform this function will protect it during the heat of summer. Perhaps you would like to plant two clematis of different colors on the same trellis to bloom at the same time, or to follow one another so that blooming time is extended. Consult your nursery for recommendations for your particular area. A lightweight trellis is adequate for clematis in most cases, for it is a lightweight vine.

Your trellis should be designed to suit the weight of the vine it supports. Style it to conform to the house or other background as in this trellis. A double clematis needs only an airy lightweight trellis—the top gracefully shaped to a point. Finials on the uprights give a final touch.

Akebia is another good perennial vine, the five-leaved variety being preferred by many who like its chocolate-colored flowers, which come in spring.

The bittersweet vine, *Celastrus scandens* for the north and *Celastrus angulatus* or *C. hypoleucus* in the south, can be kept within bounds easily and will give good results. The northern bittersweet makes a most spectacular presentation each autumn of masses of orange-colored pods. By doing your pruning each autumn, you will be able to use the cut pods indoors for bouquets each winter.

The silver lace-vine, sometimes called the Chinese fleece-vine, is a fast-growing climber. It will clothe the trellis each year with its largish leaves and a wealth of greenish-white flowers in clusters which do not belie either the lace or the fleece of its names. Cut back sharply each autumn or each spring, it will come back strongly if fed well.

For the northern sides of buildings or shady spots elsewhere, ivy can be trained over a trellis if a bit of patience is exercised. Tie it to the frame of the trellis until its rootlets attach, or until it is strong enough to support itself. Rough wood trellises will allow these rootlets to attach more readily than well-planed wood.

Climbing honeysuckle is another possible vine to use, but check first with local gardeners to see how it performs in your area. Some varieties in certain places become rampant climbers, which makes them unsuitable for small trellises, charming though the vine is.

A vine which is suitable for a trellis, whether placed on a fence, a roofed-over arbor, or even a pergola kind of trellis, is the grape. There is something rather pleasant about having a food crop climbing the trellis beside your outdoor room. It gives beauty of leaf all summer and makes a thick roof if allowed to climb on a shelter from the trellis, its ripening grapes giving off a perfume from each cluster. I remember a luncheon *al fresco* a few years ago in Italy beneath a pergola burdened with grapes, with the table laid beside a fence on which grapes also grew. It was very convenient to pick dessert without moving from my seat. But in America we must give a bit of thought to pests for which we must spray in many areas. This will discolor a painted trellis and may contaminate chairs and tables if the pesticide contains poisonous substances. Be sure to consider this before planting grapes.

The climbing euonymus, *Euonymus fortunei*, is an evergreen plant which can be kept within bounds by a bit of judicious pruning now and then. Its handsome dark-green leaves are very pleasant on white-painted trellises. It needs a good sturdy support, however, because it is a really permanent plant.

We must not forget the perennial sweet pea. This is a climber whose shoots die down annually, leaving the trellis clear for painting and other maintenance work and allowing its pattern to show and give distinction to its surroundings during the dreary days of winter. Pink, red, or white flowers are produced over a long season during the summer, the vine needing a minimum of care. They may be used as cut flowers, although they do not have the scent of their little annual sisters.

ANNUAL VINES MAY BE THE BEST CHOICE

Most trellis builders will agree that the annual vine is the best choice. There is a wide range to select from: lacy, finely cut leaves, bright green or dark green, heart-shaped or with multiples of various shapes on one stem—and in addition many colors and shapes of flowers from which to choose. Annual vines, of course, die down each autumn like the perennial sweet pea, permitting the growth to be removed and the trellis laid bare for winter maintenance and for displaying its beauty of design. Annuals grow from seeds and in most cases the growth is very rapid. In northerly regions they may be started indoors; then taken from their pots and placed in their summer location when the weather is sufficiently warm.

Possibly the favorite annual vine in America is the 'Heavenly Blue' morning glory, but 'Pearly Gates' (white) and 'Blue Star' (blue with a white star in the throat) are also beautiful. 'Scarlett O'Hara' or the new wine-red 'Darling' varieties may be used if red is desired.

Moonflower vines are nocturnal bloomers, and grow quickly to cover large areas in a manner similar to the morning glory. Their blossoms are white, opening in early evening to give forth a delicious scent, a factor to remember when you are planning a trellis beside a patio used in the evening. Planted on a trellis fence, alternating with blue morning glories, they give a day and night combination which will keep your trellises in bloom around the clock. In September, moonflowers stay open in the morning and morning glories remain open well into the afternoon, so that they bloom together in many areas at that time. Moonflowers are sometimes perennial in warm climates, and are tender and definitely only annual in the northern part of the country.

Perhaps you will want to grow sweet peas at the base of your trellis or on a trellis fence. This is a delightful idea, but in places with very hot summers sweet peas do not last beyond June, if that long. If you want to have them for the early summer only, all well and good, but be sure to have something to take over later.

Cobaea, or cup-and-saucer vine, is another annual climber which does well in many areas, its lavender-purple blossoms and rather open growth making it a good foil for a decorative trellis. It needs a long season in which to develop.

Cypress vine has very finely cut leaves and sports scarlet or white trumpet-shaped flowers. Lacy and delicate, it has the added attraction of staying below 10 feet, usually, as does its relative, the cardinal-climber. This is sometimes called 'Hearts-and-Honey' because its red trumpet flowers have a showy yellow center. These latter two vines are for decoration only, never growing thick or tall enough for a good screen or for shade.

Another dainty climber is the canary-bird vine, which has fringed, nasturtium-like flowers of rich canary yellow. It will grow in semi-shade—even prefers it—and likes a moist soil. Given these requirements it will be good for a trellis.

The balloon-vine has large, deeply cut leaves, and is more noted for its inflated seed pods than for its small white flowers.

Also more famous for its fruits than for its handsome, showy leaves is the gourd vine. It produces its fruits in a bewildering array of shapes and colors, beautiful to see on the vine and, when dried, equally beautiful and also useful for indoor decoration during the winter.

Mock-cucumber is a quick-growing native vine which will cover a trellis in no time. Although it covers thickly, it is actually a rather open plant in appearance, with lacy light-green leaves and tiny white flowers in profusion. The fruit is melon shaped, rather than long like a cucumber, and covered with soft spines all over its pale green surfaces.

Another plant which is decorative in flower is the scarlet-runner bean. It has spikes of bright red flowers and leaves somewhat similar to garden bean, though darker in color. Its relative, the lavender-flowered hyacinth-bean, is similar, producing lavender spikes of great beauty. Both will grow on strings which can be tied to the trellis, or they can be twined through the openings of a trellis.

The Japanese hop is a speedy, dense-growing vine which laughs at dry weather and heat. It will also grow in shade. A variegated form is popular in some sections and grows as well as the regular form, covering large areas quickly with decorative leaves. The fruits, or hops, are papery, resembling spruce cones.

MAKING YOUR TRELLIS

Once you have decided on the design and have considered carefully the site of your trellis so that you know what sort of vine you want to plant, you will come to the point of working out the kind and quantity of lumber necessary to build the trellis. Even though lumber is rather expensive these days, you should make the trellis heavier than you think it needs to be. It is better to err on the side of strength than to find, in a year or two, that the vine which was so tiny and innocuous has become a colossal "Frankenstein" of a vine.

Suggested dimensions and the sizes of lumber are shown in upcoming pages. Use these as guides, bearing in mind the probable weight of the vine you will grow. Also, only first grades of lumber should be used for trellises. They should be free from structural weaknesses such as knots and flaws, which may weaken the trellis and cause it to break just as your vine is getting to the point where it will be a thing of beauty. Then you would have to rebuild the trellis and spend double the time and money, in addition to waiting for the vine to recover.

Along this same train of thought, I urge you not to rush this work, either, but to take your time and cut the lumber carefully, fit it well, and put it together solidly. A job well done is done once. A job badly done must be redone, within a number of weeks, months, or years. Save on the cost of replacement and the labor involved by doing it right the first time.

Another means of saving labor and replacement costs is to use a good wood preservative (see Chapter 4) to prevent decay bacteria and moisture from entering and destroying your handiwork. Pay particular attention to those parts underground and to all cut edges, soaking the posts for an inch or two more than the depth they will be buried, even though they may be set in concrete.

Don't use creosote or any other preservative which gives off noxious gases in the soil and may injure or kill roots of vines planted nearby. Posts set in concrete are less likely to release toxic gases and cause trouble, however.

Speaking of concrete, I strongly recommend that posts always be set in a good solid base of concrete, not only to preserve the wood, but also to give stability to the trellis when the vine becomes heavy or when winter winds whip the structure about.

FINISHING THE TRELLIS AND AFTER-CARE

After the trellis is completed and the wood preservative applied (some prefer to give each individual piece its coating of wood preservative and even paint it before gluing, nailing, or screwing it finally in position) it is time to finish it with paint or stain. Follow the recommendations of the paint manufacturer as detailed on the can, or in folders put out by the better paint companies. You will find that at least two, but more frequently three, coats of good outdoor paint should be used. The first coat fills the grain, the second seals it, with the third coat completely sealing

TO AID YOU IN SELECTING ANNUAL VINES

Name of vine	*Usual height*	*Cultural notes*	*Flower color*
Balloon-vine	10′-15′	Full sun, good soil.	White
Canary-bird vine	10′-18′	Shady, moist soil.	Canary yellow
Cardinal-climber	10′-15′	Sunny, good soil.	Red
Cobaea scandens Cup-and-saucer vine	10′-30′	Sow seed edgewise; germinate quickly.	Lavender-purple
Cypress vine	10′	Soak seeds in warm water 4 hours, then plant.	Red and white
Gourd vine	8′-20′	Full sun, good soil, not particular.	Fruit various
Hearts-and-honey	10′-15′	Sunny, good soil.	Red with honey-yellow throat
Japanese hop vine	to 25′	May self-seed freely and become a pest. Variegated variety is decorative.	Papery conelike fruits are a feature
Mock-cucumber	8′-15′	Sun, any soil.	White, green fruit
Morning glory Heavenly blue Pearly gates Blue star Scarlett O'Hara Darling	10′-15′	Any good soil, full sun, soak seeds 4 hours before planting outdoors.	 Blue White Pale blue Red Wine red
Moonflower	10′-20′	Same as for morning glory.	White
Sweet pea Cuthbertson varieties	4′-8′	Early planting, cool climate best. Sub-irrigation may take them through to July.	Various

the first two and preserving them so that they will not need attention for two years. Every winter, when the vine has shed its leaves and you can see the trellis well, inspect it carefully to see if there are any sprung joints, blistering paint spots, or cracks in the paint coat where decay organisms may enter, particularly around the base.

If you find the joints sprung, try to clamp the wood back together, after filling the joint with waterproof glue mixed with sawdust. If the joint is a narrow one, fill it with either putty or caulk and let it dry for a few days before repainting it. If blisters occur, wire brush them and sand down the edges of the solid paint; then use wood preservative and let it dry for a half day or more before repainting, giving the spots two coats and repainting the entire trellis with the third coat. Where cracks occur, treat in the same manner before giving the final coat.

Each time you repaint, wait for a warm and sunny day, or at least a warm one. Cold weather slows down the absorption of paint into wood cells and may not give as complete adherence as is needed. By the time the weather has again warmed sufficiently to permit the paint to soak in, the surface paint will have evaporated and dried, decreasing appreciably the penetrating capacity of the paint and consequently its lasting qualities. Never paint unless the weather will be above 55°F during the day on which the painting is to be done. Early fall or late spring are the preferred times. Many do-it-yourselfers feel that the best time for painting is in the early days of spring, when the weather is more likely to become warmer than colder, rather than in the autumn. The paint will completely dry within a few warm days, and they claim that because the fresh paint job is spared the ravages of winter it will look smarter and better through the growing season. I believe that it is immaterial *when* the job is done as long as it is done whenever the trellis *needs* painting. If the old coat is sufficiently intact to carry it through the winter, all well and good, provided that you are sure spring garden tasks will not interfere with painting in the spring.

A WORD ABOUT COLOR

When you are considering the paint you will use and choosing the color, take note of the color of the house and its trim, of the fence, and of adjacent buildings. Consider also the color of the blossoms or the leaves of the vine you will be using. White is always a good, safe paint color, but not always the most imaginative. Some trellises, particularly those which must endure winter bareness because of the departure of annual vines, might be painted either to match the trim of the house, if the walls of the house are white, or keyed to the color of the blossoms of the annual vines. The color should harmonize with the leaves and flowers of any flowering shrubs or plants in the vicinity, too. If you have bright yellow- or blue-green-leaved plants, be sure to take this into account in choosing your color.

Occasionally a trellis may be painted with two colors, picking up the basic wall color of the house to tie it into the general effect; then using the trim color for the inner frame, for crossbars, or in some other way echoing the second color of the house without ever allowing it to become too obtrusive. Never use color for color's sake or you may find that even *you* don't like it when it is finished, let alone how it affects the neighbors! But if color is used well, you may find yourself the envy of the street, even if nobody tells you so. You'll find your neighbors copying the principle, and you'll know.

WHAT A TRELLIS IS NOT

You may well want to consider some facts of life before constructing a trellis. You will have to face the fact, sooner or later, that children live not only in the big world but in your immediate vicinity. Even though your own little angels may not be inclined to emulate Tarzan and climb up the trellis, others will. It is part of the child's nature. If this is a problem for you, then be sure to build the trellis strong enough so that it not only will support a child but can become an informal Jungle Gym if necessary. Maybe the answer will be to build some sort of climbing apparatus elsewhere for the children; and then, to make doubly sure of your trellis, if you are a demon gardener as well as a parent, plant a good thorny climbing rose on it, standing guard with shotgun or club until the rose is large enough to fend for itself.

A trellis is not a ladder, nor is it a trapeze. It should not offend the eye of the beholder, either. This is my main objection to the usual trellises offered for sale. They were never good designs and they haven't changed in fifty years or so; or if they have, it has only been in the direction of fanciness. Bad design is boring, and a million trellises of bad designs are something more than a million times as boring. You will take pride in your own trellis, on the other hand, because it is unique and was chosen to fit your house, and yours alone. It will be worth any effort you may wish to put into its building, if only for that reason.

Most of the commercially made trellises are cheap because they are badly made of too-light materials. They are too flimsy to support the weight of vines, and that is why, after a season or two of use, they sag and look so sad. The answer is to build your own trellis, choosing it for its suitability with the architecture of your house, and thereby achieving distinction.

Plastic and metal trellises are usually t be avoided, in my opinion. Aside from the un-beautiful curves and curlicues of most of them, there is the problem of heat. They are likely to get very hot in the broiling sun of summer, and certainly such heat will do the vines no good. However, some of the metal mesh or hardware cloths can be used on trellises because they are light in weight and would not hold heat for long, being made of such thin wires. They are very well suited for use with certain types of vines which like to cling with tendrils. The metal meshes which can be detached and rolled up when the house is to be painted, or when the vines have gone their way with the season, also may be worthy of consideration, but my concern is not with them.

Pipes and iron rods are not usually conducive to easy handling nor to true beauty, unless elaborate jigs and various kinds of tools are obtained in order to bend them into shape. That is why I have chosen wood as the material in designing these trellises. It is the most easily worked, least expensive, and most long-lasting material at our disposal today. You can do a good job with it, using a minimum of time and labor.

FOUR-SQUARE TRELLIS

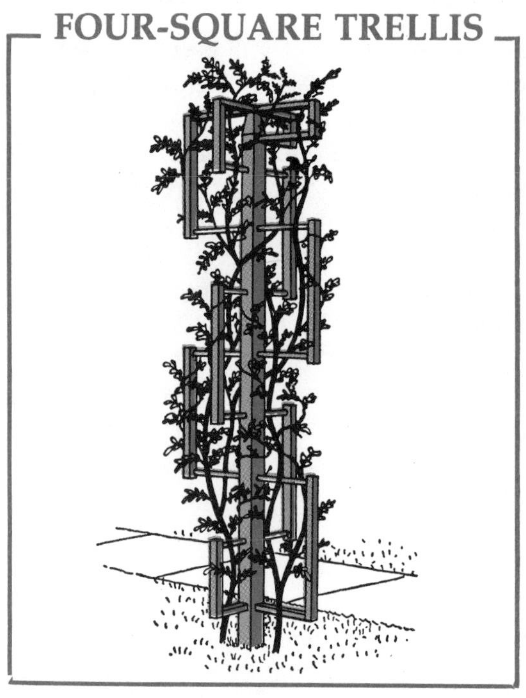

A trellis for a vine which will clothe all four sides of the central post, which will be interesting in winter because of its unique pattern and yet which will afford summer security for heavy vines, roses, or other climbing plants, is hard to find. This one will look well all year and will also be transportable—a factor for renters—if you should decide to move. If desired, of course, the central post may be set in concrete. Note that the post is tapered at the top to the width of the 5/4" × 5/4" stock used for cross pieces. They are overlapped as explained in the detail drawing and toenailed to the post where dowels are not used at base and top.

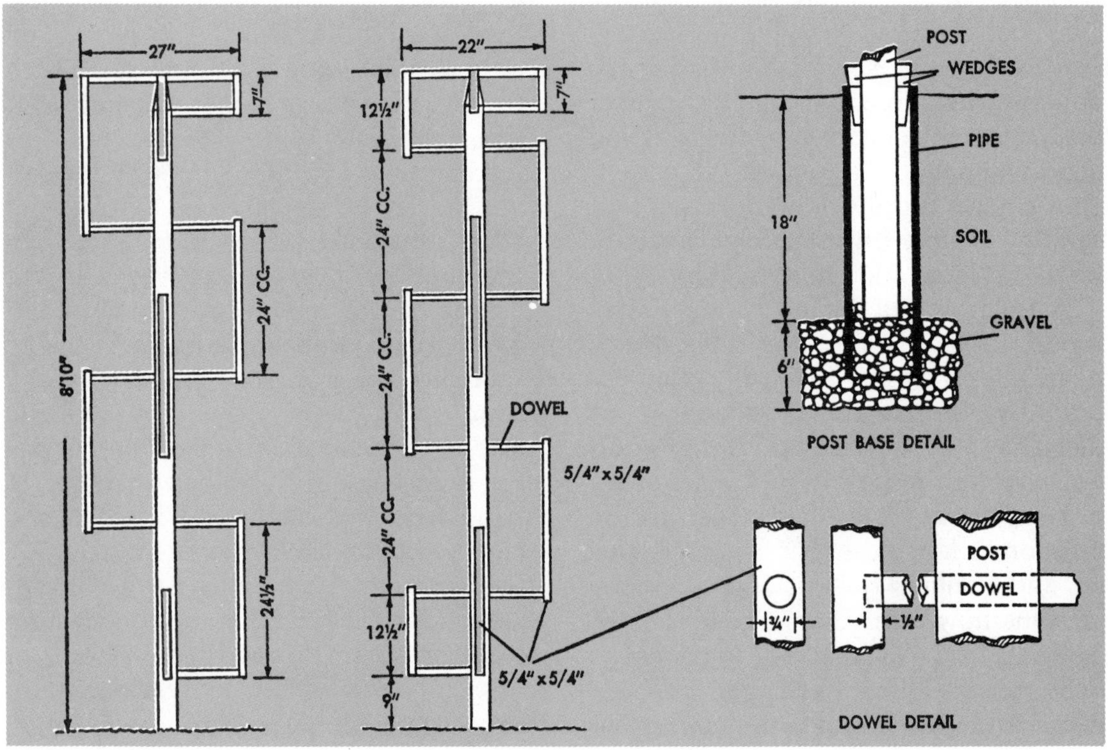

FRENCH PROVINCIAL TRELLIS

So many houses, both old and new, have taken the French provincial style for their motif of design that a trellis might well follow out the general scheme. Exterior plywood jigsawed out to the graceful lines shown in the scale detail at right makes the "window" which frames the lattice and vines. The frame of 2"×4"s is securely set in concrete, the lattice and plywood held in place by moldings mitered at corners. A 4'×8' sheet of ¼" plywood is used in this version but design may be adapted as desired. Plywood center may be used for another project if care is used in cutting. Use wood preservative on exposed edges.

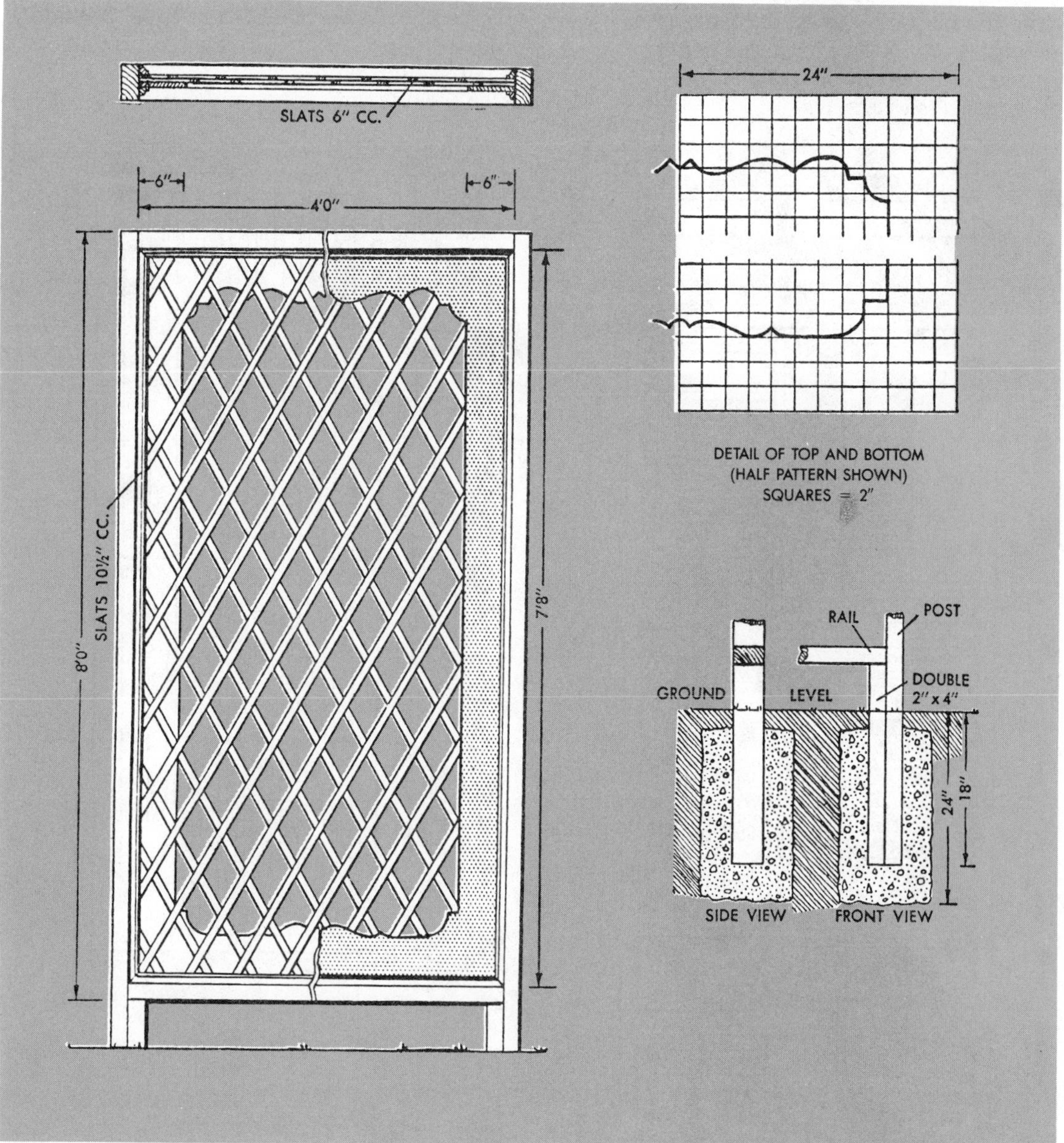

STRIPES AND RECTANGLES

This trellis combines both strong horizontals and verticals, making a good contrast to the informal, natural curves of a vine, and will give many good strong shadow lines as well as a sturdy framework to which can be fastened climbing or pillar roses, or some other vine which needs a strong support. The framework is made of 2″ × 4″s while the interior portion is made up of rectangles of 1″ × 2″s in various combinations, fastened in place with rust-resistant nails or screws.

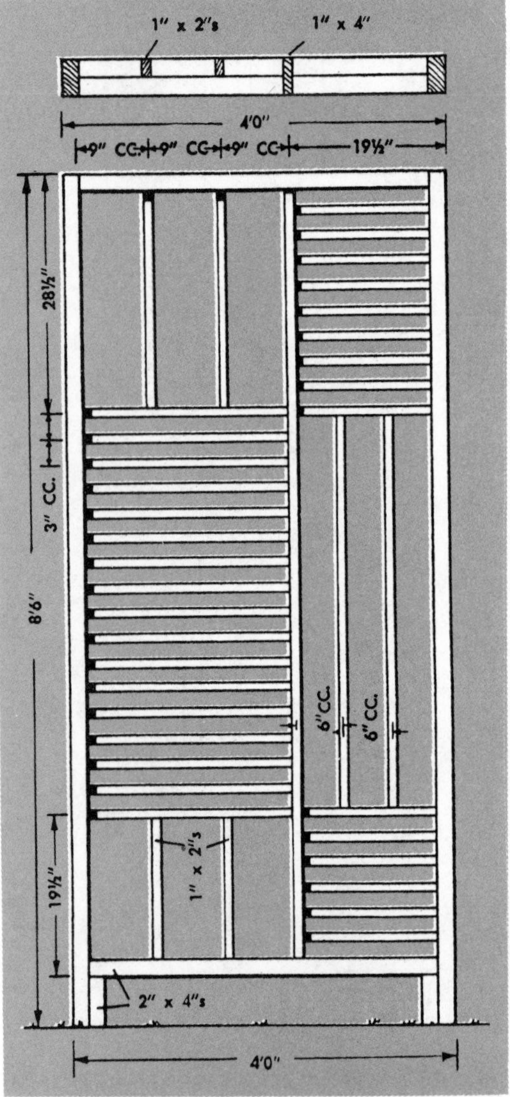

STRICTLY VERTICAL

For twining annual vines a light frame of this sort is sufficient. Morning glories, moonflower, and runner beans will twine about the vertical trellis strips nailed or screwed to the back side of the 2″ × 4″ frame with a 1″ × 4″ center bar. Frame the back side with a wider trellis strip on all four sides. Note that in both of these trellises the frame 2″ × 4″s are doubled at base, bolted together and set in concrete for protection against high winds.

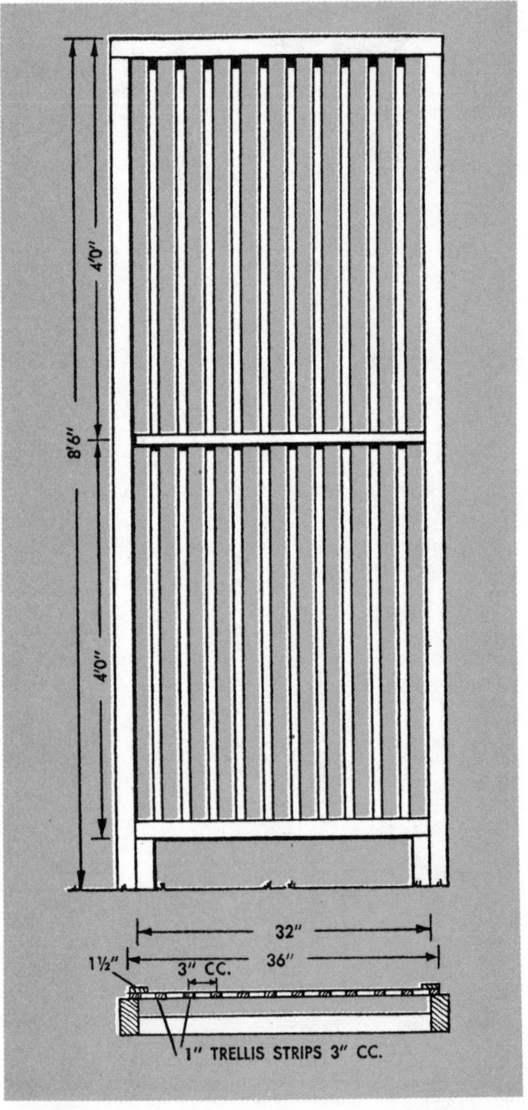

ORNAMENTAL SCREEN AND TRELLIS

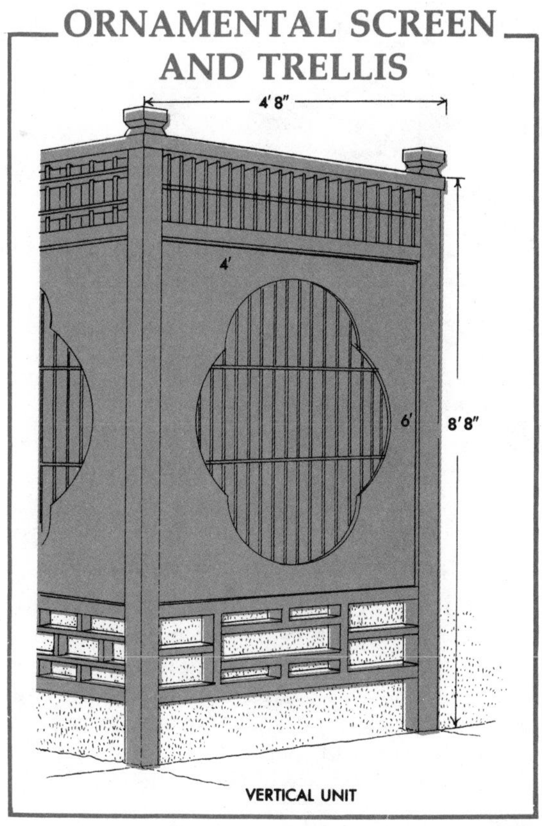

VERTICAL UNIT

To assure privacy if you have a picture window, you can make a decorative screen such as this. A woody vine with an interesting growth habit can complement the screen's delicate tracery. The screen is built of exterior plywood, cut to reveal trellis slats slotted together (see detail), screening the view and also the force of the wind, yet allowing some air circulation.

Such a structure angled in tandem as shown may also be used to shelter a valuable shrub, or may be used as a single panel to protect a door from prevailing gales. Below, the design is turned horizontally, with the slatwork still contributing a somewhat oriental effect. Slats and frame may be painted in a color that contrasts with that of the plywood.

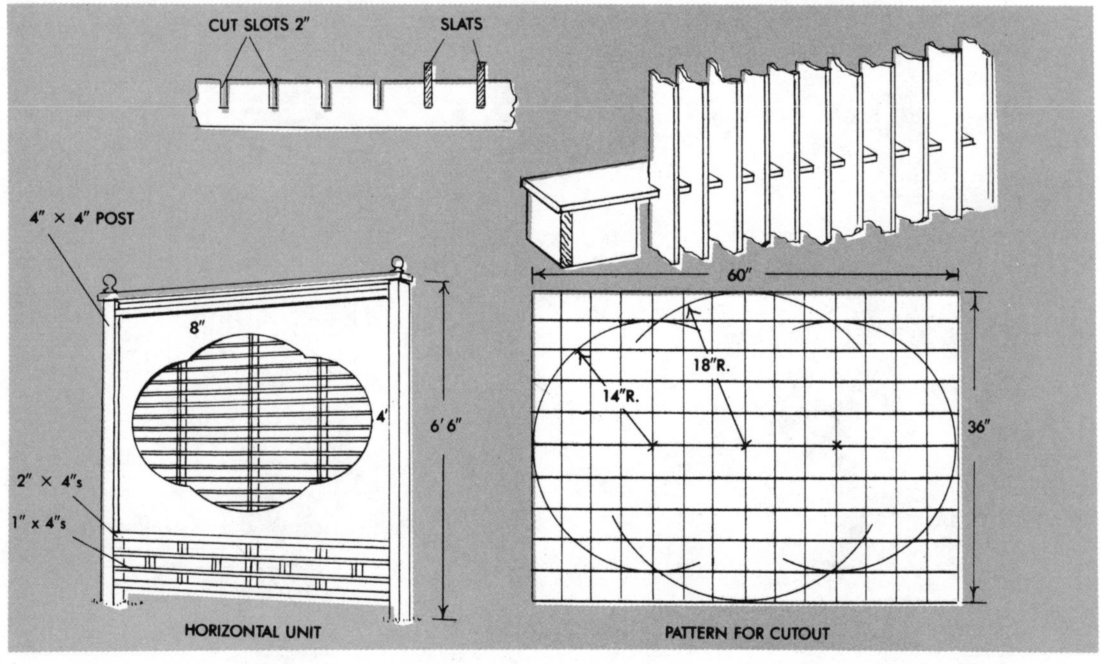

HORIZONTAL UNIT

PATTERN FOR CUTOUT

A SLATTED PRIVACY FENCE

This fence provides reasonably good visual privacy and allows air circulation, but tempers gusty winds to make a patio or deck pleasant many months of the year. The pergola-like top adds a high note of summer greenery. Keep it utterly plain and simple or, for greater privacy and to add decorative effect, consider using one of the slat patterns on the next page. The slat patterns reduce air flow but will provide better climbing purchase for annual vines. Fill the plant bed below the fence with ground-cover plants to cut maintenance. But in summer, set in pots of flowers, replacing them through the season with new ones in bloom.

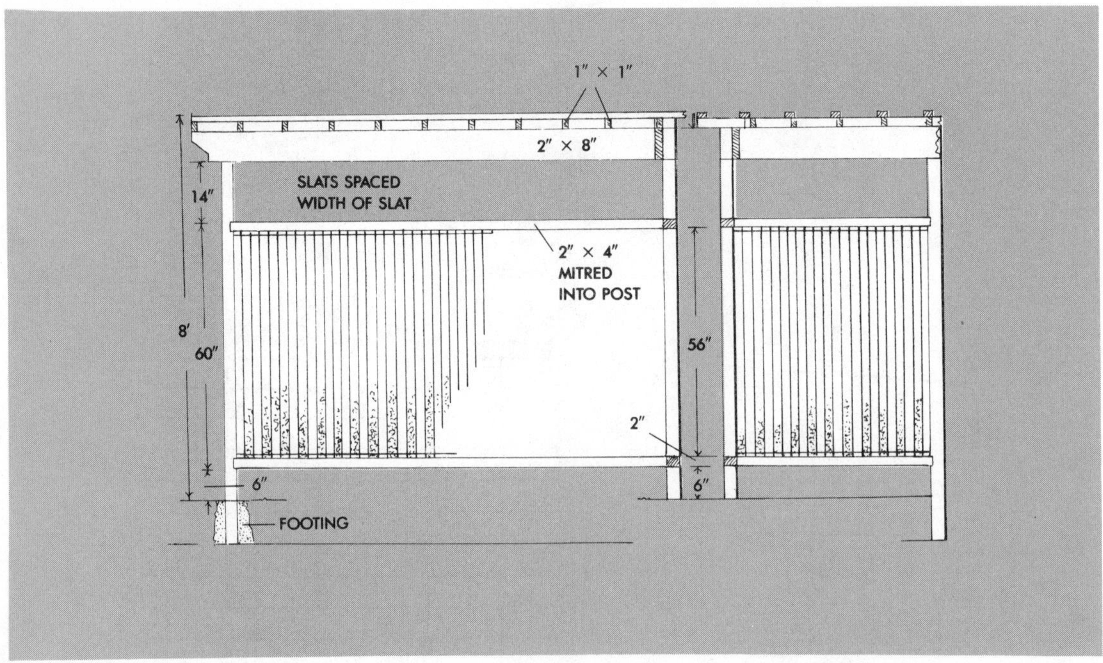

FENCE CONSTRUCTION

Ends of 2″ × 8″s may be cut square, slanted, or curved as shown.

1. Vertical slats, either 1″ × 2″s or 2″ trellis slats equally spaced, are held in place by quarter-rounds or 1″ × 1″s nailed on frame. The gate has a 2″ × 4″ frame, slatted to match the fence.
2. Diagonal lattices, either spaced to slat width or more widely, are most successful where the exciting pattern does not distract too much.
3. Horizontal lattice is calmer and may be equal-spaced in box fashion or only the upper section crossed for privacy reasons, with lower parts left open for ventilation and to vary the pattern.
4. Combination lattice uses trellis slats vertically, with 1″ × 2″s as crossbars or a mixture of 1″ × 2″s, 1″ × 3″s to provide more variety.

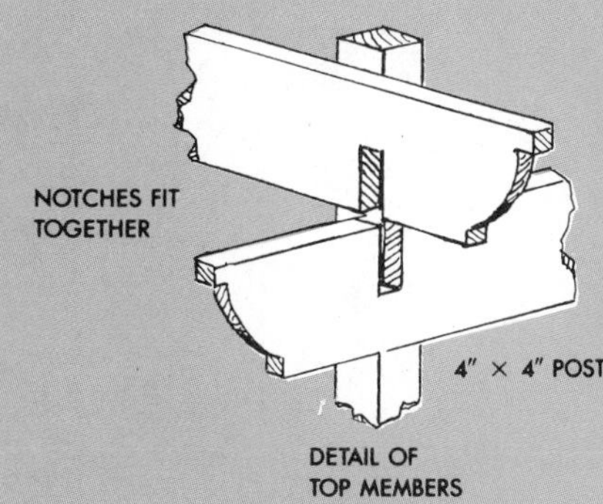

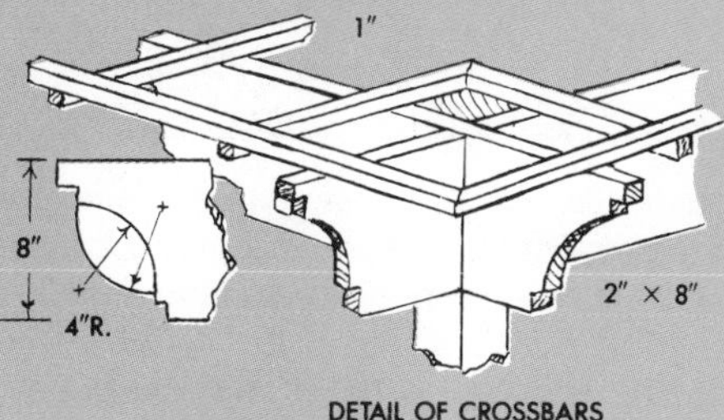

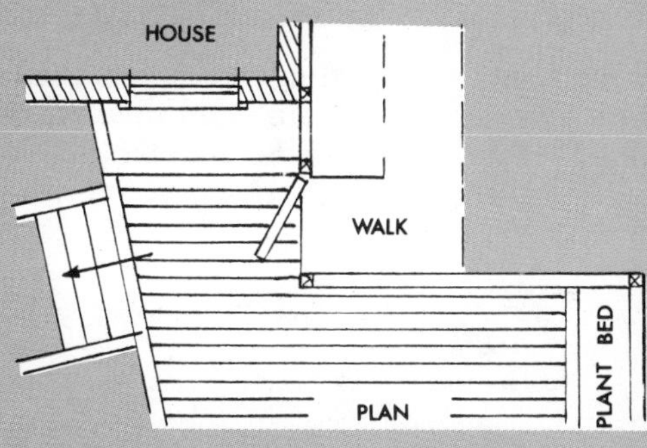

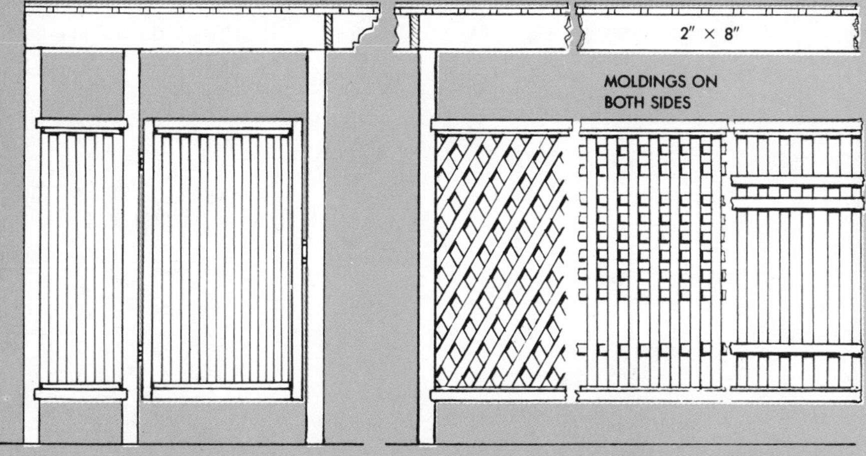

TRELLIS-TOPPED VIEWBREAKER FENCE

A simple fence to embellish patios while protecting them from prying eyes hoists the fence part to screen the eye level and leaves the ground level open for ventilation. Shown here for covering is wire screen set in plastic, but various other materials will be adaptable: 1″ × 2″ mesh welded-wire fencing, thin, wide basketwoven boards, bamboo roll-up shades, snowfencing, or woven reeds may be used.

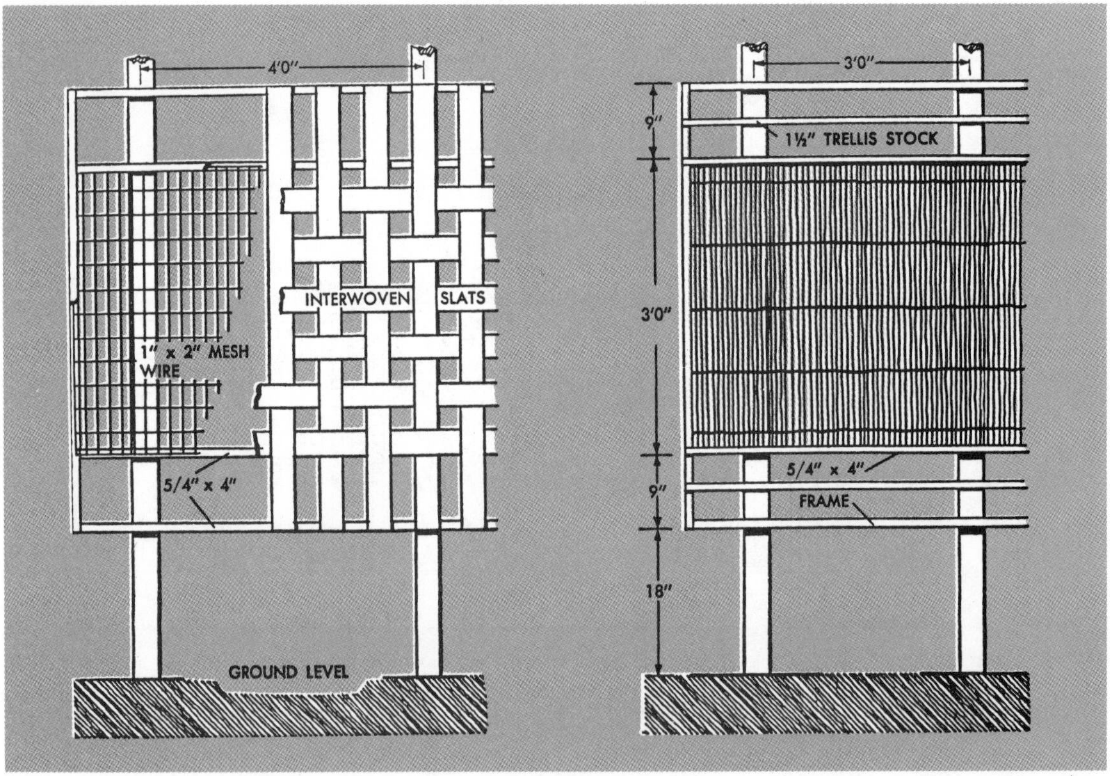

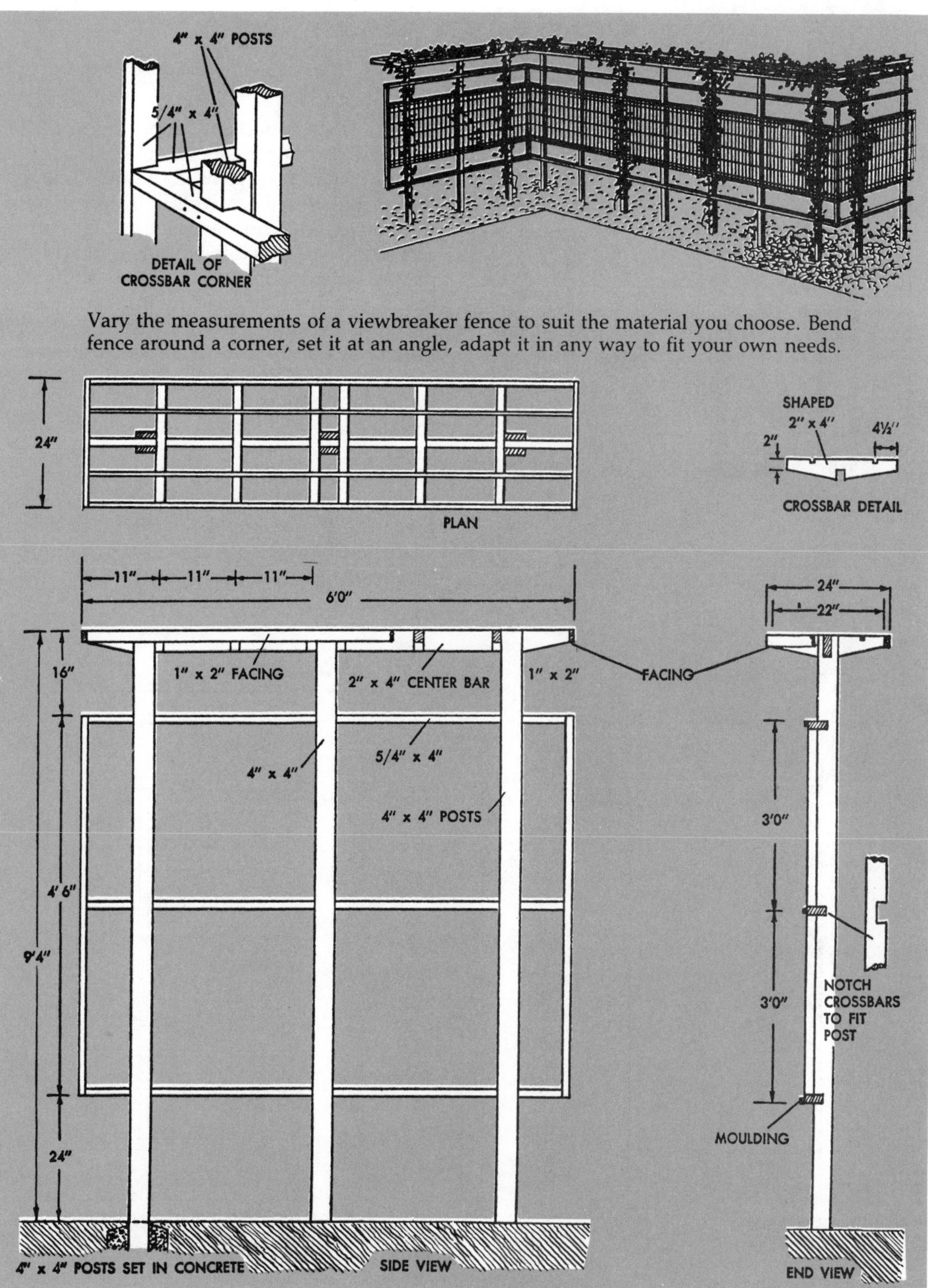

Vary the measurements of a viewbreaker fence to suit the material you choose. Bend fence around a corner, set it at an angle, adapt it in any way to fit your own needs.

THE DOORSIDE TRELLIS

Many a door is perfectly good, but dull. The addition of a trellis can make it a distinguished feature of the house. Use a design which will go well with the style of the house, and choose a vine which will stay within reasonable bounds and add its picturesque quality to the design of the trellis. All three designs are built on one basic framework of 2″ × 4″s with the horizontals and verticals inside built of 1″ × 1″s or 5⁄4″ × 5⁄4″s. Trellises can be attached to the house as shown on left, or be freestanding like those below, with the two major vertical members sunk into concrete after being carefully treated with wood preservative. The vertical at right angles to these members should have a ½″ to 1″ space left between the end and ground level to prevent moisture and rot.

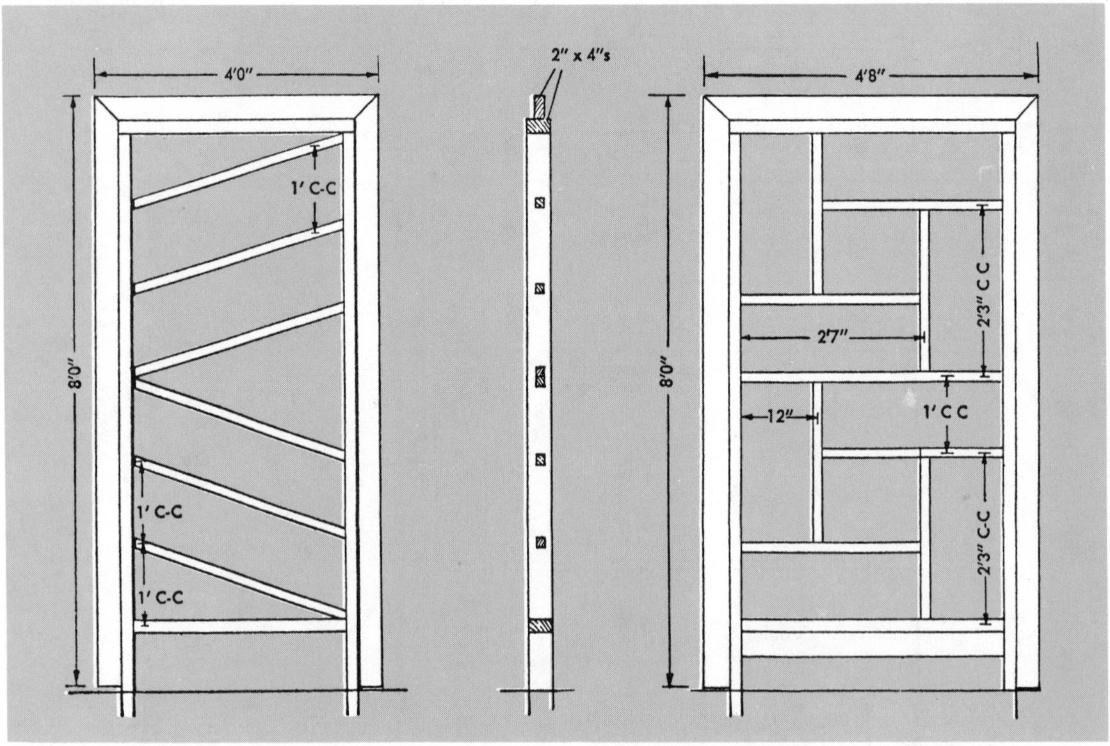

4′0″
1′ C-C
8′0″
1′ C-C
1′ C-C
2″ x 4″s
4′8″
2′3″ C C
2′7″
8′0″
12″
1′ C C
2′3″ C-C

SIMPLE DOORSIDE TRELLIS

Simplicity is the keynote of good modern design, and the crisp architectural lines of this simple trellis will complement and contrast well with the flowing natural lines of the vines that will grow on it. The two versions shown are related but give completely different effects. On the left is a design that has the slats all on the front, set into the frame and set flush with each other, while that on the right has narrow slats attached to the outside of the frame, and one set on the front, the other on the back, alternating in placement. If annual vines are used, so that trellis is bare in winter, perhaps painting slats in contrasting colors would give a gay, all-year effect, providing the colors were chosen to harmonize with summer blossom colors. Use wood preservative on exposed edges.

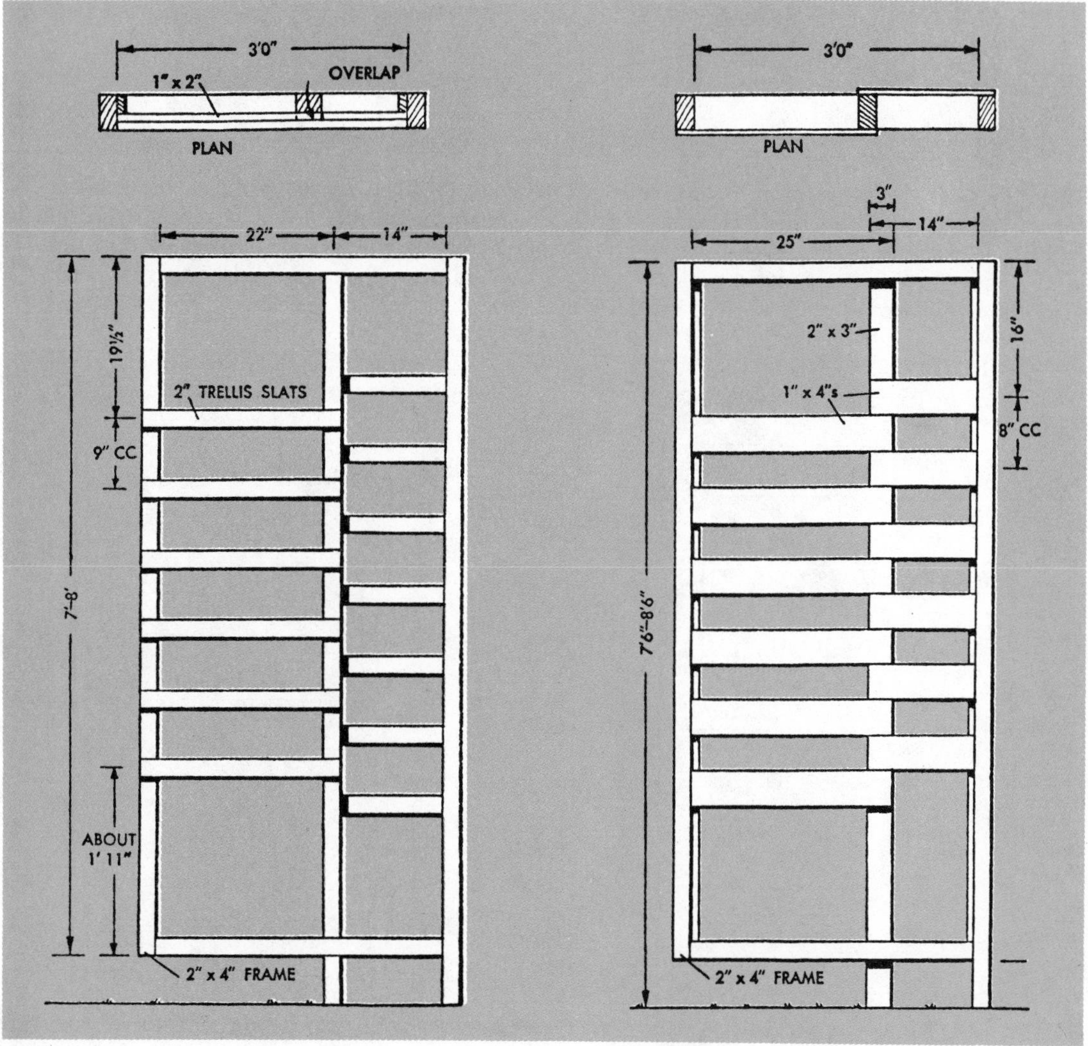

TRELLIS FENCE ENDERS

To relieve the starkness of a fence beside a bare wall, end the fence with a trellis such as these. Construction is similar to that on page 80, the top members merely being extended to meet the house and bridge the walk. The fence shown is built of grooved plywood but might be built of 1″×4″s or 6″s nailed on the 2″×4″ framing, posts sunk in concrete. Both designs below would complement modern houses.

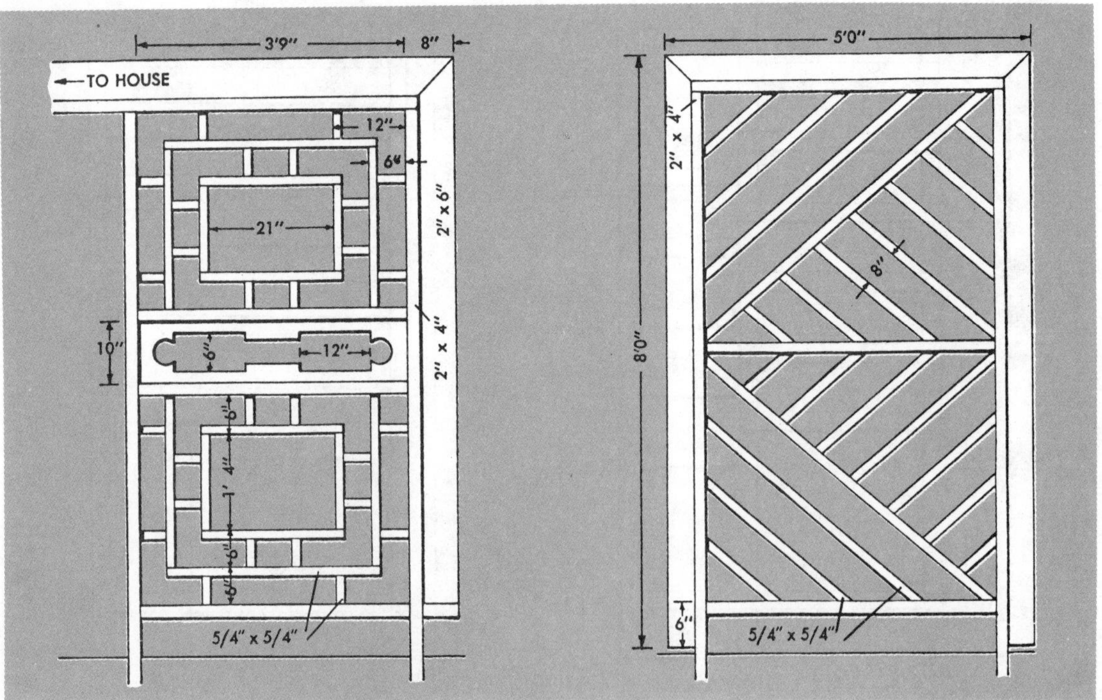

CHAPTER 7

FENCES

Sometime in the dim prehistoric days beyond the memory of man, an ancestor of the race began to cultivate the land and grow food plants. He soon found that the animals of the forest also enjoyed this food, so protection became necessary; and in order that other humans might know that these superior food products were the result of private enterprise and not the bounty of nature, some boundary line was needed to mark the limits of his endeavors. Therefore the fence came into being.

Since that long-ago time, of course, the fence has gone through many developments. It has been an important means of adding to the beauty of a garden; it has frequently provided its owner with a means of conspicuous display of wealth, as it embellished property; and, of late years (as well as earlier), it has been an important way of providing visual privacy. Sometimes the fence has served merely as a definition of the property lines, or as a kind of openwork background for a shrub border or flower bed; again, it has at times been a kind of horizontal trellis for vines, full of beauty when the flowers and leaves of the vine clothe it, and continuing through the drab days of winter to offer its own charm of architectural pattern to brighten those dismal, barren months of the year.

FENCES OF YESTERYEAR

During the Victorian era fences had developed into amazing structures, serving a function far beyond that of excluding unwanted animals or marking the boundary between the public street and the private areas of the home property. They became as elaborate, as loaded with gingerbread design, as the whatnots inside the houses. Sometimes they were built of iron, with imposing stone gateposts and with stone posts supporting the weight of the elaborate fence. More frequently, jigsawed wood attempted to imitate the whorls and arabesques of the iron fences. Even the circular flower beds in the lawns were fenced with low iron or wooden fences, and low iron fences surmounted the ridgepoles of house roofs. Eventually, of course, people tired of this nonsense and sought something new.

In America the fence began to disappear, and front yards all along the street were incorporated, visually, into the public area of the street. The resulting open, park-like look of our streets has often excited comment from visiting Europeans. They do not like the absence of fences, particularly in back gardens where fences have been omitted or wire netting used to clothe the fence frame, and their remarks on the American lack of privacy are valid. That is why there is a return of the fence today: primarily to give us privacy from trespassers and from intrusive glances of passersby.

The fence today fulfills several definite functions. It encloses the yard to keep children in and animals out; it offers, many times, an architectural finish to the home composition, enhancing the lines of the house, lengthening or shortening the property and buildings visually; and, above all, the modern fence produces the privacy that America is now mature enough to want. We are discarding the old pioneer idea that we live in a wilderness, and we are realizing that communal life in civilized areas entails a loss of that privacy which is necessary to the mature individual.

Let us take up these points and examine them further. Our small children must play out-of-doors to get healthful sunshine and air and to get them out from underfoot. Often we find that the children's play yard is enclosed beside a patio, where it can be overseen from inside the house as well as from outside. All gardeners will recognize the need for keeping animals (except one's own) out of gardens, where they may trample flowers and ruin it in other ways. Therefore, the backyard at least must be fenced. A good fence will provide a beautiful backdrop for the scene we set for our summer activities. The whole family now lives outdoors in clement weather, and eating, entertaining the family's friends day or evening in the backyard has become a way of life.

As we drive around the subdivisions which have sprung up about every city and many towns, we see how well fences can fulfill their function of extending the lines of the house, of providing an architectural finish to the property. Many a row house in a subdivision, indistinguishable from its neighbors, suddenly achieves an identity when a good fence is added which harmonizes or contrasts with the house. The use of materials which lend pattern or texture, or both, is one of the most stimulating and interesting of the many new facets of the trend in home building. Look through the designs for fences which follow this section and see how the long lines are emphasized in some; how fences are kept low to give long, wide lines to a property which may be quite narrow. If the house is one of the long, low modern homes, this will harmonize with it and produce a visual width quite at variance with the actual measurements.

PRIVACY FENCES

As plots of ground become increasingly smaller with the mushrooming expansion of suburban areas around our towns, Americans have felt a need which is met by the "privacy fence." This is not to be confused with what our grandmothers called a "spite fence"—a high fence built to show a neighbor the degree of contempt felt for him and all he represented. A "spite fence" was high, ugly, and as undecorative as possible on the side facing the scorned neighbor. It bears little resemblance to the handsome, tall, good-neighbor fences which today ensure privacy on both sides and are usually erected with mutual consent; sometimes with mutual funds. Such a well-planned fence, good to look at on both its sides, removes

Panels alternate on both sides of a 2″ × 4″ framework on 4″ × 4″ posts, overlapped 3″ to maintain privacy, yet provide for air circulation. Masonite grooved siding is moisture-resistant, yet can be painted. Note the matching gate in the fence by the house.

An attractive garden, viewed from an indoor bathroom, is surrounded by privacy fences of two kinds: redwood framed fence, right, is faced with solid light-colored boards, and redwood staves with shaped tops echo the line effect, left, of the platform outside windows.

a cause for friction immediately, and good neighbors are more likely to remain good neighbors because of it.

Outdoor privacy alone is not the entire problem. Today so many homes are being built with large areas of glass or with picture windows that interior privacy is often destroyed or made negligible. Since not everyone is an exhibitionist, it is disconcerting, to say the least, to look out of a picture window and see passersby or neighbors finding a picture from their side of the window, too. The answer is a privacy fence, one which appears as part of the overall architectural scheme and not too obviously an afterthought.

The first means of obtaining privacy is to build a high fence, tightly constructed around the entire area to be screened. But this is not always necessary. Sometimes the height of the fence need be maintained only to the far edge of the angle of vision from which the fenced area is to be screened. The rest of the fence can step down or even be dispensed with entirely. Materials, design remain the same; only height changes.

Fairly frequently it is better not to have a solid fence, for in that case it may cut off air circulation. Privacy can be gained without creating problems of ventilation in the living areas. Similarly, a fence must not create a wind trap where drafts make it unpleasant for outdoor living. Perhaps a baffle fence or a louvred fence such as those shown in these pages will offer a good solution, blocking the public gaze, but allowing free circulation of air; breaking the force of the wind where that is a problem, but letting through enough air for good ventilation. Baffle fences also have the advantage of controlling traffic through the living areas, directing it away from flower beds and terrace areas but permitting a good easy flow of air, thus adding to the pleasure of living outdoors.

Short sections of a fence may be attached to the house wall at a right angle, or at whatever angle is proper, or even curved outward, assuring privacy for

High fences can be unfriendly barriers, yet this one in a Seattle garden is not. Heavy but narrow slats are spaced about half their width apart, allowing for some air circulation, and the light natural color gives a pleasant contrast to the espaliered shrub and the fleecy junipers.

bedrooms which front on the garden and patio, and at the same time providing an excellent background for plantings alongside the paved area. These short baffle fences may be elevated to cut the line of view into the windows not only from the patio but also from neighboring yards or the street. Occasionally a tiny patio or yard will be fenced with a high privacy fence to provide a pleasant view from the house, yet permitting sunbathing in privacy.

The kind of fence chosen will, of course, be limited by the degree of privacy desired and by the factors of wind control and ventilation. Tight board fences or those made of exterior-grade plywood, hardboard, corrugated fiberglass, and other complete coverings will give the maximum privacy and protection. Wire fencing, post-and-rail, picket, and lattice fences naturally give the least privacy and wind control. Between these two extremes will be found various other fence designs, each of them with a definite function as well as a degree of beauty all its own: the louvred fences, both horizontal and vertical; closely or more widely spaced pickets of various kinds; stockade fences; woven lattice fences very closely spaced or more open in construction; and boards and trellis slats used either vertically or horizontally, in even or uneven spacing, and sometimes utilizing a variety of widths as part of the charm of their design.

Sometimes the answer will best be found in the use of a sturdy framework clothed with some more or less opaque but translucent material, such as wire screen in plastic, corrugated sheets of fiberglass or plastic, or, where there is a good view that must not be shut out, clear glass, clear Plexiglas, or acrylic. In cost, glass will be the most expensive, of course, with plastic and fiberglass costing somewhat less, and the wire screen in plastic cheapest of all. This last is light in weight and most attractive. It is not so durable

Oversized basketweave fence is easy to build, allows ventilation through openings. Inexpensively made of ¼″ exterior plywood, cut to any width that divides equally into 48″ plywood width, it is railed to alternating 4″ × 4″ posts and 2″ × 4″ divider posts.

An oriental effect is imparted by a translucent fence of Filon fiberglass panels framed by 4″×4″s and 2″×4″s. Minor decorative trim completes the desired effect.

as many other materials but, if plants are placed in beds close behind it, the sun will make very beautiful translucent shadow-pictures on the fence all day long.

Where privacy is needed only during the outdoor-living months, roll-up bamboo porch shades or snow-fencing may provide an answer to the question of what to use on the fence frame. Annual vines can augment and produce a living privacy screen; welded wire fencing of 2½″×2″, 3″×2″, or 4″×2″ mesh, 14-, 15-, or 16-gauge wire, either with plastic coating or without, provides good clinging facilities for them. In winter, when the vines have been removed, the attractive oblong-patterned mesh permits sun, air, and light to enter, which may be most desirable at that time, particularly in the modern home. Gardeners, too, will welcome such a trellis, for the vines will strip off easily once they have died back in the autumn.

FENCES FOR PROTECTION

A fence protects property in two ways. It keeps *out* unwanted animals and people. It keeps *in* your children and pets. Not all human intruders can be excluded, of course, but a fence acts as a definite deterrent to the casual trespasser. It must be remembered that post-and-rail fencing, widely spaced louvres, and fences with the lower rail set fairly high off the ground will, of course, admit small animals and permit your own pets to stray.

Cooperative fencing is often seen today, with several congenial neighbors planning their gardens so that the openness is maintained and each small plot, visually augmented by its neighbors, given an effect of space. Except for a perimeter fence, the area may be kept open, or low wire fences may be used, with posts painted deep green or black so that they disappear into the shrubbery or are inconspicuous. In this way the view is almost unobstructed but the object of the fence is achieved: pets and children are kept in the home yard.

FACTS ABOUT FROST

It will be well to consider the possibility of frost and its action in the northern parts of the country. Frosts flow down a hillside like water, collecting in low spots, being diverted around obstacles even as water flows around a log or stone in a stream bed. Realizing this, you can build

Redwood 2″ × 12″s set at an angle and overlapped make a fence that also serves as a retaining wall. The 2″ × 12″s were bolted together and capped with redwood 2″ × 6″s.

Never pass up that odd chance of dramatizing a view such as the one in this garden in Maine. Framed by the striking gateway, the sea is visible through the spaced pickets, the same as those of the tight fence placed to temper the force of ocean winds that blow across the paved area.

your fence to protect your plants. If your plot slopes, don't dam up the path of frosty air currents, but place your fences and plantings so as to keep the currents in motion down the hillside. Solid fences placed across the lower end of a hillside plot will create a frost "pool" and help to kill or injure any plants affected by frost. Instead, use an open fence which will permit free flow of air through it. If you have a solid fence creating such a gardening problem, opening up a gate in it or providing an open section in one or more places will help to overcome the frost problem.

FENCES FOR WIND DEFLECTION

Frequently the logical place for a patio or outdoor sitting room would be alongside the house except for the fact that the prevailing winds are on that facade. It is not pleasant to sit outside and be lambasted by winds; and to the gardener this may be a distinct deterrent to growing tender or fragile plants. A baffle fence or louvred fence, even a solid one with a few holes to permit ventilation of the area, can provide the answer here. Curve the fence, angle it, step it up or down to fit the contours of the location, but make it high enough to do the job.

Fences can also act as temporary or stand-in structures which will permit small inexpensive plants to grow into thick and tall windbreaks. Unless prohibitively expensive nursery stock were used, it would be many years before plants would grow large enough to become a wind barrier. Here, a fence will not only give the plant material protection while it is growing and provide proper conditions for the terrace and garden, but it will also provide a sightly background for the plants until they have reached such a size that the fence can be removed.

It is not necessary to block wind off absolutely. It can be slowed down, diverted, and guided according to the need felt. Sometimes it may be *necessary* to block the wind in a place where there is a view which you'd rather keep unobstructed. In this case clear acrylic or glass should be used. Remember that used windows may be purchased for reasonable sums from wrecking yards. Set in sturdy wooden frames, with moldings holding it firmly in place, a glass fence can be a thing of beauty. A word of caution may be in order, however. Where winds are very strong, extra-large-sized panes of glass may buckle and break under wind stress. Also be sure that no dead limbs are on trees nearby where they may be dislodged and hurled into the glass fence. Aside from these drawbacks, however, a glass-enclosed patio will permit you to enjoy a patio and garden in many problem locations.

Because of many factors, the prevailing winds may have capricious courses. Large buildings, heavy plantings of trees—particularly evergreens—the slope of the land, and the placement of buildings: all may contribute to a wind problem. Therefore you may have to keep a watch on the winds for several months, or even an entire year, to observe their action before knowing just how and where to place your fence to outwit nature.

Drive 2-foot stakes at intervals around the yard and the patio and attach strips of white or bright cloth to the tops so that you can see them easily. Taller stakes may also need to be used in extreme cases to see whether the winds vary in direction close to the ground or higher above it. Note your findings, and, when you feel you have seen enough to evaluate the problem, figure what the pattern of the winds' courses may be and plan your fence accordingly. However, this procedure is advised only for extreme cases. In most places the winds will not be strong or capricious enough to warrant going to these lengths.

CONCEALMENT FENCES

Unlovely but necessary appurtenances of modern living can be hidden from view by a fence. Garbage and trash cans, incinerators, work areas where cold frames, toolsheds, and compost piles are placed—any of these strictly necessary but unsightly objects may be beautifully obscured by a fence.

Either try to make such a concealment fence as integrated and as unobtrusive a part of the general scheme as possible, or else be bold and make it into a definite *feature* by using some contrasting material or well-planned design, thus turning the concealment of some necessity into a triumph. If possible, tie the fence in with a garage or house, or with another fence, so that it seems to have a reason for being rather than standing on its own, calling attention to itself.

A permanent viewbreaker can be constructed of pre-cast pierced concrete blocks that make an openwork pattern.

CHILDREN'S PLAY YARDS

The problem of keeping small children away from the hazards of traffic and from the danger of straying animals can be solved by constructing a play yard. Lo-

The outdoor work area of this California garden is concealed behind a tight fence. The work area has bins for soil and other potting components, as well as storage space for pots and implements below a counter that is set at a convenient height.

cate it near the kitchen or the family room, where you can keep your eye on the children as you work. In later years this may become a little private garden for herb-growing or the pursuit of some other hobby. It can be made a sun-trap where sunbathing can be indulged in privately, early and late in the season when less protected areas are not warm enough. The fence should be high, of course—high enough to prevent active young children from scaling it and escaping—and the gate should have some means of fastening it high enough that they cannot reach it, and preferably placed on the outside of the gate, so that children may be "forcibly detained" when that is desirable.

BOUNDARY DEFINER AND DOORYARD FENCES

All over the country we see a growing tendency to return to the dooryard garden, a charming area surrounded by a low fence. Where boundaries are to be defined, but where no particular purpose would be served by the use of a high fence, the low picket, wire, or board fence may be used to protect the areas. Low fences contain the plantings, giving to the outer aspect neatness and definition, which may be lacking when there is merely an edge of a lawn for a boundary. Also, a fence provides an architectural contrast for the flowers and plants used in the dooryard garden or along other boundaries, counterpointing textures with crisp lines.

ENCLOSING THE "OUTDOOR ROOM"

In a sense, a patio and even an entire yard may be an outdoor room. A fence, therefore, becomes the "walls" of that outdoor room. But unlike indoor walls, a fence need not be box-like and conventional, a squared-off structure. Fences can be built at an angle, can curve, be serpentine or zigzag, can even be freestanding structures. As with indoor walls, fences segregate living areas from service areas, giving more room by limiting each activity to its proper sphere. By clever planning a fence can make a house look longer, higher or lower, more important or less aggressive, and even help a house to settle into its site better. When materials are used which are compatible with those of the house, the whole landscape composition will be more pleasant and attractive, because all of the architectural elements "belong." A fence saves wear and tear on the yard, too, by guiding traffic into the proper channels, keeping errant footsteps from wearing out the grass and trampling flowers.

A Seattle garden with an oriental flavor has this lightweight gate offering a passage between clipped hedges. Natural barriers such as hedges often need gates to ensure privacy.

Among the pages of designs in this section you will find many devoted to "walls" for the outdoor room which are intended to serve as an inspiration and a guide rather than as something for you to copy. Improvise, adapt, and change as you wish, using materials of your own choice; or combine some elements from one design with those of another so that they will suit your location and help to solve your own particular problem.

CHECK THE REGULATIONS

There are a few preliminary matters to be settled before you dig the post holes, saw the lumber, or even settle finally on the design so that lumber can be ordered. Before going ahead with your fence, check with local building department authorities to see if there are any ordinances or regulations concerning the height, location, or materials of fences. Check, too, to be sure there are no zoning laws which may have a bearing on fences and whether or not you will need a permit to build a fence. You may inquire about this at the bank which holds your mortgage. They can tell you where to make the proper inquiries of local officials. Then, when you know the limitations, plan your fence accordingly.

For example, local rules can restrict fence height, setback, material, and maintenance. Read the fine print in local fence regulations, too. It may affect what you do. The use of barbed wire may be prohibited, as may be the setting of pieces of broken glass into the top of a masonry fence. Someone could get hurt by them. Solid fences may be outlawed, for instance, where they would obstruct the view of traffic at an intersection.

When you find height restrictions on fences, determine whether they are measured from ground level or from the center of the street, as some are. With a 6-inch-high curb plus the slope up to your house and yard, measuring fence height from street level could significantly shorten the maximum height of your proposed fence.

Some of the newer subdivision regulations forbid chain link fences higher than 42 inches unless plastic or metal inserts are used for "beautification."

Many jurisdictions won't let you expose the "wrong" or back side of the fence to your neighbors. It looks bad, and if someone must look at the lesser side of a fence, it should be the person who built it, the regulations seem to say.

A few fence regulations are so strict that you'd have to install a wooden fence at least a foot inside your property line to provide access for maintenance. Otherwise, the lawmakers assume you'd be trespassing when you go on the other side to paint it. Even approval from your neighbor may not be enough to circumvent such a regulation.

If you own a swimming pool and are fencing it off, the rules may be extra strict. As you probably know, swimming pools are thought of as "attractive nuisances," and with this derogatory term goes the legal responsibility for an accident to a youthful trespasser. Local regulations probably spell out the height and material of such a fence. If nothing else, it should be nonclimbable. A high, child-tight fence is in your favor. Even a pump house, toolshed, or ground-level solar collector may be deemed an attractive nuisance and require a nonclimbable fence or a secure lock.

You may even be restricted in the color to paint your new fence; no bright polka-dots, no alternatively painted pickets, no posters or signs. These are common proscriptions, very likely ones you wouldn't want aimed at you by another neighbor.

It is wise, too, to have the place surveyed if you are not absolutely certain of your property lines. If you build your fence so that it encroaches on your neighbor's side of the line, it becomes his property and he can remove it, paint it, do anything he likes with it. Even if it is correctly situated on your property line, it will be to your advantage to try for a written agreement with the adjoining owner as to the placement, the materials used, and, if it is centered on the property line and he pays half the cost, whether or not he will provide half the maintenance. Usually neighbors reach such agreements amicably (which is the best way), but occasionally there is lack of agreement. In this case you should reconsider to see if having a fence is more important than the hard feelings you might have to endure. If so, proceed carefully.

If your neighbor proves hostile to the idea of a fence, you may place it from 1 to 6 inches inside your property line, after you have made sure that it conforms with regulations. *Be sure* to check and double-check your property lines to avoid unpleasantness in the future. If your neighbor is amenable, or even wants to join in paying for the fence, have a lawyer draw up an agreement in writing and have it recorded as a covenant in both deeds so that it will be legally binding on future owners of the property, should either of you sell your home or should there be a change of heart later on. If, however, your neighbor is adamant in opposition to the suggestion, you may very well have other trouble with him. A fence is likely to keep that trouble at bay, and you will be able to enjoy the privacy which is the legal right of every property holder.

Sometimes in local regulations or deed restrictions you will find that it is obligatory that "party-line" fences be paid for and maintained equally by the property owners. Or it may be that, if the adjacent lot is not built on or improved as yet, there is no obligation on the part of the landowner to contribute. Then you may have to bear all of the cost yourself and, if you do, you may want to build the fence entirely on your own land. In any case, the wisdom of careful exploration of the regulations on fences has been demonstrated. Look thoroughly before you build.

HOW TO PLAN YOUR FENCE IN ADVANCE

When you have selected the design for your fence and established its location, stake out the area with relation to the property lines, as indicated above. Run a cord along the stakes so that you can see exactly what your problems may be. By measuring the distance of the run of the fence you can determine pretty exactly how much lumber will be required, how many posts to buy, and so on. It is always a good idea to draw a plan of the layout of the fence, though it needn't be absolutely accurate. It will assist you materially in determining what you need and where to put the fence. It is always easier to make revisions on a piece of paper than on the ground. Use graph paper, one or two squares or more equalling a foot. Place house, driveway, walks, and any existing features approximately where they exist in reality. It will help you to visualize the layout. Perhaps you will even find that in the plan you can figure out a better way to place the fence for greater privacy or for better traffic flow than when you are working outdoors, where you may be more confused by details.

In designing the fences shown in these pages I have tried to use stock lengths of lumber in the construction so as to eliminate as much cutting as possible. The maximum span recommended is 8 feet—in many cases 6 or 7 feet (a 14-foot-length cut will secure this) is better where the "skin" of the fence is heavy or there is some other need for shortening the span. Look into the possibility, when figuring costs, of buying the double length and cutting it, if you have a portable power saw. It could well save you money.

Check the lumber when it is delivered to see how accurately it has been cut. Sometimes the ends are cut only roughly square, but not accurately enough for use in butting two pieces together. In this case you must square and cut them to remove the discrepancy. Where a number of boards need trimming you can save labor by cutting them all at once, using a large C-clamp at both ends to hold them together accurately, thus assuring that all boards will be cut to exactly the same dimensions.

FENCE POSTS

Usually posts can be ordered already cut to the length you wish to use. For the average fence the length is from 18 to 30 inches longer than the aboveground height of the fence when finished. For heavy fences made of solid boards or other weighty materials, longer and heavier posts will be needed. For taller fences, too, where there will be more strain from wind and weather, longer posts are indicated. A 6-foot-tall fence will require posts 8 to 9 feet long; these should usually be 4″ × 4″s if the covering is heavy. Fences 48 inches tall need posts 6 feet long, and 6 to 12 inches longer than that if the material is heavy. For fences up to 3 feet in height posts may be made of 2″ × 4″s for average or light covering materials, if doubled below ground. Other post sizes which may be used are 3″ × 3″s, 4″ × 4″s, 6″ × 6″s, or larger sizes if your budget and the job warrant the expense. For dooryard or other low fences 2″ × 3″s will usually serve.

Corner and gate posts are usually made heavier (4″ × 4″ where a 2″ × 4″ is the intermediate post size; 6″ × 6″ where the intermediate posts are 4″ × 4″s) and also should be 6 to 12 inches longer than intermediate posts. If they are well set in concrete (see the "Post Base Setting" drawings below) this extra length will not

WOOD-POST BASE SETTING

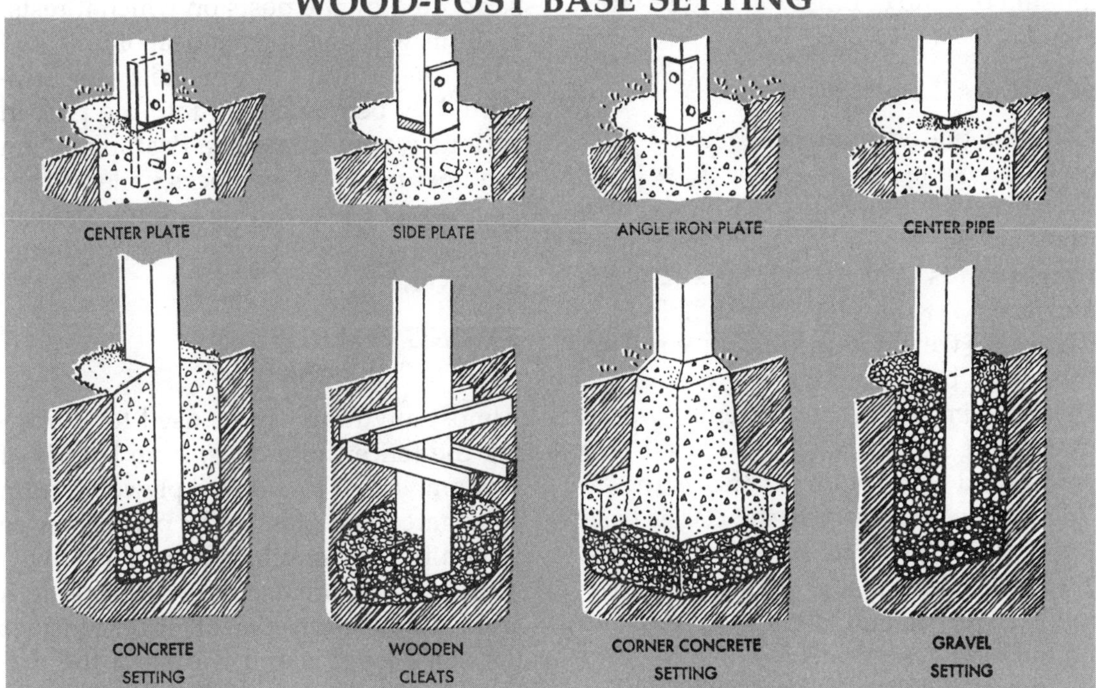

TWO WAYS TO SET POSTS TO PREVENT BOTTOM ROT

To prevent post rot, place a post support in concrete and attach the post to it. In the left-hand illustration, a steel fence post is set into the soil with the top coming an inch or so below the eventual height of the post. Hold it steady vertically with braces on at least two sides and pour concrete into the surrounding hole. Similarly, at right, a galvanized pipe is pounded into the soil and held vertically while concrete is poured around the base. The fence post has open screw holes at regular intervals (about 6 inches) with a hook for wire fencing between.

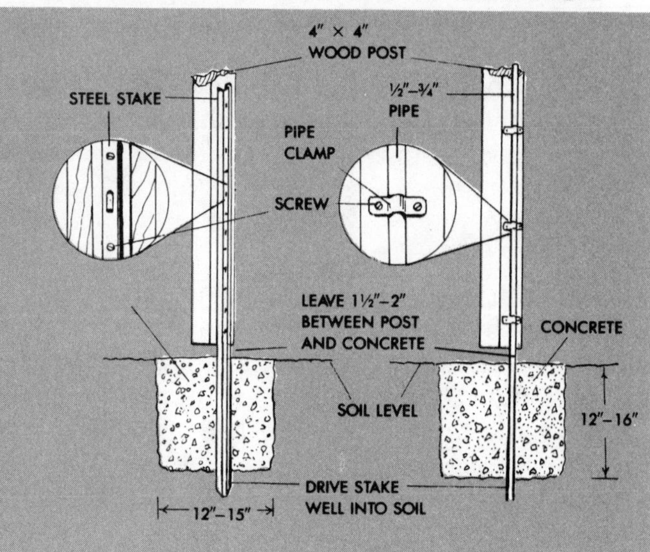

be necessary unless there is an unusual amount of wind or other strain to be withstood.

FENCE RAILS

Top and bottom crossrails should generally be made of 2" × 4"s for most types of fences. Occasionally, as in the low dooryard fences or for taller but lightweight kinds of fences, 2" × 3"s, 2" × 2"s, and even 1" × 4"s may be used. Even if there is no weight with which to contend, there may be other strains to consider—children climbing on the fence, the weight of vines if the fence is to be used as a trellis, and wind and weather stresses. You may want to stick to the classic basic frame: 4" × 4" posts for gates and corners, 2" × 4"s doubled below ground for intermediate posts, and 2" × 4"s for top and bottom and center rails.

The span of the top rail may be double that of the lower rails because it will be supported by the posts on which it rests, and this will save a good deal of time and labor in cutting. Lower rails are supported by being dadoed into the post in various ways (see "Fence Post Joints" on the next page) or by blocks nailed to the post under the rail. This latter is less satisfactory and less sightly than dadoing, however.

FACING BOARDS AND OTHER "SKINS"

Almost anything can be used for surfacing the fence these days, from boards of random widths to grooved plywood, from corrugated fiberglass or flat plastic to wire screen in plastic, which comes in rolls.

When you are deciding on the length and height of each span of fence, consider the stock lengths and widths of the materials and save yourself much labor by using fractions or multiples of these stock sizes. For instance, plywood comes in 4′ × 8′ sheets (other stock sizes are made but are not always readily available), and so do such materials as hardboard. If you can adjust your fence units to this module or fraction of it, you can build your fence with little trouble. It may be possible to have the lumber yard cut the materials on their power machinery to whatever sizes you need, if the job is large enough to warrant the added charge they will make. This will save much wear and tear on your shoulder muscles. It will also eliminate the need for having another person help you wrestle with the large sheets, for it is not always possible for one person to handle them alone.

Boards, where used for the "skin," are economical, particularly when random widths may be employed. Instead of using the more expensive grooved exterior plywood, it is possible to use grooved siding, shiplap, or some other stock lumber and save a bit on it. But you will probably feel that the extra cost is justified when you compare the time consumed in cutting a large number of boards with the convenience and saving of time effected when a piece of plywood is used. Consider the surface interest and textural beauty achieved when plywood is used with various slats or 1″ × 1″s in patterns applied to it. This is a field which is new, so you may want to develop your own patterns.

FENCE POST JOINTS

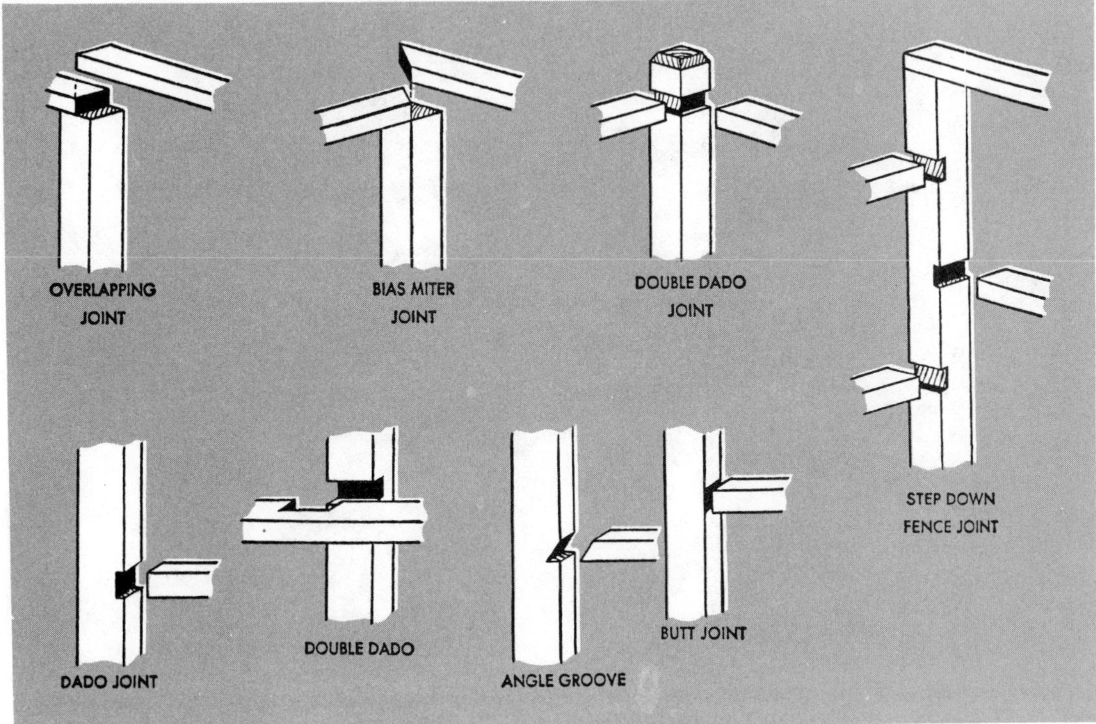

A handsome fence stepping down a slope in a Seattle garden is made of random-width boards closely placed. This makes a compatible background for the variety of textures in the naturalized plantings.

Where strength is not mandatory, or where the fence is to be used as a kind of horizontal trellis for light annual vines, lighter weights of wood may be used. Because of their lighter weight they will cost less, but they will not stand up as well as more sturdily built fences. They must be used with discretion, therefore, but with the knowledge that in many places nothing will ever give the same effect as the lacy, trellis-like fence. On the other hand, a good, sturdy, blocky fence has its uses, too. It will complement certain houses as no other fence can, lending a solidity which is most attractive and correct for a particular kind of house and location. And, of course, for privacy this type of fence is ideal.

PICKET FENCES

The picket fence, traditional as it is, has a rightness and a very pleasant quality with traditional homes. Certain types are adaptable to more modern structures, too. It is possible to purchase pickets already cut in various decorative traditional shapes of suitable lengths in many parts of the country and from the large national mail order houses. However, for those who wish to make their own pickets, I recommend using stock from 1¼ to 4 inches in width and from ½ to 1 inch in thickness, the length of the picket depending upon the height of the fence. Note, in the pages of designs which follow, the details of how to cut pickets, and also the various designs given which can be adapted as you may wish for your own fence.

Square pickets may also be used, 1″ × 1″, 5/4″ × 5/4″, 1½″ × 1½″, or even 2″ × 2″ if you wish a very heavy fence. Round pickets may be made of dowels of ½ inch in diameter upwards, but ¾ or 1 inch is preferred. Larger sizes of dowels run into considerable expense, but if you wish to use clothes pole stock, which is about 1¼ inch in diameter and comes in various lengths, you may be able to cut down the cost considerably.

HOW TO MAKE PICKETS

While pickets may be simply square or flat boards, many traditional houses seem to demand shaped pickets. Most of these can be made by a bench saw or sawed by hand, but pickets B and D require a scroll- or jigsaw to shape their curves. Cut picket boards to approximate length and clamp several together so you can saw them simultaneously. Bore holes while clamped (B, C) and after sawing and boring, file with a rasp and sand down to remove unevennesses. For C, a board a little more than twice the width may be used, holes bored, then ripsaw to finished widths, reclamp, saw angle end.

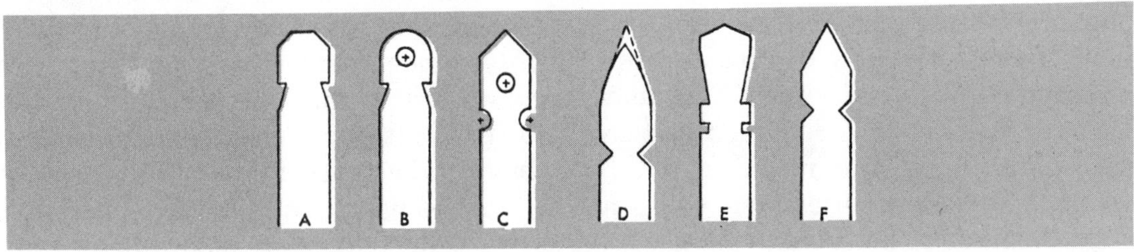

UNUSUAL MATERIALS GIVE UNUSUAL EFFECTS

In some sections of the country various unusual materials are available locally. For instance, on the West Coast, grape stakes may be purchased. They are rustic, rugged and good-looking, and may be driven into the ground, mounted on or between rails, and used in many other ways. By driving them into the ground to an even height, placing them in serpentine curves, semicircles, squares, or in any pattern you wish, you can make a very unusual low fence.

A material which is available nationally from mail order houses is snow-fencing: rough-sawn pickets or boards ½″ × 1½″ × 4′ spaced 2 inches apart and held by several double strands of twisted wire. They are cheapest when bought in 50-foot rolls from Sears or Montgomery Ward, but sometimes in local supply houses shorter lengths may be purchased. They are used by highway departments for protecting the roads from drifting snow, but when mounted on a fence they are very good-looking. Usually they come stained a pleasant soft red, but they may be painted any color. Round or square posts with 2″ × 4″s for rails permit the fencing to be easily mounted.

Picket fencing, with pointed pickets 1″ × 3″ of various lengths—36 or 48 inches—and mounted on a unit 8 feet long are widely available. These lend themselves to a variety of uses as demonstrated on upcoming pages. They may be cut in half for low dooryard garden fences, with extra rails nailed in place, upended to make trellises, and you can probably think of other adaptations. As fences, they can be mounted on steel fence posts driven in the ground with brass screws inserted through the holes in the post to secure the rails to the fence.

Where privacy is needed without cutting off all light, translucent fences may be made of corrugated or flat plastic, fiberglass, or some other translucent material mounted on a wooden frame. Steel posts may be driven into the ground and strips of flat plastic woven between them basket-fashion, making an absolutely rot-proof fence, and a good-looking one. A less permanent, but equally good-looking, fence for view-blocking without loss of light can be made of plastic-encased wire screening, using steel or aluminum wire. This tough, durable plastic will last for a number of years in most climates and, being fairly inexpensive, will cost little to replace. Where high winds are encountered it is not advocated, because it is likely to whip loose under the stress. It can be cut with tin snips or strong shears, and it generally comes in 36-inch widths. However, mail order houses may list additional widths of 28 and 48 inches in 4-mesh, 9-mesh, and 14-mesh screen, the price increasing with the density of the screen. Moldings or wood strips are used to hold the material in place on the fence frame. Similar materials are sold under various trade names, such as Cel-O-Glass and Sun-Ray Wire.

Bamboo roll-up blinds or porch shades also make interesting textures on fences and may be used for many other purposes, too. Being woven together with cotton string, they are not eternally durable, but they are cheap enough so that they can be replaced every few years. It is wise to watch end-of-season clearance sales, when stores are disposing of summer stocks. Sometimes you can find slightly damaged odd lots which you can buy and cut to fit your spaces. They are usually 6 feet long and come in widths of from 2 to 12 feet. Their pleasant color and texture, even when weathered, make them desirable in many locations.

Woven reeds, used by nurseries to cover cold frames, are also offered widely in rolls of various widths and lengths. Not as long lasting as more permanent materials, they still have pleasant textures and are suited particularly to oriental-style gardens and bamboo frames.

CHAIN LINK FENCE

Basically designed for security, a chain link fence serves well for making a tight enclosure. Neither people nor animals can get through it easily. In heights up to about 42 inches, it can be an attractive, permanent fence for residential use, especially when it is softened by shrubbery. Beyond that height, chain link fences are for industrial and commercial use.

Consider the use of metal or plastic inserts in the mesh to create a woven appearance and add to privacy. If painted, aluminum is a popular color. Green can look more natural.

A chain link fence requires concrete footings for the pipe posts, and much stretching, so the installation is best left to experts. However, you can do it yourself if you wish. Some fencing comes vinyl-clad for low maintenance.

ROLL-WIRE FENCING

Wire comes in many interesting patterns. It is ideal for use where annual vines will clamber on the fence to clothe it for the summer months. Welded wire fabric, usually made from rust-resistant copper-bearing steel, comes in various square inches, ¼″×¼″, or ½″×½″, up to 1″×1″; and in oblong meshes 1″×2″, 2″×2½″, 2″×3″, or 2″×4″, the oblongs running with the length of the roll. This pattern is particularly good with modern, simple homes.

Although considerably cheaper, chicken and rabbit wire is not so attractive. It might, however, be adaptable in some places, particularly if it backed up an attractive wooden frame.

STOCKADE

A stockade fence is constructed of approximately round 3-inch poles of even height, pointed on top. It makes an excellent fence, but one that should be utilized judiciously. It offers a high degree of privacy. Still, it can look out of place in some neighborhoods. Cedar, which weathers to a warm golden or grayish tone, is ideal for this fence and white spruce is also used. Varying heights of pickets across the top can create a sweeping effect. Use special devices to attach flowerpots and ornamentation to the pickets. A stockade makes a good background for roses and shrubs.

A stockade tends to be expensive but is well worth the investment if it serves its designed purpose and is not put up as a spite fence. It is best installed by a homeowner on posts attached to the back with the help of a friendly neighbor. Sections 4′×8′ and 6′×8′, are offered preassembled.

FIBERGLASS PANELS

One of the newest of fencing materials, fiberglass panels offer either total privacy or see-through patterns. Translucent material lets light through, creating interesting silhouette effects. Fiberglass for fencing is available in flat or corrugated sheets and in flat rolls. It comes in several colors and stripes, too, if that's what you want and local regulations allow them. The minimal maintenance of fiberglass will please you.

RAIL FENCES

For rustic charm and where lot size is ample, nothing beats the post-and-rail fence of either solid or split-rail variety. A unit is priced usually to include one post and the number of rails to go with it. Two-, three-, or four-rail types can be made with round, square, or split rails. The steeplechase or hurdle pattern enhances this type of fence. It is best used for country estates, wooded lots, or homes of Early American, rustic, or ranch architecture. You can do the installation yourself with a posthole digger. Select the finest materials your budget permits.

LIVING FENCES

Hedges offer a gracious means of enclosing and defining properties and many may be shaped to any height or width you desire. The history of hedges includes the use of Osage-orange trees to enclose farmland of the pioneers on the plains. Today subdivision developers are cursing as they try to tear out those rambling, thorny, tall hedges. One factor concerning hedge use which might be considered is that they never need to be painted, merely periodically pruned, sheared, and shaped. Some plants to consider are yew and hemlock, both of which take to shearing very well; the deciduous golden privet and Amur privet; Russian olive, cherry-laurel in the warmer areas, rugosa roses, southern yaupon of the holly family, holly of several kinds, and a number of barberries, deciduous or evergreen. Some of these may best be left to grow more or less naturally, some take well to shearing or pruning. One notable variety of alder buckthorn is 'Columnaris' which is commonly offered in the trade as 'Tallhedge' or 'Tall Hedge.' It is narrow-growing, needs little side clipping, and only occasional shearing and cutting of the top to keep it informally even and neat.

At all costs avoid the "fabulous rose hedge" offered by nurseries for a low price. It is said to grow "horse-high and hog-tight," but is also impervious to efforts to get rid of it when it spreads to 12 feet wide and each cane is studded with thorns. It is extremely hard to remove when you find out how unsuitable it is and want to replace it with a fence.

A FENCE CAN BE A WALL

Not all fences, baffles, and enclosures are made of wood, of course. In the past most boundary fences were built solidly and securely of stone or other masonry. Chapter 24 on walls and enclosures, retaining walls, and view-blockers may also be of interest. Often masonry can be combined with wood construction to produce the desired effect, adding a difference in texture that will be most welcome and attractive. For instance, where a bank has been cut away to level land on which to build a patio, a permanent retaining wall to hold the cut soil may be necessary.

At the same time it may be desirable to have a fence to block the view, to protect the patio from wind, or to provide a background for plantings placed atop the wall, at least in some portions. Brick, concrete, block, or stone masonry may be employed to give the permanent holding quality, the face of the masonry contributing either a formal, smooth appearance, if that is desired, or it may be textured for a rustic natural surface if a more informal or rugged look is indicated. The fence tied into such masonry may likewise be formal and architectural, light or heavy, finely finished and painted or rugged and rustic in appearance, to make the total effect exactly what the builder feels is best with the surroundings.

NOW IT IS UP TO YOU

In the following pages are a good many designs for fences from which to choose. You will find low fences, high fences, open fences, solid fences, privacy fences, and fences I call "bikini" because they define the property without interfering with the view. Among them we hope you will find the fence that is right for you. Feel free to improvise, to adapt and revamp any of them to fit your location and your taste, bearing in mind that a *good* fence is a *simple* fence; that only occasionally is there a place for an ornate fence. Bizarre, gimcracky effects are to be avoided at all costs because they grow tiresome sooner or later. Materials cost too much in these days of inflation to be used for anything which you will regret and, in a few years, want to replace. The good, simple, architectural pattern, on the other hand, is always tasteful and always pleasant.

FENCE FUNCTIONS

Fence Type	*Privacy*	*Security*	*Esthetic appeal*	*Hide clutter*	*Deaden sound*	*Create porch*	*Shrubbery background*	*Trellis, support for vines, roses*	*Windbreak*	*Safeguard children, pets*	*Delineate boundaries*	*Increase property value*	*Protect lawn, garden*	*Enclose pool, pond*	*Relative cost*
Screen	✓	•	✓	✓	✓	✓	✓	✓	✓	✓	✓	•	✓	✓	Variable
Picket	•	•	✓				✓	✓	✓	✓	✓	✓	✓		Moderate
Wood board	•	•	✓	✓	✓	✓	✓	✓	✓	✓	✓	✓	✓	✓	Mod. to high
Post-and-rail		•	✓				✓	✓		•	✓	✓			Moderate
Chain link	••	✓	••		••		✓	✓	••	✓	✓	••	✓	✓	Moderate
Brick, stone, concrete block	•	•	✓	✓	✓	✓	✓	✓	✓	✓	✓	✓	✓	✓	Mod. to very high
Woven-wire		•	•					✓		✓	✓	•	✓	•	Low
Living fence	•	•	✓	✓	✓				✓	•	✓	•	•		Low to high

✓ Usually serves well • When properly selected and erected •• When used with metal or plastic inserts

NOTE: *Dimensions given in all plans are nominal* not *actual*. Therefore, consider *actual* dimensions and adjust as necessary in planning and cutting. See Chapter 3 for actual and nominal measures.

PEEKABOO PICKETS

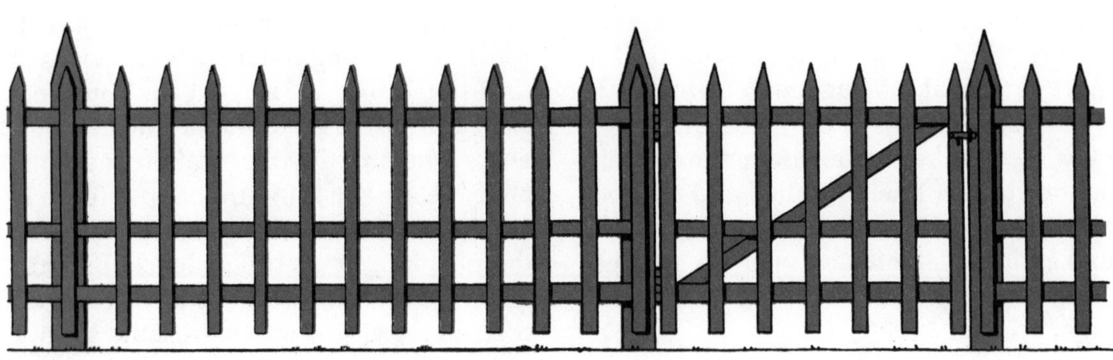

Lightweight fences give an effect of airy charm because of the flowers seen peeping through them. They protect but do not interfere with the view, the wide spacing of the pickets giving plenty of ventilation, too. The 2″ × 2″ frame is dadoed into the post, crossrail between being nailed to the front of the post. Joinings of the rails on the post are hidden by pickets on posts. Note that pickets echo "tent" cut of posts.

PEEKABOO GATE CONSTRUCTION

Note that 2″ × 2″ frame is not dadoed into 4″ × 4″ posts at gate. Instead, half-lap cut is used. Center rail is nailed to front of posts as elsewhere. Allow some space between posts and gate for hinges and clearance for frame to swing.

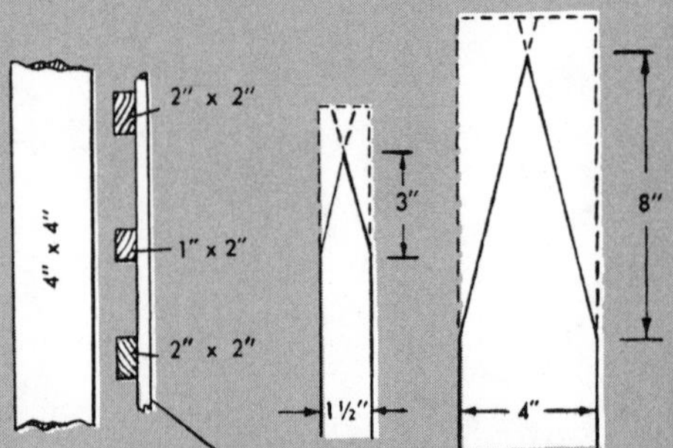

SIDE VIEW ½″ PICKET 4 x 4 POST

SECTION THROUGH GATE

PLAN

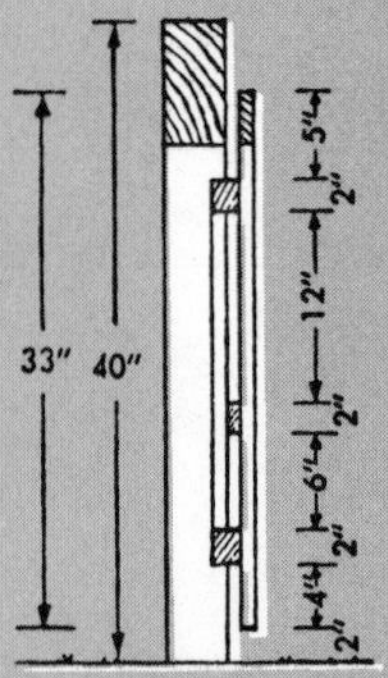

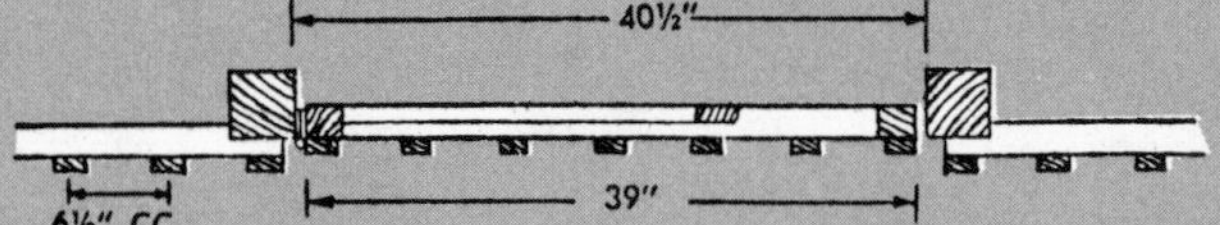

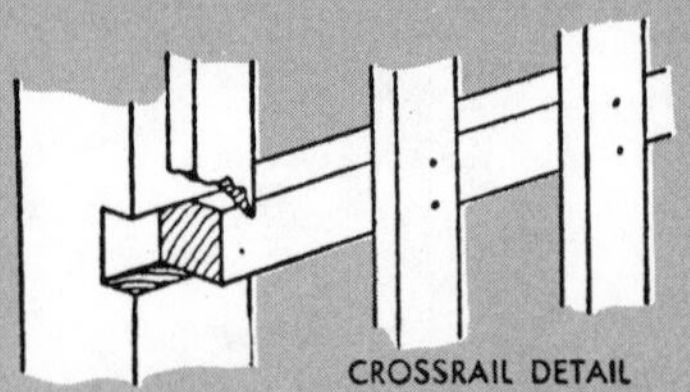

CROSSRAIL DETAIL

ROUND-TIP PICKETS

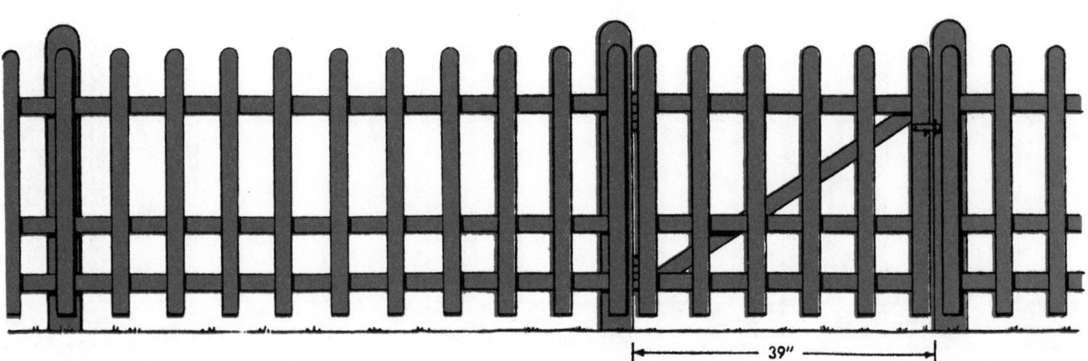

A pleasant variation in the top cutting of pickets is this semicircular-topped style, the posts also being given a "barrel" cut. To make posts, draw semicircle with compass and then saw to rough shape, rasp file to finished size, and then sandpaper smooth. Cut all pickets to rough size, allowing extra wood for waste. Clamp several pickets together, draw semicircle, rough saw, rasp, and sandpaper smooth.

ROUND-TIP GATE CONSTRUCTION

Gate frame is made of 2″×2″s with corner half-lap joints (see detail, right) and with crossrails dadoed into the frame. The diagonal brace is set into corners, crossing behind center crossrail.

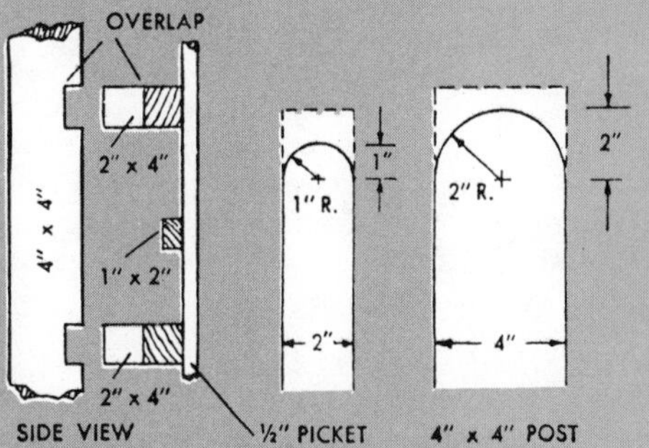

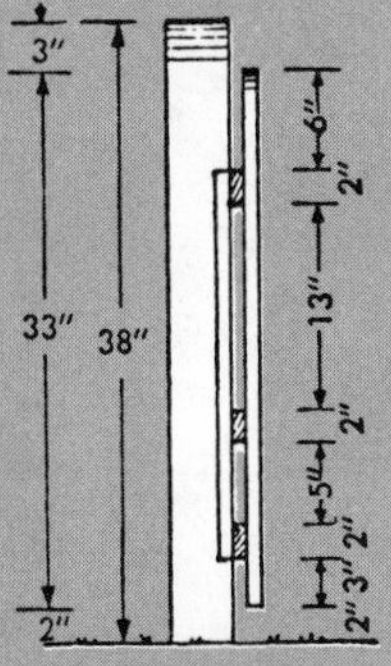

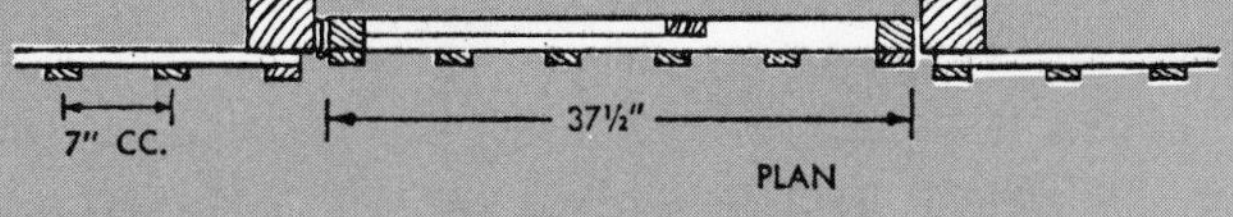

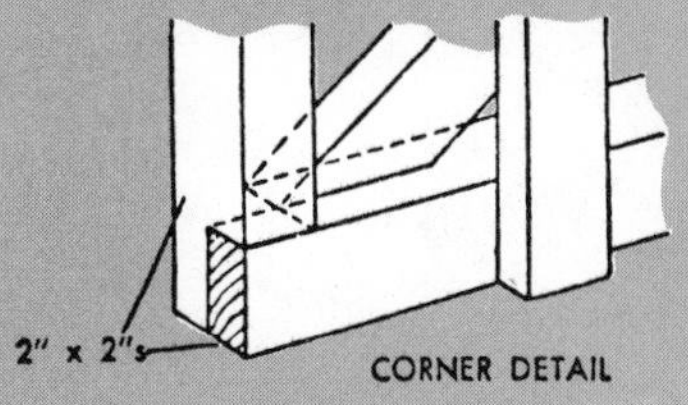

WIDELY SPACED PICKET FENCE, POINTED POSTS

An open design which defines the extent of the property beautifully, this fence utilizes 5/4" × 5/4" pickets set on a 2" × 4" bottom rail, with the tops held by moldings. The well-braced gate is made of 2" × 4"s and carries the lines of the fence through. Note details of the top rail above, and that the gate sides have been dadoed on front.

HOW TO ASSEMBLE PICKETS

Pickets may be square on top or pointed to conform with the posts, cut at 60° angle as in Picket B or at a 45° angle as in Picket A (above). By cutting and clamping several pickets together angle cuts may be done on bench saw to cut down labor. Note detail at right of the fence assembly, dadoing of bottom moldings firmly in place against post.

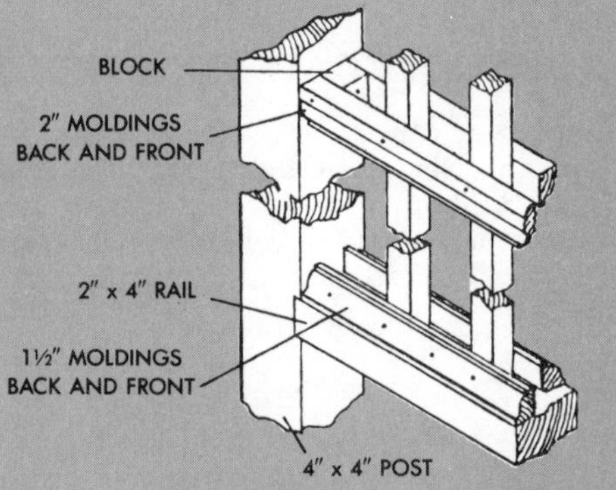

BLOCK
2" MOLDINGS BACK AND FRONT
2" x 4" RAIL
1½" MOLDINGS BACK AND FRONT
4" x 4" POST

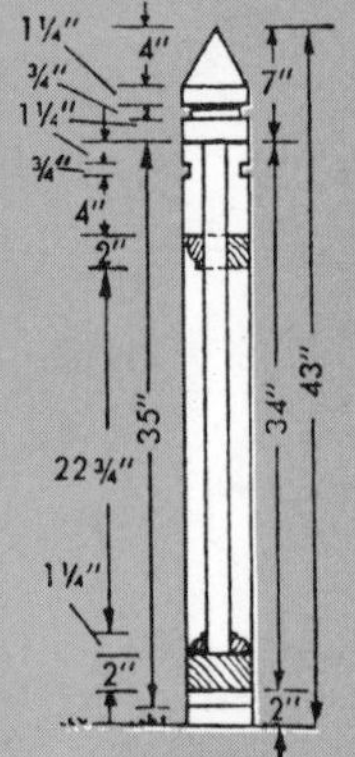

SECTION OF GATE

6" CC.
2" x 4" CUT DOWN TO FIT
MOLDING

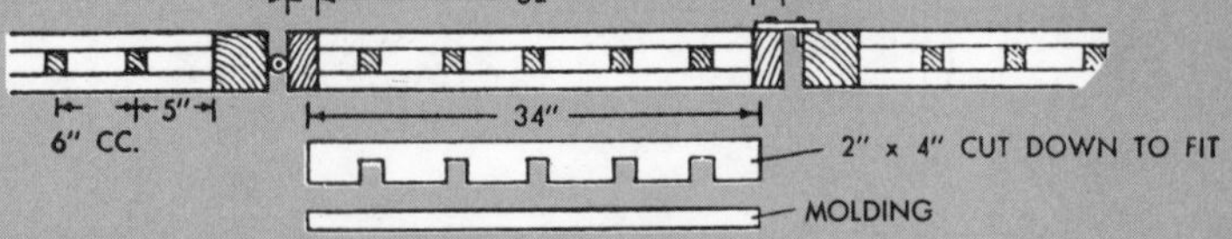

SLIGHTLY PUNCTUATED

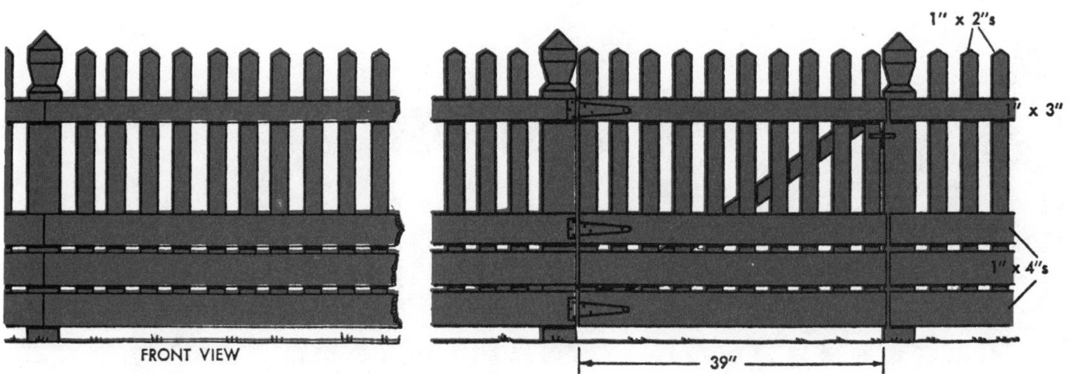

A variation of punctuated regularity uses posts with interestingly cut tops that do not protrude very much above the fence line. Also, the rails have a variation in size as well as in number. The top rail is doubled here, and bottom rail may be doubled or not, since the three rails will give fence rigidity.

GATE CONSTRUCTION

Again the gate follows in general the same construction as the fence. Note, however, that the top and bottom rails are doubled, using the same size wood as front rails, the diagonal brace being cut to fit between the rails. Either barn-door hinges, concealed, or more decorative wrought-iron hinges with a matching latch may be used.

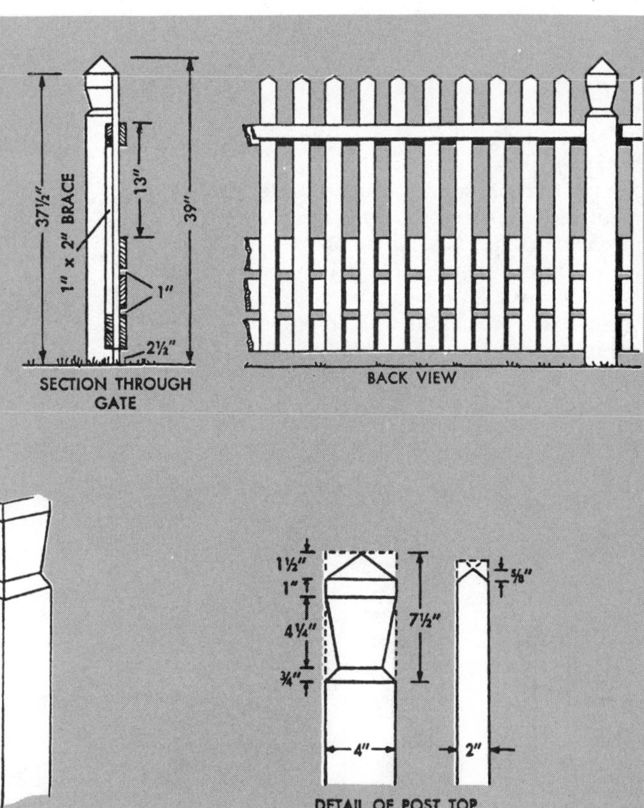

4"CC.
1" x 2"s
1" x 3"
1" x 4"
DETAIL OF FENCE

PUNCTUATED REGULARITY

1" x 2"s
1" x 4"
1" x 4"
38"
FRONT VIEW

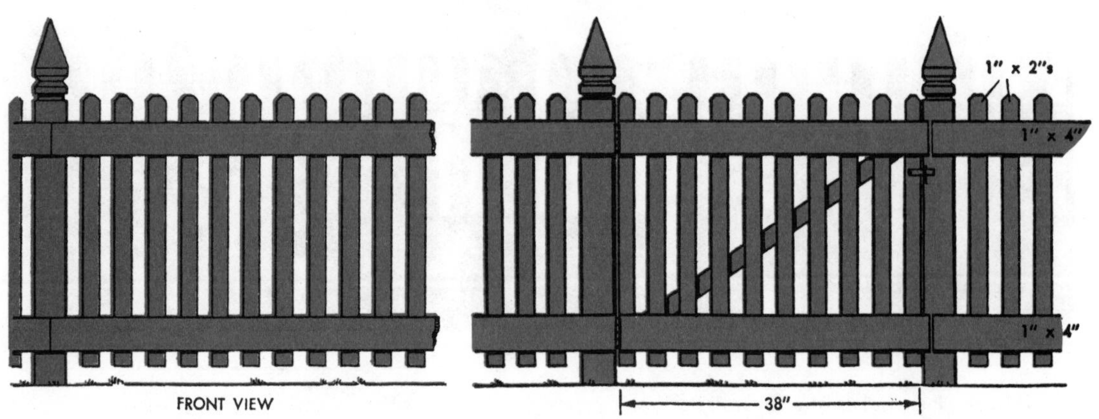

A straight picket fence with no variation of height or spacing can be deadly dull. By emphasizing the posts, shaping the tops in an interesting way, and breaking the line of the fence, dullness is avoided. Top and bottom rails are overlapped on fronts of posts, fitted between on rear, pickets being held securely between the pairs of doubled rails.

GATE CONSTRUCTION

Gate is constructed in the same manner as the fence, with the diagonal brace applied on the back side of top and bottom rails (see detail at right). Note that rails overlap on one side of gate to prevent gate from swinging both ways. Use either concealed hinges shown here or barn-door type.

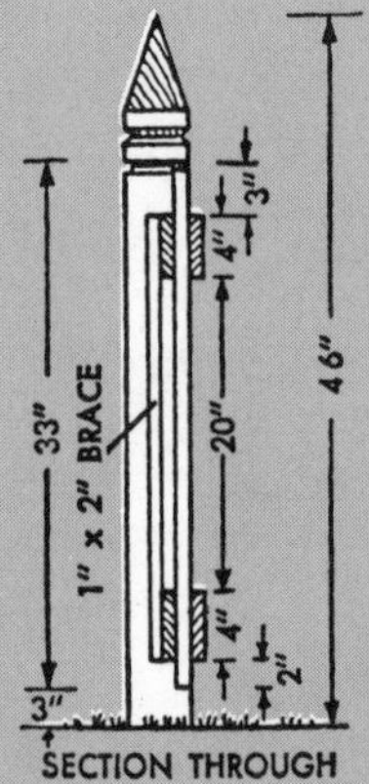

33"
1" x 2" BRACE
3"
4"
20"
4"
2"
46"
3"
SECTION THROUGH GATE

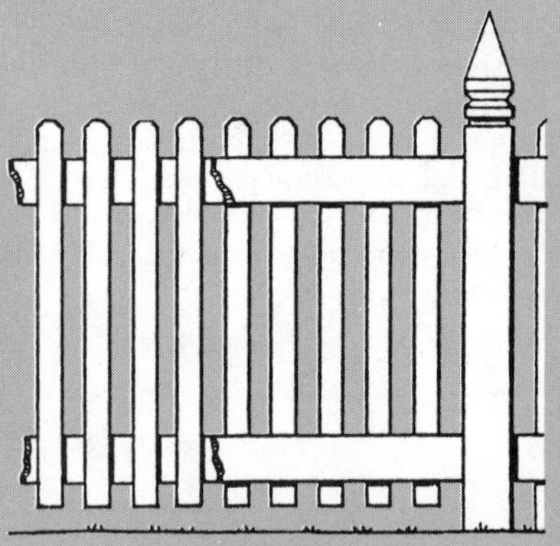

BACK VIEW

CROSSRAIL DETAIL

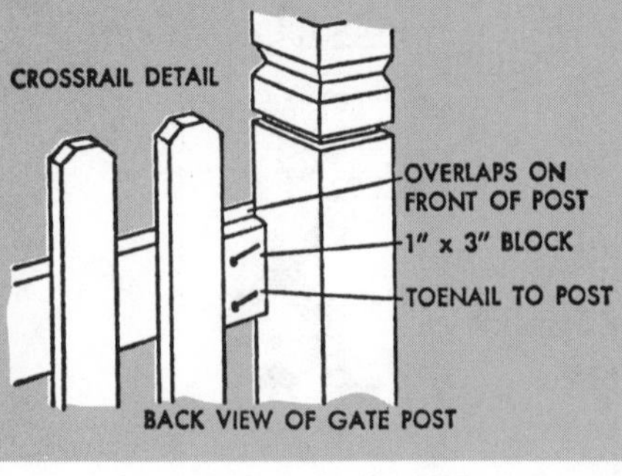

OVERLAPS ON FRONT OF POST
1" x 3" BLOCK
TOENAIL TO POST
BACK VIEW OF GATE POST

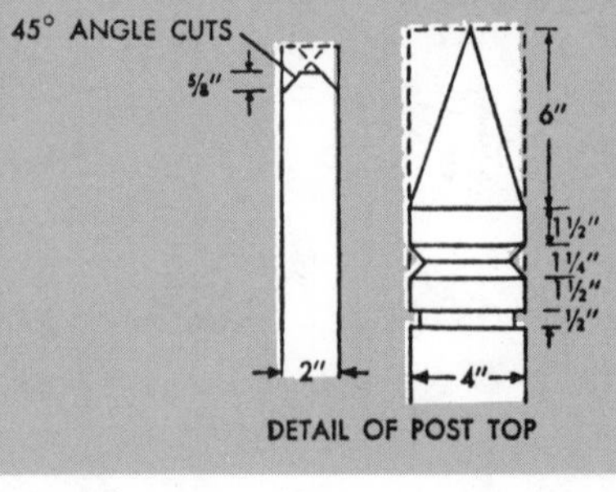

45° ANGLE CUTS
5/8"
2"
6"
1 1/2"
1 1/4"
1 1/2"
1/2"
4"
DETAIL OF POST TOP

GATE AND FENCE OF WIDE PICKETS WITH CUTOUTS

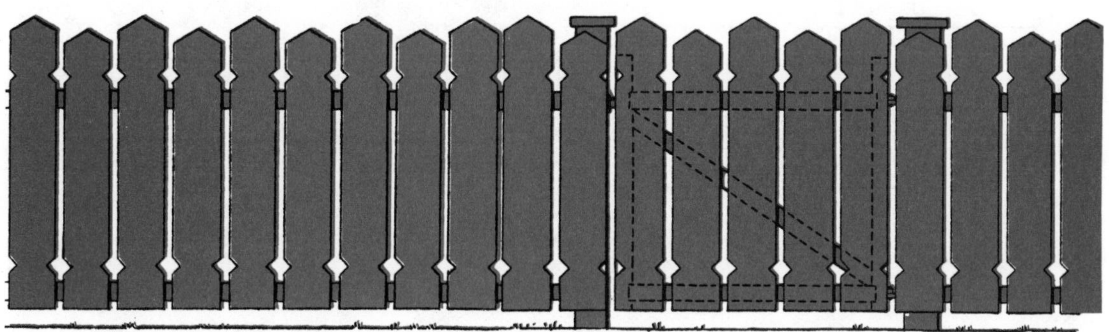

A simple but effective pattern is achieved with little work, the "pickets" being 1" × 6" boards on a 2" × 4" framework, the posts being 4" × 4"s. All boards on both fence and gate may be made of even height or they may be of two heights, alternating as shown here. Note framework pattern in dotted lines on the gate, all frame being 2" × 4"s.

HOW TO MAKE PICKETS

Cut all boards for the two sizes needed, allowing about ½" extra in length for each. By clamping several boards together and sawing them simultaneously, the work can be cut down and precision maintained. Use one of the boards already cut for pattern to trace on cuts for all the rest of the pickets.

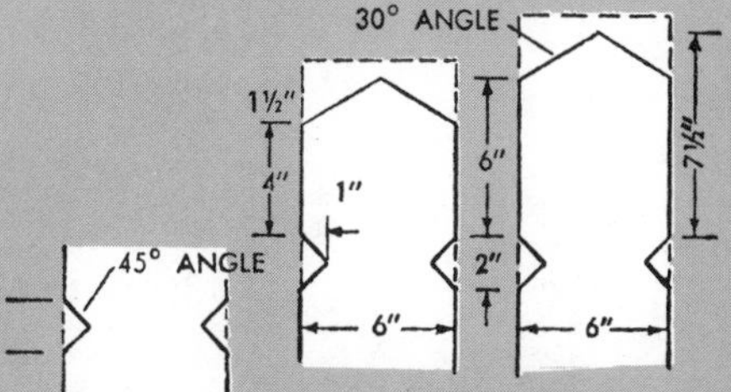

30° ANGLE
1½"
4"
1"
6"
2"
7½"
45° ANGLE
6"
6"

DETAILS OF CUTS FOR PICKETS

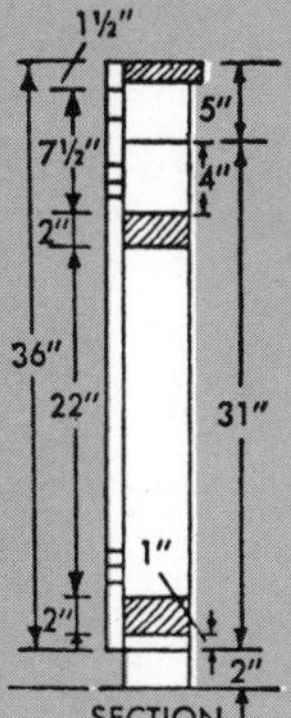

1½"
7½"
5"
4"
2"
36"
22"
31"
1"
2"
2"

SECTION OF GATE

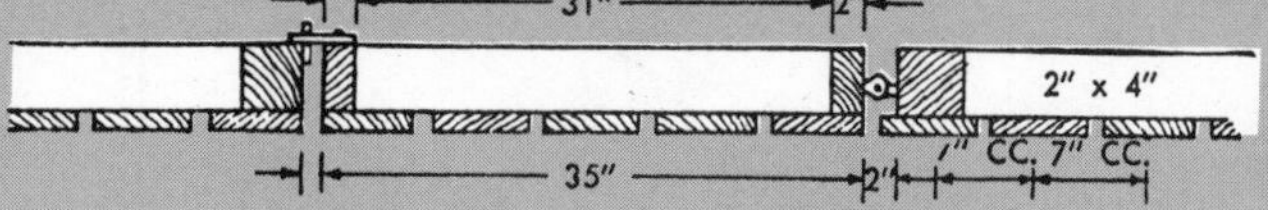

31"
2"
2" x 4"
35"
2"
7" CC. 7" CC.

THE VERSATILE PICKET FENCE UNIT

Already assembled picket fence units come in 8′ lengths, 3′ or 4′ high. Sold in most lumber yards or building markets, they are inexpensive, especially during clearance sales. You could hardly duplicate them for the price of the wood, let alone the hours of labor saved. Most have pointed pickets and are made of lower grades of wood, acceptable if painted. But they have potential for uses other than as conventional fencing.

Cut to half height (as shown below) with points cut off and extra 1″×3″s added for rails as needed, the units make excellent low dooryard fences when capped with a 1″×3″ or 1″×4″ piece and supported on 2″×4″ posts.

Upended strips cut to proper width form the unit, and with rails added make an interesting arbor or gateway. If you attach pickets to an adequate framework (see detail at bottom) you can use them for roofing and gabling, too.

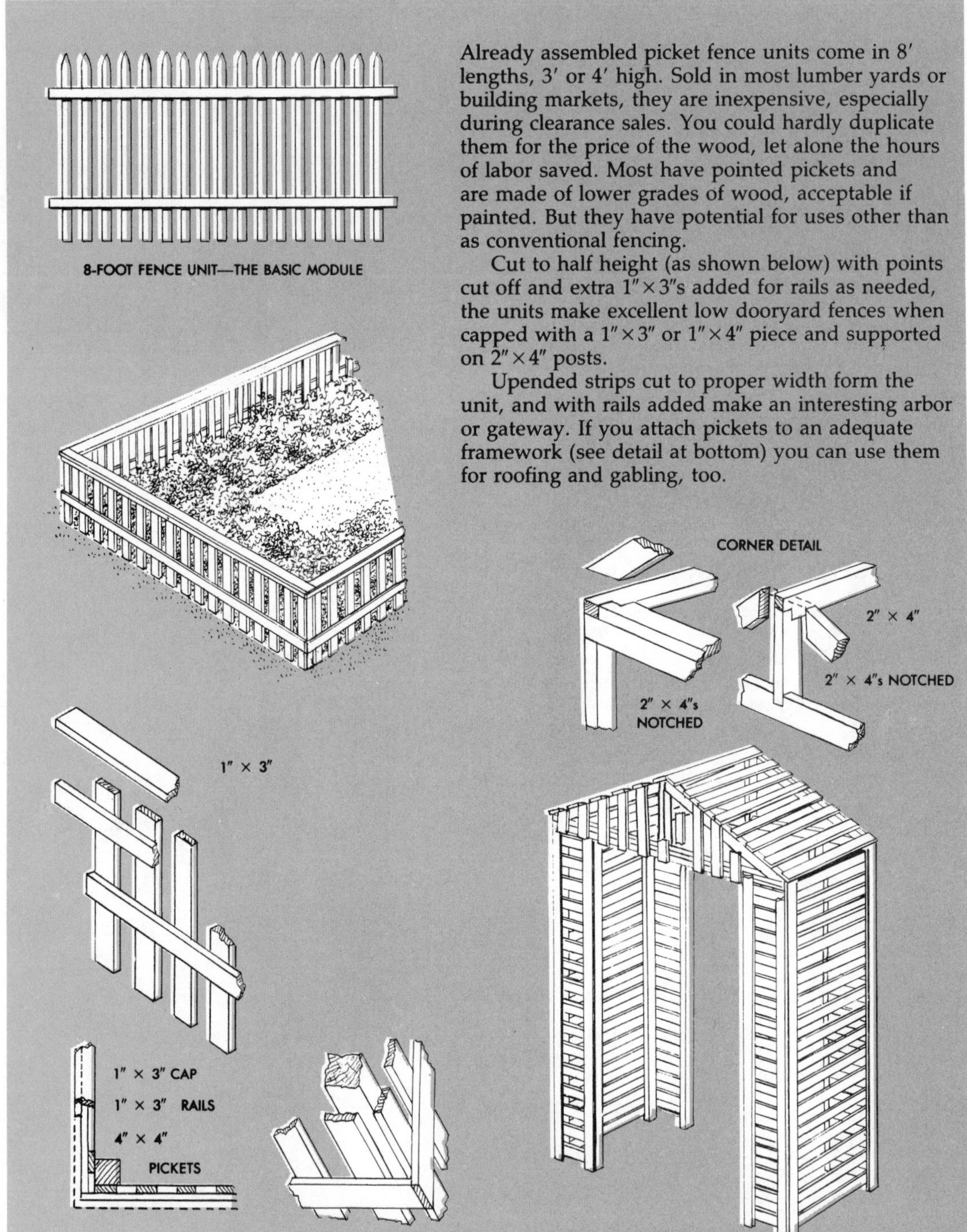

PICKET FENCES SET ON END

Picket units may be employed for uses other than fences if they are set upright. At right, mounted picket to picket and with the pointed ends lopped off and fastened to 2″×4″s, they are topped by shaped pieces to form a trellis, screen, or viewbreaker, their origin disguised. Similarly, twin trellises may be cut from units to fit the space, flanking a doorway and echoing its lintel with their top pieces—ideal for clematis, roses, or light vines to grow on. Below right, a zigzag fence is made from sections of fence of suitable height, mounted on 2″×4″ posts and capped with 1″×4″s that will give a touch of originality to many kinds of houses.

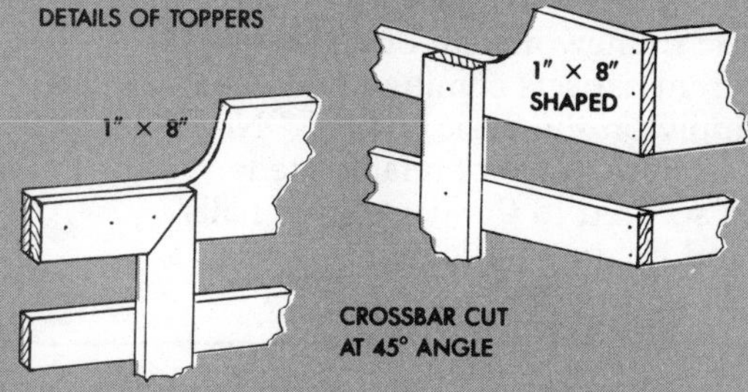

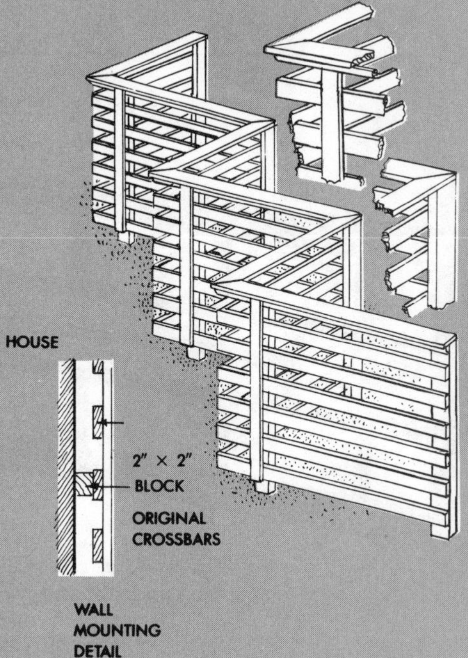

BASIC FRAME TO USE WITH DIFFERENT COVERINGS

THE BASIC FRAMEWORK

In contrasting fences, the same basic framework can often be used in a great variety of ways, the different aspects coming about from the kind of "skin" you choose to apply on the basic "bones." Note that in all these fences the central section may be prefabricated in the shop or on the ground, then secured to the posts with nails or screws, the top railing bracing and holding all together.

STRETCHED "H" FENCE

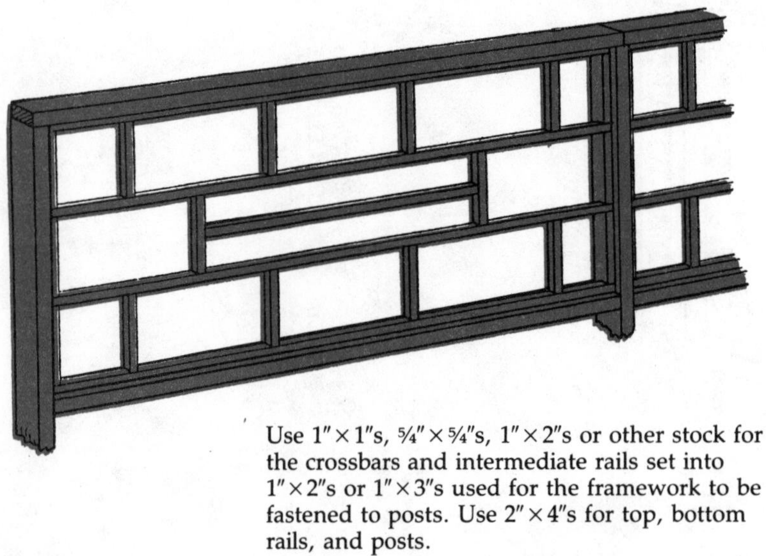

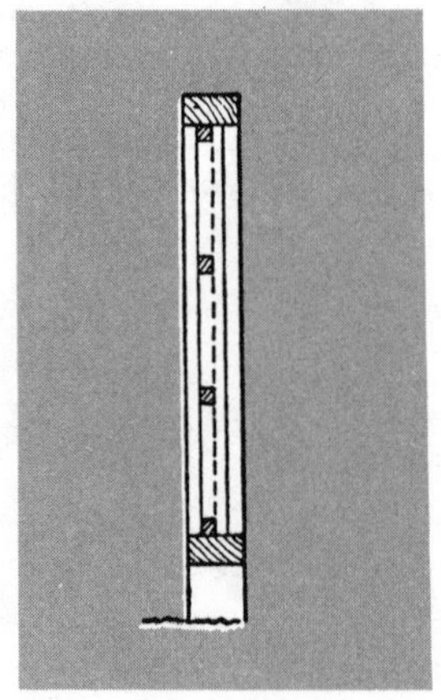

Use 1″ × 1″s, 5/4″ × 5/4″s, 1″ × 2″s or other stock for the crossbars and intermediate rails set into 1″ × 2″s or 1″ × 3″s used for the framework to be fastened to posts. Use 2″ × 4″s for top, bottom rails, and posts.

STAGGERED PANEL FENCE

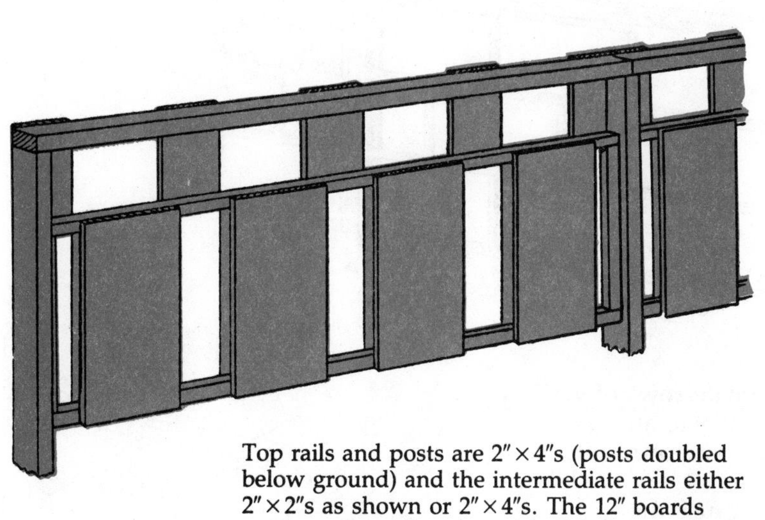

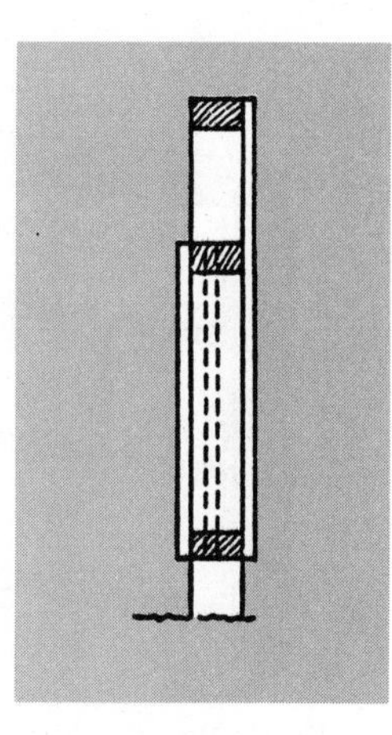

Top rails and posts are 2″ × 4″s (posts doubled below ground) and the intermediate rails either 2″ × 2″s as shown or 2″ × 4″s. The 12″ boards on fence front alternate with 6″ boards on back.

UP AND DOWN FENCE

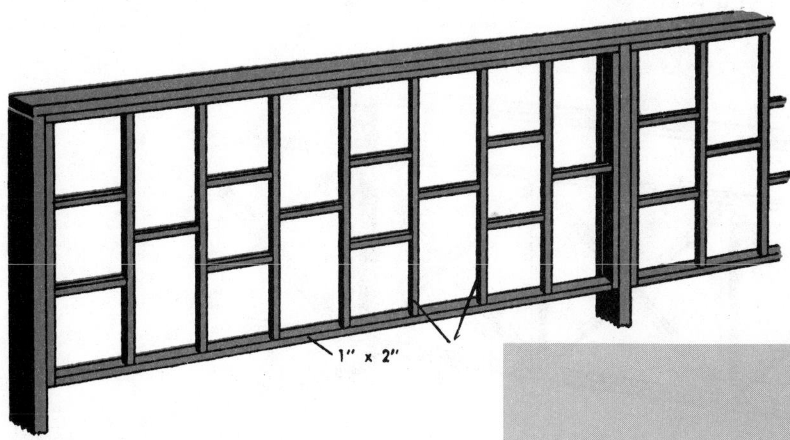

Alternating square and oblong patterns are interesting even without vines twining through them. The 1″ × 1″ verticals and horizontals are framed by 1″ × 2″ stock, but 2″ × 2″s or 2″ × 4″s might be used if a stronger fence should be desired. Use 4″ × 4″ corner and gate posts, 2″ × 4″s for intermediate posts set firmly in concrete.

1" x 1"s
SCREW
SCREW
1" x 2"
2"x4" POST

ALTERNATING OBLONGS

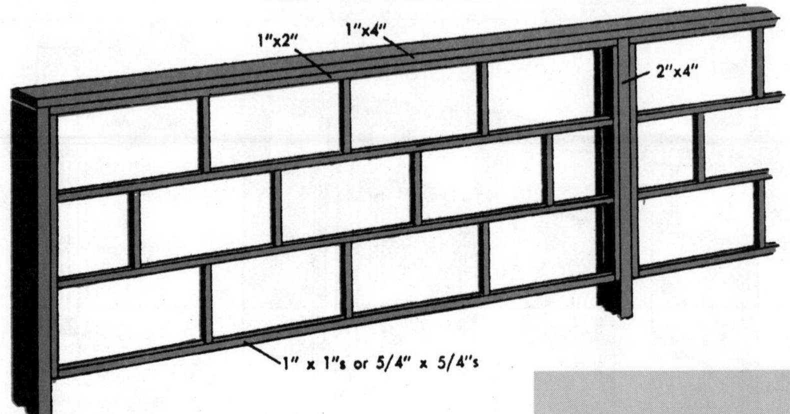

By centering the alternate rows of vertical pieces on the oblong above, an interesting and stable pattern results. Probably this is the simplest of the bikini fences to construct because the alternating placement allows nails or screws to be driven with the greatest of ease. Heavier materials may be adapted to this design, as indicated in the previous design, if you wish.

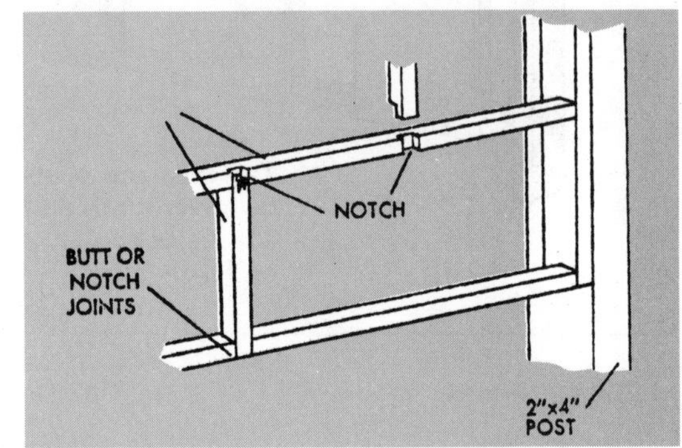

SQUARES WITH DIAGONALS

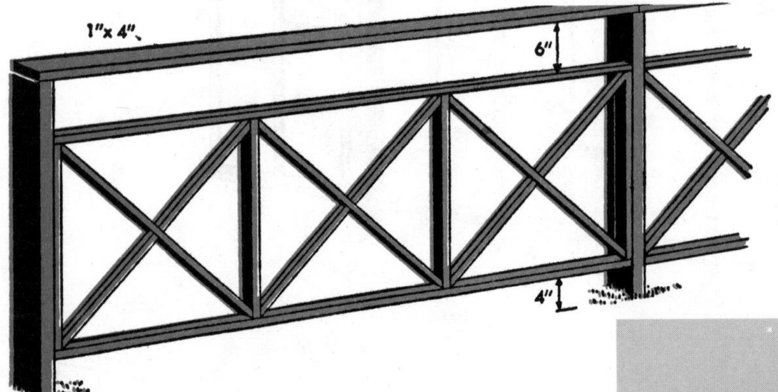

The lines of this fence are strong and simple and although it is of light construction it has considerable strength due to the use of the diagonal strips. The diagonals are fitted together with double dado joints and all cuts are simple 45° angles at the ends, simple and easy in either miter box or power saw set to proper angle.

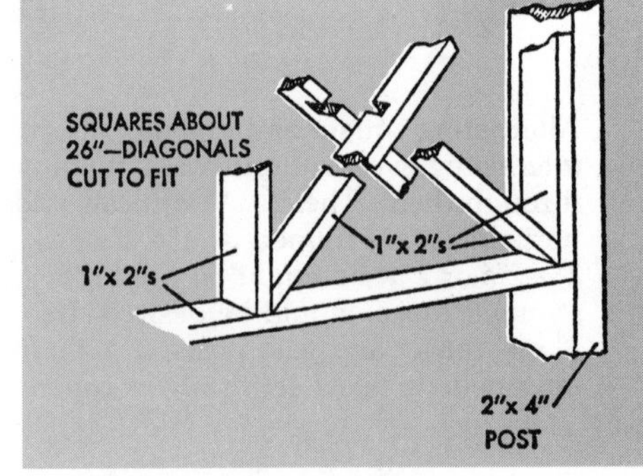

ANIMAL-RETAINER FENCE

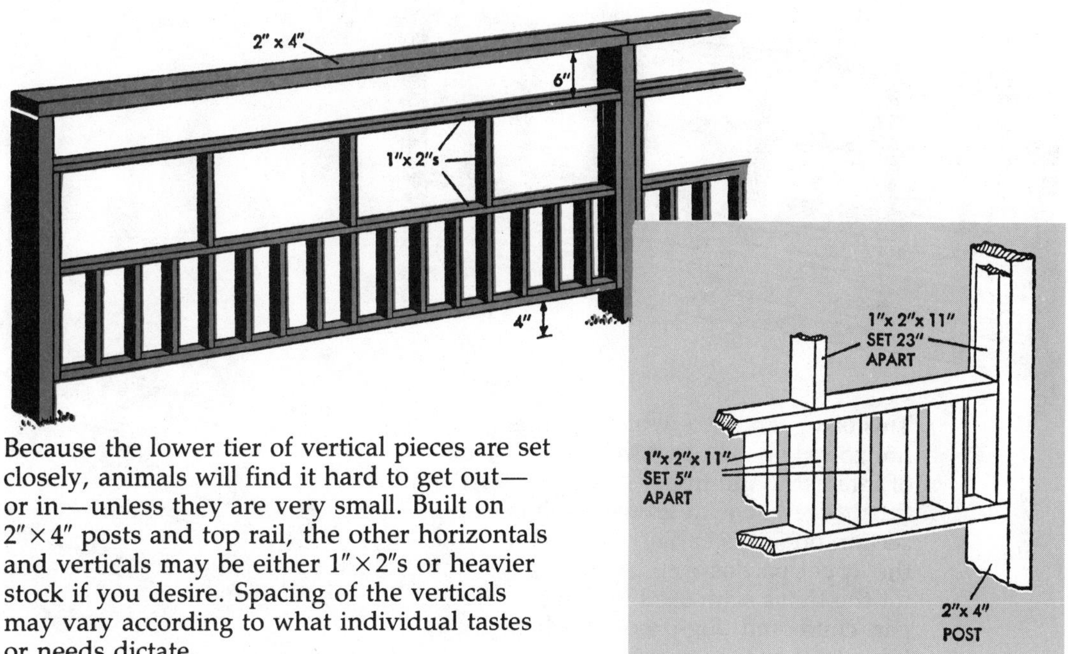

Because the lower tier of vertical pieces are set closely, animals will find it hard to get out—or in—unless they are very small. Built on 2″ × 4″ posts and top rail, the other horizontals and verticals may be either 1″ × 2″s or heavier stock if you desire. Spacing of the verticals may vary according to what individual tastes or needs dictate.

RIBBONS AND BARS

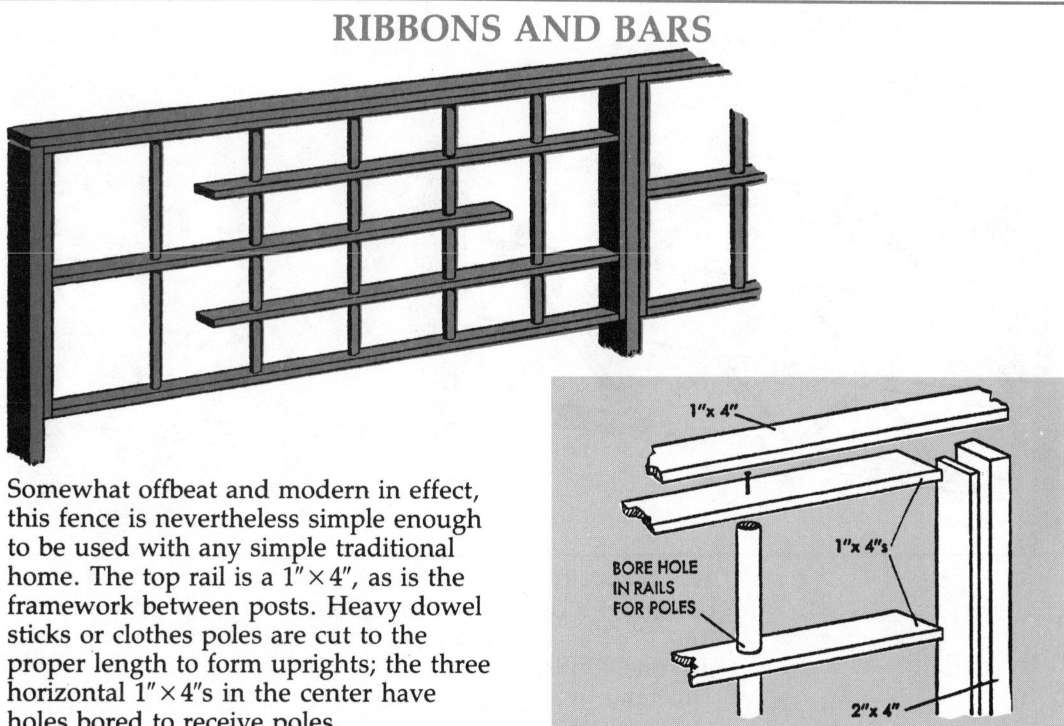

Somewhat offbeat and modern in effect, this fence is nevertheless simple enough to be used with any simple traditional home. The top rail is a 1″ × 4″, as is the framework between posts. Heavy dowel sticks or clothes poles are cut to the proper length to form uprights; the three horizontal 1″ × 4″s in the center have holes bored to receive poles.

MAINLY HORIZONTAL

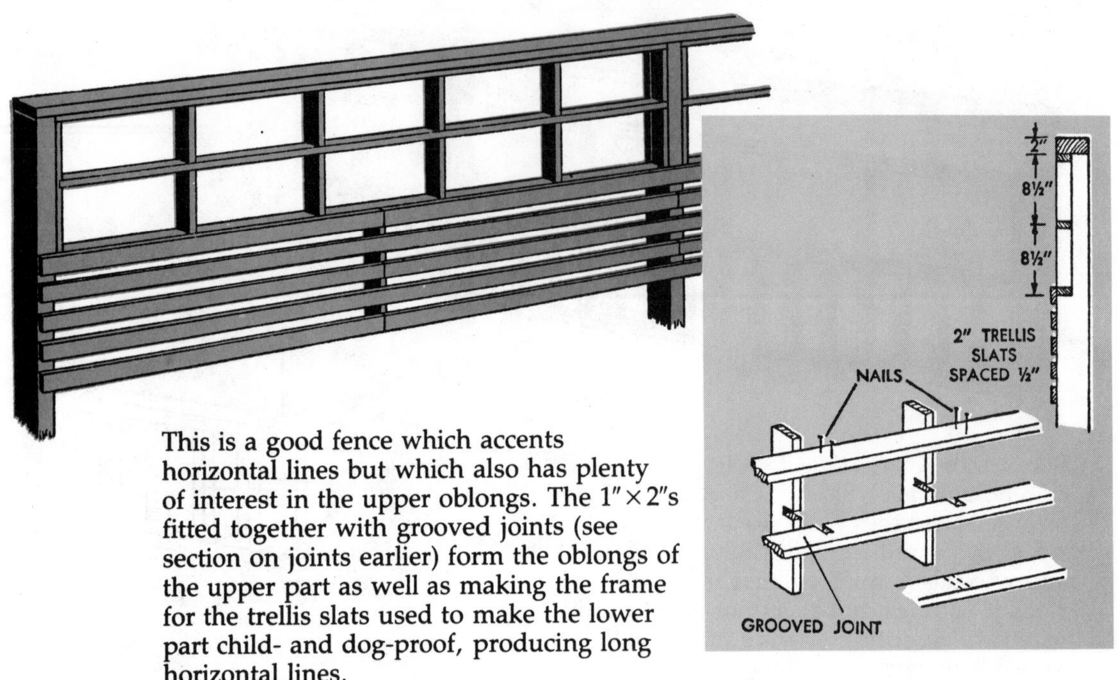

This is a good fence which accents horizontal lines but which also has plenty of interest in the upper oblongs. The 1" × 2"s fitted together with grooved joints (see section on joints earlier) form the oblongs of the upper part as well as making the frame for the trellis slats used to make the lower part child- and dog-proof, producing long horizontal lines.

DIAGONAL SQUARES

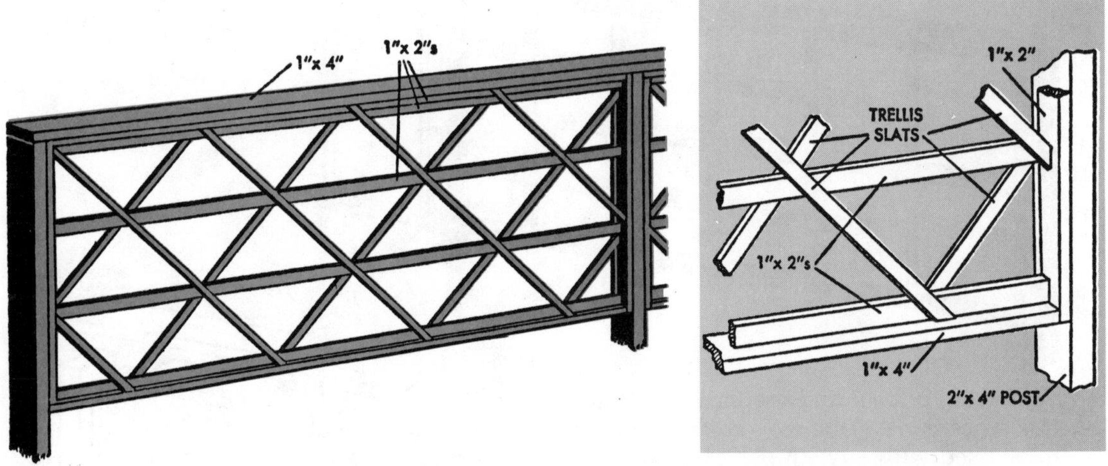

The diagonals used in this fence give strength as well as producing a certain excitement of line. The 1" × 2" frame has the four 1" × 2"s set in groove joints in the side pieces, and the diagonal trellis strips are nailed in place on either side of them. This fence would be a good one for clematis or roses or any of the good, lightweight vines to climb on.

SPINDLE FENCE

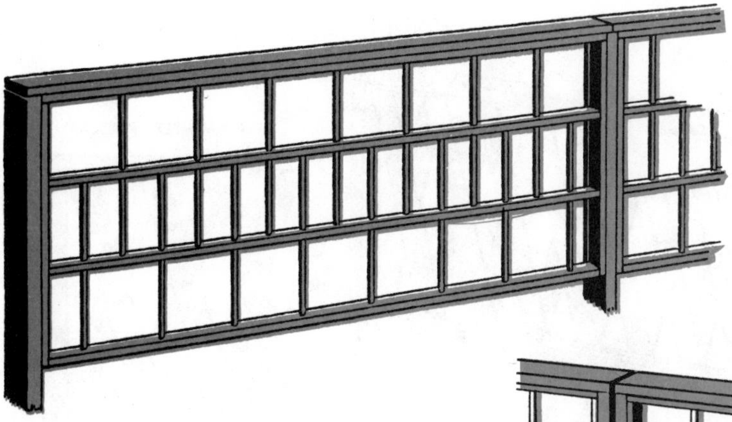

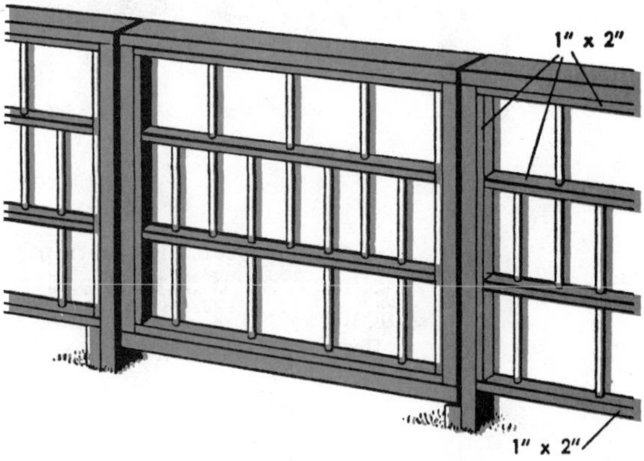

Relatively simple to construct because it is possible to cut several pieces at once and to bore the necessary holes for the dowel sticks used for the spindles, this attractive fence is particularly interesting because of contrasting round and squared stock. It may be adapted to heavier construction by using 2″ × 4″s and round clothes-pole stock.

SPINDLE FENCE GATE

The framework of the gate is all 2″ × 4″s, with the framework holding the dowels made of 1″ × 2″s with holes bored through where dowel penetrates, bored ⅜″ to ½″ deep to admit dowel on alternate spaces, a nail or screw being used through remainder of rail to hold dowel firmly in place. Use wood preservative over all, especially cuts.

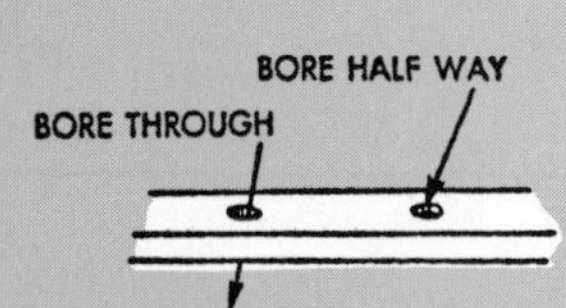

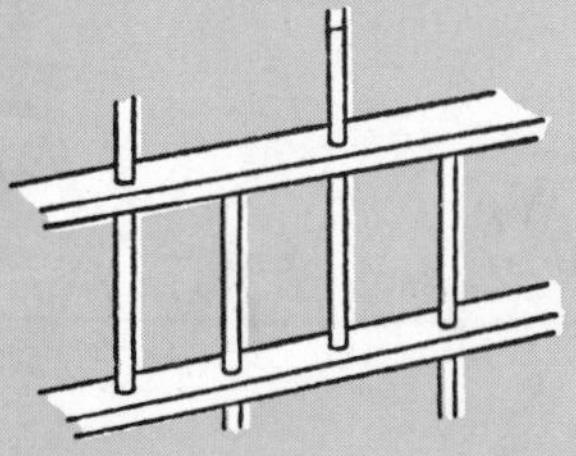

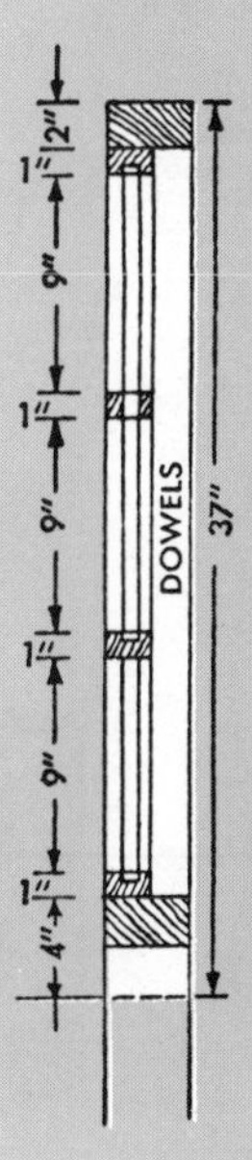

CROSSING THE BARS

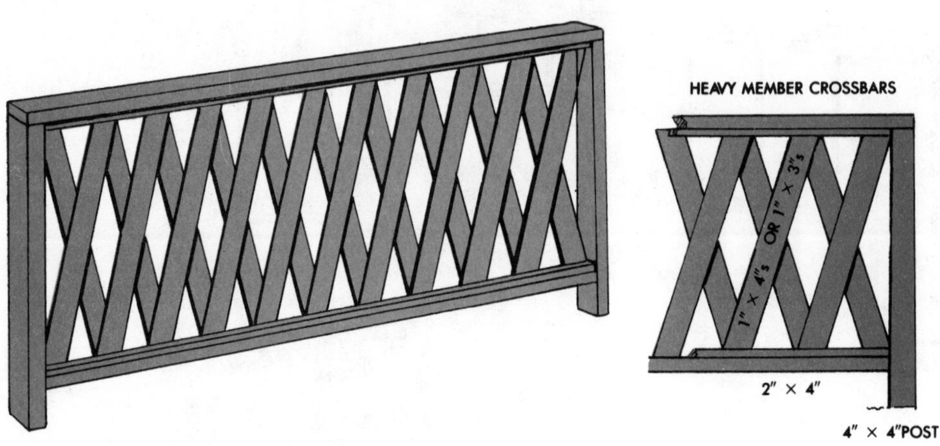

Crossed diagonal members make fences of unusual visual interest, whether formed of heavier 1" × 4"s, or lighter 1" × 3"s or 2"s, or delicate ¼" × 1¼" lattice slats. Excitement and movement are built in. Four variations are shown, each suited to a different situation.

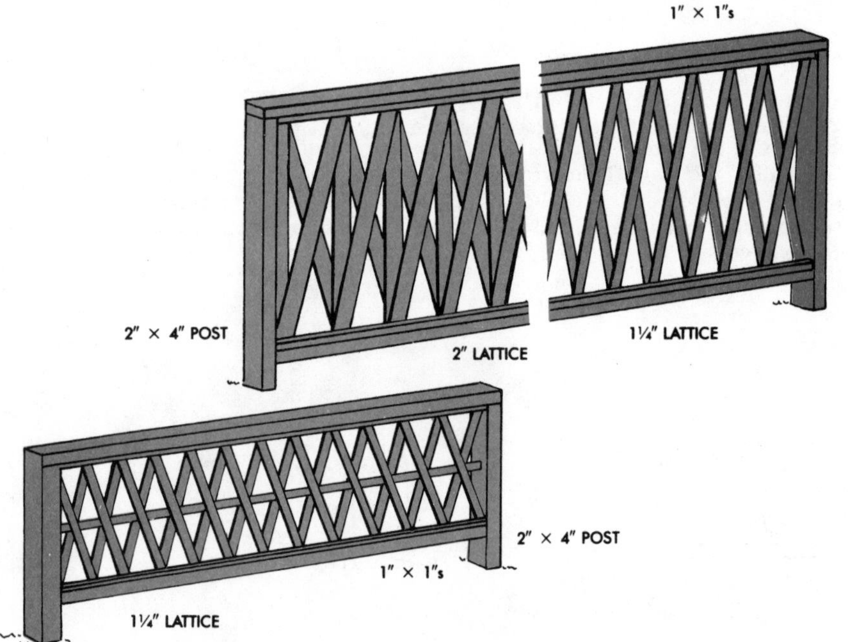

WOODEN FENCE, BRICK STYLE

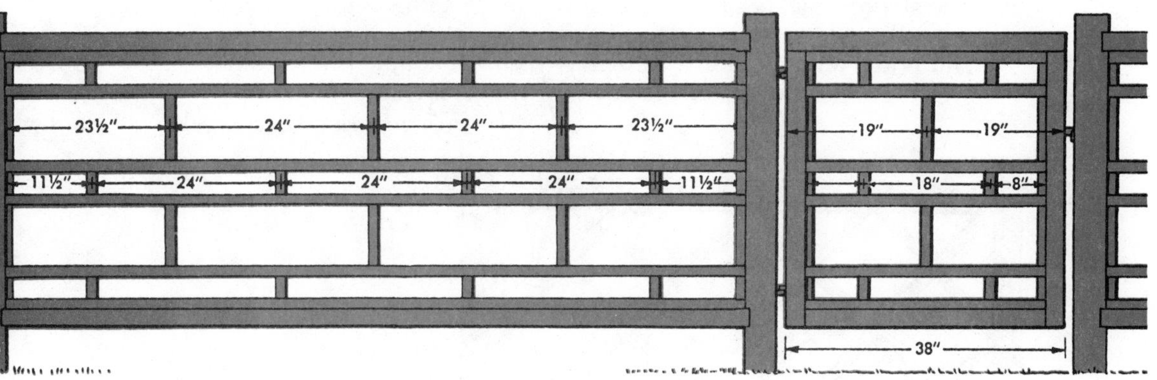

Although this fence is built of wood, it takes its design cue from brick bonding, the bands of wide and narrow oblong openings being set between top and bottom 2″ × 4″ rails dadoed into the 4″ × 4″ posts, the fretwork of the fence behind made from 1″ × 2″s, 1″ × 1″s or 5⁄4″ × 5⁄4″s. Horizontal bars are dadoed into stock at ends, which is nailed to the posts.

BRICK-STYLE GATE CONSTRUCTION

Top and bottom rails of this gate are butt-joined to the sides, with the interior fretwork being constructed in all particulars in the same manner as that in the fence itself. Gate posts are 4″ × 4″s raised like the corner posts 3½″ above the level of the top rail. Should it be felt necessary, a diagonal may be inserted behind fretwork to act as a brace.

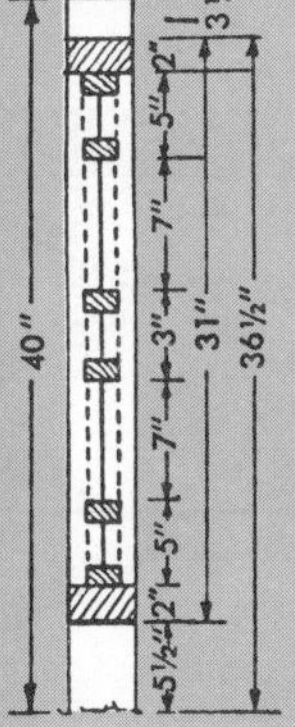

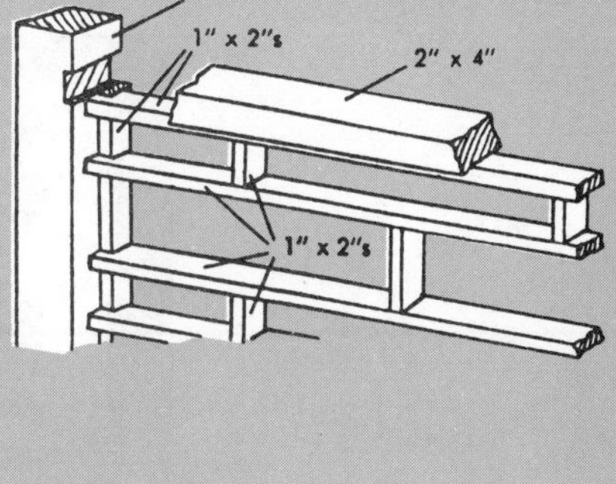

ADAPTED FROM DESIGNS OF THOMAS JEFFERSON

The stark formality of classic architecture in 18th century America was relieved by the addition of gallery balustrades, roof railings, and porch railings similar to these which are adapted from some which Thomas Jefferson designed for the University of Virginia.

(Continued on next page)

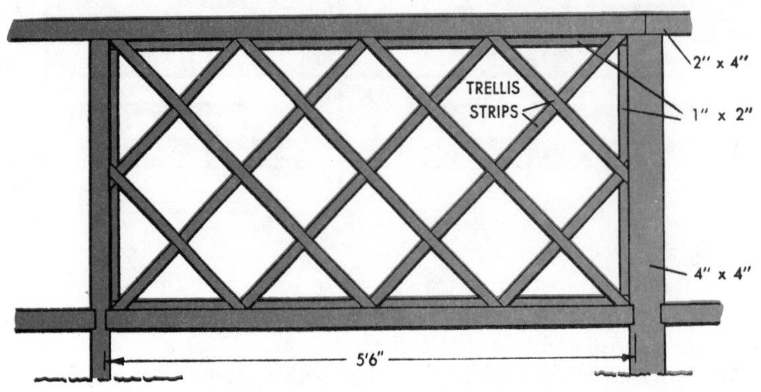

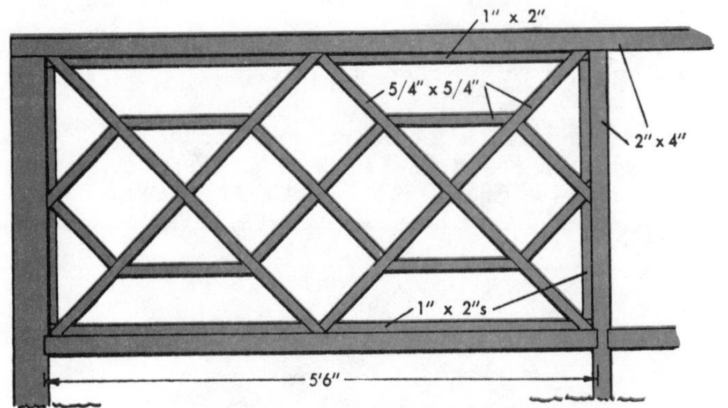

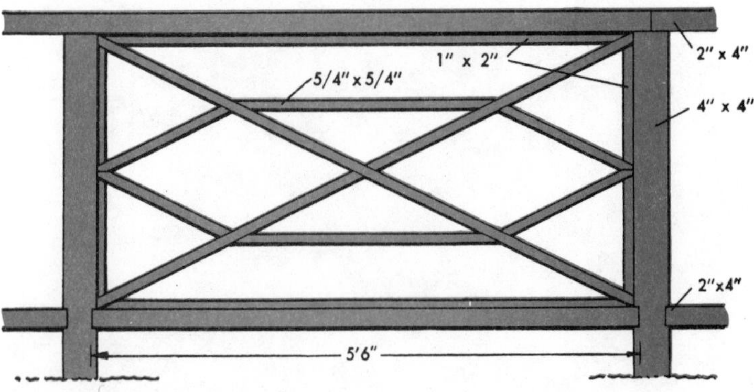

They fit well with the colonial style, but because they were adapted by him from oriental sources, many, especially the simpler ones, will make good fences for modern homes. They may be varied to fit longer or shorter spans, turned up on end and used as trellises. Vary angles of diagonals as necessary, add design units to fill out and fit space you use.

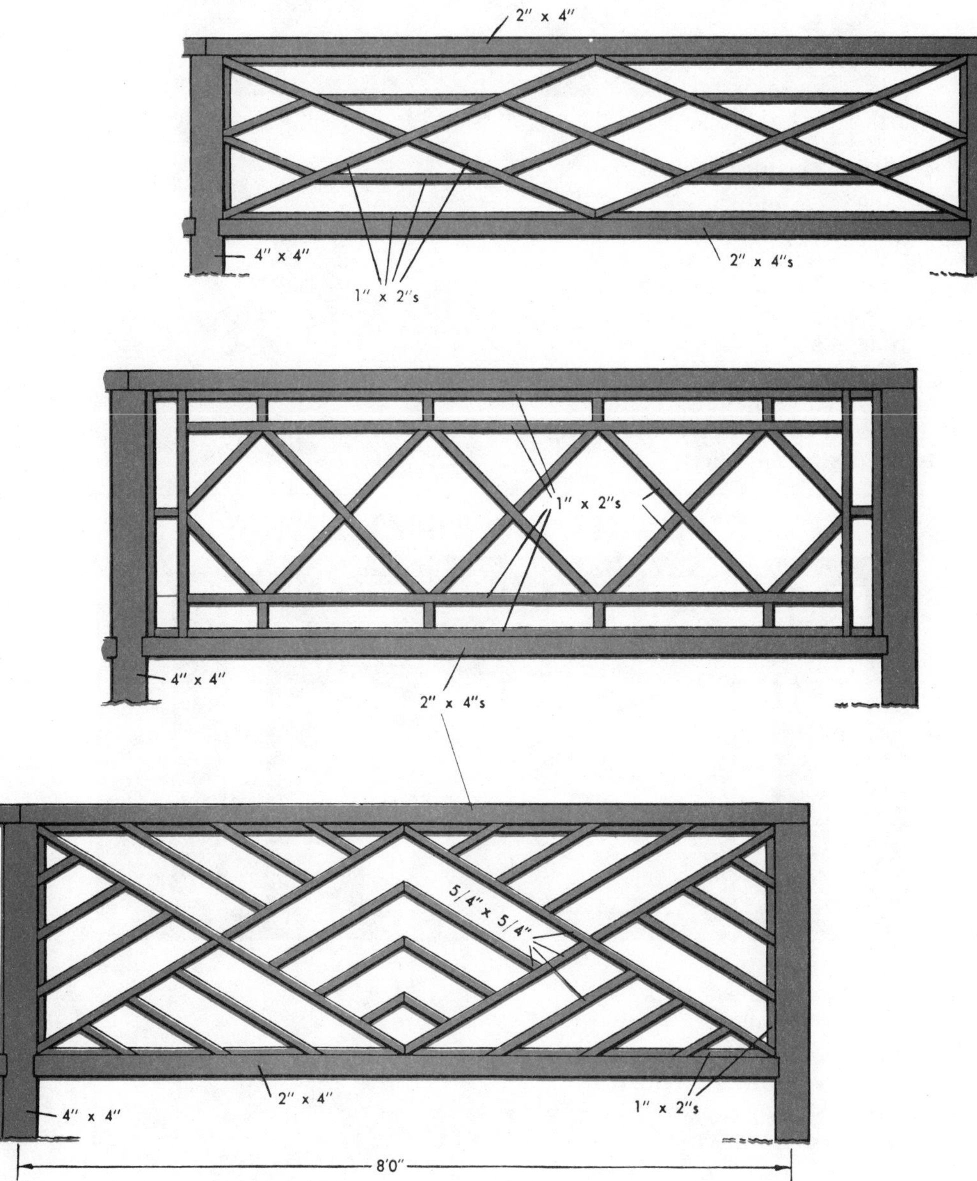

INTERLOCKING BLOCK PATTERN

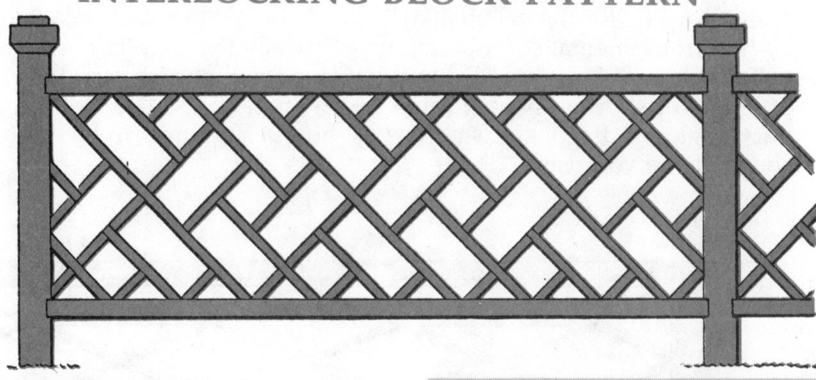

A varied pattern, featuring broken diagonals, makes a handsome yet simple fence. Since all cuts are 45° angles, ease of making is guaranteed. Use 1″×1″s, 5/4″×5/4″s, or 1″×4″s for the center; top and bottom rails being 2″×4″s; posts 4″×4″ with caps 6″×6″×2″ supported by moldings. Trellis strips may be used if a light fence is desired, nailing them to back of rails or using a plywood backing with the trellis strips applied.

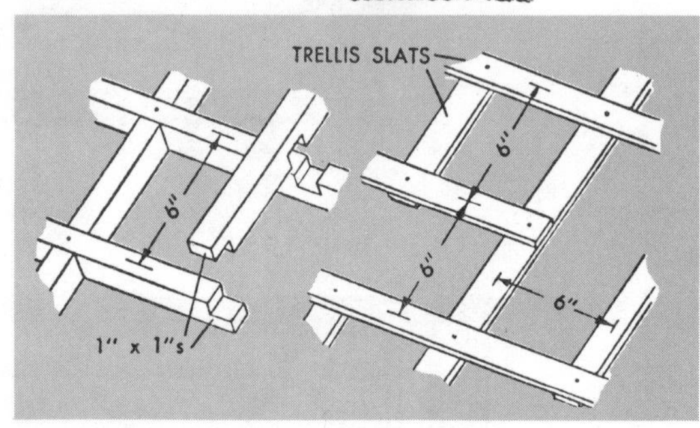

ORIENTAL PEEKABOO FENCE

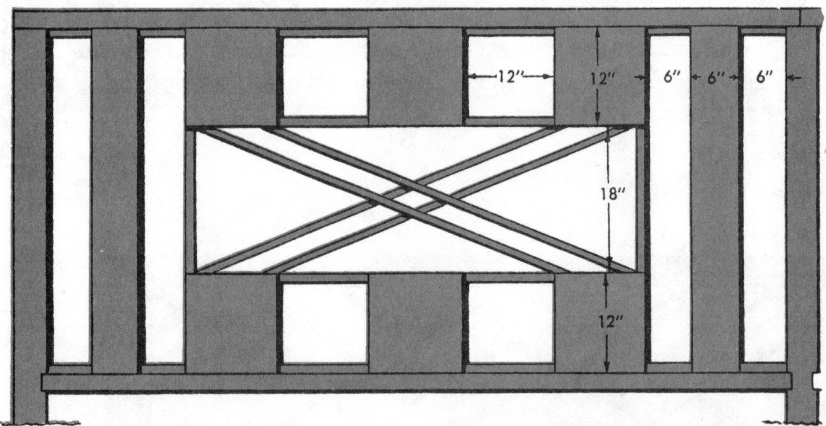

Adapted from the Japanese, this fence has posts of 4″×4″s, rails 2″×4″s with 1″×2″s used as nailing strips for vertical members. The "window" is framed with 1″×2″s, diagonals being narrow-cut trellis strips nailed to the back of the frame. If complete privacy is desired, baffle the fence by applying vertical members in all the openings (on the opposite side of the fence) and do not use "windows" or use them only for some exceptional view.

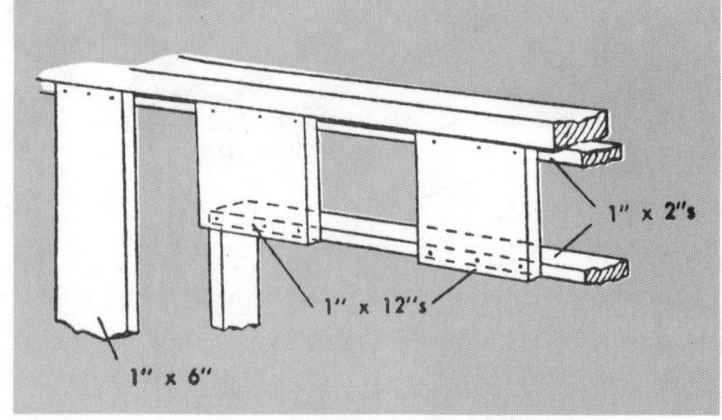

OPENWORK GATE AND FENCE

For a severely plain house or one with an oriental flavor, a fence and gate that lends pattern to the landscape, limiting the line of the property but not blocking the view, is a good solution. In the Orient, the juxtaposition of the natural informality of plants with the formal or geometrical brings an enchanting piquancy to the garden scene. In this adaptation of a traditional oriental pattern, weighty structural members are used, allowed to weather to a natural gray or painted a color that echoes the house trim.

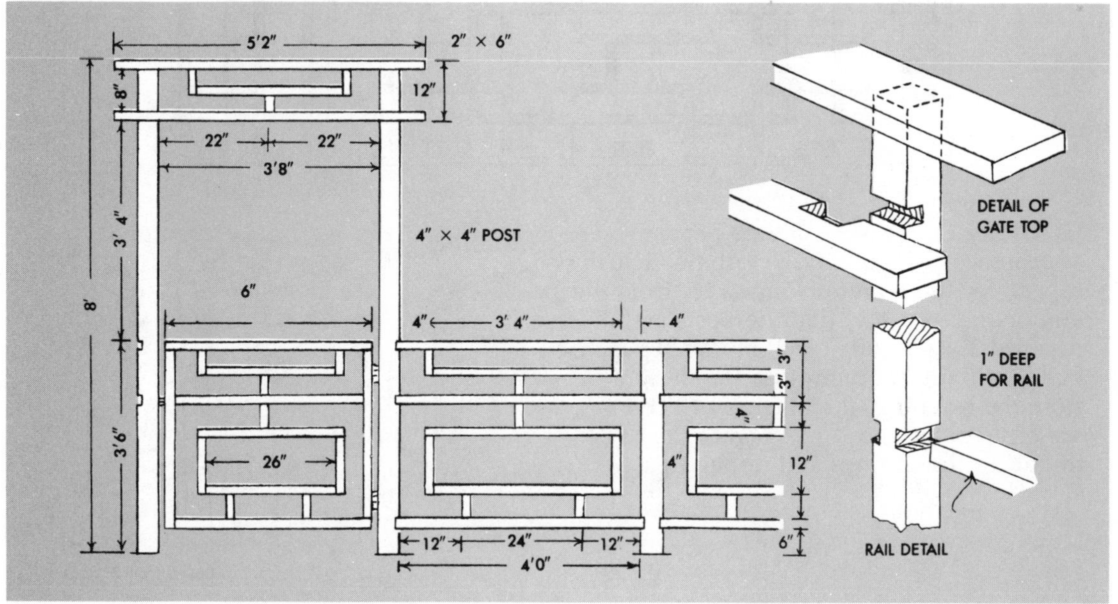

INTERLOCKING SQUARES

The fascination of pattern which is regular in its repetition, yet irregular in division of space is quite apparent in this design. Light in weight and airy in feeling, it is a fence which proclaims protection of an area, yet does it in a most gracious way. The design could be adapted to heavier-weight materials than the 1″ × 1″ strips and frame of 1″ × 2″s used here, but would be less airy in effect.

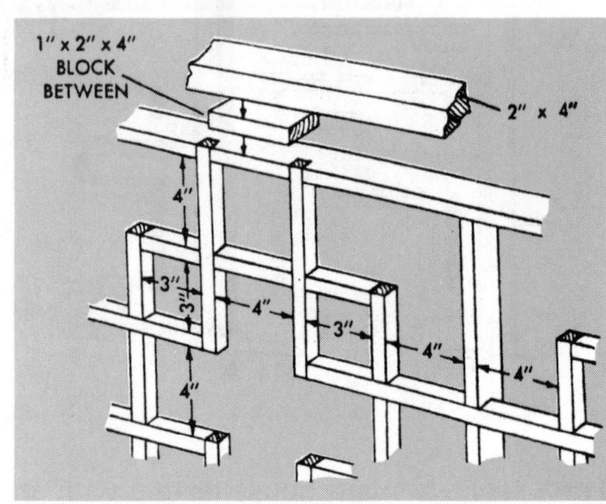

INTERLOCKING OBLONGS

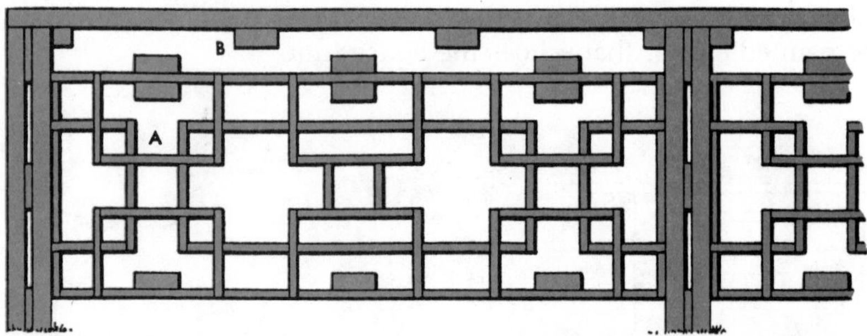

Gracefully interlocking, the oblongs give the appearance of regularity, yet do not actually repeat, for the center oblongs vary from the end ones. Note, too, that the posts are doubled 2″ × 4″s with 1″ × 4″ blocks between, giving still further interest to the design from the resulting slots. Blocks of 1″ × 4″s are centered on the 1″ × 2″ frames in the middle of the oblongs and upper area.

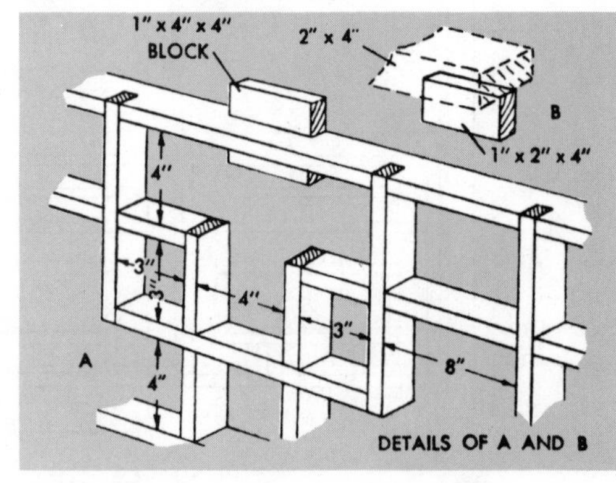

CONCENTRIC OBLONGS

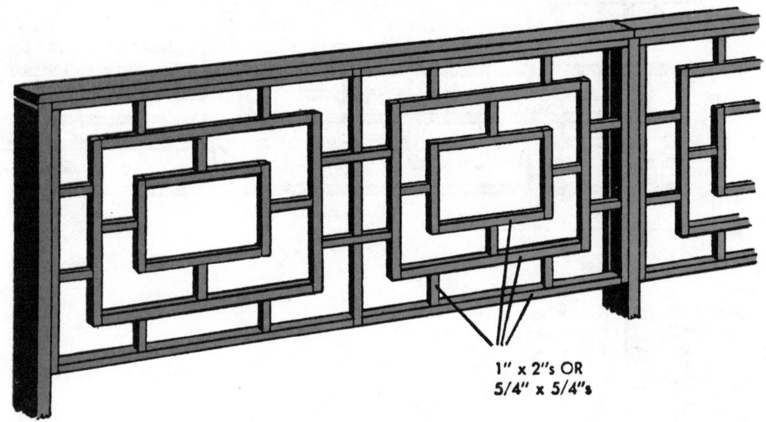

Restful but with considerable interest inherent in its design, this fence uses oblongs to good effect. By centering the short connecting pieces on the center oblong and placing the short pieces on the outer oblong even with the sides of the inner oblong, variety is introduced with no sacrifice of design stability. Easily built because of straight joints.

CONSTRUCTION OF GATE

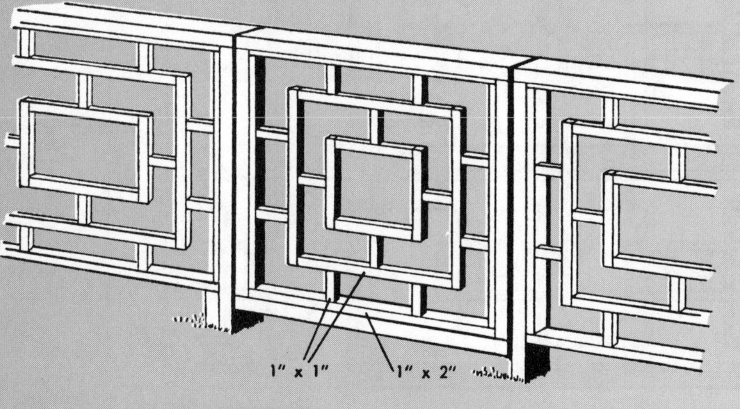

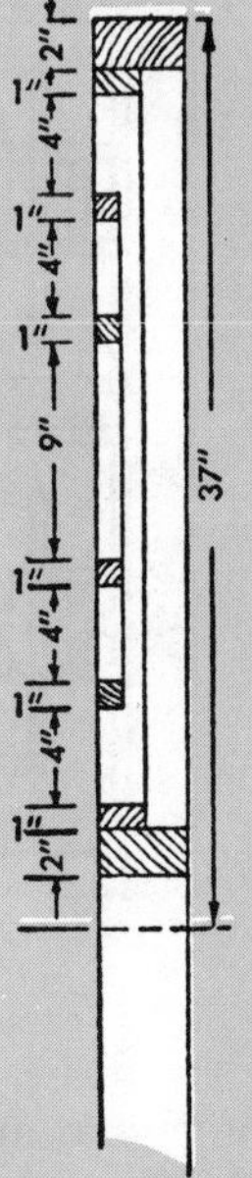

This gate is constructed similarly to that above, with a 1″ × 2″ frame inside containing fretwork made of 1″ × 1″s or 5/4 × 5/4″s. All fretwork is made with butt joints held by nails or screws and butted to frame. Set frame flush with fence front.

INTERRUPTED HORIZONTALS

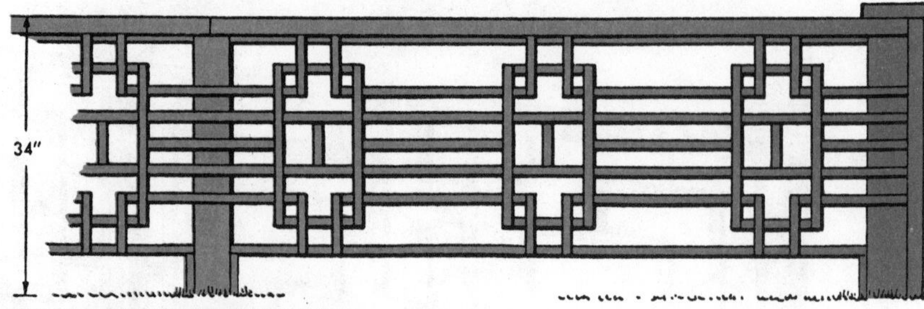

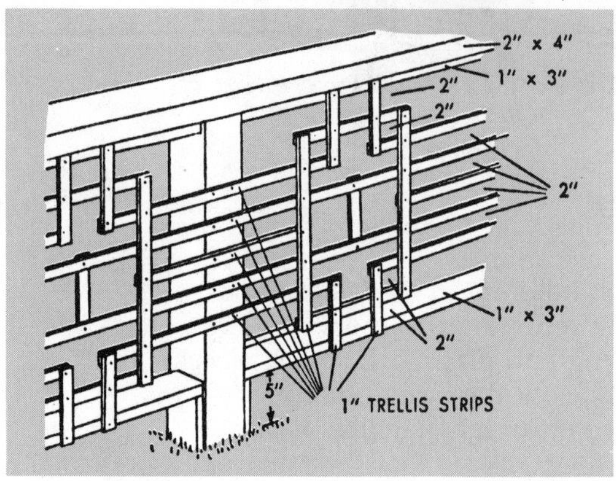

Although it may look intricate, this fence is actually rather easy to make, especially for the possessor of a power saw. It is neat and gives the effect of being rather strong, yet is actually light in weight. Posts are 4" × 4"s but might be 2" × 4"s except for corners and end or gate posts. Bottom rail might be a 2" × 4" if desired, reversing the order of top rail and setting it in a groove joint in post.

SQUARES AND OBLONGS

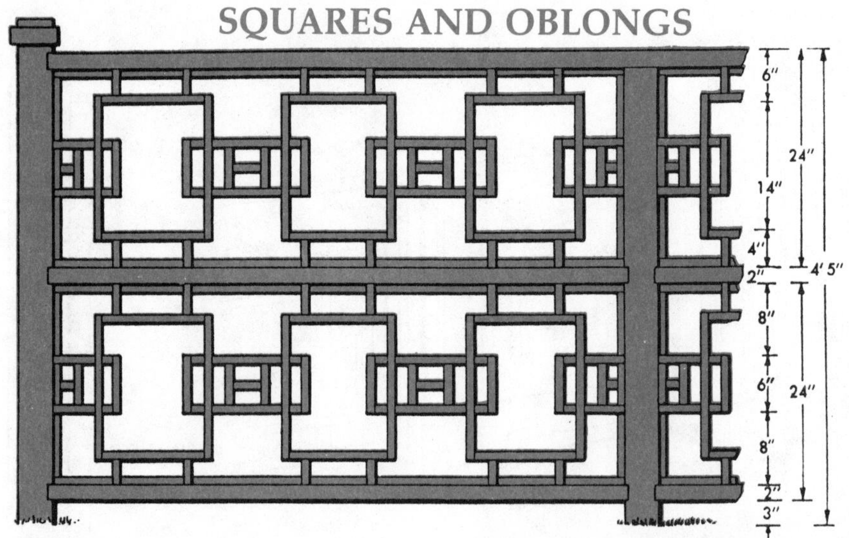

A somewhat more elaborate fence which would go well with a traditional or modern house where extra decorative effect is desired can be prefabricated in frame, set in.

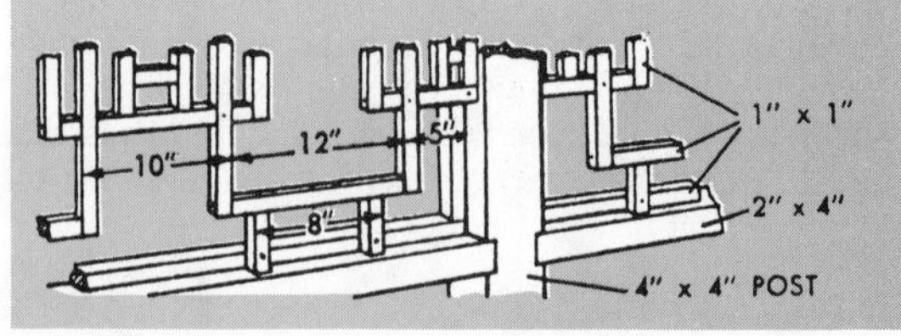

WHIRLING OBLONGS

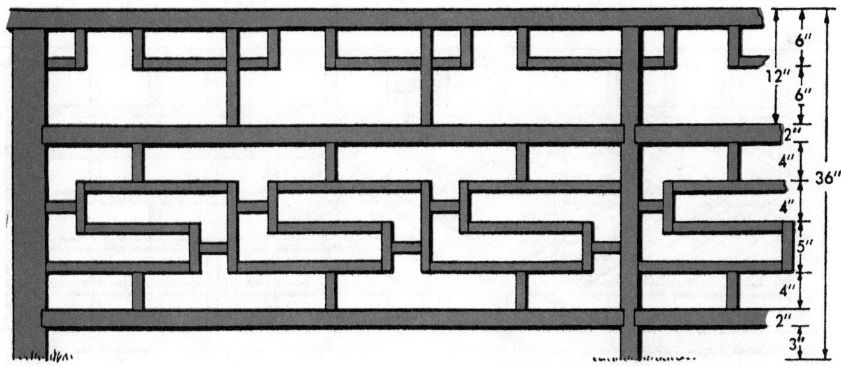

Suitable for either a modern or traditional home, this fence has a lower part which will keep out animals and keep children in, but the upper part is open. The effect is light, airy, and off-beat enough to be most interesting. The end and corner posts are 4″×4″s with intermediate posts either the same or 2″×4″s; all posts are set in concrete. Top, bottom, and intermediate rails are 2″×4″s set in groove joints in posts.

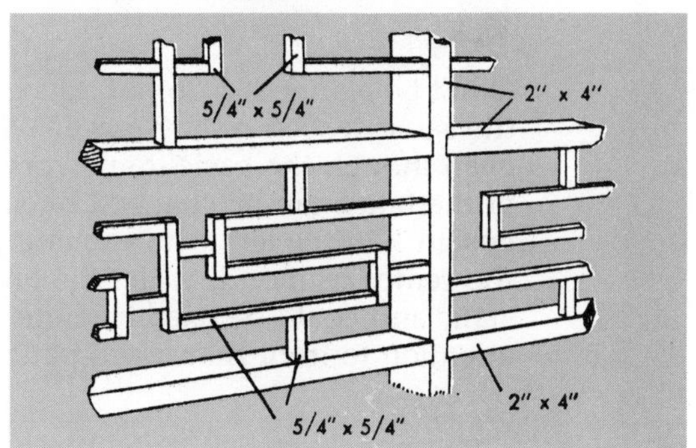

DIAMONDS AND OBLONGS

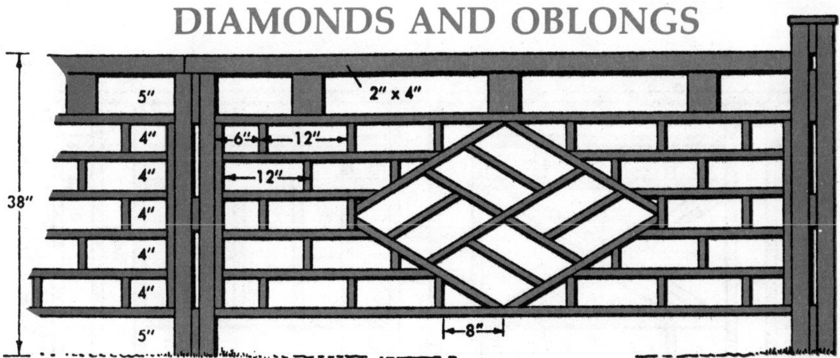

Strong horizontals lend serenity to this fence, but the diamond pattern gives it sufficient interest to keep it from being dull. The frame is entirely constructed of 2″×4″s with doubled posts held apart by 1″×4″ blocks to make interesting slots. Although this is less easy to construct than some, it is not beyond the do-it-yourselfer's scope, particularly if angular cuts are made by preset power saw.

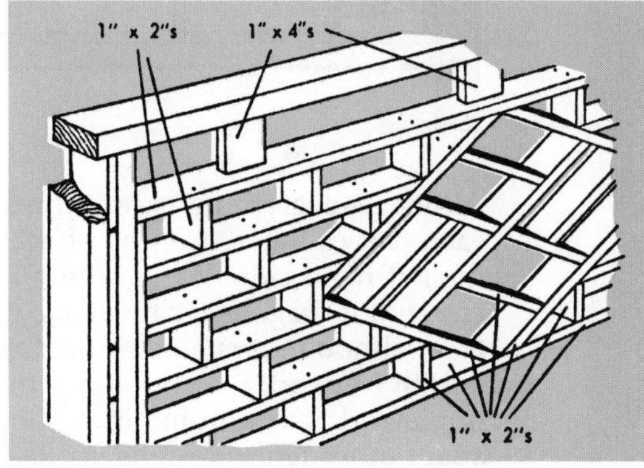

SAME FENCE, DIFFERENT TREATMENT

Don't be alarmed. I do not advocate using two unrelated patterns in the same section of any fence. What I am attempting to show is that even though the basic framework may be the same, the whole effect of the fence can be changed by varying some portion of the interior design. On the left is an exciting treatment with diagonals paralleling the center diamond, while the one on the right is rather quiet and static and could be used in more places, because it would draw less attention to itself than vivid pattern might.

RIGHT-HAND OR LEFT-HAND DESIGN?

Although everything except the small central oblong is the same in each half of this fence, the effect could hardly be more different. In the left-hand side the "window" has interwoven 1" trellis strips, crossing it diagonally, breaking the space and giving excitement to the area, although it is a quiet excitation. Or, as an alternative design, fill it with fretwork which follows the verticals and horizontals of the framework surrounding it as shown in the right-hand side. You can adapt other fence designs similarly, varying them as necessary.

DESIGN WITH MOVEMENT

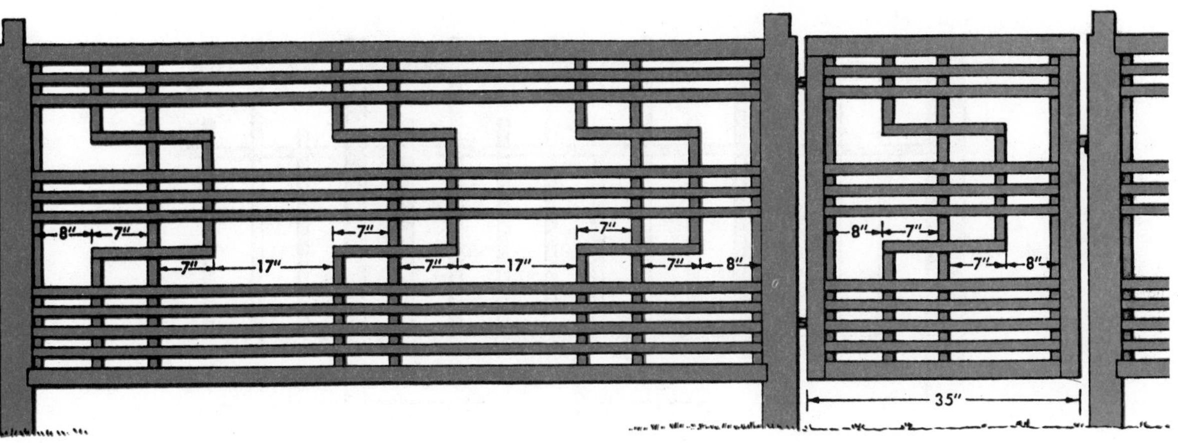

Although the various members of this fence are of necessity static, there seems to be considerable movement due to the design. Posts are 4″ × 4″s, rails 2″ × 4″s dadoed into the posts, and the interior members are 1″ × 2″s with butt joints except for horizontal crossbars which are double dadoed into upright members. The horizontals are 1″ trellis slats.

GATE CONSTRUCTION

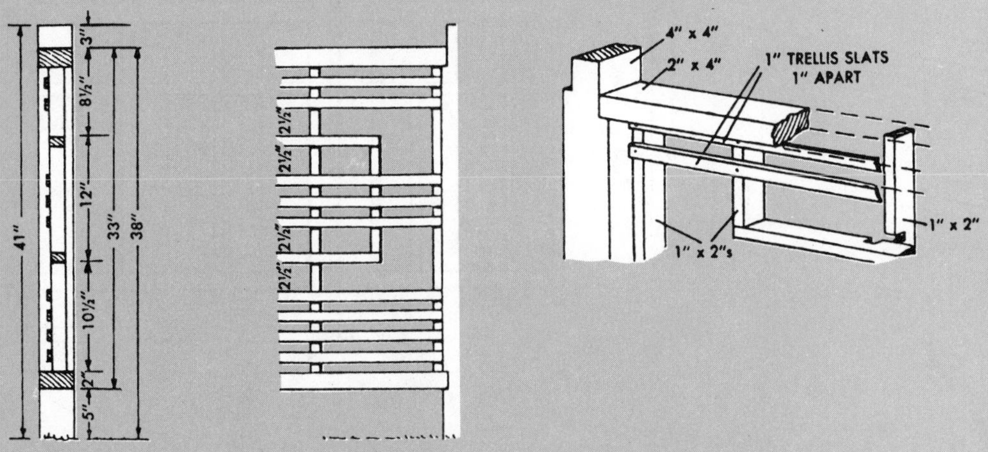

One unit of the fence design is adapted to the gate, the construction being exactly the same as that used for the interior members of the fence. Use butt joints for the rails and sides of the gate frame. Dado the fence rails into the 4″ × 4″ gate posts, notching the tops of all posts as shown, the extenders being held 3″ above the level of the top rail of the fence.

LONG AND SHORT DOWELS

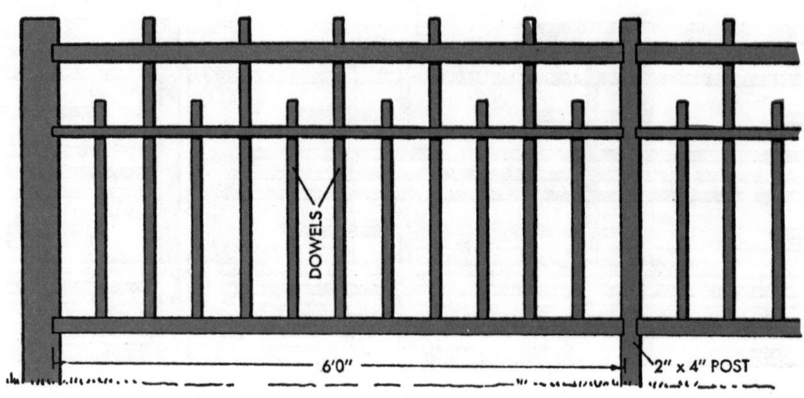

Pickets with a difference that will fit in with the most traditional house and go well with the intermediate modernized styles, too, are seen in this fence. Posts are 4" × 4"s for corners and every other post, intermediate ones 2" × 4"s with top and bottom rails 2" × 4", and 1" × 4" center rail dadoed in. Holes are bored in all rails to admit 1" dowels to penetrate.

GATE CONSTRUCTION

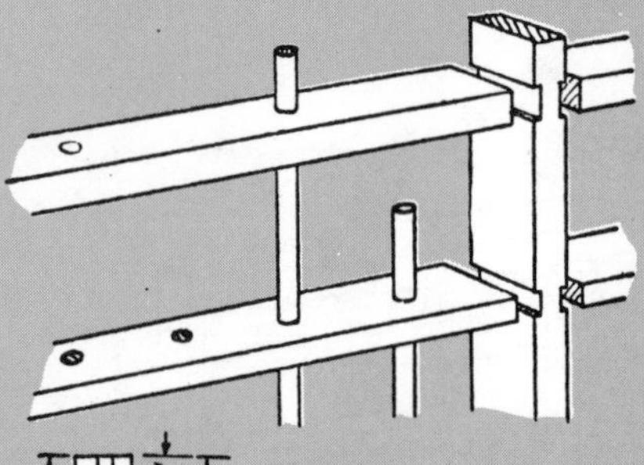

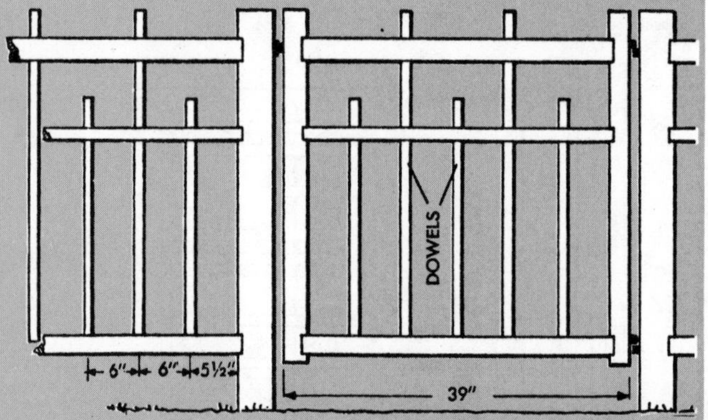

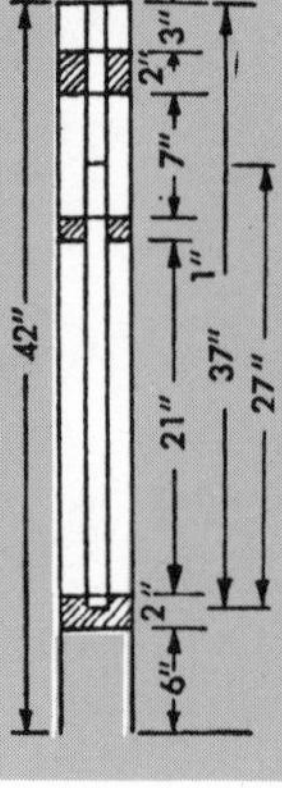

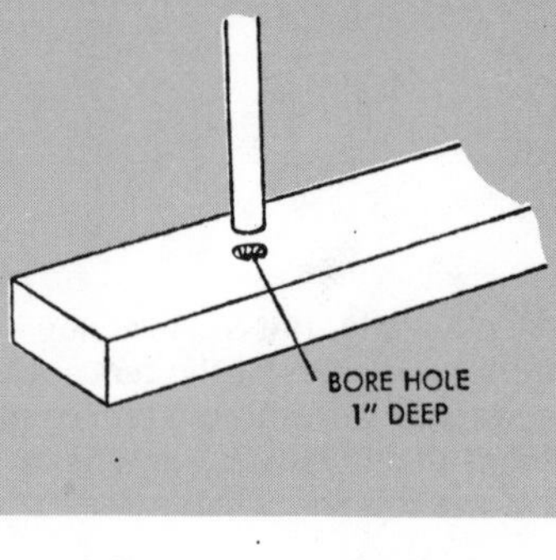

Framework is all 2" × 4"s with center rail a 1" × 4". All rails are dadoed into sides of the gate. Dowels can be set closer together if desired, but they should not be placed at wider intervals or the fence and gate will look too stringy and proportions be in bad scale.

AN INTERESTING DOWEL PICKET FENCE

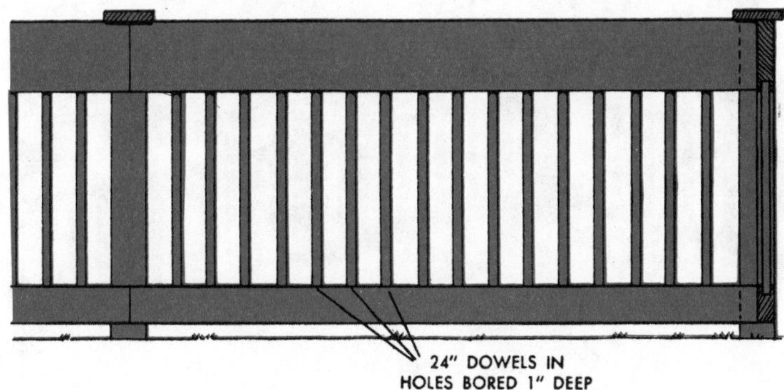

Strongly constructed of 2″ stock with holes bored to admit dowels, this fence and gate (below) have a directness of design that will go with many kinds of homes. The gate has a top rail of a shaped 2″ × 8″, with an iron rod bent into shape to hold a pot of flowers, the rod being threaded and held in place by nuts countersunk into the back side of the rail.

HOW TO BUILD THE FENCE

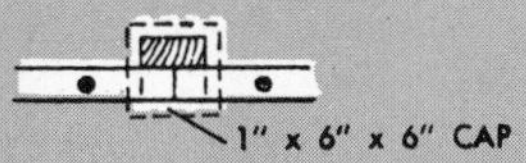

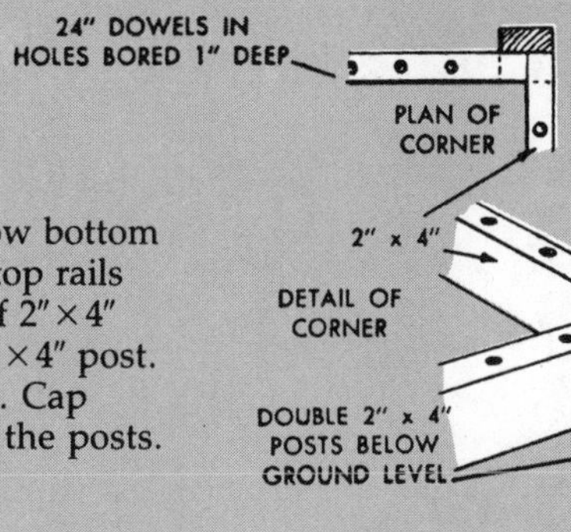

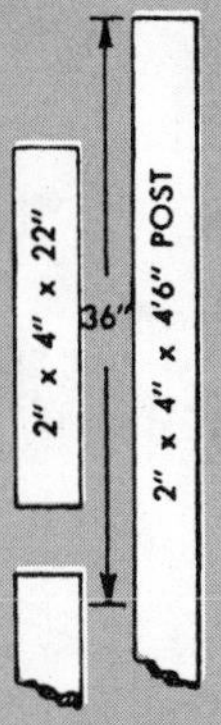

All posts are 2″ × 4″s, doubled below bottom rail, the 2″ × 4″ bottom and 2″ × 8″ top rails being set in place, then a length of 2″ × 4″ fitted between to make a strong 4″ × 4″ post. Note detail of corner post of fence. Cap blocks are 1″ × 6″ × 6″s centered on the posts.

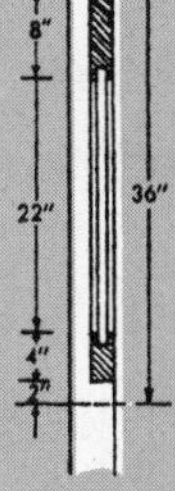

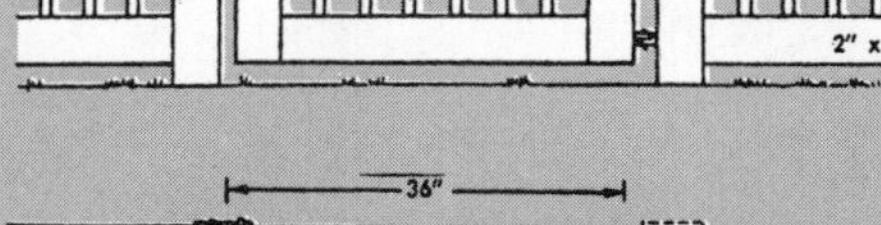

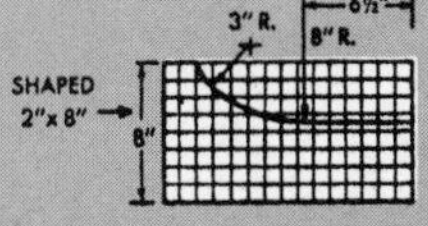

UNPRETENTIOUS, YET FULL OF CHARACTER

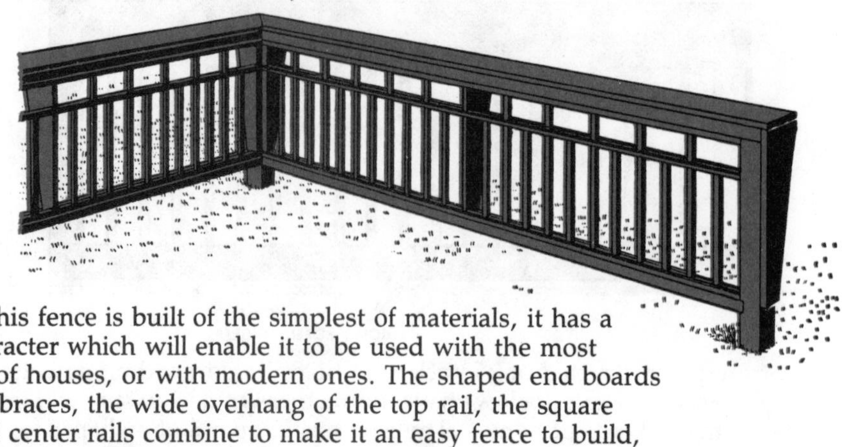

Although this fence is built of the simplest of materials, it has a certain character which will enable it to be used with the most traditional of houses, or with modern ones. The shaped end boards and center braces, the wide overhang of the top rail, the square pickets and center rails combine to make it an easy fence to build, too. The openings of the top can be varied (see below) with every other or every third picket cut full height.

TOP RAIL

PLAN OF CORNER

3″

1″ x 1″s

DETAIL OF BOTTOM RAIL

8″

1″ x 8″

SHAPED 1″ x 8″

4″ x 4″ POST

END POST

2″ x 4″

1″

2″

4″

1″

36″

20″

31″

1″

2″

4″

SECTION THROUGH

29″

CENTER BRACE

8′0″

29″

36″

7′11″

8′0″

FRONT VIEW OF FENCE WITH THREE VERSIONS OF TOP SPACES

STRIP AND STRIPE

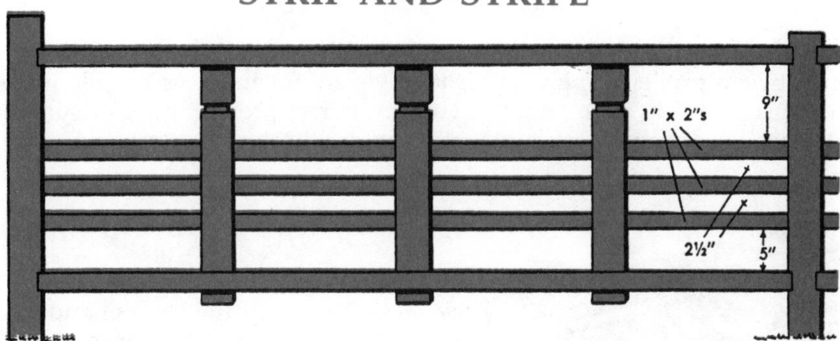

Sturdy, yet with delicacy of pattern, this fence fits well with modern, but is conventional enough to enhance traditional homes as well. Intermediate verticals are 2″×4″s with a decorative dado cut; horizontals are 1″×2″s screwed or nailed to the back of all uprights, including 4″×4″ end and unit posts. Both the top and bottom rails are 2″×4″s.

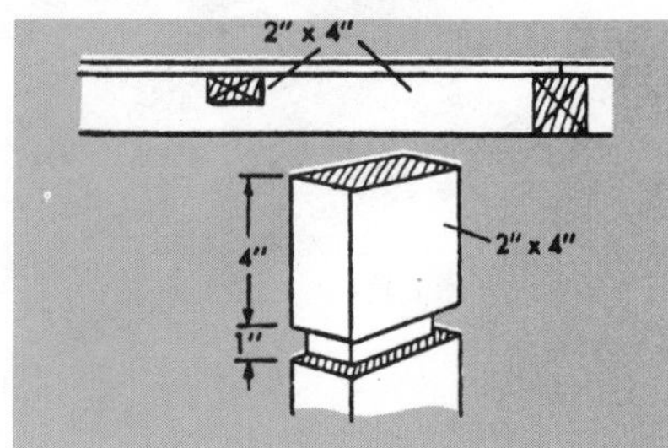

BAND AND BAFFLE

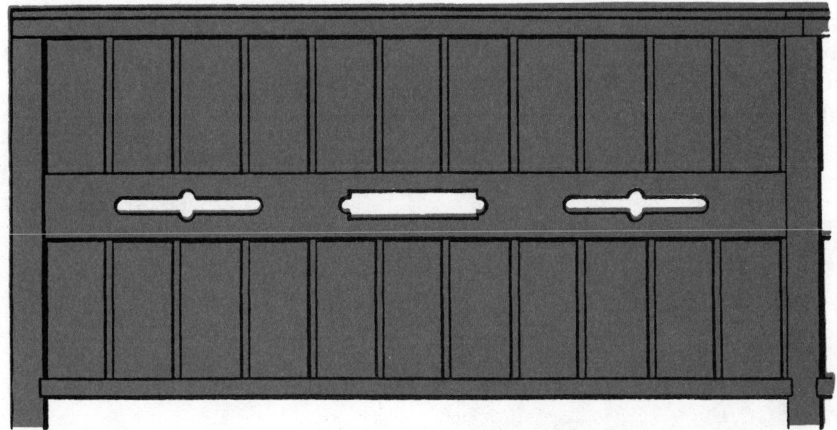

Although the effect of this fence is rather oriental due to the center band with its cut-out pattern, a plain wood band or two or three strips of 1″×2″s or trellis stock would give the same effect and perhaps allow it to fit in with more kinds of houses. The 1″×6″ uprights are fastened to backs of 2″×4″ rails and are protected from the weather by 1″×6″ caps.

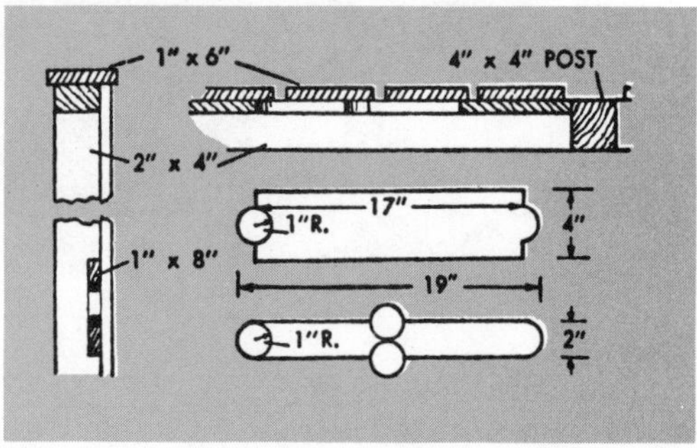

FENCE ENDERS

Today, not all fences are total enclosures. Some merely run beside the house to be lines of demarcation between properties, giving visual division. Such fences usually just stop, but they can end in such a way as to enhance your property, providing real visual interest, furnishing a place for a vine, or perhaps giving an architectural pattern.

ANGLE ENDER

Give the fence a forward thrust by bringing out the top rail and angling back the end of the fence to the bottom rail. The evenly spaced thick and thin strips of the fence boards are cut back to follow the end angle.

PAINTED SPACE DIVISION

This fence ender uses a square framework of 2″ × 4″s like that of the fence, backed by 1″ × 8″ vertical battening. Short 2″ × 4″s divide the ender into areas which are each painted in different colors for modern effect.

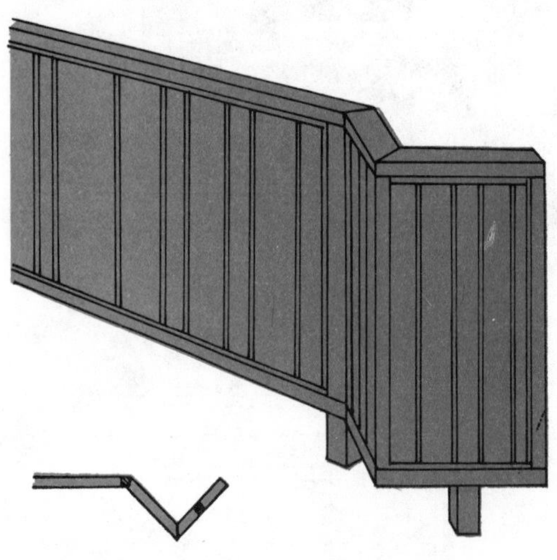

FENCE WITH A WAGGLE

A double-angled ender makes a feature of a fence. Simple and good-looking, it makes use of several random widths of vertical batten boards—1″ × 4″s, 8″s, 12″s—for facing the fence, including the angles at the end.

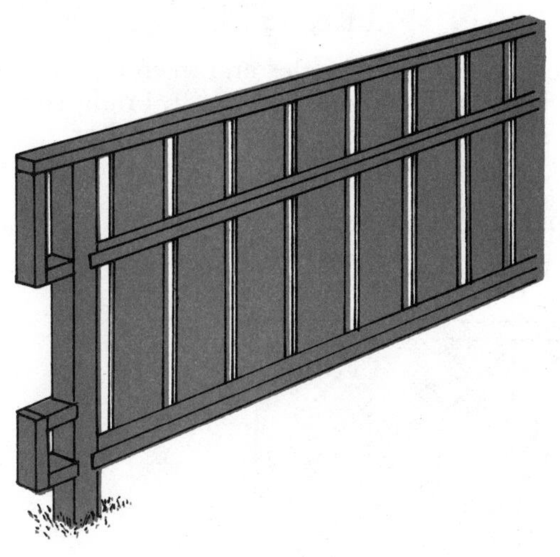

RAIL TERMINALS

The top, bottom, and intermediate rail lines are extended, the top two forming a boxy oblong, the bottom line finishing with a boxy square. Scraps of 2″ × 4″s are used. The fence is faced by 1″ × 8″s spaced 2″ apart.

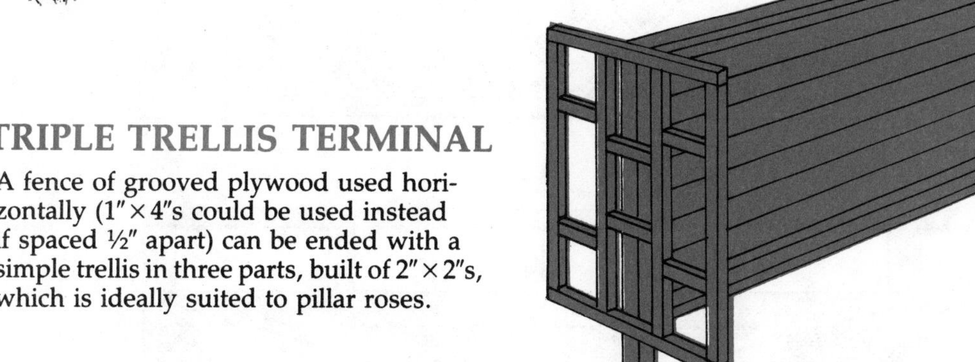

TRIPLE TRELLIS TERMINAL

A fence of grooved plywood used horizontally (1″ × 4″s could be used instead if spaced ½″ apart) can be ended with a simple trellis in three parts, built of 2″ × 2″s, which is ideally suited to pillar roses.

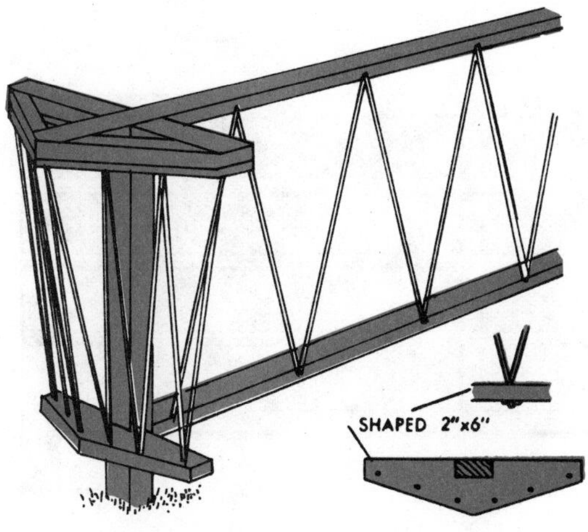

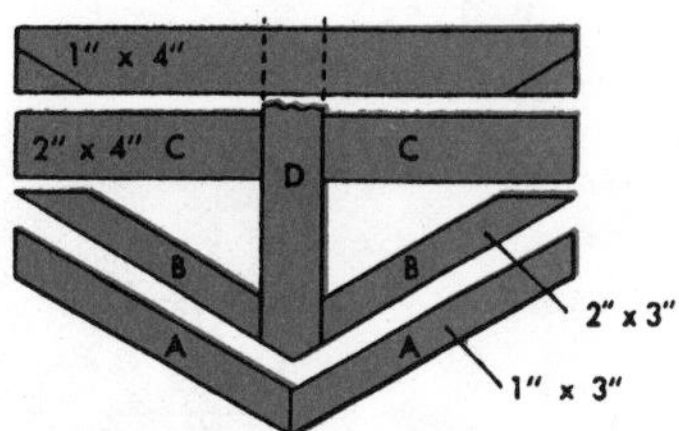

TAPERING TRELLIS

A good vine fence is made on a simple frame of 2″ × 4″s laced with plastic-coated wire clothesline. The triangular trellis ender, also laced with clothesline, tapers and gives good verticals for climbers.

USE IMAGINATION AND MAKE AN INTERESTING FENCE

TOP: Narrow trellis slats form the basis of this design, set at 45° angles and overlapped to give added shadow effects. Paint the frame and slats white, background a soft, bright color.
CENTER: Sometimes fences may be faced on the near side. Here grooved plywood or matched boards face the fence, open top showing brightly painted 2″ × 4″ framework and 1″ × 1″ decorative appliqués.
BOTTOM: Heavy full-rounds or half-round moldings are nailed or screwed to the near side of the frame, the far side of the fence faced with plywood for privacy.

USE GARDEN TIMBERS FOR FENCES

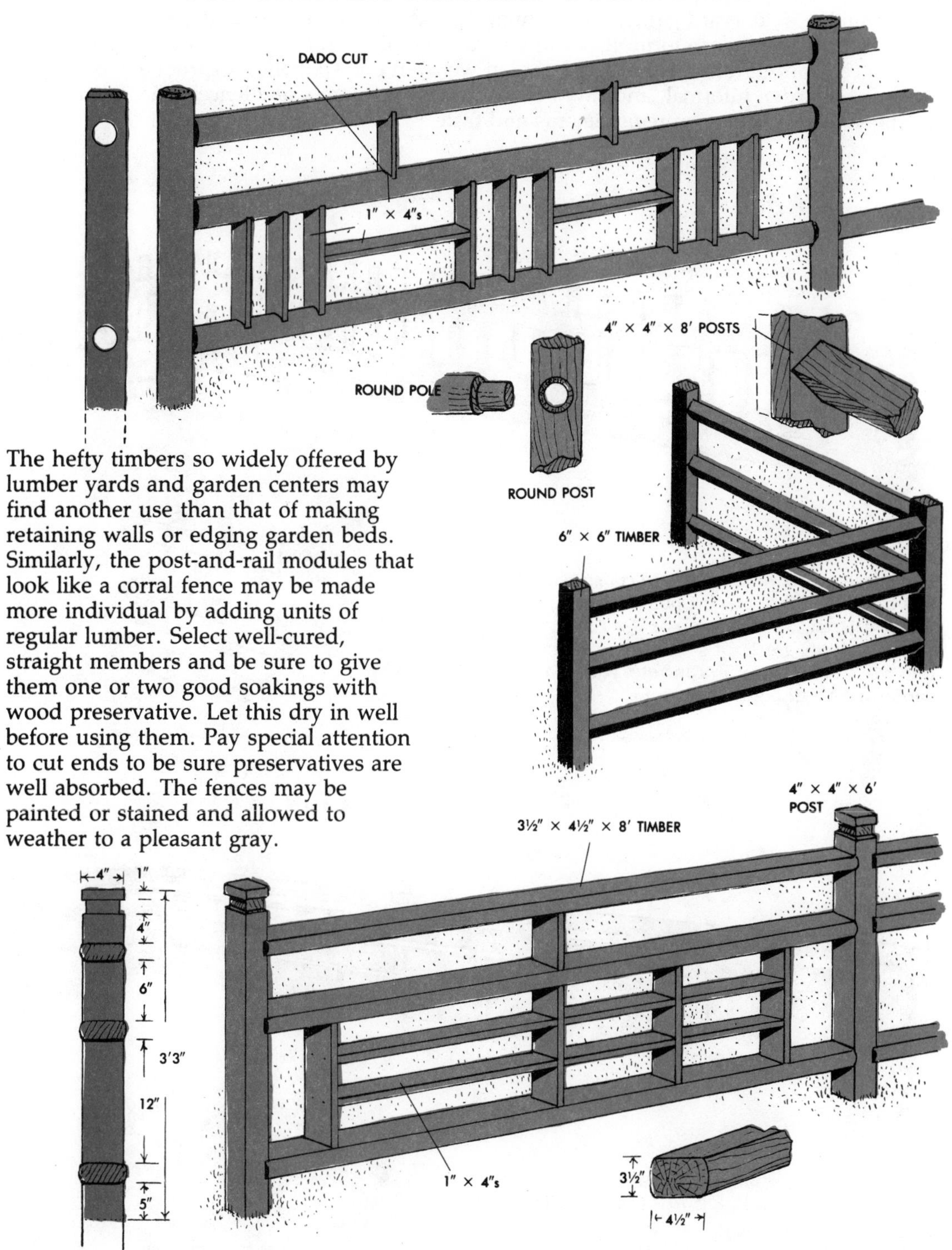

The hefty timbers so widely offered by lumber yards and garden centers may find another use than that of making retaining walls or edging garden beds. Similarly, the post-and-rail modules that look like a corral fence may be made more individual by adding units of regular lumber. Select well-cured, straight members and be sure to give them one or two good soakings with wood preservative. Let this dry in well before using them. Pay special attention to cut ends to be sure preservatives are well absorbed. The fences may be painted or stained and allowed to weather to a pleasant gray.

LOW FENCES FOR DOORYARDS

Grandmother's dooryard garden, a charming old-fashioned idea, is having a considerable success today in modern form. It is a tiny garden beside a front or back door, enclosed by a low fence. Concentrating bloom (and garden work) in one spot allows gardeners to keep the rest of the garden informal, and saves work. Shown here are a few fences; adapt others in the book to suit your own requirements and taste.

SQUARE PICKETS

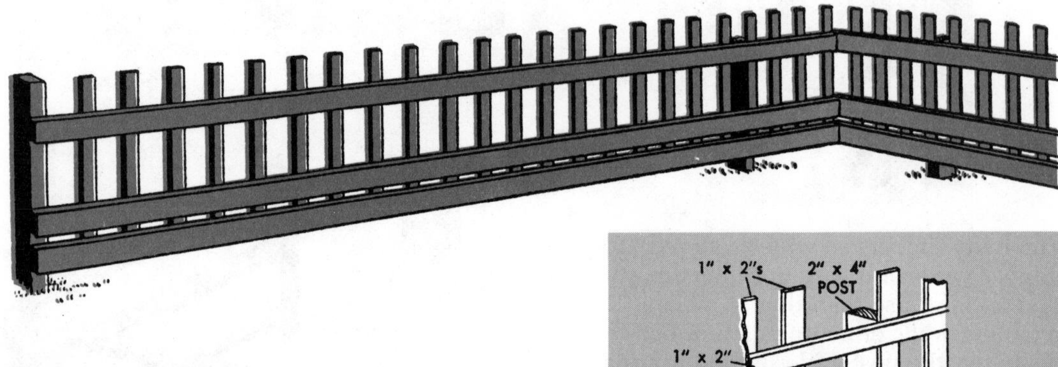

Inexpensive, and little trouble to construct, this dooryard fence may be built of 1"×2"s or trellis slats, pickets the same or 1"×1"s, 5/4"×5/4"s. Posts are 2"×4"s or 2"×3"s driven into the ground or set in concrete. Note how corner joins without corner post.

LONG LINES, GRADUATED BOARDS

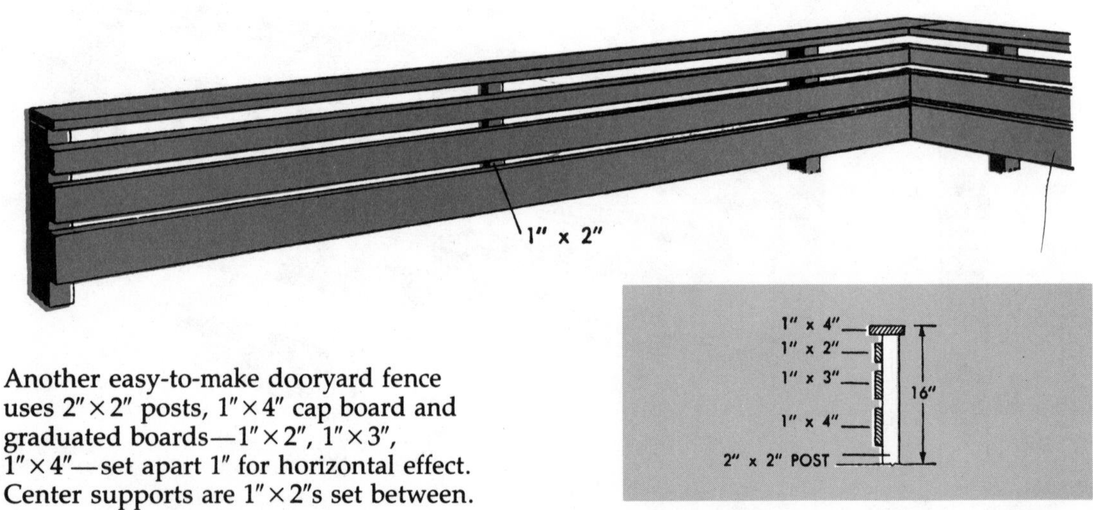

Another easy-to-make dooryard fence uses 2"×2" posts, 1"×4" cap board and graduated boards—1"×2", 1"×3", 1"×4"—set apart 1" for horizontal effect. Center supports are 1"×2"s set between.

LIGHTWEIGHT DOORYARD FENCE

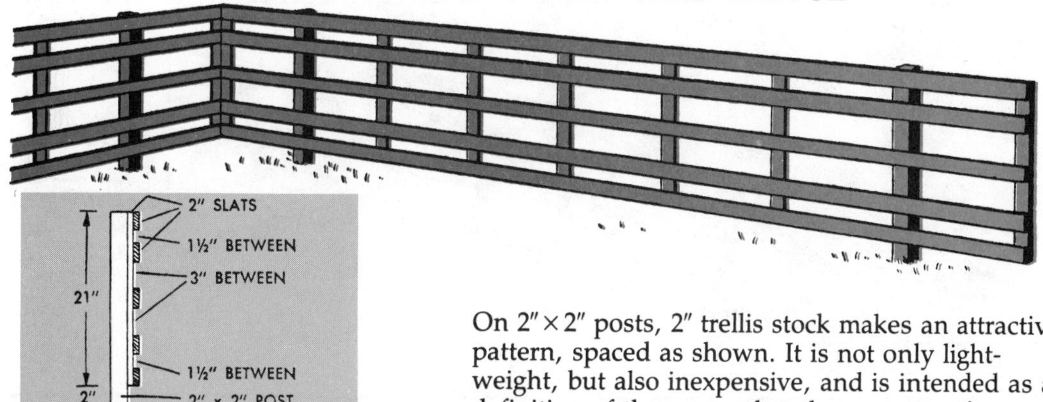

On 2″×2″ posts, 2″ trellis stock makes an attractive pattern, spaced as shown. It is not only lightweight, but also inexpensive, and is intended as a definition of the area rather than a strong fence.

DOWEL PICKETS, POINTED POSTS

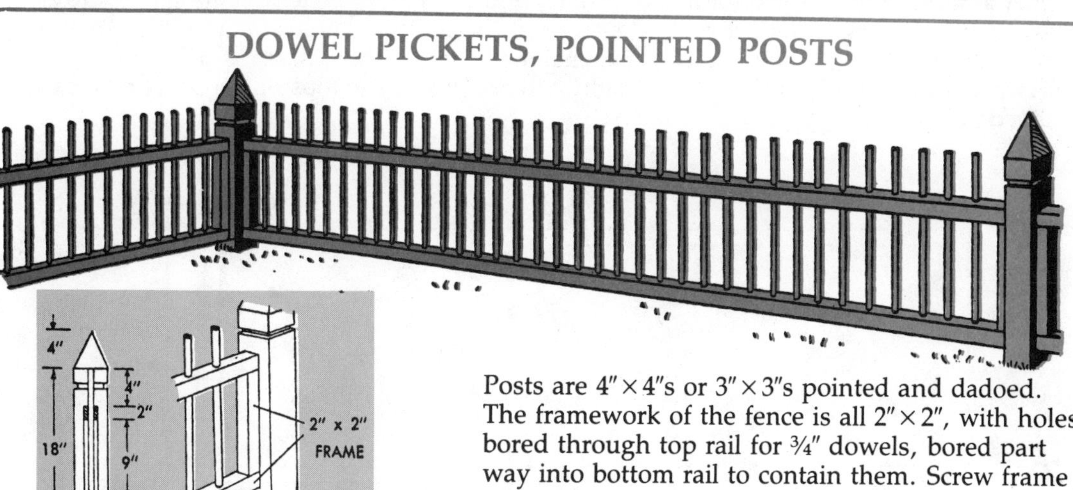

Posts are 4″×4″s or 3″×3″s pointed and dadoed. The framework of the fence is all 2″×2″, with holes bored through top rail for ¾″ dowels, bored part way into bottom rail to contain them. Screw frame to posts; use wood preservative over all, particularly cuts.

SQUARE PICKETS AND MOLDINGS

Moldings dress up top and bottom rails of this dooryard fence which features square pickets. Trellis slats, 1″×2″s, or other shaped pickets may be adapted for use. Note that top rail and molding are narrower than bottom. All posts are 2″×4″s set flat side to fence.

A STRONG FENCE OF CROSSED DIAGONALS

Either as a fence or adapted for a deck railing, you can hardly better this design. Sturdy posts and crossbars contain crossed 2″×4″s or, if there is to be little strain on the structure, 1″×4″s may be used. Fasten the two diagonal members firmly at the crossing with brass screws and be sure the ends are fixed tightly to the posts. The tops of the posts may be shaped or squared, topped with a block.

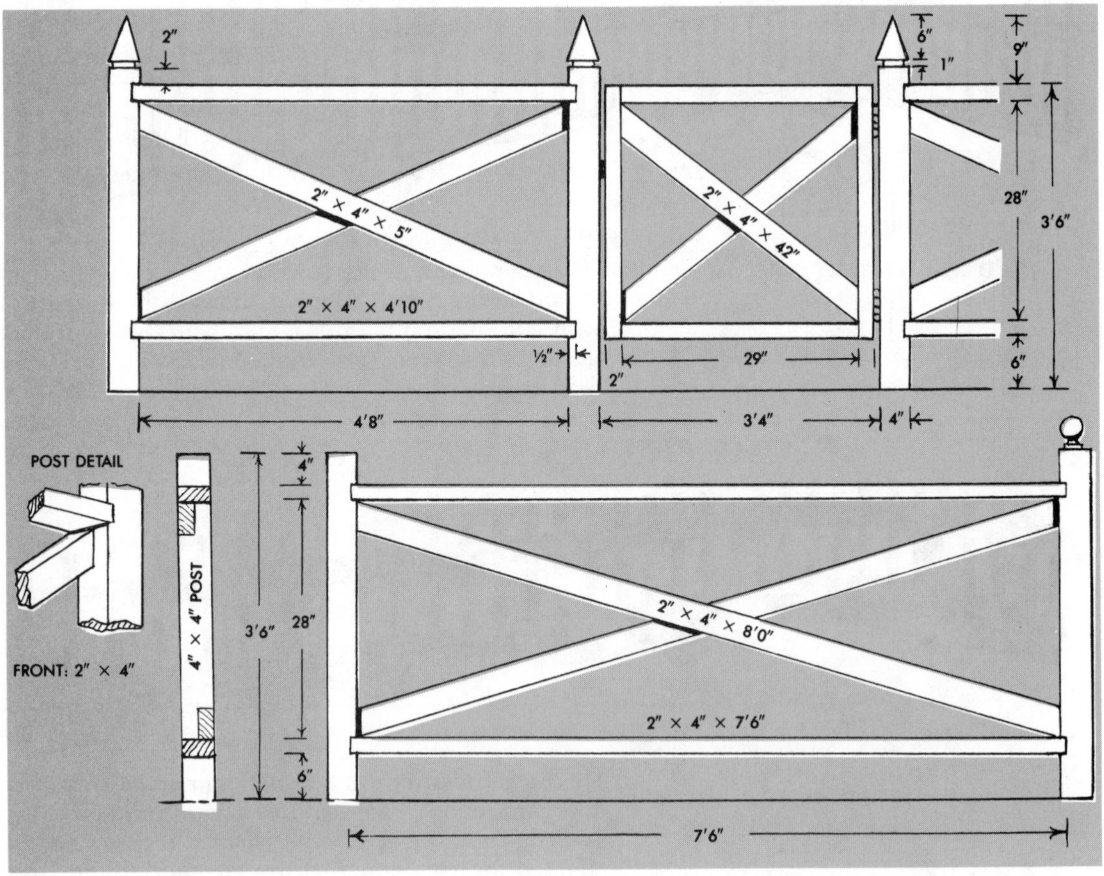

2″
2″ × 4″ × 5′
2″ × 4″ × 4′10″
½″
2″
2″ × 4″ × 42″
29″
6″
1″
9″
28″
3′6″
6″
4′8″
3′4″
4″
POST DETAIL
FRONT: 2″ × 4″
4″ × 4″ POST
4″
3′6″
28″
6″
2″ × 4″ × 8′0″
2″ × 4″ × 7′6″
7′6″

DECK AND FENCE CONSIDERATIONS

This drawing shows a number of the problems that can be solved by building a deck. Note the gate that provides access from the walk alongside the house. Also there's a fence enclosing one side to give privacy from a neighbor's house. Such a fence, even slatted or louvered will also give protection from prevailing winds and deflect a certain amount of noise, further dampened by tall, thickly foliaged shrubs outside the fence. The door shown replaced a window. The steps lead down to the garden.

COMPLETELY BAFFLED

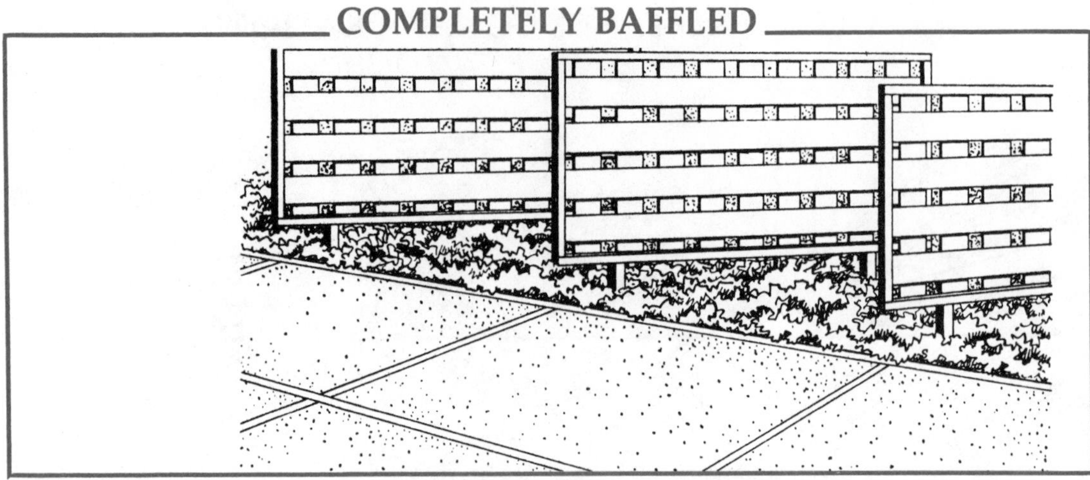

Where the view from the house or patio includes some undesirable feature, but where ventilation or passage is needed, a baffled fence may be the answer. The sight lines, indicated on plan below by dotted lines, are blocked by the fence, which makes a very decorative background for plants or which may be under-planted with ground cover.

Vines may be trained on it, too, but whatever the plantings, it will be an effective year-round baffled screen. If you wish, you may adapt other fence designs, shown elsewhere in the book, in place of this up-and-down-and-across pattern which is detailed.

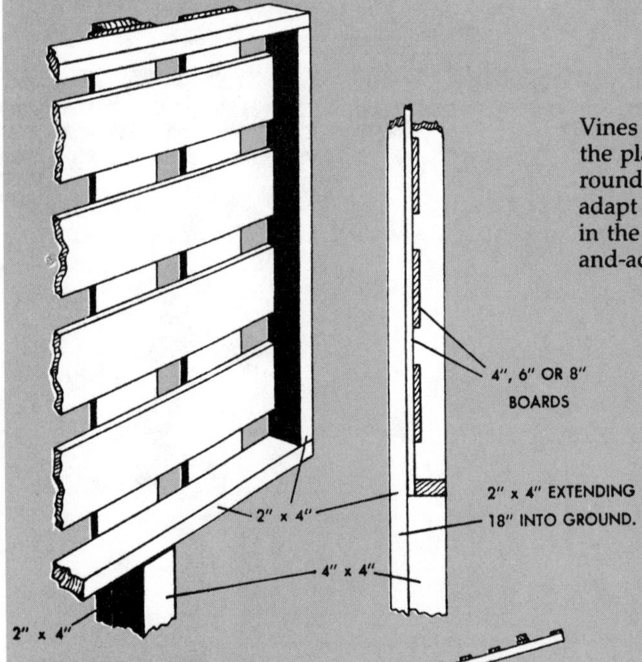

4", 6" OR 8" BOARDS

2" x 4" EXTENDING 18" INTO GROUND.

2" x 4"

4" x 4"

2" x 4"

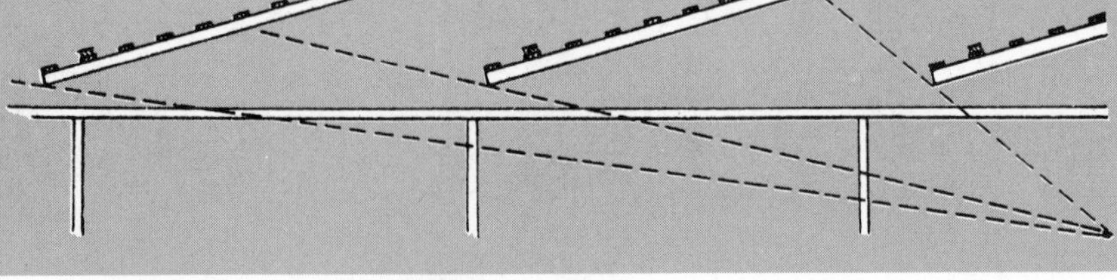

CORNERED AND BAFFLED

An area which is all too public can be kept from prying eyes of passersby with a baffled fence at the entrance as shown here in a horizontal stripe pattern. If you want a completely horizontal pattern, paint the posts a dark green or black, the fence boards a light color, and watch how the posts disappear.

Boards may be spaced more closely or more widely according to how you want to use the leaf patterns of shrubbery planted on the back side of the fence. By adapting a design of some other fence in this book you can achieve a totally different visual effect while retaining the baffle fence privacy.

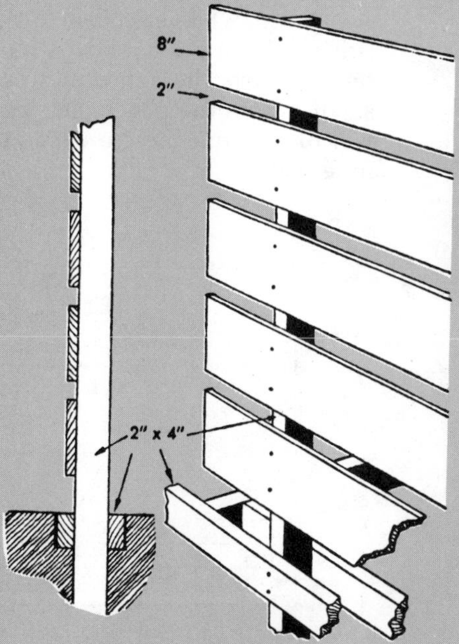

8″
2″
2″ x 4″

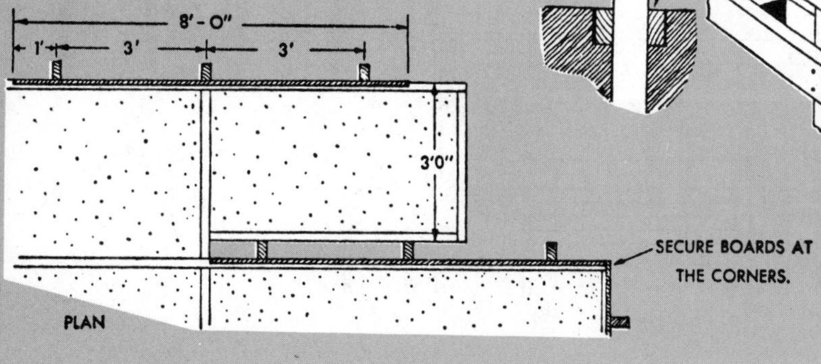

8′-0″
1′ 3′ 3′
3′0″
SECURE BOARDS AT THE CORNERS.
PLAN

BAFFLE FENCE PLANT BOX

A patio may be very close to the street or the neighbors and still be private if a low plant box is built incorporating a seat and baffle fence. Note the light fixture set in box end to guide night traffic safely across the pavement. Vines on the side street give a warm welcome, while a picturesque pine and a carpet of flowers dress up inner side.

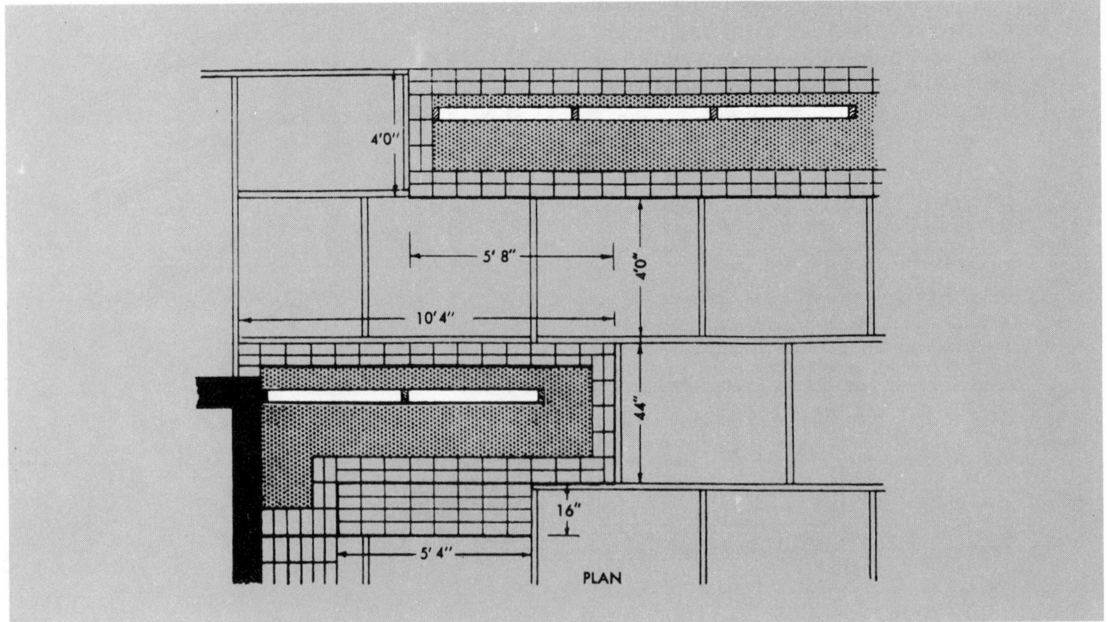

COMFORT AND PRIVACY

Cold winds may destroy the pleasure of sitting outdoors; so can the prying eyes of passersby.

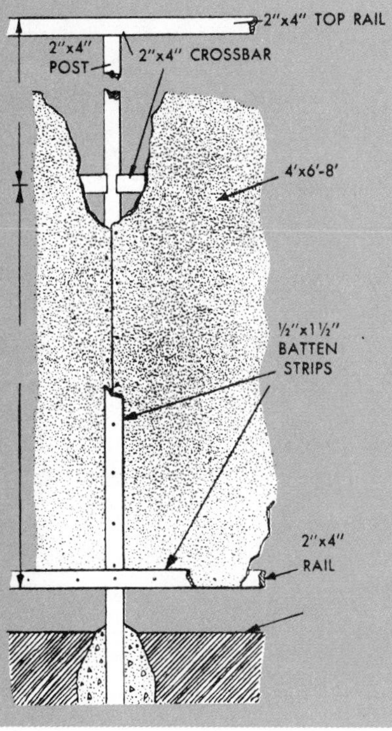

Protect your sitting-out area with a tall frame made of 2"×4"s, corner and end posts 4"×4"s, and clothe it with exterior plywood or hardboard, shiplap or corrugated fiberglass, or louvre boards. Set 1"×2"s or other widths of board at evenly spaced intervals to break the force of the wind but allow ventilation.

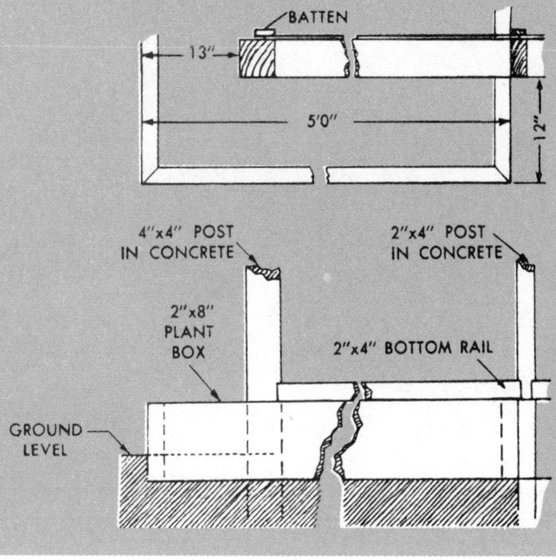

A VARIETY OF MATERIALS CAN CLOTHE THE SHELTERS

Wood laps of various types can be used. Or as below, you can achieve translucence using fiberglass reinforced plastic.

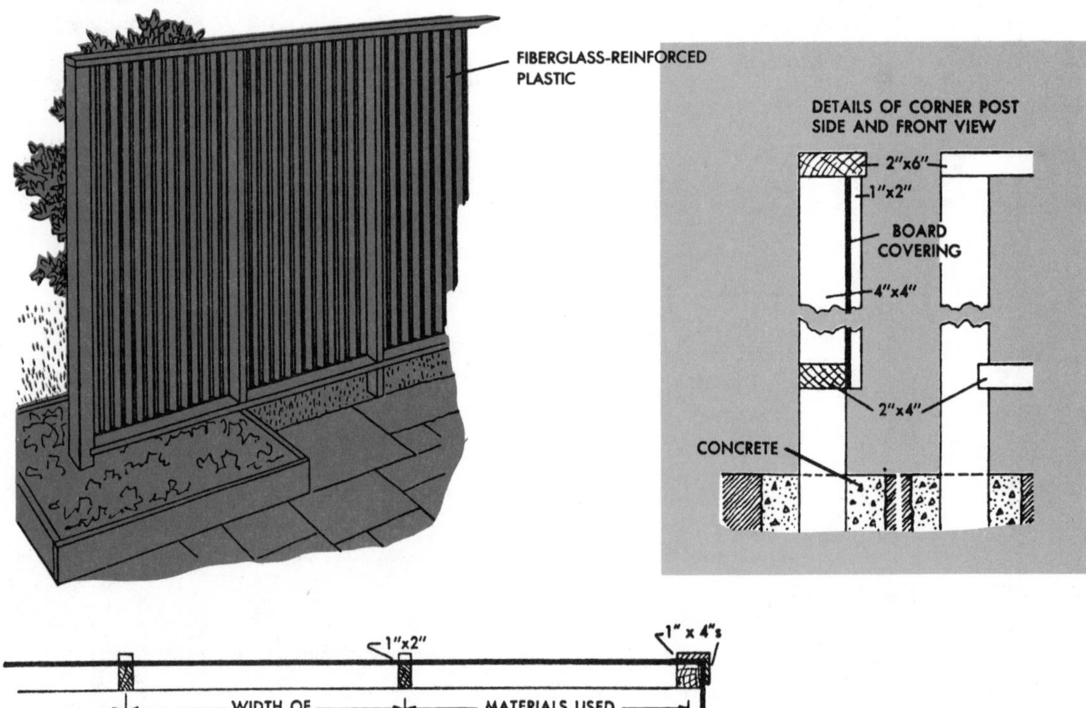

CHAPTER 8

YARD SHELTERS AND DECKS

Today we find that the activities within many a house have overflowed into the yard, making it a roofless outdoor room, so that most home owners will welcome some sort of shelter to add comfort to outdoor living. In moist climates a shelter not only adds a place outdoors in which to escape from sudden showers but also provides a place in which to sit for an evening and be protected from falling dew.

There are many shelters to choose from today. No longer need they be formally placed on the axis of the principal room of the house and have surroundings planted with overwhelming dignity, as in the past. Then the effect was impressive and beautiful but hardly invitingly cozy. Today's shelters are usually placed where they are *needed* and are casual and informal. Sometimes shelters will be found at the end of the garden, sometimes attached to the house, and sometimes freestanding along one side of the garden border—in fact, they will be placed wherever they are found to be most useful. They are practical, then, built for use as well as beauty. That is, perhaps, the outstanding universal thing about today's shelters.

Some of them bring a certain architectural significance to an ordinary development house, extending its lines and making it look larger, while giving it a distinctive appearance which divorces it from the factory-made appearance of its fellows on the street.

Many of the designs shown later in this chapter are founded on a basic size or module. To make a larger shelter, double the dimensions to make a longer shelter, or adapt according to the space you must fill. Note, too, that there are in many cases alternate "skins" for the walls, giving you a greater choice of clothing the sides and roofs of the basic structure.

Sometimes the shelters are solidly roofed; sometimes they have crossbars for a roof (the so-called "egg crate" style); and sometimes they are roofed with laths or trellis slats, with sunbreakers of snow-fencing, or bamboo shades which can be rolled up in the autumn and stored in-

A garden shelter need not be elaborate—it may be as simple as you like. Consider this A-frame, made of redwood planks set in concrete embedded in the soil. Latticed roof uses 2″ × 2″ strips to shade the brick floor set on sand. Railroad ties form the rustic steps leading to it.

doors or in the garage during those months when light and warmth in the shelter are needed. Increasingly, however, you will find shelters becoming half-and-half structures—partly roofed and partly open or covered with sunbreakers. This type will provide shelter from sudden storms under the roofed part, while the sunbreaker or open part will be pleasant for those who like the sun, either tempered a bit or full strength. Or it may be that patio paving will extend out beyond the structure of the shelter so that it is possible to move furniture into the sun when that is desirable and to pull it quickly under the sunbreaker or solid shelter when protection is wanted.

A revival of the old-time gazebo is now well established. These shelters were sometimes roofed, sometimes covered with slats or *treillage,* a crisscrossing of trellis slats that leave openings that are square, diamond-shaped, or oblong. There is much to be said for the gazebo—it is a pleasant and private place to retire to for a small gathering, to sit in and read or converse with a friend, to have a small luncheon or supper party of four or six, according to the size of the structure. In areas that are plagued with insects, the gazebo can be screened and a screen door fitted to give protection from these pests. An electric light can also be installed so that one may enjoy the outdoors and summer cool in the evenings, as well as in the daytime.

Today there are numerous companies across the country offering precut gazebo packages that can be erected according to the directions for assemblage included. Some are very handsome—and usually the better the design the more costly the package—among the various styles offered by the manufacturer. None, however, is inexpensive even before shipping costs are added. Therefore the do-it-yourselfer can build one of the gazebos or shelters shown in upcoming pages which are fairly easy to build for far less than the manufactured packaged product. And a dividend will be the satisfaction of having done it to fit into the home place, a creative activity.

Some of the designs will readily adapt to use for the basic structure for gazebos; note the Rose Arbor on page 166 which will adapt by being doubled in size or made more compatible with the space you have to use by adjusting the dimensions and by paving or gravelling the floor. The design for a Lath House Pavilion on page 168 might be used in its original dimension or another module added on each side and the roof rafters increased accordingly; the laths could be more closely spaced or crisscrossed in *treillage* fashion if greater privacy were desired. However, the classic gazebo was open at least on the sides where a good view was to be obtained, with windows or other openings giving out on that view. To shelter the interior from wind or from view, certain sides were enclosed. The Shelter in a Corner on page 182 is perhaps closest to the old-time gazebo and could easily be adapted. Note the seats, a desirable built-in feature which could be incorporated in any of the other designs mentioned above. All in all, the gazebo idea can be most successfully adapted to modern outdoor living by using one's imagination and ingenuity.

In the designs which follow I have tried to provide a wide range so that you will find one which will harmonize with your house or which can be adapted to it. Even old houses are being brought up to date these days, with the addition of a garden house or shelter attached to the house or garage, or placed elsewhere in the yard, rejuvenating the whole site. A little remodeling of the yard to bring the landscaping up to date, to open it up, and to simplify it so that it is easier to take care of, and perhaps also installing a picture window to look out upon this new vista, will help to make an old house more pleasant to live in as well as more salable, should that necessity arise.

By taking into account your hobbies, your family life, your climate with its prevailing winds and other pertinent features, and the situation of neighboring houses, you can place your shelter where it will do the most good and add to your use of your yard, even improve your plants' chances for survival. For instance, if you live in areas where strong sun makes it difficult to grow camelias or other broad-leaved evergreens, you can give them the needed protection by placing your lath-roofed shelter so that its shadow is cast over adjoining beds, or extend the lathed roof to give broken shade. This will enable you to plant your favorites alongside your outdoor entertaining room, making a real conversation piece of this exhibit of your plants.

By using a slat-roofed shelter, too, you will achieve privacy from above, where neighbors have second-floor windows overlooking your patio or where a street or path overlooks it from a hill. A solid roof offers complete protection, of course, but it is surprising how much protection a slatted sunbreaker will give, how it can hide the view, especially when reinforced with vines in summer. It will not cut off all the light from the rooms of the house, should the patio be placed alongside it; and, if you want the warmth of the sun and more light in the house in the winter, the slats can be placed on a frame which is removed each winter for storage and replaced before the sun gets too hot, or as soon as you begin to use the patio in the spring. They may be alternated in direction—vertical or horizontal.

If you want protection from the eyes of observers but like to sit in the sun, the entire shelter need not be covered: part of it may be solid, another part slatted, and part of it left open so that you have three choices; and the divisions need not always be rectangular, either, but may be at an angle if you wish. Snow-fencing, bamboo, and basswood porch shades or roll-up blinds can also be used for slatting, being rolled up for storage in winter and held in place by 1″ × 2″s or other light wood strips screwed in place on the shelter during the summer. This will prevent their being blown off or damaged by summer winds.

WHICH SHELTER FOR YOU?

To assist you in choosing the kind of shelter most suitable for you, how big it should be, where to put it, and so on, I suggest that you study Chapter 15, "Planning a Patio." This will aid you in making your decisions, for a shelter is usually used in connection with a paved patio, and many of the same considerations must enter into the planning. It is logical to place the shelter on a paved area, because it will be used so much that the maintenance and repair of a lawn beneath it would be a

A fanciful and pleasing octagonal garden shelter that is a modern descendant of the Victorian gazebo is open on two sides, windows are seen on two others, and the slatted sides give it textural interest, provide climbing support for vines to give privacy.

factor to reckon with. Also paving will make it more usable in rainy weather.

There is a preliminary consideration, however, which you must take into account. What do you need shelter from? Is it the sun, the wind, the prying eyes of neighbors and passersby? Once you have decided this question you will have a very good idea of where it would be best to place the shelter and what you will need in the way of screening.

Next you must decide on how permanent you want the shelter to be. Is it to be a freestanding one which will be a stand-in for a young tree still too small to give shade and visual privacy from upstairs windows or adjacent houses? A lightweight but well-built, sturdy structure would be indicated so that it would last until the tree took over.

Is it to be a really permanent shelter? Then there must be even more care given to its planning and construction so that it will withstand the stress of all-year weather and storms, and it should be well designed so that it will be a permanent asset, a credit to both the house and the yard. Don't rush things at this point, for the shelter must stand the test of future years, which makes the preliminary thinking of primary importance. The permanent shelter should have permanent paving; its posts should be firmly embedded in concrete; and if they are of wood they should be treated with wood preservative before being set. All parts of

A translucent fiberglass privacy wall shields bathrooms from the swimming pool, yet allows light through to the house.

Where outdoor space is very limited, it's difficult to enjoy nature and still maintain privacy. Here it's done with a wall of milky glass fiber panels framed in 2″ × 4″s on 4″ × 4″ posts.

wood structures outdoors will last indefinitely if they are thoroughly treated with wood preservative, as discussed in Chapter 4. Proper advance consideration and lucid thought will give you the kind of sturdy structure you will use with pleasure and no regret in future years.

SIZE AND HEIGHT

In general, with today's homes being built long and low, it will be a good plan to echo these proportions in other structures. The average height of indoor rooms today is 8 feet. Outdoor rooms may not *need* to be higher than that, particularly those with open or slatted roofs, but, architecturally speaking, most shelters attached to the house or another building look better when they have their roofs or trellises placed at, or just below, the eaves of the adjacent roofs, usually 9 to 10 feet above ground level. Attach the stringer enough below the line of the gutter so that crossbars or other superstructure may be placed on top and it will still come below the gutter. If this is too high, any normally visible architectural division of the house—the eaves of a low ell, the strong line of a tall picture window or door—may be your cue for measurement. If not, then place the shelter so that the lower side of the rafters will clear the lintels of doors and windows of the shelter by at least 6 inches or even a foot.

PLACEMENT OF POSTS

Similarly, in deciding on the placement of posts or other uprights, it is obvious that they should never be placed in front of a house door or window bisecting it, obscuring the view from indoors or impeding direct entry into the house. It is also apparent that in attaching a shelter to a building it should not end inside the vertical lines of a window or a door opening, but should come at least to the edge or, better still, should extend beyond it by 6 inches or a foot, if possible.

Frequently there is an ell or a jog in the house wall which will make it convenient to place your shelter in the corner formed by the two walls, provided that this location will work out from the practical standpoint of use, and also that it will look well in the yard. If it gives you privacy and protection from wind, and if

What appears as merely a pleasant jog in this fence is really a complete tightly roofed tool storage house. See next page.

it is where its use at night will not disturb sleeping children or elder members of the family, you will find that the use of two existing walls will cut down on the labor required for building and also the expense of materials for construction, saving the cost of several posts and their setting. Jogs or breaks in roof lines also make good places to start or end shelters.

OTHER FEATURES

Frequently two or more useful functions may be combined in one structure. For instance, it may be possible that in building your shelter you will make a screen for a service yard where compost heaps, clotheslines, trash and garbage cans, and other un-beautiful but necessary adjuncts of modern life are congregated. This can be done by merely adding a solid wall to the back of the structure, if it is freestanding in the yard, or else the wall may be backed up by a toolshed, an outdoor potting bench, or a garden storage house. The shelter wall may also be used as a place to display and shelter summering houseplants if shelves are built for the pots. They should be conveniently placed for necessary watering but also with an eye to showing off the potted plants in a

The same boards and spacing of the fence on the previous page are used on 4″ × 4″ and 2″ × 4″ framing. Padlocked doors keep everything safe.

to knit the family together and make it a unit. When the children have gone to bed, it becomes a refuge for the adults on pleasant summer nights.

MATERIALS

In general, any wood which is used structurally in building houses may be employed for outdoor shelters. (See Chapter 3, "Choosing Lumber.") Certain woods are favored because they are less susceptible to decay than others when used outdoors. Cedar, cypress, and redwood are the most prominent on the list, but almost

A flat-roofed exterior-plywood-covered storage unit houses not only the garden tools but also furniture and barbecue equipment, bicycles, and other possessions. It even has a place for logs and garbage cans. Shaped built-up roof beams are made of doubled 2″ × 8″s.

decorative manner. The plants will thrive beneath a lath roof where they get enough light but are protected from the burning rays of the sun.

A shelter is a good play-place for children, too. With their vivid imaginations it can become a castle, a pirate ship, a prairie schooner, or the most modern of space ships. They can play in its shade all day long during the dog days when heat stroke stalks the open lawn. They will remember it with pleasure in adult yers as a place where lunching and dining outdoors during the green seasons helped

A screened backyard shelter features removable siding panels that provide protection during bad weather and enclose it over the winter. The 4″ × 8″ sheets of Masonite are mounted on storm window hangers on three of the four walls. They are removed to expose the screened backyard hideaway. The interior of the 16′ × 16′ structure is big enough for a food-preparation counter and large picnic table for insect-free dining and entertaining.

any good, sound wood, well treated with wood preservative before it is painted, would last for many years if given yearly inspection and repaired and repainted as often as needed.

In some areas bamboo poles are cheap and available. They may be used as crossbars or set closely together as slats for viewbreakers, or they may be used in conjunction with bamboo porch shades. It should be realized, however, that bamboo is not noted for its long-lasting qualities and that it will need periodic renewal. Reed mats, available through nurseries which use them as cold-frame coverings, are also available in many places. They may be used as viewbreakers on fences fastened on the fence framing or as shelter roofs, and may be rolled up and stored over winter. They do not cost very much, and it may be that their cheapness will make them attractive enough to compensate for their not lasting more than a few seasons.

Trellis slats in conventional 1½- to 2-inch widths, ¼- to ½-inch in thickness, will last for many years if painted and properly prepared. A labor-saving device when cutting slats is to clamp a half dozen or more together and saw them all at once. Then unclamp them and stand them in a can containing about 4 inches of wood preservative. Soak the other ends too, letting them stand in the preservative for two to four hours or more; then remove them and let them dry well. Paint with undercoat on all sides and ends and with a final coat of exterior gloss paint. When that has dried install them on the trellis using copper, galvanized, aluminum-alloy, or other nonrusting nails, and give the entire shelter a second coat of exterior gloss paint, paying particular attention to filling well any joints or nail holes with paint. If there are any larger gaps or knotholes, fill them with caulk to prevent moisture from entering and then paint over them. This will preserve the shelter from rust stains and will cut down on the number of times it must be painted to keep it fresh-looking.

SPARE THAT TREE

If one of your prized large trees should die, don't feel that you must immediately have it cut down. Instead, as demonstrated on page 185, remove as many limbs and branches as may be necessary to prevent their breaking off or being blown off in storms and causing trouble. Plant a small tree nearby to give shade in future years, and then bolt long rafters of 2-inch lumber to the trunk of the dead tree (at least 2″ × 6″ lumber should be used), using 6- to 10-inch bolts to secure them. Keep rafters level and parallel to each other, using blocks if necessary to keep them equidistant. Eyebolts in the trunk at a distance of several feet above the rafters will hold cables to support outside corners of the structure. If you want to plant your new tree almost on the spot of the old one, support the middle of the rafters on the trunk and at the far end on posts.

A vine, either perennial or annual, or a combination of the two until the perennial vines grow large enough to mean something, will quickly cover the trellis and add shade-giving qualities, and will even climb the trunk and remaining limbs of the tree, preventing it from looking quite dead. Peeling the bark from the dead tree will prevent termites for a time from doing damage to it. If you want to paint it a soft silver gray or a pale pastel color it can become a feature of your garden. Or, if you want to minimize it, paint it black or a soft dark green. Either way it will add distinction to your garden until the replacement tree is large enough. Then the shelter can be removed for its shade will no longer be needed.

To digress from the use of a tree as a shelter, perhaps you will want to use it as a trellis for a vine if your dead tree has a picturesque shape which will compose well with a fence, a shelter, or some other feature. I have seen in this country large dead trees ablaze with wisteria bloom and, later in the season, feathery and lovely with the pale green leaves of that vine. In England and in the forests of France I have seen dead trees spreading their limbs in interesting patterns, their trunks and limbs clothed with the glossy leaves of ivy. It takes some years for ivy to grow that big, of course, and it won't grow in many places in this country; but other vines can be substituted, even annual ones, to make the dead tree a center of interest in the yard. At the base of the trunk a trellis may be built to support the vines and help them to reach the lower limbs.

GARDEN HOUSES AND GAZEBOS

There has been a recent surge of popularity in garden houses and gazebos, with examples of the latter now offered in kit form, often at rather fancy prices. Some kits result in sturdy structures, but some do not. The answer may be to build from scratch and save money, while assuring a strong, durable structure.

The gazebo was one of the appurtenances of the proper Victorian and Edwardian garden. Some were quite amazing examples of the art of the jigsaw. Others were quite chaste and well proportioned. A few were so plain or nondescript that they could be mistaken for a well or spring house.

There might at first glance seem to be little difference between a gazebo and a garden house. But a gazebo is defined as an isolated structure offering a wide view of the landscape or the garden surrounding it, indicating to me that it is an open-sided building, and it usually had a solid roof that might be square, octagonal, or hexagonal. A garden house, on the other hand, may be defined as a structure that might be attached to a house wall or a fence, or freestanding but enclosed on at least one side for privacy as well as shelter. The sides may be solid, latticed, or formed of cutout plywood; most likely the side facing the garden or the lee side of prevailing winds will be left open. There may or may not be a paved area associated with it.

One reason for today's popularity of gazebos and garden houses has been the growing appreciation of our heritage of Victorian architecture. The best examples are no longer frowned on. Rather they are admired. Also, as the trend of purchasing houses is now turning to the near suburbs or toward the rehabilitated central city itself, more older houses are being bought and lovingly restored by the wise buyers. These people realize that restoration enhances property value. When a garden house is added, privacy is obtained and the small garden is enhanced.

The perceptive owner of an older house may look to the house for orna-

A garden-house gazebo of unique design is constructed throughout of long-lasting Western red cedar. The 2″ × 6″ posts are bolted to U-straps of steel set in concrete footings, with 2″ × 2″s centered on each side of the posts. Seats and backs are 2″ × 4″s; flooring as well as framing, 2″ × 6″s.

ment or details to copy or adapt to the new construction. By using a basic modular unit (such as I present here), you can create a harmonious and truly individual structure by using options such as these: enclosing it with lattice work, using plywood or whatever siding best ties in with the design of your house, or merely adding ornament to the posts and leaving the walls open. Best of all, such a structure probably will cost less than one of the assembly-line kits that are less distinguished.

Make sure that the wood used, particularly those pieces closest in contact with the soil, is rot-resistant or at least pressure-treated to prevent early decay. It is a good idea to soak lower wood members in an approved wood preservative, especially on cut ends. Also be sure to support the aboveground structure on a proper foundation, which is capable of supporting the weight, thereby avoiding sagging or collapse. Follow these precepts of the Victorian gazebo builders and you will have a garden house that will endure for a hundred years or so, as theirs have, needing only minimal maintenance or replacement repairs as time and the elements take their toll.

A SUNBREAKER SHELTER

Many picture windows are so placed that the glare of the sun cuts down their usefulness. A simple framework with posts securely placed on concrete and with the top rails attached to the house can hold snow-fencing, as shown here, which breaks the glare and heat in the summer and can be rolled up, stored in winter, when the sun will be welcome. Bamboo roll-up blinds, cut to fit, may also be used, or a more permanent trellis of slats, fiberglass, plastic aluminum screen, dowel rods, placed on basic frame.

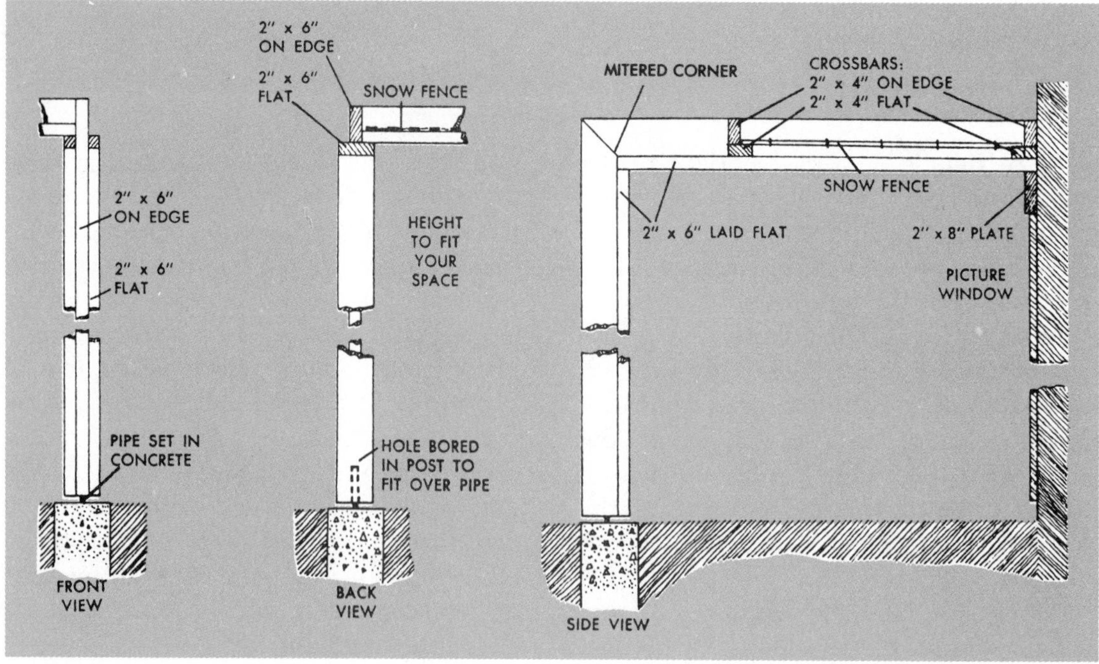

HALF-AND-HALF, SUN AND SHADE

Roofed with a 1″ × 2″ trellis supported by a 2″ × 4″ frame and sturdy posts set in concrete, this patio cover provides shade on hot days in summer, or warmth of the sun on cool days in spring and autumn. On two sides the neighbors are kept at bay by a raised fence faced with exterior plywood louvers or spaced trellis slats.

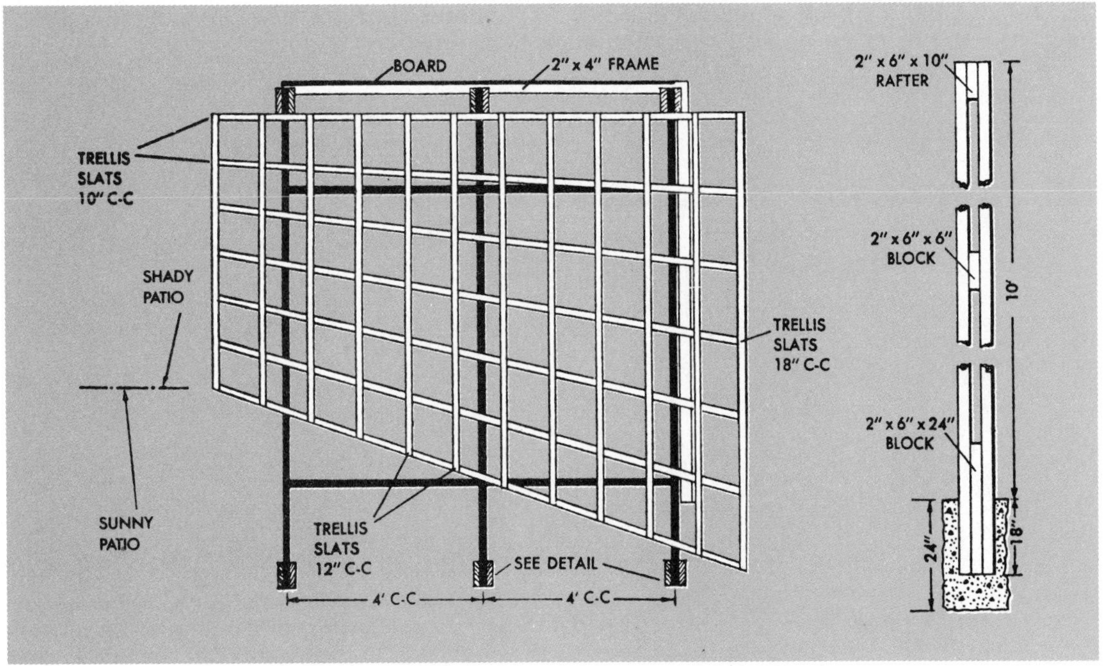

MAKE A TRELLIS ROOM BESIDE THE HOUSE

A good-looking and sturdy trellis covering a patio alongside the house will add an outdoor room to your living space. Piers of blocks support the center stringer; uprights alternate full-length pieces with short uprights resting on the horizontal crossbar. A low plant bed constructed of flat blocks surrounds the paving, giving further sense of enclosure. In this sketch, note that the back stringer is attached to the house, but it is possible to build a free-standing room by using upright construction on both sides.

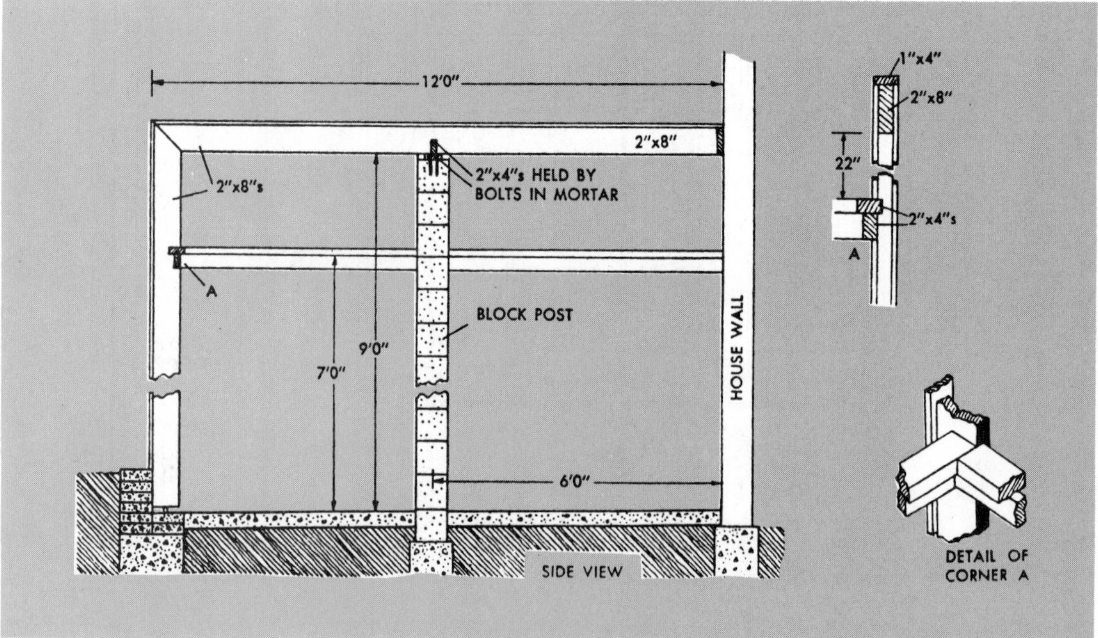

CONSTRUCTION DETAILS

The block piers should be given good strong footings so that they will not settle and fall out of line. Dig down at least 18″ in ordinary soil, deeper if the soil is light and sandy or if you do not pave the patio (which would protect foundations from frost). Footings should extend 5″ on each side of the block; but if the soil is very light, increase them to as much as 10″ or 12″ on all sides to give a proper base. The holes in the top blocks should be plugged to prevent moisture damage in future. Put a wadded-up newspaper well down in the block and then fill to the top with mortar. Bolts, with which to secure the stringer, can be inserted in the mortar while it is still wet, and secured.

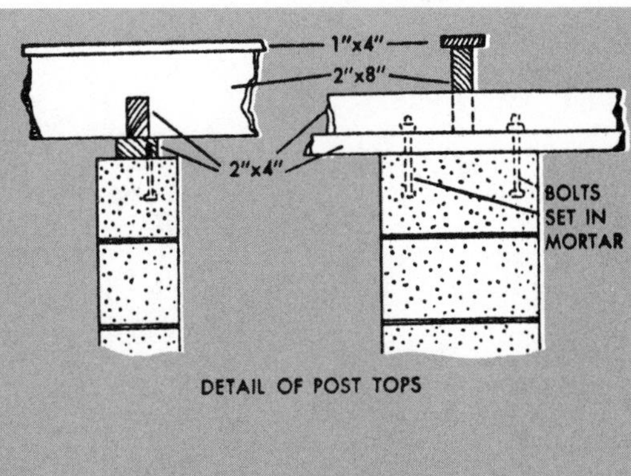

DETAIL OF POST TOPS

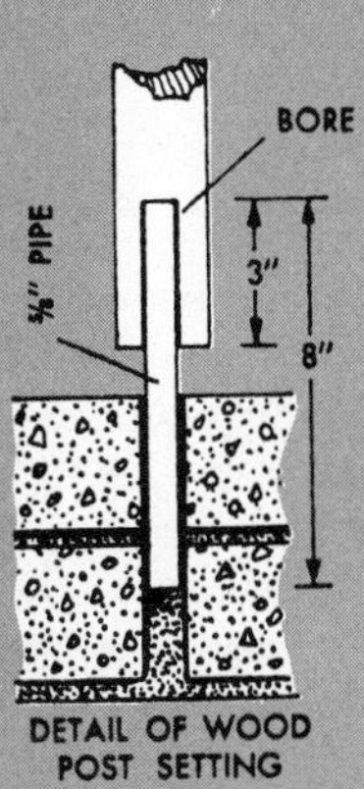

DETAIL OF WOOD POST SETTING

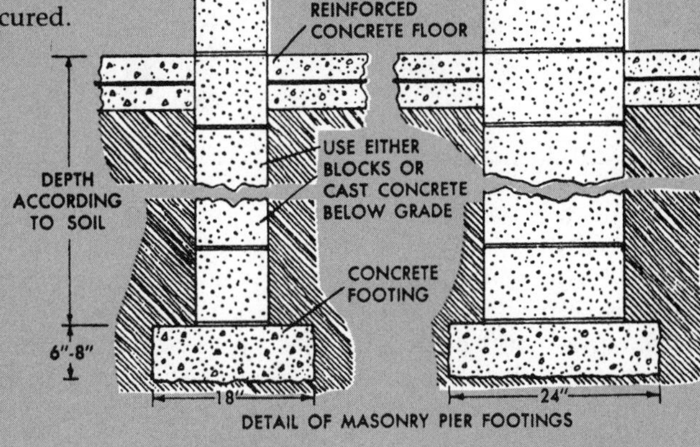

DETAIL OF MASONRY PIER FOOTINGS

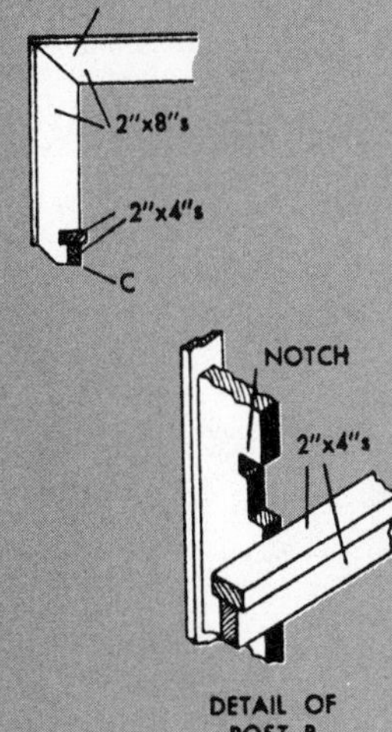

DETAIL OF POST B

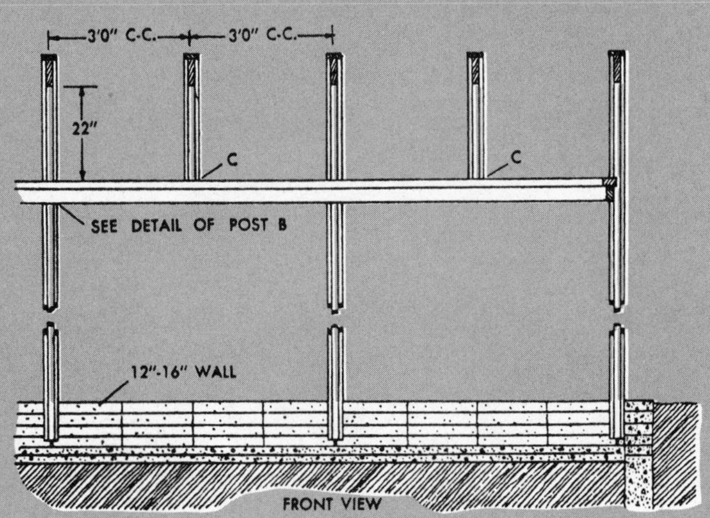

FRONT VIEW

A MODERN CLASSIC ROSE ARBOR

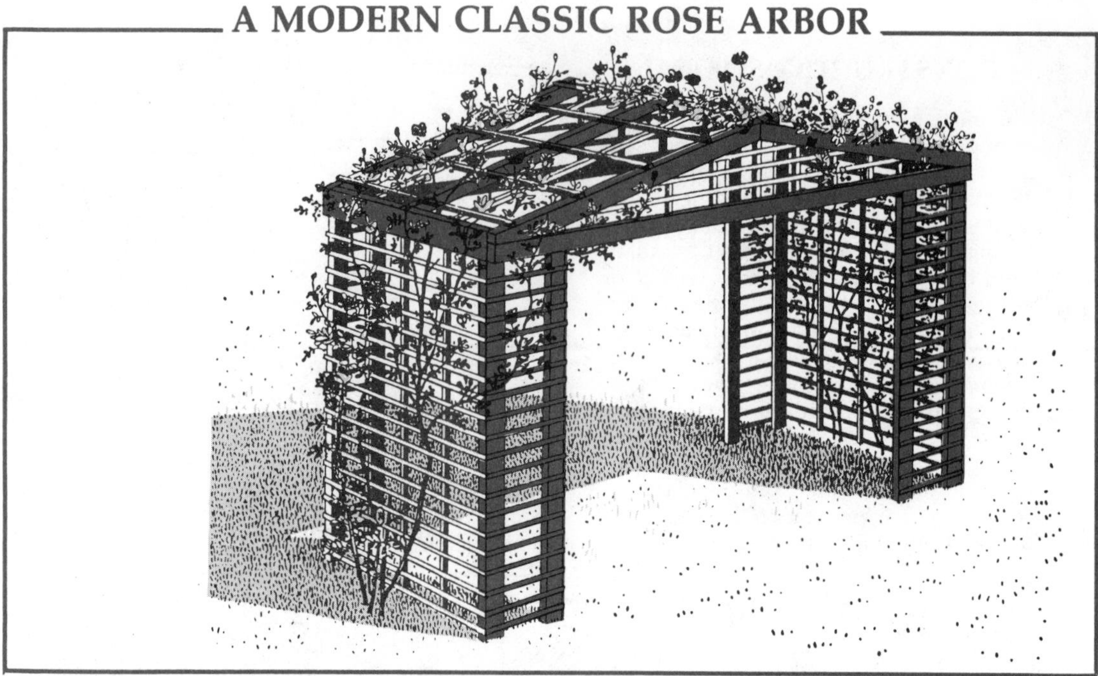

Adaptable to many uses, this arbor will go well with may traditional houses, yet it has a modern flavor, too. It can be set in the open as shown here, used in connection with a fence of similar design, be attached to a house or a garage to roof a patio with suitable regard for harmonizing the roof lines with those of the building. Its charm lies in the airiness of its proportions, its form being geometric yet open enough to complement the wayward, natural curvature of the climbing roses or vines, and at the same time sturdy enough to bear their weight when, in future years, they will need firm support. Use preservative on cut ends before painting.

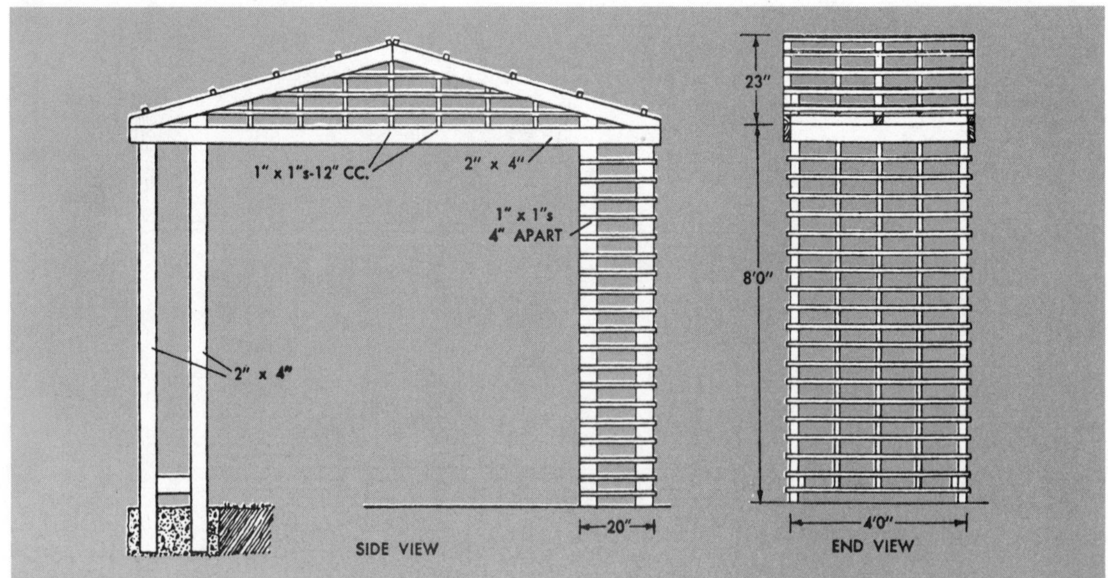

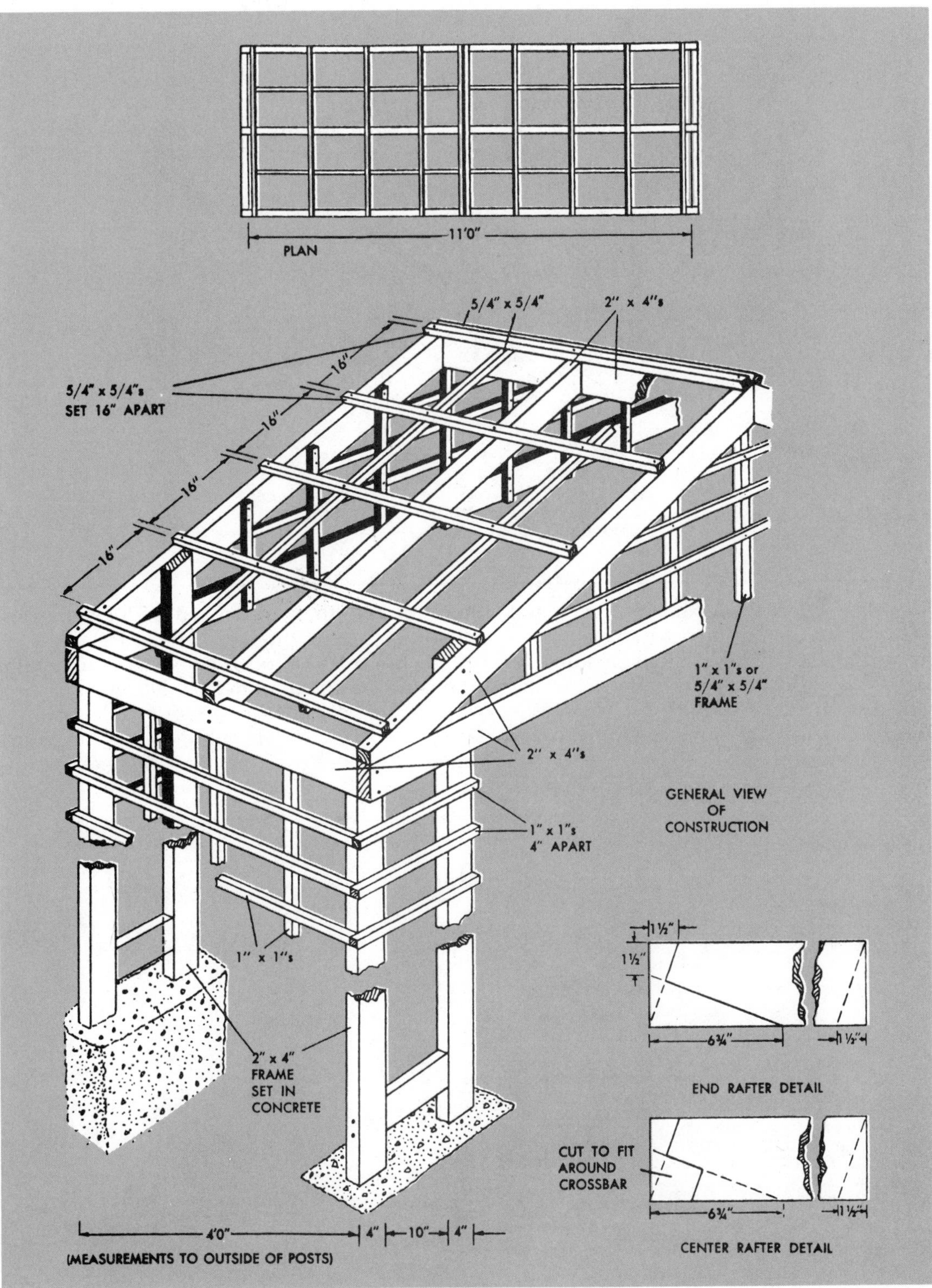
11'0"
PLAN
5/4" x 5/4"
2" x 4"s
5/4" x 5/4"s
SET 16" APART
16"
16"
16"
16"
1" x 1"s or
5/4" x 5/4"
FRAME
2" x 4"s
GENERAL VIEW
OF
CONSTRUCTION
1" x 1"s
4" APART
1" x 1"s
2" x 4"
FRAME
SET IN
CONCRETE
1½"
1½"
6¾"
1½"
END RAFTER DETAIL
CUT TO FIT
AROUND
CROSSBAR
6¾"
1½"
CENTER RAFTER DETAIL
4'0"
4"
10"
4"
(MEASUREMENTS TO OUTSIDE OF POSTS)

THE LATH HOUSE PAVILION

A garden house which combines the better features of both the modern and traditional styles will give any garden a real focus as well as providing a useful outdoor living area. The corner "house" part is made more interesting by the use of 4″×4″ posts cut to taper to a point and rabbeted for decorative effect. The flat portions of the structure may be left open or roofed with laths, like the hip-roofed corner house. Note how laths are used on sides as viewbreakers and give privacy to the corner where they overlap. The entire area of the patio under the structure may be paved, or only that under the house part, the rest being gravelled or kept in lawn.

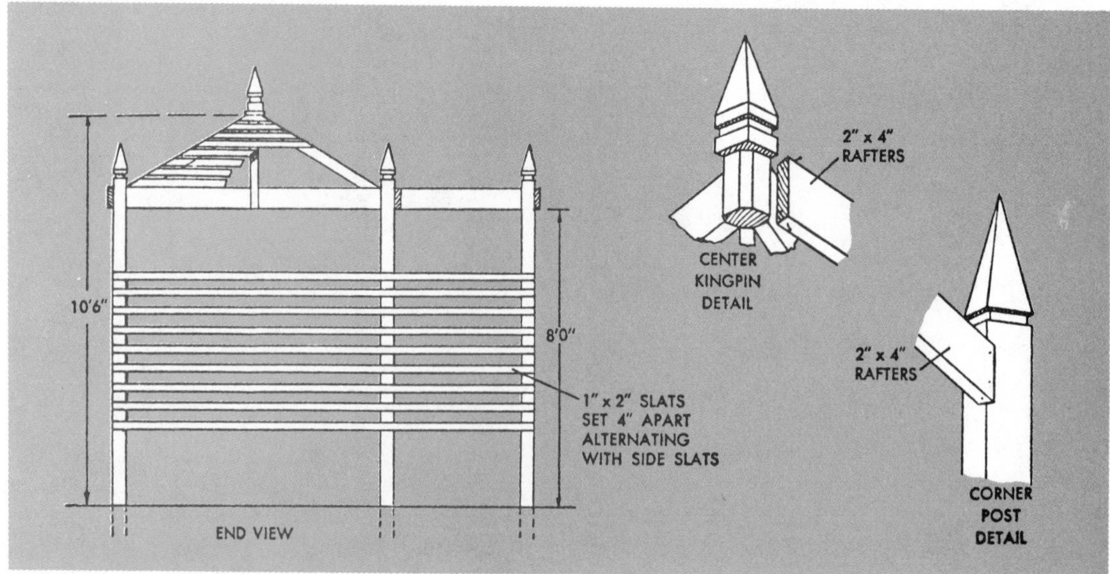

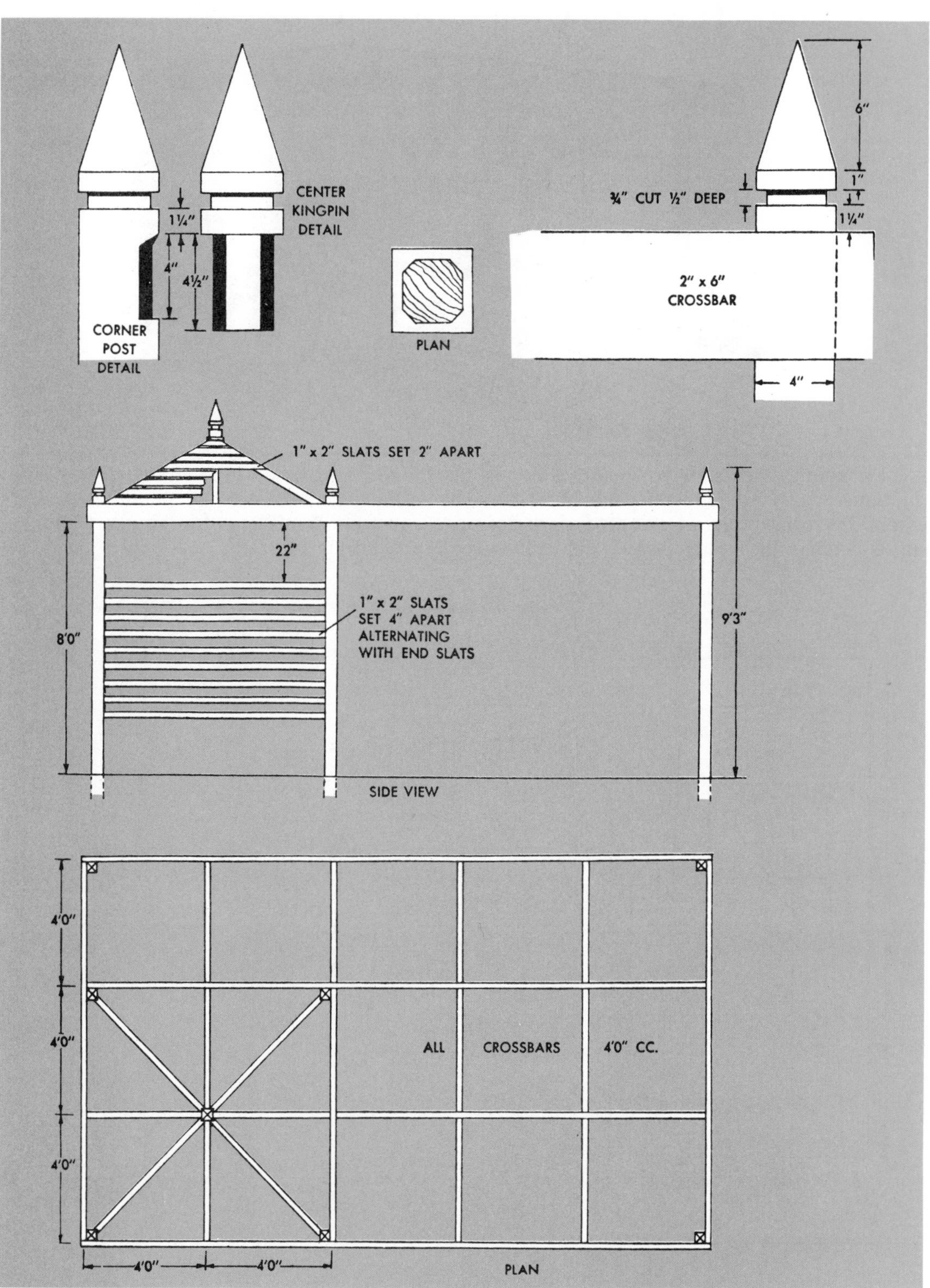
1¼"
4"
4½"
CORNER POST DETAIL
CENTER KINGPIN DETAIL
PLAN
6"
1"
¾" CUT ½" DEEP
1¼"
2" x 6" CROSSBAR
4"
1" x 2" SLATS SET 2" APART
22"
1" x 2" SLATS SET 4" APART ALTERNATING WITH END SLATS
8'0"
9'3"
SIDE VIEW
4'0"
4'0"
4'0"
ALL CROSSBARS 4'0" CC.
4'0"
4'0"
PLAN

A TRELLIS ROOM BESIDE A WINDOW

A little "room" with leafy walls and ceiling outside a window adds to the attractiveness of the house, both outside and inside. Privacy is also achieved, and shade for windows placed where the sun produces unwanted glare during the summer months; yet in winter, when sun is needed for heat and light, the leafless trellis will admit it.

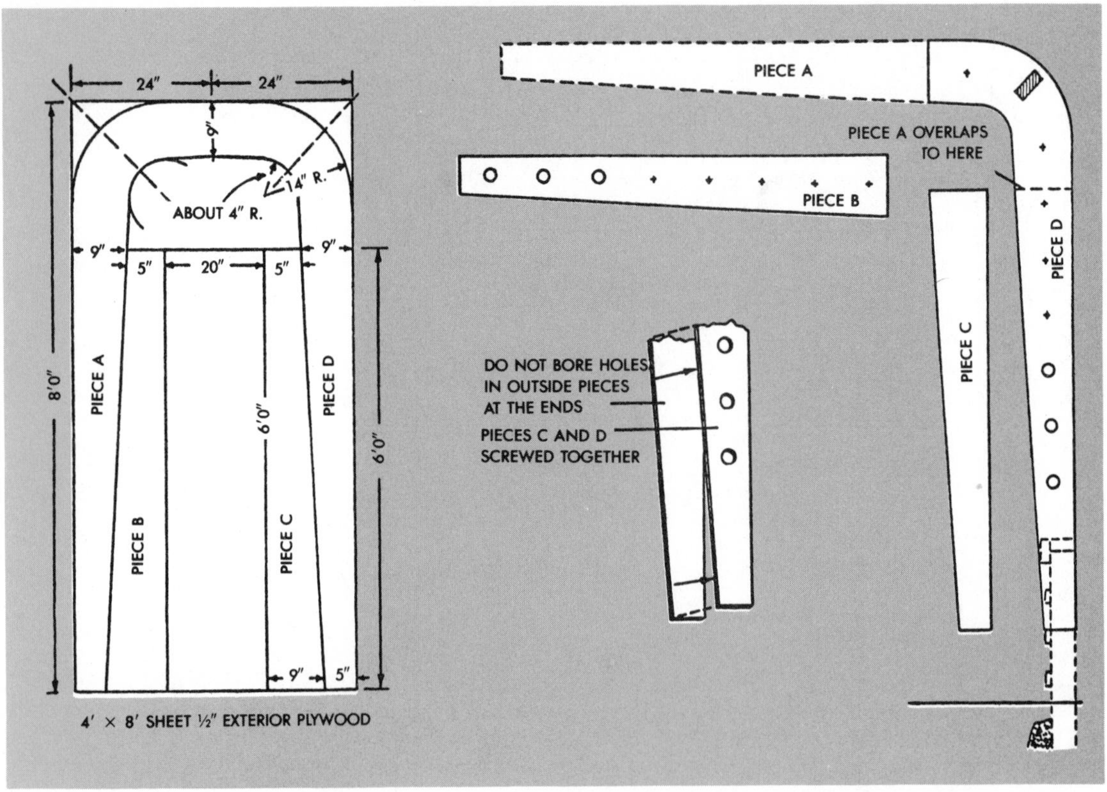

24" 24"
9"
14" R.
ABOUT 4" R.
9" 9"
5" 20" 5"
8'0"
PIECE A
PIECE B
6'0"
PIECE C
PIECE D
6'0"
9" 5"
4' × 8' SHEET ½" EXTERIOR PLYWOOD

PIECE A
PIECE A OVERLAPS TO HERE
PIECE B
PIECE C
PIECE D
DO NOT BORE HOLES IN OUTSIDE PIECES AT THE ENDS
PIECES C AND D SCREWED TOGETHER

CONSTRUCTION DETAILS

Pieces A and B, C and D (below left), are cut from a single piece of 2" exterior plywood, leftover pieces being utilized for other projects requiring exterior plywood. Use 1" × 2"s and 1" × 4"s to make the fence at trellis base, crossbars being clothespoles inserted through holes bored through the plywood (after it has been put together with aluminum screws) on each side of the angle. Frames for the fence are 2" × 4"s, doubled to make the posts, set in concrete; and 2" × 4"s are also used for spacer bars at the angle of plywood posts.

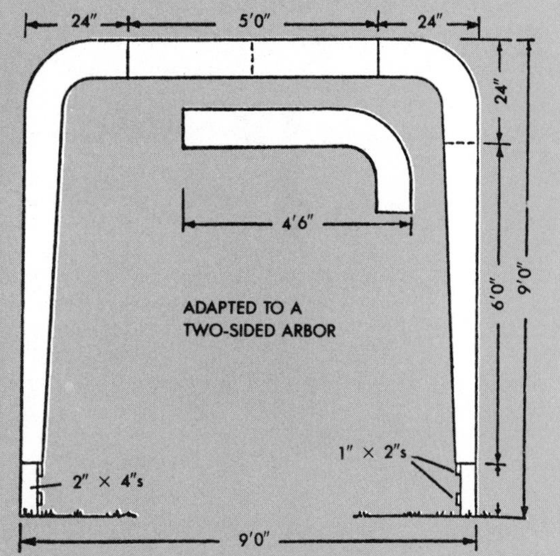

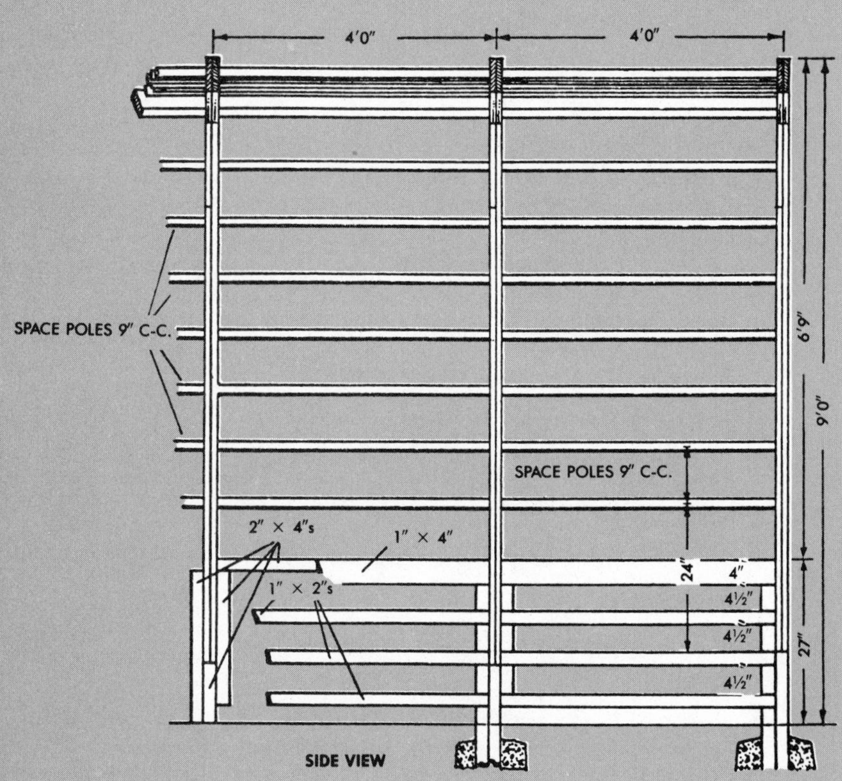

SLIDING SCREEN WITH BAMBOO

Bamboo porch shades are cheap to buy, can be fastened to basic framework as shown below (basswood detail), finished off with moldings. When sun or more view is desired, screens slide aside easily on marbles in a rabbeted channel cut into the bottom piece.

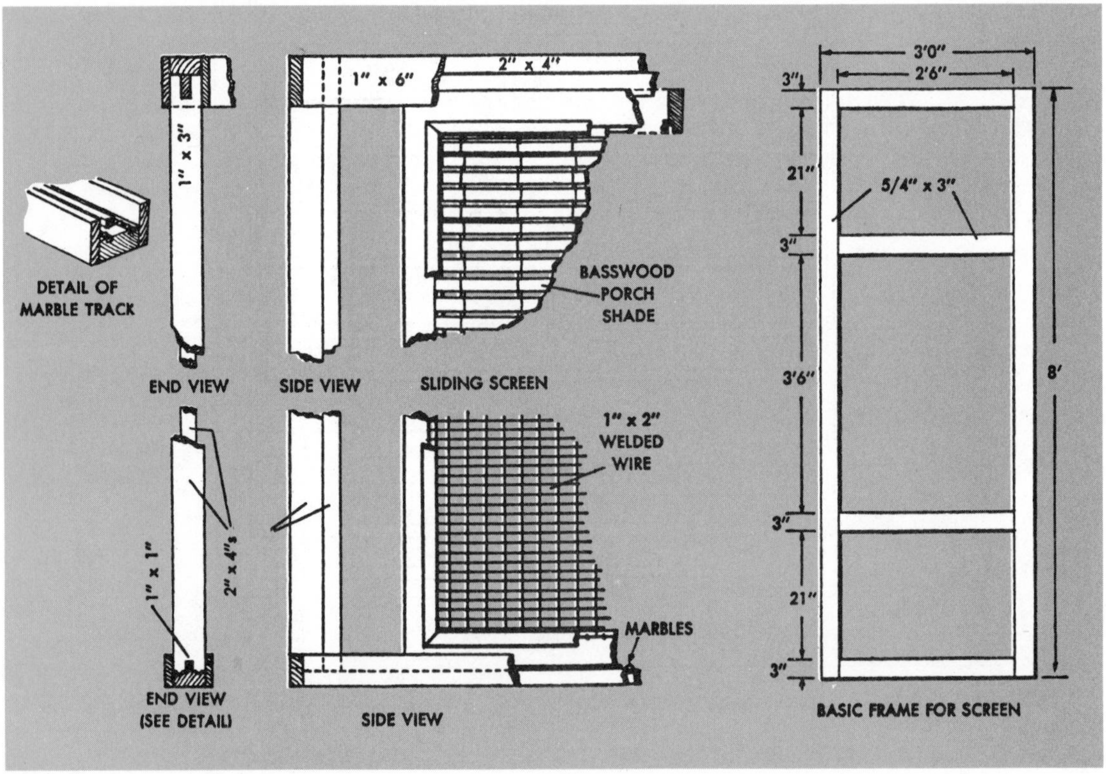

DETAIL OF MARBLE TRACK

1" x 3"

END VIEW

1" x 6"

2" x 4"

SIDE VIEW

BASSWOOD PORCH SHADE

SLIDING SCREEN

1" x 1"

2" x 4"s

END VIEW (SEE DETAIL)

1" x 2" WELDED WIRE

MARBLES

SIDE VIEW

3'0"

2'6"

3"

21"

5/4" x 3"

3"

3'6"

8'

3"

21"

3"

BASIC FRAME FOR SCREEN

SLIDING SCREEN FOR PRIVACY

Picture windows bring problems of privacy and frequently too much sun. One way to solve both problems is to use sliding screens mounted on a sturdy framework. They can be painted to contrast with or to match the house, stained or allowed to weather. Many materials can be used—bamboo or basswood porch shades, wire hardware cloth, trellis slats, snow fence, corrugated fiberglass, or plastic—and many other coverings can be applied on the basic framework shown below. With bamboo and basswood shades, a groove should be cut deep enough to admit the shade, which is tacked to the frame and a molding applied to give a neat finish to the edge. With corrugated plastic, hardware cloth or wire, material can be stretched firmly over frame, molding applied on top if a finish is desired. An interesting new variation on the permanent slat idea is the horizontal slat set straight, which shades and does not impede the outward view, but breaks the inward view. Permanent slats can also be set at an angle, as seen in lower version. The molding gives a neat-looking finish to the dadoed slat inserts.

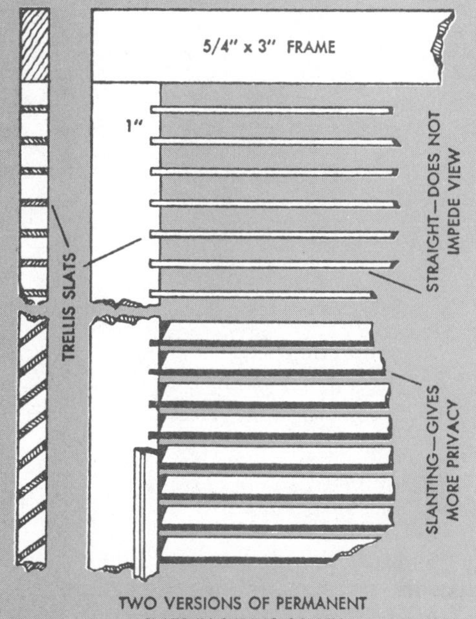

TWO VERSIONS OF PERMANENT SLATS IN SLIDING SCREEN

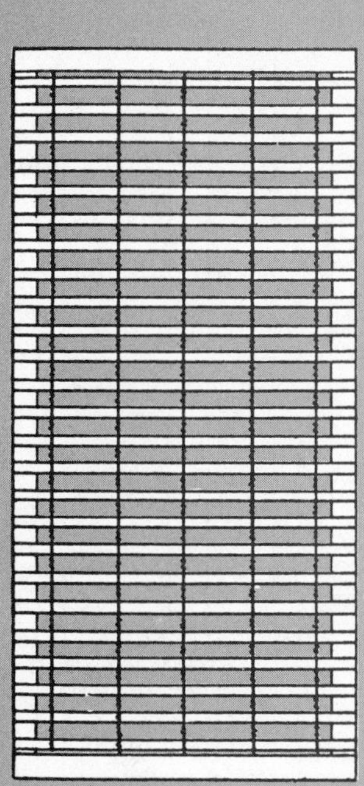

SNOW FENCE

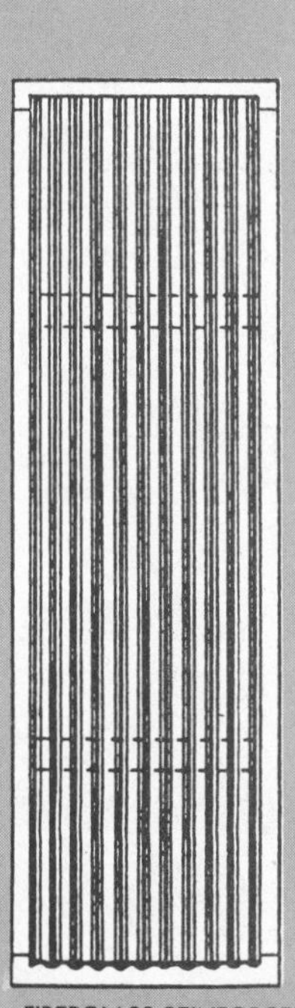

FIBERGLASS-REINFORCED PLASTIC

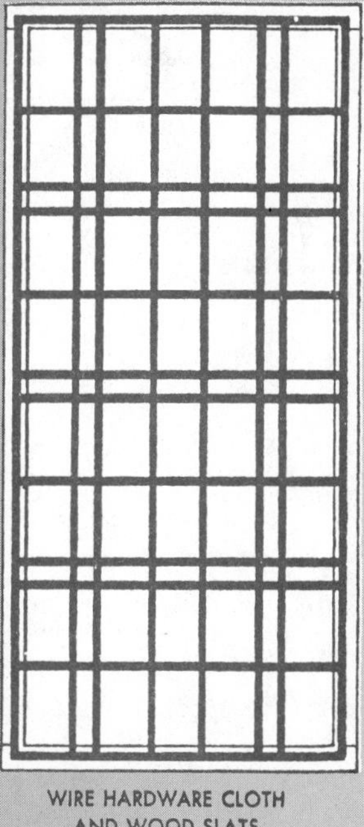

WIRE HARDWARE CLOTH AND WOOD SLATS

A SHADOWPLAY SHELTER

This quadrangular shelter is a little off the beaten track, with its seat roofed over and its trelliswork casting shadows of ever-changing patterns on the gravelled area. It adapts itself to many yards.

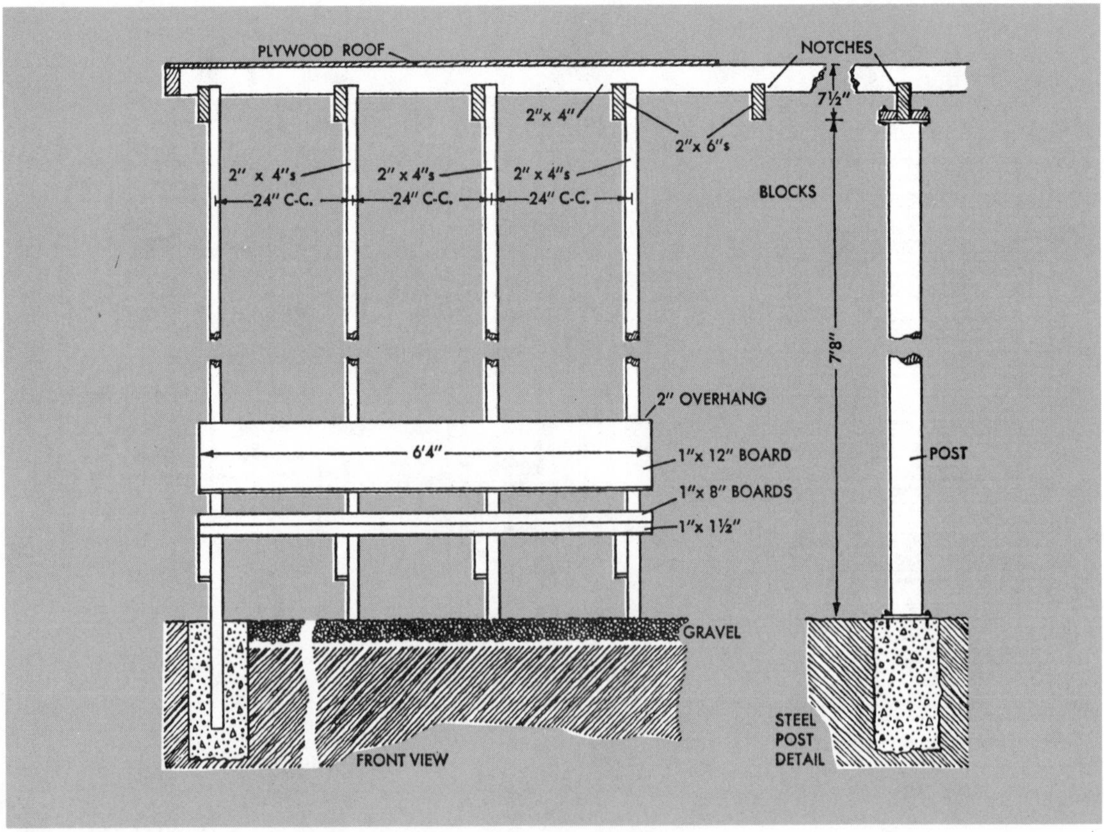

PLYWOOD ROOF
NOTCHES
2"x 4"
7½"
2"x 6"s
2" x 4"s
2" x 4"s
2" x 4"s
24" C-C.
24" C-C.
24" C-C.
BLOCKS
7'8"
2" OVERHANG
6'4"
1"x 12" BOARD
POST
1"x 8" BOARDS
1"x 1½"
GRAVEL
FRONT VIEW
STEEL
POST
DETAIL

DETAILS OF POST AND SEAT

2" OVERHANG
1"x 2"x 2" BLOCK
2" OVERHANG
1"
2"x 4"
1½"
24"

SEAT BRACKET DETAIL

NOTCH
2"x 4"
2"x 6"
1½"

TRELLIS DETAIL

FURTHER DETAILS

Basically the shelter is simplicity itself, consisting of four upright wooden posts set in concrete on one side, supporting trelliswork and seat, while on the other side three steel basement columns, bolted to a concrete base, hold up the front, giving unobstructed views of the garden. Wooden posts (4" × 4") could be substituted if desired. Only the area over the seat is roofed over with exterior plywood. But it needs sloping from front to back to provide quick drainage and thus preserve the roofing material. The 2" × 4" frame for the roof is notched to fit over the trelliswork frame, and nailed in place. Vines which climb on the trellis give adequate shade in the summer; and when they are leafless in spring and autumn, sufficient sun enters the trellis to make it possible to sit outdoors.

½" PLYWOOD
SEAT
PLYWOOD ROOF AREA
SEAT PLAN
PAVED AREA
STEEL BASEMENT COLUMNS (OR 4"x 4"s)
6'0" C.C.
24"

2"x 4" FRAME
4'0"
8'2"
2"x 4"s—16" C.C.
2"x 6"s—24" C.C.
ROOF PLAN

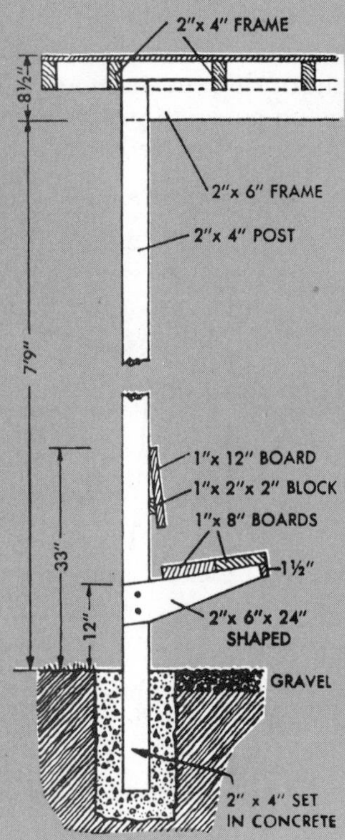

GARDEN HOUSE WITH A MODERN FLAVOR

Informality is the keynote of this structure with its seat along the back wall and the poles on the sides giving it strength and a feeling of enclosure without restricting outward view. Annual vines can clamber up the poles toward the shingled roof to make dining under cover a delight during the summer. The paving is set into the soil here, but a concrete or a brick- or stone-on-concrete platform would be equally acceptable. Similiarly, in place of the dwarf trees in pots, plant beds could be let into the paving and made gay with annuals.

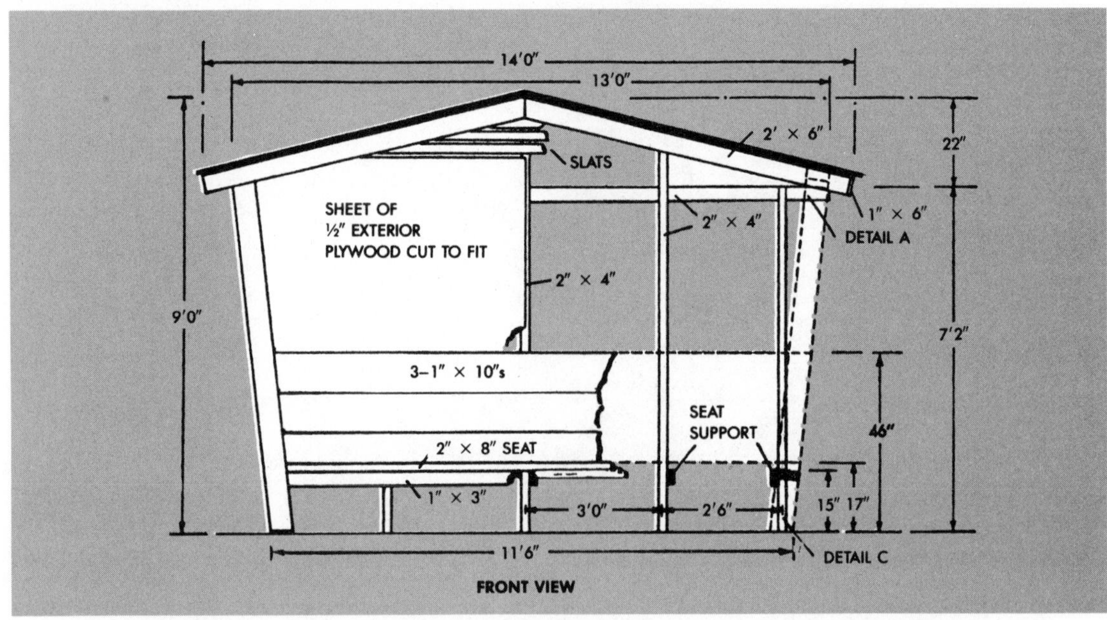

GARDEN HOUSE CONSTRUCTION DETAILS

Shingles for the roof should be heavy, thick-butt type, applied on exterior plywood roof. Rafters are notched to admit the supporting rails and the bracing members "B" are either nailed or bolted to post. Place 65" members first, then cut angle supports accurately to fit spaces, secure them to post and ridgepole.

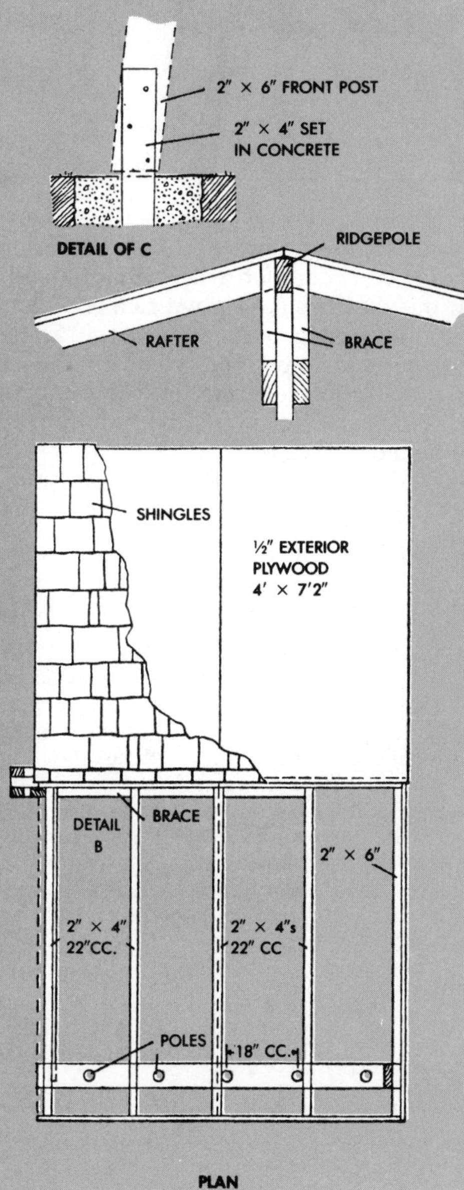

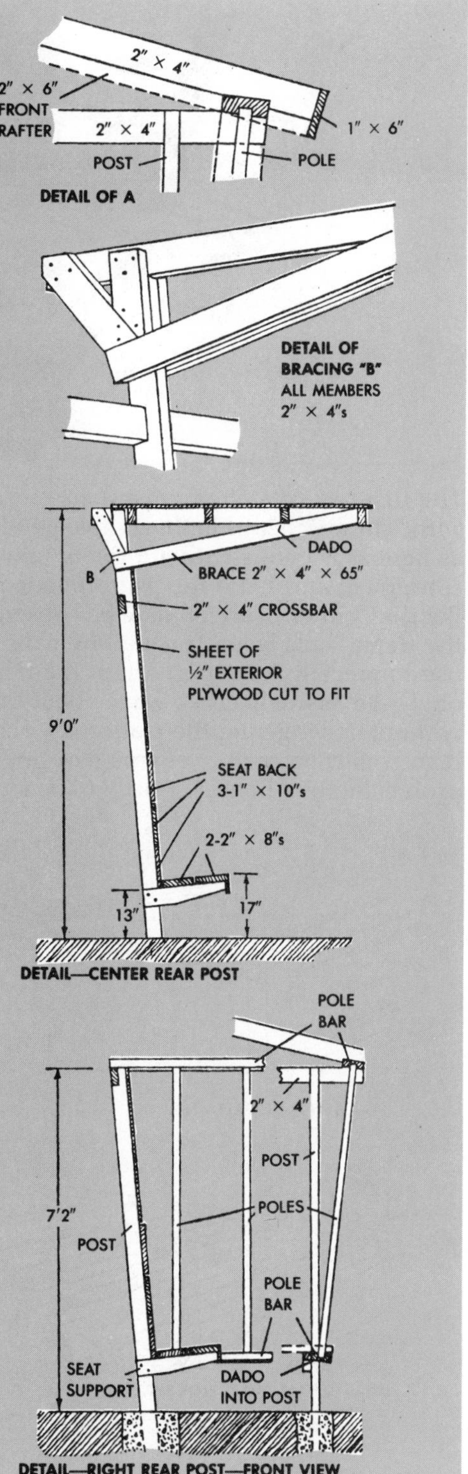

A TREE HOUSE FOR CHILDREN

The first requisite of any tree house is, of course, the tree. Choose a good strong one with a sufficient number of limbs to give good solid support to the framework. Keep the frame as light as is consistent with safety (always the prime consideration where children are concerned) and brace the platform adequately. In the sketches are shown two types of flooring, either of which may be chosen. Note that the upright posts are securely bolted to the frame, rails being fastened by nails. Hinged "gate" rail is lowered when tree house is in use to prevent accidents. Adapt the frame to the limb structure, securing it to the trunk only—limbs are likely to wave about in the wind. Holes in floor permit them to move without endangering the platform. Crossbars are bolted to tree trunk with 6" lag screws, braces notched to fit over crossbars and nailed. NOTE: Some towns have ordinances prohibiting tree houses. Check to be sure they are permitted in your area before you build.

FLOOR DETAILS

Conventional floor boards, 1" × 6" or 1" × 8", may be utilized or ½" exterior plywood laid on diagonal subflooring of rough or scrap lumber. Alternative flooring (below) may require more work but it will last indefinitely, making a rigid framework and providing perfect drainage in wet climates. Use 2" × 4"s for its outer framework, 1" × 3"s separated by 1" × 3" × 3" blocks, all bolted together with steel tie-rods through holes bored through boards and frame, giving rigidity.

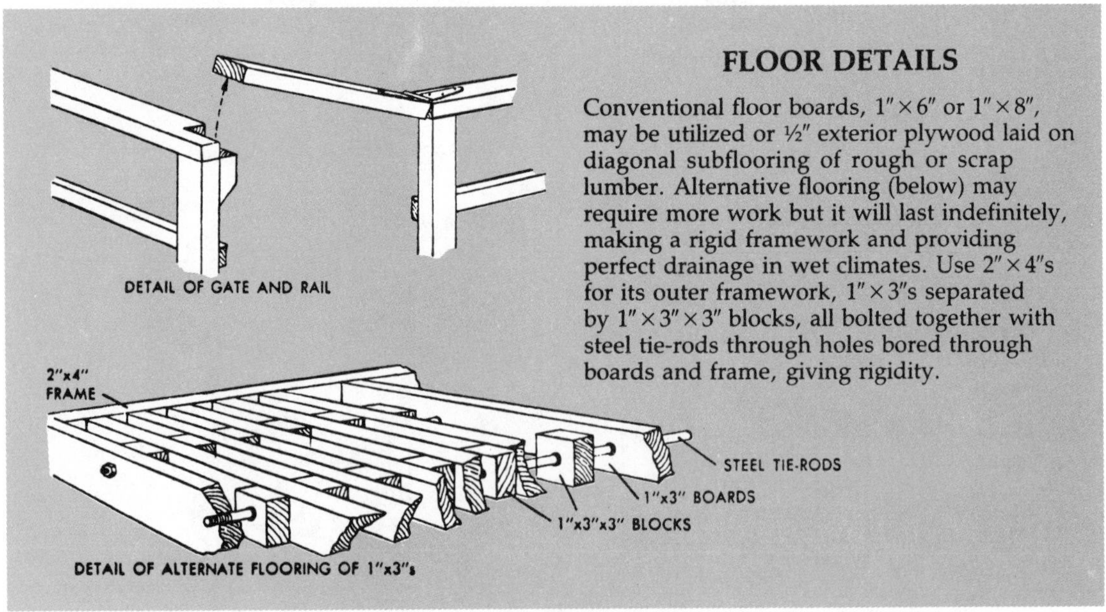

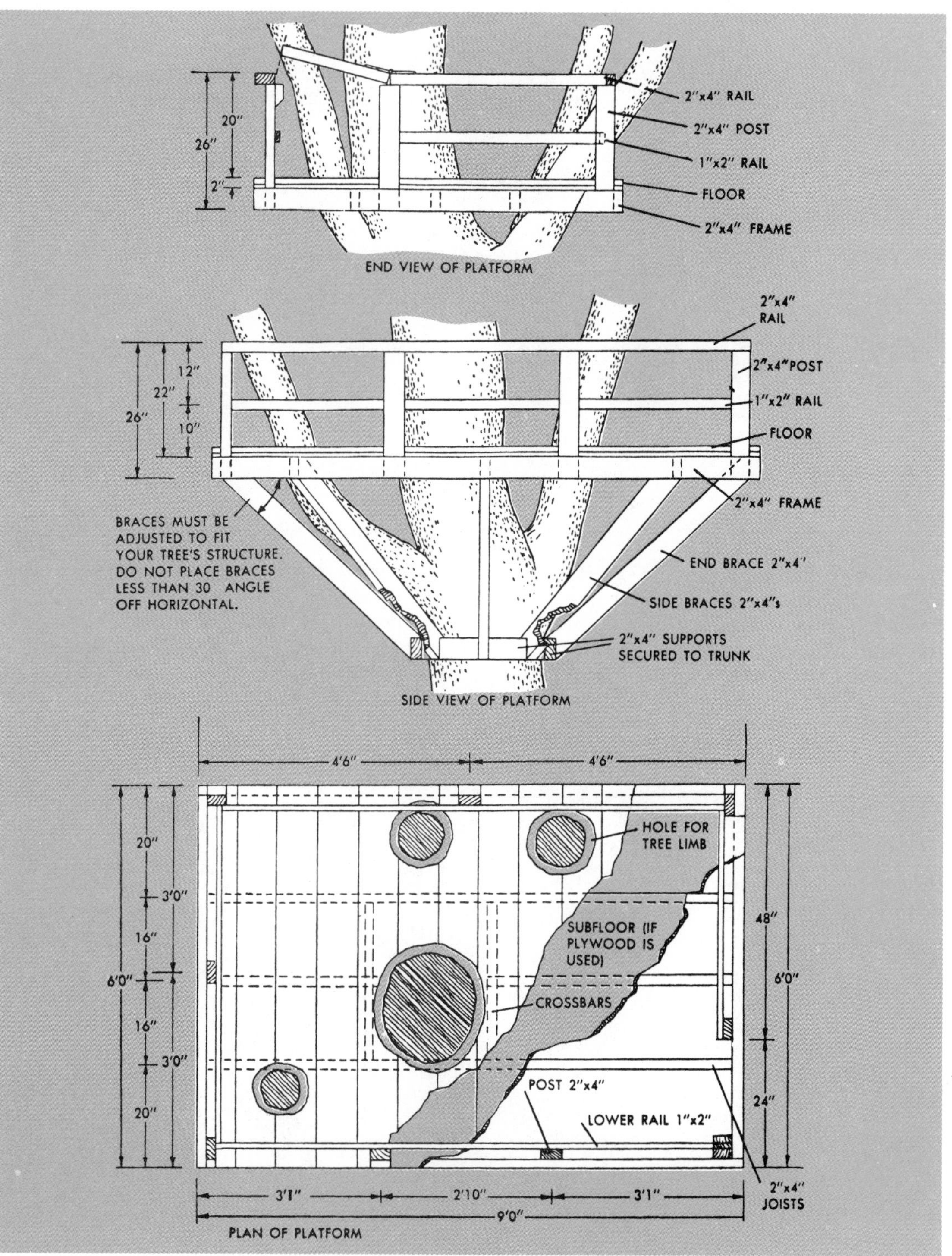
20"
26"
2"
2"x4" RAIL
2"x4" POST
1"x2" RAIL
FLOOR
2"x4" FRAME
END VIEW OF PLATFORM
2"x4" RAIL
12"
22"
26"
10"
2"x4"POST
1"x2" RAIL
FLOOR
2"x4" FRAME
BRACES MUST BE ADJUSTED TO FIT YOUR TREE'S STRUCTURE. DO NOT PLACE BRACES LESS THAN 30 ANGLE OFF HORIZONTAL.
END BRACE 2"x4"
SIDE BRACES 2"x4"s
2"x4" SUPPORTS SECURED TO TRUNK
SIDE VIEW OF PLATFORM
4'6"
4'6"
20"
3'0"
16"
6'0"
16"
3'0"
20"
HOLE FOR TREE LIMB
SUBFLOOR (IF PLYWOOD IS USED)
CROSSBARS
48"
6'0"
24"
POST 2"x4"
LOWER RAIL 1"x2"
3'1"
2'10"
3'1"
9'0"
2"x4" JOISTS
PLAN OF PLATFORM

A NEW ANGLE ON TRELLISES

Even if a patio is quite tiny, it can still have charm—in fact, the smaller it is the more it *needs* charm. An unconventional trellis which fits well with a traditional house, such as this one, lends piquancy to the home scene. Blocks form a low plant bed, give year-round definition to the patio which in summer is graced with potted plants; annuals are used with shrubs in the beds. The trellis breaks the sun's rays, providing a place for annual vines to climb on. The clapboard fence continues lines of the house.

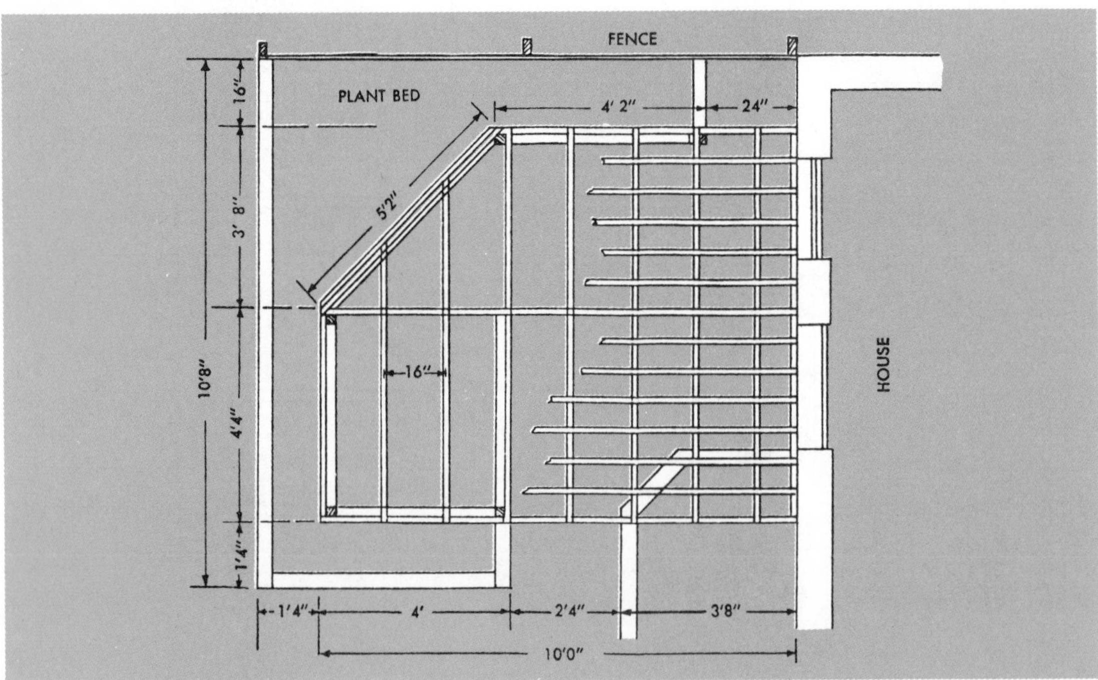

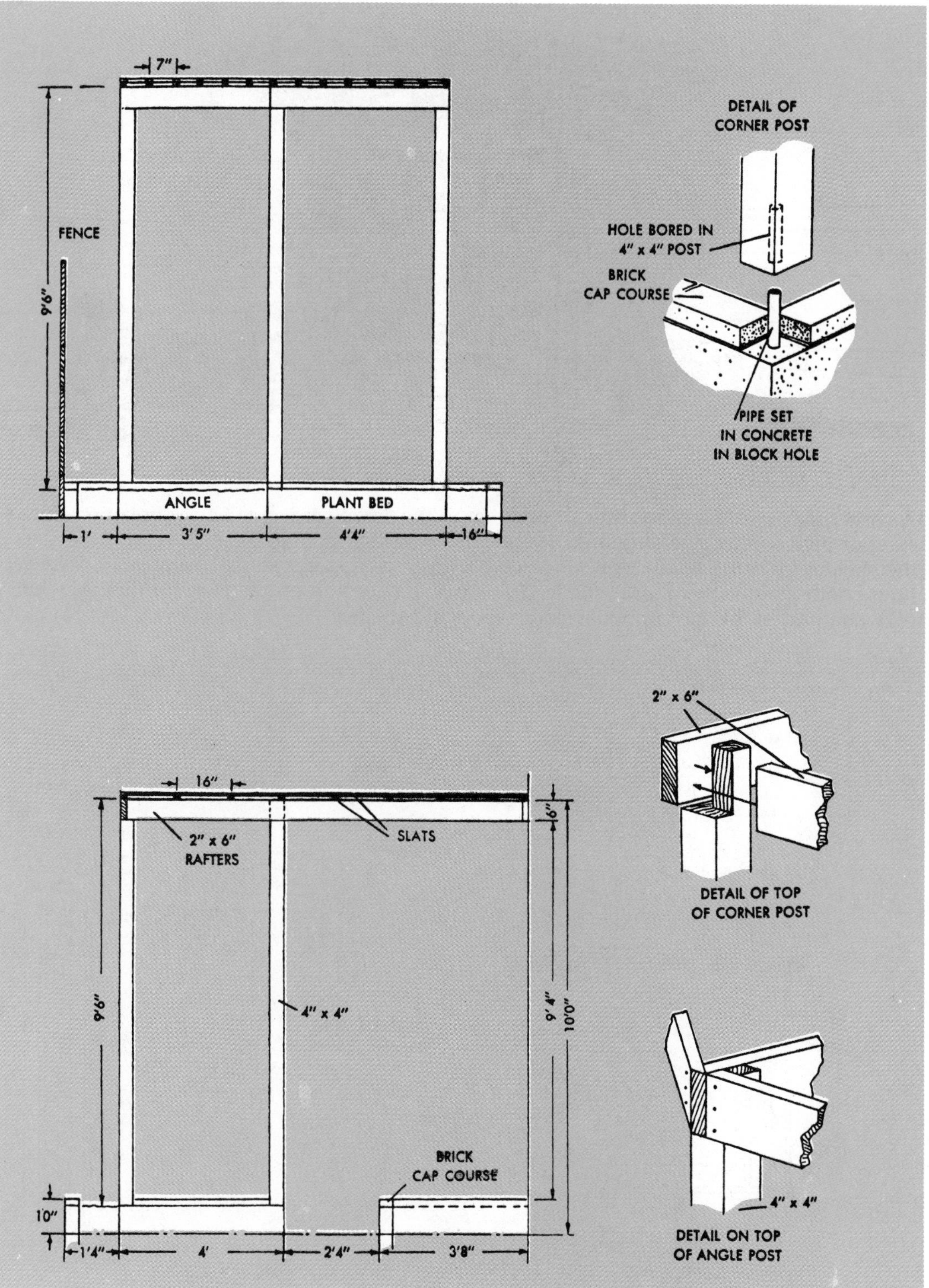
7"
FENCE
9'6"
ANGLE
PLANT BED
1'
3' 5"
4'4"
16"
DETAIL OF
CORNER POST
HOLE BORED IN
4" x 4" POST
BRICK
CAP COURSE
PIPE SET
IN CONCRETE
IN BLOCK HOLE
16"
2" x 6"
RAFTERS
SLATS
6"
9'6"
4" x 4"
9' 4"
10'0"
BRICK
CAP COURSE
10"
1'4"
4'
2'4"
3'8"
2" x 6"
DETAIL OF TOP
OF CORNER POST
4" x 4"
DETAIL ON TOP
OF ANGLE POST

ATTRACTIVE SHELTER IN A CORNER

A corner may create a most difficult problem in the small yard. By using shiplap or scored exterior plywood to give long lines to the fence and by echoing those lines with the slats of the shelter, by using boldly opposing vertical lines to support the roof, you create a garden house both good-looking and unique. The seats add comfort and a place for dining, while the plywood part of the roof provides both shade and shelter.

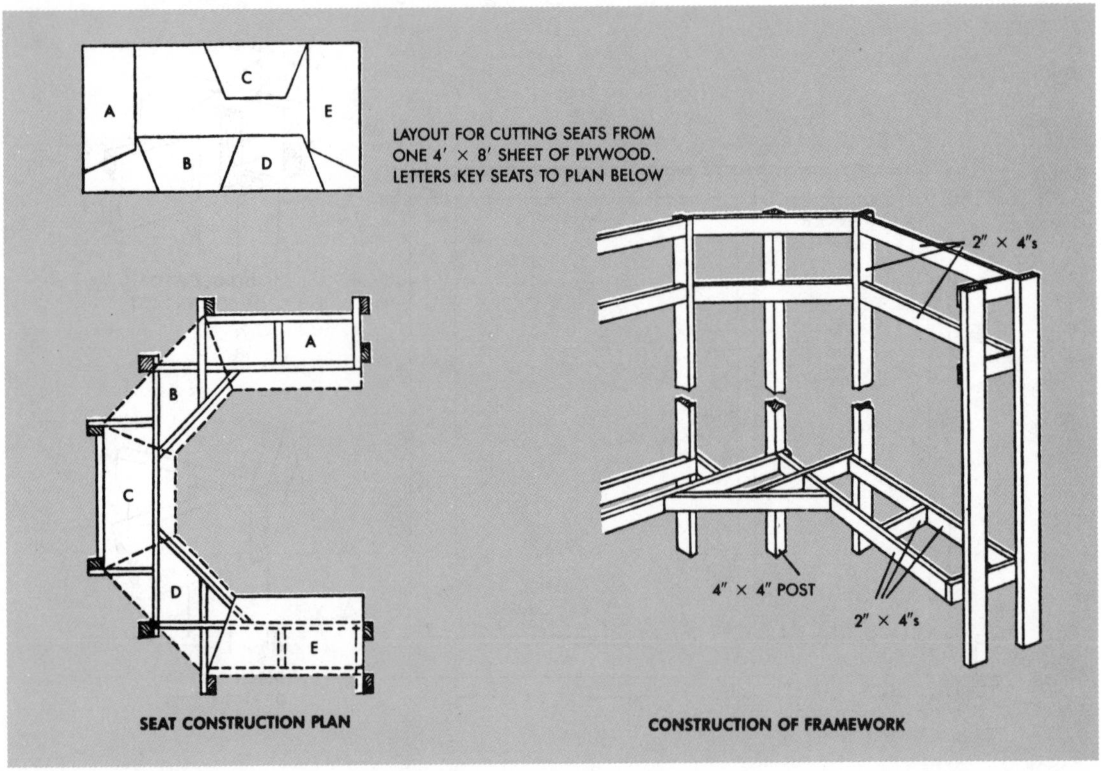

A C E B D

LAYOUT FOR CUTTING SEATS FROM ONE 4′ × 8′ SHEET OF PLYWOOD. LETTERS KEY SEATS TO PLAN BELOW

A B C D E

SEAT CONSTRUCTION PLAN

2″ × 4″s

4″ × 4″ POST

2″ × 4″s

CONSTRUCTION OF FRAMEWORK

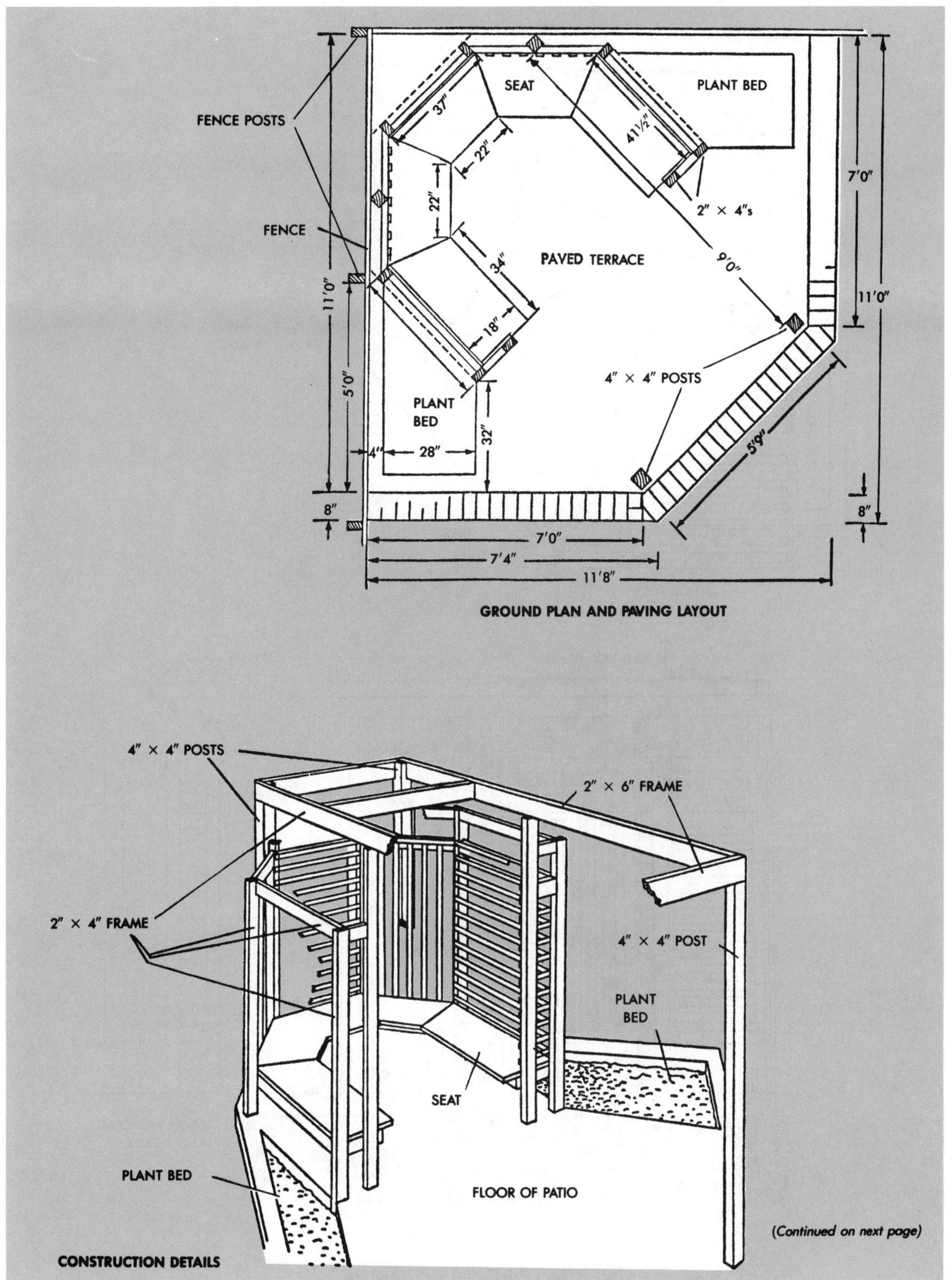

GROUND PLAN AND PAVING LAYOUT

CONSTRUCTION DETAILS

(Continued on next page)

(Continued from previous page)

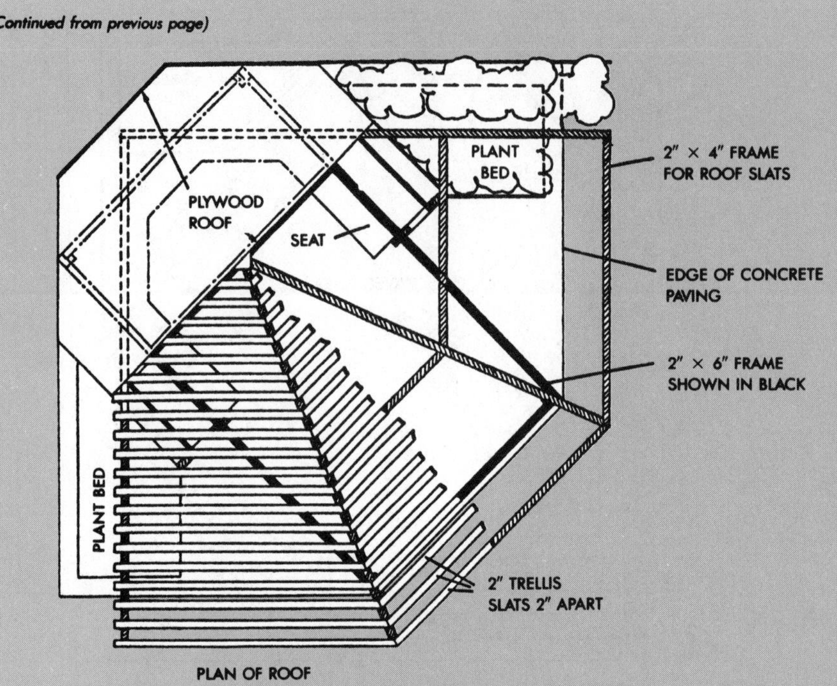

PLAN OF ROOF

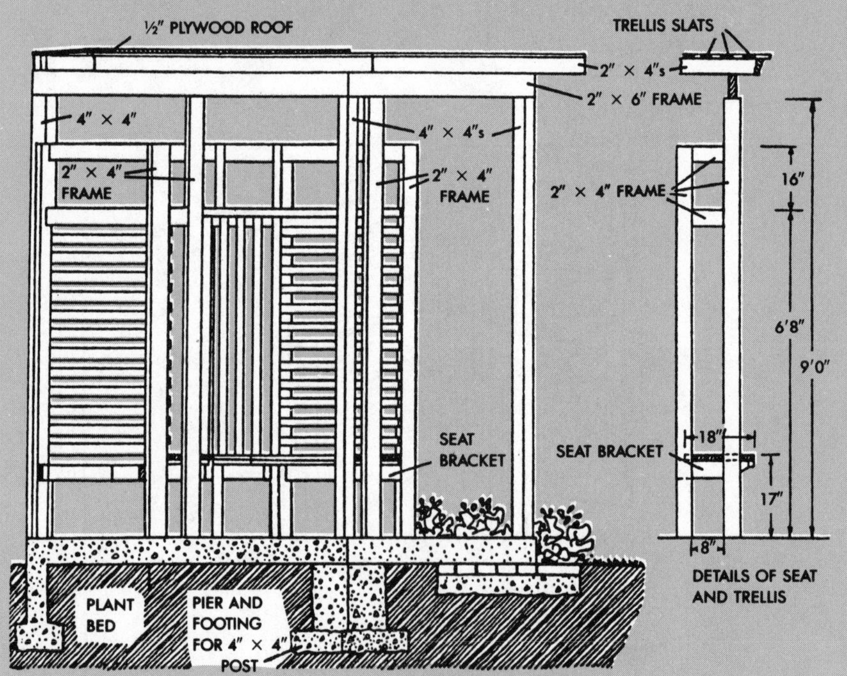

SHADE AFTER A TREE DIES

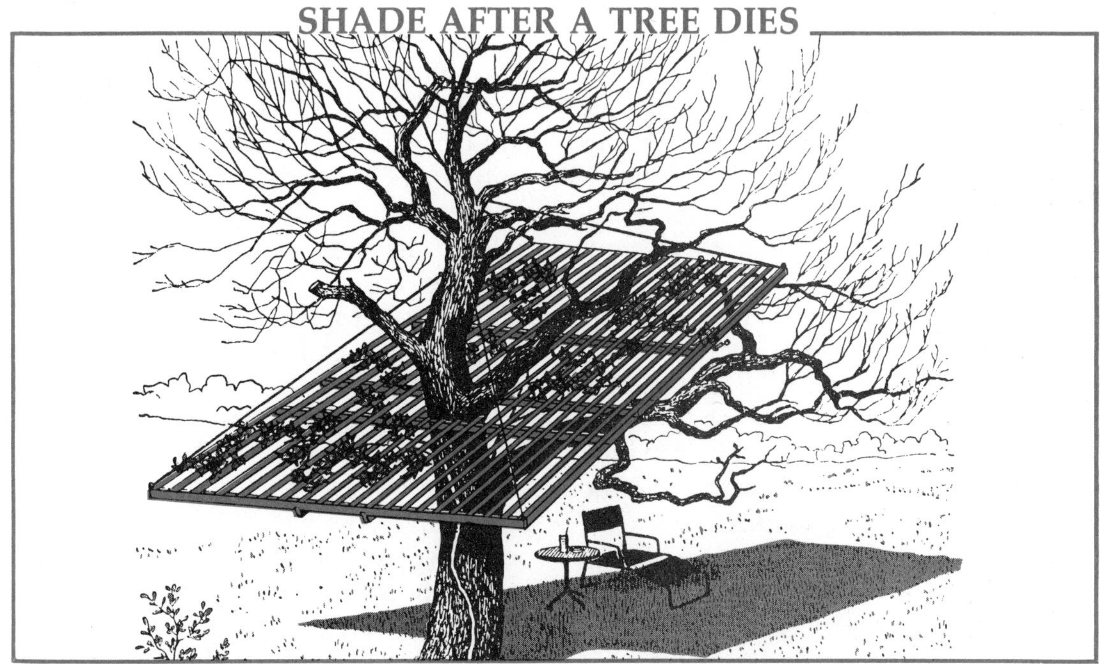

Regrettable as the loss of a large shade tree may be, the death needn't rob you of shade completely. It is possible to utilize the tree as a source of shade for some years more until its replacement grows big enough to contribute sufficient protection. Cut off all limbs and branches likely to be dislodged by the wind, bolt the center 2″ × 6″s to the trunk, then attach the 2″ × 4″ frame members securely and apply the trellis strips. For complete support, use steel cables through eyebolts to four corners. A wisteria or some other permanent vine planted at the trunk and trained up to cover the shelter will eventually clothe it and even the trunk and limbs of the tree. Meantime plant quick-growing annual vines (see Chapter 6) for thick cover, yearly shade. You may wish to peel the bark off and paint the tree a pleasant, soft color or stain soft green or brown.

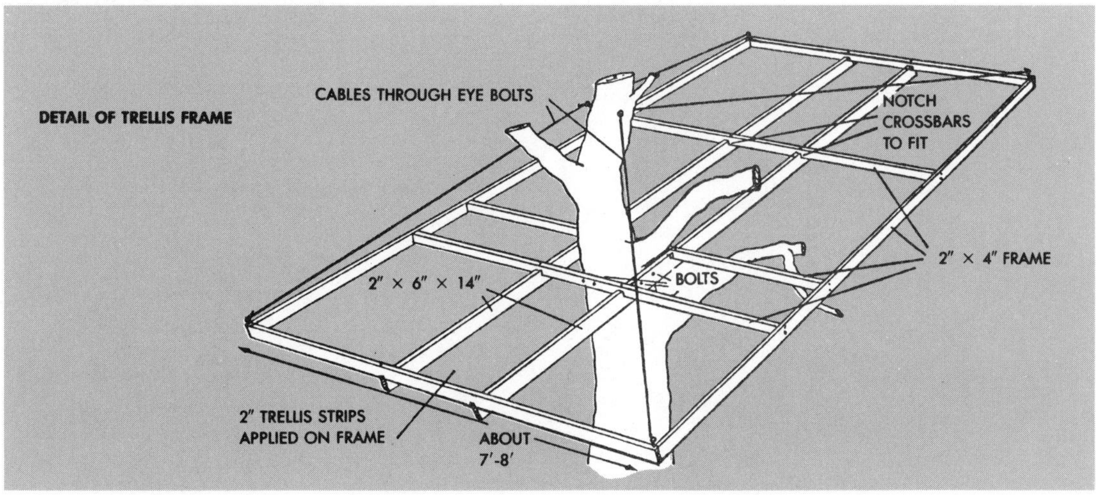

A BASIC UNIT FOR GAZEBOS

In formulating a useful, simple plan for a backyard gazebo, it seems wisest to steer clear of octagonal and hexagonal kinds, charming as they may be. Much more cutting and fitting is required to produce them, because of the angles involved, than for a 90° square cornered type. Also the average do-it-yourselfer's time is in shorter supply than talent and most people want to get on with the job, finish it, and start enjoying the use of its product. A square basic unit or module has the added virtue of being adaptable to extension and improvision in more ways than the octagonal sorts.

Using a basic structure, 8′×8′ and square cornered (or 10′×10′ if you need more space and your plot permits it), you can make it oblong by adding a quarter to its length, a half, or double it for a king-sized gazebo. By using these measures you will avoid a lot of sawing and cutting, for standard lengths straight out of the lumber yard save hours of cutting labor and time. Obviously not all pieces can be used exactly as they come—and it is a good plan to measure them before assuming they are the correct length, too. But enough pieces will need no cutting to make the job go like a breeze.

On this basic framework will be applied the "skin" of slatting or whatever, achieving privacy as well as the decorative effect you desire. Bracing is needed for strength. Note the detail of the corner-to-corner top bracing in the drawing. Joists under the wood floor also help to keep it stable, but don't forget to see that they are well impregnated with wood preservative (Chapter 4) to prevent rot from entering. It is possible, too, to floor the gazebo with concrete as for patios, or with

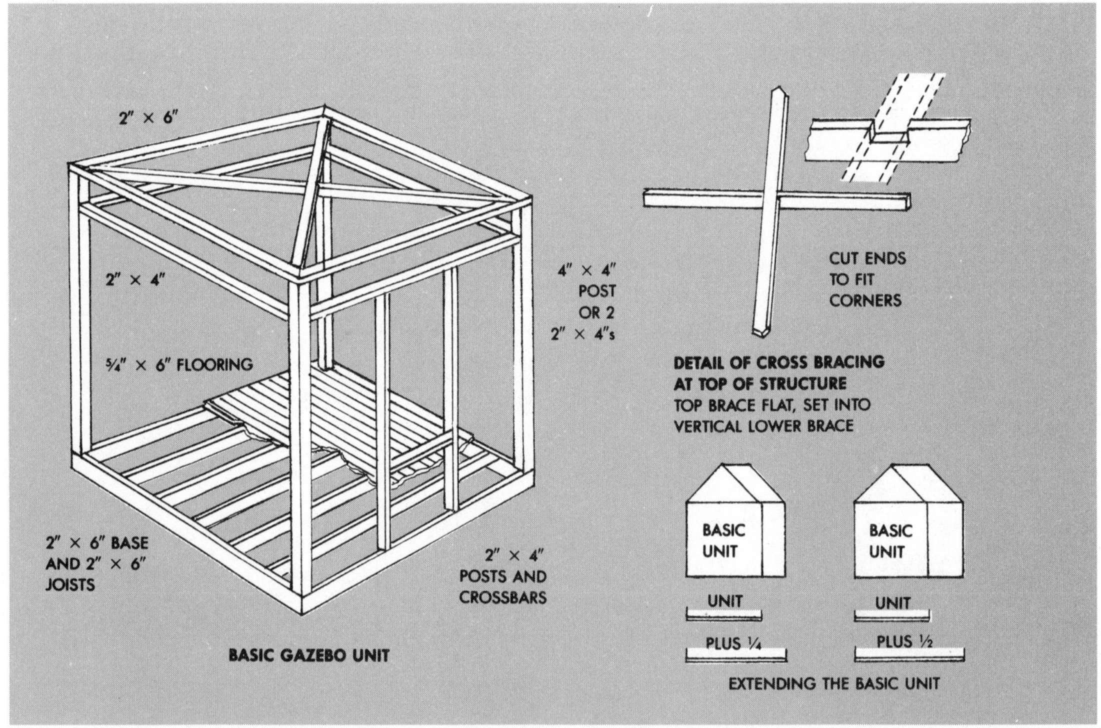

CLASSIC OR VICTORIAN GAZEBO

A classic roofline in the two versions, below left, shows how slats achieve varying effects. At right, the lower panel is plywood with molding applied to carry on the motif already visible in the doorway with its arched cutout frame. The steep-roofed Victorian style at right with its gothic arched doorway sports a further bit of fantasy with a finial above the typical Victorian gable. Vertical slats are used here but crossbar style (slats set at angles) is also a Victorian motif. Note that the 2″ × 4″ doorposts in both designs run to the roof rafters, helping to stabilize the structure which is open to the roof in the manner of the old ones.

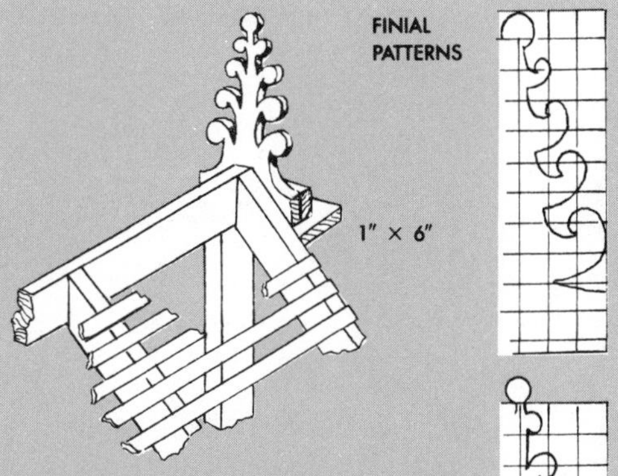

FINIAL PATTERNS

1″ × 6″

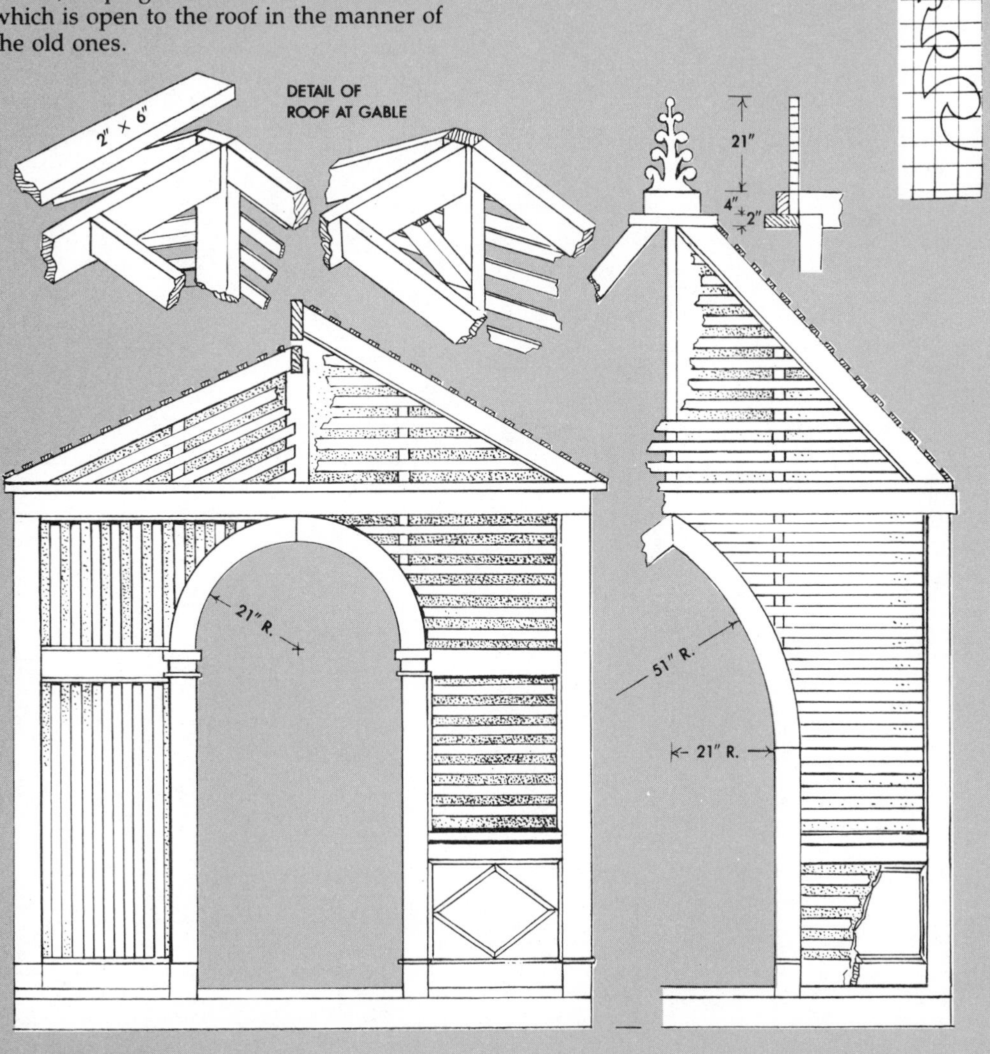

2″ × 6″

DETAIL OF ROOF AT GABLE

21″

4″

2″

21″ R.

51″ R.

21″ R.

bricks laid on sand or mortar, or any other alternative according to your desires and tastes.

Build your gazebo as you would a house—sturdy, long-lasting, useful, and above all good looking so it will be a delight for your family and friends in the years to come.

GAZEBOS WITH VARIED COVERINGS

Just about anything goes for patterns on gazebos, achieved by applying slats. The upper parts may be left open—with only those parts below windowsill height covered—or the whole wall may be slatted. Even the windows and doors may have slatted shutters and doors, paneled and with slats applied in a manner consistent with the slats on walls. Gazebos in the past were quite varied.

Left, below, chevron patterns carry over to frame the doorway top, also the diamond pattern that echoes the cutout plywood triangles of the cornice. At right, the excitement of crossbarred slatting contrasts with the serenity of horizontal slatting. Roofs echo the motifs. Detail sketches show how the rafters join to support the pointed finial that adds so much to the style of the gazebo. Of course the roof might merely end in a pyramid, omitting the finial, if desired.

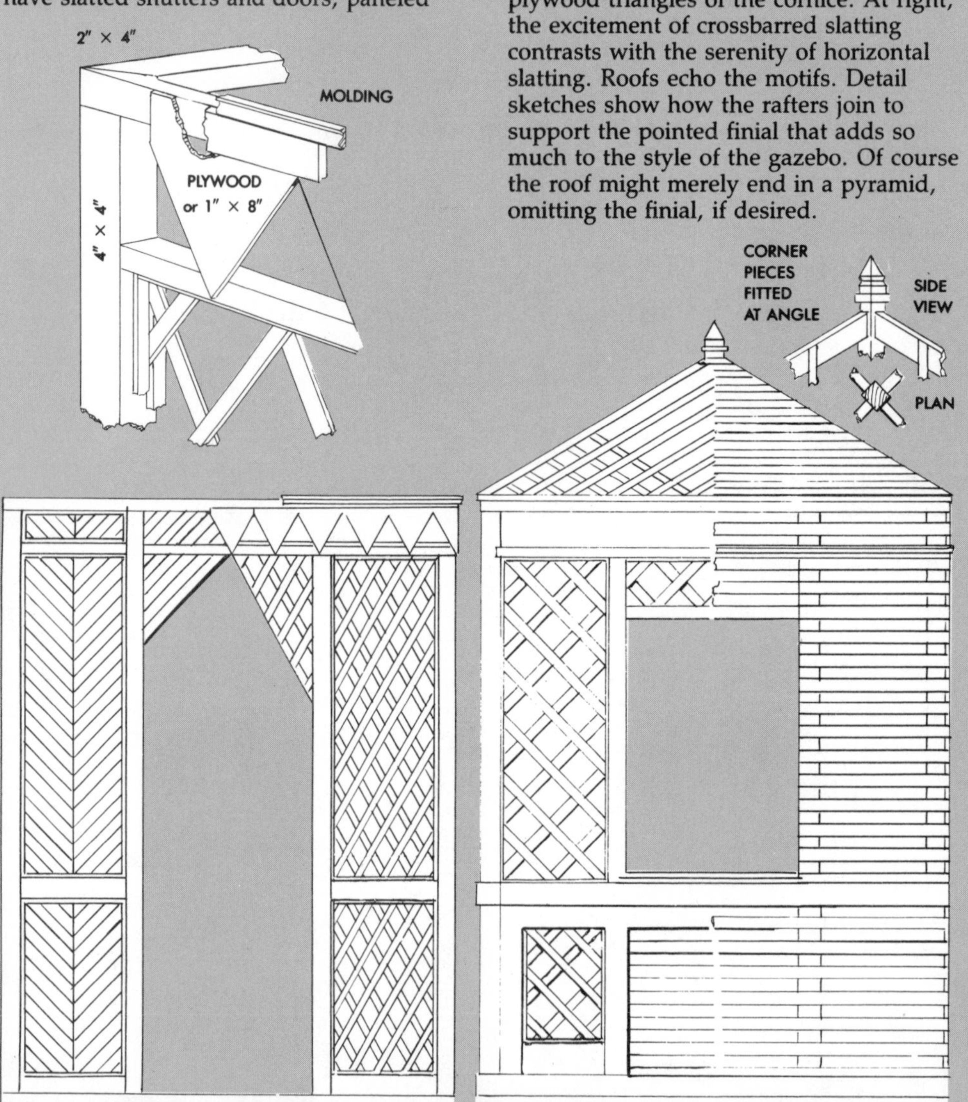

VICTORIAN OR ORIENTAL GAZEBO

Adapt a gazebo to the style of the house or to lend a touch of pleasant fantasy to the garden. Below, left, are two versions adapted from Victorian models—one with a dished roofline, the other improvising on the Mansard roofline, and both with gothic doorways; each has its own kind of slatting. Doors are framed with 1" lumber cut from wide widths. At right, below, the style is more oriental looking in the way the slats are assembled—one severe and simple, the other more ornate. The roof is built up with wide moldings around the edges and may be solid on top or slatted. Both styles may have an open window in the sides, using the same construction as for a door but with sill.

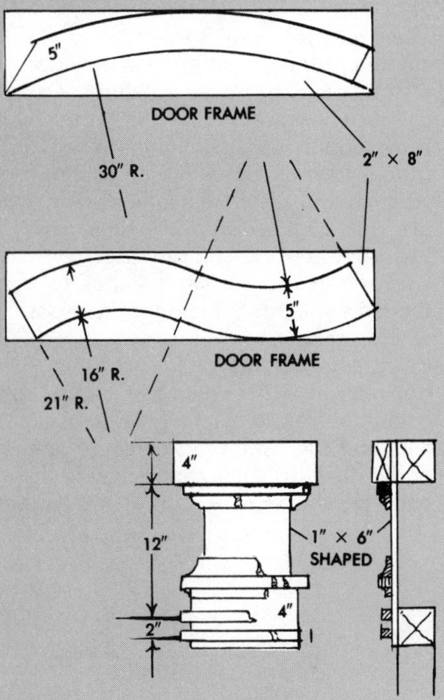

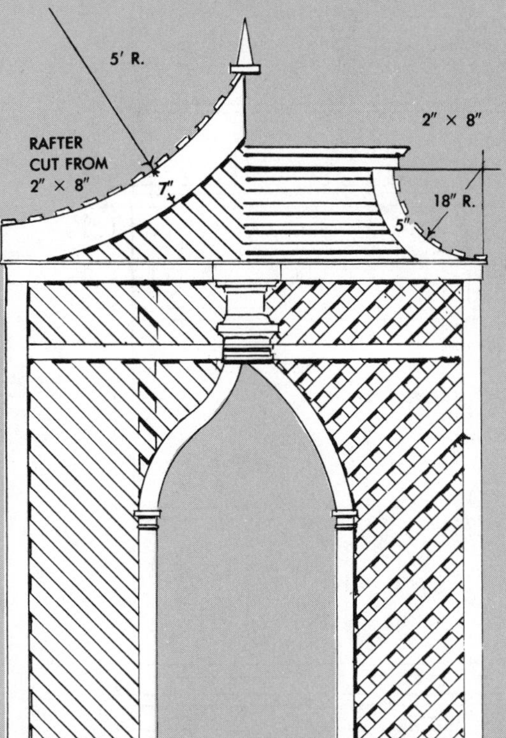

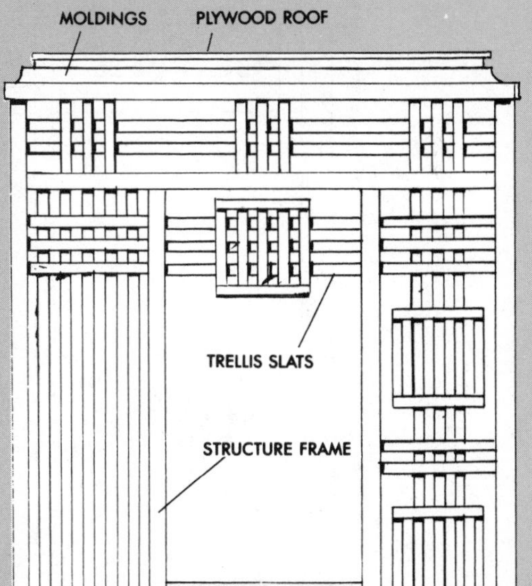

A VERSATILE CLASSIC-LOOK GAZEBO

The decorative motifs supplied by the cutouts in the exterior-grade plywood parts give this garden house an almost oriental simplicity, making it eligible for use with a stark modern setting. Yet it was adapted from a 19th century German design for a stairway rail. Its classic look also suggests use with 18th century as well as early Victorian houses. The roof may be enclosed or left open and slatted to give filtered sunlight. Screening and a door would make it a refuge where insects called "no-see-ums" are a problem. Consider also the use of the cutouts for edging a deck or balcony, perhaps adapting the structure to enclose one end of the deck or placing it alongside the patio for shelter from rain or hot sunlight.

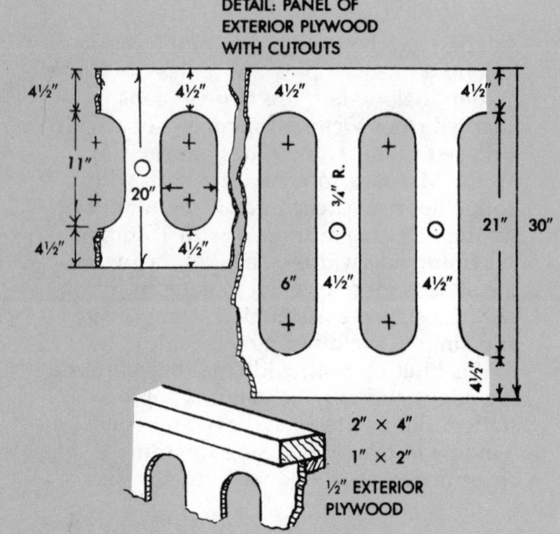

CLASSIC GAZEBO

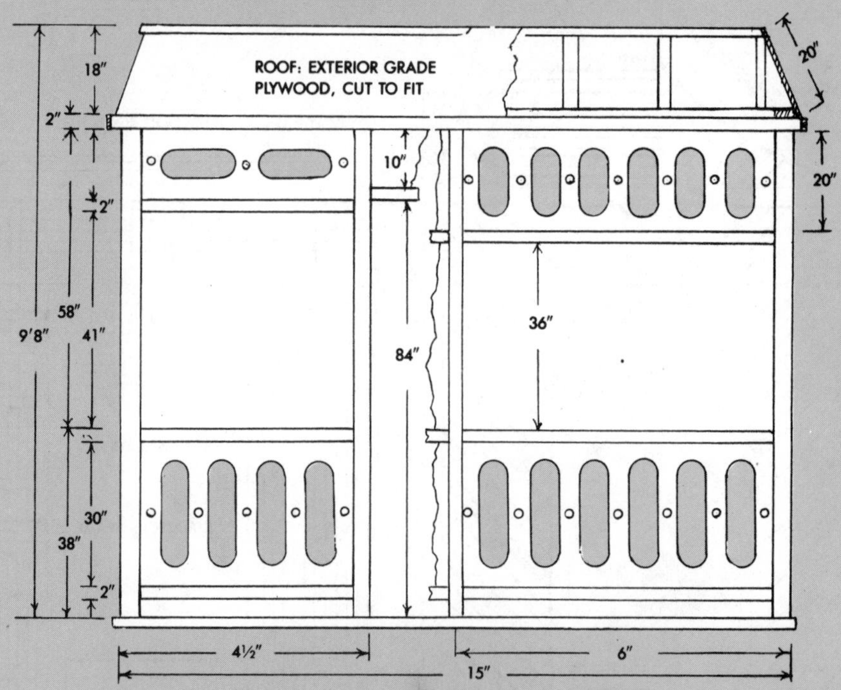

JIGSAW ORNAMENT GIVES A HOUSE A PERIOD LOOK

There is a growing appreciation of Victorian design, and even though many vintage houses are not of landmark quality, they are being bought and restored. Also, other people now buy what were once disparagingly called "carpenters' houses"—perhaps because they were so honestly foursquare and plain. These can be discreetly decorated with some jigsaw ornament to bring up the general feeling of the period.

On some of the more decorated houses, people are no longer pulling off and discarding the "lacepaper" Victorian ornament if some of it is broken or missing. Pieces are carefully removed and copied to fill out the missing parts which, in addition to being a charming restoration, will protect the investment in the house and make it more salable. But the plain, overly simple house may also benefit from a little ornament. For instance, if a sagging porch must be replaced, consider using one of the corner scrolls shown. Or use the baluster spacers to dress up a porch or balcony balustrade or a stair handrail. The swag pattern opposite was adapted from one on an early 19th century house on which it ran along the eaves and up and down both gables. Such touches used with restraint will give the house individuality and distinction.

If you have an old house (or even a new one), consider building a gazebo or garden house that echoes the lines, emulates the decorative details of the house. If there are no details from which to adapt, perhaps one of the ornaments opposite could be used.

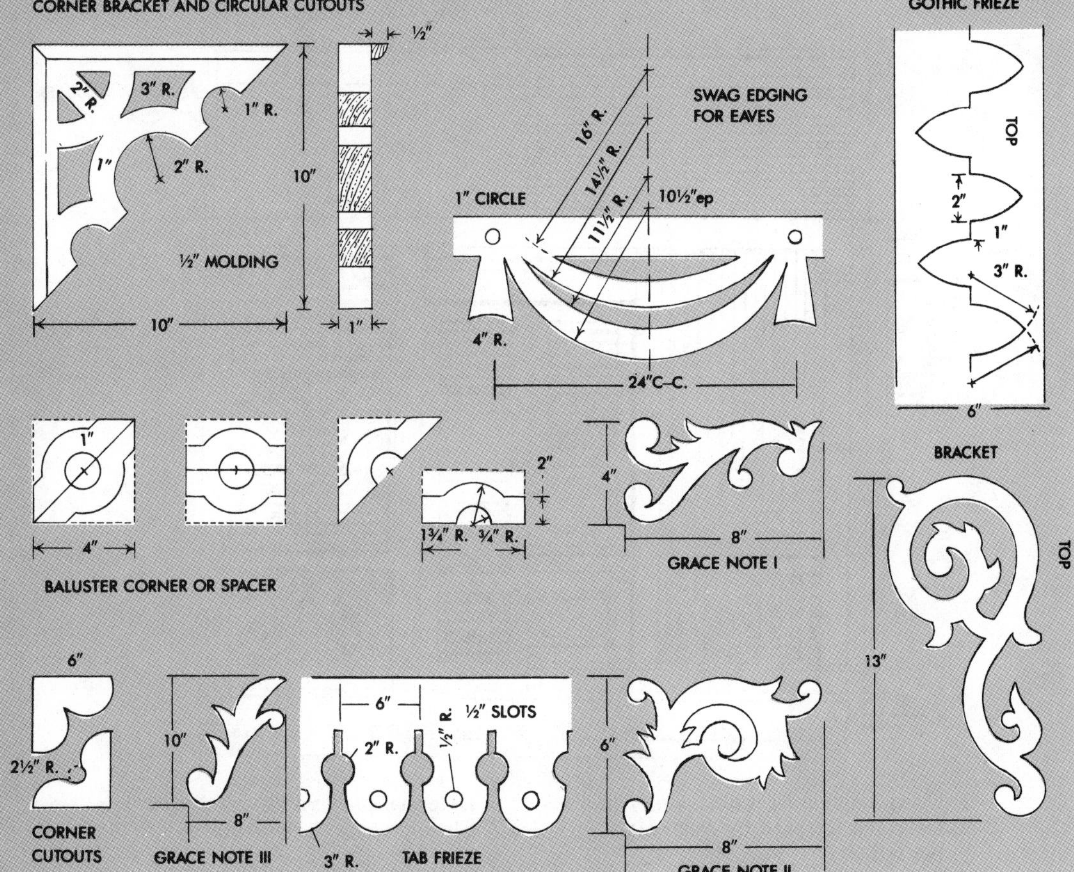

USING SLATS FOR PATTERNS

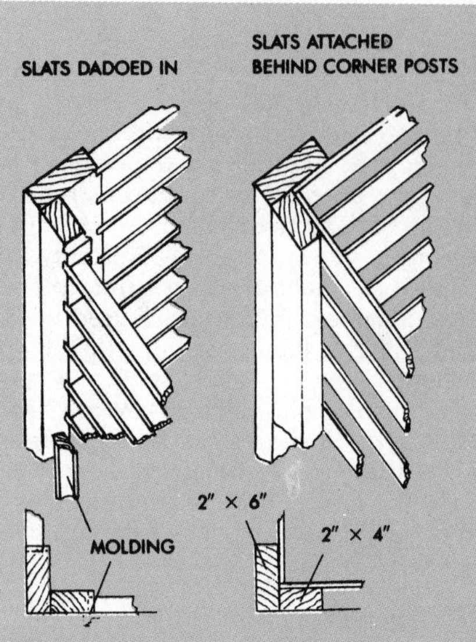

There seem to be unlimited ways to combine and space trellis slats, obtaining privacy as well as enhancing the general appearance of the gazebo. Slats are generally offered in two widths but if a heavier effect is desired, use 1"×2"s or 1"×3"s, making sure that the weighty appearance is in keeping with the proportions of the structure. A few of many combinations are shown here.

In the detail, left, and in the doors below, horizontally placed slats are dadoed into the frame at intervals. They prevent direct sunlight from entering, yet permit maximum ventilation. Where insects and even small "no-see-ums" are a problem, fiberglass window screening may be applied to the inner side. Its gray color is unobtrusive and pleasant. Shown in the other detail is the method of applying slats inside the frame. A quarter-round molding in the corner may be added if desired.

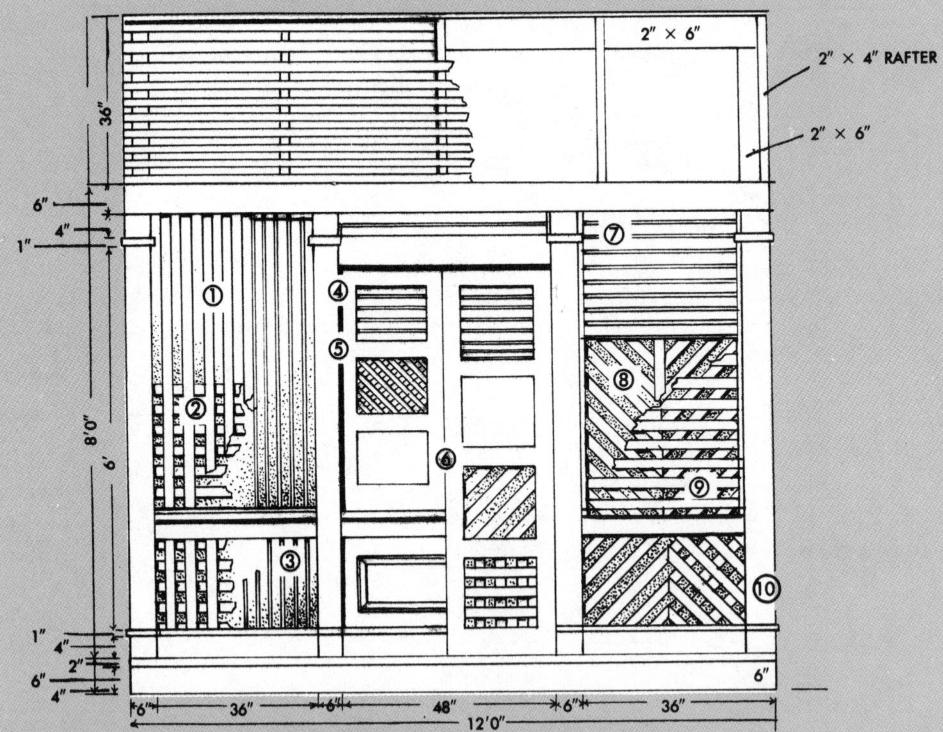

1. Used flat against inner side of frame
2. Used flat, crossed by other slats behind
3. Set vertically, narrow side facing out
4. Dadoed into frame, see Detail
5. Cut in half, crossed, for finer effect
6. Diagonal placement, full width slats
7. Closely space, half-width or less of slats.
8. Diagonal, chevon pattern
9. Chevron with crossbar horizontals
10. Crossed diagonals, full width slats

A gazebo with bonus garden storage starts with a deck framing of 6″ × 6″ posts, 2″ × 6″ joists and headers, and 2″ × 4″ decking, all in pressure-treated fir or pine. The 4″ × 4″ posts for the 14½′ hexagon are angled, sawn, and notched.

Temporary cross-bracing during construction is replaced later with 2″ × 6″ collar rafters bolted to ridge rafters. Cedar shingles are applied over black roofing paper with 1″ × 2″ nailing strips.

The completed gazebo has a hexagonal floor plan that measures 14½′ across. The rear half features a counter with lockable storage cabinets above and a tool shed entered behind.

THOUGHTS ON DECKS AND PORCHES

With extended leisure time and the awareness of the importance of the environment in fostering good health came greater use of the outdoor areas of the home grounds. Many gardens now have more than one "sitting-out spot," often geared to seasonal weather patterns—paved patios for some uses but wooden decks, too, that give an illusion of living in a treehouse while utilizing an area too costly to grade and pave. Each makes a unique contribution to the joy of life.

Another development is the revival of the old-time stoop, an uncovered porch that gives grace and importance to the front or back door. Added, too, to a venerable older home to keep its period character or attached to a modern row house in a development, a stoop adds a bit of charm and distinction—not to mention the platform to stand on while searching for your keys on stormy nights.

This entertaining deck has an original curving-front floor made of 2″ × 4″s set ½″ apart. It may be precut to curve, or roughcut, nailed in place, and the curve cut with a saber saw. The shelter has a center roof of opaque plastic for diffused light.

Ideal for a beach house but adaptable anywhere, a redwood deck features planks set on the bias in alternate directions; plant beds and barbecue pit may be let into the deck, raised seats on the side might have hinged tops, making equipment storage boxes.

The strong directional lines of the floor of this deck give it a crisp contrast to the natural curves of the plants. Douglas fir 2″ × 4″s set on edge ½″ apart are framed by mitered 2″ × 4″s. A step or two similarly styled leads down to the sloping ground.

A wooden deck need not be square and blocky. A curving free-form edge is most effective—even steps may be rounded. Redwood floor is echoed by step, both edged with ½″ boards kerf-sawed at intervals of ½″ to ¾″ and bent in shape.

A strong curve is saved from harshness by the material—redwood—and the linear effect of the floorboards. Beams supporting it rest on small concrete piers sunk in the ground. The fence is also framed in redwood, and bamboo (which is replaceable) gives a light, airy texture.

An oriental simplicity suffuses this garden scene, with its wooden deck of Douglas fir 2″×3″s, its wooden access ramp, and its use of container-grown plants. Silhouetted foliage casts alluring shadows on the semi-opaque plastic covering the high privacy fence.

Any sitting-out space is welcome in warm months, but one that is for both sun and shade is doubly valuable. A sturdy redwood trellis above a pool and a 2″×4″ floored area can be vinecovered in summer. Wood-floored decks in two ascending levels behind provide sunny sitting.

BUILD A DECK OR PORCH

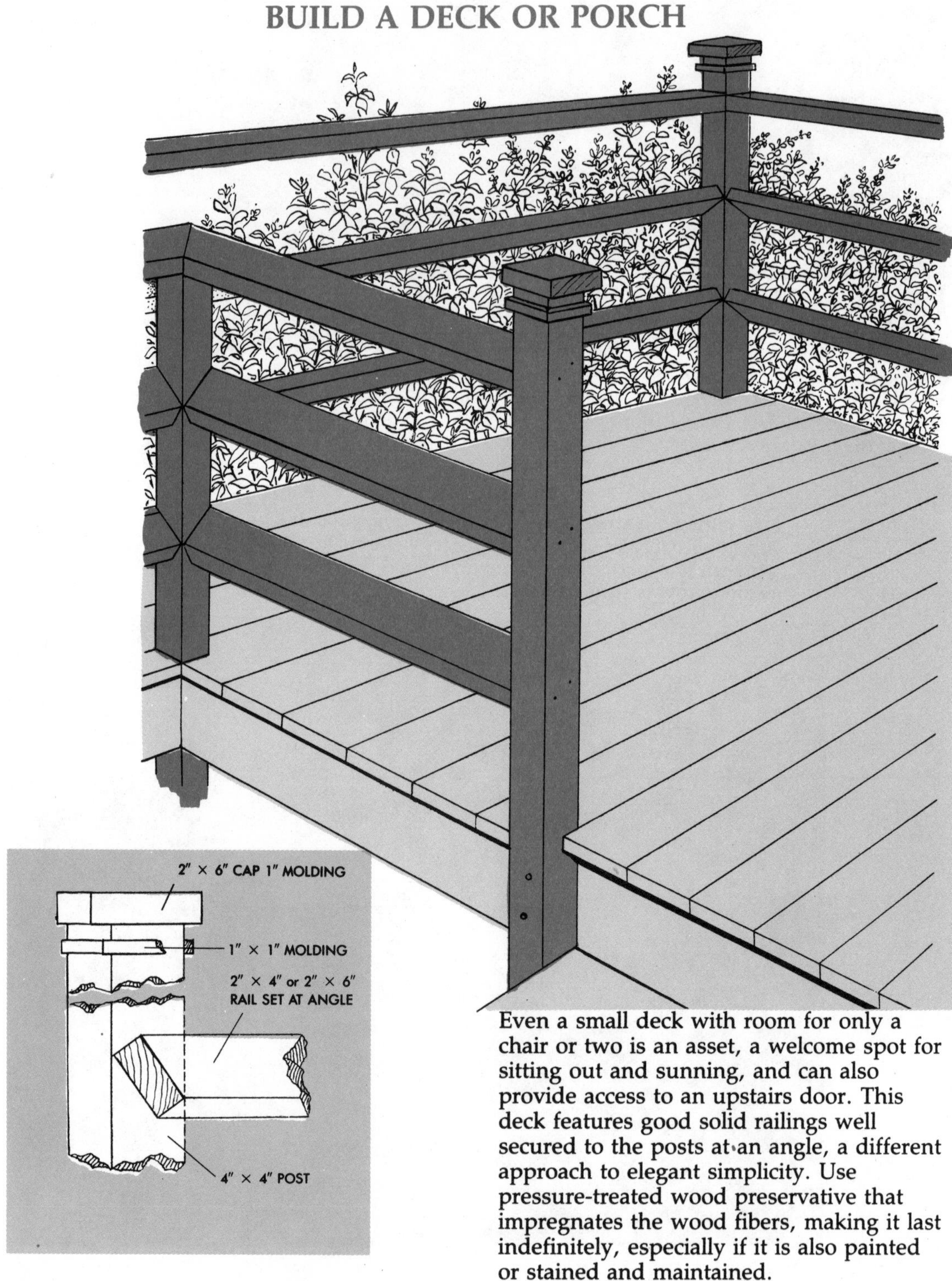

Even a small deck with room for only a chair or two is an asset, a welcome spot for sitting out and sunning, and can also provide access to an upstairs door. This deck features good solid railings well secured to the posts at an angle, a different approach to elegant simplicity. Use pressure-treated wood preservative that impregnates the wood fibers, making it last indefinitely, especially if it is also painted or stained and maintained.

PORCHES WITH CHARACTER

Adding a small porch to a run-of-the-mill house immediately lifts it into individuality and enhances its value. At right, the railing is topped by a cutout Victorian wood scroll, such as might go well with an older house or embellish a new one that lacks character.

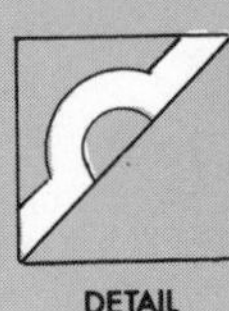

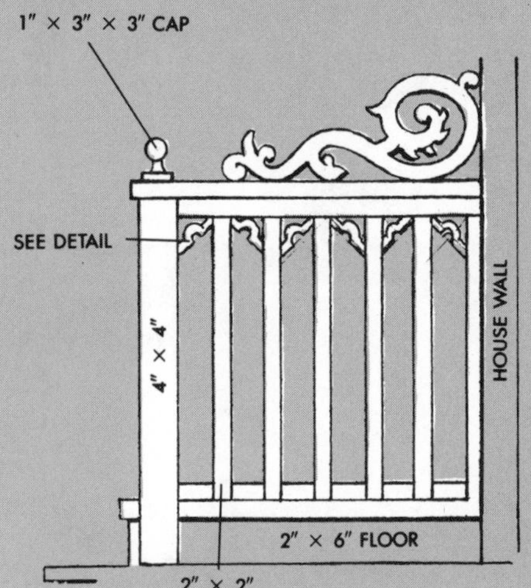

An Early American motif of weighty railings dadoed into the pointed-topped posts gives a welcome solidity so appealing in oldtime houses.

Deck and stacked-plank seating were built with economical garden grades of redwood. This deck hugs the ground and so needs no railing.

WOOD AND STONE COMPLEMENT EACH OTHER

The crisp lines of planed wood against the natural informal lines of rubble stone laid in a low wall above a gravel patio will give a visual contrast. Steps should be set on a concrete footing to prevent sagging; a bolt anchors them against downhill thrust. Leave ½″ between boards, slope steps to ensure drainage.

BOARDWALK STEPS

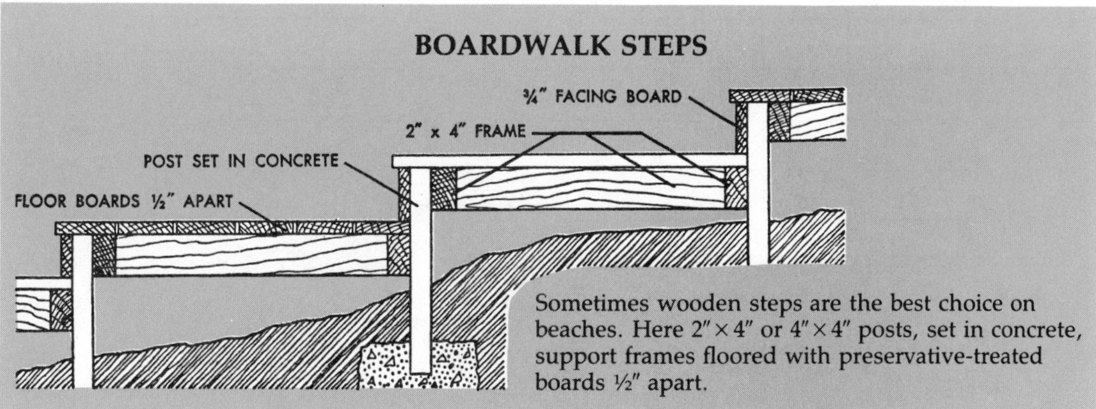

Sometimes wooden steps are the best choice on beaches. Here 2″ × 4″ or 4″ × 4″ posts, set in concrete, support frames floored with preservative-treated boards ½″ apart.

TIES THAT BIND WALLS AND STEPS

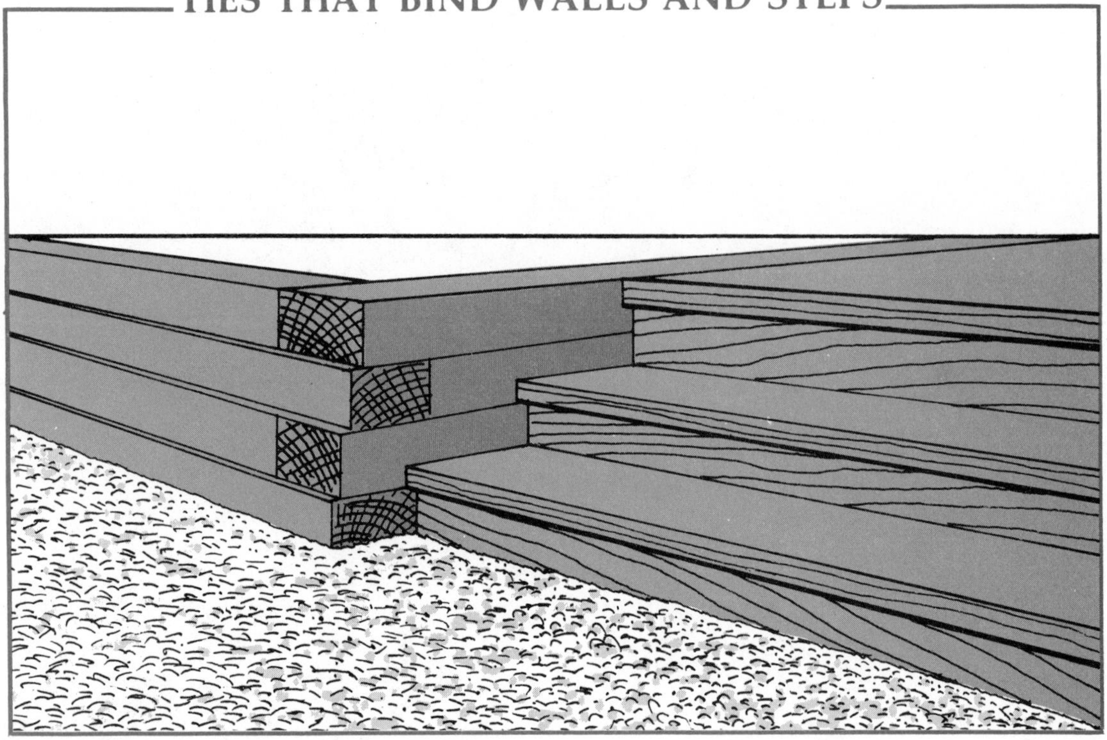

Pressure-treated timbers can last many years in your garden. To make a wall, lay them up tier after tier, stepping back slightly as shown, or keep perpendicular. To prevent frost's thrusting them out of line, bore holes and insert steel tie rods. Use 2″ planks to surface steps and prevent wear.

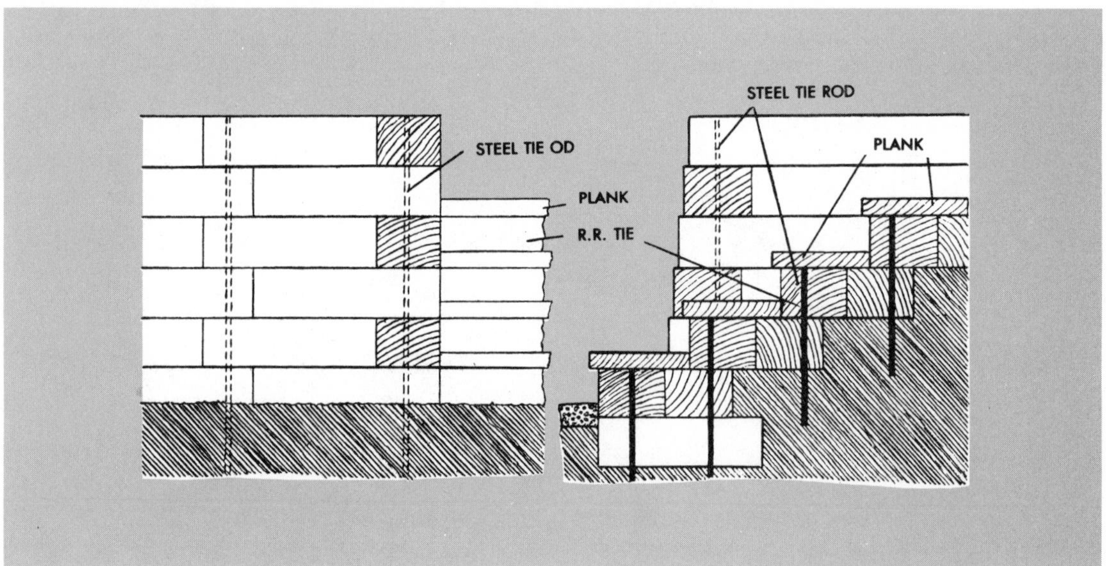

STEPPING DOWN A HILLSIDE

As more and more houses are built on hillsides necessary access must be provided by steps. A more graceful and individual means than the straight up steps usually seen is a series of "deck platforms" placed according to the vagaries of the slope and made of pressure-treated lumber. Here, 6″ × 6″ × 8′ garden timbers frame the platforms of 4″-wide boards set ¼″ apart and supported either by concrete blocks or garden timbers set upright. This design may be adapted to suit slope and location, varying lengths.

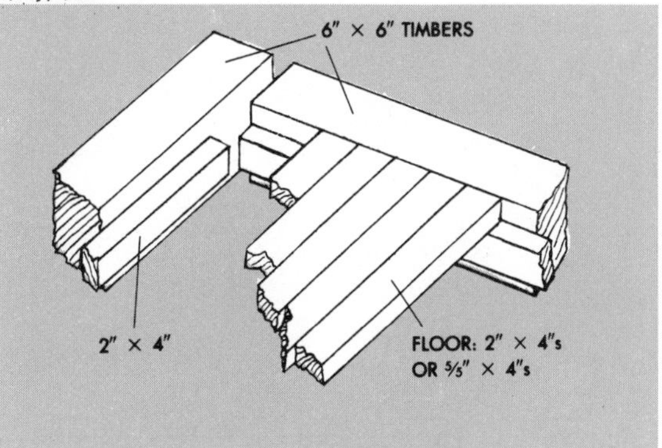

CHAPTER 9

OUTDOOR FURNITURE

With life becoming more informal every day and with outdoor life an accepted part of the American scene, there are many good reasons for building your own furniture. Use it for sitting outdoors, for entertaining on your patio—take full advantage of all the possible delights offered—and have furniture which is of a different character from that run-of-the-mill stuff one sees so much of today. While there are many kinds of inexpensive outdoor furniture which can be purchased for use on the patio, some of it rather good in design, there is an increasing need for good *permanent* tables and for seats which are strong and may be left outdoors the year round. Also, with the small quarters and changeable climates many of us live in, there is usually need for a good *demountable* table.

Therefore presented in this section are a number of simple designs which almost anyone will find easy to construct, for furniture which will add to the joy you take in your yard. Some is modern in character, so it will fit more comfortably with the modern home in good taste than will commercial furniture with its shrieking colors, its machine-made curves and angles. Other pieces will fit well with traditional homes, and several of the designs will integrate with either modern or traditional styles.

One of the main drawbacks to commercial furnishings is the impermanence of the pieces offered. Cheaply constructed, they are so light in weight that they won't last long, are never satisfactory to use, and when the final analysis is made of costs, they prove not to have been so inexpensive after all. The furniture shown here is planned to withstand ordinary weather, so that it can be left outdoors; it need not be whisked under cover at the approach of every storm. It will take its beating from children's (ab)use and still look all right, for its simple, good-looking lines, its rugged character are *designed for use*. And it will age well. If you should ever need to replace any parts for any reason, you will find them either in your wood scrap box or at your nearest building supply center. Can commercial furniture offer this advantage?

SPECIAL FEATURES

Note that the seats and tables I call "demountable" have tops which can be taken off for storage in the garage or cellar during the inclement months, leaving only the masonry parts to bear the brunt of ice

A built-in seat utilizes the guardrail of the deck for attaching its slanting back members, giving stability. The deck is made of Douglas fir 2″ × 4″s set on edge, while the seat has them laid flat, both on seat and back, spaced ½″ to assure drainage.

and snow during the winter. Those made entirely of cinder blocks and stone slabs can, of course, be left outdoors and used on those few bright days of winter when the sun lures you out for a quick picnic in the sparkling air. These, too, can be called "demountable" because they can be moved from one spot in the yard to another if you wish—from the open patio into a sun-trap in a corner, from the patio alongside the house to another place where you may have an outdoor fireplace for cooking. But they are rather heavy and you won't want to move them too often.

Consider the tables which fold down from a porch or deck railing and those which lower from a kind of outdoor "breakfront." With one of them you can have a good-looking piece of furniture which does not take up a great deal of space when it is not in use.

In addition to these features you will find a number of designs for seating pieces. Note in the previous chapter how seats have been built in as integral parts of the shelters, and, in the upcoming chapter, "Versatile Walls," how low walls are shown used as seats, too. These will "come in very handy," as my mother used to say, when you are entertaining the family or large numbers of people on the patio for luncheon or for cocktail parties, or other gatherings.

The primary consideration in choosing outdoor furniture, whether you build it yourself or buy it, is that it should be practical and useful. Secondarily, it should be good-looking and simple, so that it fits well into its surroundings and is a part of the general picture—an unobtrusive part. You will find that the natural qualities of weathered wood, stone, and building blocks used for furniture will help keep it in the background and in harmony with the house and natural parts of the yard. If the materials must be painted, use soft colors, never bright or dominant ones, *never* hard reds or bright oranges, or even the hard unnatural greens.

Before designing outdoor furniture, consider the recommended heights and other measurements indicated on the next page.

TABLE OF MEASUREMENTS AND HEIGHTS: FURNITURE FOR ADULTS

Seats	*Height*
Floor to seat	16″-18″
Floor to shoulder rest	36″-37″
Seat to head clearance	2′ 11″ min.
Width, side to side, minimum	15″
Depth, back to front, minimum	15″
Clearance, top of seat to table	11″
Clearance, top of knee to table	5″
Clearance, seated people, elbow to elbow	27″ min.
Clearance, kick space from stationary seat to table upright	19″-20″
Clearance, space in front of knee	7″ plus 12″ foot-space
Clearance behind heel, legs vertical	7″
Stationary seats should extend no more than 2″ to 3″ under table line.	
Tables:	
Width, table used one side only	22″-24″ min.
Width, table used on both sides	28″-30″ min.
Table height, top to floor	29″
Clearance for knees, seated, min. height	24″
Clearance for seated people, elbow to elbow	27″ min.

CHILDREN'S FURNITURE HEIGHTS

Height of child	*Seat height*	*Table height*
3′ 3″	1′	1′ 10″
4′ 0″	1′ 2″	2′ 1″
4′ 4″	1′ 3″	2′ 2½″
4′ 8″	1′ 4″	2′ 4″
5′ 0″	1′ 5″	2′ 5″
5′ 4″	1′ 5″	2′ 5″
5′ 6″ and over	1′ 6″	2′ 5″

NOTE: All the above measurements can be varied to suit the uses of the child and the adult. If you want to experiment to find out what is the best height for you, measure various tables and sitting pieces in your home, using the measurements of those pieces you find most comfortable. The above table was compiled on the basis of average measurements, that is, tall- to average-sized people.

A curved seat is supported at ends by bolted multiple 2″ × 4″s with others flat against the curving back at the corners. Sabersaw a hefty wide plank in the desired curve, place the two straight sides together, and attach them to end cleats fastened to end supports.

Portable painted bench has a seat formed of three 2″ × 8″s screwed to a 2″ × 6″ crossbar and supported by three 2″ × 8″ legs that are overlapped 2″ each side of center space. Note how legs are angle-cut for tight fit, how crossbar is beveled to meet leg line.

A bench may be used for sitting or to display a bonsai tree. Made of redwood—2″ × 8″ planks for seat, invisibly attached with epoxy-glued dowels set in holes bored in seat planks and in crossbars that, like legs, are 4″ × 4″s. Dado crossbars 1½″ into legs.

POTTING BENCHES

Although perhaps not strictly furniture, potting benches are a part of the garden picture, and the ones shown here can also be built into basements, garages, or toolsheds. The rolling potting bench will be trundled out on the patio frequently, so it may be included as a part of the furniture section.

Every gardener has difficulty with storage—where to put stakes, where to put hand tools and all the various useful things which make such clutter when left about the house or garage or out in the garden. These benches will help to organize things and make them orderly and useful. For the indoor gardener, a potting bench is the answer to a prayer when it has storage bins for soil, peat moss, sand, lots of shelves, and plenty of storage space for pots. Outdoors, too, where people are using more potted plants to get quick color, such a potting bench with a shelter built over it will be most welcome in many a garden.

With this section, as before, I suggest that you look at the designs and, if they do not exactly meet your needs, adapt them as you see fit. Change merely for the sake of change is not what I mean, of course, but change for improving the use of the piece so that it adapts to fit your specific needs will give you a taste of the creative experience which is one of the most satisfying joys of craftsmanship. Your furniture can express *you* as much as any other part of the garden does.

A potting bench provides a potting surface, adequate bins for soil, sand, and peat moss, shelves for pots and other needs. Exterior plywood is used in ¾″ thickness, mounted on a sturdy framework of bolted 2″ × 4″s. Note guards on top and sides.

BENCH—PORTABLE OR PERMANENT

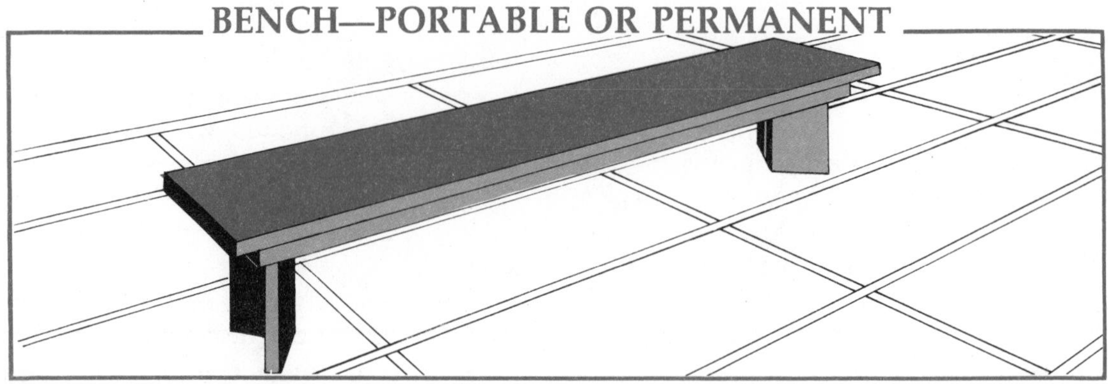

A bench of simple lines, built of sturdy 2″ stock and painted to harmonize with the house or stained a dark, woodsy color, will be a useful addition to any patio. If you wish to place it permanently, treat the posts with wood preservative, set them in concrete beside the paving or in whatever location you have chosen for the bench to be placed.

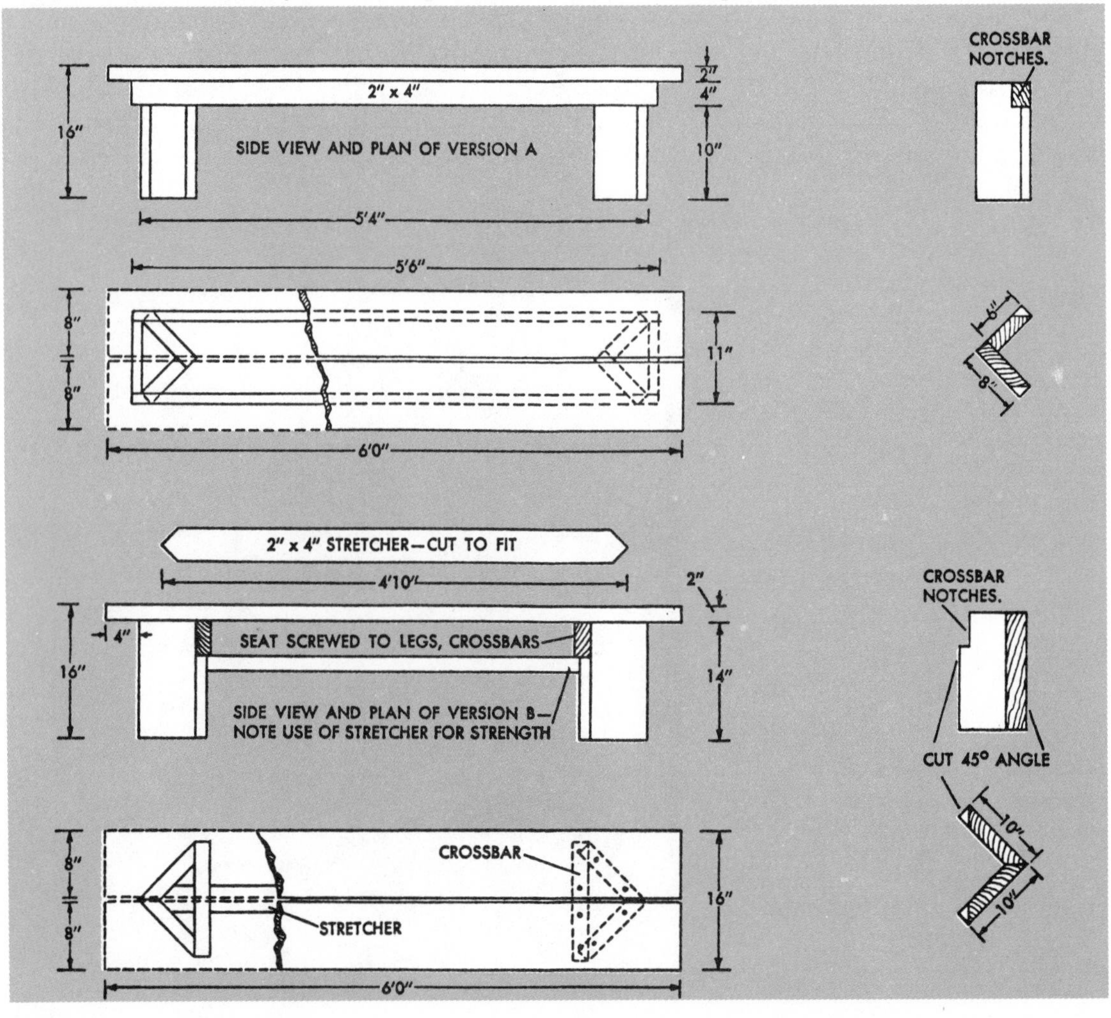

2″ x 4″
SIDE VIEW AND PLAN OF VERSION A
16″
2″
4″
10″
5′4″
5′6″
8″
8″
11″
6′0″
CROSSBAR NOTCHES.
6″
8″

2″ x 4″ STRETCHER—CUT TO FIT
4′10″
2″
4″
SEAT SCREWED TO LEGS, CROSSBARS
16″
14″
SIDE VIEW AND PLAN OF VERSION B—
NOTE USE OF STRETCHER FOR STRENGTH
CROSSBAR NOTCHES.
CUT 45° ANGLE
10″
10″
8″
8″
CROSSBAR
STRETCHER
16″
6′0″

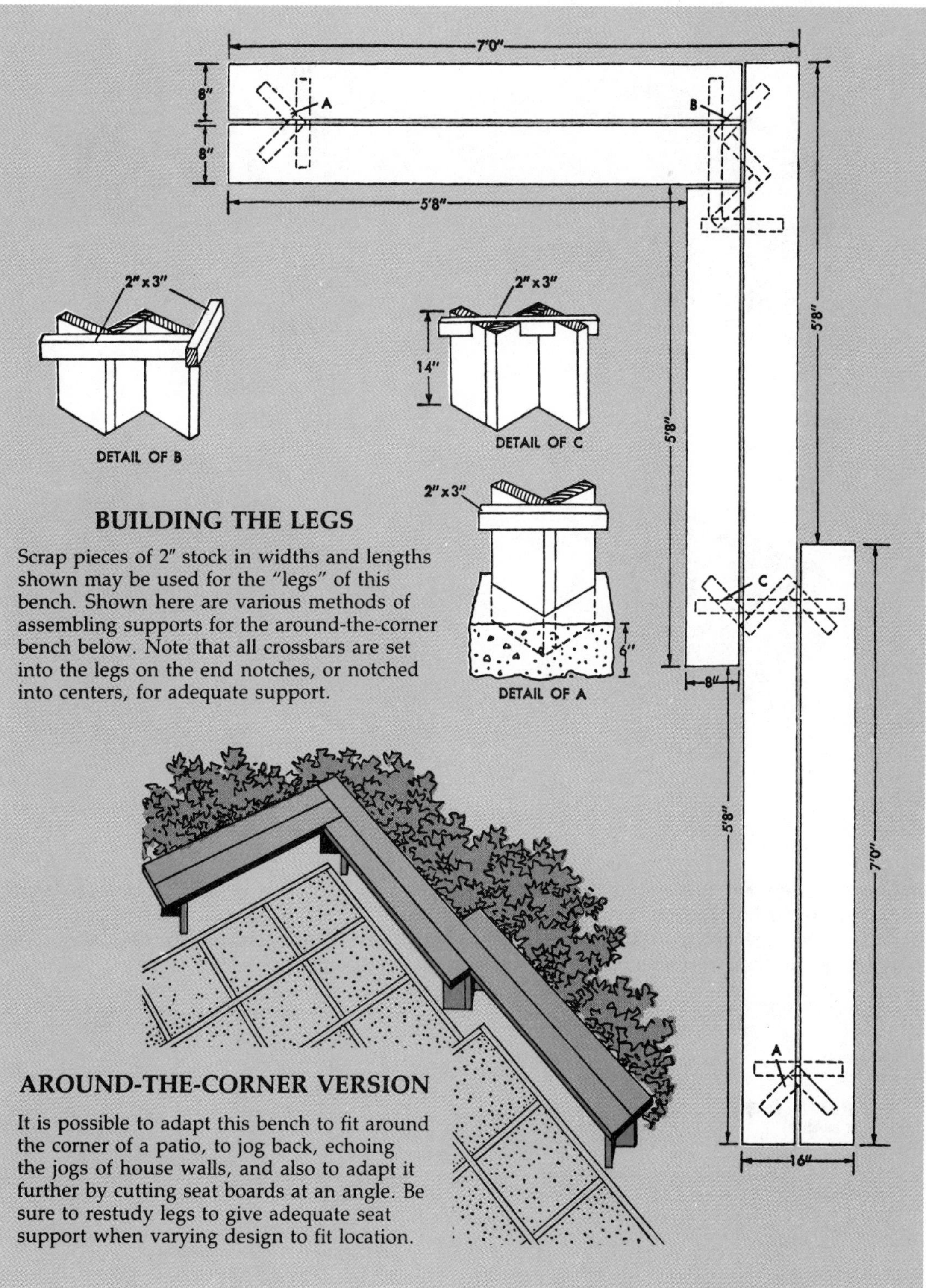

BUILDING THE LEGS

Scrap pieces of 2" stock in widths and lengths shown may be used for the "legs" of this bench. Shown here are various methods of assembling supports for the around-the-corner bench below. Note that all crossbars are set into the legs on the end notches, or notched into centers, for adequate support.

AROUND-THE-CORNER VERSION

It is possible to adapt this bench to fit around the corner of a patio, to jog back, echoing the jogs of house walls, and also to adapt it further by cutting seat boards at an angle. Be sure to restudy legs to give adequate seat support when varying design to fit location.

BENCHES FOR GOOD COMPANIONS

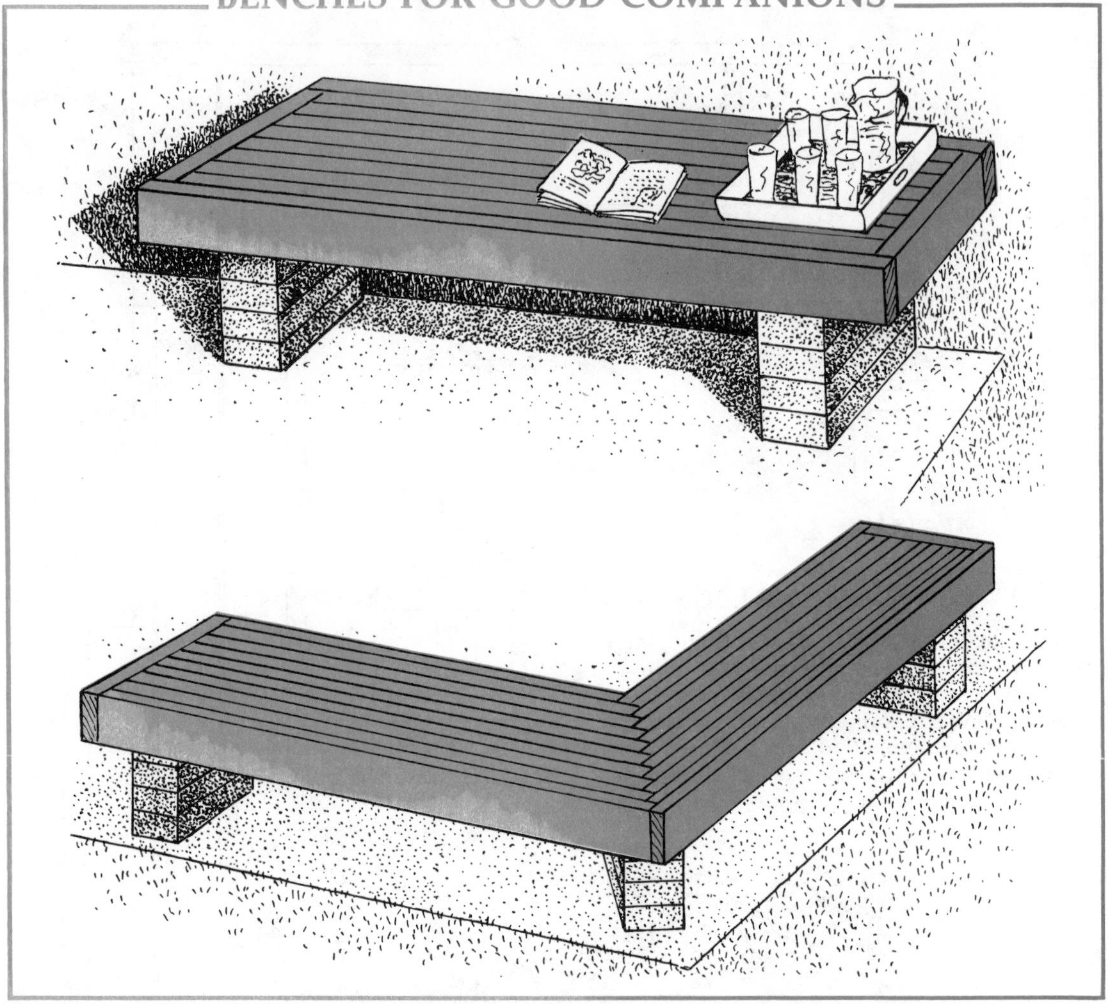

Backless garden benches are coming more and more into use. This bench can be used alone as shown in the top version, or it can be designed to angle off, following a patio boundary or one of a part-shade, part-sun trellis. Such a bench can be adapted to any site and can be portable or permanent. (See companion version on next page.)

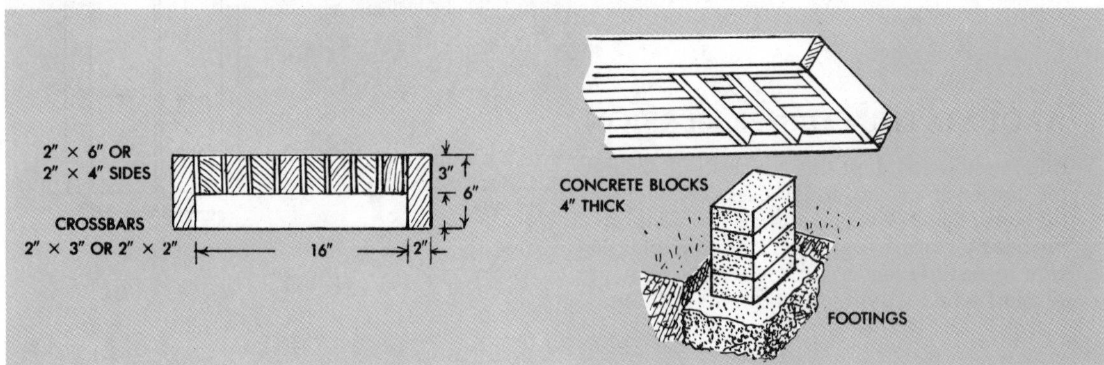

Built of 1″ × 2″s separated by 1″ × 2″ × 2″ blocks, this bench has apron boards and two center boards of 1″ × 6″s shaped at the ends to meet end aprons of 1″ × 4″ stock. Supports consist of two 2″ × 8″s shaped as shown resting on 2″ × 4″ feet which protect them from rot. (A permanent version would be set in concrete after treatment with a wood preservative.) Note that boards are butted at corners and nailed or screwed together securely, as are center blocks.

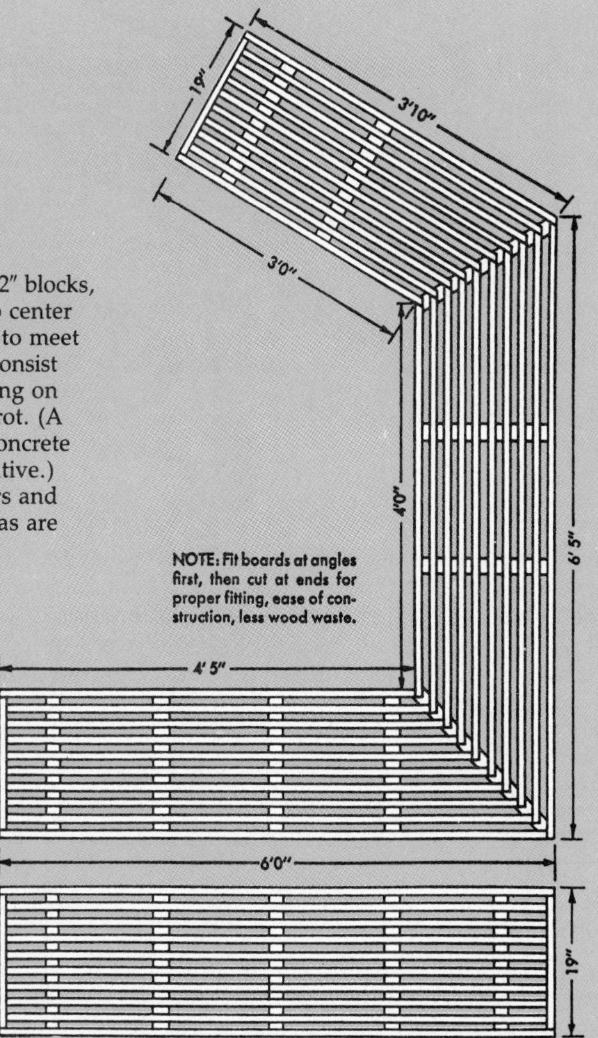

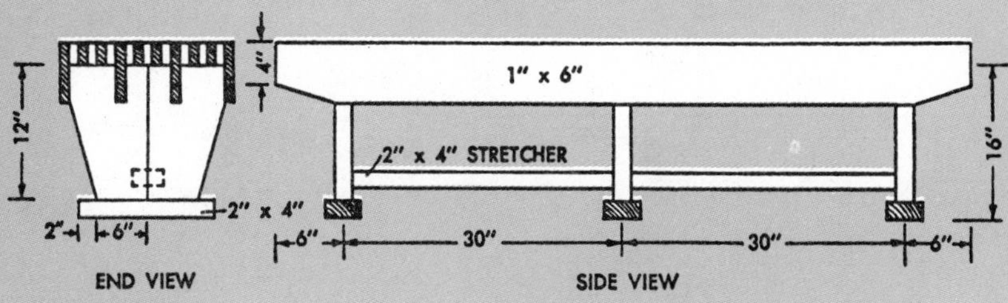

FOLDAWAY TABLE ON A BALUSTRADE OR WALL

A table which folds away when not in use, leaving precious space free, is an asset to be prized. Hinges attach the 2″ × 2″ frame to balustrade, fence, or wall; hinged legs fold up inside frame to be held by turn-buttons on a stationary block. Legs are secured by a ¼″ steel rod bent into a double hook, fitted into holes bored in leg and frame. Use ½″ exterior plywood for table top and for legs, too, if desired. Vary the dimensions to suit your needs. This table will seat five adults with good elbowroom.

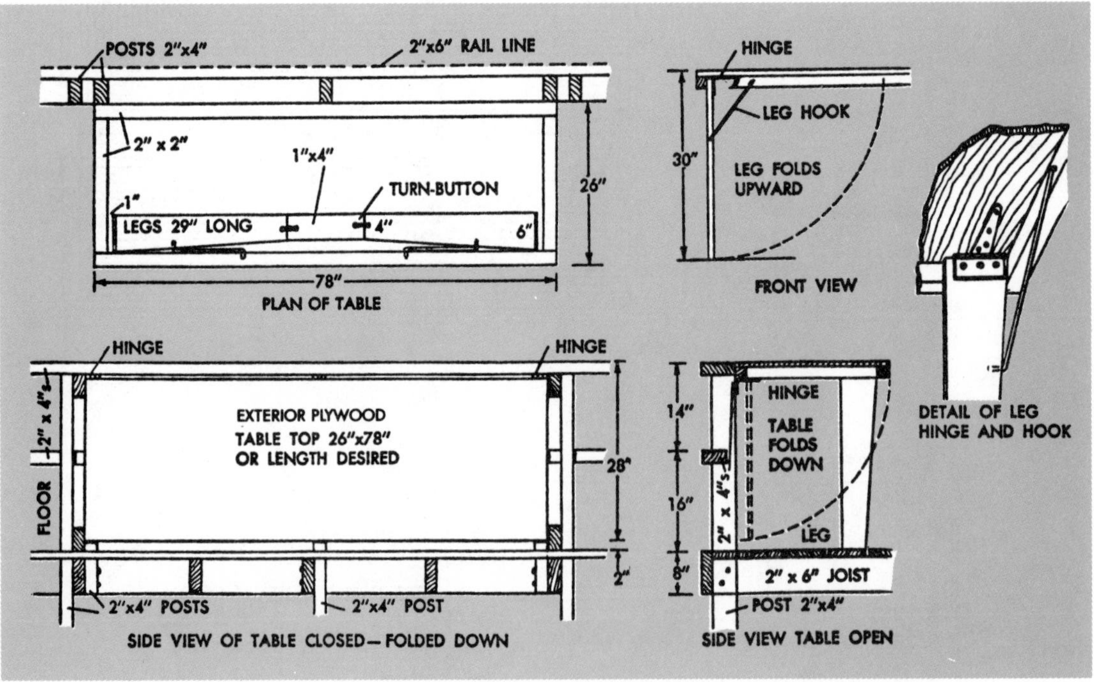

FOLDING LOVESEAT OR BENCH

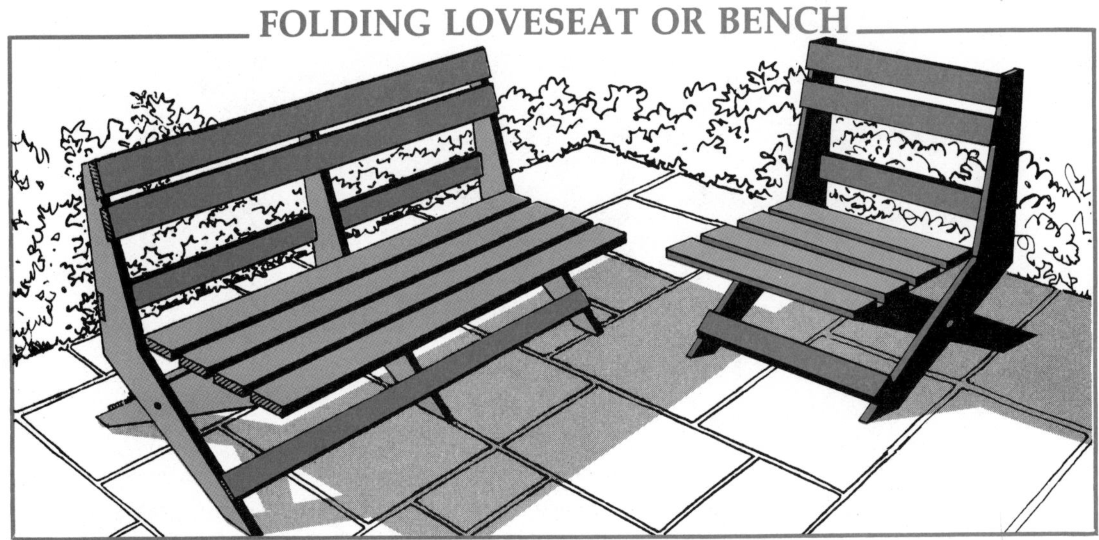

A chair and a loveseat of similar design are easy to build, easy to fold up and take in for the winter or for quick shelter from a summer shower. The boards used for seats may be 5/4″ or 2″ (the lighter weight may make them more transportable) with 1″ × 4″ stock used for backrest boards. Legs may be cut from 2″ × 10″s or heavy exterior plywood.

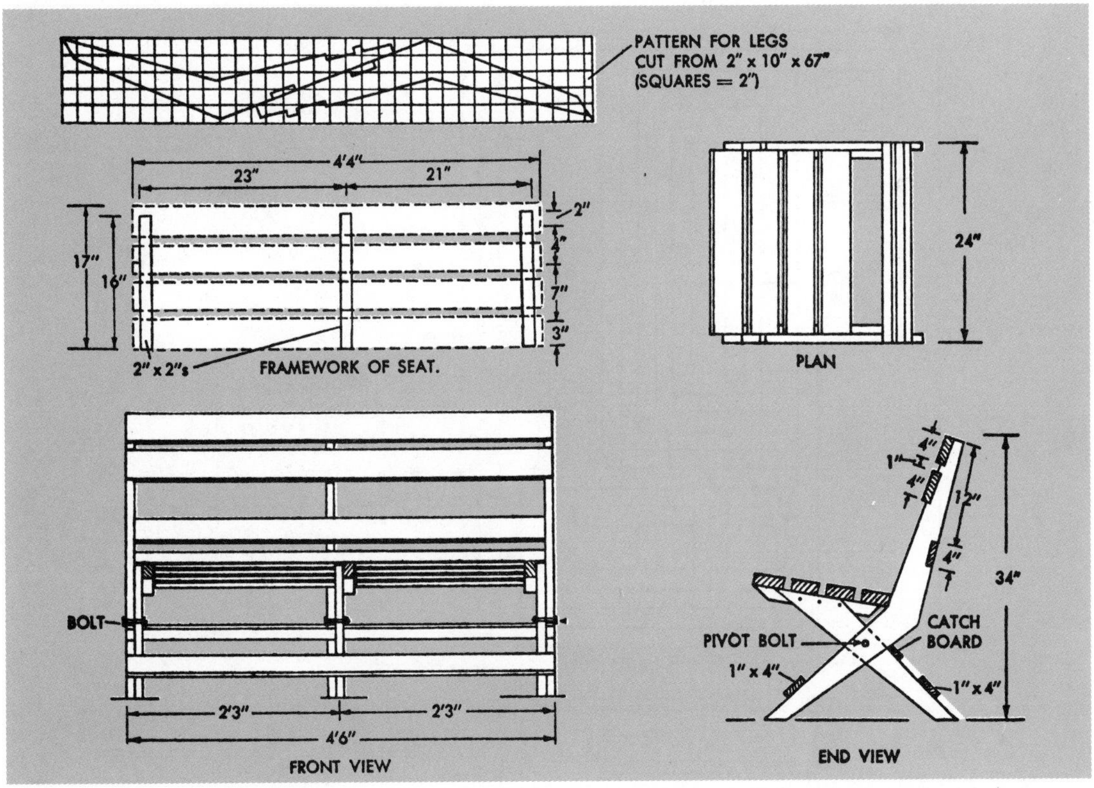

PATTERN FOR LEGS
CUT FROM 2″ x 10″ x 67″
(SQUARES = 2″)

4′4″
23″
21″
2″
4″
7″
3″
17″
16″
2″ x 2″s
FRAMEWORK OF SEAT.

24″
PLAN

BOLT
2′3″
2′3″
4′6″
FRONT VIEW

4″
1″
4″
12″
4″
34″
PIVOT BOLT
CATCH BOARD
1″ x 4″
1″ x 4″
END VIEW

CUPBOARD WITH LET-DOWN TABLE

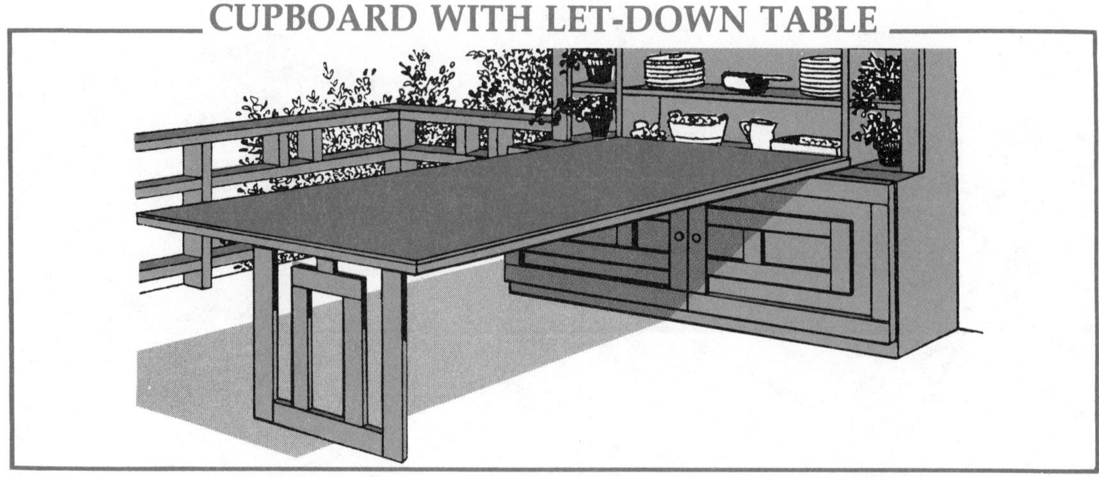

When a garden house or patio has limited space, the need is acute for a dining table which will fold away. This table, combining storage space for plates and other necessary equipment, is hinged to let down, the rear resting on the jutting lower cupboard space, the front supported by a hinged leg which is a part of the decorative frame when not in use. Potted plants grace the shelves on either side. Lower cupboards may have two doors to divide into center and two side compartments.

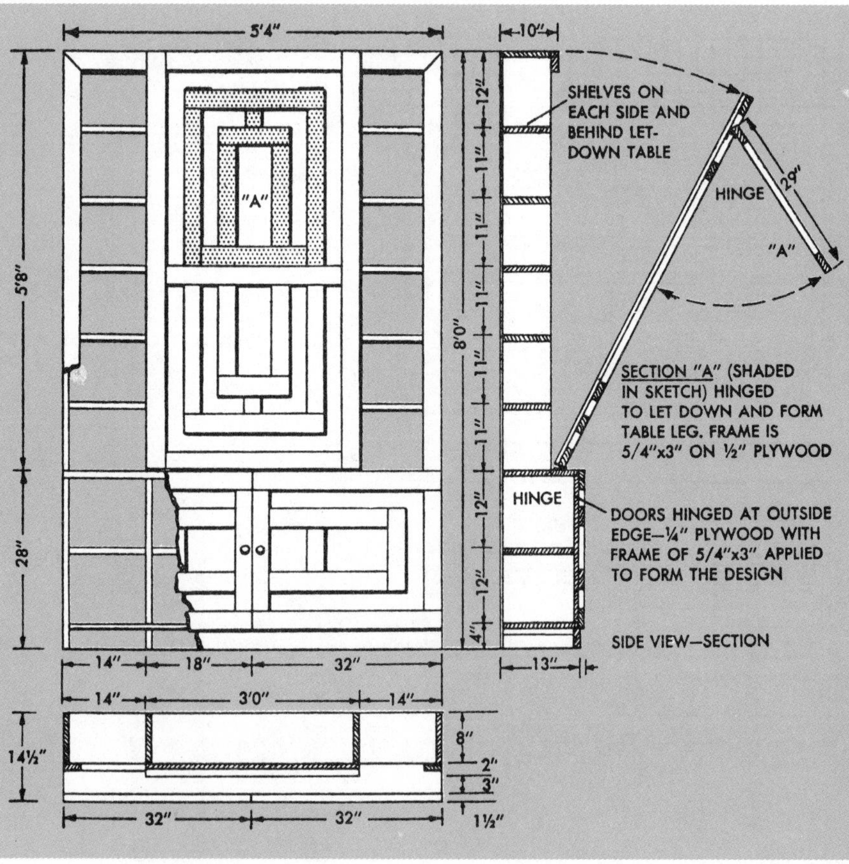
5'4"
10"
"A"
5'8"
28"
8'0"
12"
11"
11"
11"
11"
11"
12"
12"
4"
SHELVES ON EACH SIDE AND BEHIND LET-DOWN TABLE
HINGE
29"
"A"
SECTION "A" (SHADED IN SKETCH) HINGED TO LET DOWN AND FORM TABLE LEG. FRAME IS 5/4"x3" ON ½" PLYWOOD
HINGE
DOORS HINGED AT OUTSIDE EDGE—¼" PLYWOOD WITH FRAME OF 5/4"x3" APPLIED TO FORM THE DESIGN
SIDE VIEW—SECTION
14"
18"
32"
13"
14"
3'0"
14"
14½"
8"
2"
3"
1½"
32"
32"

FRONT VIEW OF LET-DOWN TABLE

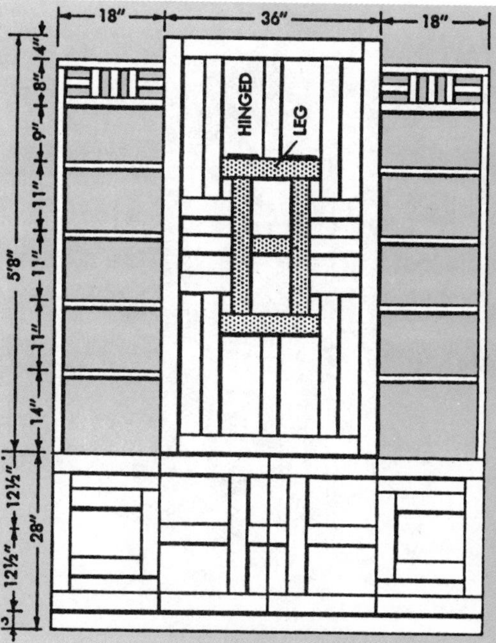

BREAKFRONT LET-DOWN TABLE SHOWN CLOSED

PRIVACY FENCE WITH LET-DOWN TABLE

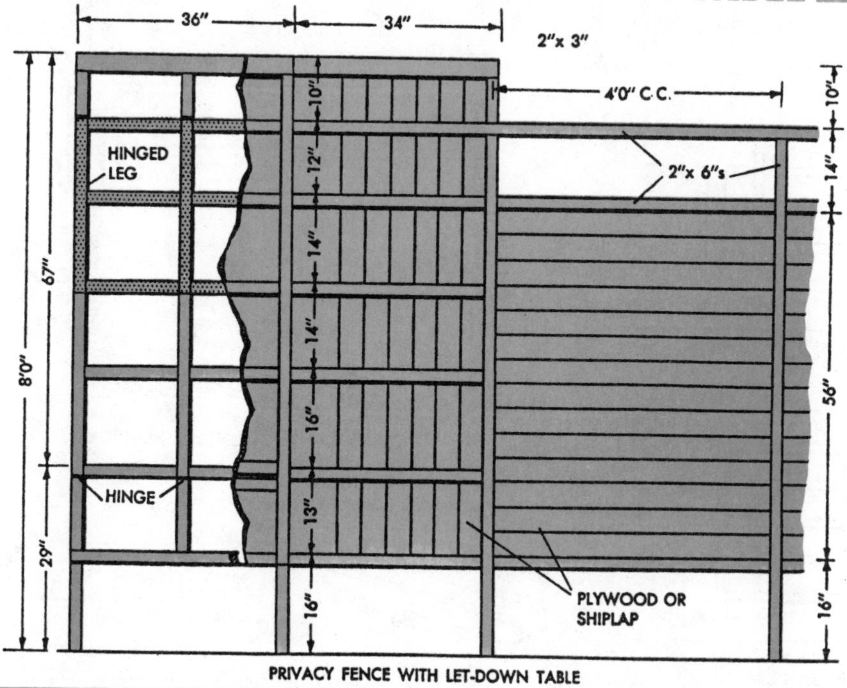

PRIVACY FENCE WITH LET-DOWN TABLE

Fence table has no lower compartment, only 2″ × 6″ shelves behind table which continue alongside to open shelves for plants. Vary cupboard and table dimensions to suit.

BREAKFRONT FOR PLANTS

A breakfront with adjustable shelves that may be used indoors or on a covered patio to summer houseplants outdoors also provides storage space below for pots, plant foods, vases, and other equipment. The shelves are made of 1″ × 2″s fitted together as shown in the details. The triangular cuts in the projecting ends fit over the dowel rod supports and prevent shelves from sliding.

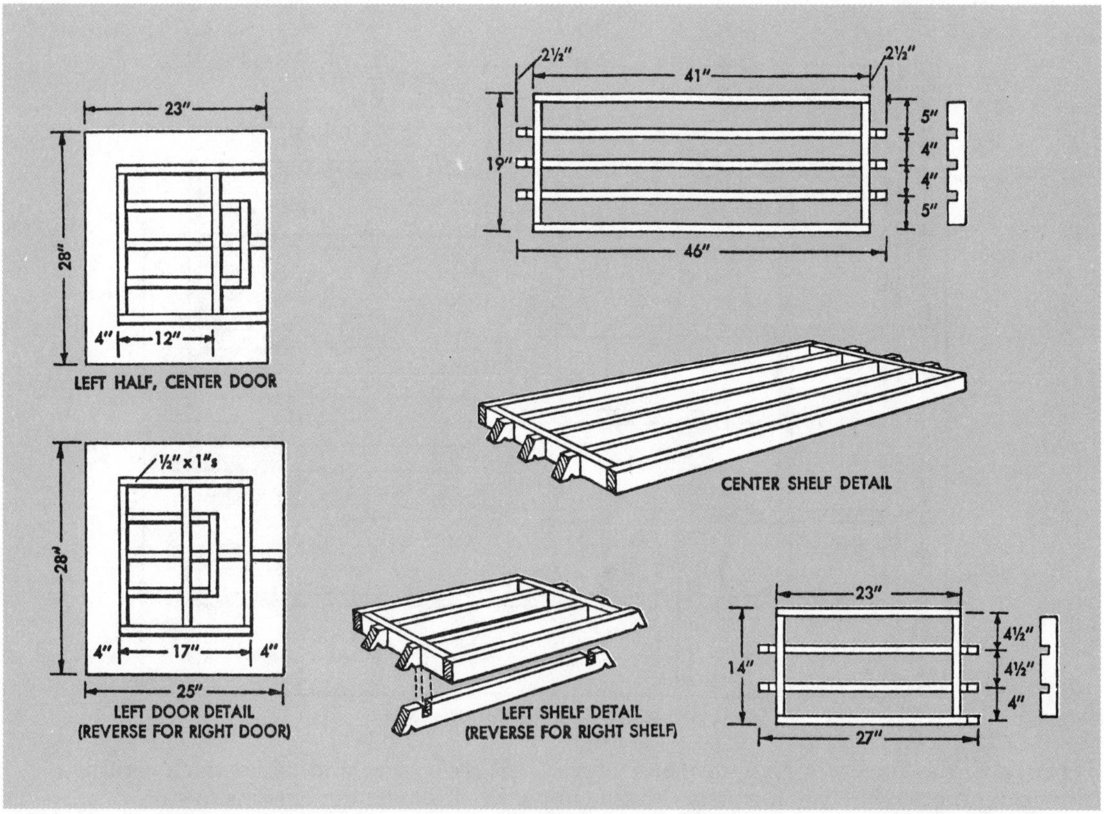

23″ 28″ 4″ 12″

LEFT HALF, CENTER DOOR

2½″ 41″ 2½″ 19″ 5″ 4″ 4″ 5″ 46″

CENTER SHELF DETAIL

½″ x 1″s 28″ 4″ 17″ 4″ 25″

LEFT DOOR DETAIL
(REVERSE FOR RIGHT DOOR)

LEFT SHELF DETAIL
(REVERSE FOR RIGHT SHELF)

23″ 14″ 4½″ 4½″ 4″ 27″

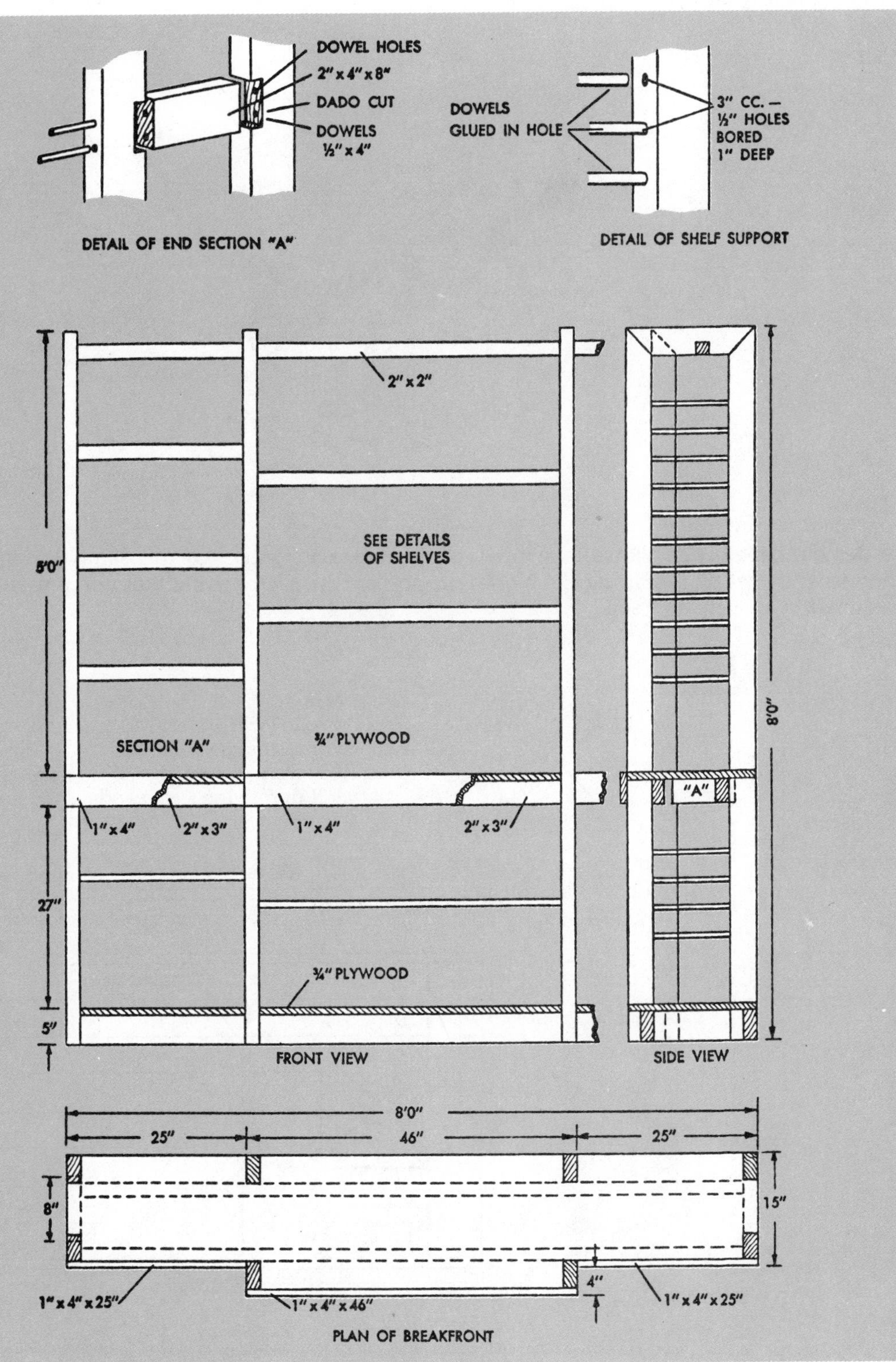
DOWEL HOLES
2" x 4" x 8"
DADO CUT
DOWELS
½" x 4"
DETAIL OF END SECTION "A"
DOWELS
GLUED IN HOLE
3" CC. —
½" HOLES
BORED
1" DEEP
DETAIL OF SHELF SUPPORT
2" x 2"
SEE DETAILS
OF SHELVES
8'0"
SECTION "A"
¾" PLYWOOD
1" x 4"
2" x 3"
1" x 4"
2" x 3"
27"
¾" PLYWOOD
5"
FRONT VIEW
"A"
8'0"
SIDE VIEW
8'0"
25"
46"
25"
8"
15"
4"
1" x 4" x 25"
1" x 4" x 46"
1" x 4" x 25"
PLAN OF BREAKFRONT

MOUNTABLE AND DEMOUNTABLE

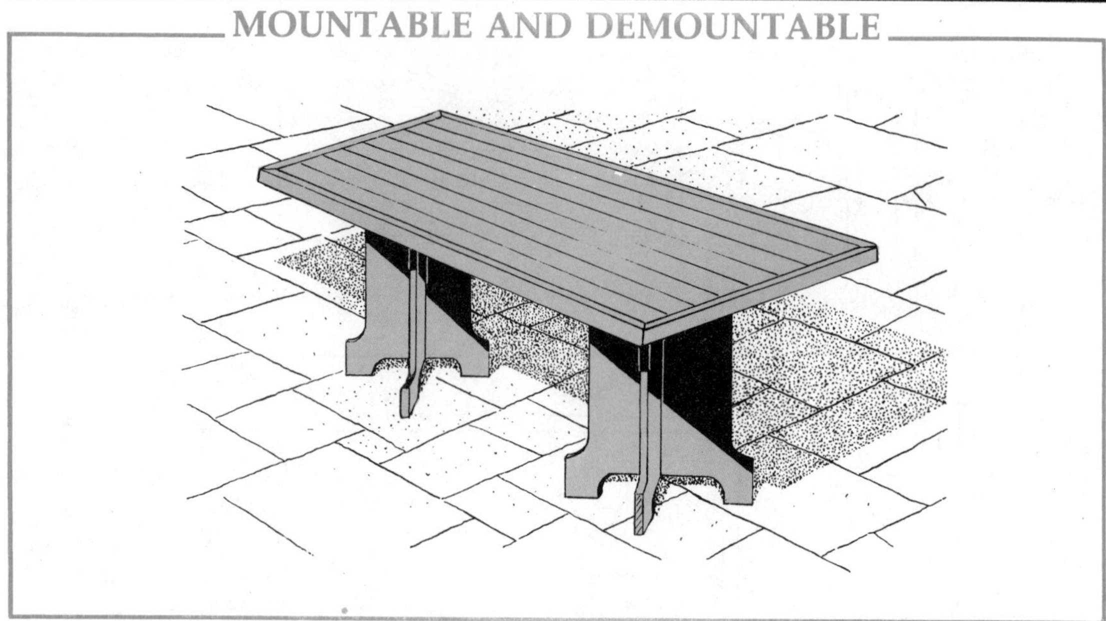

A demountable bench allows easy moving and compact storage. Or this same design may be permanently set by mortaring the blocks supporting the seat, setting them on a footing as required by climate and soil.

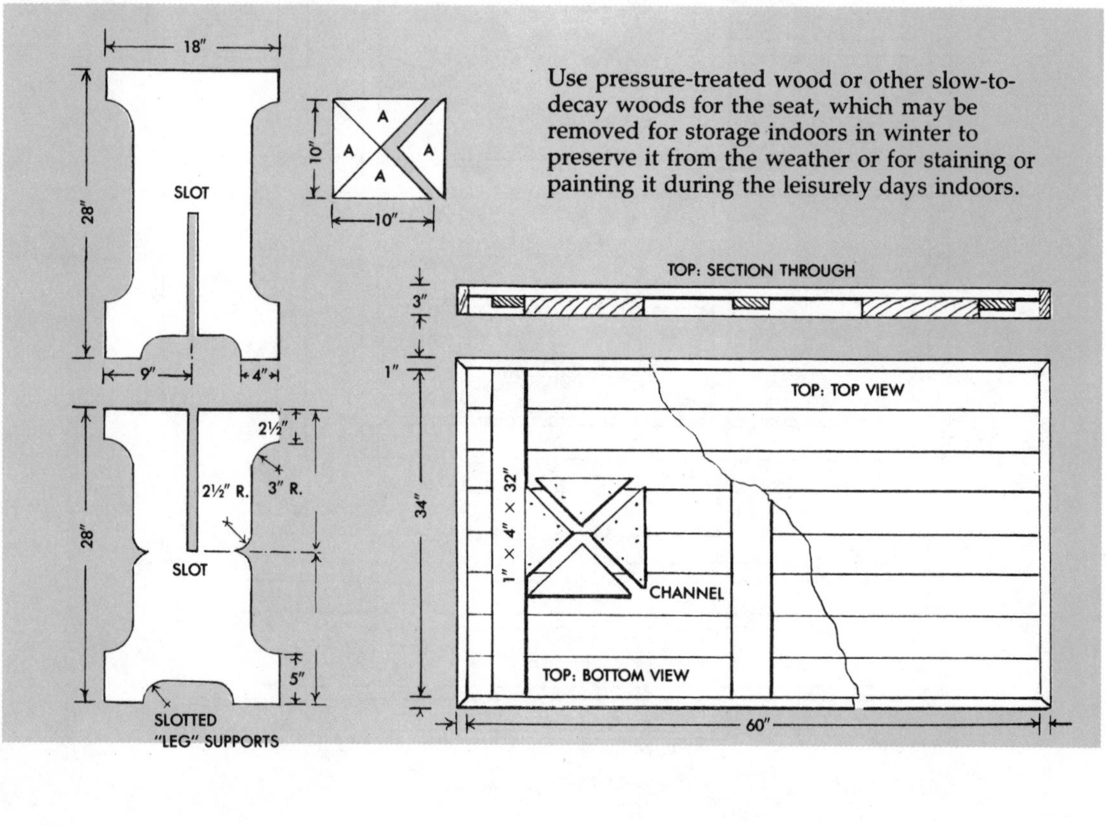

Use pressure-treated wood or other slow-to-decay woods for the seat, which may be removed for storage indoors in winter to preserve it from the weather or for staining or painting it during the leisurely days indoors.

ADJUSTABLE LAZY LOUNGE

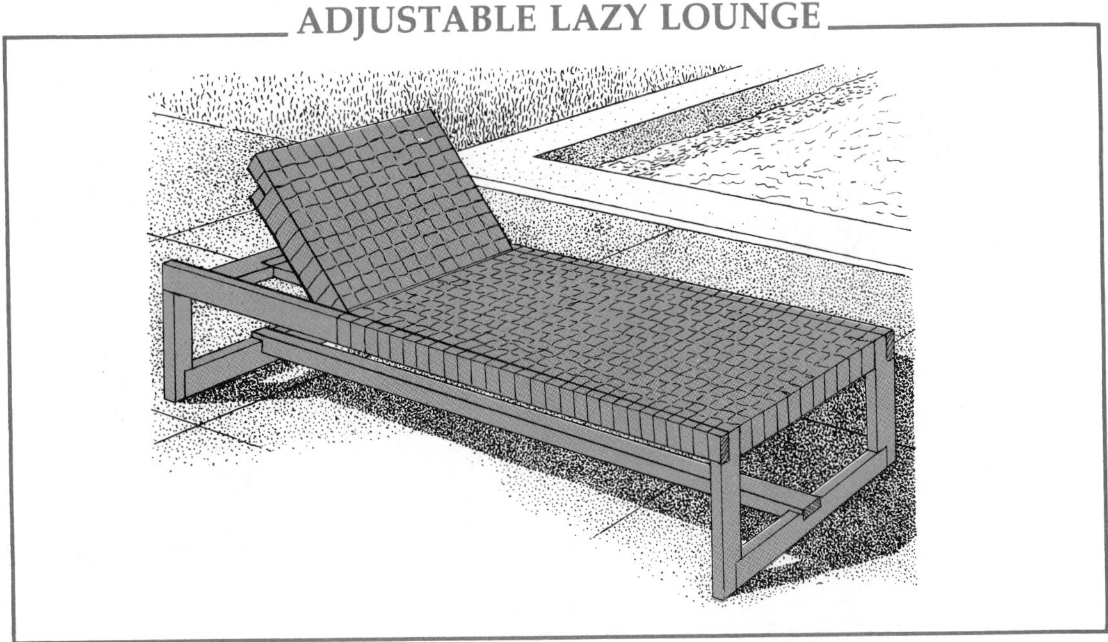

On a lazy summer day, a lounge is hard to beat. Here, a simple, sturdy frame with a hinged backrest is adjusted by inserting the plywood support into dadoed slots.

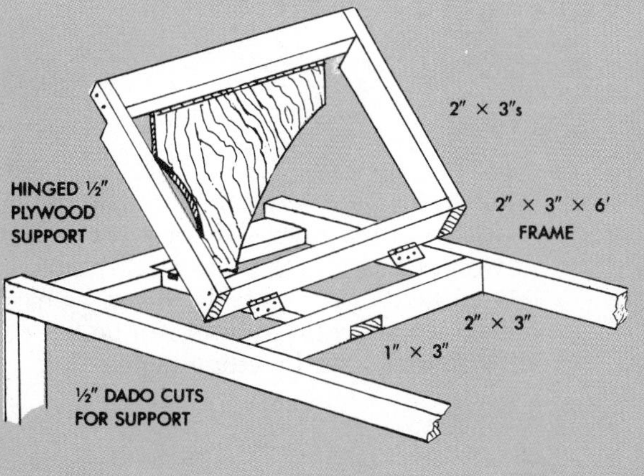

Since the piece will be left outdoors in summer, use exterior-grade glue and brass screws or nonrusting nails. Wide plastic tapes used for recovering garden furniture and available from hardware and other stores are interwoven in checkerboard fashion, using one color for each length of tape, with a contrasting tape woven across, and fastened on the inner side of the frame. Paint the wood to match or contrast with the tapes, or stain the wood and let it weather to a natural gray.

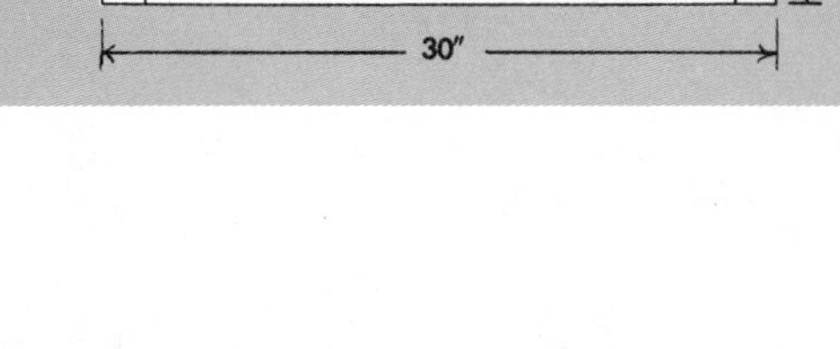

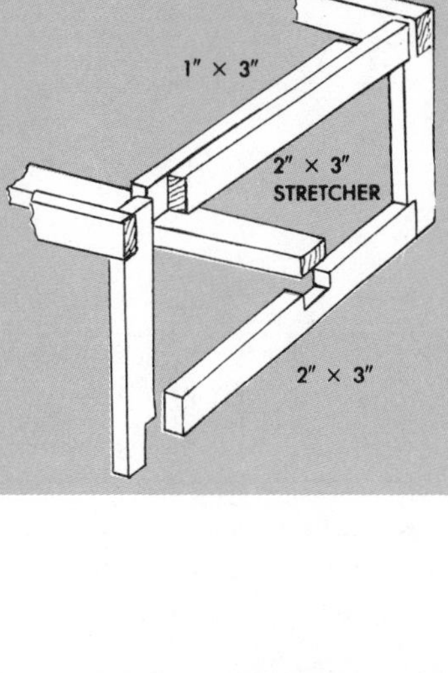

MOVE THE TABLE FOR LUNCH

With a few chimney flue blocks, an exterior plywood panel, or slab of stone, you can move your table around to enjoy various parts of your garden or patio as the sun and blossoms may dictate. Chimney flue blocks form the support here for the table and make the seats when paired. Cushions will make them more comfortable, but are not necessary.

COFFEE TABLE

An exterior plywood panel or slate top cut round or in irregular slab style set on a pair of wall blocks makes a most acceptable low cocktail or coffee table. It can be easily picked up and moved, and can be left out all winter as a bird feeding table.

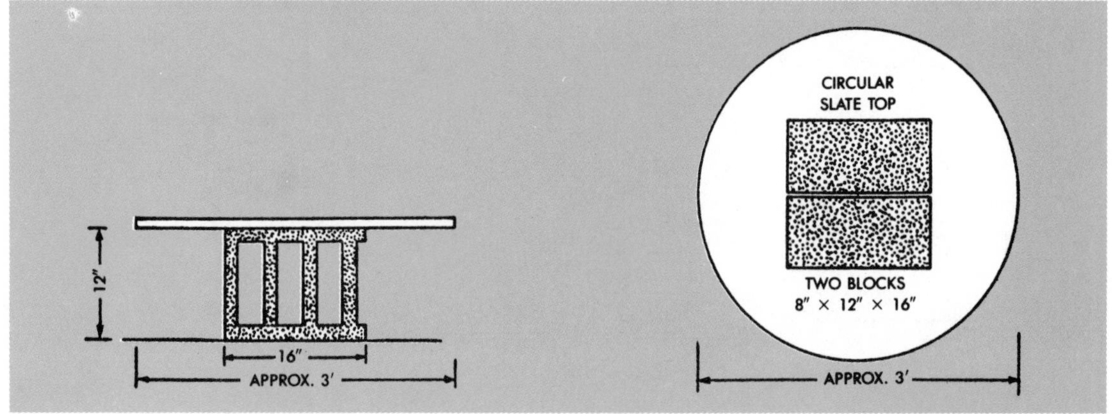

TWO INFORMAL TABLES

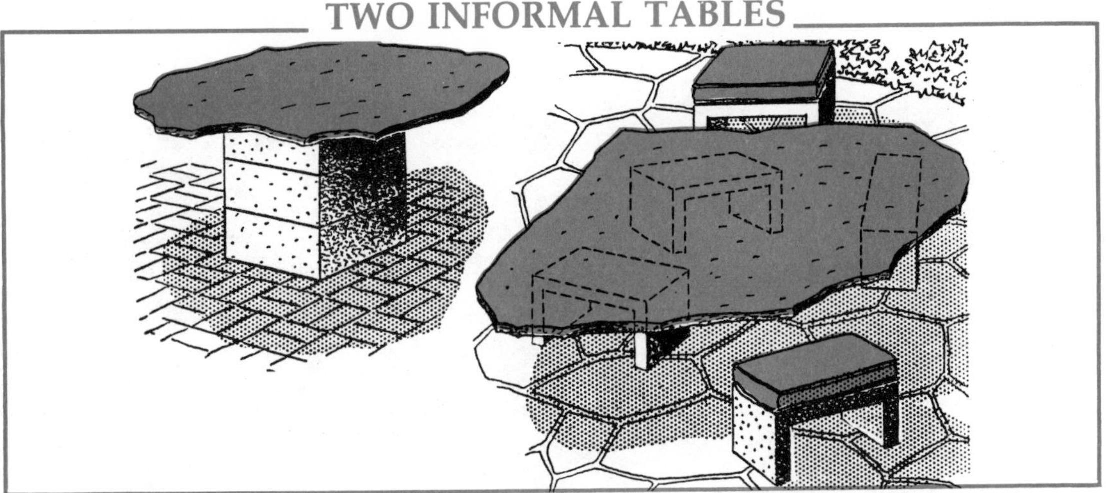

At left, a table which is demountable yet is impervious to weather can be built by stacking up three chimney blocks and placing a slate slab or exterior-grade wood panel on top. Or, use several half-blocks placed to support a larger slab or panel, at right, for a low table. Half-blocks with cushions make low seats.

ROUND COFFEE TABLE

In most areas it is possible to buy a slate top cut in a circle, or you can use exterior-grade plywood. The table shown here is either demountable or permanent and the supports are simple to assemble. A pair of half flue blocks are stacked as shown inside a full square chimney flue block.

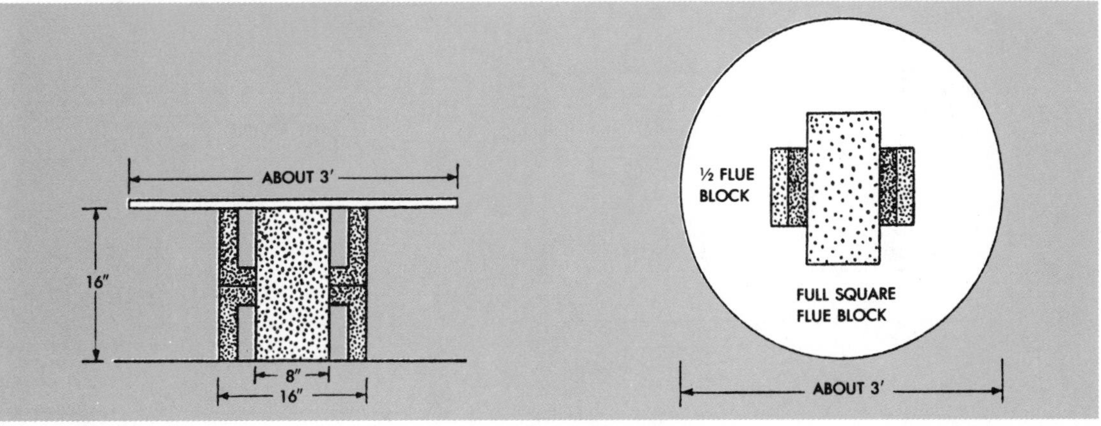

DEMOUNTABLE PLYWOOD AND BLOCK FURNITURE

An exterior plywood top screwed to a simple framework which fits around a pedestal of cement blocks mortared to a concrete foundation makes a most useful outdoor dining table. Benches on block supports are also sturdy, simple, and good looking, built of planks on a framework which also fits around blocks. Note that both the table and bench tops may be removed and taken indoors for storage or for winter protection.

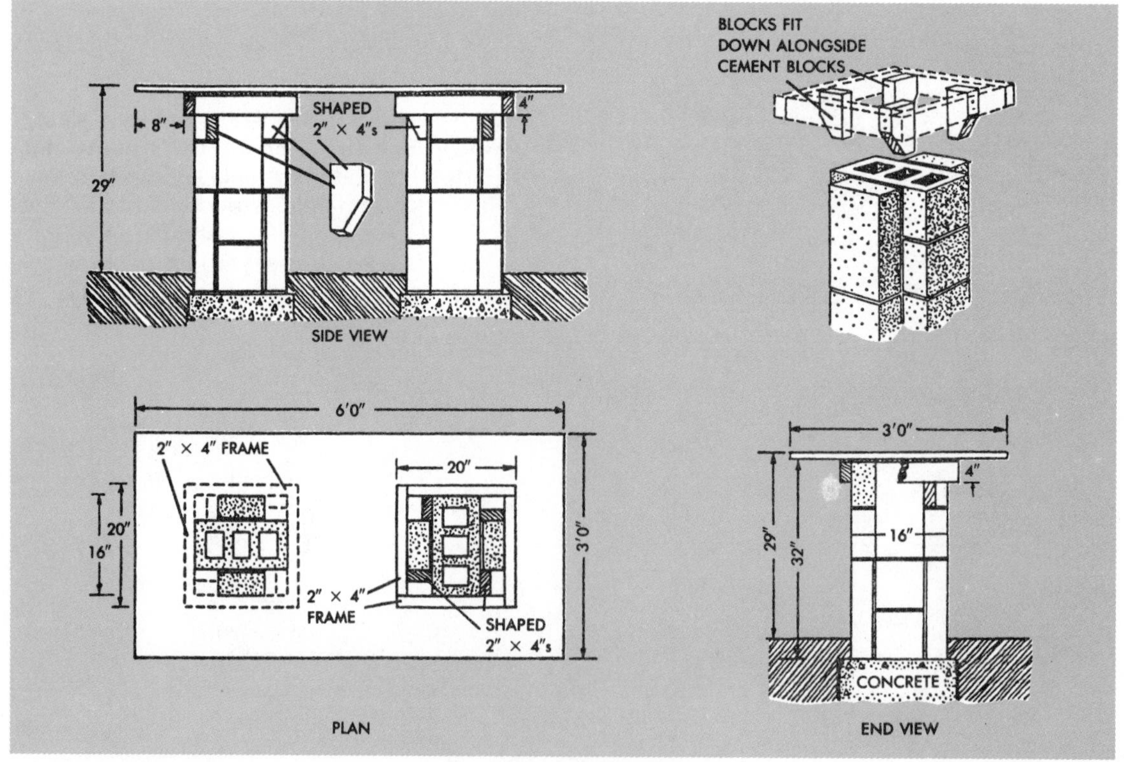

MAKING THE BENCH

The construction of the bench follows much the same lines, with solid masonry blocks being used as vertical supports, the frame of the seat with its 2″ × 4″ wood blocks fitting down over the masonry blocks. The wood part of the bench may be lifted off if you wish, for storage indoors for the winter.

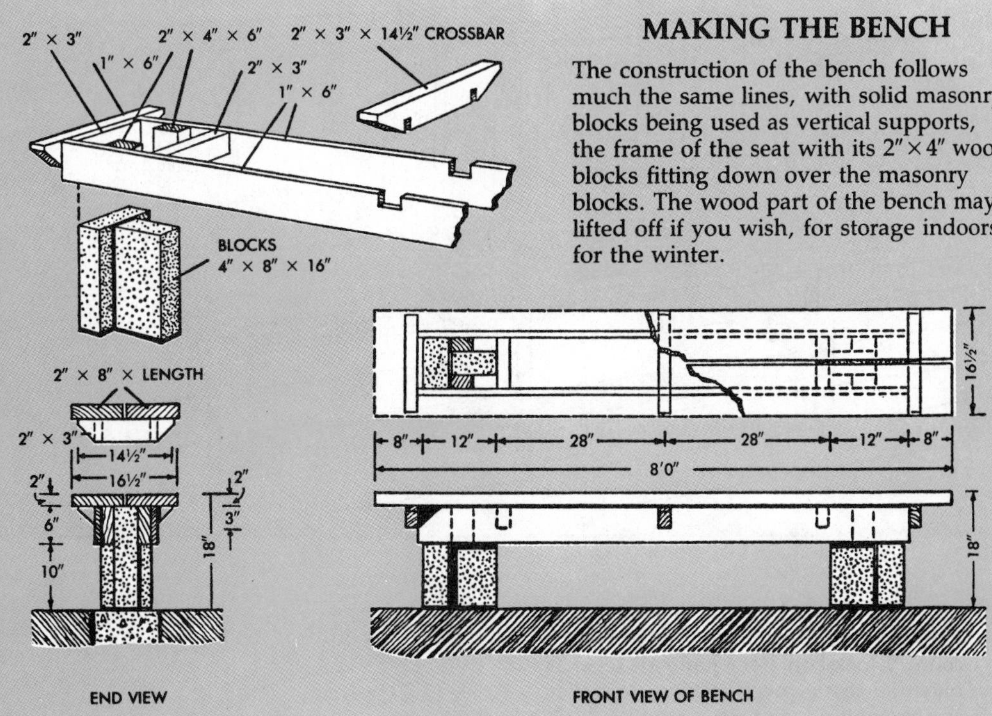

END VIEW

FRONT VIEW OF BENCH

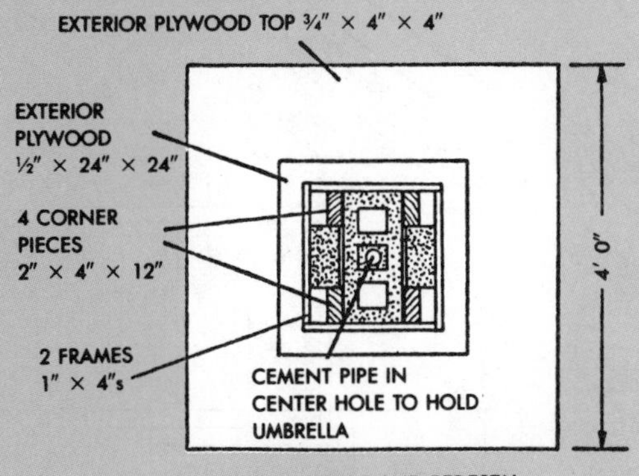

PLAN OF TABLE AND PEDESTAL

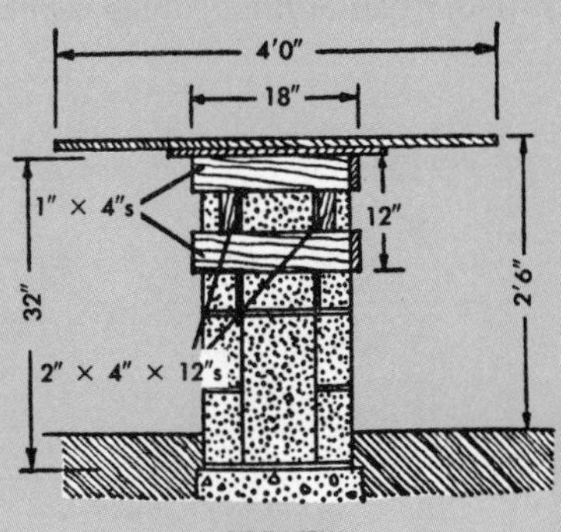

SIDE VIEW

A DEMOUNTABLE SQUARE TABLE

A square table built of exterior plywood fits on a single pedestal of cinder or concrete blocks. To keep it solid and stable, longer wooden blocks and a double banding of wooden strips are used to fit down around the masonry pedestal. Screw a 24″ square of plywood to the top of the framework, then mount plywood and framework to table top with aluminum screws, thus avoiding holes in the top surface of the table. Or 1″ × 3″ stock can be used to frame under table edges for strengthening it, if you should wish to do so.

CALL IT A CAPTAIN'S BENCH

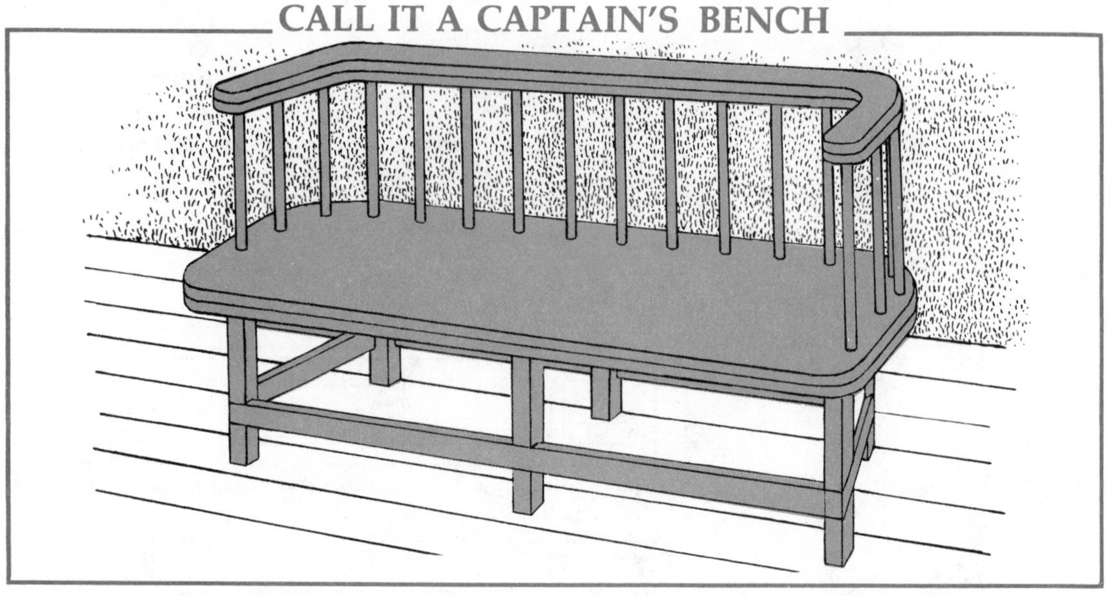

The captain's chair motif is adapted to a country-look bench for patio or deck. The plywood seat is given stability as well as a weightier look with a shaped 1″×2″ under its edges. Stretchers are dadoed into the legs and 1″ dowels are glued into bored holes in the seat and set into the under half of the doubled seat-back rail.

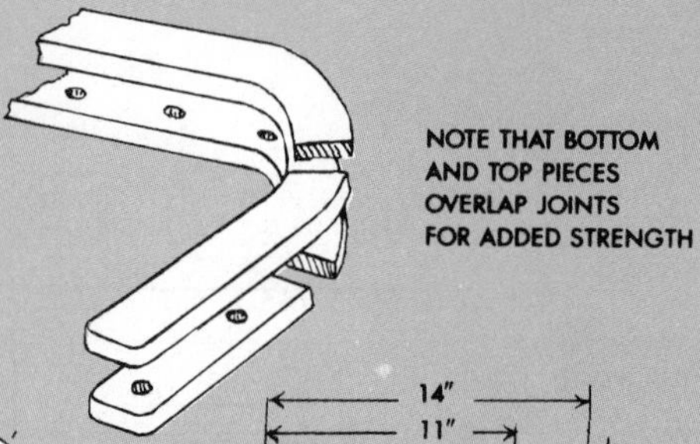

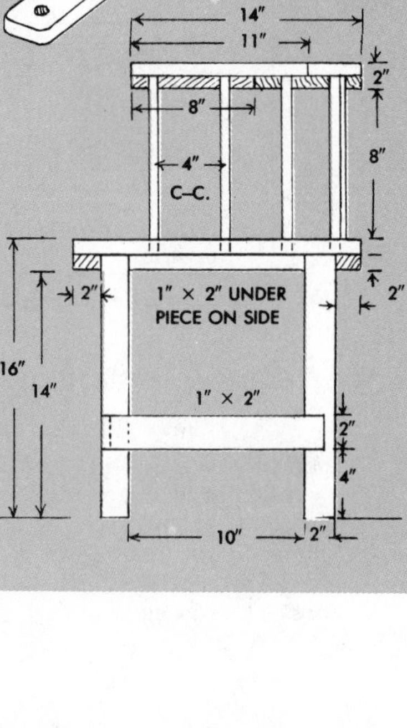

NOTE THAT BOTTOM
AND TOP PIECES
OVERLAP JOINTS
FOR ADDED STRENGTH

6″ R.
6″ R.
6″
UNDER 3″
3″ TOP
6″ R.
6″ R.
14″
18″
2″
9″ R.
2″ R.
4″
4″
LEG: 2″ × 2″
STRETCHER 1″ × 2″
28″

14″
11″
2″
8″
8″
4″
C–C.
1″
1″
2″
2″
16″
14″
1″ × 2″ UNDER
PIECE ON SIDE
1″ × 2″
2″
4″
10″
2″

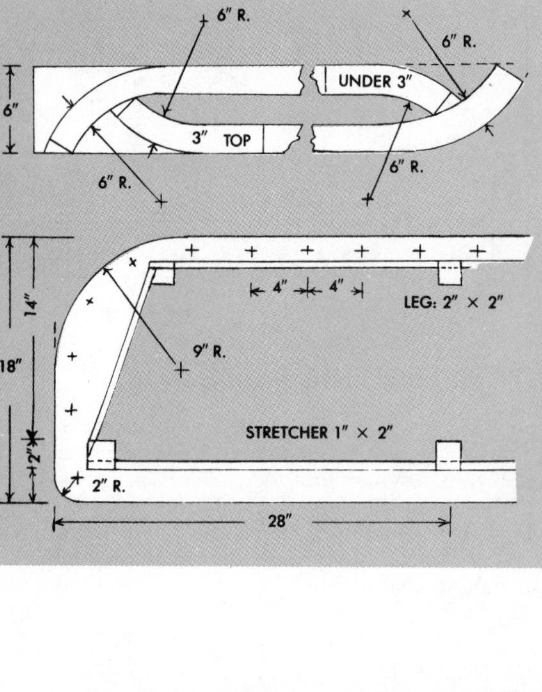

THREE COUNTRY-STYLE GARDEN BENCHES

A basic unit that maybe furnished in three ways—one without a back and two with backs—is designed in sophisticated country style. Handsome additions to a deck, patio, or garden house, they may also be used indoors. Build them of long-lasting cedar or redwood, stained or painted to fit their background. Note: Back center rail is set into ends, but the top rail is set outside to make the back slant slightly backward.

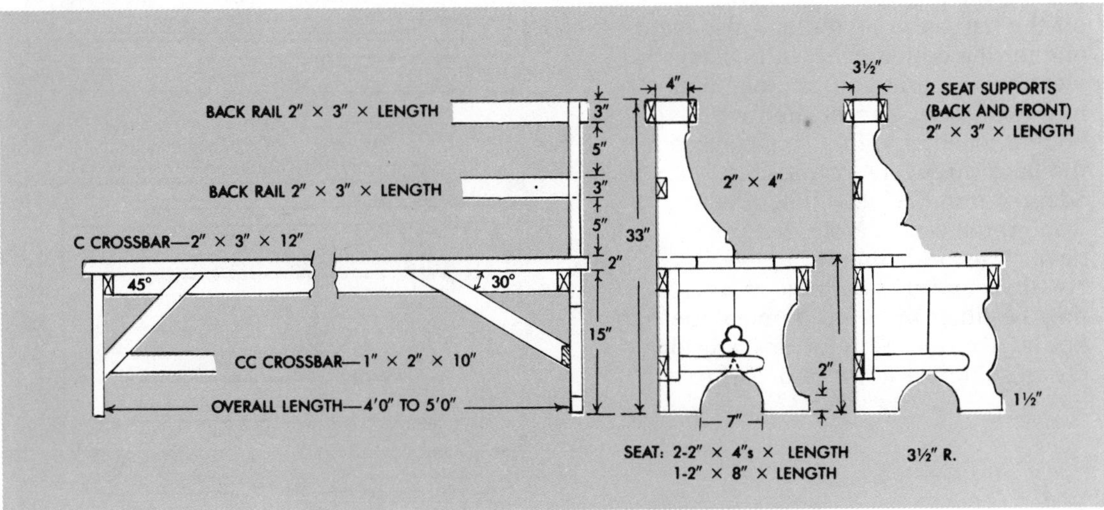

ROLL-AWAY SERVICE CART

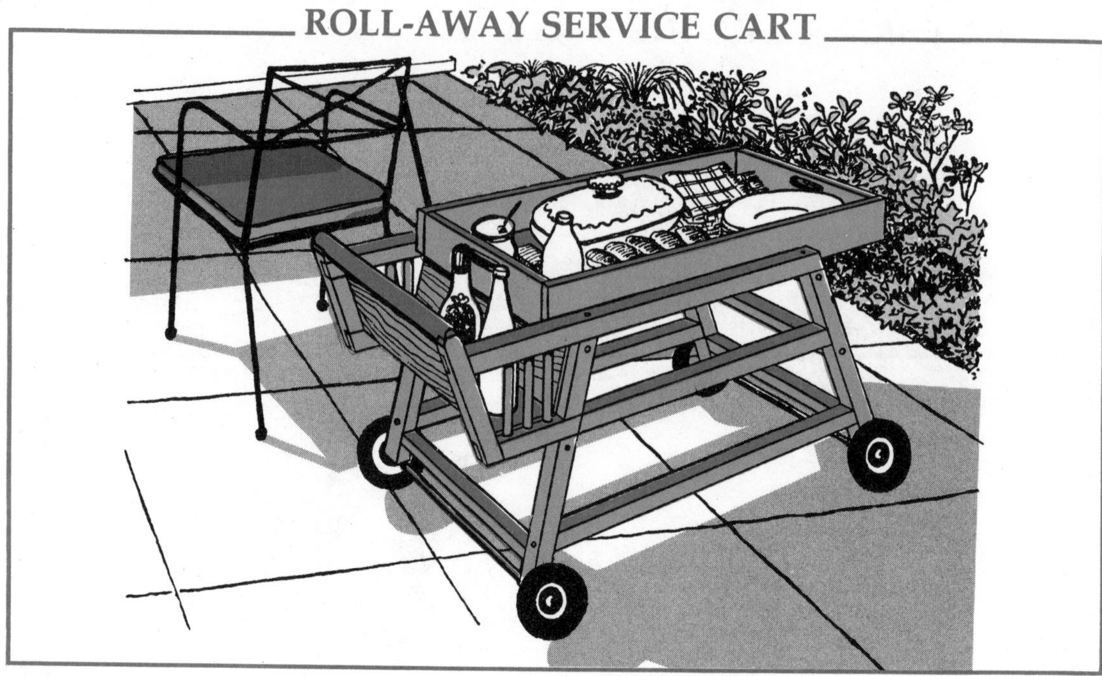

Push this attractive cart up to the kitchen door, load it with food, dishes, bottles—all the appurtenances of outdoor eating—and roll it out to your picnic table. You'll find outdoor eating work halved, cutting trips back and forth to one each way. Return the cart with dirty plates and the debris of a meal to the kitchen door, then lift off the tray on top (you may also want one for the bottom, shown in side view below), and you can take it all into the house. Rubber-tired wheels bought together with a suitable axle at the hardware store (or possibly adapted from a child's discarded wagon) roll easily. Note that trays have cleats on bottom to fit over crossbars and that bottoms of trays may be either plywood or metal mesh. Bottles stay secure in the space below the pushing bar at the end of cart.

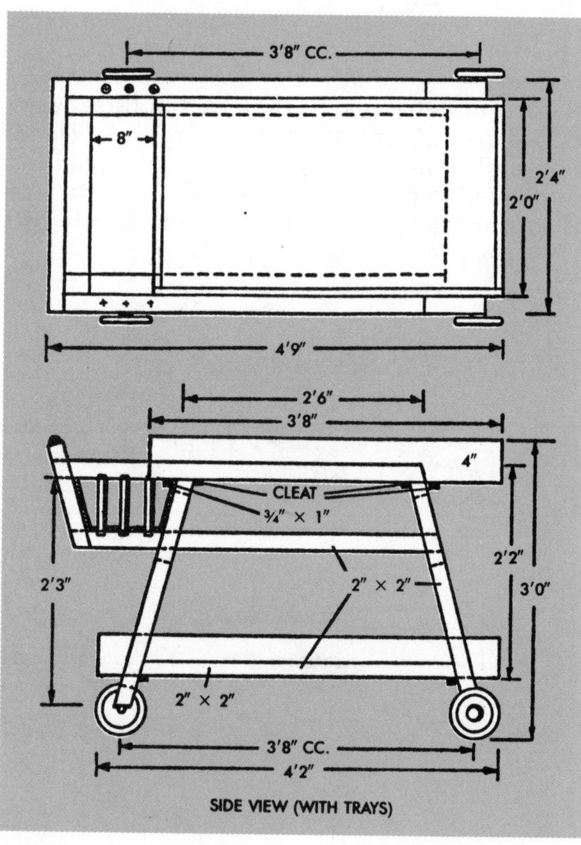

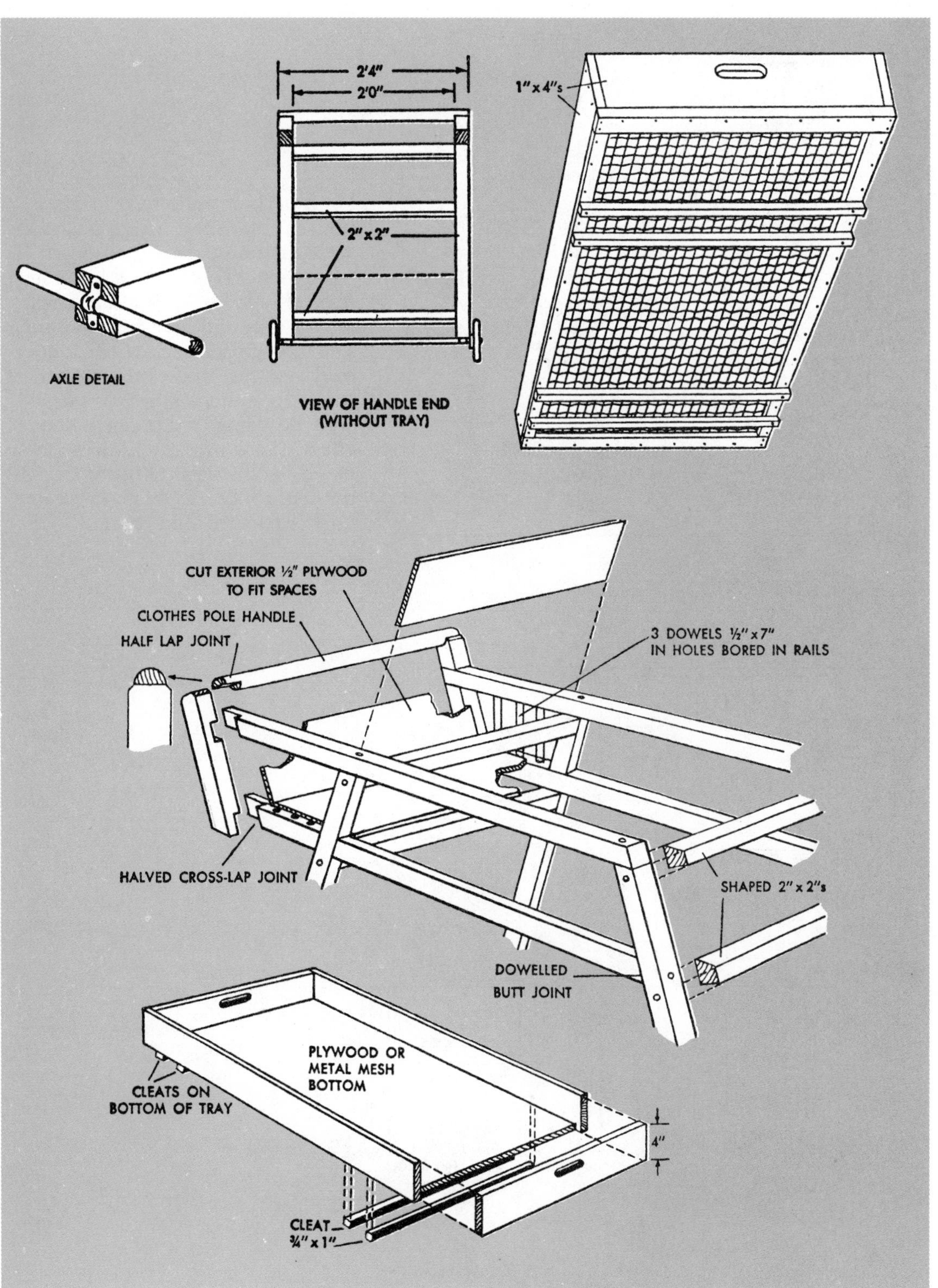
2'4"
2'0"
2"x2"
1"x4"s
AXLE DETAIL
VIEW OF HANDLE END
(WITHOUT TRAY)
CUT EXTERIOR ½" PLYWOOD
TO FIT SPACES
CLOTHES POLE HANDLE
HALF LAP JOINT
3 DOWELS ½"x7"
IN HOLES BORED IN RAILS
HALVED CROSS-LAP JOINT
SHAPED 2"x2"s
DOWELLED
BUTT JOINT
PLYWOOD OR
METAL MESH
BOTTOM
CLEATS ON
BOTTOM OF TRAY
4"
CLEAT
¾"x1"

COUNTRY-STYLE CUPBOARD-TABLE

For a deck or patio next to the house, you can use a cupboard to store dishes, glasses, and other equipment. This version has a let-down hinged front that becomes a table supported by a hinged panel. The storage area below has a door or doors that follows the pattern of the top—either vertical country-style boarding or a paneled door effect. Use a turn-latch carved from wood for the vertical board design, but use a more sophisticated catch for the paneled door design.

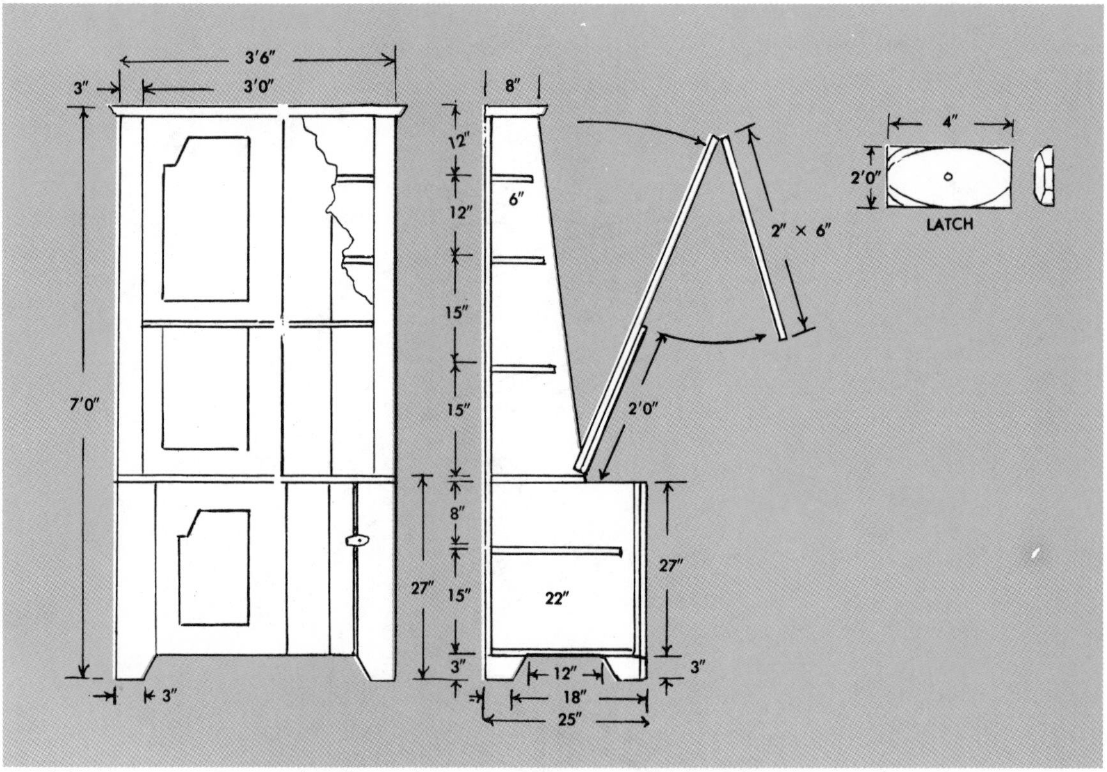

3'6"
3" 3'0"
7'0"
3"
8"
12"
12"
6"
15"
15"
8"
27" 15"
3"
22"
2'0"
2" × 6"
27"
3"
12"
18"
25"
4"
2'0"
LATCH

SATISFYINGLY SOLID AND STURDY

Portable, yet sturdy, this strong and simple design fills the bill for a garden bench. It is suited to modern or traditional houses for garden or patio. The seat is formed of two 2″ × 10″s of pressure-treated lumber with the center 2″ × 4″s of the sides set into them. The aprons and stretcher add further stability and strength and if all pieces are dowelled, as shown here, a touch of design is added as well as strength. Nails may be used instead, of course, and the bench can be painted or stained.

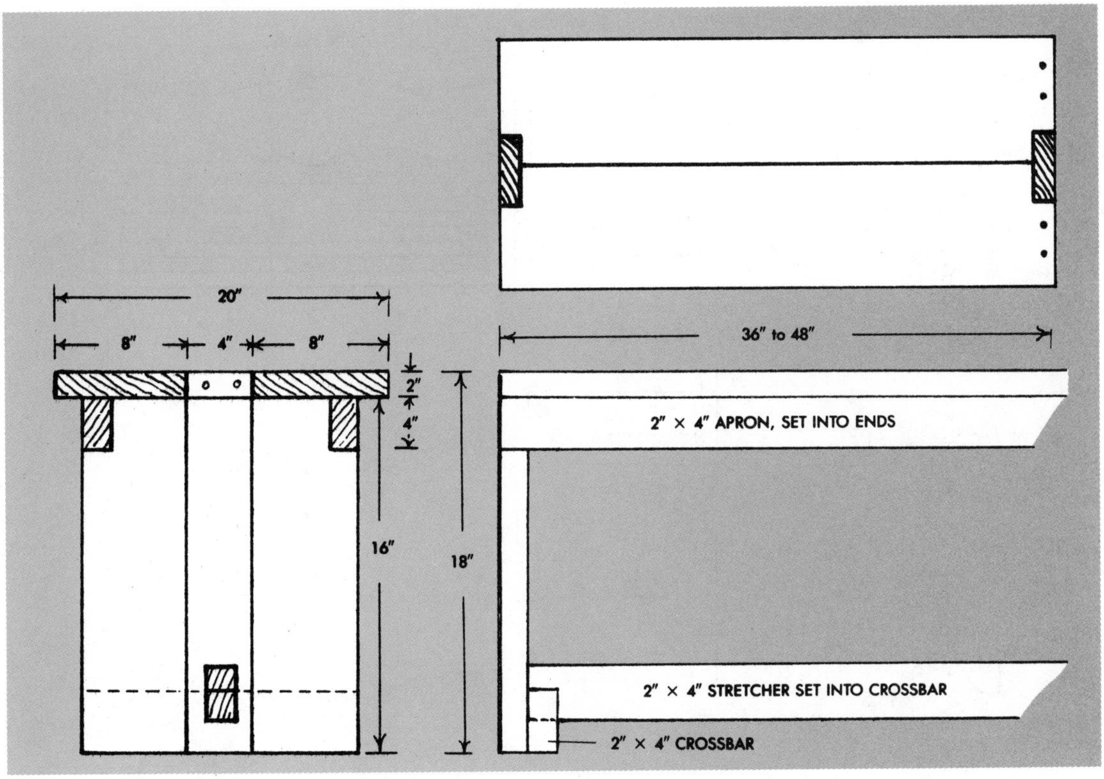

20″

8″ 4″ 8″

2″

4″

16″

18″

36″ to 48″

2″ × 4″ APRON, SET INTO ENDS

2″ × 4″ STRETCHER SET INTO CROSSBAR

2″ × 4″ CROSSBAR

PORTABLE PLANT SHELVES

Useful both indoors and out, this stand is easily transportable from sun to shade, from one garden area to another to provide color and decorative notes with its flowering and leafy plants on both shelves. Plant saucers are set on the dowel rods, permitting good drainage from overflows and allowing for ventilation. Indoors, shelves should have catch pans or they should be solid and waterproofed.

Side tops A, B, C, D, E, F, and G go with side bottoms AA, EE, FF and GG, matched by the letters. Tops B, C, and D may be paired with EE or GG bottoms. A simple gothic double curve, seen in the drawing, is another possible choice for A and D bottoms. Side pieces: Choose those that go with whatever side top and bottom is chosen.

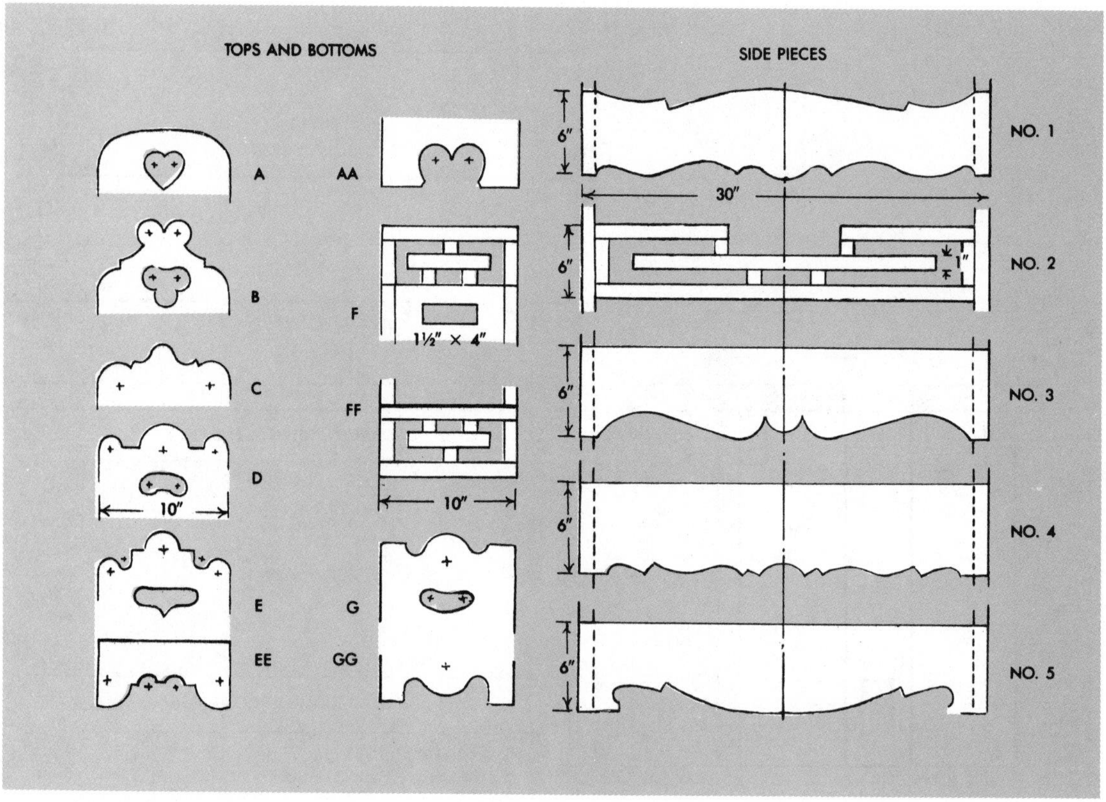

TOPS AND BOTTOMS

A
AA
B
F
1½" × 4"
C
FF
D
10"
10"
E
G
EE
GG

SIDE PIECES

6"
NO. 1
30"
6"
1"
NO. 2
6"
NO. 3
6"
NO. 4
6"
NO. 5

A "WHERE-TO-PUT-IT" GARDEN BENCH

In a small home garden, storage space for potting materials is often nonexistent. One solution is this easily made garden bench that requires only two 4′×8′s of exterior-grade plywood plus a few extra pieces of wood. The seat lifts for access to sand, peat moss, and soil compartments; hinged back pieces open to reveal adjustable shelves for packs of fertilizer, pots, and bottles. Seats may be fitted with cushions and taken indoors in bad weather.

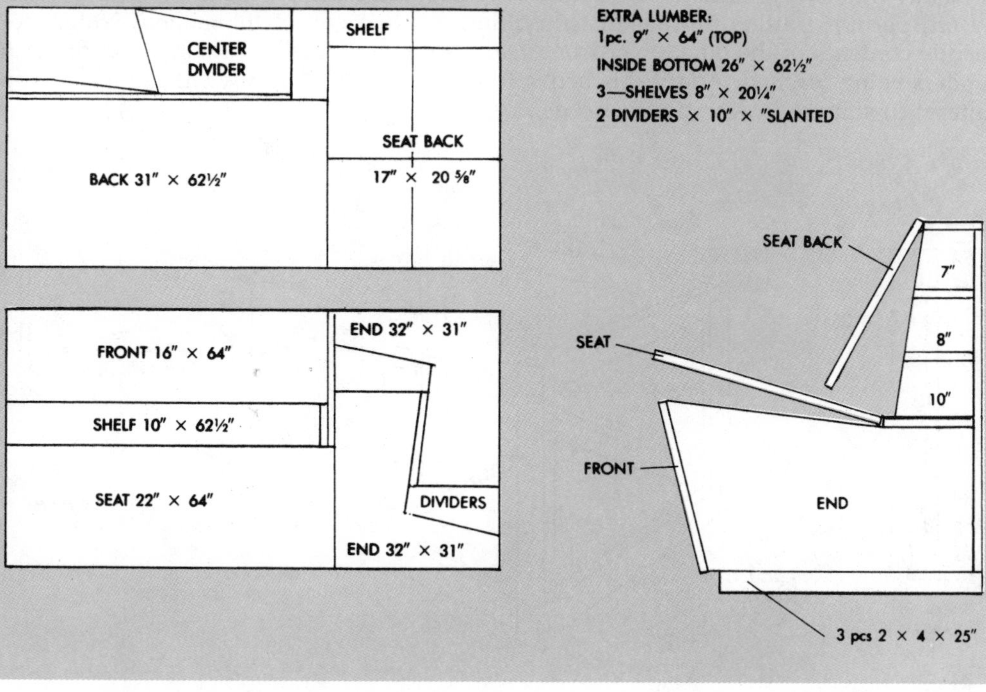

CENTER DIVIDER
SHELF
SEAT BACK
BACK 31″ × 62½″
17″ × 20 ⅝″

EXTRA LUMBER:
1pc. 9″ × 64″ (TOP)
INSIDE BOTTOM 26″ × 62½″
3—SHELVES 8″ × 20¼″
2 DIVIDERS × 10″ × ″SLANTED

FRONT 16″ × 64″
END 32″ × 31″
SHELF 10″ × 62½″
SEAT 22″ × 64″
DIVIDERS
END 32″ × 31″

SEAT BACK
7″
SEAT
8″
10″
FRONT
END
3 pcs 2 × 4 × 25″

A POTTING BENCH WITH MANY OTHER USES

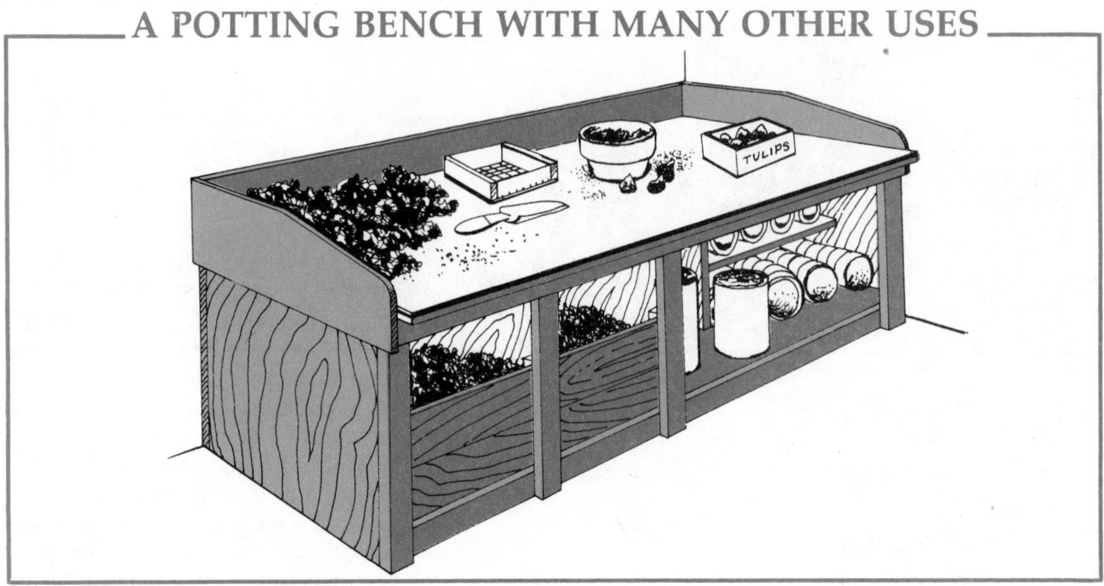

Gardeners fortunate enough to possess greenhouses or those who garden on a fairly large scale outdoors will have need for a potting bench that is sizeable. This one also provides storage bins for peat moss, potting soil, sand, and has shelves for pot storage and for insecticides, fertilizers, and such. The top is made of hardboard, exterior quality, which wears well and is relatively impervious to water. Bench may be used for other purposes in between its uses as potting bench, for cutting and arranging flowers, as an auxiliary carpentry bench, and in many other ways. The collar around the back and sides prevents soil and debris from falling off, permits putting ingredients of potting soil in a corner for mixing. Note, too, that as the contents of the bins lower from use, front boards may be removed to facilitate remainders being reached. Adapt this bench to a smaller size if you wish, to fit your space, and alter it to suit your own specific needs.

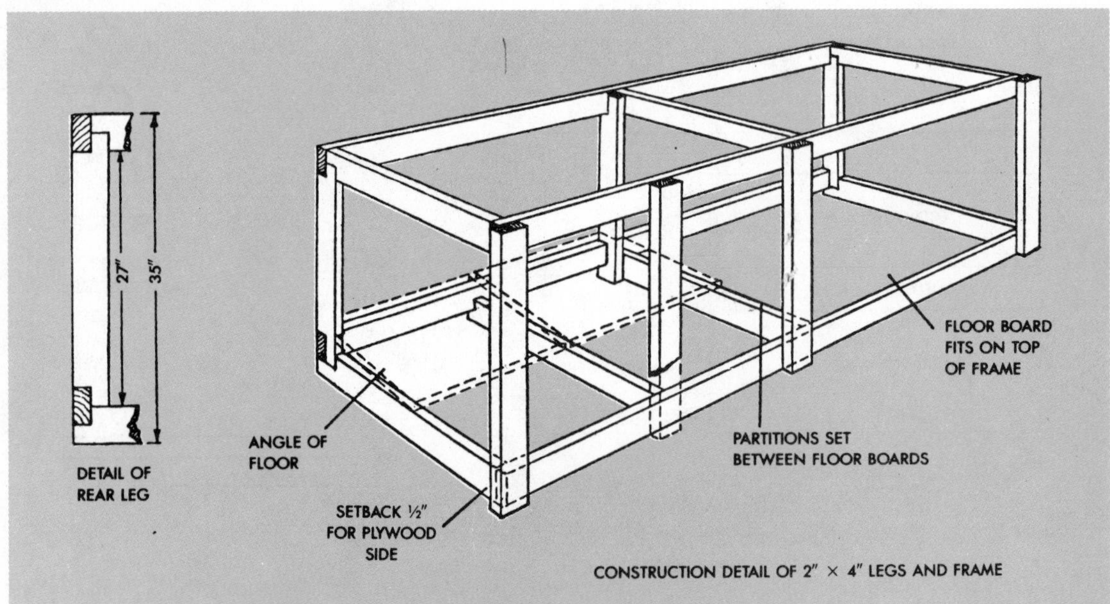

CONSTRUCTION DETAIL OF 2" × 4" LEGS AND FRAME

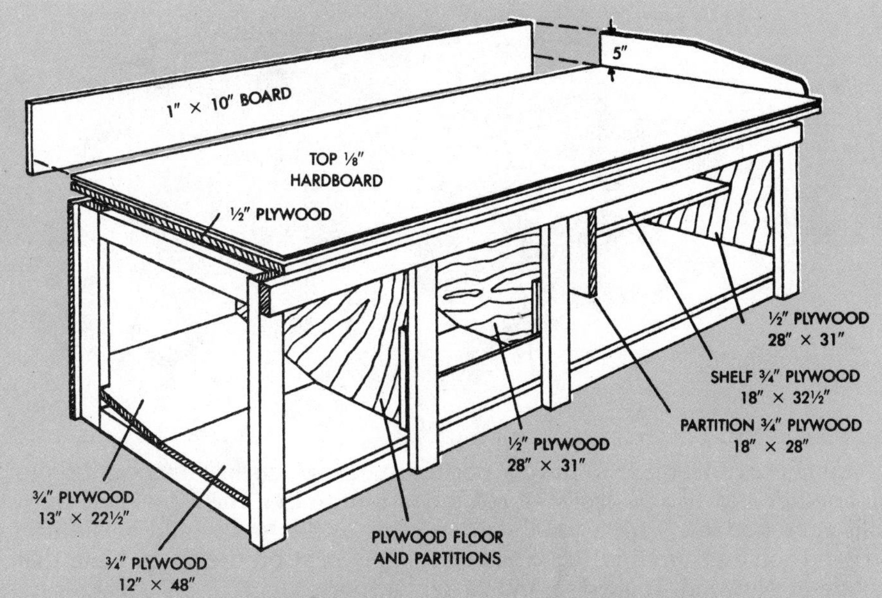

BENCH CONSTRUCTION NOTES

Note how bottoms of bins are inclined, to throw soil toward front of bench. Bins may be lined with aluminum or other sheet metal to permit storage of damp materials, if desired, and top may also be finished with metal instead of hardboard. Exterior plywood in ¾" or ½" thickness is shown, but boards of various widths may be used instead, if top is covered and bins are lined.

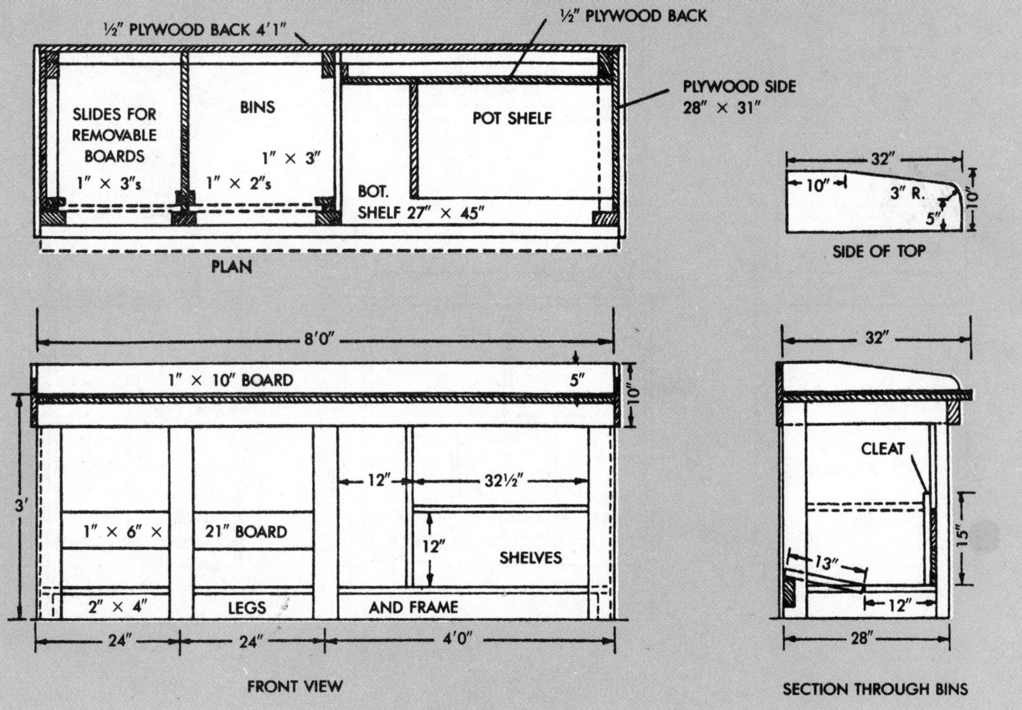

PUSH-AROUND POTTING BENCH

Sometimes it is most convenient to have a portable potting bench which can be pushed from one area to another and also be easily stored when not in use. The removable tray on top makes it still more portable—for a small garden perhaps the tray would be sufficient. Peat moss, sand, and soil are stored in the bins below, pots kept on the shelf. Note that the outer parts are made of plywood, the frame and caster supports are of 2″×4″ stock. If desired, use tempered hardboard for topping the bench and tray.

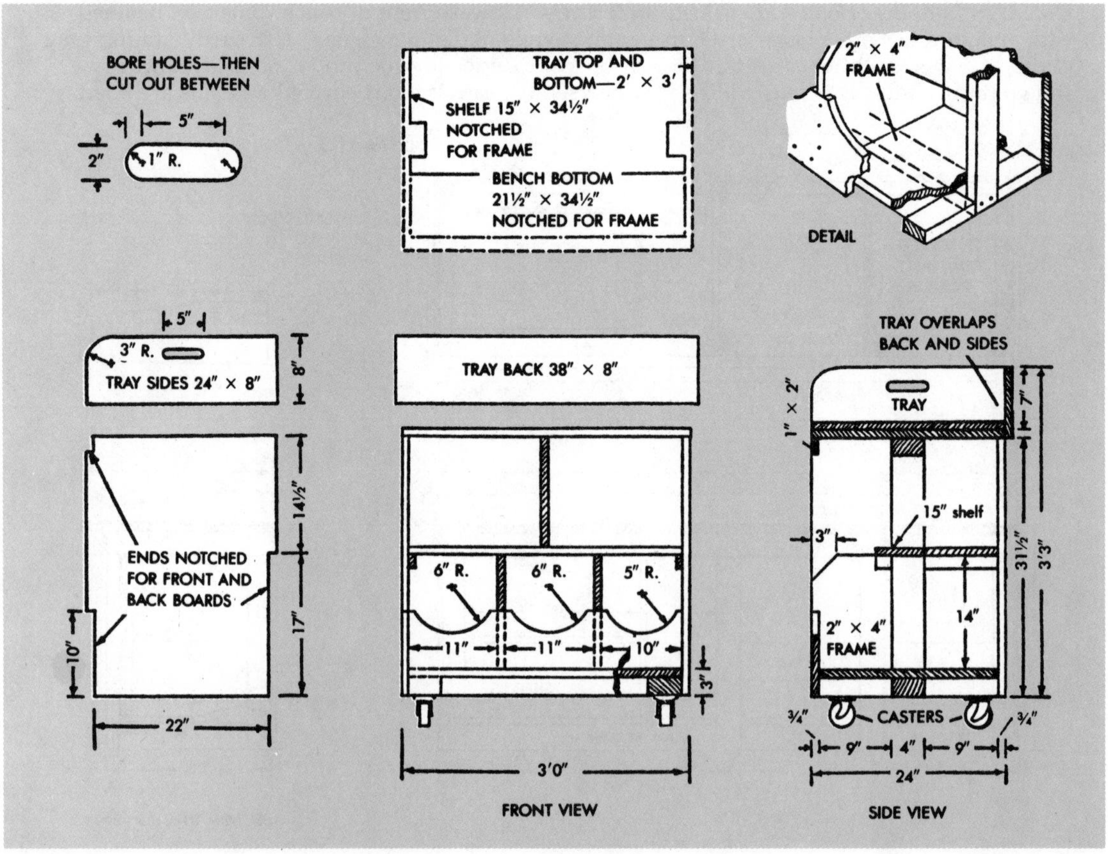

BORE HOLES—THEN CUT OUT BETWEEN
5″
2″
1″ R.

TRAY TOP AND BOTTOM—2′ × 3′
SHELF 15″ × 34½″ NOTCHED FOR FRAME
BENCH BOTTOM 21½″ × 34½″ NOTCHED FOR FRAME

2″ × 4″ FRAME
DETAIL

5″
3″ R.
TRAY SIDES 24″ × 8″
8″

TRAY BACK 38″ × 8″

TRAY OVERLAPS BACK AND SIDES

ENDS NOTCHED FOR FRONT AND BACK BOARDS
14½″
17″
10″
22″

6″ R.
6″ R.
5″ R.
11″
11″
10″
3″
3′0″
FRONT VIEW

1″ × 2″
TRAY
7″
15″ shelf
3″
14″
2″ × 4″ FRAME
31½″
3′3″
¾″
CASTERS
¾″
9″
4″
9″
24″
SIDE VIEW

A PLACE FOR EVERYTHING

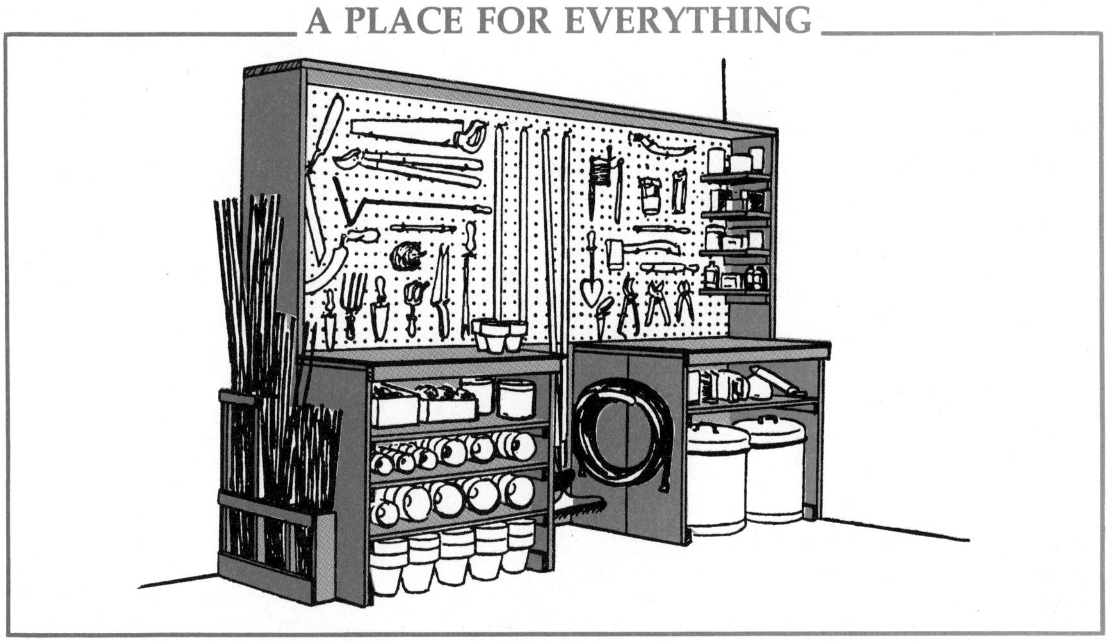

It's always easier to put a tool back when you've finished using it if there is really a place to put it. This simple pegboard arrangement adapts to the tools you now have, can be adjusted to those acquired later. Work tables are built above shelves for pots and garden equipment. Table sides are put to work as storage for stakes and hose. Note upper shelves for dusts and sprays. Garbage cans provide covered storage for soil, sand, and peat moss gardeners need for use in pots, flats.

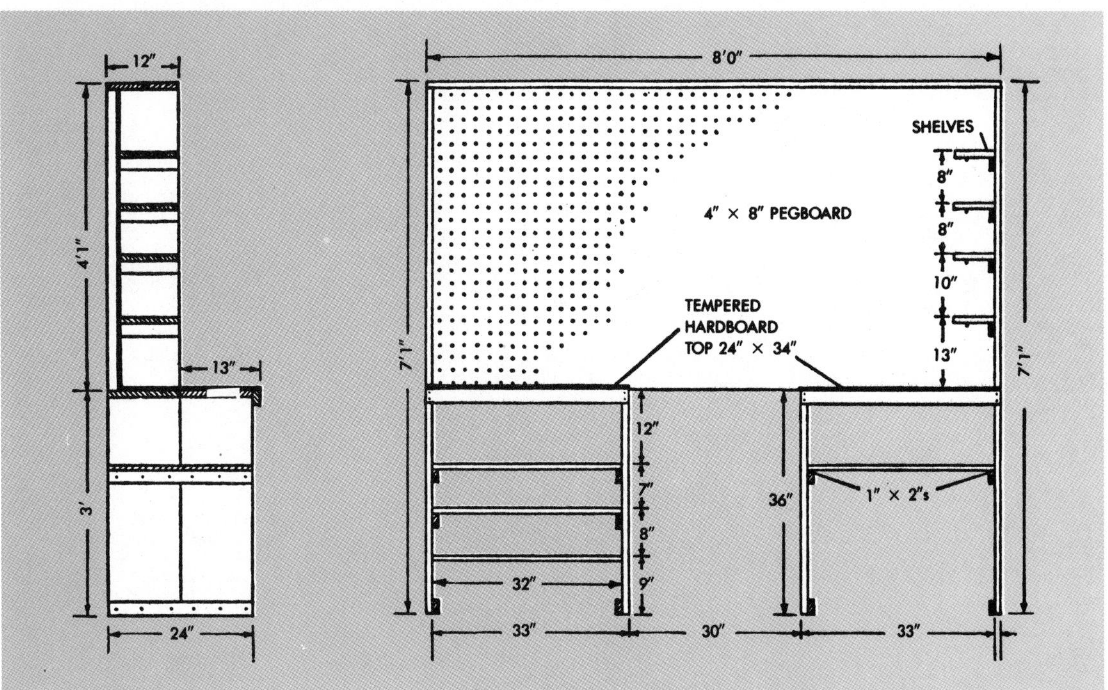

PART II

MASONRY CONSTRUCTION

CHAPTER 10

TOOLS FOR MASONRY

Any sort of building work is made more difficult by not having the proper kinds of tools to work with. No matter how small or how simple the job may seem it will go more quickly and be done better if you have the right tools and know how to use them properly.

In masonry work, as in any other kind of project, tools made specifically for the job will be required for certain operations. In other parts of the work, carpentry tools may be used, or perhaps even improvised tools, if you want to take the time and trouble to make them. It is possible to build most of the masonry shown in this book, and to get good results, by using only three or four basic tools, as many thousands of do-it-yourselfers have proved on similar undertakings. Other projects and the more ambitious designs

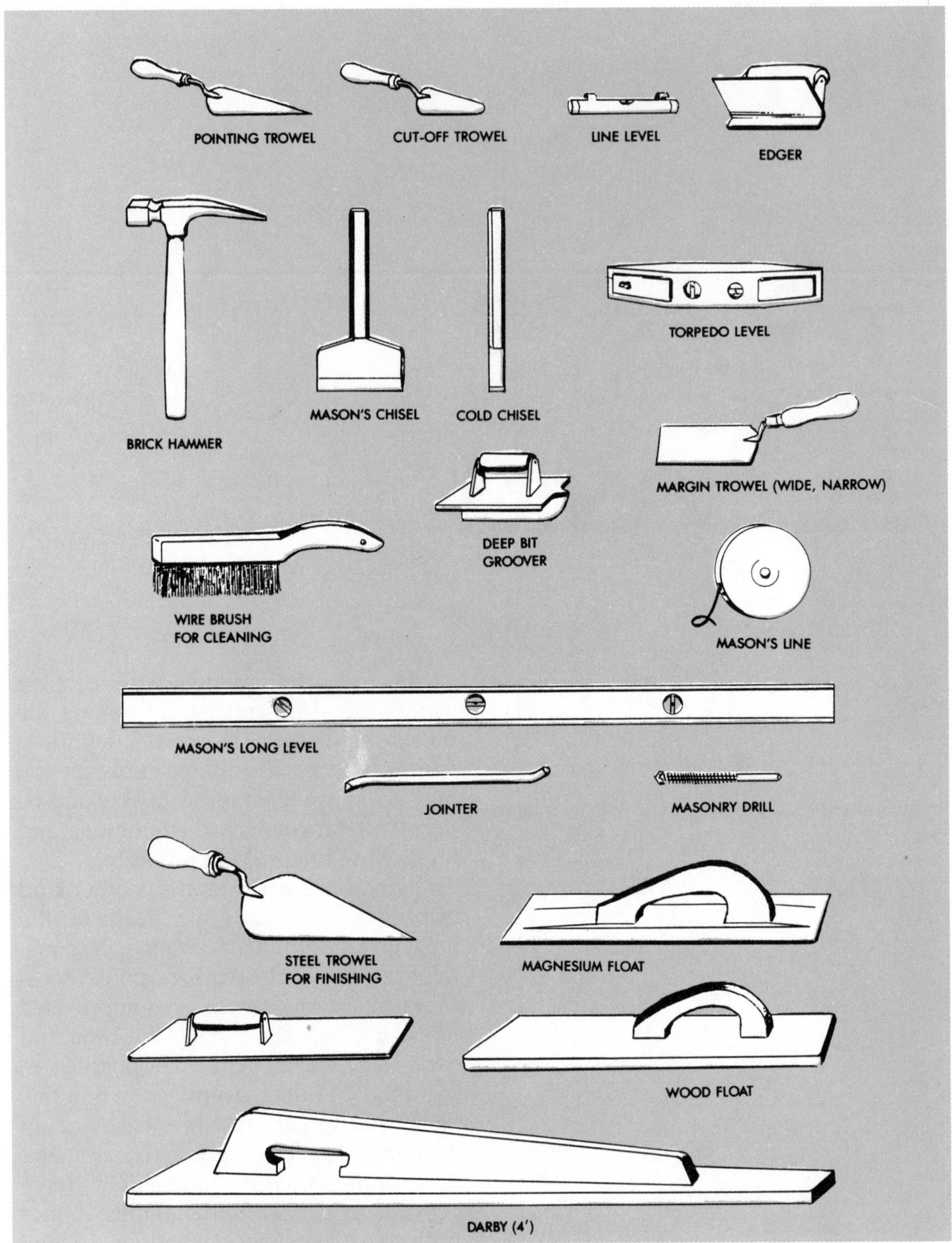
POINTING TROWEL
CUT-OFF TROWEL
LINE LEVEL
EDGER
BRICK HAMMER
MASON'S CHISEL
COLD CHISEL
TORPEDO LEVEL
MARGIN TROWEL (WIDE, NARROW)
DEEP BIT
GROOVER
WIRE BRUSH
FOR CLEANING
MASON'S LINE
MASON'S LONG LEVEL
JOINTER
MASONRY DRILL
STEEL TROWEL
FOR FINISHING
MAGNESIUM FLOAT
WOOD FLOAT
DARBY (4')

in this book may require other tools.

The implements most needed are few: a good trowel, a mason's brick hammer, a good level, and a pointing trowel. With these tools you can make do in producing most kinds of masonry work. You will also find the following tools useful when you are able to add them to your collection: a mason's chisel for cutting bricks, a rule (either a folding one or a roll-up tapeline), a ball of mason's line or cord, and a steel framing square such as carpenters use. You will probably want to add a set of jointing tools, a pointed mason's chisel, and probably a standard cold chisel 1 to 1¼ inches wide. If you are laying up a wall, you will need a plumb bob to make sure that the wall is kept vertical.

The trowels you'll need are of the two above-mentioned types: a large one with a pointed, somewhat flexible blade about 10 to 12 inches long for use with mortar when you are laying bricks or blocks; and a smaller one, called a pointing trowel, with a 4- to 6-inch blade, which is most useful when pointing up joints in constricted space and for various other small jobs. Both should have the handle shank brazed to the trowel blade or made in one piece with the blade, the wooden handle being set firmly on the shank. Good blades are scientifically heat-treated to harden the steel and good handles are made of durable hardwood. (See the accompanying drawings of tools.)

The mason's brick hammer should be well balanced so that it is easy to use, be made of good hardened steel, and weigh about 1½ pounds. The head of the usual type is square at one end and tapers to a broad, chisel-like point.

Made of wood, the mason's level differs from a carpenter's level in that it is usually longer, averaging 42 to 48 inches in length, or even more. It probably will have three spirit bubbles, one of which either is set permanently at a 45° angle or can be adjusted to various angles up to that. In a pinch, or for small jobs, it is possible to use a short carpenter's level, adapting it to use by binding a good straight board, 42 to 48 inches in length, to the side of the level with masking tape or friction tape; keep the board even with its lower edge. Be *sure* that the board and level *exactly* coincide on the bottom sides in order to be used with assurance of accuracy. If, however, you plan to do much masonry work now or later, it will be to your benefit to buy a mason's level. In some narrow spaces you will need a shorter level and for this purpose a 12-inch or shorter one will do. A torpedo level (see drawing) about 9 inches long is a convenient size. It may contain one or two spirit bubbles in the body of the tool in addition to the central horizontal one on the top side. A line level hooks onto the mason's line when it is stretched tightly between corners of bricks or blocks; it is used as a guide for the line so that courses of masonry can be kept level and straight. By using such a level you can be assured that the line is stretched properly to a true level. Actually, for most work detailed in these designs, only the large mason's level will be needed. Only when building a very long wall or some large structure will a line be used and a torpedo or line level be useful or necessary.

Brick chisels are most useful for cutting bricks squarely. The wide one shown has a blade about 3 inches wide, while the blade of the cold chisel is 1 to 1¼ inches wide.

An electric or hand drill can be used for boring holes in masonry and concrete. Use a carbide-tipped drill made especially for this purpose. When the carbide-tipped drill strikes a particularly hard piece of aggregate or a hard vein of stone, it is wise to stop drilling and use a star drill and a hand hammer to crack the hard spot until it is penetrated or sufficiently broken up to permit use of the drill again. A hammer-drill works better yet, but such professional tools cost quite a bit.

The folding rule or roll-up tapeline—for both the minimum length recommended is 8 feet—can also be used for carpentry projects, as can the steel square. The professional mason's square is somewhat smaller, but the large carpenter's square is usually adaptable for this use.

Mason's line or cord may be made of cotton, but nylon or linen cord is less likely to stretch excessively. The cord is used in laying out a project and making sure that the corners are squared up (explained in Chapter 12), as well as to keep courses straight, as discussed earlier. A pair of mason's line blocks, (see drawing) either purchased or homemade, are used to hook around the built-up blocks or bricks at each end of a wall to keep courses straight and held in place by the tension of a well-stretched mason's line between them. They are most useful.

Jointers, used for striking the mortar joints in various ways, are shaped for easy use in the hand. If you plan to make any of the fancier kinds of joints (see drawings of masonry joints), you will find that a jointer of the right type will speed your job. They come in various shapes, each especially formed to make a certain kind of joint, sometimes combining two types in one S-shaped tool. You'll use them also in certain kinds of concrete work and for striking joints in bricks or blocks used for paving.

TOOLS FOR CONCRETE WORK

You will need some other tools if you are going to do concrete work (see drawings). First used is a darby, a 48-inch-long wooden tool for the initial smoothing of a concrete slab. In place of a darby a bull float serves the same purpose. Though it costs more than a darby, a bull float lets you reach to the center of a large slab without getting onto the still-plastic concrete. Next used is a wood float with mahogany face and hardwood handle. The best tool for outdoor concrete finishes is a magnesium float with a wooden handle. One or two separate wood floatings followed each time by the magnesium float produces a nonslip textured finish quite easily. Steel troweling is not recommended. It is difficult to learn and creates a finish that may be too smooth for safety outdoors unless brushed or otherwise textured afterward to create a nonslip surface. A jointer for cutting control joints and an edger for finishing off the sides of cement on walks, driveways, or patios will nearly complete the tool list you'll probably need for most cement and concrete work.

The wood float should be about 5″ × 13″ to 14″, with a wooden handle secured at both ends to the blade. The edger and the jointer are usually slightly curved at both ends so as not to pick up or drag the plastic concrete. Both are made of metal and have wooden handles. The jointer should have a bit at least one-fourth the slab's depth: 1 inch for a 4-inch slab. You may find some newer versions of these tools made from stainless steel which is nonrusting and consequently easy to care for. This type of tool will last indefinitely.

CARE OF TOOLS

It pays to buy quality tools even though you may not be able to buy many to begin with. Cheap tools can cost more if they buckle or break in the middle of a job. They may ruin a batch of concrete or prevent you from working Sundays when stores are closed and it is impossible to replace tools quickly.

Once you have purchased your tools, be sure to arrange a place to keep them in orderly fashion, somewhere that is dry and out of harm's way. Don't just lay them on a cluttered shelf or put them in a corner of a damp basement where they will rust or get lost. Chisels and other bladed tools should be kept sharpened, and all iron or steel tools should be cleaned and wiped with an oily rag after each use to prevent rust. Well-kept tools are not only ready for use at a moment's notice, but they are the signature of a good do-it-yourselfer with respect for implements. They are good to look at and they will last for many years.

CHAPTER 11

MATERIALS FOR MASONRY

All masonry is basically the same: it is composed of units of certain sizes held apart, as well as joined, by a "bond" of mortar. The strength and durability of the wall will depend upon how good the mortar is and how carefully the units are laid. All horizontal points must *be* horizontal. The plumbness of corners and all vertical lines will depend upon the horizontals being level. Similarly, the looks of the wall depend upon the straightness and the levelness of the horizontals, the uprightness of the verticals, and the plumbness of the wall.

To avoid walls cracking or breaking from normal stress and strain, vertical masonry joints are "staggered," placed so that they do not fall immediately above each other. This added strength and durability has been achieved in various ways, often quite decorative in the patterns produced, as shown in the illustrations of bonds in Chapter 12. In Common Bond the units are placed with vertical points falling exactly in the center of the preceding units below. Staggering one-third or one-quarter is also possible and when units are laid as headers—facing end-on across the wall—the result is more engaging. See the Diaper Pattern, the English and Flemish Bonds, and Rolok.

In modern buildings Stacked Bond is often called for; that is, each unit is laid exactly above the preceding unit in the course below, with all vertical joints aligning with those below, resulting in emphasized vertical as well as horizontal lines in the pattern created by the joints. This is hard to do, and not recommended for do-it-yourselfers. Raked joints and/or colored mortars will give added pattern and textural effects. In this case, in order to tie units together, metal tie-rods, tie strips, or metal mesh strips should be inserted to bridge the vertical joints and be held in place by the mortar. Stacked Bond is most frequently employed in veneering, facing a block, concrete, or cheap brick wall with finished bricks, broken-texture blocks, and such.

Ancient bricks were handmade and varied widely in size and even in shape. They were rough and probably rather difficult to lay, yet we find them in walls which are still standing after many centuries, showing how durable masonry can be. In Pompeii, in Rome, and in other cities of even greater antiquity, we see many walls of great beauty made with sun-baked brick. With today's machine-made bricks and other precisely formed masonry units which are almost identical in shape and size, varying only a tiny fraction due to shrinkage in baking or drying, we find it quite easy to obtain walls that are pleasantly uniform and which conform to exact measurements. In any batch of bricks which are delivered to your property you may find variations of up to 1/8 inch; and in blocks, hollow tile, and other units you may find some variations of as much as 1/4 inch or so. These are allowable and should cause you no alarm, because shrinkage is inevitable in drying out or in the baking and varies from batch to batch in the same brickyard under identical conditions.

However, you may find it hard to match bricks at a yard other than that where they were made. Different factories use different machinery in making bricks and masonry units, for not all of them have as yet conformed to the modular size advocated by the industry. It will be well to check the sizes of the bricks in your present construction, if you can, before ordering to see if you can obtain new ones from the source originally used. In all the tables and plans which follow, therefore, approximate measurements are given, the ones which the industry has approved as standard. If yours do not conform, make allowances as necessary.

KINDS OF BRICK

Common brick. Made from ordinary clay with no coloring added, and no texturing or other processing, these bricks will vary in color and texture even in the same baking batch. This is something which some builders deplore and others prize, according to individual tastes and the purpose for which the brick is to be utilized. Many degrees of hardness and softness are to be found in the category embraced by the name "common brick." Those nearest to the baking fire are hardest, those farthest from it are softer, more likely to chip, and less resistant to weather and moisture conditions. The hard-burned bricks are sometimes called "clinker" in the trade nomenclature, or "hard-burned" in some sections of the trade. Where nonloadbearing walls are built with bricks sheltered from weather or from moisture and freezing, the cheapest common brick may be used. These are usually called "salmon" brick (although the color may be anything *but* salmon). For all other outdoor work and for load-bearing walls, clinker or hard-burned bricks are the best to use. Most common brick is rough in texture, relatively porous, and probably will have a slight bow in the lengthwise measure. Always place the convex bow on the *lower* side when laying up a wall.

Pressed brick or facebrick. More uniform in size, with well-squared corners, and altogether smoother and finer in texture, these bricks are usually used for facing walls, since they are more weather-resistant and also are likely to run more uniform in color. They may be used for facing any wall except one exposed to fire (such as in backing-up a fireplace) in which case use...

Firebrick. These are specially made units somewhat larger than the standard-sized brick, running to a size of about 2½" × 4" × 8". Made of a specially selected fire-resistant clay, firebrick is coarser in quality and in finished texture than other bricks. Hearths and flues or fireplaces may be lined and floored with this brick. It will resist the hottest of fires.

Unbaked brick. A recent development, these are not baked but formed in molds of cement and sand and allowed to dry out until completely set, therefore unbaked bricks are usually most precise in size and admirably square-edged. They are quite uniform in color, too, because the color can be controlled in the mixing, but to my mind they are less interesting because of this. Some types are made as substitutes for baked firebricks and seem to be quite satisfactory. The common unbaked bricks are well suited for use in walls either as backing-up or as facing bricks. To some, their texture as well as the absolute uniformity of color is less pleasing than that of baked bricks, but, if the joints are well raked and if the wall is to be painted, this objection might be overcome.

Used bricks. Provided they are well cleansed of mortar and the edges have not been too chipped or damaged, used bricks salvaged from razed buildings are perfectly good to use. Such damaged bricks are all right for backing-up if they are still sound and cleaned. It is sometimes poor economy to buy salvaged bricks when the cost of new brick is balanced against the price of salvaged brick and the effort required to clean, examine, and sort each brick for use. Of course if the brick comes from a building or wall on your own property which is being demolished, or from some structure being razed nearby where the only cost involved is the hauling, it may save considerable money to clean and re-use them.

The method of cleaning is this: Grasp a piece of broken brick about half the size of a regular brick (this is called a "brickbat") and rap it smartly against the mortar on a brick held in the other hand. This chips and dislodges most of the mortar, and the rest can be rubbed off with the brickbat. I would be the last to say it is an easy job or an interesting one, but it can save money if the conditions are as detailed above.

Paving brick. Much harder and usually larger than ordinary types of brick, all the edges of a paving brick are rounded and each face of the brick is smooth. The lengths and widths of paving bricks are designed to pattern out in even multiples when laid flat. It is sometimes possible to buy used paving brick from salvage yards for paving walks or traction strips in a concrete driveway. The bricks will be too large and heavy to use for wall-building but are perfect for paving walks, patios, and driveways.

Roman brick. Longer in proportion to its height and width than the ordinary types of bricks, Roman brick is being much used in modern construction because of the long, low lines it gives to walls. It looks particularly good as veneer in Stacked Bond with the joints raked and with a fairly rough-textured surface on the facing side.

SCR bricks. These are wider and longer than most other bricks. They can be used for garden walls, for house walls one-story high, and for various other projects. Because of their size—6″ × 2⅔″ × 12″—they can be laid quickly, reducing the time needed for the work and also saving a little on the cost of mortar. Vertical holes through the bricks permit mortar to penetrate, making a strong bond between courses. For house walls, metal clips may be inserted in the joints to hold furring strips; 2″ × 2″ stock gives space for insulation and furrs out to allow placement of wallboard, lath, plasterboard and the like to be applied for interior finishes. For outdoor use, the width allows use of a single-brick wall, particularly where frost is not a problem and especially for low walls in all regions. A cap course of solid bricks will be needed to cover the holes.

Other types of bricks. Many kinds of bricks are available by special order for particular use. Various shapes, such as round corner, coping in different shapes, molded face, hexagonal paving bricks or tiles, and many others, are made in most areas but must usually be specially ordered. They are more expensive than common bricks but they give effects which are not obtainable in any other way. Check locally for types, prices, and availability.

Features found in some bricks. Various surface textures are made, the wire-cut surface being widely used. I do not, personally, favor this type of surface because it is so full of texture as to look shaggy. Furthermore, it is likely to collect dust, grime, and soot in city areas and will be very hard to clean. A good brick wall with slightly raked joints gives a most pleasing texture in itself and no further textural emphasis will be necessary.

Today many bricks, even common ones, are found with various depressions

NOMINAL SIZES OF BRICK

(for use in figuring quantities of bricks needed for jobs)

Type of brick	*Width, inches*	*Height, inches*	*Length, inches*
Conventional	4	$2\frac{2}{3}$	8
Roman	4	2	12
Norman	4	$2\frac{2}{3}$	12
Engineers'	4	$3\frac{1}{5}$	8
Economy or modular	4	4	8
Jumbo	4	4	12
Double	4	$5\frac{1}{3}$	8
Triple	4	$5\frac{1}{3}$	12
SCR*	6	$2\frac{2}{3}$	12
Firebrick	$4\frac{1}{2}$	$2\frac{1}{2}$	9

*Note that SCR brick is 6 inches wide and 12 inches long, a factor to be reckoned with in choosing brick for one-brick-thick walls. It is sufficiently strong to build walls for a one-story house, hence it is ideal for many kinds of garden walls.

molded into the top and bottom surfaces to hold mortar and thus give a better bonding. These depressions are usually of an oblong shape and run to within an inch or so of each edge. Other types have round holes bored through the brick at intervals so that when the bed joint is laid the mortar sinks into these holes and is pushed up into the holes in the next course, thus assisting in making a strong joint. Steel rods may be forced through these holes, too, making an exceptionally strong wall even though it may be only one brick in width. The mortar in this case is forced tightly around the steel rods, of course. It's not a do-it-yourself job, however.

BLOCKS OF ALL KINDS AND OTHER MASONRY UNITS

Many types of building blocks are available in all areas of the country, some more prevalent according to local tastes or availability of materials than others. We have only to look about us to see what strong, durable and beautiful walls they make, how interesting in texture and architectural effects they can be.

Concrete blocks. Whether made of cement and any of a number of materials—cinders, scoria, pumice, Haydite, or gravel—all blocks are known by the familiar name of concrete blocks. Some are more finished looking than others, so it is well to check on the looks of the blocks before ordering them to be sure that you obtain what you desire. They come in an astonishing array of sizes, shapes, colors, and textures, some molded for use on corners, for chimney construction, for surrounding window sashes and door frames, and for other specific uses. Blocks which use cinders may contain iron particles or scraps which rust when used for facing walls, exposed to weather. Rust stains will appear, bleeding through paint, disfiguring the surface, and often disintegrating and leaving a hole.

Blocks are made by mixing portland cement with the aggregates and pouring the mixture into molds which are then

SIZES AND KINDS OF BASIC BLOCKS

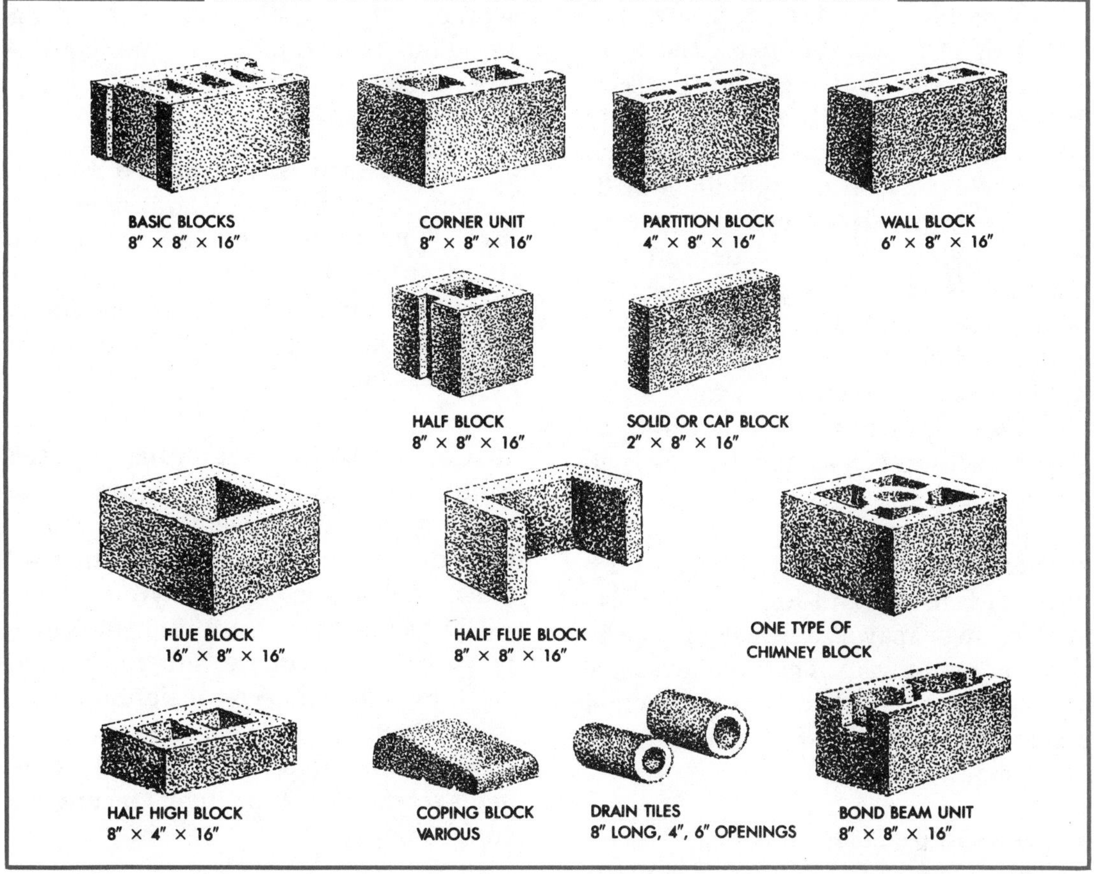

BASIC BLOCKS
8″ × 8″ × 16″

CORNER UNIT
8″ × 8″ × 16″

PARTITION BLOCK
4″ × 8″ × 16″

WALL BLOCK
6″ × 8″ × 16″

HALF BLOCK
8″ × 8″ × 16″

SOLID OR CAP BLOCK
2″ × 8″ × 16″

FLUE BLOCK
16″ × 8″ × 16″

HALF FLUE BLOCK
8″ × 8″ × 16″

ONE TYPE OF
CHIMNEY BLOCK

HALF HIGH BLOCK
8″ × 4″ × 16″

COPING BLOCK
VARIOUS

DRAIN TILES
8″ LONG, 4″, 6″ OPENINGS

BOND BEAM UNIT
8″ × 8″ × 16″

The older sorts of blocks are 3-core; newer kinds are 2-core. Wider widths of blocks used for walls and foundations may be 10″ or 12″.

shaken well by machinery to settle the mixture and release air pockets. When set and fairly dry, the blocks are removed by releasing the molds and stacked for steam-curing and drying. Because most blocks are hollow-cored, they are relatively light and strong for their size. They may be used for loadbearing walls, the size being selected according to the width needed for the load to be borne. Walls go up quickly and blocks are satisfying to work with. A complaint of some amateurs, that blocks are heavy and therefore tiring, is no longer necessarily true. The core area lightens the weight a good deal. Working with blocks is a very pleasant task and the fascination of seeing the project progress so quickly is part of the pleasure.

Split blocks. Some concrete blocks are cast two units wide, then broken. The uneven side is laid as the outer face of the wall. Most interesting textures result, a rather stonelike quality, rough-textured and pleasant in walls, breaking up large expanses in a most unusual way. Colored-aggregate and integrally colored blocks are available in an array of textures.

Slump blocks. These are cast, and before they are really set hard, the forms are removed allowing the block to "slump" or subside. The squashed effect is similar to that found in adobe brick walls, so typical in old buildings in the Southwest. Especially suited to homes with a Spanish or Latin-American look, they are also useful for garden walls, retaining walls, and other construction work where a different texture is desired. In modern design homes or where a conventional block might be cold and too smooth, slump blocks may be used with good effect.

Glazed blocks. Mostly for indoor use, where a finished and formal look is desirable, these may also be used for facing patio or terrace walls. Their extra cost may also have to be considered as well as their suitability. However, they will need little or no maintenance.

Grille blocks. This is a field that has expanded rapidly. Many ordinary blocks lend themselves to grilles. For instance, the *single-core blocks* laid horizontally or set vertically, overlapping at corners, make a good checkerboard patterned wall. *Square chimney blocks*, or those with *round cores* for use around cylindrical flue tiles, are also effective, and easy to obtain, easy to lay. Grilles may be constructed of any kind of open blocks combined with *partition blocks* or with *thinner patio-paving blocks* laid between them in double rows, projecting on either side of the wall. Similarly, *single-core blocks* may be set vertically, with two *partition blocks* laid horizontally between them, to give a kind of open-and-closed checkerboard design. Many other combinations of blocks may be used to form grilles and a truly creative worker will take much pleasure in figuring out new patterns, designing grilles from the blocks available.

Shaped-face or sculptured blocks. Coming in many styles and varied facings, these blocks give variety and textured interest to walls. Diagonal or diamond-shaped patterns fit together as blocks are laid to give directional patterns to the finished wall.

Colored blocks, aggregates selected. More frequently than ever before blocks are now offered in integrally colored concrete or with selected aggregates that will make the finished wall anything but a cliché of blocks that are dull, that must be painted, stuccoed or otherwise decorated to give architectural significance to them. Often you will be able to select from blocks with interestingly varied aggregates set in colored concrete, for complete surface finish.

Ground-face blocks. A recent development is the smooth-face block that has a look similar to that of a terrazzo floor. The finished block is placed in a machine that grinds down its surface (in a manner similar to being fed into a wood-sanding machine with an abrasive belt) to expose and also grind flat the aggregates. The finished blocks can be treated with a sealant, and this will make them attractive for indoor use, as well. Colors that contrast or blend with the aggregates used make them doubly attractive. The sealant makes them waterproof, too, so that they would be more useful than ordinary blocks for areas where moisture is a problem or for walls which would need to be washed down occasionally.

GRILLE BLOCKS

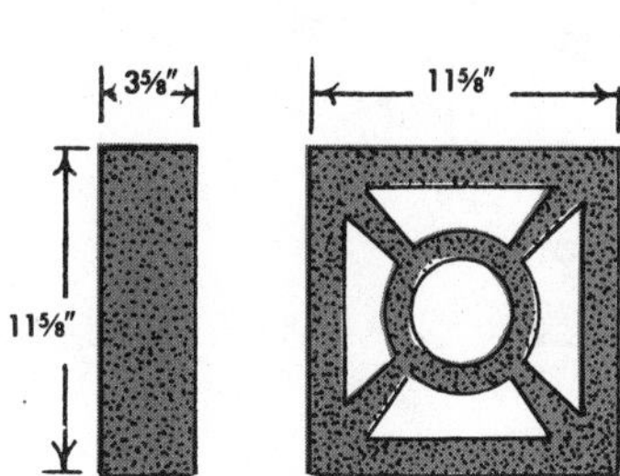

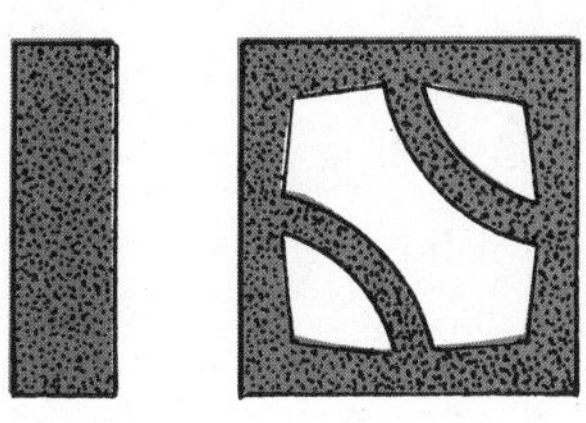

HOLLOW CLAY TILE—SOME TYPICAL SIZES

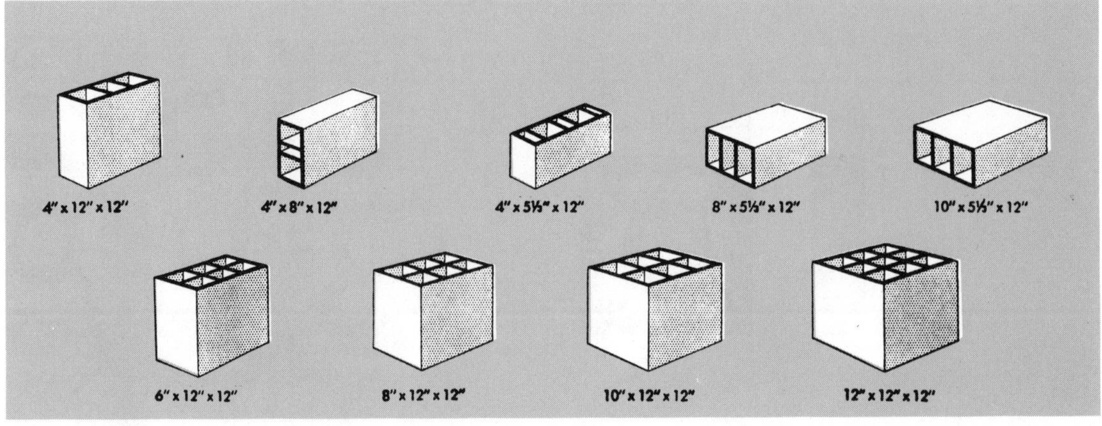

Quantities of Brick Needed for 100 Sq. Ft. of Wall Area

(Based on standard-sized brick—2⅔″ × 4″ × 8″—with a ½″ mortar joint. Overall measurement of 2¾″ plus for brick and joint.)

Type of wall	*Quantity per 100 sq. ft.*
1. Single course wall, brick set on edge	399
2. Single course wall, brick laid flat	616
3. Double course wall, solid 8″ wall	1232
4. Triple course wall, solid 12″ wall	1848

NOTE: Most brick veneers facing a backing-up course of concrete, cement, or cinder blocks, or frame construction will be a single course, laid flat, as in line 2 above. It is possible to set the bricks on edge as in line 1 above. A variation of the 8-inch wall is the Rolok or the Flemish Rolok wall (see illustrations in Chapter 12), which will make a light but strong hollow wall.

Clay tile. Favored for use as flooring and for facing pools, making wall designs, and patterned walks, clay tile had been out of fashion for some time, except for use in bathrooms and for floors in public places, but now it is definitely back in favor, with many exciting and beautiful new interpretations and many new uses being advocated. It is a most durable and permanent material; in museums we can see tile and mosaics from Roman and pre-Roman remains which are as beautiful today as they were when they were laid. Many beautiful designs can be worked out with small tiles and bits of tiles; mosaic work as fine as embroidery can be achieved by artists in this field. For tabletops, garden seats, and as inserts in walls, tiles which are glazed or unglazed, painted or molded, or in plain colors are all excellent. For anyone interested in pursuing this line I suggest research in books on Spanish and Portuguese architecture and gardens to see how interestingly tiles were used. Some of the modern books on how to make mosaic may also give inspiration and assistance in the creation of new design approaches with ceramic tiles.

CHAPTER 12

HOW TO LAY MASONRY

Because the first thing to be done after the wall units have arrived and you are ready to build your wall is to make ready the mortar, I shall consider that job first, assuming that suitable footings for the wall have been prepared. (See Chapter 14.)

Good mortar is strong mortar and therefore of the utmost importance. If it is carefully made, with the ingredients precisely measured so that the formula is correct, and the materials thoroughly blended, then the mortar should be as nearly perfect as it is humanly possible to make it. The perfect mortar should be wet enough so that the masonry units cannot rob it of too much moisture (this will be discussed later on); should contain enough lime so that it will spread well without losing its adhesiveness; and should be composed of *fresh* ingredients which are free from impurities. The water should not be heavily alkaline or contain salts, for either of these two elements will tend to reduce its strength.

MORTAR FORMULA

If you have only a small amount of masonry work to do, it may be to your advantage to buy Sakrete mortar mix or one of the other commercially prepared mixtures in which the sand and cement have been blended in the proper proportions. This way you need to buy only what you need. For all except very large jobs, it is probably best to use these convenient mixes, because of the time saved in measuring out quantities and the fact that preblending has been done by the manufacturer. All that is needed is water in quantities specified on the package and mixing according to directions there, too. A strong, durable mortar results. One sack will lay about 50 bricks.

In cases where larger quantities of mortar are needed, it will be much more economical to buy sand, cement, and lime in the quantities needed and mix it according to the formula below. That is, of course, where quantities of more than a single bag of cement are required and the aggregates or sand exceed a half load. Use portland cement for the formula ingredient. It should be fresh and clean, with the bags unbroken, and should be stored in a dry place. Be sure to keep the bags *off the floor or ground* and in a *dry building*. Bags, although fairly moisture-proof, will absorb moisture from concrete floors or from the soil and this will cause the cement to harden or to deteriorate. Should you ever find any lumps in the cement which cannot be crushed with your fingers, it will be well to discard the cement and buy some fresh bags. The sand used should be free of soil, weeds, twigs, and other plant or animal matter. Unwashed beach sand should not be used, or the strength of the mortar will be affected. Beach sand itself is perfectly good to use, provided it has been *thoroughly washed* with fresh water to cleanse it of silt and salt.

Commercial hydraulic hydrated lime should be used to increase the workability of the mortar and also to augment its waterproof qualities.

Although many formulas for mortar have been developed, the Brick Institute of America specifies this simple one for home projects. It will serve for most brick, block, and tile work. Sand should be dry, with the cement and lime free from lumps. Enough mortar will result for laying 40 bricks. That is about all you can handle in one mixing.

1 shovel portland cement
¼ shovel hydrated lime
3 shovels fine clean sand
water to achieve the consistency of soft mud

For plain (not reinforced) masonry you may use up to 1¼ parts hydrated lime or lime putty to increase cookability of the mortar. Mix the ingredients well until they have sufficiently integrated so that the mixture is a uniform brownish-gray color. Then, into a depression scooped out of the center of the dry heap, pour a *little* water; mix it in well; then add more and again mix well. *Never* add a large quantity. It may be too much and make the morter soggy and too wet. By adding water bit by bit you can get it to just the proper point and then stop. In mortar-making, unlike in concrete, you should carefully add all the water you can while keeping the mortar workable. While the water tends to weaken the resulting mortar, it increases bond, and that's even more important. The ideal mixture is wet enough to spread easily but not so wet that it is loose and will spread like cream. If it is the consistency of putty, stiff enough to stand by itself without collapsing yet wet enough to be easily spread and worked by a trowel, it will be just right. Observe professional masons at work, if you can, and take note of the look of the mortar consistency they are using.

Let me emphasize that not too much mortar should be made up at any one time because it begins to set within two hours, and in hot summer weather or warm areas it will set even sooner. Therefore you should mix only enough to use for an hour or so of work (probably two bucketfuls will be enough until you see how your speed and proficiency work out). Once mortar has begun to set, never add water to soften it or you will find that the strength is decreased and the mortar probably ruined. However, if mortar starts to stiffen because some of the mixing water has evaporated, you can retemper it by carefully adding a little more water and remixing. But if the mortar is 2½ hours old, throw it away and make a fresh batch.

Mix the mortar in an old tub, in a bucket, on a wooden platform made of scrap lumber or a piece of outdoor plywood. Best of all, perhaps, is a metal wheelbarrow, which will not be harmed by the mixing and can be cleaned afterward quite easily. Use a garden hoe in mixing if the quantity will permit it, pulling it through the ingredients to distribute the moisture and to stir up dry particles scraped from the bottom of the heap. In measuring out the ingredients it is imperative to use the same container for *all* of them, wet or dry. Let us point out, too, that the mixed quantity will turn out to be a little less than the total of the dry quantities, the reason being that the small particles of cement and lime fit in between the sand particles when well mixed and liquefied. Keep the decrease in mind when mixing any specific amount, and try always to mix a little more than is needed to be sure to have enough.

WETTING BRICK OR TILE

All brick and clay tile should be thoroughly moistened before being laid so that a minimum of moisture will be extracted from the mortar by the dry bricks or tiles, thus keeping it strong and durable. On the other hand, there should be no free water visible on the units when laid, either, or they may not bond properly with the mortar. Some pull between the two is desirable.

Stack the masonry units in convenient small piles along the site of the wall where they can be easily reached for use (the mortar may harden if you have to run with your wheelbarrow for another load of bricks to complete the wall). You may stack them loosely or merely pile them in a heap. Professional masons usually stand behind a wall when building and often stack the bricks there, but you may find it easier to reach over the wall to get your bricks until it rises high enough to make that impossible.

By placing a hose with its nozzle adjusted to a fine spray so that it will play on the brick pile for about 15 minutes before you use them, the bricks will be sufficiently moistened. Or, if it is more convenient, fill an old washtub with water and stack the bricks in it, letting them soak for at least a half hour before using them. Bricks should be removed and allowed to drain and dry a little, so that there is no free water on the units when laid, for proper bonding, as detailed above.

Concrete blocks should *never* be wet down before being laid, however, for wetting makes them expand and if laid wet, they may contract when drying out, and crack the wall. Store them where they will stay dry and can be laid up dry; buying them wet is a hazard we must face, but if they are spread out to dry in the sun for several days, with covering of sheet plastic applied if there is rain or snow and also if they are covered at night to protect them from dew, they will be dried out thoroughly before being laid. Protect a wall in progress by covering it with polyethylene plastic or strips of roofing paper or some other adequate covering, thus keeping it dry and allowing it to cure properly and avoid cracks.

FOOTINGS AND FIRST COURSES

Concrete footings should first be constructed as detailed in Chapter 14, for footings and some sort of foundation will be necessary in all cases except those where a wall is only two or three bricks aboveground. A thin footing of concrete on a 3-inch bed of tamped cinders or gravel will usually prove sufficient to support such a wall. For warm climates, running two or three courses below ground level should suffice. The foundation and footing in cold climates should run sufficiently below ground level to prevent frost from heaving the wall, and to provide a firm foundation. Use a footing where the soil is light or unstable. This will keep the wall from tilting and cracking.

The primary courses are extremely important, for unless they are kept level (unevenness occurring in casting footings can be compensated for in the first few courses by varying the depth of the bed of mortar) all of the succeeding courses are likely to be out of plumb, and may even increase the error. Therefore spend time and care on the first courses, and the others will be kept in line more easily, with the corners square and plumb and the joint lines straight and even. Decide before you begin how high the wall is to be, and set a stake marked at the proper height to act as a guide. Also consider what the thickness should be: one brick, two bricks, or whatever size of block you will need to bear loads or withstand weights and pressures (as in the case of retaining walls). Low walls up to about a foot high may be built one brick thick—except for retaining walls—but any wall of seat height or higher should be two bricks thick, or else made up of backing-up blocks, hollow tile, or concrete, which may be veneered or faced with bricks. Veneer courses should be tied in with the back-up courses by means of corrugated metal called tie strips or veneer ties. Header courses can be used to tie the back-up and veneer together where brick back-up is used. See page 260.

Walls of waist height or higher should be three bricks in thickness if they are to be retaining walls; standard 8-inch blocks may be used if they are to be the finished face of the wall. The higher the wall the greater will be the need for strength. Steel rods may be used for bracing, either by inserting them through the holes in bricks or by grouting them into the hollow cores of blocks every third or fourth core or so in high walls, thus lending strength to the wall, and assisting it to hold back the weight and pressures of soil-when the wall is a retaining wall. A single course of brick veneer facing a cast concrete backing-up will be less likely to shiftand crack if the concrete has been reinforced with horizontal reinforcing rods,or by a combination of horizontal and vertical rods. These are called *rebars*.

HOW TO LAY BRICKS

Whatever you may be going to use for building, the basic technique used in laying bricks will be your guide; for with blocks or hollow tile, or any other material, the procedure is very much the same.

First lay out a course of bricks along the foundation, which has been cast quite level and smooth. Lay them in a header course (see the upcoming joint drawings of header and stretcher courses) with about ½ inch left between bricks to allow space for mortar joints. This procedure is called "chasing out the bond" and will permit you to figure exactly the number of bricks you'll need per course. If you have a two-brick-thick wall, lay out a second course stretcher-style on top of this first one, with a back-up course behind it and centered on the facing course. This will let you figure how many bricks you will need for courses of this kind. If your courses can be adapted to even brick lengths you will save considerable time and energy by not having to cut bricks to odd lengths to fill out the courses.

If your wall is to be only a single brick in thickness, first lay a header course—bricks laid crosswise, not end to end. An exception is the SCR brick. Atop the header course and on succeeding courses, lay bricks end to end—stretcher courses—centered on the header bed course. No header courses will be necessary in succeeding courses in single-brick walls. In multiple-brick thicknesses, header courses are placed at intervals to tie the walls together and to give a certain decorative effect; or bricks may be inserted as headers in stretcher courses, singly or in multiples, for decorative patterned effects. See the illustrations for English Bond, Flemish Bond, Diaper Pattern, and Rolok walls.

In single-brick walls you can achieve the same effect by cutting bricks in half and using them in the same patterns.

After you have noted the number of bricks needed for the various courses and transported a corresponding number to the vicinity of the wall where they can be easily reached, you are ready to start the final operations. Set a stake at each end of the wall and run a mason's line between them to give you the *exact* line of the face of the wall. You can butt every course of bricks against the line to ensure straightness and plumbness in each succeeding course, raising it as each course is completed. The correctness of the succeeding courses will depend upon the correctness of this first course.

USING THE MORTAR PROPERLY

When your mortar is mixed and ready for use, place about a pailful on a piece of

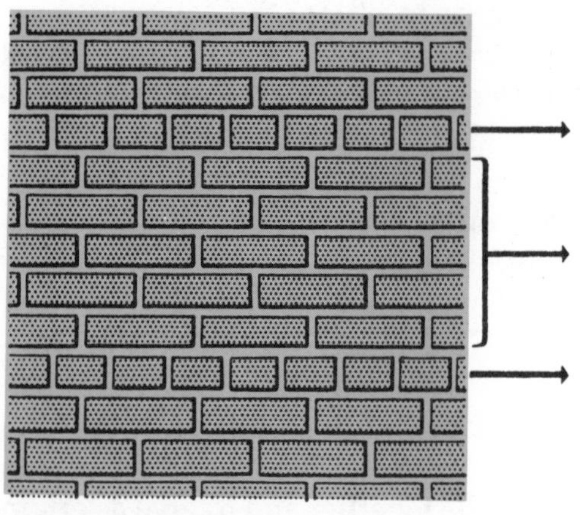

COMMON BOND

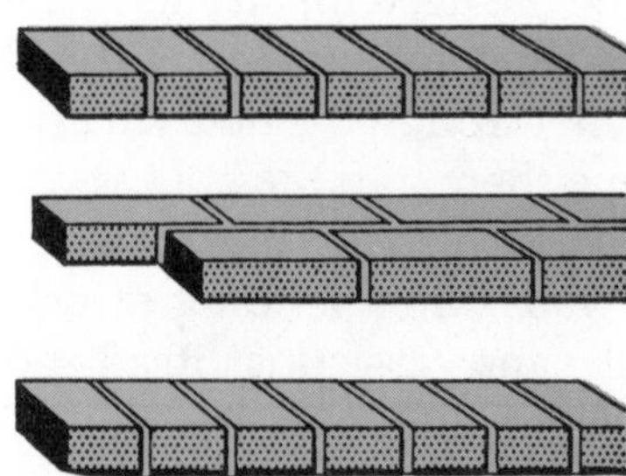

Placing header courses every fifth, sixth, or seventh course ties double stretchers together for strength. Easiest, cheapest to build.

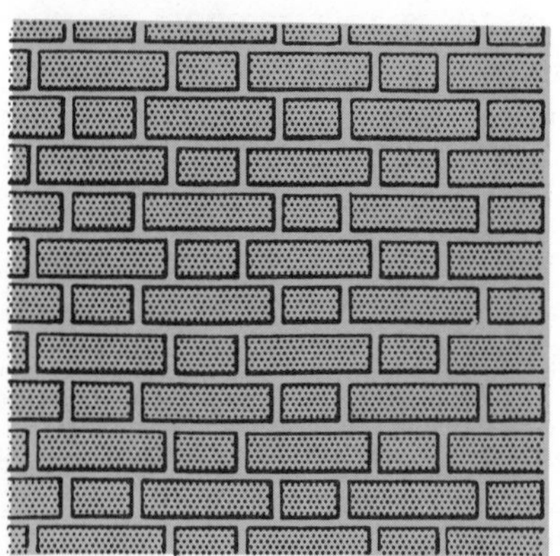

ENGLISH BOND

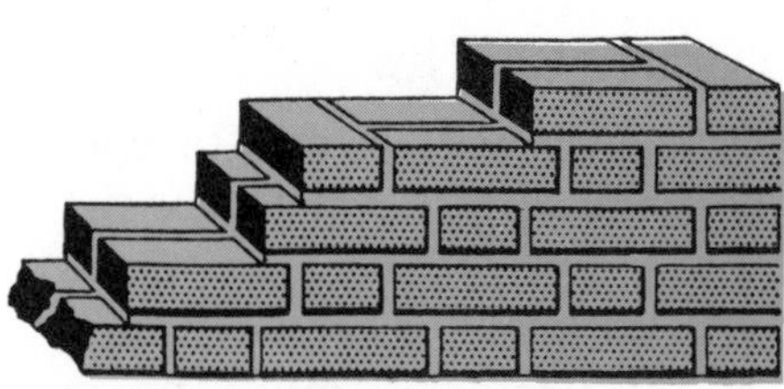

Header and stretcher courses alternate. Care must be exercised to keep vertical joints thin, to maintain proper spacing of headers.

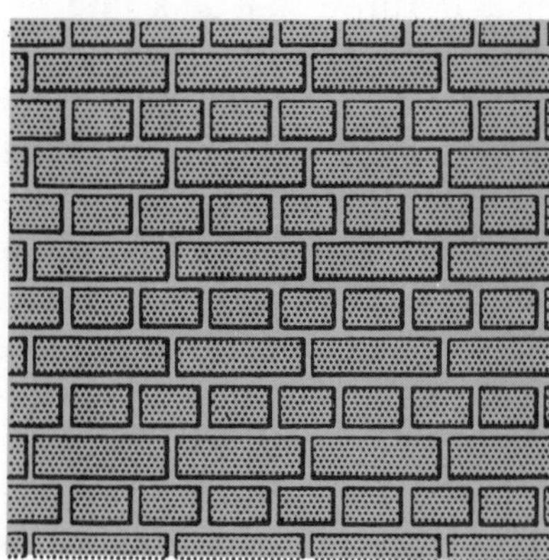

FLEMISH BOND

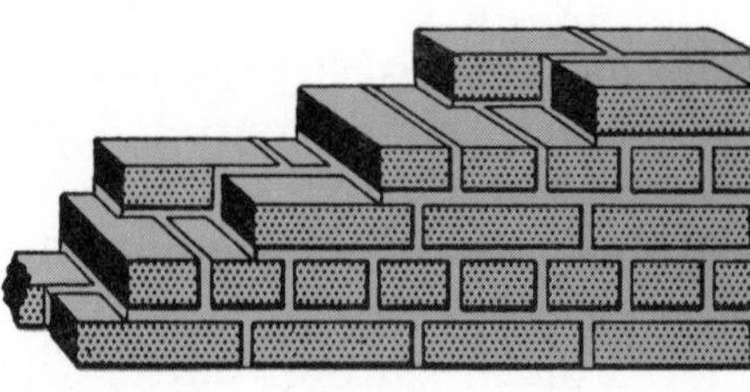

Headers and stretchers alternate in same courses, each header being centered on a stretcher above and below. Easy to lay.

DIAPER PATTERN

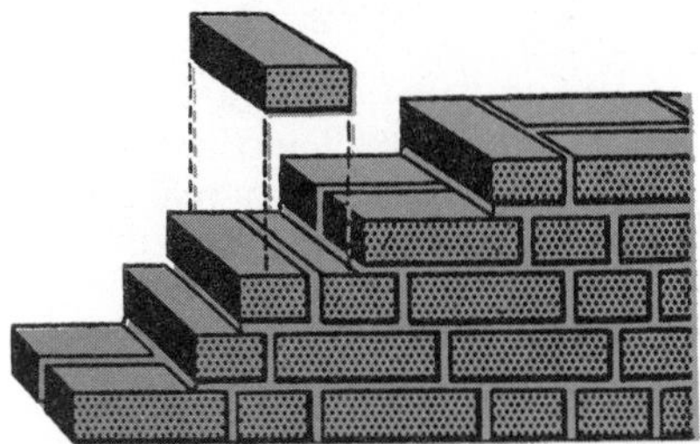

Header courses are staggered to produce the diamond shape shown here, darker or lighter headers being used to emphasize the pattern.

ROLOK WALL

The header courses are laid flat with all of the stretcher courses laid on edge leaving a generous insulating air space between them.

FLEMISH ROLOK

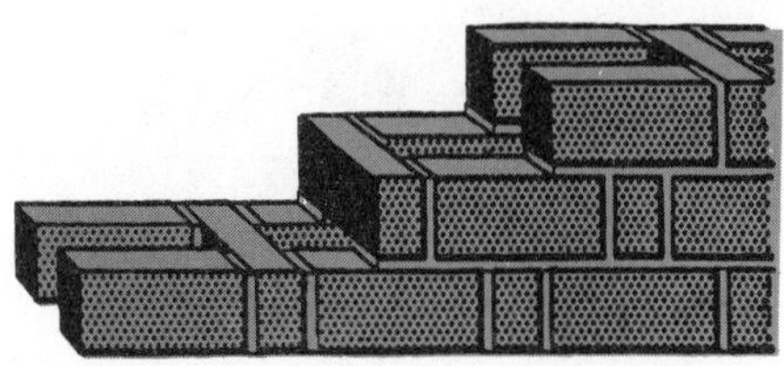

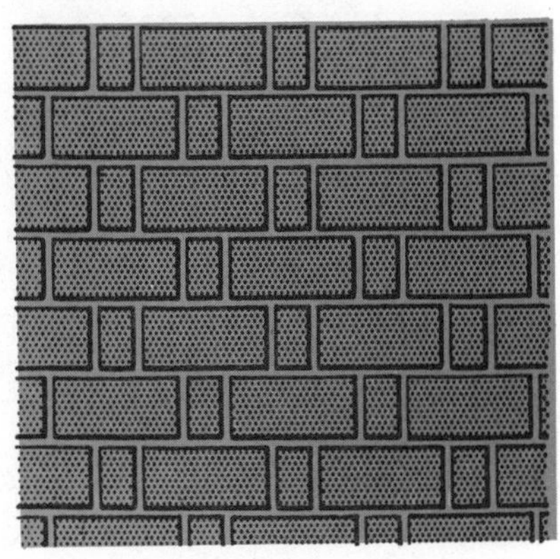

This variation of Flemish bond makes a good-looking wall, very strong and with the added value of insulating air between stretchers.

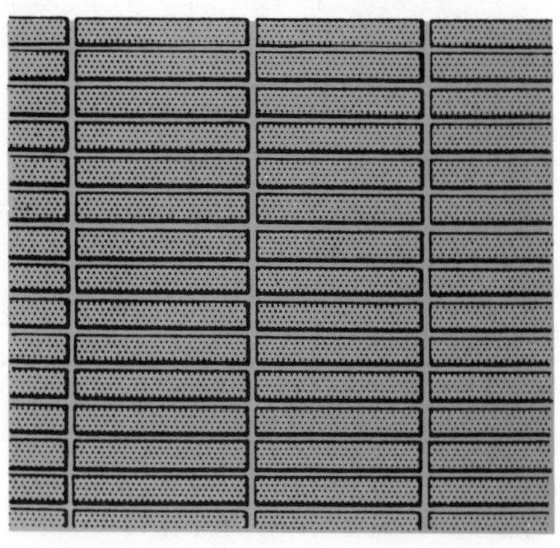

ROMAN BRICK

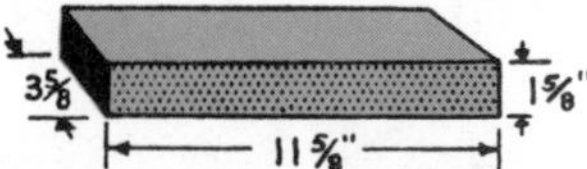

Increasingly popular is the use of Roman brick, a longer, shallower unit patterned on bricks used thousands of years ago in Rome. Although sizes vary with manufacturer and material, dimensions will be near those shown.

STACKED BOND

Bricks set above each other; although interesting in pattern, vertical joints need to be tied together frequently to obtain strength.

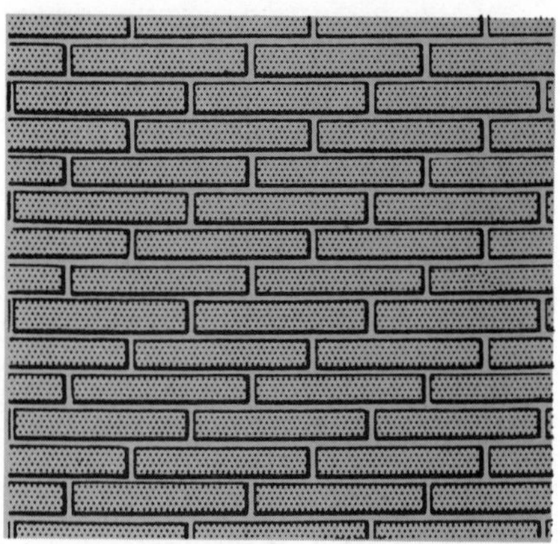

ONE-THIRD BOND

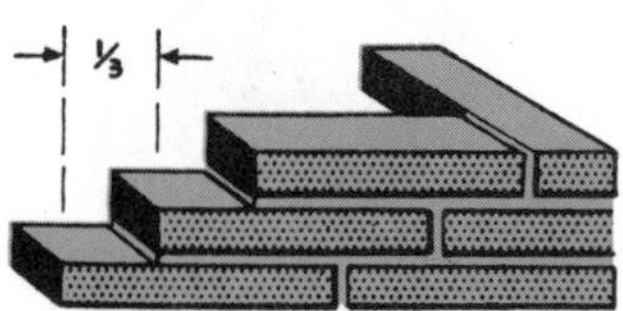

Bricks laid with each succeeding course one-third across from those in original course; joints make a pleasing diagonal line in wall.

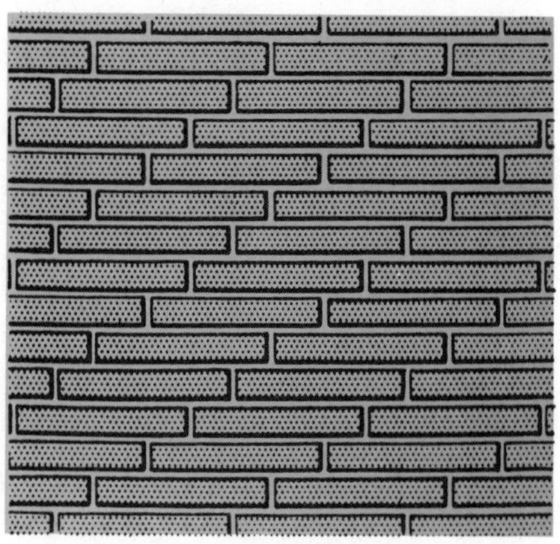

ONE-FOURTH BOND

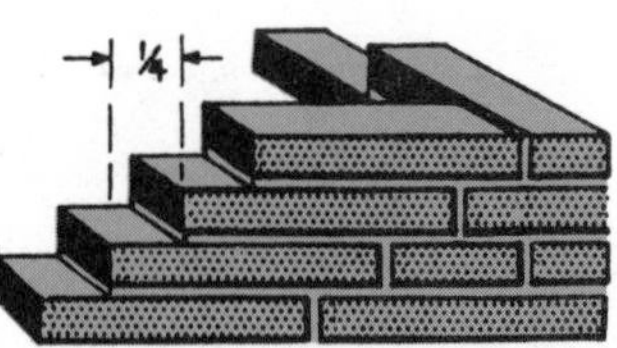

Bricks laid with each succeeding course one-quarter across from that of original course, the joints forming a steeper diagonal line.

plywood 20 to 24 inches square and set it on a box or on the ground where you can easily reach it with your trowel. Scoop up a trowelful and begin at one end of the wall (removing the first course of the dry run of bricks as you go) to spread a layer of mortar about ½ inch or so thick on the foundation or footing for about the space (for a header course) of four or five bricks—from 20 to 24 inches along the foundation. This is called a bed joint and mortar should be spread so that it centers on the foundation or footing. Modern techniques call for a flattish mortar surface, perhaps tapering a little from side to side, to give a firm bedding. In succeeding courses, never spread more mortar than you can quickly cover with the bricks—20 to 30 inches, depending on your speed, skill, and weather conditions—for mortar begins to set very rapidly, especially in hot, dry weather. Bricks laid on a partially set mortar bed may make a weak bonding with it.

Then put the corner brick in place, setting it so that the face is laid squarely against the stretched line. The second brick to be laid, and all succeeding bricks in each course, will require one other operation. They must be "buttered" on one end before being set in place so that the vertical or "head" joint is filled with mortar. The method is simple: Simply scoop up enough mortar on the tip of the trowel to cover the side or end of the brick with about ½ inch of mortar and wipe it off the trowel onto the brick. After a few tries you will find out which is the best way to hold the brick, to fill the trowel tip with mortar, and to slide it off on the brick. Only experience can perfect your technique. Buttering will be used in all kinds of masonry work, and it should be perfected and made efficient so that you can swing into the work and complete it with dispatch and precision.

Once the brick is buttered, it should be slipped lightly into place on the mortar bed with a kind of swinging motion to butt it against the previously laid brick so that the mortar is squeezed out and the joints—both bed and head—are about ½ inch thick. Never place the brick on the bed mortar and then attempt to force in mortar for the head joint—it will never be easy or successful, although outwardly it may look so for a time. Also, if the brick is not successfully bedded the first time, do not remove it and then just replace it. Either add fresh mortar to the packed-down bed joint or scrape off the bedding mortar and replace it with a fresh lot, rebuttering the end on the brick, too. Not replacing the mortar or freshening it can only lead to failure of the joint—and any wall is only as strong as its weakest joint.

If, however, when the brick is swung into place and laid, it is slightly out of line or a little high at one end, it can be tapped lightly with the handle of the trowel to bring it into place. A little practice will give you the feel in your wrist of how hard to tap the bricks to bring them into place without dislodging them or squeezing out so much mortar that the brick is then too low.

When the wall is about half laid, move operations to the other end and begin there, laying the bricks in reverse order, working carefully and keeping the faces butted against the stretched line until only one more brick remains to be laid in the center. This is called the closure brick. Butter both ends of that final brick and gently slide it into place, tapping it lightly down with the trowel handle until it is

HOW TO MIX MORTAR AND LAY BRICKS

The simplest way to make good mortar is to use a ready-packaged mortar mix. First, mix dry in a container such as this single-project cardboard mortar box, using a hoe. Add water in the amount stated on the package.

Mix in the water until the mortar is uniform in color and consistency. Mixing may be done on the push and the pull strokes of the hoe. Unlike concrete, mortar needs as much water as it can take, yet still remain stiff enough to support the units.

Mixing may also be done in a wheelbarrow or on a concrete slab. Form a pocket in the center of the pile for the water before adding the water and then mixing it.

A five-gallon-pail power mixer is a good size for making mortar without hand-mixing. Add the dry materials first, then add the water while the drum rotates. The pail lifts out for carrying mixed mortar to the mortarboard.

When using mortar from the mortarboard, periodically slice through it with the mason's trowel to keep it soft and workable. Scooping it up and throwing it back onto the mortarboard also helps restore workability.

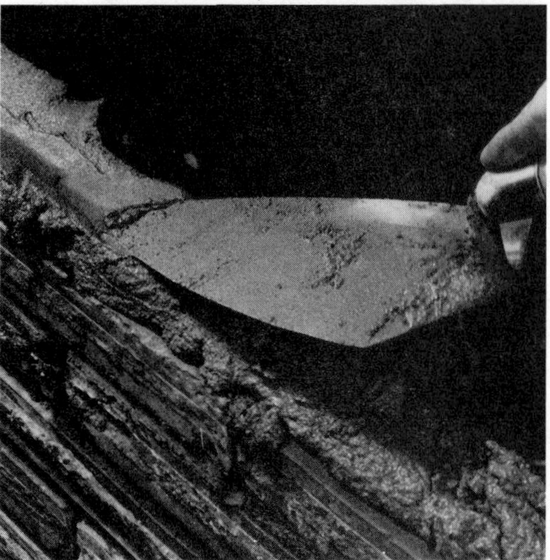

To lay bricks, place some workable mortar on top of the last laid course and furrow it with the point of the trowel. Furrowing concentrates the mortar at the edges, ensuring full bed joints.

Then with the trowel held at an angle, slice off excess mortar along both sides. Mortar sliced off may be returned to the mortarboard for another use.

(Continued on next page)

Now you can lay bricks in the freshly placed mortar bed. Tap each brick down until it is level across and its top edge is aligned with the string. Finally, scrape off the excess mortar flush with the wall.

In bricklaying, the corner bricks are laid plumb, one above the other, and used as guides for laying the in-between ones. Stretch a taut stringline between two corners.

A brick wall is only as strong as the bond between mortar and bricks. To check the bond, remove a brick about an hour after laying it. If the brick breaks cleanly away from the mortar, the bond is poor.

For a stronger bond try using the mortar with a wetter consistency and dampening the bricks shortly before you lay them. If the break comes in the mortar itself (more like this), you're getting a better bond.

A pair of mason's blocks is handy for holding the stringline at the corners. The blocks may be made of metal, plastic, or wood.

You can make your own joint-raking tool from a wood block and a 16d common nail. Rake the nailhead in the mortar joint to scrape out mortar to nailhead depth.

bedded properly. Be sure that the head joints are filled and tightly packed.

With the blade of the trowel, trim off the excess mortar squeezed out in bedding the bricks, so that the joints are flush with the bricks. Don't tool the joints immediately, for the mortar may be too wet and fresh to hold the shape given it by the tool. On the other hand, don't wait long or the mortar may have set too firmly to be successfully and easily tooled. This is a part of masonry work for which no exact time limit can be given, because of climate, weather, season, and other intangibles. Trial and experience will guide you to the exact time for tooling; but it may comfort the novice to know that there is usually plenty of leeway for tooling before the mortar is too set to allow it to be done. Tooling will not only shape the joint and remove excess mortar, but it will also compress the remaining mortar, making a good, weather-tight joint which will add to the textural beauty of the wall. (See illustrations in Chapter 13.)

Header courses and soldier courses necessitate a slight change of operation. Header courses are those courses in which the ends of the bricks face the finished face of the wall, as noted earlier, with the wide measure of the end laid *horizontally*. Soldier courses are those in which the wide measure of the end of the brick is laid *vertically*, or those in which the brick is stood up on its end when laid. In both of these instances the buttering will be done so that the side of the brick which butts against its neighbor is covered and makes a head joint.

HOW TO CUT BRICKS

Occasionally it may be necessary to cut a brick to fit a particular space in the wall: either to fill the final space between the last two bricks in a course, or to space out a course so that it ends properly for a window, a door, a gate, or some other opening. There is a good and a bad way to do everything. The bad way to cut a brick is to hit it with the mason's hammer and hope for the best. While some professionals become very adept at this, the amateur can waste a good many bricks and consume a good deal of time trying to learn the trick. Instead, I advocate the following method, which will cut bricks evenly and with little danger of their breaking and wasting good material.

Score the brick all the way around to a depth of about ⅛ inch at the juncture desired for the cut. Use a cold chisel for this and use a carpenter's try square, if you wish, as a straightedge. Then put the brick on a flat, firm surface, place the broad mason's chisel vertically on the scoring, and rap it smartly with the hammer. This should cause the brick to break evenly and squarely along the scored groove. For rough work, such as for cutting a brick for a backing-up course, you may use the mason's hammer to strike the brick and chip off a portion of it, but this is seldom precise and is never as satisfactory as the scoring method for facing courses. Should there be any excessive irregularities on the broken-off brick, they can be chipped down by using the chisel-like blade of the mason's hammer.

SUCCEEDING COURSES

Always start at each end of the wall and build up four or five courses tapering up to the corners; then lay the courses in the intervening areas. When the wall is about level, build up the corners again for a few courses and repeat until the eventual height of the wall is reached. When a course is laid between corners, it should be kept level by using the mason's line as a guide. Always check corners with the mason's level as they are built up, or use a plumb bob to keep corners and wall vertical. To keep horizontal courses level, attach a line level to the tautly stretched line in the center, thus preventing the need for frequent use of the mason's level. Always, when moving the line up to the next course, be sure that it is securely fastened to the corner pieces and is tautly stretched and level, so that the succeeding courses will be straight and true. Check the face of the wall and the corners frequently to be sure they are kept in plumb, for slight leanings have a way of becoming exaggerated as the wall grows higher.

Should you be called away in the middle of the job or have to stop when the light fails in the evening, be sure to tool the joints and to clean off all mortar first so that you can make a good fresh start with the bed joints next day. Cover the wall with sacking or building paper, weighting it so that wind will not dislodge it. If you have to leave without tooling the joints, wet a burlap bag or other cloth with water and cover the wall to prevent the mortar's drying too quickly. But don't delay any longer than you must, for mortar sets quickly and you may not be able to tool the joints cleanly if you procrastinate. Keeping a bucket of water handy so that you can wash off the tool and keep it wet will help to give good, cleanly tooled joints. Always try to finish a section of wall completely, having bricks bedded and set, joints tooled and finished before leaving the job. Then you will have a good, clean, well-built wall.

When you have finished the final course—usually a cap course or soldier course—finish the tooling of joints; then use the side of the trowel blade to scrape off any bits of mortar which may have dropped or splashed onto the face of the wall. Do this while they are still fresh and can be easily removed. Then let the wall cure for about two weeks before the final process.

CLEANING THE WALL

Clean excess mortar and splashes from faces of all walls as you go along. A bristle bench brush will probably do it while mortar is fresh. Later, a wire brush will be required. Stubborn smears on block walls can be removed by rubbing with a piece of broken block. Brick walls may be completely cleared of mortar stains (and also of the white efflorescence that sometimes appears later on brick masonry) by applying a wash of hydrochloric acid—also called muriatic acid—in a *mild* solution. *This should be handled with care*: in its undiluted state it will dissolve and injure concrete and mortar and even in dilution will eat holes in clothing, damage painted surfaces, eat paint film, and puncture galvanized pails and other metal receptacles. Therefore it should be mixed in a plastic pail. Wear old clothing, rubber gloves, and eye-protection. Should the solution be spilled, immediately flush the area with plenty of clear water. Hosing it down will be best, if this is possible. If any splashes come in contact with the skin, they should immediately be rinsed off with lots of water and a saturate solution of bicarbonate of soda applied. To the cautious worker this would indicate the need for having a hose, a bucket of water, and some bicarbonate of soda handy while the acid is being used, just in case they might be needed.

The strength of solution recommended is 10 parts of water to 1 part of acid. Use a stiff old broom or a rag tied to a stick to apply the solution to the predampened wall. When the entire wall has been washed down with the acid, begin hosing it down with water, flushing it well from top to bottom. Should any blobs of mortar or splashes of cement still show, spot treatment with the acid will eventually remove them. Remember that mortar joints may also be affected by this acid solution if it is allowed to stay on them for very long, weakening them and leaving them open to weathering damage. Therefore it will be well to do any large walls in sections, hosing down before going on to the next section. If efflorescence reappears in a few months or a year, you can give the wall another bath of the acid solution, which should clear up the trouble and prevent its happening again.

FINAL TIPS ON LAYING BRICKS

Where walls of two or more bricks in thickness are to be laid, the back-up courses are always staggered so that the head joints do not coincide with those on the face course. (See Common Bond drawing earlier in this chapter.) They are usually centered on the face course so that at the end of the wall or on corners the bricks will fit neatly and require a minimum of cutting. Succeeding courses are staggered similarly, with no head joints, or as few as possible, running through the width of the wall. Headers, as well as header courses, are an exception to this,

Specially cast blocks can be found for almost any purpose. These shown are made for building round columns with four blocks and rounded-corner walls using one block.

of course. Half bricks are used in the back-up courses where individual headers are called for by bonding pattern, being placed on either side of the header so as not to upset the staggering.

Back-up courses are buttered both on the end for the half-brick header and on the side which is adjacent to the facing course. Some professional masons butter only the end, and after the brick is laid and head joint set they throw in a little thin mortar to fill the intermediate joint between facing and back-up courses. I do not advocate this procedure because I feel it is not reliable; and in addition it requires the mixing of a second, thinner batch of mortar. I feel that the method detailed above is better; any mortar which is squeezed out from the head joint or the intermediate joint can be left to become part of the next course's bed joint, provided that more mortar can be laid on to make the bed before the squeezed-out mortar sets.

You may not wish to buy the line blocks given in the tool list (Chapter 10), and you may in this case use nails shoved into the bed joints near the corner on which to attach the mason's line for keeping courses level. This method is more trouble, but it can successfully be used.

When laying bricks in a curve or in a

small circle with a short radius, it may be necessary to cut the ends on an angle to avoid wide, ugly head joints. Therefore it is a good plan not to use too small a radius for the curve line unless it is absolutely necessary. It will be even worse when you reach the cap or soldier courses, for here the problem will be magnified if the entire length of each brick must be cut. About 3 feet would be the minimum radius recommended; a greater size would be preferable.

HOW TO LAY BLOCKS AND HOLLOW TILE

Even though the various blocks and hollow clay tile are much larger than bricks and differ in having hollow cores, the basic method of laying is really quite similar. Because they are larger units you may find them easier to lay in some ways, and the wall will grow much faster than is the case when bricks are used, due to their large unit size. They are usually set in single stretcher courses with a simple running bond—courses overlapping by half with the head joints centered on the block in the course below. Decorative patterns may be achieved by varying the laying or by using various-sized units, as shown in the accompanying illustrations.

Unlike bricks, concrete blocks have tapered inner cores, the top side being thicker-walled than the bottom side. Blocks are usually shipped and stored right-side-up, but if not, you should invert them for easier handling. The center web of the block, when the thick part is topside, makes a neat "handle" for lifting it.

Blocks are actually ⅜ inch smaller in each of their three dimensions than their nominal size indicates. Thus an 8″ × 8″ × 16″ standard concrete block ac-

HOW TO LAY BLOCKS

1. Mortar stiffened by moisture evaporation should be reworked; add water in small quantities, mixing and testing before adding more. Discard all mortar not used within 2½ hours of original mix at temperatures over 80° F; within 3½ hours when temperatures are below 80° F.

2. Professional masons always make sure that mortar is sticky enough to adhere to concrete blocks being laid in walls. A quick vertical snap of the wrist makes mortar stick to trowel, keeps it from falling off the trowel as mortar is applied ("buttered") on edges of block.

(Continued next page)

BLOCK LAYING *(Continued)*

3. Concrete blocks have tapered inner cores so that every block has a top and a bottom. The bottom (left) has thinner walls than the top (right), which presents wider spaces for laying mortar. Also, the center web is thickened at the top forming a "handle" for lifting and placing the block.

4. The first course of blocks should be laid out dry (without mortar) on the footing with its end joints spaced ⅜ inch apart. A piece of plywood that thickness makes a handy spacing tool. Dry layout ensures that the wall comes out the right length and permits joint adjustments, if necessary.

5. Check the layout of wall by setting out blocks first for accuracy of layout and dimensions; then spread a full mortar bed, wider than wall, and furrow it with trowel as shown to ensure plenty of mortar for blocks to rest on, complete coverage, and a good tight joint.

6. Carefully position the first corner block in mortar bedding and tap it down level in both directions and to proper height. Tapping may be done with the trowel handle (but mortar falls onto your hand) or the hammer handle.

7. An aid in getting corners to the desired elevation is a marked stick called a story pole. Make story pole marks exactly 8 inches apart to place block courses at those intervals. This allows for ⅜" mortar joints.

8. Subsequent blocks are buttered with two strips of mortar along each outer edge. The strips stick better if you slice the trowel downward across the block's edge.

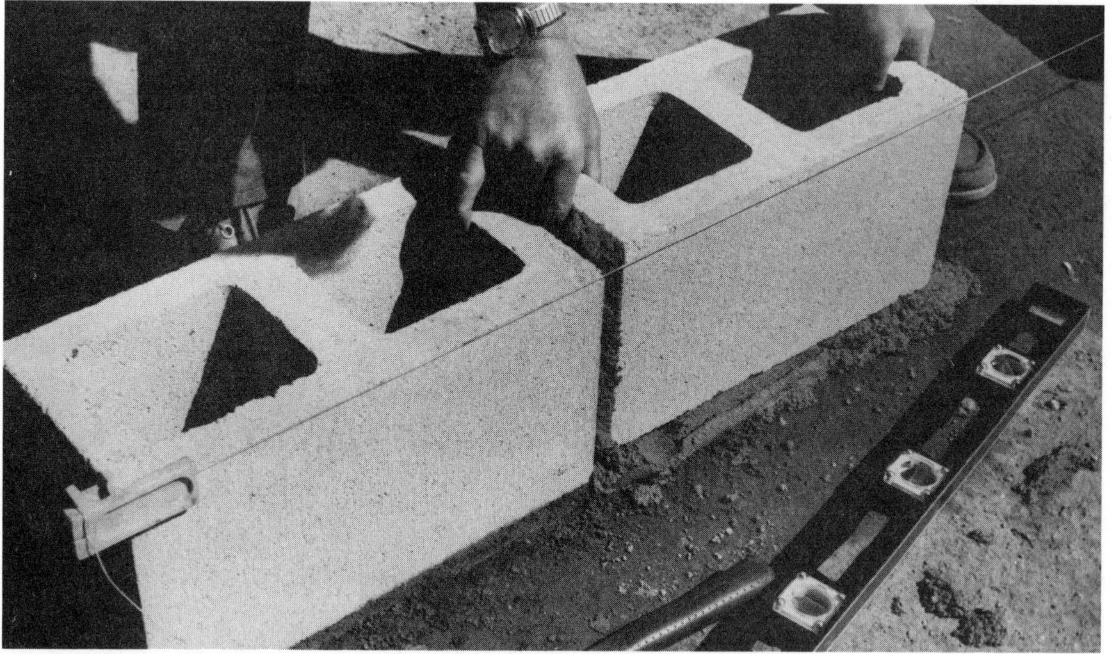

9. Then lay the block against the corner block, pushing it well down into the mortar bed as well as against the corner block to leave a ⅜" end joint. Tap it down level and aligned with the stringline between corner blocks.

(Continued next page)

BLOCK LAYING *(Continued)*

10. In building up corners several courses ahead of the in-between blocks, use a level to align blocks. Tap gently with a mason's hammer to nudge the blocks into position.

11. After the block is aligned, tap it down level with the corner block. Once the stringline can be set up, it takes the place of aligning and leveling the blocks lengthwise.

12. Even though laid to a stringline, blocks need to be leveled across. Place the level as shown and tap the block to center the bubble. If the block sinks below the stringline, pull it out and lay it again with fresh mortar. With some practice you can level a block both ways at once.

13. Blocks in succeeding courses are placed to overlap joints in the course below. Set ribbons of mortar on the tops of blocks below, working only one or two blocks at a time so the mortar doesn't stiffen before you lay a block in it.

14. Lay and align the second-course corner block with the corner below but at right angles to it. This way, corner blocks interlock for strength all the way up the wall. If the corners are plumb, the whole wall will be plumb.

15. Lay up corners first, four to five courses, checking each corner at each course for horizontal alignment, for horizontal level as above, and for plumb. Work courses from the corners to make sure blocks are in the same vertical plane.

16. The secret of good masonry is continual checking to make sure the wall is plumb. Check corners at every course, plumbing both sides of the wall. Between corners, use either a level or a straightedge as courses are laid to make certain blocks are kept in the same plane.

17. In building corners, step each course back half a block—that is, the end of each course has the next block laid crosswise. Check horizontal spacing by placing level diagonally across corners of blocks to be sure that they align.

(Continued next page)

BLOCK LAYING *(Continued)*

18. To complete courses, a final *closure* block must be laid between corners. Butter all four edges of block ends, also those of blocks on either side, to make doubly sure of a tight joint. Place the closure block. If any mortar falls out, remove the block and repeat the operation.

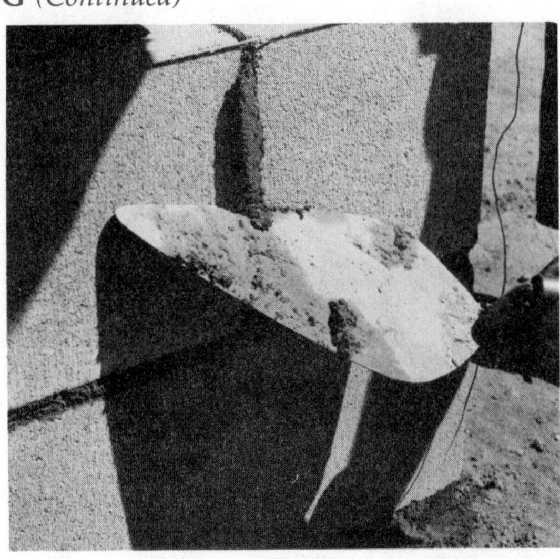

19. Cut off the excess mortar that squeezes out of the joints, using the trowel at a slight angle to the block faces. Excess mortar, even though it is dry, can be retempered with water and reused by returning it to the mortarboard. But ensure that it's not more than 1½ hours old.

20. Tool mortar joints soon as they become "thumbprint" hard. First tool the vertical joints, then the horizontal, using a long blocklayer's jointing tool. These tools come rounded (like this one) or with V-joints. Here a course of cap blocks tops off a low block wall.

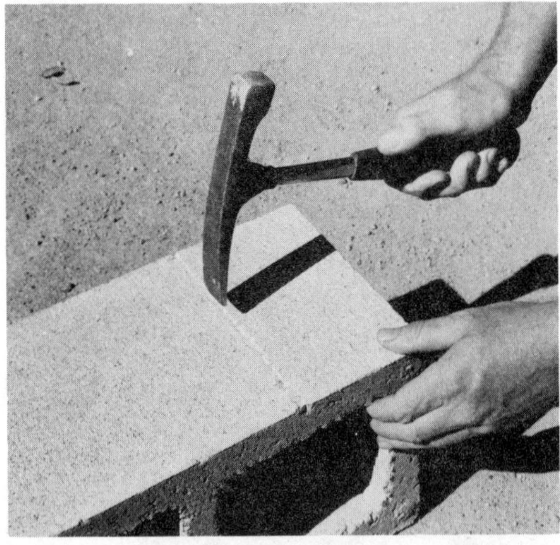

21. Try to design your projects so you can build them from full blocks and half-blocks. However, if you must, you can cut a block by first chipping score-lines opposite each other on the back and the face. Keep chipping back over the lines until the block separates. (Wear eye protection.)

22. Long block walls need control joints at about 18′ intervals. These are continuous joints all the way up the wall. To tie the separate walls together, lay pieces of ¼-inch wire mesh in each course across the vertical joint.

23. Where block cores are to be grouted, fill with concrete containing ⅜″ maximum size aggregate and strike it off on top of the wall. Grouting gives added strength to the wall and is often used in combination with vertical reinforcing bars.

24. To tie nonbearing block walls into intersecting walls, place strips of metal lath or ¼″ metal mesh across the joints in alternate courses of wall; apply mortar over it. If one wall is to be built first, place strips in the wall; then tie into the second wall as courses are laid.

tually measures 7⅝″ × 7⅝″ × 15⅝″. The difference is made up by the ⅜-inch mortar joints to make the space taken up in the wall by one standard block equal its nominal size. Thus when laying blocks, always aim for ⅜-inch mortar joints all around.

The first course of blocks should be laid on the concrete foundation on a full bedding or mortar the same as for bricks. Sometimes the first course of blocks is laid directly in the fresh footing concrete and tapped to align with a stretched string. This gives them a good deal of resistance to being pushed off the footing, as the concrete wells up inside each core to lock footing and blocks together.

The second course should be laid in a full bed of mortar, just as for bricks, except that the ends are buttered only on the outside edges. Likewise, only the front and back edges of the bedding course need be buttered, ignoring the transverse webs or partitions of the blocks. Joints may be finished off by merely scraping off excess mortar flush with the face of the wall. After the mortar has stiffened a little, the joints may be lightly tooled, as with brick joints. The V-joint is most frequently preferred for both hollow tile and cinder and concrete blocks.

Build up the corners with three or four blocks, tapering downward to the foundation, checking carefully with the level to make sure they are plumb. Stretch the mason's line well and lay each course carefully. With their greater weight, blocks are more difficult to lift and set properly, and constant vigilance must be exercised lest the wall sag or belly outward. Because of their larger unit size the chances of error increase rapidly.

Finishing the top of the wall may pose a problem because of the hollow cores in the blocks. These should be covered with a coping course of thin solid blocks called cap blocks, or with a soldier course of bricks. Coping blocks may also be used if they are obtainable; or it is possible to make a form of wood on top of the wall and cast your own coping of cement or concrete. All coping courses should overhang by 1 inch or more to carry drips out beyond the face of the wall and prevent their deteriorating or defacing it. With solid block, coping blocks, or cut stone there is no problem about finishing the top of the wall, for the front and back webs of the blocks are buttered as with any other course, and the coping course is buttered at the ends which butt against the previous block. But if brick is used, a different method may have to be employed to ensure success.

Where the wall is constructed of 6-inch blocks, the soldier course of a single row of bricks will give sufficient overhang, but where walls are wider it may be wise to use a brick and a half or Roman brick for the coping course. Where a brick and a half are used, the joints will be staggered, naturally.

MORTARLESS BLOCKS

If you've ever tried laying concrete blocks, you know that it takes patience and practice to be able to butter and lay each block and get it properly aligned in the wall with all the other blocks. It's much easier, though, with mortarless blocks. Mortarless blocks are laid dry, directly on top of each other. No mortar is used.

Modern concrete blocks are highly uniform products, made by sophisticated, computer-controlled machinery. They fit together with virtually no gaps between. Heretofore, most mortarless block systems have tried to take advantage of this uniformity by using specially shaped units with projections to lock them together in the wall. However, no system has enjoyed much success simply because the projections create immense manufacturing and shipping difficulties.

A new system of mortarless blocklaying works with regular blocks—the standard 8″ × 8″ × 16″ units that are locally made and available all over the U.S. and Canada at reasonable cost. What makes regular blocks layable without mortar are hoop-like plastic positioning devices called "yotas." Yotas fit into the block cores between courses to align and hold the blocks in the wall. When the wall is topped out, some or all of the block cores are then grouted with liquid concrete (grout and pump mix from a ready-mix producer or home brew). The yota system also works with half-high and bond-beam units, split blocks, patterned blocks, and more, as long as the blocks have two cores and are 8 inches wide. (See next page)

To build a mortarless block wall with yotas, you simply start with a level cast-concrete footing, setting ordinary concrete blocks one on top of another. Yotas fit into the block cores between courses. Later core-grouting unites the wall into a solid structure. The 5″ × 6″ concrete cores form sturdy spines up and down the wall to hold the blocks together into a structural system akin to that used in ancient pagodas. Engineers call it *concrete stud* design. It makes a wall that is able to flex without breaking.

Anyone who can heft blocks can lay up a mortarless block wall. The yota's cost per piece is very low, making the material cost run only about 20 percent more than for a wall made with mortar. Labor savings, though, are substantial. Core grouting and vertical and horizontal rein forcing requirements are the same as for a wall laid up with mortar between the blocks. The large 4½″ × 5½″ open centers of the yotas permit easy reinforcement and grouting.

The first course of blocks is set directly on the concrete footing. Yotas are then snapped into the cores of all first-course blocks. Then the second course of blocks is set on top of the first, and so on all the way up the wall. Bond-beam courses, if used, and the last course do not get yotas.

Yotas are tools, not structural members. Yotas do not support the blocks; the blocks support themselves. Mortarless block construction using yotas meets building codes as long as the wall is engineered according to concrete stud design (See Section 15 of *Reinforced Concrete Masonry Handbook*, by J. E. Amrhein, third edition, published by Masonry Institute of America). But before you work on a project that falls under a building code or inspection requirement, it's a good idea to check with your local building inspection department. Mortarless block walls are covered by building codes.

Footing irregularities do not reflect up the wall, according to the yota's inventor. He says that he has never run into a problem from starting mortarless on a properly built concrete footing. Slight irregularities in the footing can be accounted for by filling low spots with sand, but that is rarely needed. If a block should not align with its neighbor in the wall, a

MORTARLESS CONCRETE BLOCKS

Mortarless split-block wall built by inventor Jim Sexton is strengthened by polypropylene plastic insert rings Sexton calls *yotas*. The yotas hold the blocks in alignment until the block cores are later grouted.

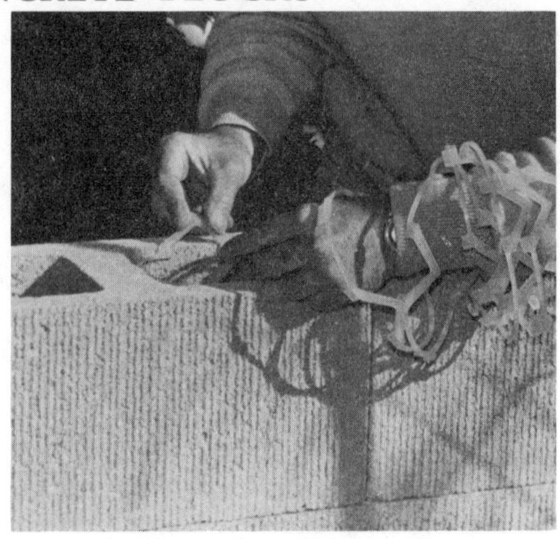

With a supply of yotas on one arm, snap a yota into both cores atop each block. The wall's strength grows as it goes up. Mortarless wall-building takes about one-third the time required when mortar is used.

The yotas make contact at six points around the block cores while their ears stick up to engage the cores of the blocks above.

The awaiting yota ears guide each block into exact alignment with those below. Later, grout will be placed around the vertical rebars.

small chip of flash could be the cause of the problem, making it fail to seat on the block below. Removing the obstruction lets the errant block drop back into line. And while the unmortared joints will let water leak through the wall, no concrete block wall is watertight without cement-plastering and waterproofing. If waterproofing is necessary, this can be done with stucco. The process is no different than for a conventional block wall.

Yotas may be found at local concrete block dealers or ordered from BondX, Inc., PO Box 1771, Fallbrook, CA 92028. (Send a stamped, self-addressed envelope for information and order sheet.)

STONE MASONRY

In working with stone, either natural or cut, the method of using the materials and mortar changes somewhat.

Uncut or natural stone may have many varying heights and lengths and contours that are nowhere near flat. If the stone comes from stratified deposits, the height is likely to be constant, though varying widely from piece to piece. These may be laid by fitting together the various units as shown in the two illustrations of Ashlar masonry on upcoming pages. Cut stone, unless coming from a used-materials source, is likely to be very expensive and not within the scope of the average do-it-yourselfer. It, too, may be laid in Ashlar combinations.

Other natural stones, with irregular faces and varying even more in size and shape, should be laid with the flattest portions facing outward so the wall is roughly flat on the vertical side. These variations may make a most charming wall with interesting effects, as seen in old stone walls in fields or stone-built houses around the world. Provided not too many dissimilar kinds of stones are employed, the effect can be unusual and will fit well into the site.

Caution: Avoid setting the longer stones vertically, since they do not occur that way in nature. You might end up with something resembling fangs or teeth (see illustrations "Errors to Avoid in Stone Masonry" on page 283).

Care must be exercised, too, in using mortar, particularly if the stones are roundish or very uneven. A fairly stiff mortar should be employed to prevent its oozing out in setting, making a messy, drippy joint.

Smooth the joint and slightly indent it to give the wall a little texture from the projections of the stone. Then clean up the wall as directed for finishing brick joints and faces.

Avoid using a conglomeration of oddly, differently shaped stones, those of varied colors, bizarre striations, and rounded boulders set into stratified stone walls. The wall should not become an outdoor whatnot or a crazy quilt of oddments thrown together. A tasteful stone wall calls attention to itself quietly and only for its harmony of slightly different elements put together with competent craftsmanship. A haphazard combination of totally unrelated forms and colors calls attention to itself for a totally different reason.

Boulders, those rounded stones frequently encountered in glacial regions, are a problem because they are so hard to set in mortar and difficult to fit into wall structures. Larger ones, of interesting shape and texture, as well as properly

STYLES OF STONE MASONRY

FITTED NATURAL STONE

Carefully chosen pieces of natural stone, cut to shape as necessary for fitting and mortared evenly will make a strong, long-lasting wall.

RUBBLE STONE

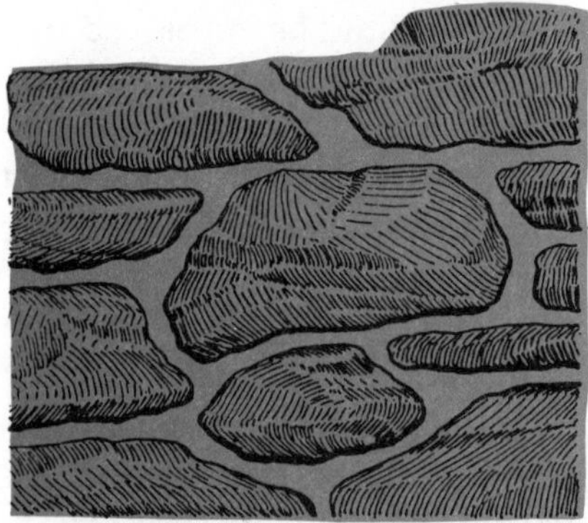

Uncut stones, uneven in size and shape, are called rubble stones. Laid so that their longest dimension is roughly horizontal, they'll give a more natural effect.

NATURAL STONE

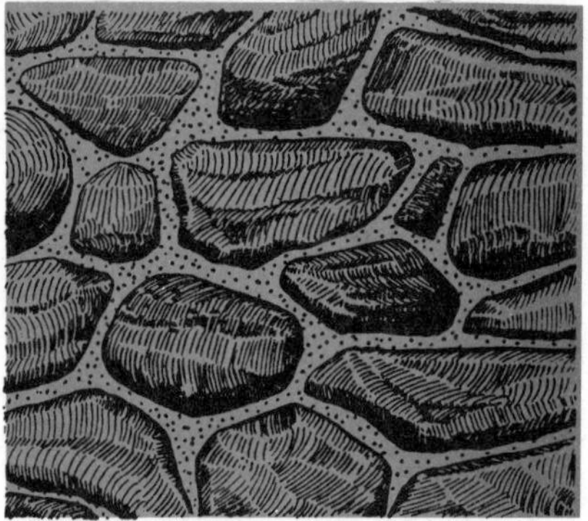

Stones selected to fit together and also to keep the face of the wall reasonably flat are pleasantly informal, interesting in texture.

COMBINING MATERIALS IN WALLS

When there is an outcropping of rock to be connected to a wall of brick or other man-made material, knit them together with stones of related color interwoven and laid flush with the courses of brick. Don't, however, place stones at random in brick walls or allow them to overhang—too frequently a warty look will result.

COURSED ASHLAR

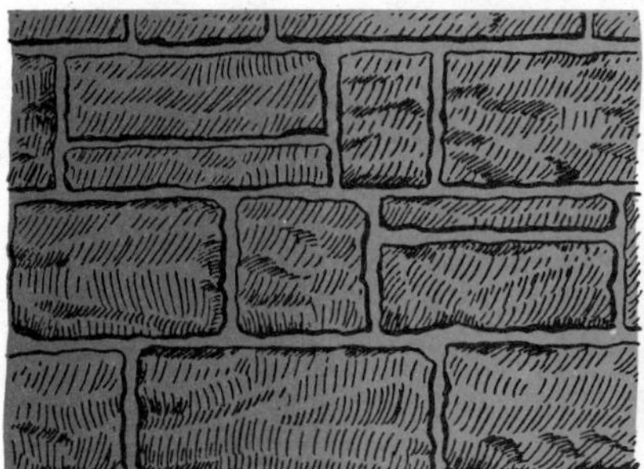

RANDOM ASHLAR

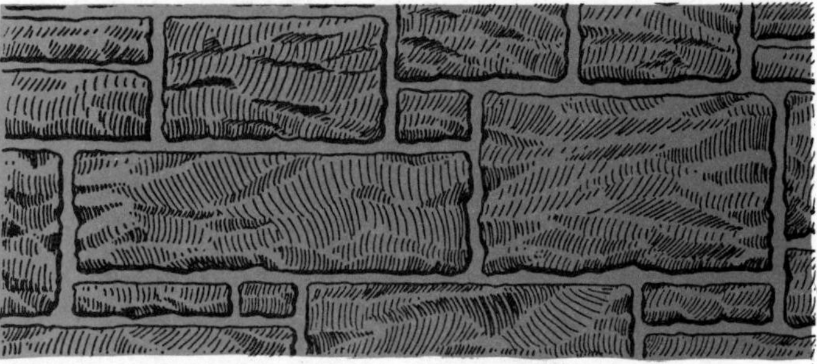

Ashlar masonry is built with stratified stones or those cut and roughly dressed to a squarish shape. Shown at left is a method to lay stones in informal courses. At right, the roughly squared stones are of various sizes, and although the joints are fairly regular no attempt is made to form regular courses. Fit them together so that a pleasing sequence and variety of sizes occurs; get variety, too, with colored stones, but keep the colors close in tone to avoid a checkerboard look.

ERRORS TO AVOID IN STONE MASONRY

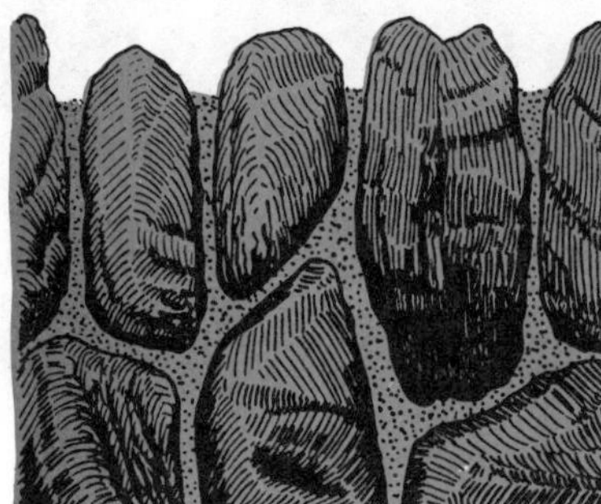

Don't set stones upright—you won't find them set upright in nature.

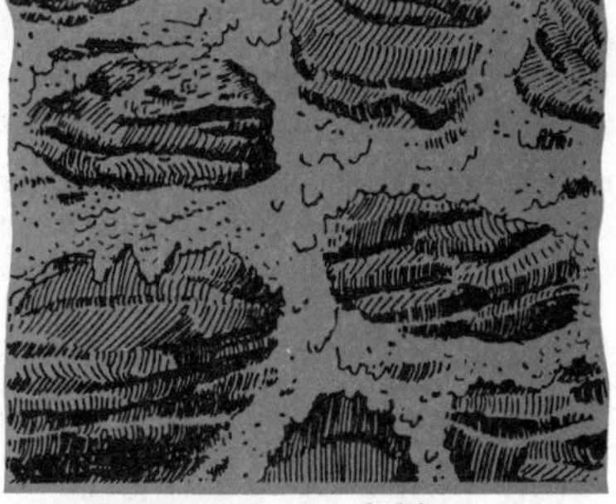

Don't set stones in slobbery mortar like raisins in a rice pudding.

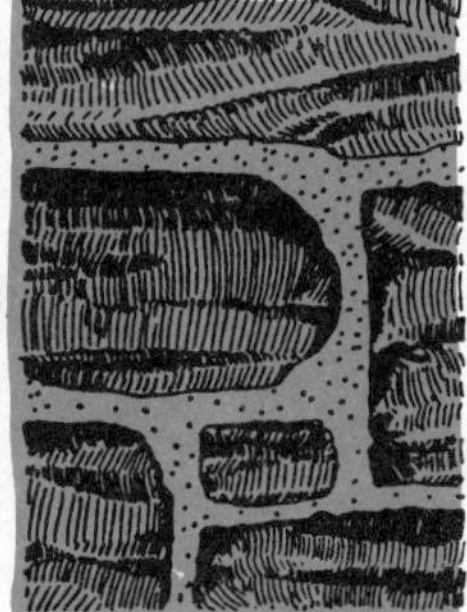

Don't let stones project beyond the wall face unless there's reason.

Don't use too many kinds of stone or you'll get a haphazard effect.

Interesting for its combination of materials as well as its design patterns, a streetside cut-stone wall in Athens, Greece is topped by an open fence weighty enough to go with stonework. The gate combines the fence weight with vertical round bars, adding to the air of pleasant protection and privacy.

colored, may be split by striking properly to rive the stone along a stratum. These can then be used either to face the wall or to be laid flat on a flattish stone with the rounded part projecting a little. Beware of the use of too many rounded projections, or the wall may resemble peanut brittle.

In my own garden, while having a slope bulldozed for paving, we encountered a huge stone. The dozer could only make it tremble, not move. So we left the stone with its small depression in the top to serve as a birdbath, while the slope was cut away in a wide S-curve beginning at the steps by the house and swinging around the pavement then back to end at the stone. An 18-inch brick wall was built to retain the soil of the slope with a wide coping to be used as auxiliary seating for outdoor luncheons and parties. To integrate the formal brick wall with the utterly natural stone, a few stones of suitable size were incorporated into the brick wall, as is shown in the drawing on page 282. This seems to unite the two elements successfully.

Incidentally, a low wall of this sort is useful in that it allows a weeder to sit on a cushion and perform weeding chores in comfort, reaching well into the flower bed above the wall.

CHAPTER 13

MASONRY JOINTS AND PAINTING

Perhaps the most important choice, next to selecting the masonry material you will use for the wall you are going to build, is that of the kind of joint you will use to bring out the inherent qualities of the wall materials and show them to their best advantage. Often masonry alone will have a beauty in itself quite aside from any architectural or plant embellishments, merely by an unusual choice of material and by thoughtful choice of the proper joint to show off the masonry material. The wall itself can be the showpiece and the planting merely the grace note.

Joints will create an interesting texture with sunlight, making shadow-effects that form a constantly changing and ever-fascinating pattern on the wall. Various textural effects can be obtained by the way in which the joints are shaped—by raking out the joints to get an indented shadow, or by squashing out the mortar in the joints and then either leaving them as an informal, irregular mass or shaping them so that they are extruded but formal. Even the color of the mortar can influence the final result. For instance, mortar which is dark in color will cut down the shadow effect on medium- to dark-colored walls. Conversely, white or light-colored walls with darkened mortar forming the joints will produce a far stronger pattern than if pale or white mortar is used. Dark masonry units with light-colored mortar will also have an impact because of the contrast of color. And all this is quite aside from the three-dimensional patterning caused by raking or otherwise shaping the mortar joints.

Where walls face the sun a good part of the day, more shadow texture will be apparent than on walls which receive only light reflected from the sky or from other buildings, as on north-facing walls. Therefore, if you wish to emphasize texture on northern walls the raking should be a little deeper, the shaping intensified, in order to obtain the proper joint shadows.

Sometimes, particularly where a very formal or refined sort of masonry work is used in modern or fine traditional architecture, it is attractive to have no joints showing at all or to subordinate the joints to the texture of the masonry units themselves. In that case, a flush joint is the answer. You may even tint the mortar to approximate the masonry unit color if you wish to pursue the flat effect to its final conclusion. Thus, by using flush joints with mortar in a related color, a very subtle textural effect with a subdued pattern is produced to make a unique architectural contribution to the general picture.

VARIOUS JOINTS AND HOW TO MAKE THEM

After the masonry units are laid and just before the mortar finally sets, the mortar joints are ready to be finished. This merely means that any loose mortar which was squeezed out when the masonry units were set in the mortar bed should now be removed. The trowel is usually employed to remove the major excess and final tooling is done with various tools which may be purchased or made in the home workshop.

A good, neat, well-made joint will finish the wall properly so that it has a professional look. A ragged, sloppy joint will make the wall look amateurish and bedraggled, reflecting no credit on your craftsmanship or on the home which your craftsmanship should beautify. Therefore, you should exercise care and precision in striking the joints in walls you build, observing the basic rules and practicing them to achieve a well-built, good-looking, durable wall.

Hold the blade of the trowel at about a 30° angle from the wall, one edge of the blade resting flat against the wall so that it will scrape off the blobs of mortar that have squeezed out. Using a quick motion, holding the trowel so that it stays in approximately the same position in relation to the wall, scrape off the mortar and dispose of it by a quick jerking motion of the trowel or by tapping it lightly against some firm object. An occasional dipping of the blade in a bucket of water or a quick rub with a wet rag will keep it clean and prevent any mortar from adhering to it. Once the excess mortar is removed from the wall you are ready to proceed with the finishing work of tooling.

The head joints (vertical ones) are always tooled first, whatever method of tooling is employed. Then the bed joints (horizontal ones) are struck; and then comes the final removal of any blobs or other accidentally left mortar which can be whisked off with the tip of the trowel blade. Certain of the joints may be finished with the point of the trowel, too. The flush joint, the struck joint, and the weather joint may be finished this way, and the trowel is also used for the final finishing of the tuck joint.

Flush joint. The reason for all tooling is to compress the mortar somewhat and to remove any excess mortar from the finished wall. In the illustrations on the next page, note how the edge of the trowel scrapes along the wall and removes the mortar until it is even with the surfaces of the masonry units. This joint is usually used with cement or cinder blocks; often it is employed on brick work where a smooth effect is desired.

Struck joint. In this case the point of the trowel is inserted at about a 30° angle and run along evenly to compress the mortar and at the same time expose the upper edge of the lower course of brick. Vertical joints are either lightly raked (see raked joint) or kept flush for an even effect.

Weather joint. The trowel point is again employed at about a 30° angle, this time to expose the *lower* edge of the *top* course of brick, the method being merely reversed from the proceeding detailed for the struck joint. Vertical joints are finished in the same way. This is one of the best joints to give texture, especially in severe climates or those which are exceptionally damp, as this joint will shed water better than any of the others, except possibly the flush joint. It will give nearly as much shadow effect as a raked joint without any of its drawbacks.

Raked joints. This makes one of the handsomest of masonry effects. If regular, even-sized modular units are employed, it will produce a good deep

The raked joint in bricks is one of the best looking and easiest to make. In severe climates, however, flush-tooled joints will prove more weather-resistant.

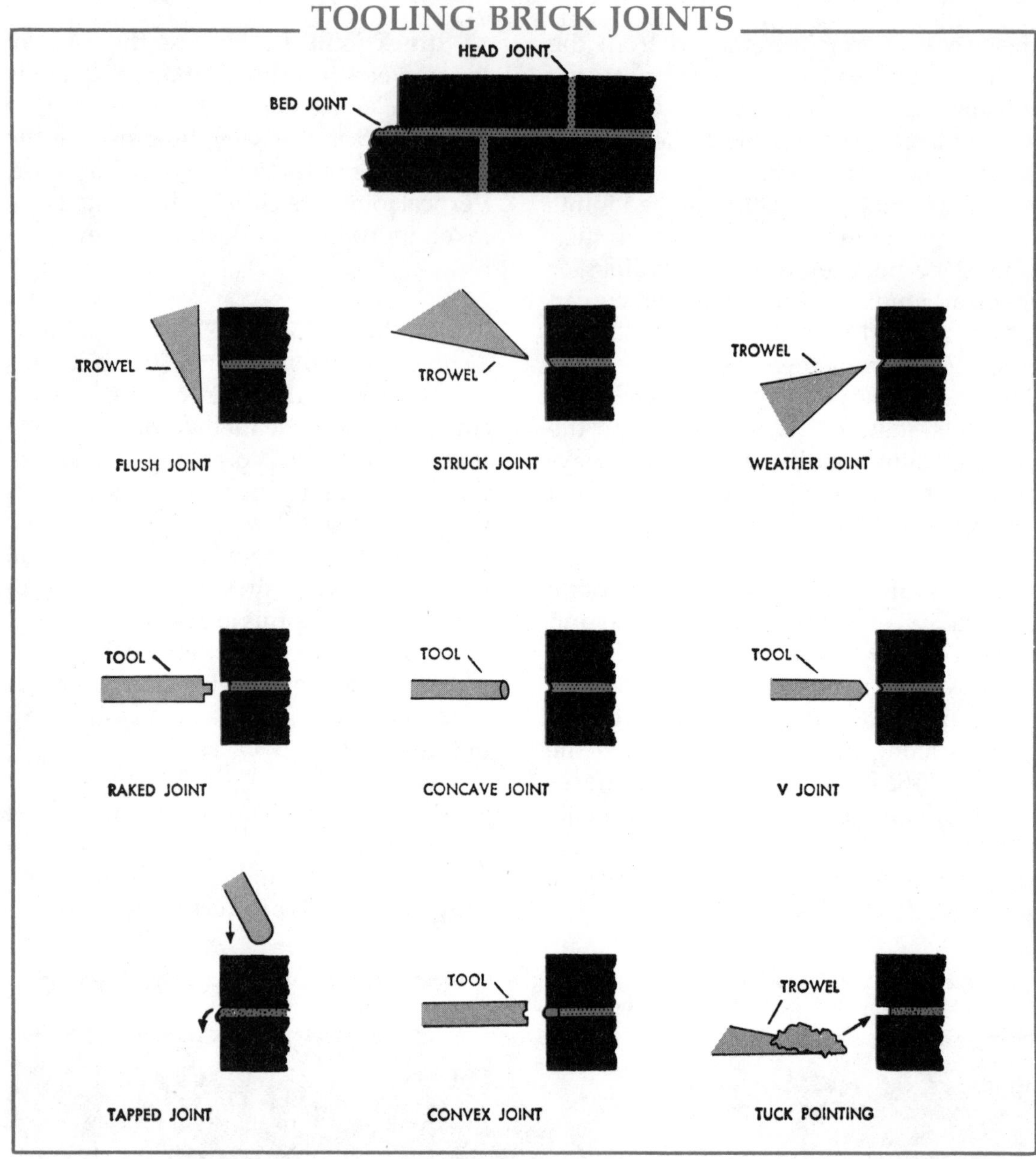

shadow line, emphasizing the geometric pattern pleasantly. It may be painted or left in its original finish, as you desire. However, in some climates it may have certain drawbacks. It will retain moisture, ice, and snow, and if the brick or other units are porous it may lay them open to cracking from freezing and other moisture deterioration. Where no insulation or moisture barrier is used on the walls of a house with raked joints, the inside walls may become rather damp. It may require more repointing than other types of joints (all joints may need repointing after a good many years of weathering); but even with these drawbacks, which do not obtain in all climates, it is still my favorite joint and one of the most beautiful and most satisfying.

Concave joint. As weather-impervious as the flush joint, this one is made by using a short length of pipe or a round iron rod to shape the joint. Hold the pipe or rod level with the joint at an angle so that the rounded side of the end fits into the joint. Draw the tool along, holding it always at the same angle. You should choose whether you want a deep concave or a shallow one and hold the tool at the proper angle to achieve it. The closer to the wall the shank of the tool is held, the deeper will be the joint, for the round end will fit more deeply into the area between the masonry units. A ¾-inch rod or pipe is about the right size to use for finishing a ½-inch joint. If joints are wider, larger-sized pipes should be employed. For concrete blocks, a jointing tool should be a minimum of 22 inches long, allowing for bridging irregularities.

V-joint. This joint can be made with a purchased tool; but if a homemade tool is desired, a length of strap-iron can be ground down to produce the V, or the point of a trowel or the corner of a board may be used. Whatever tool is employed, however, the main danger to avoid is that of getting the joint uneven. A proper V-joint centers the point of the V between courses of masonry units.

Tapped joint. A bit of practice will be necessary in order to produce the proper effect in making this joint. It depends upon the mortar bed's being just the right thickness so that the right amount of mortar is squeezed out when the masonry unit is tapped with the handle of the trowel. It should not be too thick, or too large a blob of mortar will be forced out, making the joint uneven and slobbery. A little practice will enable you to judge just how much mortar to use when laying the bed joint and when buttering the end of the unit to get the proper final effect. Correctly made, this joint gives a very interesting rough-cast appearance which is most attractive in the proper setting. It is not the most weatherproof of joints, but it will last about as long as any of the open joints.

Convex joint. For finely finished masonry work, such as fitted stone masonry, this is most useful. It is half-rounded and protrudes beyond the masonry line, giving a rather interesting line texture to a smooth wall. It is frequently used on semi-dressed or cut-stone walls, too. The tool may be used before the wall is scraped and cleaned, or the joint may be raked and refilled and the tooling done afterward. (See tuck pointing.) Due to the extra care necessary and the extra compression, this joint will probably be as long-lasting as any, particularly if tuck pointed.

Tuck pointing. The joints are raked as detailed above for raked joints, and then, by the use of a specially prepared mixture of mortar made with extra-fine sand, the joint is refilled. This must be done, of course, before the original mortar has set, so that the two will bond together successfully. Use the point of the small pointing trowel with a small quantity of mortar and avoid dribbling it or splashing it on the masonry units. You may finally tool the joint flush or use the finishes for any other joints except the raked joint.

This method may also be used to repair a wall which has weathered to the point where mortar is softening and beginning to fall out. First clean out the old mortar well with an old chisel or sturdy screwdriver, then tuck point and tool to the desired finish.

PAINTING MASONRY

Often the texture of masonry walls can be enhanced by painting them. New additions to old walls will be integrated with the old walls by covering up color differences with paint. Similarly, stone walls which have wildly unrelated colors can be pulled together and given dignity and greater effectiveness by being painted. A stone wall will lose that plum-pudding or raisin-bread appearance and become a coherent architectural mass, a thing of beauty and a joy for as long as the paint lasts. Old houses can be made to look fresh and modern when dismal, dark masonry walls are covered with light and appealing pastel colors, or with white or medium tones which will dispel the gloom and bring the house up to date. This is not a new idea, of course, for painted masonry and color-washed walls have been used in many parts of the world for centuries, and we have many examples of their use in our own country in the past.

Paint protects walls, helps to weatherproof them, and cuts down the need for repointing mortar joints and filling weather-induced pockmarks and holes. Some paints especially formulated for masonry use do not seal the pores in the ordinary sense, according to the claims of the manufacturers. They allow the masonry to "breathe," prevent condensation of moisture on the inside of the wall and also keep it from collecting behind the paint film, thus avoiding blistering with resultant peeling off of paint films. Possibly in retaining walls, garden walls, and such, the condensation factor is less important than in house walls, but it should be considered for it will affect adherence of paint to the masonry and consequently call for more maintenance, repainting, and added work.

Paints with an oil base. These are still available and used for masonry although other more recent introductions have cut into their use. I suggest that you read all the details of paints in this chapter, consider the various attributes of each kind, and then make your choice. In oil paints, either gloss or flat-finish paints may be used for brick, stone, or block walls, as well as on stucco. Porous concrete or cinder blocks may need a little special treatment before the final coating. All surfaces must be thoroughly dry before being painted so that the paint will bond properly and not blister or flake off later on. It is always well to make a test of the wall surface by painting a square yard or so of wall with the primer coat to see if there are any alkaline places on it—what painters call "hot spots" because they seem to burn the paint. If blisters or discolorations appear, wire brush the wall over them and give two more primer coats to seal them off. If not, the wall can be safely painted after two or three days have elapsed without "hot spots" appearing. This alkaline test is necessary only on new walls; old walls which have weathered will presumably have dispersed the alkalinity. On most walls a single coat of primer, followed by a finish coat when the primer has thoroughly dried, will be all that is necessary. If you are using a colored finish coat it will be well to tint the primer to a hue approaching the color of the finish coat. This will prevent streakiness and thin spots in the final coat. If any appear, let the first finish coat dry well for several days and then follow it with a second coat to flatten out and give an all-over smooth and even coat.

Cement-base paints. These were formerly offered by a number of manufacturers and were much used. They come in dry form, to be mixed with water and applied with a brush. However, with the emergence of the newer synthetic-base paints, and the ease of using them as well as the greater range of color, the long life, and lack of maintenance required, I no longer feel that cement-base paints can be as fully recommended as in the past. The acrylic latex, alkyd, polyvinyl acetate, and latex bases are so versatile, so easy to use that I believe the do-it-yourselfer can choose them with assurance and use them for many kinds of projects. Most in their favor is that many types can be used on wood, both siding and trim, on shingles, shutters, and on primed metal as well as on masonry, something that cannot be said for cement-based paints.

If a cement-base paint had been used on an old wall that is now to be repainted, be sure that it is thoroughly cleaned off—powdery old paint wire-brushed and washed away—and the surface thoroughly prepared with a sealer coat. Consult your paint dealer for his recommendation on a sealer that will meet your needs. Do not expect any paint that is applied over peeling, powdering, or loosened coats of old paint to adhere and give a long-lasting, maintenance-free job. A little extra work in preparing the surface will save much labor later on of redoing an unsatisfactory job—unsatisfactory because the paint will not properly bond with the surface.

Latex paints. These offer the do-it-yourselfer much else of advantage. A wide range of colors is available, from pale pastel to deep tones, also many of them are recommended by the manufacturers for use on quite a variety of materials—wood siding and shingles, shutters and other trim, primed metal work (gutters and downspouts, for instance), as well as for all kinds of masonry, including stucco. Add to these virtues another solid advantage—easy application and quick drying—and the crowning virtue of all, quick and easy cleanup of applicators with water and soap, and you have something approaching the ideal masonry paint. Most of them can be applied with a brush, a roller, or be sprayed on. However, I am old-fashioned in that I believe in the first coat being brushed on, so that all pores are well filled and the paint better bonded than is sometimes the case when a roller or other applicator is used. These paints dry within 30 minutes, for the most part, under ideal drying conditions, or a bit more than that depending on weather or climate conditions. But once on, they quickly harden and cure into a perfect coat. Should succeeding coats be needed—and new work frequently will need two to three coats because of the porous nature of the surface—they may be quickly applied without waiting hours and days as with other kinds of paint. These paints dry quickly to a splendid flat sheen and insure that dust pick-up and bug trapping in the paint surface will be practically eliminated. Paint dealers caution against use when the temperature is below 55° F.

The "breathing" action mentioned above is a distinct virtue in that it allows air to penetrate and condensation is virtually eliminated. Moisture is usually the cause of blistering and consequent peeling off of paint films from walls, and condensation on the inside of walls may cause trouble indoors, as well. A tough film of paint that will dry to a flat, velvety sheen, will resist cracking, blistering, peeling, will provide a water-resistant surface (even in driving rains, snow, and ice), one that is also practically impervious to ordinary dirt and stains, chemical fumes, sea air, and smog—such a painted surface is the aim of all painters and these paints come very close to providing it.

Most of these paints can be thinned with water, but be sure to *read the directions on the can carefully* and follow them to the letter. It is usually recommended that the first coat be used full strength in order to fill the pores, priming the surface and providing a proper base for succeeding coats.

Masonry should be examined and repaired before painting. Look for breaks, cracks, holes, and voids in joints and fill them either with mortar mix or use a "block filler," purchasable at your paint store and probably manufactured by the paint company whose paint you will use. Allow repairs to dry thoroughly before painting the masonry, and be sure to remove all loose dirt, all splashes or drips of mortar, grease, oil, loose paint, and surface dust. Also make sure that the wall is dry.

Surface preparation caution. *Do not use acid washes or zinc sulphate to neutralize the surfaces to be painted.* Instead, use water, either hosed or brushed on, and if this does not clean the wall—possibly where grime and dirt are embedded in the pores—scrub with a household detergent dissolved in water to loosen and remove the dirt and oily substances. Then rinse down the surface thoroughly with plain water.

Where moss, mildew, or moldy spots are present, remove them by a scrub-down with a solution of household bleach (such as Clorox) in the proportion of a gallon of water to a pint of bleach. Afterwards, rinse the surface thoroughly with plain water. *Never use acid washes* for removing moss or mildew.

The cleanup of rollers and brushes or sprayers is very easy with latex paints. Merely wash them well with warm water and strong detergent, then rinse them under running water from the tap and they will emerge as good as new within a short time.

These are the principal kinds of paints recommended for use on masonry. Look into them and see the colors and kinds available before you decide against painting the walls. However, should a natural color of brick or block be desired—or where blocks have been chosen for their color quality, for the aggregates exposed, or for some other quality—look into the clear sealants or silicone-type sealants that will close the pores without changing the colors appreciably. In any case, whatever your final choice, you will be pleased that maintenance is cut down, that color has been added (if that is your choice), and that the beauty is enhanced.

CHAPTER 14

MAKING AND USING CONCRETE

Concrete is an excellent material for do-it-yourselfers, when it is properly made. You can make it to suit your purpose, in quantities large or small; and it may be used in so many ways and for so many purposes that projects designed for concrete or adaptable to it would fill several volumes the size of this one. It is a very durable material. Because of our modern formulas with their exact measurements; because we have developed good methods of finishing concrete; because it can be adapted to very intricate casting forms; and because, finally, it can be reinforced so that it will bear heavy loads without cracking or danger of collapse, we have at our fingertips probably the most useful, permanent, and relatively low-cost plastic building material the world has ever known.

Not so long ago concrete was relegated to small areas or used for only workaday projects, but today it is used much more imaginatively. There are so many textural treatments possible, ranging from very rough pebbly surfaces—with the aggregates exposed and pebbles tamped into the wet surface of fresh concrete—to the very smoothest surfaces, which can be waxed and used as dance floors. With these possibilities and the use of coloring materials to give life and beauty to the concrete, we may well call it the most versatile of materials.

Concrete can be used in the old humdrum ways, or it can be employed in stimulating, creative ways to give piquancy to whatever is made of it and to heighten the effect of the outdoor picture. It has so much more to offer than just its commonplace and worthy qualities of permanence and durability that it should be considered for every possible project in the yard.

Before we take up ways and means, the formulas for mixing, and so on, let us look into the methods of handling it which may be employed by the do-it-yourselfer. Mixing and laying quantities of concrete is heavy work. Let's admit that immediately and proceed to see what can be done to lighten the tasks connected with its use. By planning your job so that it can be done in segments, none of them a large, back-breaking project, you can manage things so that it won't be too much for you to handle even though it may take you some time to achieve your goal. For instance, in building a patio you can cast it in sections, rather than in one piece. It is better to do this for many reasons, one of which is that contraction strips are needed to allow for contraction and expansion due to heat and cold. If these strips can be made with 2″ × 4″s, which may be left in the patio or removed after the patio blocks have been cast (the areas can be filled in with soil and planted with grass), you can do several squares at a time, and let them cure while you are going on to the next strip of squares. Your patio will expand as rapidly as your time, your energy, and your enthusiasm will permit. Also it will present less strain on the pocketbook when taken in segments.

Walks and driveways may also be built in sections, and, although steps are usually better poured at one time in one piece, it is possible to cast them in sections if they are properly tied together with reinforcements which extend between the two units. It may be possible, of course, to enlist your family or to hire a couple of strong-armed men for a day or two to help you do large projects if you feel they're too much to attempt alone. Concrete mixers can be hired by the day in most places; they will cut down the labor of mixing large quantities of concrete such as will be needed for patios or driveways, particularly if you have been able to hire a worker to do the shoveling and hauling so that you can do the finishing and lighter tasks.

READY-MIX CONCRETE

You should look into the possibility of buying concrete already mixed if you need a sizeable quantity. It is called ready-mix concrete. Many building materials dealers sell it by the truckload. Large truck-mixers keep the mix spinning and churn-

Using ready-mix concrete for projects larger than several cubic yards is efficient. While the mix comes down the chute of the truck-mixer ready to use, be sure to have enough help on hand to finish it.

ing as it is driven from the batching plant to your home. You'll need a couple of wheelbarrows to haul it from the place the truck parks at your home, unless it is adjacent to where the concrete is to be used, in which case it may be channeled from truck to project by a metal chute.

Ready-mix concrete offers many advantages; not least is the price, when compared with that of do-it-yourself mixes, particularly when the quantity desired is for more than a few yards of concrete. Very probably you will find that the ingredients alone will cost as much as, or more than, the price of the ready-mix, and there will be the labor of shoveling, thoroughly mixing, and final handling of the concrete yourself to add to that when you are considering the two methods. For someone with limited time, even if the price were a good bit more, it seems to make excellent sense to buy ready-mix concrete because of the time saved as well as the labor avoided. You will find that read-mix producers are, in general, quite used to supplying moderate or small quantities needed for average jobs such as a walk, a patio, or a short run of retaining wall.

Order ready-mix the right way, to be sure of getting the most from the knowledge your dealer has about his concrete. When you call him, be ready to give the following information: (1) the quantity needed; (2) the time and place of delivery; (3) maximum-size coarse aggregate—one-fourth the thickness of the project, generally; (4) minimum portland cement per cubic yard (see accompanying table, "How to Order Ready-Mix Concrete"); (5) maximum water content (from the table); (6) percent air entrainment (from the table); and (7) maximum slump, a measure of the concrete's workability. According to experts, ready-mix with a maximum slump of 5 inches should be specified for hand methods of placement. If you should specify a compressive strength, make it at least 3,000 psi. Anything less than that is not quality concrete.

Be sure to order your ready-mix at least a day before you'll need it. For small jobs have at least one strong person there to help you when the truck-mixer arrives. For large projects, have two or more helpers on hand, more if fancy finishes are planned. And if the mixer cannot dump on the subgrade and the mix must be wheelbarrowed in, plan on needing still more helpers, at least two more, and extra wheelbarrows.

Do not add water to the ready-mix that arrives unless it's impossible to place and finish as you receive it. Added water weakens the mix. If water must be added, put in up to 2 gallons per cubic yard in two steps, mixing and testing after each. No more than that.

Perhaps you will want to canvass the possibility of having concrete laid by contract, if you feel the project is beyond your abilities. Get one or two contractors to estimate on the work—be prepared to find that it will cost up to twice the amount you'd pay if you did the work yourself and bought only materials. It may well be worth it. However, you may still be able to pare the cost a bit if your contractor will allow you to do the necessary digging out and grading, and he may even let you build the forms if you can convince him you are competent. These pos-

HOW TO ORDER READY-MIX CONCRETE

Exposure	*Max.-size coarse ag.*	*Portland cement (lb./cu. yd.)*	*Max. water (lb./cu.yd.)*	*Air-entrainment (% by vol.)*
Severe: many freeze-thaw cycles per year; deicer chemicals used on slab in winter.	1″	564	254	6-8
	¾″	586	264	6½-8½
	½″	640	288	7-9
	⅜″	660	300	7½-9½
Moderate: few freeze-thaw cycles per year; deicer chemicals not used.	1″	520	260	5-7
	¾″	540	270	6-8
	½″	590	295	6½-8½
	⅜″	610	305	7-9
Mild: no freeze-thaw cycles; deicer chemicals not used.	1″	520	*	†
	¾″	540	*	†
	½″	590	*	†
	⅜″	610	*	†

*Water limited by compressive strength needed for service.
†2% to 3% to improve cohesiveness and reduce bleeding.

CONCRETE FORMWORK

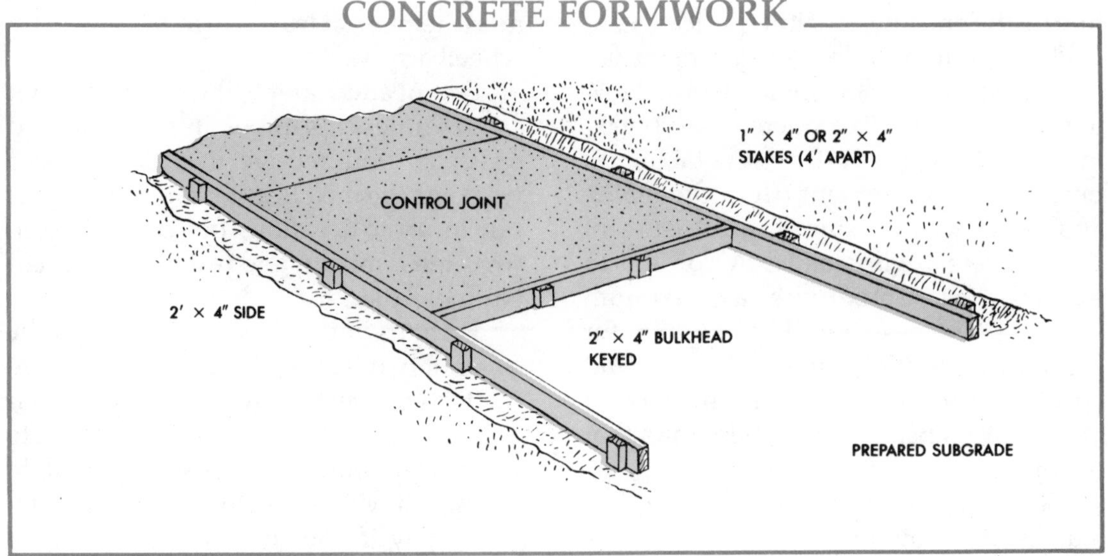

sibilities will depend upon the goodwill and cooperativeness of the individual contractor, of course.

In the event that he will let you do something, it is a good plan to have a written contract specifying clearly what are the contractor's responsibilities and what you are to finish. In this way neither of you will be expecting more than should be required, and unpleasantness can be avoided. Sample contracts of this sort may be available from branch offices of cement manufacturers, or you may write to the Portland Cement Association, 5420 Old Orchard Road, Skokie, IL 60076, for information on contracts and specifications for concrete work. This association also offers some helpful booklets which give pictures of projects, tables of quantities needed for formulas for various projects, and other useful information on concrete and how do-it-yourselfers can employ it to improve their homes and yards.

"YOU-HAUL" CONCRETE

Another method to consider is haul-it-yourself or "you-haul" concrete, becoming available in an increasing number of locations. Consider it particularly if your job is from half a cubic yard to 2 cubic yards. (A cubic yard is 27 cubic feet.) Haul-it-yourself is offered in three versions:

CONTROL JOINTS

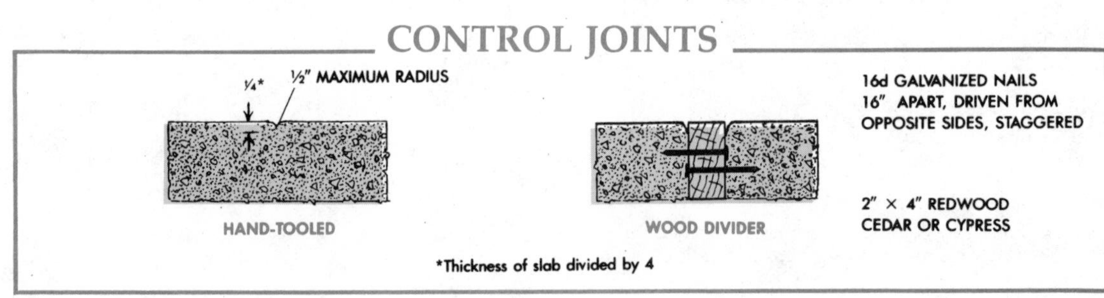

hopper-trailer, trailer-mixer, and pickup-mixer.

Hopper-trailer-hauled concrete is batched and mixed at a central plant located in the yard of the dealer where you buy it. Then the mix is dumped into the box of a trailer attached to your car. The big drawback to hopper-trailer concrete is that the concrete's ingredients segregate or settle out during the haul home. The heaviest ingredients—gravel and sand—settle to the bottom of the hopper. The lighter ones—the water and cement—come to the top. The people who sell hopper-trailer mix claim that they put something into the mix to prevent segregation, but there probably is no such thing. What they use is an air-entraining agent. This is fine—most concrete benefits from air entraining—but it still settles out and segregates. The air-entraining agent slows segregation only slightly. If you want good, quality hopper-trailer concrete, you must have it made very stiff. According to a Portland Cement Association engineer, you should insist on getting a 2- to 3-inch slump.

Note that slump is a measure of concrete's stiffness or wetness. For most uses concrete works well at about a 5-inch slump. This means that a specially compacted cone-shaped pile of it will slump from a foot high to only 6 inches high when the forming cone is gently removed. Concrete with only a 2- or 3-inch slump is so stiff the mix stands up in a pile. Power spreading and finishing equipment is advisable for handling it. A mix this stiff wouldn't flow out of the hopper's foot-square dump door. It would have to be shoveled out of the hopper.

Thus, if you use hopper-hauled concrete and want quality, you'll have to find a dealer who will actually make the properly stiff mix. Then, back home, you'll have to fight it into the forms and coax a finish onto it. None of that will be easy.

An easier solution is to find a dealer who offers trailer-mixer or pickup-mixer equipment. This contains a portable concrete mixer that keeps churning the concrete on the trip from central plant to home. Throw a lever and the mixer reverses direction and discharges the load. Segregation cannot occur. Slump can be a correct 6 inches for good workability. Locate dealers offering trailer- or pickup-mixers in your local Yellow Pages directory under "Concrete, Ready Mixed." Most dealers who've invested in the costlier equipment will advertise this fact.

Another potential problem with haul-it-yourself concrete is that the dealers may know little about designing, selecting, proportioning, or mixing concrete and its makings. It's far from a simple process. If your project's success is important to you, you need to be confident of getting quality concrete, which never comes by chance. Your dealer should know and understand the *rule of sixes* for quality concrete: 6 inches slump; 6 sacks of portland cement per cubic yard of concrete; a maximum of 6 gallons of water per sack of cement with the water that's already in the sand accounted for; and 6 days of wet-curing. The last is your responsibility as the builder, of course.

Too few haul-it-yourself dealers actually measure the water into the mix. Most measure the aggregates by the loader scoop, which is hardly accurate. Well-made concrete develops a compressive strength of 4,000 psi. Anything less is bound to develop problems such as cracking, crazing, dusting, and scaling, none of which will make you proud of what you build with it. So choose your haul-it-yourself dealer very carefully. A good dealer will furnish trailer- or pickup-mixers for hauling, will meter the water into the mix, weigh-batch the cement and aggregates or use sacks of cement, six per cubic yard and he will also weigh out the sand and stones. In other words, he will do the same things that a ready-mix dealer does, only on a smaller scale.

A fully loaded trailer-mixer with one cubic yard of concrete weighs 6,200 pounds. The concrete alone weighs almost 3,800 pounds per cubic yard in the plastic state. Any trailer heavier than 3,500 pounds is supposed to be towed with an SAE Class 3 load-equalizing hitch with 2⅜-inch ball. Yet trailers are set up for 2-inch hitch balls common with Class 2 hitches. So, with a trailer-mixer, right off the bat you're inadequately hitched. Remember that as you pull away from the yard. And in no case should you try to haul one of those hippos with a clamp-on bumper hitch, or any Class 1 hitch. A car's bumper is not that strong. You can haul a cubic yard behind any full-sized car or pickup. A minipickup can handle it, too. If all you have available is a subcompact or intermediate sedan or wagon, you'd better plan on renting an adequate tow vehicle along with the trailer-mixer, or find a pickup-mixer you can rent. Drive carefully and slowly. Start, stop, and turn extra gently. Be careful where you go with the trailer, too. Don't drive in anywhere that you can't get out of.

Hauling it yourself can be a good way to use concrete in medium-sized amounts, provided you investigate before you invest. Most dealers permit ample time for dumping and clean-up before charging any trailer or pickup overtime.

The pickup-mixer is easiest to manage for it is merely a mixer similar to the latter type mounted on a pickup truck chassis. You hire the whole thing for a fee, including the concrete, and drive it to where you are to use it, maneuver it into place, dispense the concrete, then return the equipment. It may be the best answer for many jobs.

In all three cases, the cost of the concrete is a little less than that of the ready-mix, but not enough to make much difference unless you have a large job such as a driveway or a huge patio to pave. You may feel it is not worth the extra trouble and labor involved in picking up the mix and transporting it yourself. In *all* cases, be *sure* that you have everything in readiness and the site completely prepared before the concrete arrives—forms in place and braced, ground leveled and filled, fill tamped—in short, be *completely ready*. There will be no time for adjustments and extra work to be done when a batch of concrete is waiting to be used and probably already beginning to set as it waits.

PUMPED CONCRETE

Perhaps the best way to use concrete in any amount more than a couple of cubic yards is to order pumped ready-mix. This relieves you of all the problems of hauling and placing concrete. A ready-mix truck pulls up to a convenient spot near where you want the mix and a concrete pump on the pickup truck or trailer backs up under the mixer's dump chute. The mixer

Pumped concrete eliminates the time and energy otherwise needed for the hauling of ready-mix to the forms.

discharges into a hopper on the concrete pump and the pump squeezes the mix through a long hose to place it right where you want it in the forms. With pumped ready-mix there's no hauling, little shoveling. Your first job is to start finishing the mix.

The pump's hose can reach through a door, over a fence, wherever a 2- or 3-inch-diameter hose can go. Concrete comes out its end like toothpaste from a tube. The cost is only a little more than for the ready-mix alone. In some cases pumping is cheaper than holding a waiting ready-mix truck on overtime while you wheel concrete in with a wheelbarrow. Hose-reaches of up to 250 feet are standard procedure.

The concrete for any around-the-house project can be pumped. It's highly practical whenever the truck-mixer cannot dump its load directly between the forms. Moreover, it keeps those heavy monsters off your driveway where they could crack the concrete or make ruts in a blacktop drive.

A special pumping mix is required when a concrete pump is being used. If you do not order the pump through your ready-mix dealer, be sure to specify that a *grout and pump mix* is needed. This contains a smaller maximum-size aggregate for easy flowing through the pump and hose. Pumping does concrete no harm; in fact, it actually adds to its strength. Renting a concrete pump and doing your own pumping is not recommended. Some mixes become "constipated" in the hose if not kept moving fairly steadily. Then the hose has to be taken apart at joints and the mix washed out to get things moving again. It can be hard work. It's much better to have a pump operator along with the pump, for he takes care of any problems and cleans up his equipment before returning it and you can concentrate on your project without worry. Like the ready-mix driver, the pump operator will expect to be paid—a check is often okay—before he leaves the job.

Even with a concrete pump on the job, you still need plenty of help for finishing the concrete. Don't try to skimp on that. The mix that's placed almost all at once will tend to set up almost all at once. You must be able to get the desired finish on it before it does. Nevertheless, pumping saves so much work that practically all concrete contractors use it for backyard projects. You can benefit as they do. Most pumping contractors charge by the cubic yard, with a minimum charge for coming out and setting up. A pumping mix usually costs slightly more than a regular mix, but the work saved more than pays the added costs for pumping. For a pumping contractor, look in the Yellow Pages under "Concrete Pumping Service" or ask your ready-mix dealer.

PORTLAND CEMENT

Portland cement is usually specified for general construction work. It is so named because, after it has been liquefied, cast, and cured, it is said to resemble a kind of limestone from the Island of Portland off the English Coast. It is a *type* of cement, *not a trade name.* Several manufacturers make it, using the fixed standards of the U.S. Government and the American Society for Testing and Materials (ASTM). It is usually packed in paper bags weighing 94 pounds, each equalling 1 cubic foot, dry measure. Although it is often obtainable also in barrels containing the equivalent of 4 sacks, these are seldom practical for do-it-yourself use.

Cement must never be stored in damp places, on concrete floors, or on the ground. It may absorb moisture through the bag even in comparatively dry basements. Opened bags allow the cement to take up moisture even more quickly, absorbing it from the air, which will make the cement lumpy or solidify it altogether, thus rendering it unfit for use. Even unopened bags will become lumpy or solidify if not used within a reasonable length of time, particularly in humid climates; so it is a good plan to figure carefully and not order more than can be conveniently used at one time, and thus avoid the perils of storing it. On the other hand it is downright disconcerting, to say the least, to run short of cement if you are a weekend do-it-yourselfer. It is better to have an *extra* bag in case it may be needed late on a Saturday afternoon, a Sunday, or a holiday if you are working then, for those are days when it is usually impossible to find a place from which it can be bought. If it is not used, you can always put it to good use the next weekend or the following one.

Any leftover concrete can be poured into the forms for stepping-stones and paving blocks (Chapter 19) if they are kept in readiness. This will prevent waste by using every bit of excess concrete after any project, and you can utilize a partly used or full bag of extra cement by putting it to use this way, too. If you have a partly used bag which must be kept for a while, get a polyethylene plastic trash bag and use it to encase the cement sack. Using a hot electric iron over a folded piece of aluminum foil will seal a seam in the plastic. The top can be left open if you wish, merely by folding or rolling it several times to make a tight joint, and then using the hand-tie to hold it tightly closed. This will preserve the cement and keep moisture from it for a long time.

AGGREGATES

While the cement and the water—of the four ingredients in concrete—come to you ready to use, the aggregates—coarse and fine—are found in a variety of forms. Some are good for making concrete, others are not. The kind of sand that's best for making concrete contains particles in various sizes from ¼ inch on down to dust-size. This is called *uniform gradation.* Also, the sand particles have to be hard enough to withstand exposure to freezing and thawing without breaking up.

Sand is the fine aggregate, while crushed stones and naturally occurring gravel is the coarse aggregate, and both need the same qualities: cleanliness, uniform gradation, and hardness of particles. The smallest coarse aggregate particles should reduce in size to meet the largest particles of sand, that is, ¼ inch. The largest size of coarse aggregate to use in a mix depends on the dimensions of the project you are making. If it is a slab—sidewalk, driveway, patio, floor—the

The aggregates in concrete are coarse (stones, bottom) and fine (sand). It is important that the particle sizes be evenly graded from smallest to largest, not all of one size. Stone and sand should be clean, discussed in next caption.

To check the suitability of sand for making concrete, put a 2″ layer in a glass or jar with water and shake. If, after settling, less than a ⅛″ silt layer is left on top, the sand's clean enough.

largest pieces of coarse aggregate should be only one-fourth its thickness. If it is a wall, the largest aggregate should be only one-fifth the narrowest dimension between sides of the form. If you use pieces that are too large, they will get in the way of placing and finishing. Smaller than maximum sizes are all right; however, it is those larger pieces that make for an economical mix. They help to fill out the volume of the mix at the least cost. In some parts of the country, good aggregates are tough to find. It's best to buy yours from a dealer who is attuned to what it takes to make good concrete.

WATER

The water used in mixing concrete and cement is exceedingly important, for if it is unsuitable it may have an adverse chemical reaction and weaken the mixture. It must not contain alkali or oils—don't use old gasoline or oil cans for measuring it unless they have been *thoroughly* washed out with a detergent—nor should it be very acid, since all of these will react adversely against the cement, preventing it from achieving the proper strength. Nearly any water which is suitable for drinking can be used in mixing concrete, provided it is clean and has no silt or vegetable matter in it. Always wash out pails or other receptacles for measuring water before using them to prepare concrete.

CONCRETE FORMULAS

The Portland Cement Association has devised new directions for proportioning concrete to get workability, quality, and durability. The instructions which follow reflect those. The size of batch you can make at one time depends on your concrete mixer's drum capacity. You can probably rent a gas- or electric-powered mixer, whenever you need one, much cheaper than you could buy one. They're available in drum sizes from ½ to 7 cubic feet. The actual mixing capacity is about 60 percent of the drum volume. With a decent-sized mixer you can figure on an output per day of about 50 cubic feet per person. This is just for the mixing. Recruit more help for the placing and finishing operations.

The quality of the cement paste, water plus portland cement in the plastic mix, directly governs the strength and durability of the hardened concrete. Thus correct proportioning of ingredients—especially the water and cement—is vital to quality. The tables on page 306 give a desirable water-cement ratio of about 6 gallons of water per 94-pound bag of cement. Less water makes for stronger concrete, but reduces workability. More water improves workability, but cuts down on strength and durability.

While the most accurate way to proportion concrete is by weight, you may prefer to batch by volume. Shovel-batching is volume proportioning. That's okay. Both by-weight and by-volume tables are given. When you proportion by volume rather than by weight, remember that the volume of each batch is always somewhat less than the sum of the volumes of the ingredients. This is because the smaller particles fit into the spaces between the larger particles. On the other hand, material weights always add to the total weight of concrete.

Trial mix. Since sand and coarse aggregates are variable, depending on where

BATCHING CONCRETE BY WEIGHT

The most accurate batching of concrete ingredients is done by weighing them out. A bathroom scale and three pails will let you do it with accuracy. Support the batch cans above the scale's platform and zero it with the cans empty. Get proper weights from the table on by-weight batching.

Once you've weighed out every ingredient, made a successful trial mix, and adjusted your ingredient weights to it, you can switch to easier by-volume batching by marking level lines on batch cans where the weighed-out ingredients reach. The scale is then no longer needed.

they come from, the accompanying tables have been based on average sand and average coarse aggregate found around the nation. They may need a little adjusting to suit the actual material you work with. Here's how to do that:

Make your first batch a trial mix. Use the figures from the appropriate table, correcting for water contained in your sand. (See accompanying photos.) Then examine the resulting trial mix for stiffness as well as for being too sandy, too gravelly, or just right. Adjust as follows:

• Too wet: Add about 3 pounds of dry sand at a time for each cubic foot in the batch. Examine each time after mixing. When the trial mix looks right, record the total weight of sand added. The resulting trial mix may then be used in the project. In proportioning later batches, cut down

PROPORTIONING CONCRETE

By Weight (air-entrained concrete)

*Maximum coarse aggregate**	*Cement (lb.)*	*Sand (wet, lb.)*	*Coarse aggregate (lb.)*	*Water (lb.)*
⅜ inch	29	53	46	10
½ inch	27	46	55	10
¾ inch	25	42	65	10
1 inch	24	39	70	9

*If crushed stone is used, decrease coarse aggregate by 3 lb. and increase sand by 3 lb.

By Volume (air-entrained concrete)

Maximum coarse aggregate	*Cement (lb.)*	*Sand (wet),*	*Coarse aggregate (lb.)*	*Water*
⅜ inch	1	2¼	1½	½
½ inch	1	2¼	2	½
¾ inch	1	2¼	2½	½
1 inch	1	2¼	2¾	½

Among concrete's ingredients, the sand varies most. Adjusting for water contained in it will make your mixes come out with uniform stiffness. To judge wetness of your sand, squeeze some of it in your hand, then release. If the sand falls apart (top photo), it is dry. If it forms a cast but leaves no excess water on your fingers, it is average wet sand (center photo), the way most sand comes from the pile. And if it forms a cast and leaves water on your fingers, it is very wet. Adjust your concrete proportions accordingly. (See table at left.)

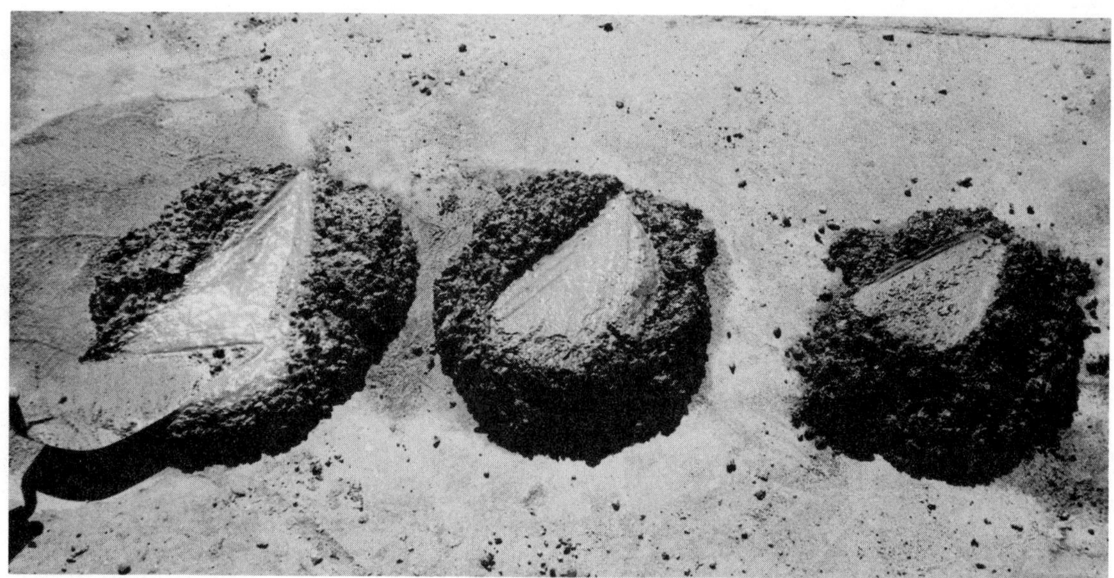

Concrete stiffness (also called slump) is an indication of its workability. The water content of your trial mix should be adjusted to make concrete of about 5″ slump, as shown in the center pile. The concrete on the left contains too much water for maximum strength. The concrete on the right would be strong, but it is too stiff for hand methods of placing and finishing.

on the water 1 quart for each 10 pounds of dry sand that you had to add to the trial mix. Use the *original* quantities of sand and coarse aggregate from the table.

• Too stiff: Cut back on the amount of coarse aggregate in the next batches and adjust your figures for the new weights. No water adjustment is necessary. You can save the trial mix for use by adding both cement and water to it in the proportion of 1 quart of water for each 4 pounds of cement. This maintains a water-cement ratio of about 6 gallons of water per sack of cement.

• Too sandy: While a sandy mix works easily, finishes well, and is good for making finely detailed concrete castings, it is not an efficient use of materials for larger projects. To correct it, add 3 pounds of coarse aggregate per cubic foot. Mix again and examine. If need be, add coarse aggregate in 3-pounds-per-cubic-foot increments and remix until it looks right. Then adjust your figures for subsequent batches. The trial mix may also be used in the project.

• Too stony: In the next batch, cut back on the amount of coarse aggregate and increase the amount of sand equally. Note the new sand and coarse aggregate figures for subsequent use. You can adjust the trial mix for use by adding sand to it.

In every case, keep a record of the proportions used in your good mix. Afterward—as long as you can use the same sand and coarse aggregate—the proportions should not need changing, except to adjust for variations in water in the sand.

• Sand moisture: Most sand contains

Another adjustment to make to your trial mix is for coarse aggregates. The left-hand pile is too rocky for successful finishing. The pile on the far right contains too little coarse aggregates for efficiency. The pile in the center has just the right blend of coarse and fine aggregates.

some water. When proportioning, this must be counted as part of the mixing water. The tables assume average *wet* sand. (See photo on page 306.) This is the way sand is usually found on the job. If your sand is different, adjust as described in the photo caption. If you use volume batching, forget the wetness adjustments. This method isn't accurate enough to bother with them. But because sand bulks (increases in volume) as much as 1¼ times its dry volume, try to volume-batch with *wet* sand.

AIR-ENTRAINED CONCRETE

Practically always you will want your concrete mix to be what is called air-entrained, also for ready-mix, haul-it-yourself, or pumped concrete. Air-entrained concrete contains millions of microscopic air bubbles that serve as safety valves for expansive pressures when absorbed water freezes inside the concrete in winter. Air-entrained concrete can take freezing, thawing, and deicers far better than plain concrete can. For this reason, it's recommended that you gear up to make air-entrained mixes. Even if you live in a freeze-free climate, you still need the other benefits of air-entrained concrete: cohesiveness and freedom from bleeding. Bleeding occurs when excess water in the plastic concrete rises to the surface soon after placement. Finishing operations must be delayed until bleed-water evaporates. Because it does not permit bleeding, air-entrained concrete can be finished much sooner.

Air-entrained concrete is made by using either air-entraining portland cement Type I-A or Type II-A (the A means air-entraining), or by mixing an air-entraining agent (such as vinsol resin) into the mix. Do-it-yourself dealers and concrete

products outlets seldom stock either one. Ready-mix dealers have them in bulk, but probably won't want to sell you a small amount. One place to get some is from a U-Cart haul-it-yourself concrete dealer. They call it *Free-Flo*. A quart should be enough. Ask the dealer for the price. Bring your own container; the dealer's supply will be in a 55-gallon drum. Get directions on how much to add to a batch to get the desired air content. Hand-mixing is not vigorous enough to entrain air into the mix. Only machine-mixing will do it.

PREPACKAGED MIXES

The task of selecting and proportioning the separate ingredients for mix-it-yourself concrete can be bypassed when you use prepackaged concrete mixes, ideal for small projects, a timesaver for big ones. These come in 80- or 90-pound bags. Each makes about ⅔ cubic foot of concrete. You can get them either with or without coarse aggregate. The former is called *gravel mix* or *concrete mix*. The latter is called *sand mix* or *mortar and topping*. Use concrete mix for projects thicker than 2 inches. Use sand mix for thinner projects. Be sure that what you buy contains no lime or other plasticizers. While these add to the workability of mortar, they weaken the product too much for use as concrete. The amount of water to add to a bag of mix is shown on the package. Prepackaged mixes do not make air-entrained concrete unless you add an air-entraining agent.

A metal wheelbarrow is convenient for mixing up a concrete batch. Waterproof and impervious to scraping with the hoe or shovel used in mixing, it has the additional advantage of being transportable so that you can wheel it to the sand and gravel piles, and measure them and the cement directly into it; after the water has been measured and mixed into these, the wheelbarrow can be wheeled back to the job. Or it can be filled with the dry ingredients and the water mixed in at the site where the concrete will be used.

You will need a shovel and a hoe. A square-ended shovel or garden spade is the best to use, but any shovel can be used if you haven't either of these. A garden hoe can be used, although a mason's hoe, which has holes in its blade, will more quickly mix ingredients.

The procedure for mixing concrete is as follows:

Measure out the sand and place it in a ring in the wheelbarrow, or on a large piece of exterior plywood if you are not using a wheelbarrow. Then measure out the cement and place it in the center of the ring. Thoroughly mix the sand and cement with the shovel until the whole mass is a uniform brown-gray with no streaks of either sand or cement visible.

A five-gallon-pail mixer is handy for small jobs and for mortar-making. With extra sets of pails, it can even be prebatched. The batch sizes it makes are ideal for casting a few small stepping stones at a time. Over the course of a month many stepping stones can be made this way.

Next, measure out the gravel or other aggregate you are using and spread it on top of the mixture; then turn it again with the shovel to distribute the gravel evenly throughout. When this has been done, make a hollow in the dry ingredients and pour in a little water, mixing it and turning the dry ingredients into it with the shovel or the hoe. Add water, a little at a time, mix, and then add more water, until all of *the proper amount of water* has been used. You may use less than is prescribed in the table if the mix seems to be of the proper consistency, or just a *little* more if it is too stiff, but be careful in adding water lest you use too much.

Keep mixing the concrete until it is thoroughly blended, scraping up every bit of the dry ingredients which cling to the bottom of the wheelbarrow or mixing platform and working it in. Practice will enable you to use less muscle without any less thorough mixing, perhaps, but never skimp on the mixing. Better sore muscles than a weak batch of concrete, a mixture which may fail to do its job properly. Use the concrete within a half hour of the time you finish mixing it.

Always mix the ingredients in the order given above: sand and cement, then gravel, and finally the water, whether you are using a mechanical mixer or mixing by hand; and you will be assured of proper blending.

HOW MUCH TO MIX

That will depend upon what you are doing with the concrete, on the depth of the paving, on the width, length, or height of the wall, and on other factors. Paving for patios and for walks should be a minimum of 3 inches thick, or, even better,

EASY-ORDER CHART FOR CONCRETE USERS

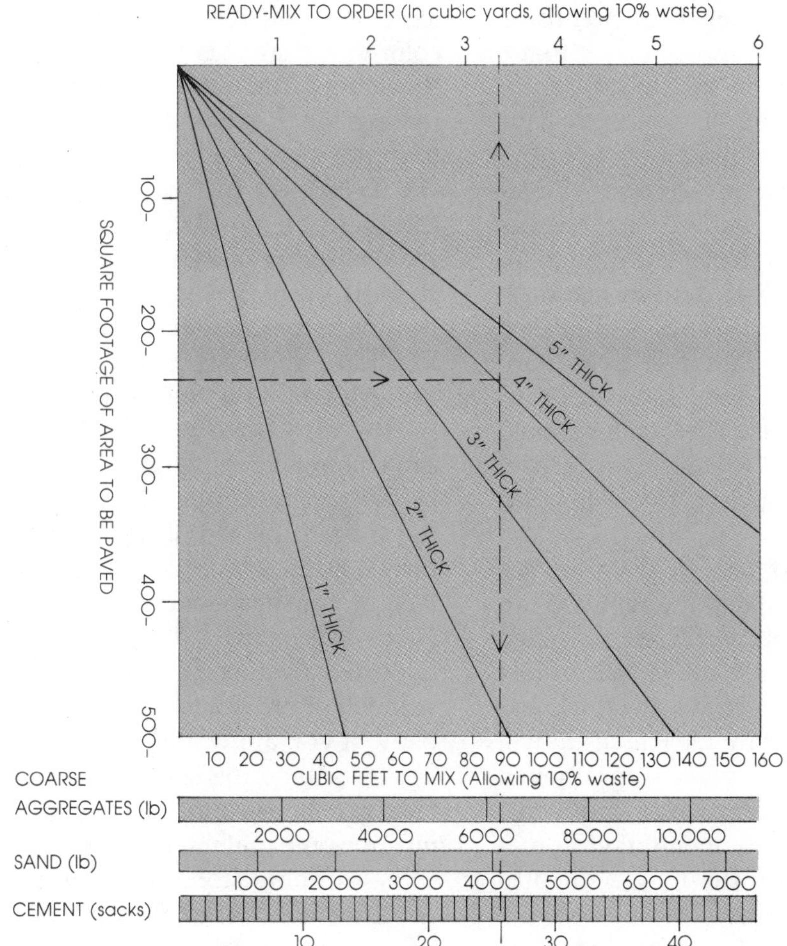

How to use the chart: Start with the area that you wish to pave, measured in square feet. For example, a 4-inch-thick patio that is $12' \times 20'$ gives a total area of 240 square feet (dotted line). Find the *240* at the upper left of the *area* scale. Then draw a horizontal line to the right until it intersects the diagonal line representing the thickness of your project, in this case 4 inches. Then, to find the cubic yards of ready-mix concrete required, go up to the *ready-mix* scale. It shows that 3¼ cubic yards of ready-mix would be needed. To find how much mix-your-own concrete you'd need, go down to the *cubic feet* scale. This indicates that you'll need some 88 cubic feet. To find how much of each ingredient to get, continue the line down through the *ingredient* bars. A bit over 6,000 pounds of coarse aggregate; slightly over 4,000 pounds of sand; and 26 sacks of cement.

3½ to 4½ inches thick. Driveways should be not less than 4 inches thick, according to many authorities, and I believe that 6 inches should be the minimum depth. Even though you don't expect to have heavy oil trucks or other heavy equipment on the concrete when you are building it, future necessities may require otherwise. Thinner slabs may be reinforced with welded-wire mesh made especially for this purpose or with ½-inch steel reinforcing rods. In frost areas, reinforcing will help to keep slabs intact as will contraction joints. These latter should be placed at 9- to 10-foot intervals, closer in narrower slabs such as for walks. (See page 329.)

If the square footage of the area of a projected concrete slab is known, you can easily figure how much concrete is needed for a project. Multiply the length in feet times the width in feet times the thickness in inches and divide by 12. The result will be cubic feet. Add 10 percent for uneven subgrade and spillage waste. From this it's easy to figure how much of each material to order using the by-weight proportioning table shown earlier and the maximum-size coarse aggregate you'll be using. Divide the final weight of cement by 94 to arrive at the number of bags needed. Sand and coarse aggregate are ordered by the pound. Use of the table does away with the calculations.

COLORING CONCRETE

Coloring concrete will give added interest to paving, a floor, steps and steppingstones, and you even simulate natural stone colors that will allow concrete to harmonize with natural stone used for walls and garden features. The main criticism (and all too often justified) about colored concrete is that it is too bright, that the end result is often garish, dominating the scene and making it difficult to create a harmonious color scheme that will include the house, flowers, and other garden features. Although concrete colors may fade a bit and tone down with aging, there is no reason why colored concrete cannot be harmonious and natural-looking. Care and taste must be exercised to achieve a natural, subtle effect.

There are three methods by which you can color concrete: 1. Mix coloring agents in the concrete itself. 2. Spread the coloring agent on top of fresh concrete and trowel it into the finish. 3. Color the surface of finished concrete with a dye, a stain, or a paint.

You can mix the colored concrete yourself or order it from a ready-mix company, if you are willing to accept the limited colors and the uncontrolled effect you may get. If you mix it at home, you can mix up some preliminary samples and cast some stepping stones or other paving to get some idea of what result you will obtain, adjusting the final colors accordingly. One cannot tell from wet concrete mix or even uncured concrete what the final color will be. Only when it is thoroughly dry is the result truly visible. But with preliminary experimentation, you will have a fair idea of the final color.

The coloring agents most frequently employed are usually mineral oxides, especially prepared for this use, and available through your cement supplier. The usual colors are: red, black, green, blue, yellow, and brown. By mixing two or more colors in varying quantities you can achieve some wonderful hues. For instance, by mixing a bit of black with the red you will get brownish and chocolate tones, with deeper tones appearing as you add more of the colors. Blue and green will give a deeper blue-green color which can be toned down and made more harmonious with the surroundings by killing the brightness slightly with a bit of black added. Yellow added to red will produce orange-red tones, and blue added to red will give a cooler, more purplish tone. Again, by adding a bit of black you can tone down the brightness.

It is generally believed more tasteful to use only a few or closely related colors in paving—that is to say, don't use red, blue, green, *and* orange blocks in a single area. Rather, use blues and greens together, reds and oranges, reds and blacks with greys, chocolate and brown tones. Observe nature and see how successfully colors are blended together in rocks and how they seem to occur naturally in related hues with many subtle variations.

Some authorities recommend using white portland cement rather than the normally gray-colored cement in order to get "clearer, brighter colors." If you want brilliant, circus-toned paving, by all means achieve it this way, but if you want a pavement that does not draw attention to itself, that lies flat on the ground, unobtrusive as a tasteful rug, I suggest using the gray-colored cement and toning even that down a bit with a little black coloring matter.

For the most intense colors use coloring pigment up to 10 percent of the weight of the cement. Use no more than that, as it overly weakens the concrete. Full-strength pigments will usually produce good colors when 7 pounds of pigment is mixed with one sack of portland cement. Use 1½ pounds per sack for pleasing pastel colors. This reduces to about 2 pounds of pigment in a cubic foot of concrete, 50 pounds in a cubic yard for full strength colors; 6 ounces per cubic foot, 10 pounds per cubic yard for pastels. Always use the minimum pigment necessary to get the color you want. Pigments may be natural or synthetic, but use only those intended for concrete. They're available where concrete products are sold. Add an air-entraining agent to get surface durability.

COLORING GUIDE FOR CONCRETE

Color	*What to use*
Black, dark gray	Black iron oxide, mineral black, carbon black
Light gray	Normal portland cement
White	White portland cement, white silica sand
Brown	Burnt umber or brown oxide of iron (use yellow oxide of iron to modify the color)
Buff	Yellow ocher, yellow oxide of iron
Rose	Red oxide of iron
Pink	Red oxide of iron (small amount)
Cream	Yellow oxide of iron
Blue	Cobalt oxide, ultramarine blue, phthalocyanine blue
Green	Chromium oxide (use yellow oxide of iron to shade color)

MIXING COLOR IN CONCRETE ITSELF

Color mixes must be blended more thoroughly and mixing should take longer

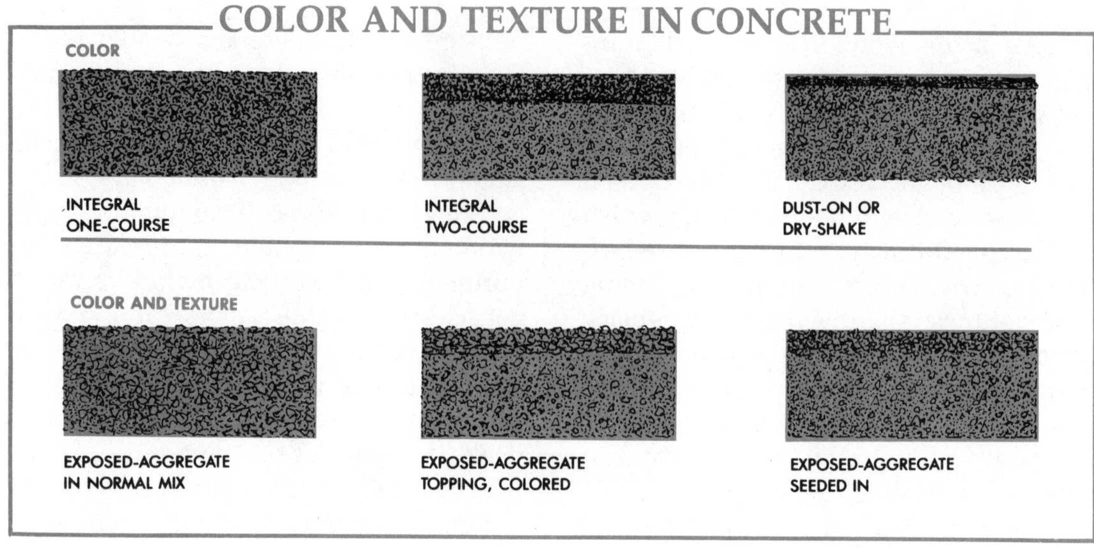

than for ordinary concrete mixtures. Don't skimp on mixing or you may have streaky uneven colors in your paving. For thin pavement—stepping-stones and the like—you may want to color the entire mix but, because of the cost of the coloring ingredients, for larger areas and for thicker pavings particularly, you may want to consider two layers of concrete: a base layer with a color layer laid on top. Mix regular concrete with a variety of aggregates and pour it into the forms to within an inch or even a half-inch of the top, or final surface level, and level it fairly well. Allow it to set till surface water has disappeared, then pour in the colored concrete mixture.

This mixture should be made *without* coarse aggregates, though the proportion of cement to sand and water should be approximately the same. Level to the tops of the form, then complete the process of finishing, floating, and troweling in the same manner as for other concrete. Cure the slabs carefully, protecting them from spotting and staining during the process.

TROWELING IN COLOR

This method is about as reliable when properly done as the above method and certainly easier than mixing the concrete in two coats or layers. Mix and pour regular concrete level with the top of forms and strike off; level with a bull or hand float, after the free water has evaporated from the surface. The dry color agents are then sprinkled or shaken over the surface, care being taken to spread as evenly as possible. "Dry-shake" colors are offered ready for use, packaged by the manufacturer. A dry-shake mix is made using two parts fine mortar sand and one part coloring pigment.

Allow the dry-shake to absorb moisture from the surface of the concrete for a few minutes, then, with a hand float, float it into the concrete surface, blending it in thoroughly. Repeat the process of spreading the dry-shake but this time use only about half the quantity, and then float it into the surface again in the same manner. Trowel the surface at once; then, after it has set up sufficiently, a fine steel-troweling should be given (followed by a *final* steel-troweling if a very smooth surface is desired). For most floors and pavings, a light brushing of the surface with a push broom will make a little surface "tooth" or texture, giving traction for wet weather use and not unpleasant in dry weather. You need 50 pounds of dry-shake coloring for each 100 square feet of surface to be colored.

PAINTING, DYEING, STAINING

These require a different approach and are usually done only on old or finished concrete. If the floor or paving has previously been painted, it must be thoroughly cleaned and then repainted. Dyeing and staining will not work satisfactorily on previously painted surfaces, no matter how well you think you have removed all paint. Paint may be applied by brush, roller, or spray, and formulas specifically made for use on masonry should be used. A formula which incorporates epoxy is long-wearing and has proved satisfactory for most uses.

For a concrete slab, unpainted, unfinished, whether new or old, dyeing and staining will be possible and give satisfactory results for a number of years. It can be redyed or restained and brought back to life again, if you wish. These two methods wear longer than paint, require less upkeep, and give pleasing effects because the colors are absorbed into the pores of the concrete, creating a more stonelike natural effect. The floor or paving should be thoroughly cleaned, scrubbing it with a solution of 1 pound of trisodium phosphate to 1 gallon of water. This should be flushed or washed off thoroughly with clear water. Grease spots or oil stains (particularly on pavement that has had cars standing on it or where cooking has been done) should also be removed to insure even coverage of the colors. A solution of lye—1 pound to a gallon of water—poured on sawdust or shavings and allowed to stand overnight or at least several hours will usually lift the spot. *Handle the lye solution with care.* Lye is strong and dangerous skin and eye burns can result from splashes or careless handling. Wear gloves and clothing covering arms and legs. Also protect the eyes. If one application of lye does not entirely remove the grease stain, repeat the application one or two more times. Scrape the stained spot with a putty knife after the sawdust is carefully removed and disposed of, then flush with clear water.

Next apply an acid etch to open surface pores so that the dye can penetrate deeply, and to remove any further impediment to absorption. Again, protective clothing and caution will be wise. One gallon of muriatic acid combined with 2 to 3 gallons of water in an enamel pail—note this carefully, for the acid will eat unprotected metal—will give the proper solution. Brush it on the slab generously and scrub it in, letting it stand till all bubbling ceases, then work it into the slab, brushing it up and down and then across till there are no slick spots left on the surface. Flush the slab with clear water to remove all acid; then let it dry *thoroughly* before applying color.

Stains may be applied with a roller or a brush and you have a choice of greens, grays, reds, and browns in a variety of tones. For porous surfaces, two coats may be necessary, with a day elapsing between coats to allow drying. Concrete floor wax toned with the color you used may be used to finish the surface, if you wish, but this is usually only done on interior work.

Dyes are applied with a stiff brush. Sometimes a second coat may be required for a final dressing. Colors come in the same range. If some spots are lighter, or glossier, scrub them more vigorously till the tone seems the same as elsewhere on the slab.

One final caution: Always read manufacturer's directions on the packages and follow them completely to insure good results. The above are the best general directions I can give; specific ones must come from the maker of the products.

ALLOWING FOR SUBSURFACE DRAINAGE

All grading, leveling, and construction of forms must be done before concrete is mixed or poured. Where there is any likelihood of subsurface seepage or excessive moisture, it is well to excavate 2 to 3 inches extra to accommodate a layer of tamped gravel or cinders. This will insure subsurface drainage and prevent any sinking or heaving of the slabs from frost or bogginess. Concrete needs uniform support. In bad cases of subsurface moisture, drainage tiles laid under the paving to carry away the excess moisture will suffice, provided that there is some place to which the water can drain from the tiles. If any filling needs to be done, it should be well tamped, wet down, and, when its surface has dried, tamped again. The process should be repeated several times until a good firm surface is obtained. Allowing several months or a year of settling before casting a slab on fill will also do the trick. If your slab must cross a recent excavation for a gas or water line, reinforce the slab above this fill, for cracks and sinking are sure to occur, particularly if your project is a driveway, which must carry heavy weights. Such trenches should be soaked and exceptionally well tamped before the slab is cast over them.

Note: In digging out for wall footings, make sure that the footing is below the frost line in cold areas. The usual recommendation for measurements of wall footings is that they should be the same depth as the measurement of the wall width, and twice as wide as the width of the wall. Thus, if your wall is 12 inches wide, make the footing depth 12 inches and the width 24 inches, with the wall centered on it.

BUILDING FORMS

If your project is the paving of a patio, a walk, or a driveway, it will probably require only the simplest of wooden forms. Sometimes forms may even be incorporated into the paving by using redwood, cypress, cedar, or some decay-resistant wood which has been well treated with wood preservative (Chapter 4). For paving patterns which are obtainable by using this method and from which you can adapt your own design to fit the space you are to fill, see the illustrations on page 394.

On the other hand, you may want to cast your paving and remove the forms, using them elsewhere for further casting and saving the cost of further forms, as in the case of building a long walk, or in casting a paved patio in rows of units.

SLAB DESIGN

Type of slab	*Nominal thickness*	*Width*	*Slope*	*Control joint spacing*
Driveways	4″ (cars) 5″ (heavy trucks)	8′-9′ (1 car) 15′-18′ (2 cars)	¼″/foot drainage 14% max. grade	10′ max. (across) 12′ wide (or more) needs a center joint
Sidewalks (and walks at spots traffic crosses)	3″ (foot traffic) 4″ (cars) 5″ (heavy trucks)	2′-3′ or more	¼″/A. drainage	40″ max. (across) (2′ width) 5′ max. (across) (3′ + width)
Patios	4″ or more	larger the better	¼″/A. drainage	10′ max. (each way)

Note: For pre-casting paving blocks, as well as for casting slabs in place, a stiff mix of concrete with a minimum of water will allow the forms to be taken off very soon after casting for reuse. For paving blocks, cast them on a plywood pallet leaving them on it to cure and harden; or they may be cast as specified in Chapter 19. Wrapping the members of the form with waxed paper, rather than oiling them (as often advocated), will keep the wood clean. Razor-blade the wrappings and remove the form easily. The waxed paper can be torn off or left to disintegrate.

It will be well, in fact, to plan the patio paving or walk so that it can be paved in units; then you can do only as many units as you may be able to handle in a day. About all that the do-it-yourselfer can expect to accomplish in one day is about 50 square feet of 4-inch-thick paving. If you can break this up into 4- or 3-foot squares (or oblongs of the equivalent square footage) you will find that you can do about three 4-foot squares or five to six 3-foot squares per day. In the beginning, have as many forms built for the squares as you think you may be able to accomplish in a half-day's work—say two 4-foot or three 3-foot. Use selected 2″×4″ stock which is straight and clear grained for the forms. If they are to remain as part of the paving, use wood preservative on them.

Stakes set outside the forms will hold them solidly; crosspieces in the forms should be securely nailed into place. Start with one end of the form and nail the stake securely to it so that the top of the board will be level with the soil, or with whatever level you wish the concrete to attain. Place the other end of the form on a stake and secure it, using the mason's level or a long carpenter's level.

Let me digress to point out that patios, driveways, and walks all need a slight pitch to enable moisture to drain away. Patios are pitched away from the buildings they adjoin; driveways are crowned so that they drain from the center to both sides, unless there is some good reason for draining to only one side; and walks also are usually crowned. On occasion it will be advantageous to pitch driveways to drain in the center so that the water will be led down to an outlet or sewer. About ½ to ¾ inch per 5 feet of length is

A PATIO FORM LAYOUT

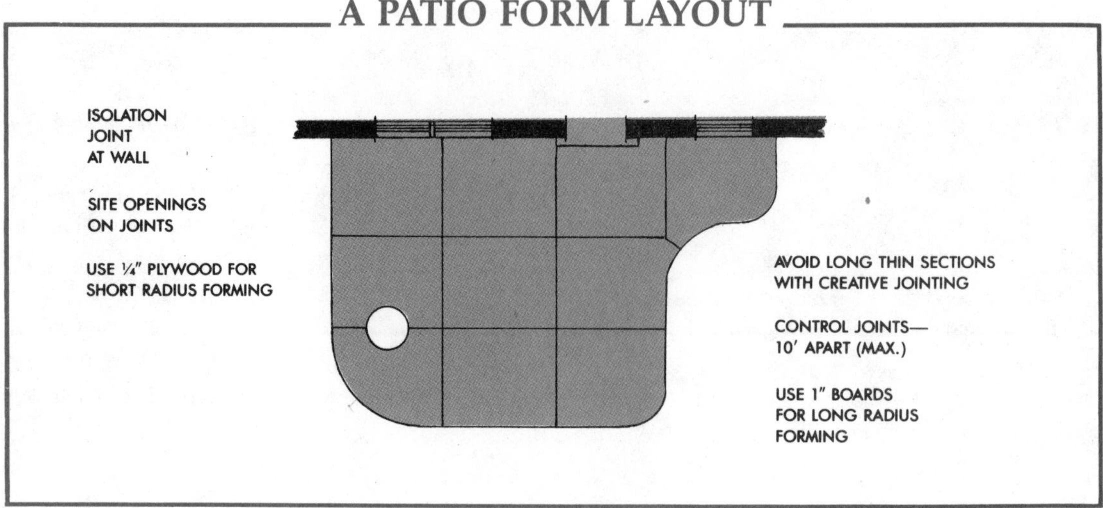

usually sufficient drop for drainage on patios, and a little more can be used for driveways and walks.

To return to the building of forms, be sure to use good sturdy stakes that are long enough to anchor firmly in the soil. Brace the forms against other objects, or use several heavy building blocks to hold them if you are not certain the stakes will hold, as may be the case in sandy soil. Use as many intermediate stakes as may be indicated by the length of the forms. Wet concrete is very heavy and may burst out of the forms or push them aside if they are not securely anchored. If you wish to cast concrete with a long curving edge—as on a patio, a driveway, or a walk—thin plywood may be used for the form, or hardboard, cut to proper width. Double or triple the boards and you'll have fewer stakes to set and the form will be strong and pliable. Or use 1-inch boards of suitable width, making saw cuts a third to halfway through to allow them to be bent. Cuts are made at regular intervals, a few inches apart, with cuts farther apart for arcs with a larger radius. Whatever the form material used, make sure that the curve is a true arc with no bumps or jogs or "corners" occurring anywhere. Stake well so that the forms will hold the concrete and not be pushed out of place, thus assuring a long, flowing curve.

POURING THE CONCRETE

When your forms are ready, water the area inside them, soaking it well on the evening before you are to pour the concrete. This will prevent the soil (or dry gravel if you are using a drainage layer) from pulling water from the concrete and weakening it. Early morning is the best time to pour concrete in hot weather, because heat makes it set quickly, sometimes preventing proper finishing and curing. The ideal time for concrete work is cool or moderately warm weather, so it is best if you can schedule your work to take advantage of this. If the temperature is likely to go below freezing, it is not wise to attempt a concrete job because freezing will weaken and destroy it.

HOW TO LAY A CONCRETE SLAB

1. Excavate to required depth—base plus thickness of concrete slab—roughly leveling soil. Remove all sod and vegetable matter, digging out soft and muddy-moist spots and refilling with sand or gravel. Also loosen hard, compacted spots; tamp well to give uniform support to slab.

2. Build forms of straight kiln-dried or seasoned wood, staking on outside of forms at intervals to brace and hold firm. Drive stakes in straight to ensure that forms are plumb and true. Level forms, using a carpenter's or mason's level both lengthwise and crosswise.

3. After it has been poured into the forms, chunk the concrete with a flat-ended shovel to further consolidate it. Chunk along the forms, too. This mix is about the right stiffness (slump) for good workability. If concrete flows into place, it contains too much water.

4. Striking off is a two-person job, one on each end of the strikeboard. Make two complete passes with the strikeboard, sawing it across the tops of the forms and moving it ahead a little at a time. Keep a little concrete ahead of the strikeboard to fill in low spots.

5. For a large slab, where you cannot reach all of it from the edges, a bull float is best for initial finishing. Raise and lower the handle a little on push and pull strokes to keep leading edge of the blade from digging in.

6. When you can reach all parts of the slab from the edges, a darby makes an excellent initial finishing tool. Hold it with both hands and work in overlapping arcs. Note that the first finishing step begins immediately, even before the ready-mix truck has cleaned up and left.

7. After the water sheen has disappeared, float the slab with a wood or magnesium float. The metal float works better on air-entrained concrete. One or two floatings produce a gritty-textured finish that is ideal for outdoor slabs.

8. Edging is done along with jointing and floating to put smoothly curved fillets on the top of the slab. It looks good and keeps edges from being chipped once they harden. An edger with a ½" maximum radius is best.

9. Steel-troweled finishes call for a number of trowelings, each after concrete has gained additional stiffness from the time before. Final troweling, shown here, takes considerable pressure with the trowel held at a steep angle. The trowel rings against the slab. A steel-troweled finish is not recommended for outdoor do-it-yourself finishes.

10. Another way of curing a slab is to paint on a membrane-forming curing compound, available at concrete products suppliers. As you can see, even this clear compound discolors the surface. In about two months, after concrete has thoroughly cured, the coating will degrade in sunlight and disappear.

11. After concrete has hardened sufficiently not to be marred, remove coverings and replace with a layer of sand or straw for at least three days, keeping it moist by sprinkling with water regularly. Or build earth dikes around edges and fill with 1" of water.

Place a plank over soft ground so that you can wheel up your barrowload of concrete and pour it into the forms, dumping it with ease. Concrete should be used within a half-hour of mixing for best results. After it is in the forms chunk it with a shovel. Pay particular attention to the corners, ramming the concrete in to be sure no air holes remain. The next pouring will be placed adjacent to it, not on top of it (unless it is the finish-coat pouring). Then quickly mix the next batch before the first sets. Don't make what are called "cold" joints in concrete. If you are unable, for any reason, to finish the entire slab, install a keyed bulkhead in the form and finish to it. The tapered keyway is made by ripping a board on an angle and nailing it onto the bulkhead with the smaller side facing out. Then, before pouring the next time, remove the bulkhead and keyway. The fresh concrete will then form itself into the keyway, tying the two old slabs together.

PRELIMINARY FINISHING

You have about 1½ hours after mixing to place and start to finish a concrete slab. Dampen the subgrade before putting concrete on it. Don't, however, place concrete on mud, snow, ice, or soft spots. Use a rubber-tired wheelbarrow to transport concrete from a ready-mix truck or mixer to the forms to prevent segregation. You can rent it if you do not have one. Always dump concrete full depth against the forms and work backwards, dumping against either a form or the previously placed concrete. This helps to compact the concrete in place. You can chunk the mix with a shovel to compact it against the forms. Never add water to the mix to make it flow into the forms. That weakens it, as explained earlier. Spade the concrete to consolidate it. A short-handled square-ended shovel works fine for this.

Strike off the surface of the concrete with a long, straight 2″ × 4″ strikeboard or screed. It takes two people to do this. Seesaw the strikeoff back and forth, moving it ahead a little with each cycle. Strike off twice.

If you have a bull float or darby (shown in Chapter 10), you can do the initial floating immediately with it. A bull float has a 4-foot-long wooden blade that smooths any irregularities in the surface. Its long handle permits early use without going onto the still-soft slab. A darby is an extra-long wood float that likewise smoothes irregularities. The bull float is pushed and pulled across the surface from outside the slab. The darby is worked in overlapping arcs, and may require getting onto the slab with a pair of kneeboards. Work backwards so that you finish over the marks left by the kneeboards.

Next cut the slab away from its forms with a trowel. Ideal for this is a narrow-bladed margin trowel, but a bricklaying trowel will do. Then wait for all the bleed water to evaporate from the surface and for the concrete to stiffen slightly. When there's no free water on it and it will hold your weight with only a ¼-inch-deep boot impression, you can begin the rest of the finishing process. Eliminate the impression immediately, of course.

Start your final finishing by floating and edging all around. Edge with a curved-blade edging tool. Cut control joints along with or just after edging. These are needed to give a big slab a place to crack that will forestall random shrinkage cracking. (Concrete shrinks on setting, and unless heavily reinforced it will crack. Control joints control shrinkage cracking.) Float the surface with a magnesium flat (air-entrained concrete) or a wood float (non-air-entrained concrete).

At this point, the surface is not what could be called *smooth*. If you like the texture but not the float marks, you can remove them by a light brooming. The roughness after brooming will depend on how soon you broom and how stiff the broom's bristles are. For a smoother finish, give the slab a second edging, jointing, and floating after the water sheen has disappeared again and it has gained additional stiffness. Use the wood float again or magnesium float for go-around number two, also. Follow by brooming. Steel-troweling, though widely used as a final finish for floors, is too smooth and slippery in wet weather for most outdoor uses, and is not recommended. It is important to keep from overfinishing concrete, that is, working too much of the cement paste to the top. Overfinishing leads to dusting, crazing, and scaling. If you follow the steps above, you will not be overfinishing your slab.

The tool that you use for cutting the control joints should have a deep enough bit to cut them at least one-fourth of the slab's depth. Thus, on a 4-inch slab, 1-inch-deep control joints are needed to control cracking. Another type of joint, called an *isolation joint*, is made with ¼- to ½-inch-thick composition strips. These can be purchased where concrete products are sold. The dealer will likely refer to them as "expansion joints." It's an inaccurate term, since concrete does not to expand beyond its original dimensions. Isolation joints are needed where one type of concrete construction meets another; for example, between a patio slab and the house foundation, or between a sidewalk and a driveway. They keep differential movements in the constructions from affecting each other.

Control joints should be a maximum of 10 feet apart in both directions. A driveway wider than 12 feet calls for a longitudinal control joint down its center to keep a random crack from forming there. This can be formed in or made during finishing. In any case, the two slabs thus created should be tied together by a row of ½-inch-diameter 3-foot-long reinforcing bars on 40-inch centers across where the joint will be. Transverse control joints need no such tying together.

Clean all tools immediately after completing the job, using water. Dry and oil them before storing them.

It is essential that all concrete be "cured" so it can gain sufficient strength before drying out. Minimum curing time is 5 days. Seven days is better, especially in cold weather. "The longer the stronger" is a good rule to remember about curing. Curing can be by membrane-forming curing compound, which can be purchased from concrete products suppliers, continuous sprinkling, waterproof covering, wet burlap, or ponding. To avoid a splotchy appearance in colored concrete, do not use plastic coverings to cure it.

After curing, all newly placed concrete needs at least 30 days of air-drying before it can stand up to deicing chemicals. So you should complete all your concrete projects at least a month before the first bitter cold weather.

Because concrete is an alkali, avoid prolonged skin contact with cement or plastic (unhardened) concrete mixtures. It's a good idea to wear protective clothing while working. Rubber boots will let you walk in the plastic mix without harm, but do not go barefoot. Skin areas that have been exposed directly or through saturated clothing should be washed thoroughly with water. Adding a cupful of cider vinegar to a gallon of water for a final washing will help skin to recover its normal acidity. Eye protection will guard against blowing cement dust and spattering concrete.

HOT WEATHER CONCRETING

Most likely you will not feel like working on concrete when the weather is too cold for the usual procedures to be used. But during hot weather concrete needs special attention. Make your plans to provide the treatment needed. Work in the early morning or start later in the day after the sun is off the project. Build sunshades, windbreaks. Keep the aggregate piles damp and cool. Consider using crushed ice to replace part of the mix water to help cool the mix, making it slower to set. Sprinkle subgrade or subbase and forms with water before placing concrete against them. Have plastic sheeting on hand to cover the poured surface until just before you are ready to finish it. Then remove the covering. Arrange for plenty of help so you can begin finishing as soon as the bleed water has left the surface and complete it as rapidly as possible. The concrete's set must not get ahead of your finishing crew. Finally, begin the cure as soon as the surface has set enough to take it without being harmed.

Taking these steps will let you get your concrete laid and finished the way you want it before it becomes too stiff.

EXPOSED AGGREGATES

This extremely rough, but durable, finish is obtained by using a stiff coarse-bristled brush and water to scrub away the surface concrete, removing the small aggregates and cement to expose the larger aggregates. The final surface layer should contain only sand and uniform aggregates of the size which it is desired to expose, chosen for color as well as for uniformity of size. This layer is finished by initial floating and allowed to harden for about four to five hours in average weather, or longer in cool weather, less time in hot weather. A surface which has hardened too quickly due to hot weather may be scrubbed with a bristle brush (not a wire brush), and hydrochloric (muriatic) acid, in a solution of 1 part acid to 5 or 6 parts of water. Rinse and hose down with water after the aggregates have been sufficiently exposed, to keep the acid from continuing to eat away the concrete.

This rough surface, attractive though it is, has some disadvantages. It is not a good play surface for children, being extremely abrasive, and it may also prove inconvenient to use with some kinds of furniture. It will hold dust and dirt and is not easy to sweep, so that hosing and an occasional scrubbing may be necessary to keep it clean. However, its attractiveness with informal structures and even fairly formal ones (it mates particularly well with modern architecture) and its compatibility with rough-sawn boards facing houses and fences will recommend it to many. It provides excellent traction

These photos show effects obtained by using exposed aggregates of ½″ or less and 1½″ or more. Techniques for laying exposed aggregate walks are shown on upcoming pages.

FINISHING EXPOSED AGGREGATES

1. Exposed-aggregate finishes are colorful, agreeable in texture, give a rustic effect that is most decorative. Choose aggregates uniform in size and compatible in color, not less than ½″ to ¾″ in diameter. Distribute them evenly on top of concrete immediately after screeding.

2. Embed aggregates initially by patting them in gently but firmly with a flat board—a 2″ × 4″ is a good size and weight—resting it on both sides of form so that surface remains flat and even. Be sure to work in well until aggregates are thoroughly embedded.

3. As soon as concrete is firm enough to support a man on a board, hand-float the surface using a metal floater. Make sure that all aggregates are embedded just beneath the surface so that grout completely surrounds them, with no holes or openings left in the surface of the concrete.

4. Allow surface to set for an hour or so, and test; then expose aggregates by brushing with a stiff-bristled pushbroom or a straw broom, hosing surface as the work is done. For large slabs, do-it-yourself use of a retarder is not recommended.

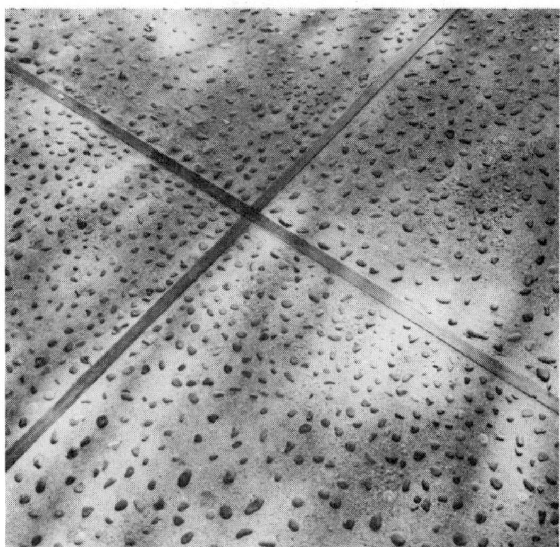

5. Exposed-aggregate concrete with pebbles loosely spread and form boards left in creates an outdoor surface of lasting beauty. Another advantage of leave-in forms: one square can be done at a time, cutting the job down to a more manageable size.

in all weather and looks attractive even in very large areas of paving. It is best used for paving patios, walks, and steps.

REINFORCING THE CONCRETE SLAB

Most paving around the house benefits more from a little extra thickness of concrete than it would from the addition of steel reinforcing. And the extra thickness of concrete usually costs less than the steel might. Still, three kinds of home projects call for reinforcement: (1) light reinforcement—usually with welded-wire fabric—to keep normal cracks in concrete from widening; (2) heavier reinforcement to buttress concrete against tensile forces, such as slabs in spots where the soil has been filled or is unstable, and where strain occurs from weight, as in heavily trafficked driveways; and (3) engineered reinforcement to build safe, loadbearing structures. Lacking an engineer's directions to reinforce, that leaves two reasons.

Light steel reinforcement can be used to build a concrete wall or slab without control joints. While it will still crack, the cracks that do form will be held tightly together and won't develop into ugly, wide ones. Concrete floors that are to be tiled need this treatment. Crack-containment steel mesh is marketed according to spacing and gauge of the wires it's made of: common is 6″×6″ mesh in 6-, 8-, or 10-gauge, heaviest to lightest. Sometimes the wires running in one direction may be of a heavier gauge than those in the other direction. Easy to use, welded-wire fabric comes in rolls and (for the heavier gauges) sheets. Roll it out and cut it off with nippers. Mesh isn't costly,

The simplest reinforcing to use is welded-wire fabric, also called steel mesh. Rolled out on the subgrade and supported at mid-slab height, the mesh provides enough reinforcing to keep concrete's shrinkage cracks from opening up beyond hairlines.

Devices to hold steel reinforcing at proper height in a slab are called "chairs." This was made from a block of concrete with tie-wires sticking out of it. Laid beneath the steel, its wires were twisted together to hold it in place during casting. Plastic "chairs" are available too.

Another way of positioning the reinforcing at proper height is two-course casting. The first course is struck off at the desired elevation and the reinforcing laid on it. Then the top course is spread over the steel.

either. Crack containment calls for about 0.15 percent cross-sectional area in steel. A single layer of mesh in a slab provides that. This is nowhere near enough reinforcement to strengthen concrete completely.

If strength is needed, forget mesh and add an extra inch of thickness to the concrete. Form control joints to take care of shrinkage cracking. But a garden pool, low garden wall, swimming pool, and those onground steps can all benefit from true steel reinforcing for strength. To get this, use either steel reinforcing bars (called rebars, for short) or multiple layers of welded-wire fabric. It takes some 0.3 to 0.5 percent cross-sectional area in steel to do the job. How much steel to use depends on the span, the distance between supports. Long spans need a higher concentration of steel than short spans. The 0.5 percent steel figure is not too conservative for home-project reinforcing.

On the other hand, designing true structural concrete that might fall and cause injury is no do-it-yourself project. Don't try to dope out your own reinforced concrete beams, columns, and elevated slabs unless you're an engineer. Stick to safe, low-down, and smaller projects.

Concrete rebars come in two styles, smooth and deformed. Those less than ⅜ inch are smooth, usually. Larger bars are deformed, containing lug-like ridges to help increase bond. They're sold by steel and concrete products dealers. Bar diameters come in multiples of ⅛ inch, designated by number. A No. 4 bar is 4/8, or ½ inch in diameter. A No. 5 bar is ⅝ inch. Bars come 20 feet long, usually. Most dealers will trim bars to the length you ask for, even bend them if you tell them what you want. Iron and steel scraps

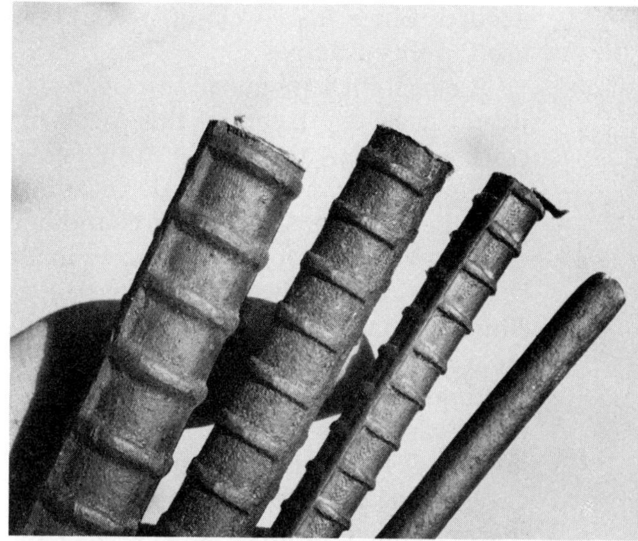

Steel reinforcing bars vary in size to let you select the needed amount of reinforcement. Shown are (left to right): deformed No. 5 (⅝″), No. 4 (½″), No. 3 (⅜″), and smooth No. 2 (¼″) rebars. Strengths of the steel they're made from vary, too, but for home use the lowest strength is often ample.

found around the workshop—pipes, angles, channels—can be pressed into use as concrete reinforcement provided they're free of heavy rust, grease, oil, and such bond destroyers.

The formula for figuring how much steel needed is: $A = \frac{12tP}{100}$. *A* is the steel mesh cross-sectional area in square inches. Get it from the "Cross-Sectional Area of Welded-Wire Fabric." The *t* is your project's actual thickness in inches. And *P* is the percentage of steel required (0.15 for crack containment). Running out the figures for a 4-inch-thick nominal (3½-inch actual) slab on your calculator gives: A = 12 × 3.5 × 0.15 ÷ 100, or a steel cross section of 0.063 square inches. Looking in the table on mesh, you find that 6″×6″ No. 6 mesh provides 0.058 square inches per foot, almost what's

CROSS-SECTIONAL AREA OF WELDED-WIRE FABRIC

Fabric style	*Longitudinal or transverse steel area (A) (sq. in./ft.)*
6″×6″ No. 6	0.058
6″×6″ No. 8	0.041
6″×6″ No. 10	0.029

SIZE AND CROSS-SECTIONAL AREA OF REBARS

(Most rebars come in 20-foot lengths)

Rebar	*Dia.*	*Area (A) (sq. in.)*
No. 2	¼″	0.05
No. 3	⅜″	0.11
No. 4	½″	0.20
No. 5	⅝″	0.31
No. 6	¾	0.44

needed. Since it's so close, it could be used in this example.

A 6-inch-thick (nominal) driveway slab would need two layers of this mesh for crack containment.

Figuring for rebars is harder than for mesh because bar spacing adds another variable. You can avoid using higher math by assuming a convenient rebar size to eliminate that variable. The following formula makes this easy: $S = \frac{100A}{Pt}$. *S* is the spacing between bars in inches; *A* is the trial rebar's cross-sectional area in square inches. Get *A* from the table "Size and Cross-Sectional Area of Rebars." The *P* is the percentage of steel desired (0.15 for crack containment, 0.5 for reinforcement). And *t*, as before, is the actual thickness of the slab or wall. The formula presupposes a single layer of rebars. For a double layer, multiply calculated bar spacing by two. Place rebars running in both directions at the calculated spacing.

For example, in designing a 4-inch-thick garden pond with steel to resist ice pressures in the sides and bottom, say you pick a convenient rebar size of No. 3 and run through the formula. It becomes: $S = 100 \times 0.11 \div 4$, or a 5½-inch bar spacing for 0.5 percent strength-adding steel.

If you end up with a way-out spacing like 24 inches, simply run the formula again using a smaller bar size. Should the spacing work out too close, try a larger bar size. Maximum rebar spacing is three times the actual thickness of a wall or slab. For example: 10½ inches for a 3½-inch-thick slab. Minimum is enough to more than clear the largest aggregate size you'll be using in the concrete mix. For practical purposes, avoid spacings of less than 3 inches. Precise spacing of the bars in a reinforcing gridwork is not critical. What is important is getting the required number of bars in place without leaving any out. Slight shifting of bar positions is okay. The normal tolerance of bar placement is plus or minus an inch. Don't however, cut any bars to clear pipes or other obstacles. Go around them instead, or else avoid them.

Steel rebars may be spliced within a project by overlapping them at least 24 bar diameters and tying with wire. Thus a ½-inch bar should be overlapped at least 12 inches. Splices should not be lapped less than 12 inches, either, regardless of bar diameter. Smooth rebars should be lapped twice as much. Stagger the laps in parallel bars so none occur in the same part of the casting.

Welded-wire fabric needs to be over-

To make a strong saddle tie at rebar junctions, loop soft No. 16 mechanic's wire and hook it beneath the lower rebar as shown. About 1½" of wire should stick up for easy twisting with pliers when finished.

lapped at least one whole grid spacing, plus two inches. Thus, two pieces of 6″ × 6″ mesh should be overlapped 8 inches. Rebars need to be tie-wired where they intersect to keep them in place while casting. Do it with No. 16 mechanic's wire, one wrap at each bar intersection. Use three tie wires at bar splices.

Steel for crack containment should be positioned about one-third of the way down in a slab—1¼ inches below the surface of a 3½-inch-thick slab. This may be done in a two-course operation, striking the concrete off below the top, laying the steel, then pouring more concrete over it. Or the steel may be supported on stakes or pieces of concrete or brick wired under it to hold at the right height. Pre-built "chairs" for supporting reinforcement are available where you buy the rebars. At least two supports are needed for each rebar. Never lay mesh on the ground, pulling it up as you pour. It's better to "walk" the mesh in from the top. Neither method ensures accurate positioning. Reinforced concrete needs extra-careful placement. Tapping the forms with a hammer after a pour helps to bond the concrete and steel. Maximum aggregate size should run not more than three-fourths of the least spacing between neighboring bars or bars and forms. One-inch maximum-size aggregate is a common requirement with reinforcing.

Any concrete slab that's built on more than 12 inches of earth fill becomes a structural slab, one that needs 0.5 percent steel reinforcing in it. For people-only, such slabs use No. 3 bars on 7½-inch spacing. For on-fill driveways that must carry heavier loads, cast 6½-inch-thick slabs reinforced with No. 5 rebars placed 8 inches on centers in both directions.

One final thing: Reinforcing steel—bars or mesh—in concrete needs protection from weathering, which causes corrosion. For this reason minimum distances between steel and the surface of a concrete wall or reinforced slab have been established by the American Concrete Institute. These are shown in the table "Minimum Concrete Coverages." For slabs and walls, such as you'll likely be building, it's ¾ inch. That is, any steel used in a reinforced slab or wall should not reach to within ¾ inch of the surface on any side. Footings need more coverage because they are buried below ground level.

MAKING FOOTINGS

Concrete footings for brick or block walls as well as for cast concrete walls are usually specified as twice as wide as the wall centered on it, and the depth of the footing the measurement of the width. Thus, an 8-inch wall would have a footing 8 inches thick and 16 inches wide. No forms need be built unless the soil is very sandy and loose, trenches usually being sufficiently squared off to be used for forms. Footings should be reasonably level on the top though they may be slightly rough, because block or brick walls need a base that is level enough so they can start the ground courses at true level and maintain it to the top of the wall. Footings should be placed below the frost line in soil.

Where foundations are poured as well as footings, consider pouring (after filling in with soil) an extra 4 to 6 inches of foundation in front of the wall, to be used as a mowing strip if lawn is to be brought

FREESTANDING CONCRETE MASONRY WALL

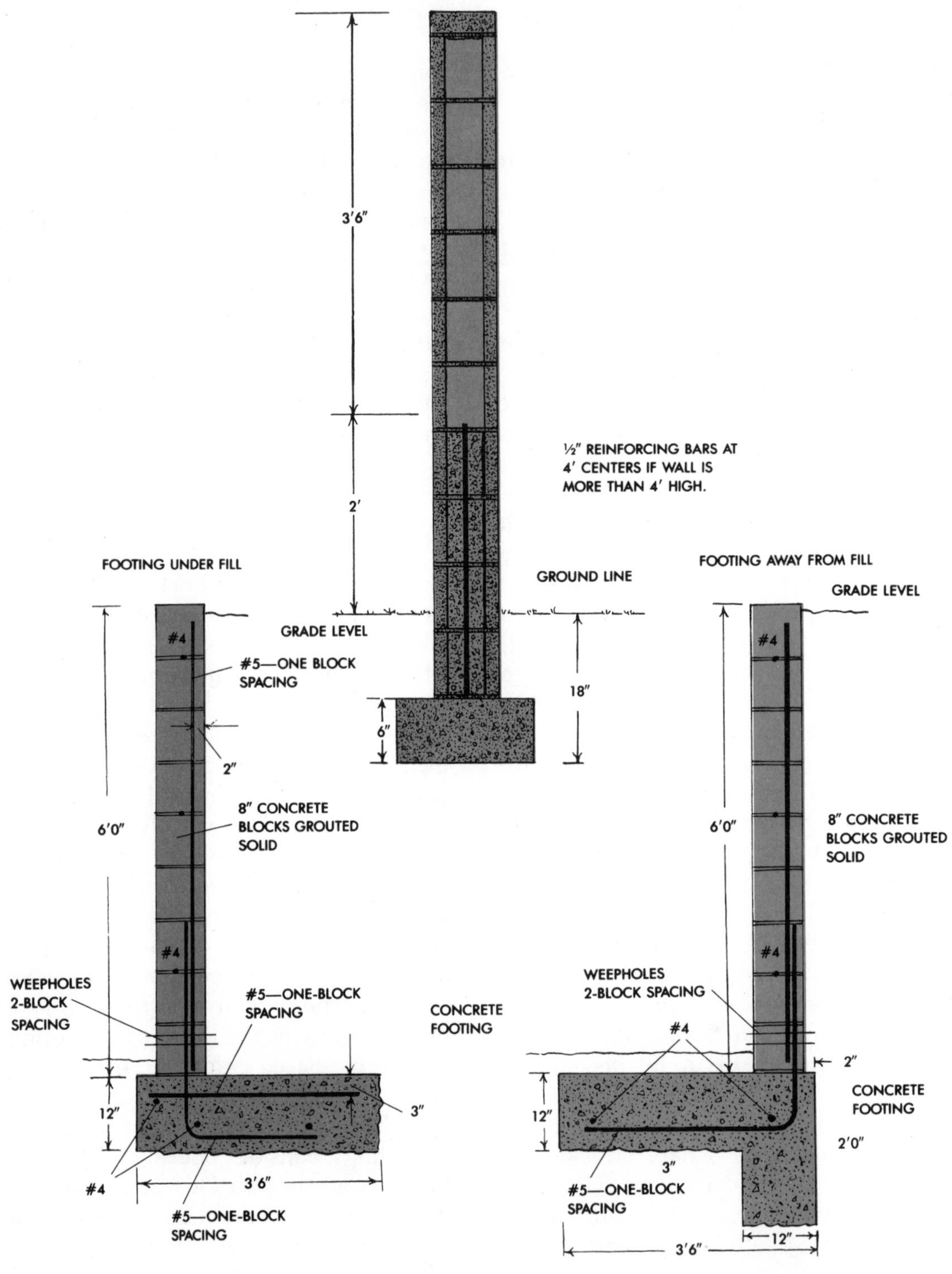

CONCRETE BLOCK RETAINING WALLS

up to the wall. This will eliminate hand cutting and trimming, and still give a neat, easily maintained edge to the lawn. Similarly, where a walk is to abut a wall it may be poured with an isolation joint strip between wall and walk.

POURED CONCRETE WALLS

These walls give you great leeway in design, for anything which can be built in wood as a form can generally be cast in concrete. Concrete is a plastic, fluid material admirably suited to construction work in the yard.

If poured concrete walls are to be high—even if they are retaining walls—they may prove very heavy work for the amateur; but if they are of seat height or less, they are not too ambitious a project. High walls require not only more elaborate forms and better bracing and reinforcement, but also ramps or some system to transport barrow-loads of mixed concrete up to where they can be poured into the forms. This is less of a problem where a retaining wall is being built, because the barrow can be wheeled up the hill, and planks set out across the excavation to the forms for pouring the barrow-load of concrete. Low walls require less elaborate forms and can be poured by tilting the wheelbarrow directly from the ground, or by setting a plank on a concrete block or two if a higher vantage point is needed.

Build all forms and do all excavating necessary, piling the soil nearby for refilling once the project is completed, before beginning to mix the concrete. Do not rush things. Be certain everything necessary is completed and ready before going on to the final step of mixing and pouring.

Forms may be faced with exterior plywood or hardboard to give aboveground walls a smooth face. Where that is not desired, any lumber 1 inch or more in thickness can be used for the forms. The main thing is to use strong lumber with no knots of a size to weaken it; use straight, unwarped boards. For making curved wall forms, 1″ × 6″s may be used, with saw cuts every few inches halfway through the boards. For large curves, every 6 to 8 inches will do, and for small curves, every 2 to 3 inches. Wet the board

MINIMUM CONCRETE COVERAGES

Project	*Min. cover*
Footings	3″
Slabs and walls	¾″
Footings	1″ or more

Source: American Concrete Institute

Concrete is a fluid medium that will take on the shape and texture of whatever it's cast against. This panel was poured into forms lined with a sheet of sandblasted plywood. It came out looking like a piece of petrified plywood.

thoroughly before bending and securing it to the framework. It is also possible to use a framework of 2-inch lumber cut to the curve desired and face it with thin exterior plywood or hardboard (¼ inch), being sure that the frame is well braced to withstand the weight of the poured concrete.

While pouring the wall, spread each layer over as much length as possible, making layers 6 to 8 inches deep, and tamping them into place with a board to force out air holes and compact the concrete. A smooth-surfaced wall is assured if a flat shovel is forced down between the form and the concrete to remove air bubbles and pockets from the surface. Build up the wall with these 6- to 8-inch layers and, when you reach the top, level it off and finish it with the screed board; then float, edge, and finish-trowel it.

Forms should be left in place on poured walls for at least a week after the walls are completed. Place a canvas or building paper cover over the wall so that it is protected from too-fast drying and curing.

FOUNDATION FORMS

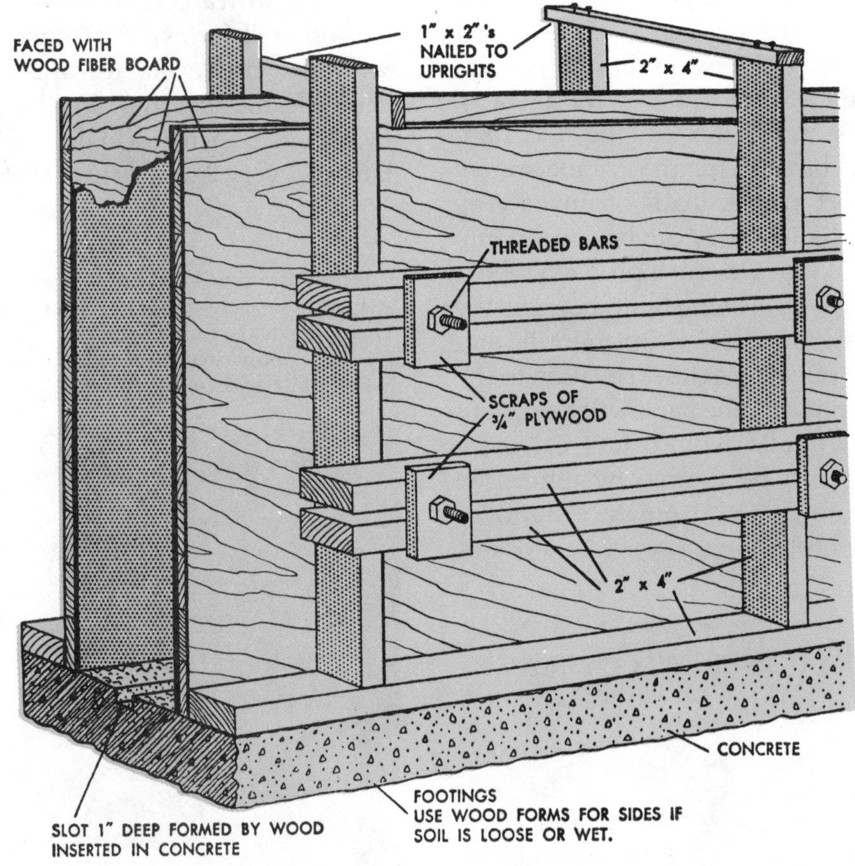

Remove it, sprinkle the wall daily with water to keep it damp through the curing period, then replace the coverings.

Contraction joints. Necessary in unreinforced walls as well as slabs, contraction joints will be placed vertically every 10 to 12 feet. So that strength is not lost, the wall should be keyed to preserve unity, being cast with a kind of tongue-and-groove effect vertically; or it may be cast with a piece of plywood secured to the form where the joint is desired, with reinforcing rods extending from section to section through holes bored in the plywood. Rods should be placed every 3 inches in the wall's height at this point.

Reinforcing rods. Walls over 2 feet in height and less than 8 inches in thickness may need to have steel reinforcing rods inserted horizontally and vertically. For size and spacing information, see the section on "Reinforcing the Concrete Slab," earlier in this chapter. Overlap so that no part of the wall is weakened by having all the rods end together at one point. If your wall is large, perhaps you will want to look into hiring a concrete mixer or buying ready-mix concrete.

Capping. Finished walls should be capped to prevent them from weathering and to give them a finished look. Bricks in a soldier course, thin concrete blocks, coping blocks, tiles, or wooden seats may be used to top the wall and protect it. If the wall is to have a wooden seat on it, be sure to insert the bolts in the still-wet concrete so that you can later attach the seat with ease. Bolts should be sunk at least 4 inches into the concrete and should project high enough to allow a nut to be placed on the threaded shank without its showing above the seat's surface. Holes are countersunk in the wood of the seat to accept the nuts.

PLANNING FOR MOISTURE

Where a poured wall is used as a retaining wall, remember that moisture from the hillside will collect behind it and cause pressures, unless you insert weep holes every 6 feet or so to allow the water to drain out. Or you may insert a line of drain tiles behind the lower part of the wall to carry away excess water, arranging for it to exit at the end of the wall where it can drain away. A gutter is sometimes provided at the foot of the wall face to carry away water which may come out of weep holes or flow down from the hill over the face of the wall, preventing its running across walks, lawns, and patios below.

Walls may be extended by casting an overlapping pier on the back side, or by drilling into the existing wall and inserting reinforcing rods to tie the two together. By painting, stuccoing, or plastering them, the extension can be made almost unnoticeable. Cast concrete walls may be painted with masonry paint, stuccoed, plastered, or left with the grain of the wood forms showing, if you fancy that and if they are worthy of being exposed. Sometimes striated or sandblasted plywood is used for the facing of the form to give the striated or "driftwood" texture to the finished wall. The wall may be painted if you want a colored finish. (See Chapter 13 for information about masonry paints.)

WALLS TO RETAIN TREES

With hillside sites being used more extensively every year, we find that we must grade to make level living areas, and this means that we must either destroy trees or find some way to retain them and their roots. The intelligent thing to do is to keep some trees for shade in the living area, building a retaining wall out near the perimeter of their roots. Such a wall is best kept low, about seat level or a little higher, so that less damage is done to the roots and so that the wall need not be made exceptionally strong, merely strong enough to hold the hill and to withstand pressure from roots in future years. It should be fairly waterproof, because the roots of the tree will have to be watered for several years to assist them in getting over the shock of being cut for the building of the wall, and to enable them to reestablish themselves and send their new roots downward.

Where it is necessary to fill in around existing trees, *always be very careful.* Hundreds of trees are killed each year by people who foolishly believe that they can fill 2, 3, or 4 feet over roots of trees and still have them live. Trees *won't* accept this treatment because their feeding roots near the surface need air and moisture; when this is shut off they have no recourse: they die. If you must fill in over a tree's roots, put an 8-inch layer of heavy crushed rock down, out to the perimeter of the outermost branches; put 4 inches of gravel or sand on top of this; and then fill in with soil, leaving a well around the tree with openings into the stone and gravel layer to permit water to go out to it. Make such a well at least 4 feet in diameter (larger if possible), and try to avoid having the fill be more than 2 feet in any place.

Young trees adjust better to having roots amputated than do older ones. Therefore, if there is a choice to be made between saving a young tree or an old one for shade, choose the younger. If you must use an old tree, leave as much root anchorage as possible. Sometimes when you are digging footings you will encounter a large root below ground. While a small one may be safely cut, any large root should be saved. Dig the footings about 6 inches away from the root on each side to allow for expansion, running them 12 inches deeper, for about 12 to 18 inches outward, than the rest of the footing. After footings are cast and cured, lay a pre-cast window or door lintel across the root to carry the wall's weight. Allow for 2 to 6 inches of expansion room above the root, too, or it may exert pressures as it grows which will crack and upset the wall.

It is possible to resist the pressure of a hill on a retaining wall by methods of construction, too. Use vertical reinforcing rods bent to an L-shape, letting the lower angle extend out into the footing, and fastening the uprights to horizontal rods with wires. Extend the footing on the face of the wall to 8 to 12 inches beyond the face so that the "foot" will help to resist outward presures. The face of the wall should slant back or be "battered" from the base to the top, making the wall in profile slightly wedge-shaped. About 1 to 2 inches per 2 feet of height is a good ratio for slanting the walls.

REPAIRING CONCRETE

Should concrete become damaged by winter freezes or develop cracks and chips from any other source, patch it promptly when the weather permits. This can now be done with much less work and far less trouble than was once required. New compounds with additives in them make the job easier than using conventional portland cement and sand mixtures. The quick-drying latex-, vinyl-, or epoxy-fortified compounds will make a stronger patch than ordinary cement-and-sand, performing in ways that it cannot, and on all but very large patching jobs will certainly be the answer to your prayer. They are, of course, more expensive, but their advantages far outweigh the price.

Latex patching cement. The latex type comes packaged in two separate components—a powdered cement and a liquid latex. Mix the two, blending them into a smooth and workable consistency according to package directions. This will harden in a half-hour to an hour, so do not mix more than is needed for the minimum time span of drying. Although package mixing directions can be used in general, for various purposes you can vary to suit the job at hand. For building out a broken corner, for instance, keep the mixture thicker so that it can be molded and will hold its form. For small chips and fine cracks, make it thinner so that it will flow easily. Latex cement can be spread as thinly as 1/16 inch, may be "feathered out" on the edges to meet existing surfaces. Conventional concrete mixes must be used at least a half-inch thick and this usually means chipping and cutting out old concrete to make room for it. The thin latex mixtures are also excellent for patching hairline cracks. They are also splendid for smoothing the pitted and the pockmarked concrete.

Epoxy patching cement. Because epoxy is the same adhesive used in the powerful epoxy glues, it is tough and has the strongest possible bonding strength. Not only can it be used for patching, it may also be employed to set brick, tile, flagstones, and slate; for bonding glass, steel, and ceramic tile, too. It comes in kits with two bottles—one is emulsion, the other a hardener—and a bag of dry cement. The liquids are mixed according to proportions detailed on the package, then stirred into the dry cement. It may also be "feathered out" in thin layers so that there is no need to chop out concrete or to prepare it in any way other than to clean it well with a stiff brush of all dirt, and remove grease or oil from the surfaces before beginning to patch. Be sure that you fill all cracks and depressions well and tightly pack them to ensure a good bonding.

Vinyl patching cement. This comes already mixed in a dry compound. All that is necessary is to add water and mix well, then use it. Like latex cement, a layer as thin as 1/8 inch may be applied, making it ideal for pockmarked or rough concrete. It has greater adhesive strength than conventional sand-and-cement mixtures and it can be used to set brick, tile, stone, and even glass. It is not affected by winter freezes and thaws in cold climates, and it resists chipping and cracking.

Remember that all of these compounds set very quickly, so that no more than the amount that can be used in something under a half-hour should be mixed at one time. Divide larger jobs and do one part with the first batch, then mix another and patch the next part.

For large patch jobs, particularly where a section must be replaced entirely, the conventional concrete-and-sand mixes may be used, and probably should be, because of the price difference and also because of the quick-drying qualities of the additives in the patching cements. In that case, you'll want to use a bonding agent. Commercial patching compounds are formulated with bonding agents in them. When you use anything else to patch with, it will help to brush on a bonding agent. An ordinary cement-water slurry may be used as a bonding agent, too. Mix portland cement and water to thick cream consistency and brush the slurry onto all surfaces to be bonded. Then, while the slurry is still wet—and before it turns white—lay in your patch. Cement-slurry bonding works well on rough surfaces and those that have been acid-etched to provide "tooth" for the slurry to grip. Do not try to use it on smooth concrete without first etching.

CHAPTER 15

PLANNING A PATIO

A patio, according to the traditional Spanish definition, is a paved, usually unroofed area enclosed on two or three sides, usually with a wall on the unenclosed sides. In America today, however, "patio" is accepted to mean any outdoor space that is paved, whether or not enclosed, either adjacent to the house or placed elsewhere in the grounds wherever suitable.

There are many people who choose their patios merely by thumbing through glossy magazines. When they find a glamorous picture, perhaps something planned for quite a different kind of climate and different sort of house, they think, "That's pretty! That's for me," and then proceed to have some version of that patio built in their garden. But a patio is far too expensive and permanent to be chosen so lightly or so frivolously. There are a good many practical considerations which enter into the choice; they should be taken into account and used in the planning *before* the patio is built, and not afterward when regrets set in.

Among the factors which should come under scrutiny are:

- What is your climate?
- What size is your family?
- What are their interests and inclinations? Their ages?
- What do you expect as to durability, function, future use?
- What can you spend for a patio?

This latter factor is a vital one for it is the kingpin, often, of the whole matter. The pocketbook usually settles a good many things about our way of life, and this is no exception. A patio should not be too elaborate for its surroundings. It should not overpower its setting, but it should, on the other hand, be adequate. It is an outdoor room and as such it is "capital improvement" which will add to the value of your property if you ever wish to sell it, provided that it is properly planned and durably built. Also, sometimes it is possible to start out with both a small and a big plan, adding pieces each year until it is the size you really want it to be. Perhaps it can start out as a gravelled area and then, when it is possible, concrete, stone, or brick can be laid on the gravel. If you want to do it or have it done all at once, you may want to take out a loan and spread the payments over several years. If you do it yourself, adding

Contrasting lightly textured patio paving and steps with raked-joint retaining wall is an effective means of using textures in masonry. Broad, easy steps lead to the landing and then carry down to the lower level from there.

to it year by year, you'll have the use of the patio as it expands; you will spread the work over several years and the cost, too, saving loan interest charges.

First of all, a patio is for use. What do you want from yours? Is it to be an outdoor room where you will entertain, eat, sit, and where the children can play in clement weather? What time of day will you be using it most? If it is to be used at night, can it be lighted? If it is to be used a for eating, how close to the kitchen is it; or do you want to put cooking facilities beside it?

If you have children, the patio is a good play-place for them. It may be that it should be placed adjacent to the part of the house where someone is most likely to be at work, so they can supervise and watch the children play. Perhaps you can satisfy two requirements, that of eating outdoors and that of supervised play, by placing the patio adjacent to the kitchen, where food can be passed outdoors from a window or from a convenient door to be served before it cools.

Should you wish to use the patio for evening entertainment or for sitting outdoors to watch television after the children and older members of the family have retired, the patio is best placed away from the bedrooms, so that the noise of conversation or entertainment and the lighting of the patio will not disturb the sleepers. Alongside a detached garage, or perhaps an attached one which extends away from the bedrooms, would be a good location. This would give a chance for plantings near the house, as well. Some people prefer to divorce the patio from the house and place it in a corner of the property, using high fences to give it privacy; while others prefer to have it attached to the house for easy traffic into and out of the dwelling.

The weather and the sun must also be taken into consideration when you are planning your location for the patio. Remember that the afternoon sun is hottest about three o'clock, and that a patio on the southwest or west of the house is likely to be unpleasantly hot during the afternoon—even into the early evening if it is paved—and it retains the heat unless it is very well shaded. Even if it is shaded, it is usually hotter during those hours of the late afternoon. Many people today are locating patios on the east or southeast side of their houses, even though that side may face the street or be close to a neighbor's house. Devices such as privacy fences and baffles will protect them from passersby and from the neighbors.

On the other hand, if the only logical place for your patio is the southwest or west, making use of a large existing tree to shade it or planting a good-sized one to grow up and give you shade during the hottest hours may be the answer. Until trees get large enough, and even afterward, annual vines on a framework covered with trellis slats will give enough shade to make the patio pleasant. When the trees get large enough to shade properly, the trellis slats may be removed and the vines dispensed with. You may leave the trellis framework, or take it down, as you wish. It is also possible to use roll-up materials for temporary shading. Snow-fencing, bamboo or basswood porch shades, and other materials can be rolled up and stored indoors during the winter, when any light and heat will be welcomed indoors and on the patio. They

WAYS TO ACHIEVE PRIVACY ON SMALL PROPERTIES

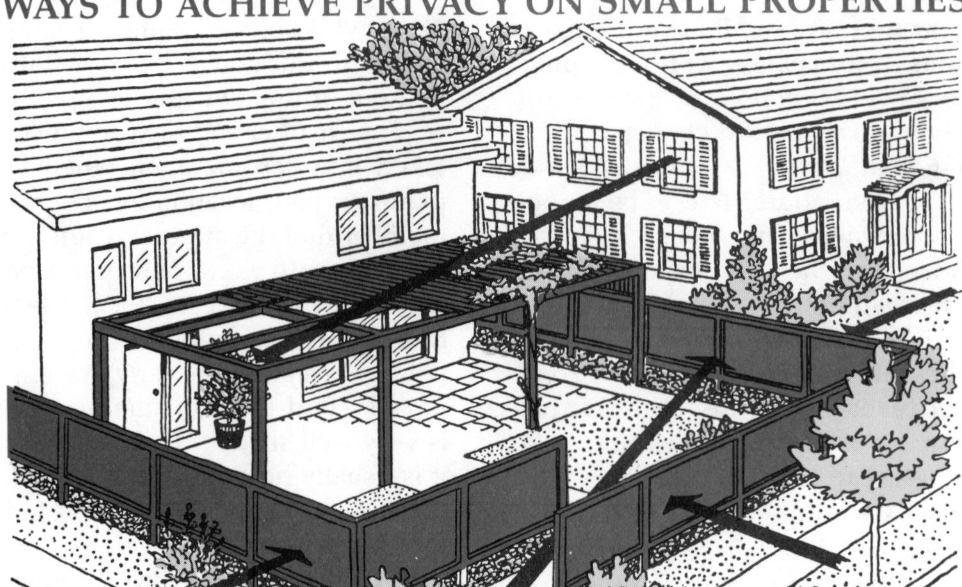

In many neighborhoods it is difficult to get privacy because houses are close together and because upstairs windows overlook living areas of neighborhood yards. By careful planning, by taking into account all factors involved, it is possible to assure complete protection from all angles. Below are shown several methods. The fence which surrounds front yard has a baffle entrance rather than a gate, thus assuring protection of the living patio from observation by passersby as well as from adjacent properties. The patio shelter is partly roofed over with slats to give summer shade as well as protection from eyes on upper floor of house next door. Black arrows show sight lines.

can be lashed to the framework during summer so that winds and storms will not dislodge them.

Take into consideration the prevailing winds, too. In many places a cold wind, a strong wind, or a hot, dry wind may make the vulnerable side of the house less desirable than the side which is sheltered. It is sometimes the case that this windy side is the only possible location, due to the layout of the grounds. In this case you may want to have wind barriers erected in the form of baffle fences; louvred fences; fences with plate glass inserted where there is a view to be preserved but a wind problem to be overcome; or fences with wind-directing tops, which will cause the wind to leap over the terrace before sweeping to the ground again. Plantings, too, may be installed, with evergreens preferred, but with quicker-growing deciduous material also a good possibility. This living wind-break will be very effective when it has grown to proportions large enough to prevent the wind from sweeping over the patio.

Is your climate variable? If sudden showers are likely to come up without warning, perhaps a covered or a partially covered patio may be the answer to this problem. Terrace furniture can be quickly wheeled or carried under cover and, when the shower is over, brought out again for use. If your climate is cold, it is possible to tuck a patio in the angle of two walls which face the sun, so that you will have a protected warm spot in which to sit early in the spring and late in the fall, when other parts of the property may be too cold for comfort. This brings us to another point which you may wish to consider.

MULTIPLE PATIOS

A trend of the past few years is toward more than one paved area. In view of the points brought out in the discussion above you can see why this has come about. If the property is large enough or if the pocketbook can stand it, several would seem to be the best possible answer for all the questions.

A patio on the eastern side of the house is pleasant for breakfasts before the sun gets up toward its zenith and becomes too hot for comfort, and the same patio can be used for cocktails in the afternoon and for evening entertainment. Patios on the west or northwest can be used for morning, noon, and evening entertaining. They are also pleasant in the off-seasons when a bit of warmth in the afternoon is welcome, provided that wind does not interfere with the pleasure of sitting out. A small patio outside a bedroom is an agreeable place in which to sit in dishabille or even to sleep, privacy being maintained by a high fence. If there are older members of the family, such a patio outside their rooms would provide a pleasant refuge when the younger family members might be monopolizing the main patio for their own entertaining. It would also provide a place in which to entertain their own friends in peace and privacy. Parents of teenagers who allow their children to entertain extensively at home will appreciate such a refuge during the green season when the youngsters are in possession of the main patio.

Multiple paved areas extend the pleasures of living and give a richer expression to healthful outdoor life. Having the children's sand box next to it makes the patio a play-place for them during the day; and then it can be taken over by the parents at night. When the children grow up, the sand box can become a plant box or a pool, or the area turned into a flower bed. One patio may be a covered one or have an enclosed porch or a garden house placed alongside it, while another may be left open to the sun to give you a choice of sitting-out places for all kinds of weather, as well as all times of day.

All of these considerations and any others which occur to you should be carefully evaluated and worked out so that you can make the most intelligent choice possible. Probably you will have to compromise somewhere along the line, for practical considerations must always shape the ideal and will influence the placement, the construction, and the embellishment of your patio.

PROBLEM SITES

Not so long ago patios were never built on anything but level, flat land, and, if a house had to be built on sloping land, a patio might be considered but would probably not be built, due to the expense of excavation. Today, however, patios can be built anywhere and everywhere, even on very sharply sloping hillsides where houses have been perched to take advantage of the view. In such extreme cases the "patio" may become a wooden deck built on posts and joists and fitted around existing trees whose branches have been trimmed to the proper level, thus taking advantage of the shade while opening up enough space for use around them. If the trees are surrounded by the deck on a very high level, sufficient space must be left open around the trunks so that they can sway with the wind without endangering the structure.

On less violent slopes, a space can be made by excavating with a bulldozer or by hand (depending upon the extent of the work and the energy of the builder), the excavated soil being used as fill on the downhill side, probably behind a retaining wall. The fill should be well soaked with water, tamped, and allowed to settle for some time before it is finally paved, to avoid cracks. If the uphill side of a patio is more than a foot or so high, it may also require a retaining wall where the excavation has taken place. If there are existing trees on the site the retaining wall may be curved, square, or triangular shaped to save the trees and contain the important roots. It is dangerous to fill in around a tree more than a few inches, for roots need air as well as water. The fill may cut these off and smother and kill the tree. Thus, if your tree is on the downhill side, it would be well to curve the retaining wall around it to leave four or five feet of clear soil at the original level about the trunk.

Very frequently such retaining walls can be the real feature of a patio rather than a regrettable necessity. If the wall is a low one, it can be utilized as extra seating space for parties and picnic luncheons for large groups. A pool or a raised flower bed can also add to the interest and beauty of a retaining wall when it can be incorporated. Often two retaining walls—one on the edge of the patio kept low for seating purposes and to contain a flower bed, and another one higher up on the hill to hold back the rest of the bank—will be a better solution than one high wall would have been. The pressures will be distributed over two walls instead of concentrated on one, and the wall will look less forbidding and be less of a problem to plant and make attractive.

The vogue for houses of the split-level, tri-level, or whatever they may be called, variety seen everywhere nowadays brings in new problems of patio placement, but offers excellent opportunities for using the patio to tie the house to its site and keep it from looking peculiar, as so many houses of this type appear. It is possible for the patio to be built to give living space outside the living room on a raised, intermediate plane, tying in the wing and its two stories with the other section of the house; bringing them into scale with each other; thus making them more interesting architecturally, a function which was performed to a certain degree by the porch on Victorian houses.

Speaking of old houses and porches, many an old house can be made to look up-to-date and to perform today's functions well if the porch is removed and a patio built to replace it. Most old porches are too narrow and skimpy for today's uses and they are seldom well planted or screened for privacy. Sometimes the porch can be left, if it is in good condition and looks well on the house, with the paved area built out in front of it and at its level, the floor being of wood to match or to replace the wooden floor, with the new joists being set on a masonry foundation. This will not only make it possible to enjoy your home more, but it will add to its value and enhance its salability should you ever wish to dispose of it.

Frequently a patio with its fence, its trellis, or view-breaking structures can integrate an unrelated pair of structures, such as a house and a detached garage, or a house and a tool shed or other building. The breezeways, so popular in recent times, can also be brought into use by adding patios to them. Too small to be used as a sitting place and too wide to be considered merely a passageway from house to garage, the breezeway becomes a real feature when it includes an outdoor patio, and has a function beyond that of connecting the house and garage.

HOW TO LAY OUT YOUR PATIO

Once you have determined what your problem is, you are on the way to solving it. Pace off and measure the area you have decided to use for the patio. Perhaps if you drive stakes on its perimeter and run a cord around them you can visualize better what the area is; assess its qualities and its drawbacks. Outdoor furniture can be placed in position within this area, or boxes and other makeshifts if you don't yet own the outdoor furniture you'll be using on it. Test it to see if the furniture is out of the way of traffic from the house across the patio. See if it is large enough for the uses you plan for it and also whether its shape and outlines are pleasant to view from the house as well as from the patio itself. Then, if you want to make revisions in size, shape, and even in placement, you can do so without any more trouble than taking up the stakes and trying them elsewhere.

When, finally, you have come to the conclusion that you have the ideal solution to the problem, it will be possible to begin the excavation, the building of retaining walls, the laying of the drainage beds, and the other preliminary operations, and eventually to finish the patio. These preliminary skirmishes with the problem may sound a little unnecessary; but if you have any confusion of mind, they are the way to resolve and clarify anything which has bothered you.

WHAT MATERIALS TO USE

The determining factor of what materials to use in paving the patio may well be their expense, but other factors should not be ignored. The suitability of the materials, their color, texture, and durability should also enter into the choice. What you use for retaining walls, what kind of fencing and shelter or trellis are also factors to take into account.

Paving. There is such a wide choice of materials here in such an array of colors and textures that all you must determine is which is best and what you can afford to pay. If you feel that you do not want to go into permanent paving, you can employ gravel, bluestone, marble chips, brick dust, granite chips, beach sand, or choose from many other substances. All have their merits and most of them are relatively cheap and widely available. A well-kept lawn may be the answer in some places, although it will require constant repair and upkeep due to the wear it will receive. Also, chairs and tables will punch holes in turf after wet weather, and it will be less possible to use a lawn during rainy weather than quick-draining, quick-drying stone materials.

In modern use, the loose materials are usually contained within areas defined by wood boards, masonry, concrete edgings, or metal lawn edgings. They have many advantages; but the main disadvantage is that they are not permanent. Weeds root among the particles and require constant vigilance; children love to play with gravel and other stone chips, throwing it at each other or the house, even taking bucketfuls of it to dump on the lawn, where it does the lawn mower little good. In wet weather particles will adhere to the soles of shoes and be tracked into the house, where they will injure polished floors and linoleum. But for all these disadvantages there are many assets: advantages which will probably far outweigh all the drawbacks. The textures are very pleasant, and the variety of colors available in the materials makes it possible to complement any setting. Sometimes these loose materials are used in conjunction with other paving: gravel or crushed bluestone may be used to surround stone or concrete stepping-stones, or a rectangular terrace may have some squares paved with permanent materials and other squares with loose stone chips or brick dust. Brick dust or colored stone chips make a very attractive border around a patio, or a definition line across it, one part being paved with permanent mate-

The paving pattern is individual and unusual in this charming garden. Behind, a brick wall succeeds in seeming to be airy, yet manages to be graceful and substantial.

rials and the other floored with gravel.

Permanent paving is, of course, ideal. Its expense will range from a moderate price for bricks laid on sand to sizeable sums for tile or mosaic laid on concrete. At any price, permanence is desirable.

Bricks. Laid on sand or set permanently on concrete with mortar, bricks give a chance for a variety of patterns and colors and have a pleasing texture. They are among the most versatile of paving materials, lending themselves to many uses because of their small modular size, which allows them to be used in sweeping curves, to be laid flat or on edge, to be set into other materials to form paths and thus direct the flow of traffic across a patio, as well as to lend spice and variety in a number of other ways. Note the patterns shown in Chapter 18 and consider them for the patio you are planning; brick may be the best choice for you. If so, be sure to order hard-burned brick because it will wear better than common brick, which is softer and will disintegrate after a few years of hard use.

Concrete blocks. Either those especially made for paving, which come in a variety of sizes and colors, or the type used for building walls, are adaptable for use. Either the 2-inch or the 3-inch thickness will serve equally well. In many parts of the country a large 24-inch square block, often in colored cement and about 3 inches thick, is now available, and in some parts various other sizes of this same kind of block may be had. You may also cast your own blocks (see Chapter 19), either in their permanent location or elsewhere, to be assembled and laid when you have the requisite number for the job.

Blacktop. This can be used for paving and has the advantage of being inexpensive, reasonably permanent, and not bad looking. It has an odor for a time after being laid, particularly in hot weather, and in addition it is also likely to dent from chair or table legs. Because it is dark it will absorb heat more than light-colored paving does, and will hold it into the evening on really hot days. It is best installed by professionals, although some ama-

ASSORTED PAVING BLOCKS

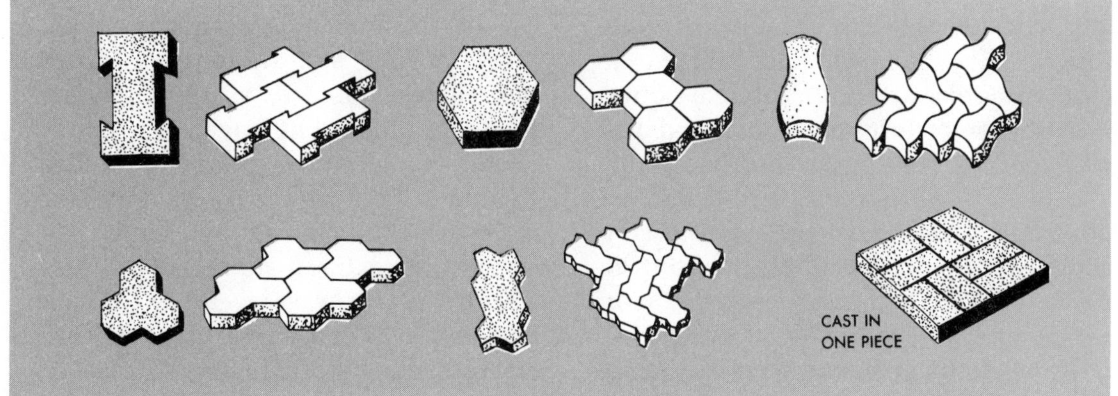

teurs find it not too difficult to do. My own feeling is that it needs the small but heavy powered rollers which professionals employ to flatten it and make it level.

Concrete. One of the best and most adaptable of materials for paving terraces. It can be used as a base for brick, slate, or other stone, and when used by itself can be cast in any shape, combined with other materials, and colored in a variety of pleasing shades. (See Chapter 19.) By varying the finish of the surface, anything from a finish as smooth as slate which can be waxed for dancing to the nubbly texture of brushed aggregate can be obtained. Properly made, concrete is absolutely permanent, and will last and wear well for a lifetime.

Many effects are possible with concrete. I refer you to Chapter 14, "How To Make and Use Concrete," for the various methods of achieving these effects. The most recommended surface is the medium-rough finish for it has sufficient "tooth" to make it safe for walking on in wet weather, yet is smooth enough to have a refined texture, if that is what you feel is best for your patio. The combed rough finish and the exposed aggregate finish are both interesting textures and give considerable traction, being quite rough. They are especially suitable to modern homes and to traditional homes in rustic or picturesque styles and will give contrast to smoothly finished walls.

Concrete with redwood, cedar, or other durable wood between areas of concrete used as forms and left there for division lines is a modern interpretation which makes a patio very interesting. Sometimes the areas are squares, sometimes oblongs, and sometimes bricks are laid in crosswise or lengthwise patterns between the cross-strips of wood, making the paving into a very interesting and unusual feature. You will see examples of all of these in Chapter 18, to give you many ideas from which to select.

Stone. There is much to recommend stone. Its texture and color and its natural beauty are only enhanced by time and weather, which makes it an ideal paving material. It is likely to be a most expensive material, particularly if it is in the cut-stone category. However, in some regions stone occurs naturally in shelving strata. If so, it may be possible to use a crowbar to dislodge pieces large enough to use for paving and to carry them home from the country. Whether you search on private or public property, naturally you must get permission first.

Slate. Available in most places, too, slate makes a handsome pavement. It is a little fragile and is likely to chip if anything hard is dropped on it, so it is best used mortared to a concrete base with the joints well finished. It may come in squarish shapes or in irregular shapes of triangles and oddments of all kinds which can be fitted together in what is called "crazy paving" style. Many people like to mix all the colors of slate—black, red, green, gray—in one pavement, but it is usually in better taste to limit it to one or two hues, because the colors of slate are vivid, especially when wet. Slate, being a very fine-textured stone, is likely to be a little slippery in wet weather. This may be a factor to consider if the patio must be crossed a good deal in wet weather.

Tile. Used extensively in many areas of the country where it is available and where it is priced within the means of the average home owner, tile may be either colored or plain, combined with brick or other kinds of paving, and is good for outlining areas of concrete. The patterning of the tile makes a pleasant relief from the usual dull all-over effects, giving the patio distinction and originality. Amateur ceramists can embellish their own tiles with fired and glazed designs to line the terrace pool or decorate a masonry seat on the patio, as in Spanish and Portuguese courtyards.

Wood blocks. These are used in many areas where they are available at a reasonable price. This subject is treated at some length in Chapter 18. But wood used for decks is something to consider everywhere. 2″ × 4″s or 2″ × 6″s on a good sturdy framework set on concrete piers firmly embedded in the ground make very handsome floors. Stock of 5/4″ × 6″ or 5/4″ × 4″ is also offered but should be laid on joists more closely spaced. Either countersunk screws or large nails fasten the boards to the framework. Wood should be well treated with wood preservatives (Chapter 4) before being laid; then a coating each year of boiled linseed oil should keep them in good shape. The wood can be stained a deep, dark color, or finished in its natural shade. The floor boards can be laid in many interesting patterns: in large squares with the direction varied in the laying so that alternate squares or oblongs are laid at right angles to each other, or perhaps diagonally across the patio or in chevron fashion. About 1/4 to 1/2 inch of space is left between the boards, these cracks allowing the deck to drain well and simplifying sweeping off dust and dirt.

Cut flagstone. This can be laid on sand, on concrete, or directly on the soil itself, although the latter is not highly recommended. Random squares—squares and oblongs of various sizes fitted together so that they give a pleasing variety of sizes but maintain a certain regularity at the same time—may be purchased and fitted together in a subtle and beautiful grouping, making a good pavement which does not draw attention to itself but is interesting to contemplate. Flagstone (usually sandstone) is never overly colorful or overly patterned and therefore stays a part of the background, unless it is somehow featured. But by itself it is never obtrusive.

Pebble mosaic. This, too, will add interest to paving. Used in strategic places, such as in front of a door as a kind of "welcome mat," to border a flower bed or a pool, or to break up a large area of flat concrete paving, it can be very piquant and add considerable interest to the patio. (See Chapter 20.) If you are very ambitious, and have available large quantities of the proper kind of pebbles, you can make a great feature of pebble mosaic, but it is not recommended for impatient people or the dilettante.

OTHER FEATURES FOR THE PATIO

The patio can be made more livable by the addition of various other appurtenances. Trellises and shelters will make it more beautiful and provide shade and shelter when needed; privacy fences and

A narrow side yard can provide a paved area for family use with a tall fence (this one is made of Western red cedar) on a sturdy frame to assure privacy. Cedar 2″ × 4″s with spacers make the seat, set on pipes in concrete, and additional cedar 2″ × 4″s are laid in the concrete.

baffle fences will give seclusion and protection from passersby and neighbors who are too near. Pools will give a pleasant, cooling tinkle of water and provide a very attractive grace note with their plantings and living sound of water. Planters of various kinds, whether built up alongside or into the paving itself, will bring color and beauty to the outdoor room that most patios become; and seats, whether of masonry or wood, whether permanent or demountable and transportable, will add to the attractiveness of the patio and extend its use. Look through the chapters which deal with all of these and see if you wish to incorporate them in your plans.

Patios not only augment the living space of your home, but they add a new kind of life to your property. I cannot recommend them too heartily, and you will take double pleasure in one if you build it yourself.

CHAPTER 16

BUILDING A PATIO

Applying what you have learned in the previous chapters about concrete, you can build a patio that will add to the enjoyment of your outdoor living. You may as well build a patio to be proud of, rather than the fairly common plain, gray contractor-built one. Use pattern, color, and texture to make yours different.

Most patios can be built right on the ground, after removing the topsoil. Only in mucky or poorly drained ground will you need to add a gravel or sand subbase. However, adding sand can greatly ease grading and leveling.

The rule-of-thumb patio size is said to be one-fifth the floor area of the house itself. Thus, a 2,000-square-foot house would get a 400-square-foot patio. But a minimum size might be $12' \times 12'$, while a larger patio can include a porch or pool

Although this looks just like a hand-set flagstone entry, it was pattern-stamped in dust-on-colored concrete to set off the rammed-earth house it serves. The random pattern has the advantage of masking misalignments of stamping lines.

deck. Arrange the patio for easy access to the house and to the balance of the yard. Orient it to the sun for maximum use depending on climate and your sun tolerance. It should slope away from the house ⅛ to ¼ inch per foot for good drainage, yet be flat enough to avoid having low spots that would collect rainwater.

Dig out the topsoil a few inches beyond the forms on all sides. This gives space for the forms when you set them. Then grade and tamp the soil. A good tamper can be made from a 4″×4″ post. Set the forms, holding them with 2″×2″ or 1″×3″ stakes driven into the ground on the outside and sawed off at form level. Stakes should be 4 feet apart or less, half that on curved sections. A level and stringline will help you set the forms at the proper elevation and in a straight line. Be sure to install isolation joint material where the patio meets other construction. Patio openings can be left wherever needed by forming around them.

HOW TO LAY OUT A SQUARE CORNER

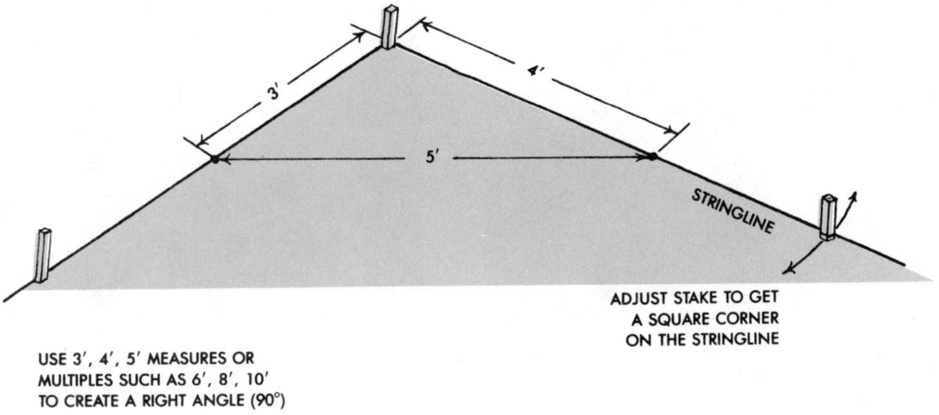

PATTERN-STAMPED PATIO

The patio shown in photos on the next pages was made with pumped ready-mix, leave-in redwood forms, and a dust-on-colored pattern-stamped finish. It has a rustic handmade look as though Mexican tile were laid on a concrete base. This would have cost far more than the pattern stamping. In fact, the cost was only slightly more than for a plain concrete patio, mostly due to the cost of the coloring pigment. It took four days to make: one day to remove the old, rotting wood deck, two to grade and form, and one more day to cast and finish. The total cost was less than half what a concrete contractor had bid for the plain gray slab with standard steel-troweled finish.

Special mix. Concrete that is to be pattern-stamped should be made of a special mix containing coarse aggregates no larger than 3/8 inch. Larger pieces would tend to get in the way of the stamp-pad bars. A grout-and-pump mix furnished by a ready-mix dealer for concrete pump use should meet these criteria. You can get additional time for stamping by having your dealer add a water-reducing retarder along with a small amount of superplasticizer to the mix. This will create a high-slump condition that lasts two to three hours and takes the pressure off the finishing operation. If your ready-mix dealer is unfamiliar with this, ask him to see National Ready Mixed Concrete Association publication No. 158. Concrete made with these additives will cost a few dollars more per cubic yard than plain concrete.

If you reinforce the slab (see Chapter 14), it need not be jointed. Otherwise,

HOW TO MAKE A PATTERN-STAMPED PATIO

1. Slope and grade the patio area using a straightedge and level. Do it with shovel, rake, hoe, whatever works best for amount of material to be moved and heaviness of soil. Use of the existing ground for the subgrade will save work.

2. Install the forms. Here garden grade redwood is painted with a preservative so it could be left in place. Use 2″×2″ or 1″×3″ stakes, nailing them with double-headed 16d form nails for easy removal later. A sledgehammer is used as backup for nailing.

3. Forms may be spliced on the inside at ends with a scrap of wood, keeping it well below the top so concrete will cover it. Use four nails for this splicing.

4. After screeding the edges of the sand subbase level, use a flat-ended shovel or the back of a garden rake to bring it even with the screeded edges. A sand subbase saves on concrete and needs only a little compaction.

5. Before pouring the concrete, dampen the sand subbase with a water hose. After pouring, strike off the surface of the concrete using a straight 2″ × 4″, as shown. Here an isolation joint and one form are used as screed guides, working around obstructions such as patio roof columns.

6. An ideal first tool for finishing large patios is a bull float, which can be worked from outside the slab. This one was made from a flat 1″ × 8″ board with 1″ × 1″ handle installed at an angle. To prevent digging in, keep the float's leading edge slightly raised.

7. After dusting the surface with a coloring pigment, float the color in, here with a magnesium float (use a wood float on non-air-entrained concrete). Apply a second, lighter coat of dust-on coloring and float it in for an even overall color. Save a little color for touch-up.

8. After the second floating, align pattern stamp pads with the longest house wall or starting line and maintain alignment as you proceed. Tap pads all over with dead-blow hammer to set them to desired depth. Start as early as possible so the final portion of the patio doesn't get too hard for stamping.

(Continued next page)

9. Two stamp pads let you stand on one while you position the other. Use your weight to help force the pads in. If the impressions are not to be mortared later (best for do-it-yourself), a ⅜" depth is sufficient. For mortaring, go full depth of the stamp bars if you can, but you'll need soft concrete for this.

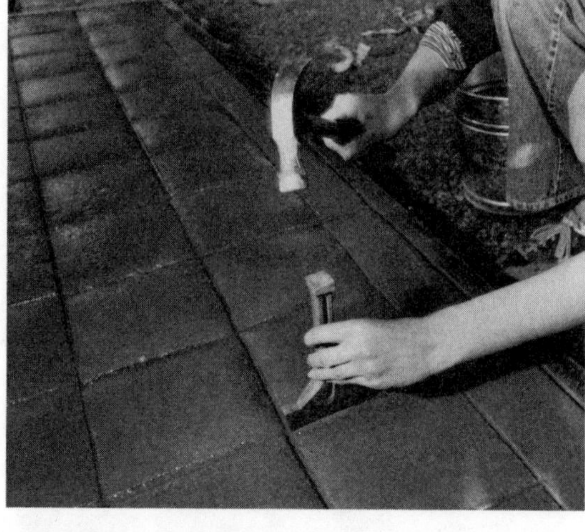

10. Edging and touching up are done with one of two hand-chisel stamps often furnished with stamp pads. Tap in the hand stamp to the same depth as pad bars went, for matching grooves. Later, you can mortar the joints flat, making them easier to clean.

control joints should be provided as discussed on page 322. As control joints might interfere with the pattern-stamp lines, reinforcing the slab or using leave-in forms seems preferable.

Forms should be built scaled to the module of the pattern, if possible, to avoid having thin "tiles" along the edges. In this, some allowance should be made for what's called "float" of the stamping pads. Figure float at about 1⁄16 inch per foot. Therefore, a 12-foot-wide patio would need to be formed 12-feet ¾-inch wide to provide for tool float. Design your patio so the long lines of the pattern will run across, not with, the line of sight. This reduces the need to be concerned about straight-line error. Some reference line is needed to start the stamping. It can be a stringline tautly stretched or the long wall of a house.

Stamping pads are plastic or aluminum. Although the aluminum ones are too costly to buy for a single use, they might be rented if you can find them. A pair of plastic stamp pads can be purchased and figured as a cost of doing the job. Later, once friends see your patio, they may wish to borrow them for making their own pattern-stamped patios.

A 400-square-foot pattern-stamped patio is the absolute maximum you should attempt to place and finish in one day. Avoid working on a hot, dry day and in the direct sun, for the concrete will set too fast to be stamped uniformly. A 3-pound dead-blow hammer is a necessity because the pads are reluctant to sink in without considerable pounding. An ordinary hammer is likely to damage the forms. Tap the forms in the center first, then all around the edges. This sets

PLASTIC STAMPING PAD PATTERNS

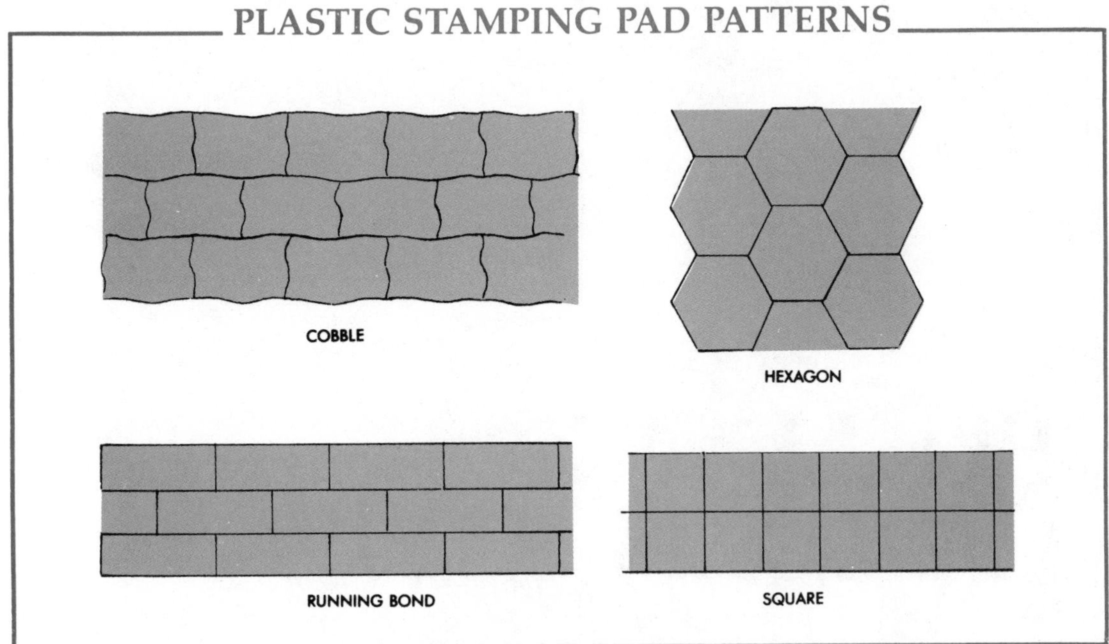

the form with the least floating. Watch for form twisting after you start pounding and adjust your tapping to correct for it.

Although a pattern-stamped patio may sound like more work than a plain one, the rustic appearance covers up imperfections such as tool marks in the finish that might otherwise show. So, as long as you get an even color over the surface of the slab, you can be less careful about floating.

Pattern-stamping creates a patio you will be pleased to tell incredulous friends that you built yourself.

CHAPTER 17

BUILDING GARDEN STEPS

A large part of the charm of the old Italian and French gardens lies in their use of steps. The change of level in Italy is made mandatory by the landscape in which hills abound; but, more frequently than not, in France the use of steps seems to stem from the esthetic theory which is so beautifully displayed in her great formal gardens.

In our country today we are using more and more hillside sites for our homes each year, carving out terraces from the slopes with bulldozers and leveling our living areas into terraces which step down from the house, from the street, and from terrace to terrace as we need more land for outdoor living. Some parts may be paved, as for patios, some turned to lawn and flowers or hobby gardens.

In the new trend in American gardens we see many more hillside plots left as

Nature made them, with wild trees and shrubs kept and others planted to complement them, and with fewer hillside lawns to create problems of maintenance. It is only the living areas around the houses which have been leveled for patios and living lawn areas. Paths thread downward through the natural parts of a hillside, with a few unobtrusive steps inserted here and there where the slope becomes too steep for a path to negotiate easily. Sometimes the paths are a series

Exposed-aggregate concrete, boxed by broad planks of treated wood, creates a formal-informal atmosphere that suits the modern house. Plantings in soil spaces beside steps and patio help to soften still further this geometric effect, making it homelike and human.

of very wide steps, a kind of ramp broken here and there by risers.

In more formal treatments, steps are used to climb up to terraced areas above the level of the house or the garden, or to descend to those placed below it. Little retaining walls are built to divide the garden into two levels, both charming the eye and giving the illusion of more space, because the division will lend a visual interest to the whole picture.

Steps, steps, and still more steps... that seems to be the order of the day in American garden design, and the choice of kinds of steps to use in your own garden has never been wider. Ramp steps for climbing long slopes gently, with the minimum effort; circular steps; free-form steps with flowing curves; wooden steps to wooden-decked balconies; water-washed stone steps laid to simulate a natural outcropping of rocks; brick-and-plank steps; cast concrete steps; concrete-and-plank or concrete-and-brick steps; cut-stone steps; steps made of square garden timbers or railroad ties—the list is practically endless. Every day more new and exciting ways to use building materials are found, bringing new changes to the classic combinations and making wonderful new combinations of materials to suit our changing styles of houses and gardens.

PLANNING YOUR STEPS

Granting the need for steps, the next question to be asked is, what kind of

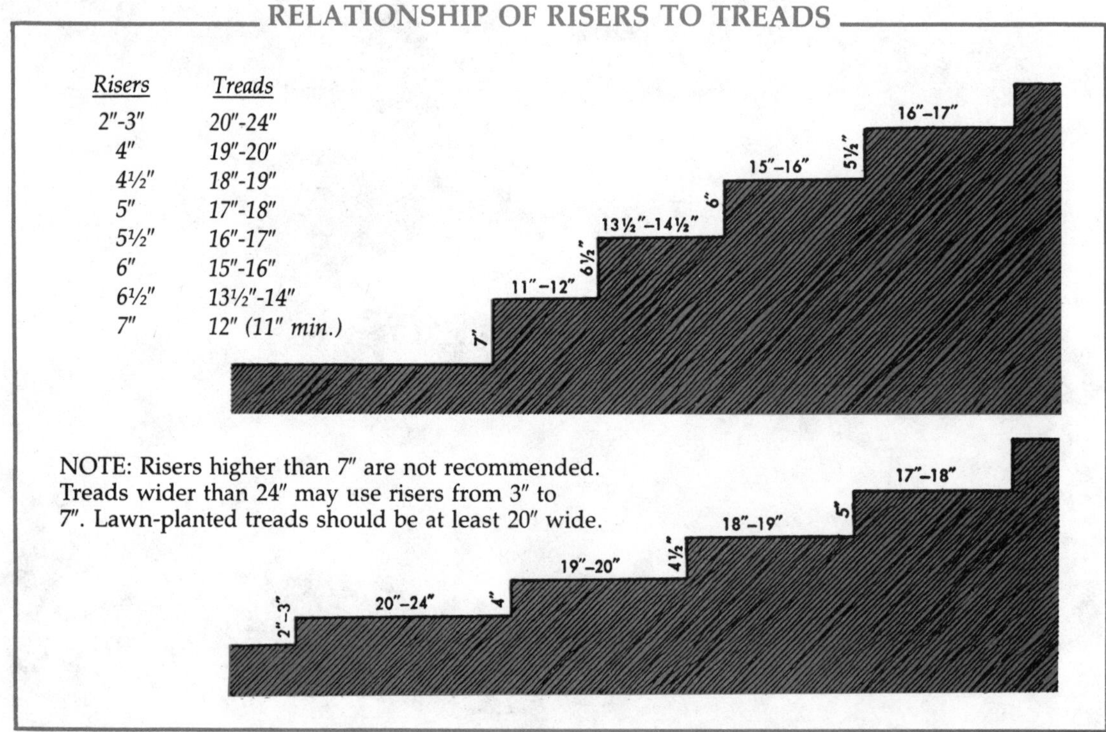

steps? How many, and where shall they be placed?

The shortest distance between two points is a straight line, but when we build steps we may find that this is not the safest way, the most comfortable, or the most satisfying in design. Steep runs of steps are frequently dangerous. They are always less comfortable to ascend and are perilous to come down. There are certain primary proportions between the width of the tread (that part on which you walk) and the riser (the height of the front part of the step). Look for a moment at the riser/tread table's giving measurements for the best proportions to use in planning your steps, assuring you a good, easy climb whether the slope is a long gradual one or shorter and steeper.

There have been tests made which show that broad treads and high risers are just as tiring and frequently as hazardous to use as the commonly acknowledged dangerous combination of high risers and narrow treads. In general we might say the rule is that the closer to a ladder steps become, the more effort must be put forth in climbing them, and the closer they come to the level, or like a ramp, the less effort will be expended in negotiating the slope.

But the width of steps is important, too, though the "elbow room" factor is often ignored in building steps. Where they must pierce a retaining wall or be built beside a wall, thus necessitating a bannister, the width from side to side becomes important. The illustration on the next page shows the minimum widths for steps to permit the passage of one or two persons, and you can judge proportions for wider sets of steps.

Even a stairway can be dramatic, making its emphatic statement in the general garden scheme. These cast-in-place steps have planting space left at the end of every other step, making a place for a fine collection of sun-loving plants needing little water.

Don't forget that garden steps must be at least as wide as stairs in a house, for gardeners are constantly toting flats of plants and other garden equipment up and down them. Lawn mowers, garden carts, and other wheeled equipment must frequently negotiate garden steps in order to be used on the various levels. Per-

RECOMMENDED DIMENSIONS FOR GARDEN STEPS

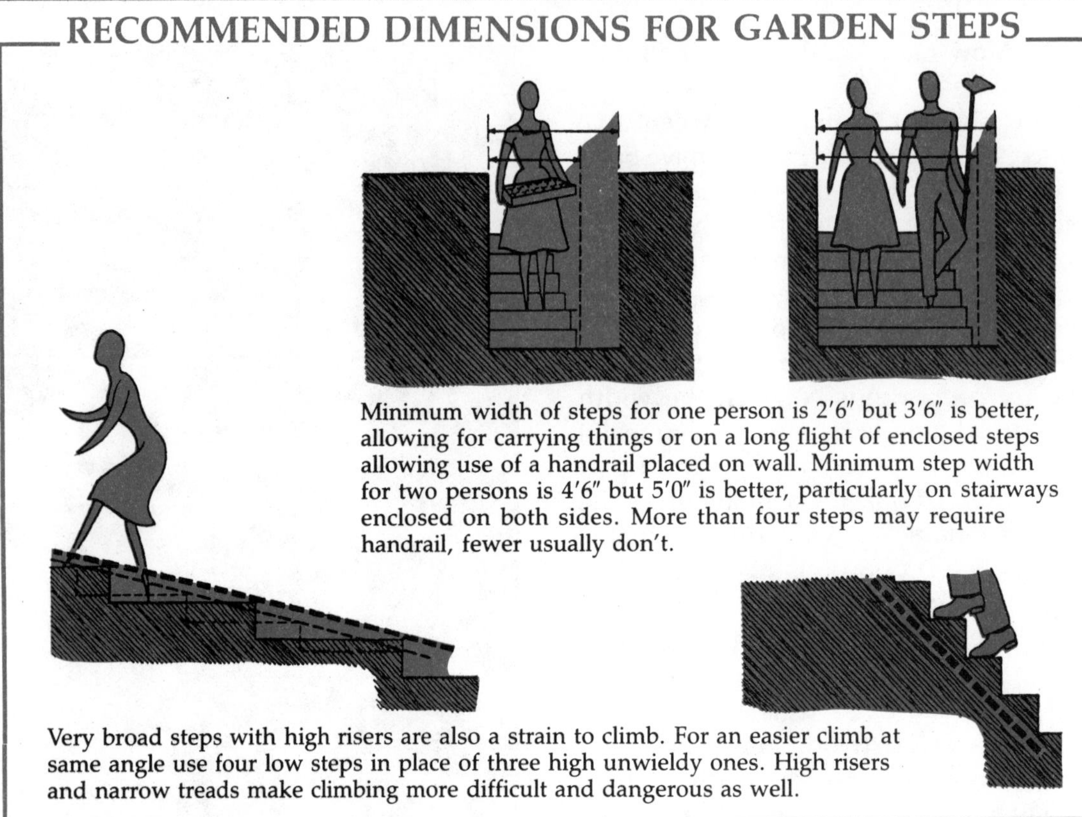

Minimum width of steps for one person is 2′6″ but 3′6″ is better, allowing for carrying things or on a long flight of enclosed steps allowing use of a handrail placed on wall. Minimum step width for two persons is 4′6″ but 5′0″ is better, particularly on stairways enclosed on both sides. More than four steps may require handrail, fewer usually don't.

Very broad steps with high risers are also a strain to climb. For an easier climb at same angle use four low steps in place of three high unwieldy ones. High risers and narrow treads make climbing more difficult and dangerous as well.

haps you might solve this traffic problem by building ramps of concrete, brick, or stone (whichever material faces the steps) alongside the steps for the gardener to use. Or if expense or lack of space rules this out, wooden ramps built to fit the steps can be put in place when needed and taken up and stored in the garage or tool shed in between uses.

MATERIALS

The choice of material will be governed by many factors. First of all the style of house and garden where the steps are to be built must be considered. The materials must be compatible with those used in the retaining walls, house walls, patio paving, walks, and other adjacent features. If the general effect desired in the garden is natural and informal, the steps may be built of rough stone brought in from fields and hills nearby or bought from stone suppliers. In this case, do not use too many different kinds of stone or too many varieties of texture, or you will end up with a little bit of masonry which looks like an exhibit in the Natural History Museum's geology section, rather than functional steps which keep their place because they are simple, quiet, and *useful.*

Stone steps may be set either in the soil—with gravel or cinders providing a drainage layer beneath them so that they will remain where they are set—or they may be laid in informally formal patterns such as those seen in "Steps with Opposing Circles" in the upcoming drawings. These are usually best laid in concrete and mortared in place. You may leave little pockets of soil here and there in which to plant small flowering plants or living material of other kinds. In Wales, at the estate of Lord Aberconway, "Bodnant," I saw some circular steps in which a few inches of soil had been left at the rear of each step except the top one. All of these were planted with rings of tiny violas and the riser of each step formed the background for a mass of lavender bloom. This charming planting idea may be adapted to your own garden, using annuals, perennials, or succulent plants.

Where ramp steps or short runs of steps are inserted in a long walk up a slope having sharp breaks, it is best to use the same material for the treads as that found in the path in which they occur. Blacktop, gravel, crushed bluestone, marble chips, rough stone or concrete, brick, or lawn—whatever the walk material may be, it can be adapted to the steps. Risers should also be compatible: wood, stone, brick, or any of the materials which are shown on the pages of drawings and plans.

Occasionally where long walks—particularly straight ones—must be used, with steps occurring only occasionally, a change of pace and texture will add interest to an otherwise commonplace and rather tiresome walk. The circular steps entitled "Break Straight Lines with Circles" (page 368) are a case in point. If still more interest is needed or desirable, bricks or stones may be set into the concrete steps in radiating patterns as shown.

A dash of spice or a pleasing bit of individuality may be given to a garden which is otherwise rather usual by angling the steps, turning the flight at a slight angle or even making a 90° turn. Look at the drawing called "Steps with Variety and Unity," which demonstrates how low steps can take a turn for the better in a small garden. In "A Better Garden Stair-

Concrete slabs cast in 2″ × 6″ redwood forms and topped with laid-in bricks without sand or mortar make attractive steps. The project was started with the bottom step, which was completed before starting the second step. That's what's called doing it in easy steps. Staggering the steps adds a striking appearance.

HOW TO BUILD FORM FOR CONCRETE STEPS

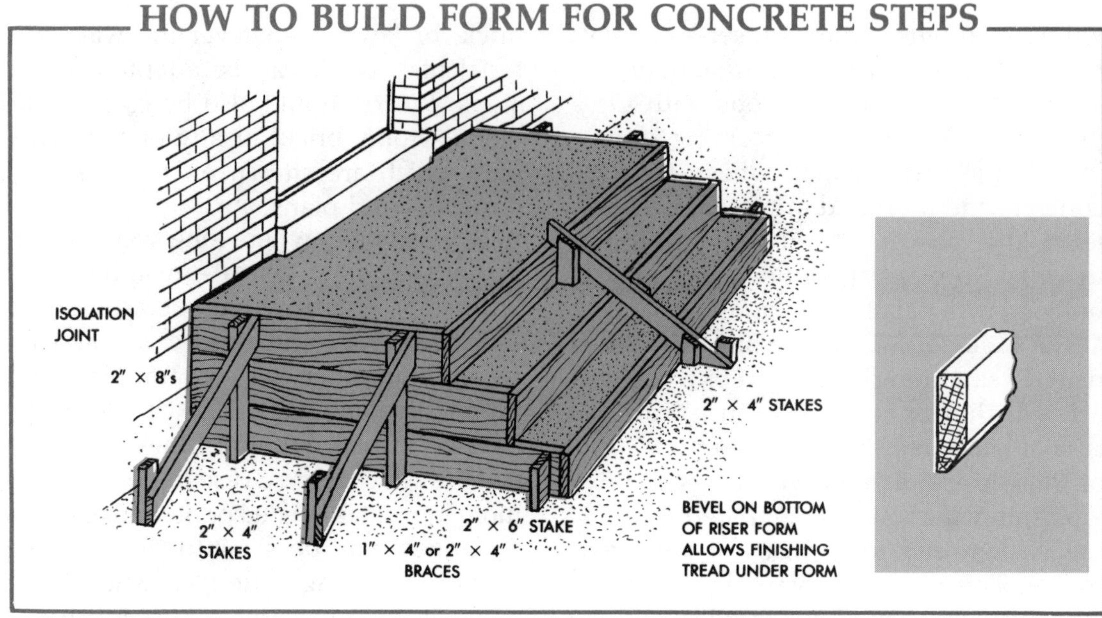

way"(page 365) you will see how to avoid making a too-long flight of steps where a considerable distance must be covered due to a sharp change of level. By inserting two landings, varying the color of the cast concrete with insertions of brick or tile paving on the landings, and making the steps still more individual by extending the risers and planting the soil boxes which end each tread with flowering or other colorful plant material, you can make a real feature out of the necessity of steps. Also, by breaking the retaining walls into sections, you avoid a high, blank, rather ugly expanse of masonry. The trick of extending the risers and planting the treads may be adapted to most of the other steps shown to give them a fresh, unusual, modern look. Or you may want to plant ivy alongside the steps, training it across the risers to keep them green throughout the year. An occasional nipping back of stray shoots will keep the ivy within bounds with very little work.

PRACTICAL CONSIDERATIONS

The practical side of building steps must not be ignored. Use adequate foundations and footings to insure the permanence of your work. A deep footing beneath the bottom steps will materially help to prevent the weight of the concrete and masonry mass from sliding down the hill, as may be the case if concrete is poured into an excavation which merely parallels the land's slope without the use of this "slide stopper." Where steps are laid on soil, without concrete, use gravel or cinders as advocated earlier, and be sure that drainage away from this layer is also provided, if possible. Such steps should be slightly overlapped so that the lower step assists in supporting the one above.

Where steps are planned to be finished and to tie in at the specific level of a wall or to match the level of an existing walk, be sure when you are planning the concrete foundations to allow for the depth of the paving or tread-finishing material plus the mortar joint. Then when the steps are completed you will have no hiatus between levels of step and adjoining wall or walk.

There are so many places in small gardens in which a few steps will make all the difference in the world, not only in comfort and convenience but also in visual effect. I urge you to look over your garden and see where steps might fit into your landscape plan. If you decide that there is a valid use for them, study the examples which follow and choose the one most suited to your purpose. But don't rush into construction until you've thoroughly studied all aspects of the problem. Make sure that your choice is right and that you know just what to do. Be sure to make the excavations for drainage and footings adequate, put the drainage layer in place, build the forms for the concrete, and then begin to move fast, once everything is in readiness.

WITH STEPS, EASY DOES IT

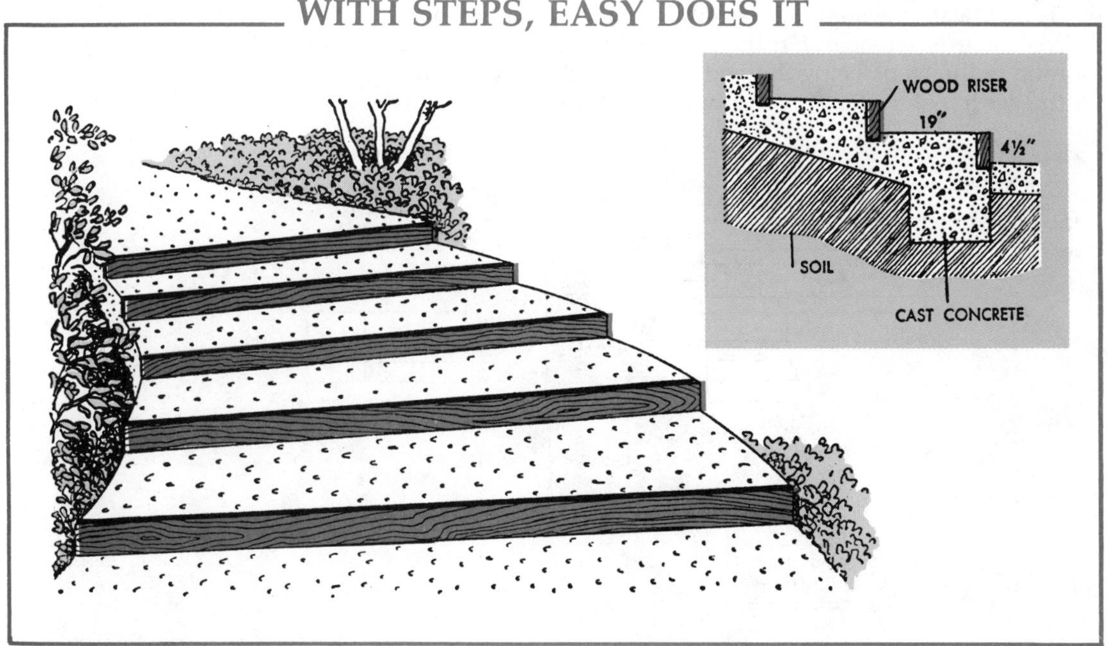

Let the slope of the land govern the kind of steps you choose. Use steeper, narrower ones where slope breaks abruptly, curving broader steps with low risers for gentle slopes. Set treated redwood risers in concrete steps for permanence. Always use a deep footing at bottom step (see side view) to prevent weight from thrusting steps downhill.

A SECRET EXIT FROM A PATIO

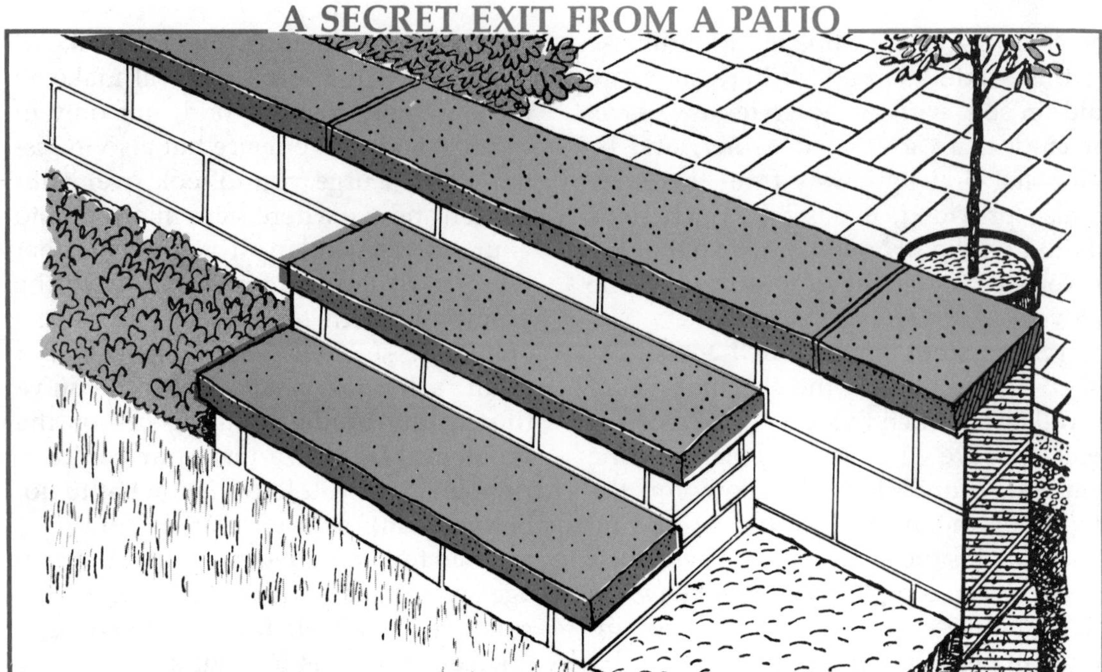

By using a wall one step high around a patio which is only slightly above the lower level, a "secret" stair is possible. On the patio side it presents the look of an unbroken wall, the location of the steps being defined by a potted plant or a flower bed let into the paving, while on the garden side steps ascend between flower or shrub beds.

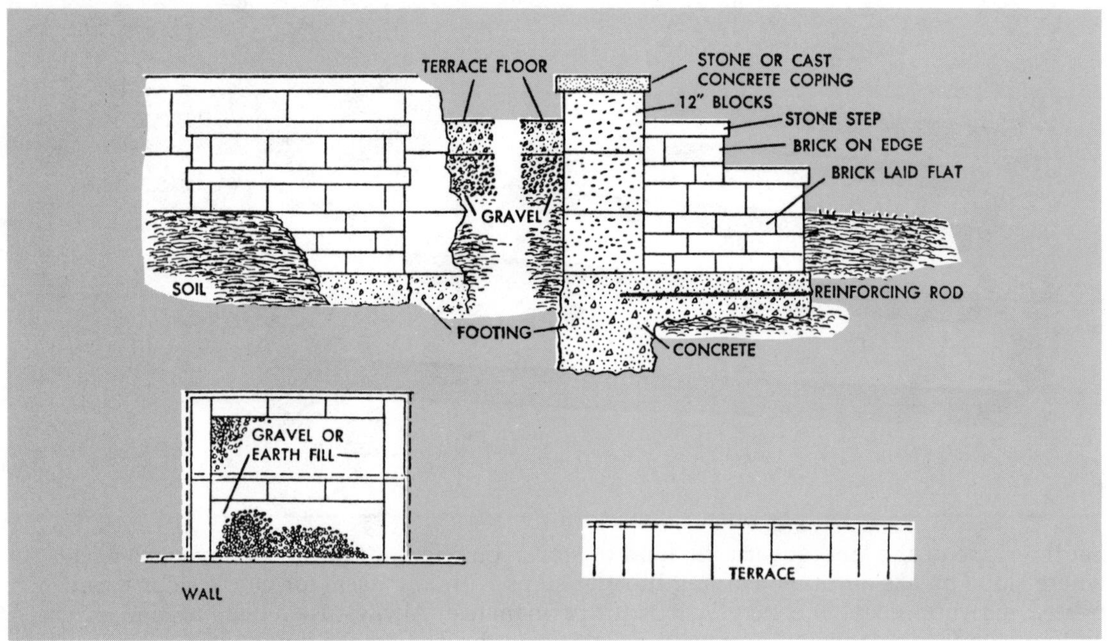

CORNER STEPS ARE INTERESTING

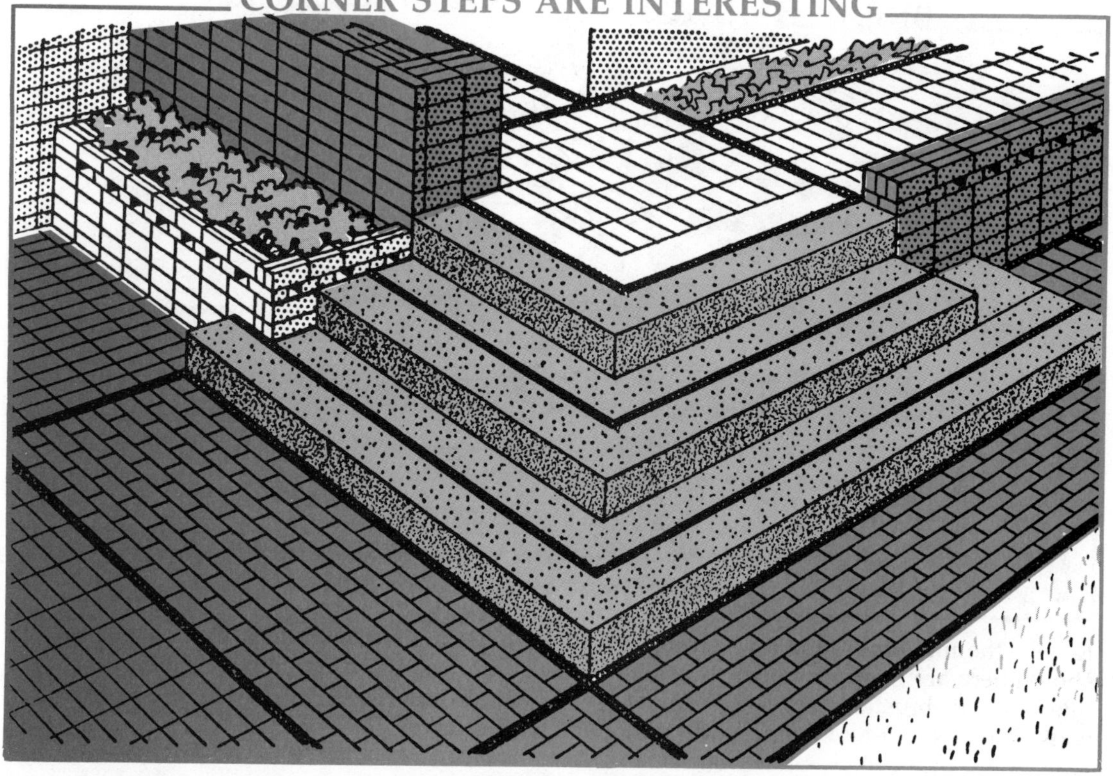

Descending from a walk which goes around the corner of this house, corner steps give easy access to the lower patio and its adjacent lawn. A raised plant bed in the angle of the patio echoes the pierced brick retaining wall—note stacked bond—and brick paving areas are defined by preservative-treated wood also set in concrete steps.

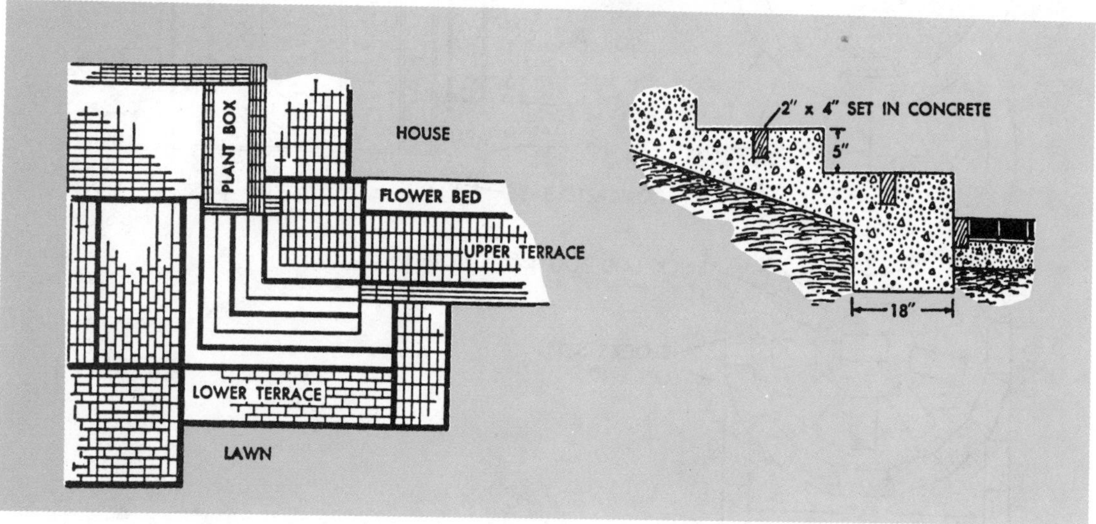

BREAK STRAIGHT LINES WITH CIRCLES

Relieve the monotony of a long, straight walk by inserting circular steps. Used in those shown here are risers of cinder or concrete blocks mortared to a concrete base before being filled in with brushed-aggregate concrete, which is also the material used in the brick-edged walk. Bricks set in a radiating pattern in steps lend interest.

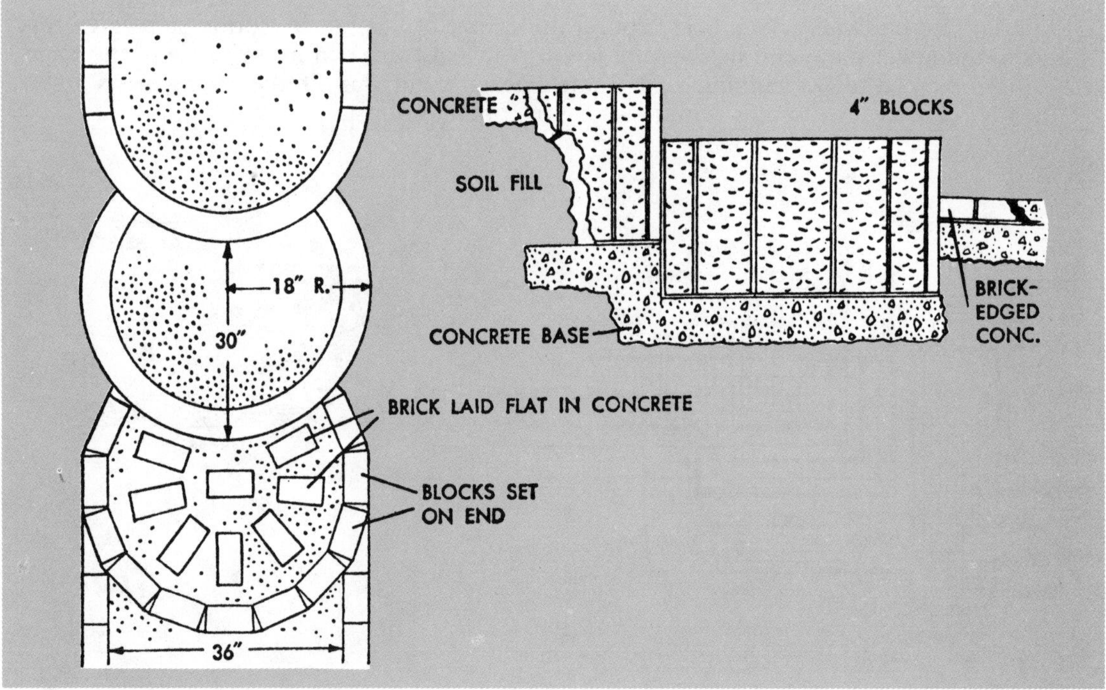

STEPS WITH OPPOSING CIRCLES

Circular steps go particularly well with formal or informal traditional architecture. Any material may be used to construct them, but fieldstone laid dry, as shown here, is informal and small plants can be grown in the cracks between stones. For the best visual effect use fewer steps above the circular landing than those descending from it.

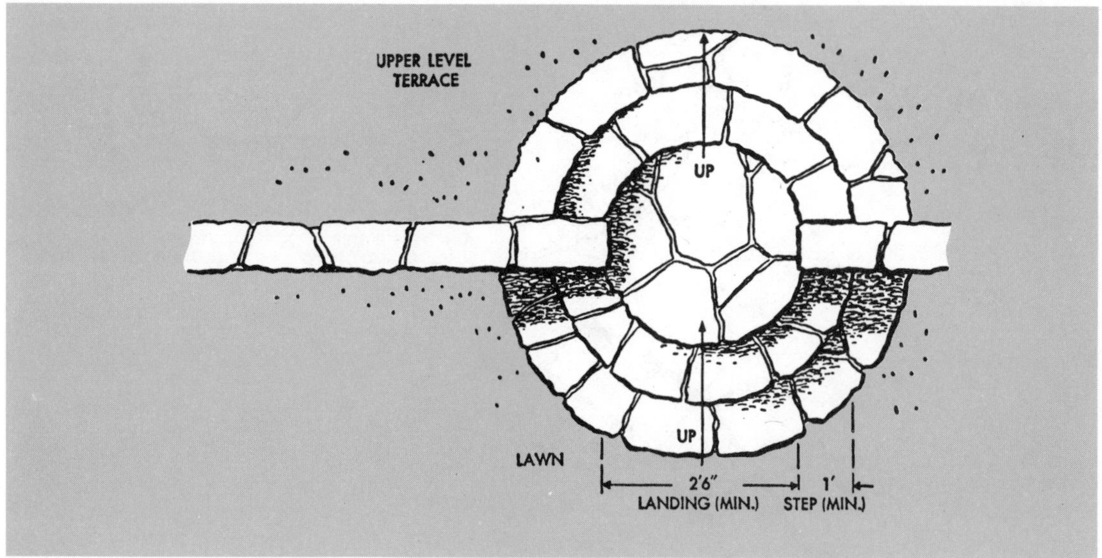

MORE OPPOSING CIRCLES

Here opposing circles of stone are used in a wild garden with a stretch of sloping path for a landing. Top steps bow toward us, the wider, shallower bottom ones bow away from us. Because these steps are informal, they may be adapted to either traditional cottages in a natural setting or modern houses which fit well in natural landscapes.

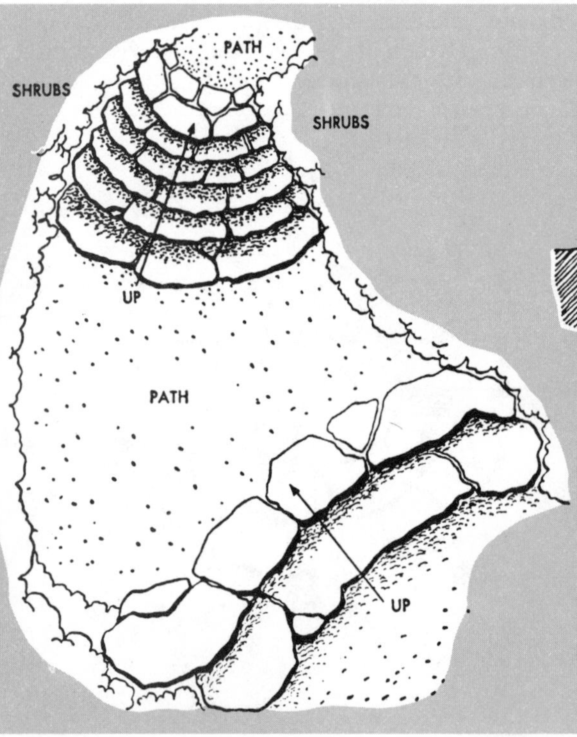

PATH

SHRUBS

SHRUBS

UP

PATH

UP

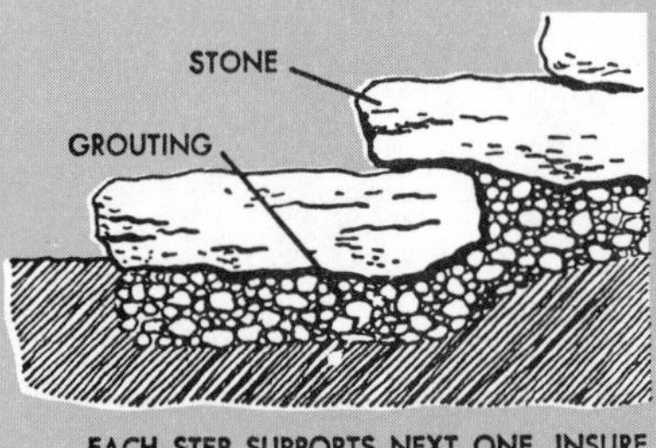

STONE

GROUTING

EACH STEP SUPPORTS NEXT ONE. INSURE DRAINAGE BY USING GROUTING BELOW

STEPS WITH VARIETY AND UNITY

In areas where ledge rock is plentiful or quantities of other masonry materials are easily available, the garden will gain in interest from changing levels of plant beds. Vary widths of the beds and heights of walls but keep unity by using only one kind of material. A flat platform by the steps encourages use of colorful potted plants.

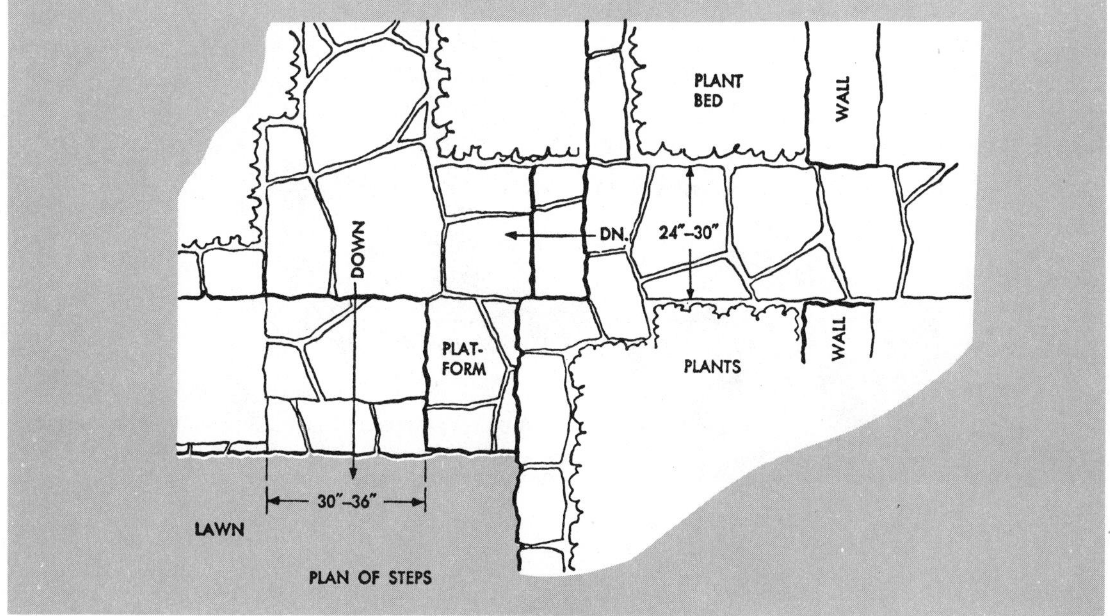

PLAN OF STEPS

USE RAMP STEPS FOR LONG SLOPES

Broad steps with low risers may be the answer on long slopes where paths are too steep for an easy climb. Break long runs of steps with a level landing or perhaps a rustic seat to rest on. Make steps 2′6″ wide with 4″ to 7″ risers; floor them with sand, blacktop, concrete, bricks, gravel, or wood, according to use, form, and cost.

WOODEN STEPS

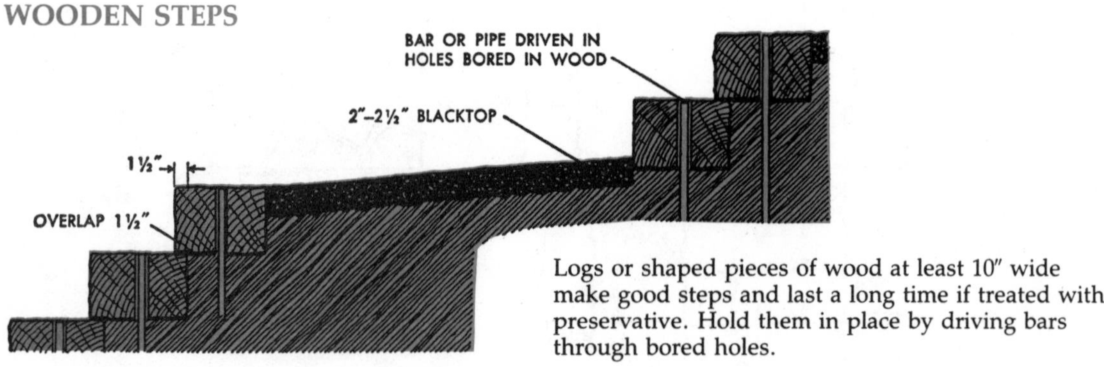

Logs or shaped pieces of wood at least 10″ wide make good steps and last a long time if treated with preservative. Hold them in place by driving bars through bored holes.

CONCRETE RISERS

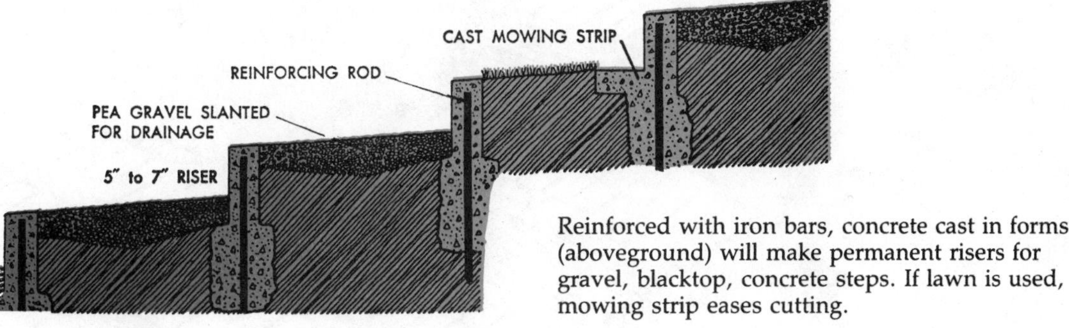

Reinforced with iron bars, concrete cast in forms (aboveground) will make permanent risers for gravel, blacktop, concrete steps. If lawn is used, mowing strip eases cutting.

BRICK RISERS

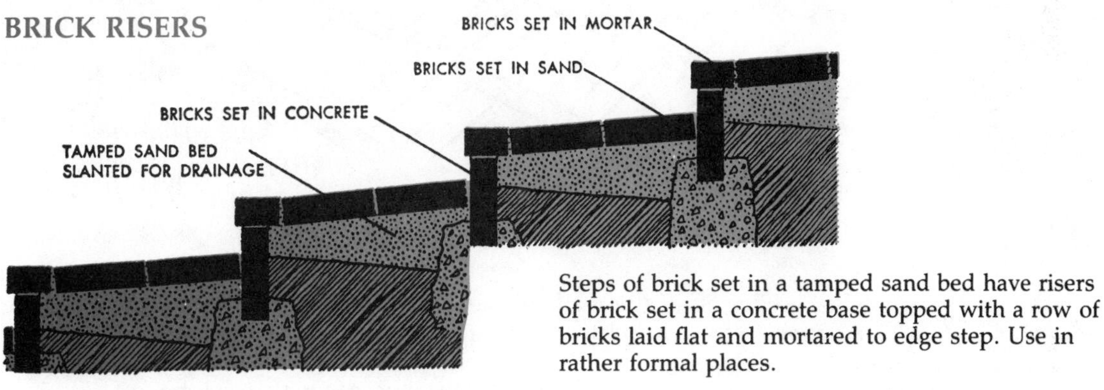

Steps of brick set in a tamped sand bed have risers of brick set in a concrete base topped with a row of bricks laid flat and mortared to edge step. Use in rather formal places.

ROUGH STONE RISERS

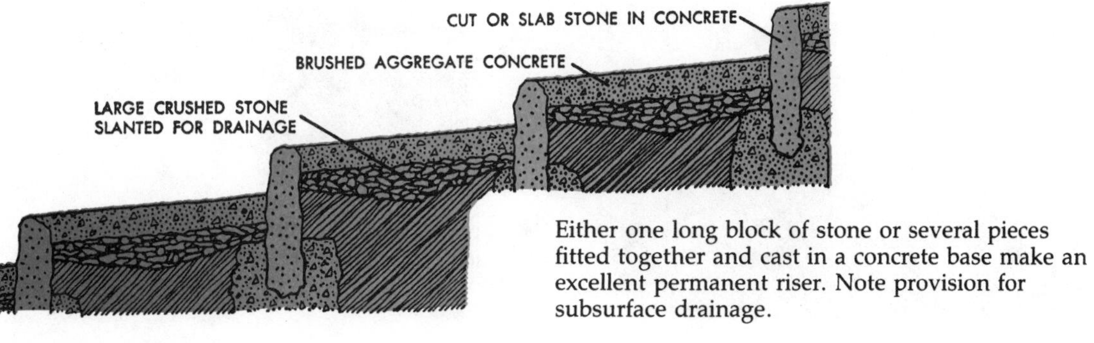

Either one long block of stone or several pieces fitted together and cast in a concrete base make an excellent permanent riser. Note provision for subsurface drainage.

WOODEN PLANKS TEAM WITH BRICKS

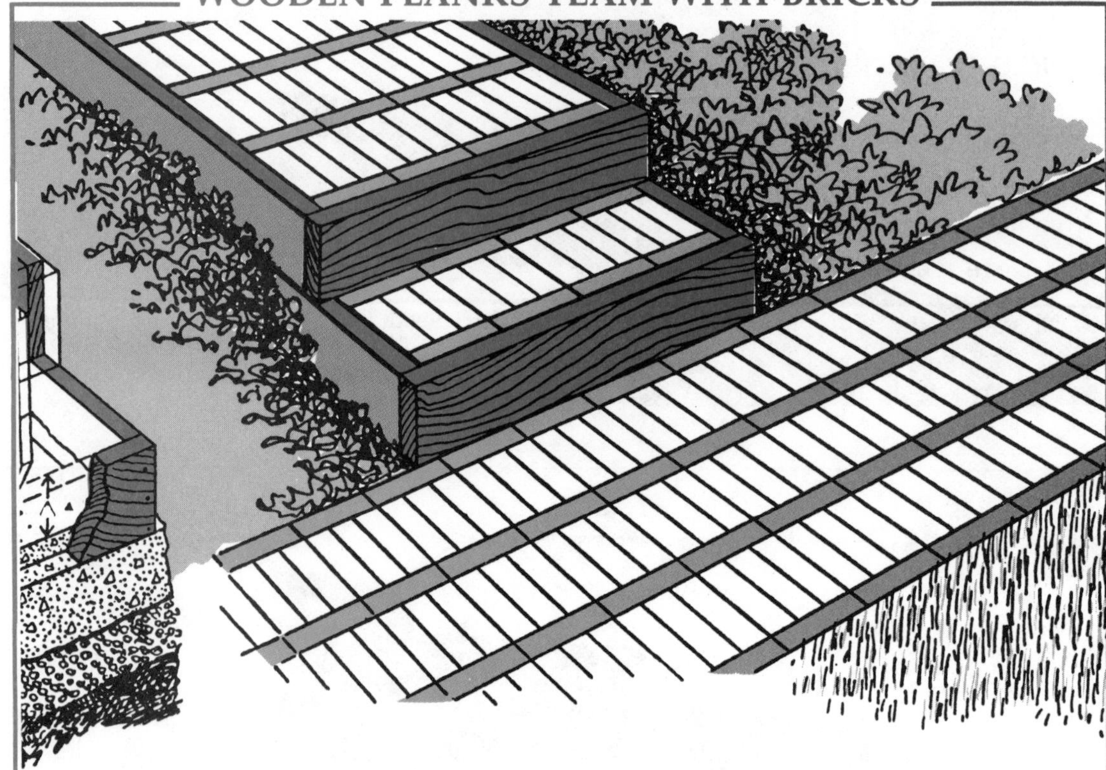

Brick steps which echo the design of the walk are held in place by 2″ × 6″ redwood planks or some other preservative-treated wood that is stained or painted, unless a weathered-wood effect is desired. Bricks may be mortared on concrete base (see side view) or laid without mortar on bed of tamped cinders or gravel. Distance A equals brick height.

STAKED WOOD RISERS

2″ x 8″

2″ x 4″ STAKE

1½″–2″ SAND

CRUSHED STONE SLOPED TO V FOR GOOD DRAINAGE

Wood planks of any depth which will expose 6″ for riser may be fastened to 2″ × 2″ or 2″ × 4″ stakes driven into soil. Steps slanted 1″ to 2″ to a 3′ step provide drainage.

BALANCED BUT NOT BISYMMETRICAL

Retaining walls beside steps need not have exactly the same treatment on both sides. As shown here, one wall can curve around to hold a plant bed on the uphill side, lower side has retaining wall above plant beds. Steps may be placed at the end of retaining wall or along it wherever there is some logical architectural or garden division to follow.

WIDE STEPS WITH CHARACTER

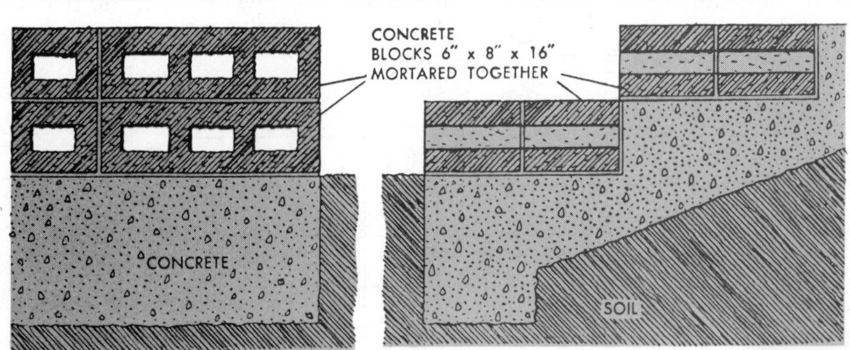

Concrete blocks are long-wearing and make steps that are interesting in texture and as unusual and unique as can be. Laid on a concrete base with a deeper footing in front (to prevent down-thrust of gravity from dislodging them) they lead from level to level with dignity and character. The holes in the front may be left open, or, if you wish, filled with pebble patterns.

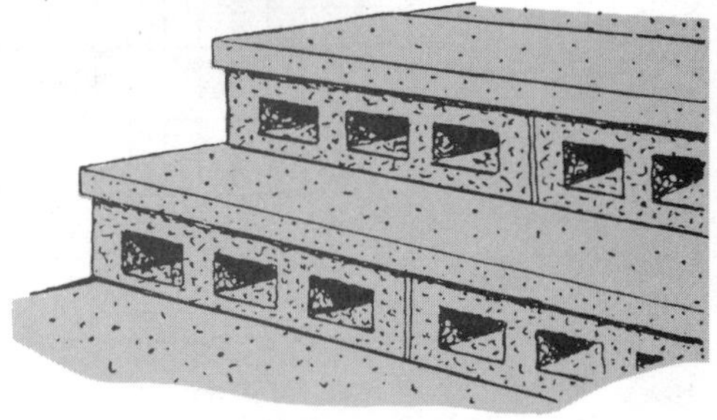

LOW, BROAD STEPS OFFER A WELCOME

Today, houses often are built on sloping land, the backyard being higher than the rear patio by the house; or possibly the front door is placed a little below street level so that the rear terrain may be used to better advantage. In most cases, broad, low steps are the most inviting, making the transition between levels agreeable, easy.

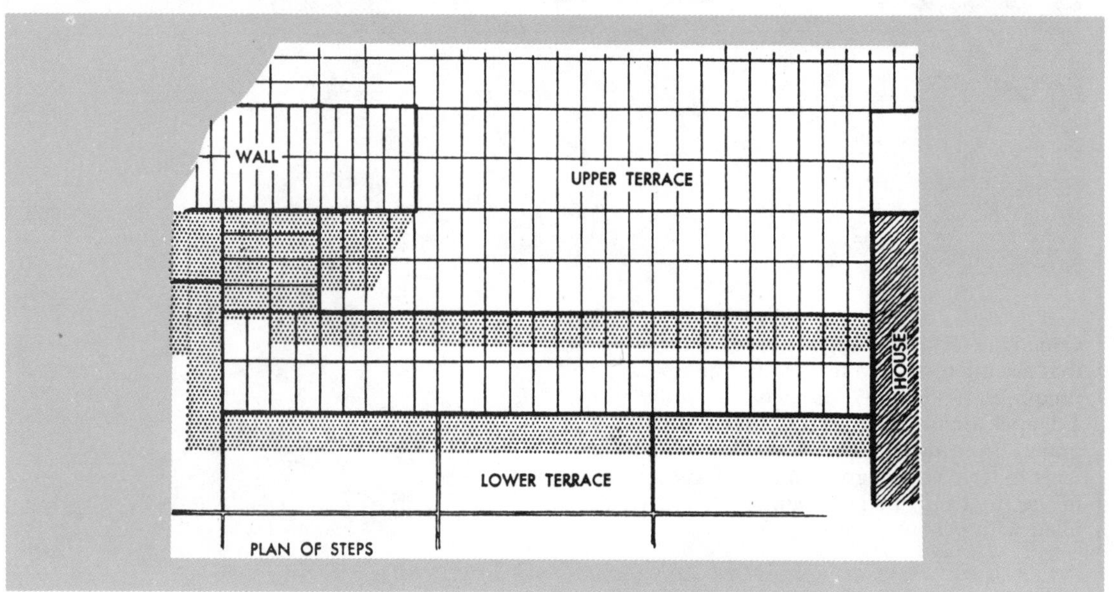

A BETTER GARDEN STAIRWAY

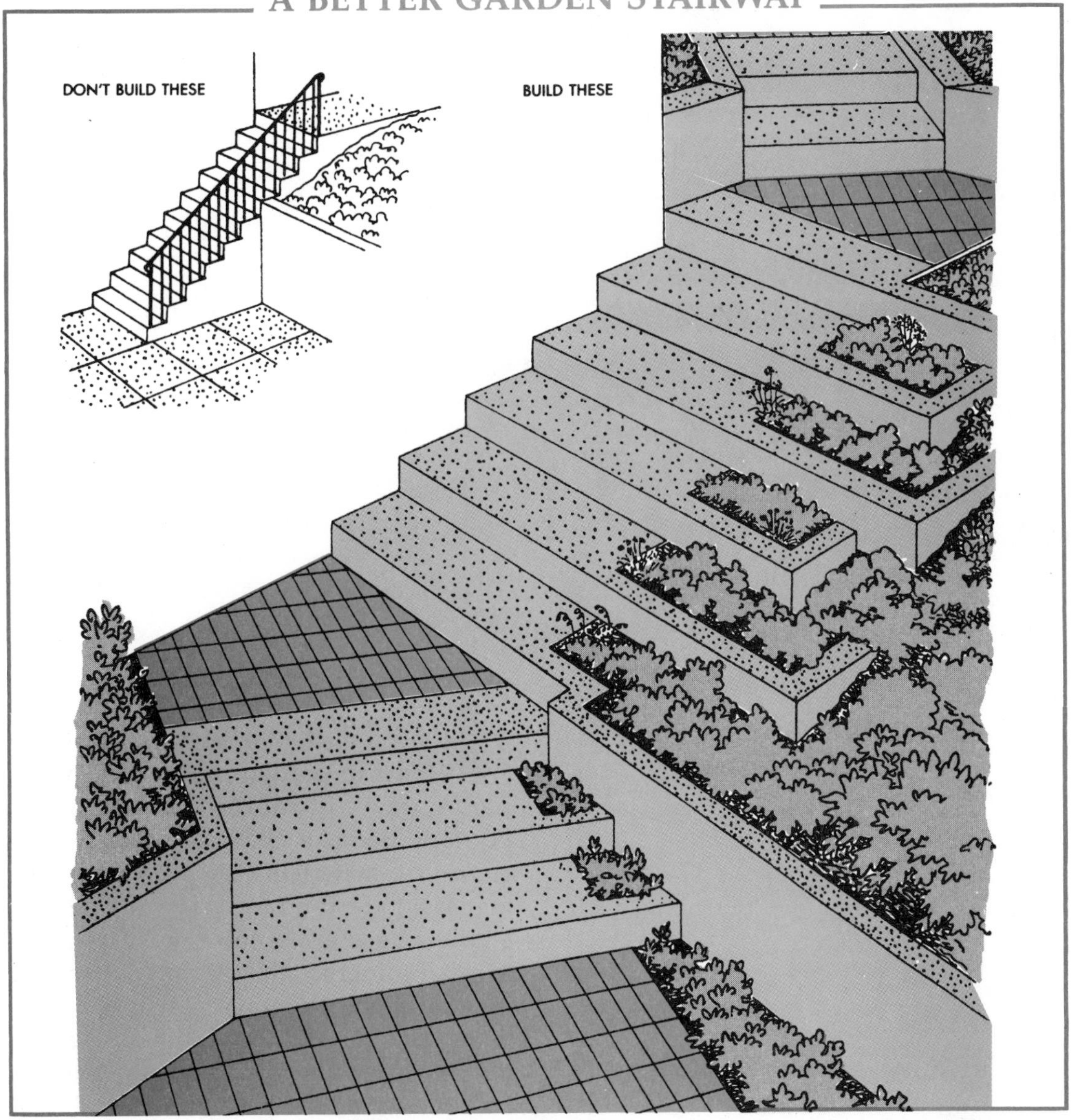

DON'T BUILD THESE

BUILD THESE

A straight line is the shortest distance between two points—and sometimes the dullest, too. Steps needn't always follow the stiff, straight side of a building; instead, give them more visual charm and make them easier to climb, too, by turning at landings placed to give a rest space for climbers. Widen the treads a little, reduce riser height a bit, and you can dispense with a handrail. Two steps placed above the corner of the house will gain space for the lower patio. Cut down height of the retaining wall so it won't be grim, plant the resulting bank with ground cover, and add some planting boxes to the end of each step. You'll have a local showpiece!

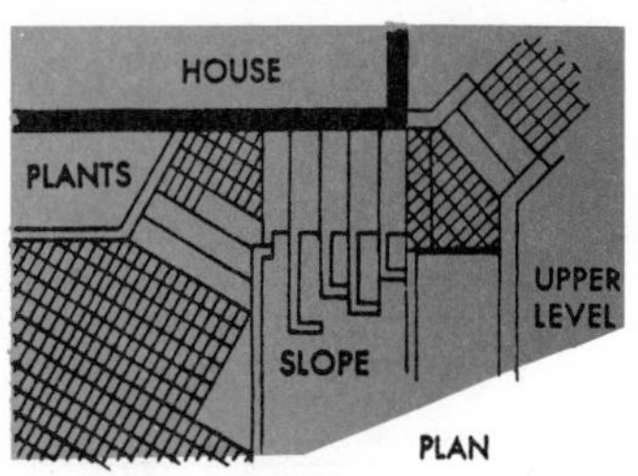

CHAPTER 18

PAVING WALKS AND PATIOS

The question of what to use for paving garden walks and patios seems to give the novice a bit of trouble, perhaps because there is such a wide choice of material. However, once the material to be used to surface the desired area is chosen, attention must be given to what underlies this paving. No matter how attractive the paving materials may be or how unusual the texture or the pattern obtained in laying down the paving, no patio or walk is more durable or better than the underpinnings on which it is laid. Therefore let us take up the question of how to lay paving materials permanently so that this knotty problem will be settled.

Paving, as much as any other element, can give the outdoor picture distinction. Therefore the choice should be made with care and discretion. Similarly, once you have chosen what is to be laid, be sure that it will be permanent, easy to maintain, and safe to use in all weather throughout the year. You can cut the cost of building a patio or a walk in half or more if you do the work yourself. It is not the easiest kind of project, but perfectly possible to achieve.

The first move is to measure the area that your paving is to cover (I assume you have read Chapter 15 if it is to be a patio), and to stake it out with stakes every 3 feet or so. It may help to run a mason's line around the stakes so that you can see exactly how it shapes up and make revisions before it has cost you any labor which may have to be put in again. When it is laid out to your satisfaction, figure out the approximate square footage to be covered; then visit your building materials dealer. Select several of the materials you like and wish to consider. If your dealer can be persuaded to lend them to you, you might take samples of the paving materials home with you to try on the spot to see how colors look with your house or any other architectural features. If not, then you will have to exercise your imagination. You will be able, once you have chosen two or three likely paving materials, to figure out comparative costs for the materials from the square footage to be covered. Don't forget to figure in the costs of the underpinnings—sand, gravel, cinders, concrete, or whatever the paving material will rest on.

Whatever surfacing you finally choose, there will be only one of two basic methods used in laying the paving: mortaring it to a concrete base (this is the most permanent and satisfactory way, and naturally the most expensive), or laying it on a tamped base of sand, cinders, or some other porous material, or sometimes on a combination of two of them. Cinders or

Brick walks laid in various patterns assure firm footing in all weathers, and here seem also to tie together the varied textures of the stones in the dry wall.

crushed rock may be used where the soil is exceptionally wet, or where it is so heavy with clay that drainage is poor when heavy rains occur. To make a good flat base for the paving material, a layer of sand on top of this coarse drainage layer will be necessary. The sand should be tamped down well to level it off.

There is a third paving material which shall be considered later on—concrete cast in place—but for the moment we are concerned with loose units of paving materials to be laid for walks or terraces. Of all the infinite number of paving patterns possible in a great variety of materials and sizes of units, all will be laid in one or another of the above methods.

SAND BASE METHOD

Because it is the simplest and cheapest method, this will appeal most strongly to do-it-yourselfers. But considerable care and skill must be exercised to obtain really good results, even though it would seem that basically all you must do is grade the soil to the proper depth, lay a bed of sand to the proper thickness, and then place on top of that the paving material chosen. If any of these basic operations is not done well, the result will be far from pleasing and will require much work for replacement and maintenance.

Remember that sand will settle even after it has been wet down and tamped. The weight of the paving material will pack the sand somewhat and the weight of use and traffic will pack it still further. This will make the level of the paving uneven, and it will be lower than you had thought it would be in the beginning. Therefore allow ½ to ¾ inch of space for settling and, when paving walks, crown the center a little so that, where the general traffic will be, repeated use will gradually pack down and level the walk. Should any particular units sink out of

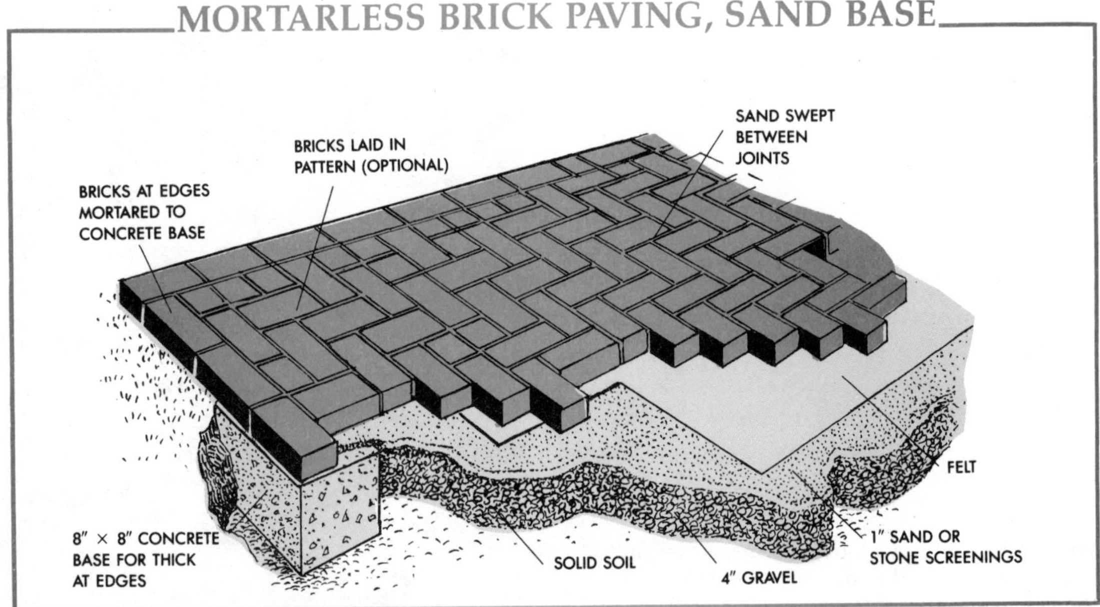

line, it is comparatively easy to pry them up to fill under them with a bit of sand and then replace them.

With both walks and terraces it is wise to start with the boundary courses. While the soil may be allowed to remain more or less roughly level, these edges must be precise and carefully placed. Usually boards are used for edge guides, nailed to the stakes and set with the aid of a level, if the walk is to be level and not slant to conform with a hillside. But a walk should be level on both its edges, no matter how it may slope, so the guide boards must be leveled.

Place the boards so that the top is exactly at the edge where you wish the paving to begin, with the stakes on the outside. After the first board is set, do a trial run with the units (I am thinking particularly of bricks, but the principle holds good for any modular unit paving material) to see how many you can place across the width of the walk with good tight joints. Then place the other board on the other side of the walk and level it, stake it, and make ready to start work. For patios or pavings broader than garden paths, you may have to set some intermediate boards to assist you in leveling; or put in stakes at intervals driven to the exact depth desired, so that the top of a stake can be the guide for a good straight board or a mason's line, which will help to keep things going well and to keep the paving level. Note that all patios should have a slight pitch for drainage in wet weather, even though the paving units when laid on sand will allow rain to drain into the joints and disperse in the sand and drainage layer below.

A minimum of 2 inches of sand should be used for the bed, placed either on the soil or on 2 to 4 inches of well-tamped cinders, gravel, or well-crushed stone where drainage is needed. Level the sand roughly with a board and then soak it thoroughly with a hose, the nozzle adjusted to a medium-fine spray so that it will not dislodge the sand too much. After the soaking it may be necessary to refill any low spots and soak it again. The sand should then be leveled with a screed board, which may be cut to rest on top of the side form boards and shaped to crown the walk, or used as a square leveling board if a patio is being laid. A 2″ × 4″ is frequently used, but a 1″ × 4″ or a 1″ × 6″ may be used if desired. The edges which project over the board will guide it and permit fairly accurate leveling. The board will be cut to scrape out the sand to the depth of the paving units that are to be used. Every now and then remove the sand which the screed board has pushed up in front of it.

LAYING THE PAVING

Now that the sand bed is ready for use, you are ready to lay the bricks or other units. The secret of success in laying paving is to be found in the constant tamping and careful fitting of the units, and in the frequent checking of levelness of the paving. Keep your level, a short board about 1″ × 4″ × 13″, and your heaviest hammer always at hand. It is possible to use the board and hammer to tamp an entire row of 3-inch-wide bricks, to set them. *Never hit the paving material directly with the hammer* or you may damage it by cracking, chipping, or gouging it. Use the board and hammer also in front of a row of units to tamp it back firmly against the previous row. If you are laying paving in hot weather, don't just leave it when you must stop in the middle for the day. Always dampen the sand base with a hose, again using a fine spray to prevent dislodging the sand which has been leveled. This will keep the sand in place and moist, so that it can be slightly dampened the following day and the next lot of units laid on it.

FINISHING TOUCHES

After all the units have been laid, place a shovelful of sand here and there on the surface of the paving and then sweep it across so that the sand fills in the cracks of the joints between units. You will find that dry sand sweeps better and will fill more compactly; and, if the cracks are well filled, there will be less shifting and set-

MORTARLESS BRICK PAVING

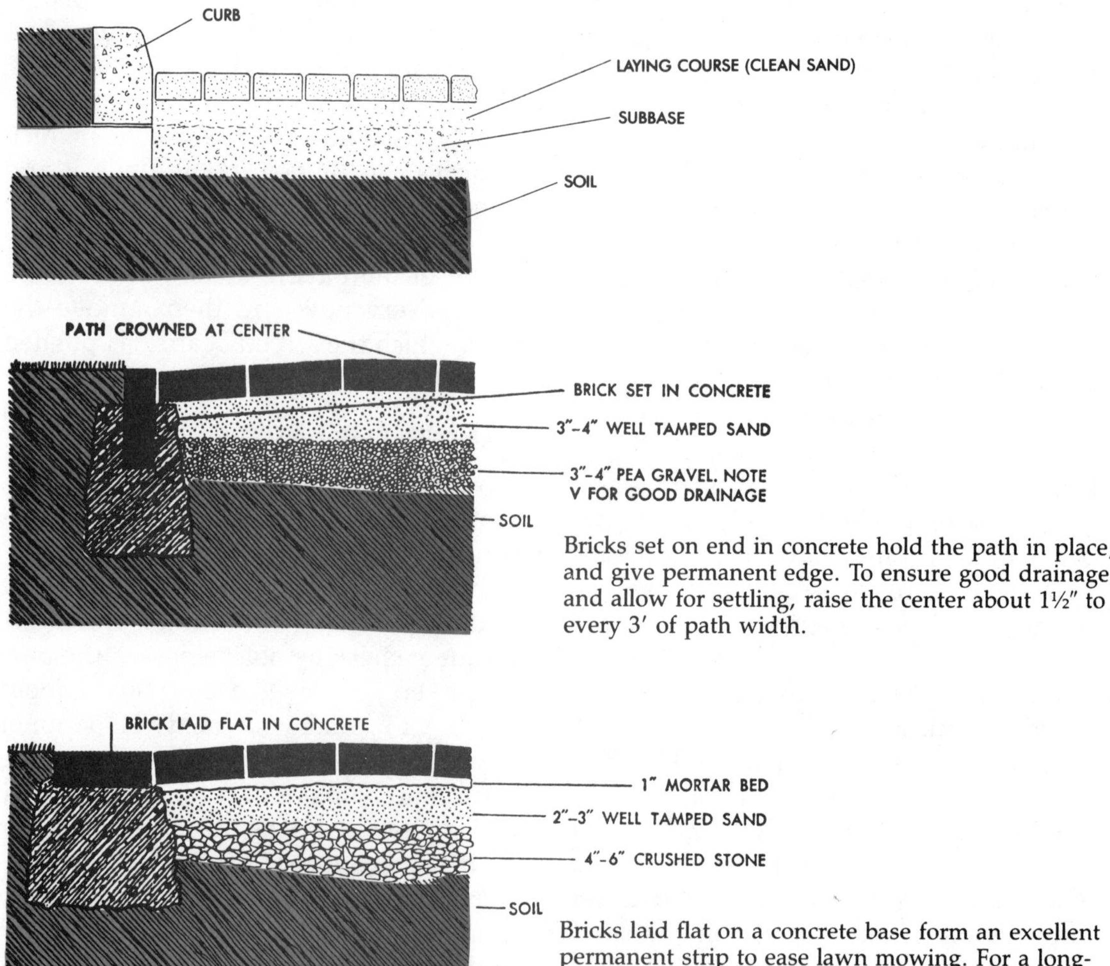

Bricks set on end in concrete hold the path in place, and give permanent edge. To ensure good drainage and allow for settling, raise the center about 1½″ to every 3′ of path width.

Bricks laid flat on a concrete base form an excellent permanent strip to ease lawn mowing. For a long-lasting walk, tamp sand hard before laying brick on a mortar bed.

tling in the future. After all the cracks are filled, use a hose with a gentle spray to wash more sand into the cracks and to settle what is already there. Then, when it has dried, sweep up the excess sand and remove it. Occasionally, for a year or so, you may want to put on some more sand and repeat this process to keep cracks full and not allow weeds and grass to take root.

The wooden edging may be left in place if desired—redwood, cedar, or cypress, well brushed and soaked with wood preservative, being best for this purpose—or the edging may be removed. In either case, fill in with soil next to the paving or edging and sow grass seed, if the paving abuts on a lawn; or fill with good topsoil if there is a flower border next to the paved area.

It may be that you will want to use a brick edging set in mortar or concrete, in place of the boards, to contain the sand and the paving material, thus making a permanent edging to the walk or terrace. (See the upcoming drawings.) The brick may be set on end on the concrete base or laid flat, with mortar between bricks in both cases. Paving bricks may be laid on a sand bed between these permanent edgings; or they may be laid on a 1-inch mortar bed on top of a well-tamped sand bed; the sand bed in both cases well wet down and allowed to settle, and then screeded to level it. These permanent edges will form the edge on which the screed rests as it is pulled along to level the sand bed. Note that paving should be set from ¼ to ½ inch higher than is eventually desired, to allow for settling.

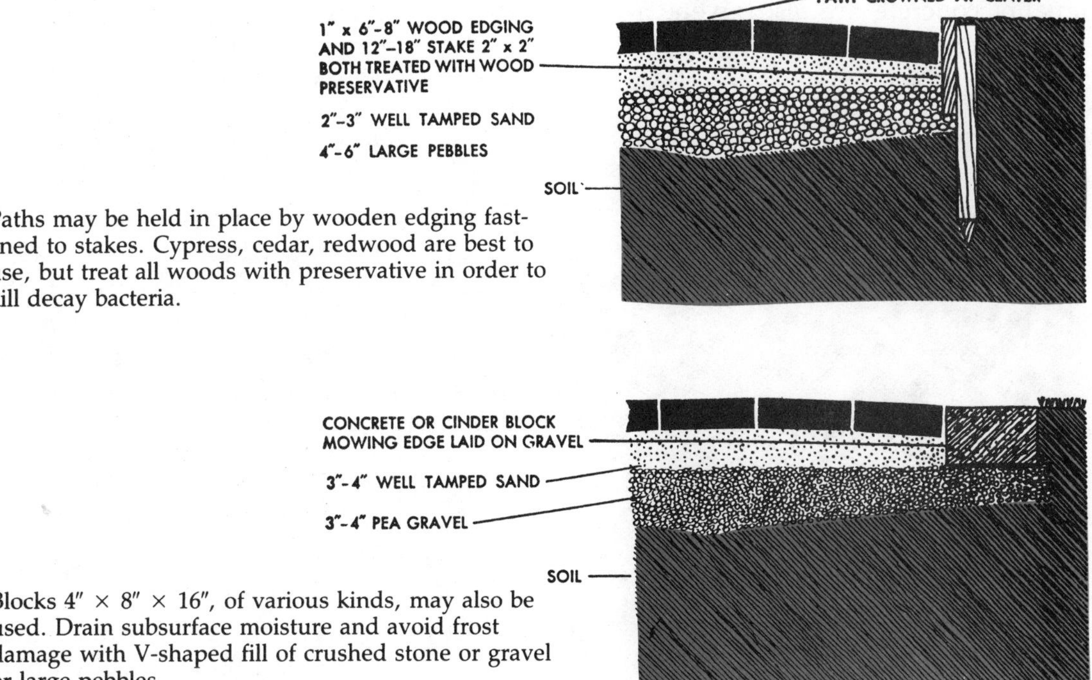

Paths may be held in place by wooden edging fastened to stakes. Cypress, cedar, redwood are best to use, but treat all woods with preservative in order to kill decay bacteria.

Blocks 4" × 8" × 16", of various kinds, may also be used. Drain subsurface moisture and avoid frost damage with V-shaped fill of crushed stone or gravel or large pebbles.

PAVING SET IN MORTAR ON A CONCRETE BASE

The most permanent bedding for pavement and the one requiring the least maintenance is, of course, concrete. The paving material is usually mortared in place on top of this concrete underlayer. Occasionally paving units are laid on a 1-inch sand bed placed on top of concrete to obtain the softer texture of the unmortared pavement. This may be desirable in many places.

Place joints between slabs every 6 to 8 feet (10 feet at the most) to allow for contraction and expansion during temperature and weather changes.

Good drainage under the concrete is essential; 3 to 4 inches of crushed rock and tamped cinders will ensure this. On top, pour the concrete in the manner described in Chapter 14, where formulas for quality concrete are also given, a 3- to 4-inch slab sufficing for this underlayer. In the case of a very wide walk or a patio, it will be well to divide it into sections and build forms for them so that they can be conveniently cast. You will have to allow for the depth of the paving unit plus mortar joint when casting, so that your paving will come out even with the soil line or whatever you have determined as the final height of the pavement. Be sure that these forms are at the height you wish to have the concrete end, so that they can be used for support for the screed. After one section is cast and set you can remove the form, and the resulting joint, when the next section is cast, can serve as a joint for the slab.

MORTAR-SET PAVING ON CONCRETE BASE

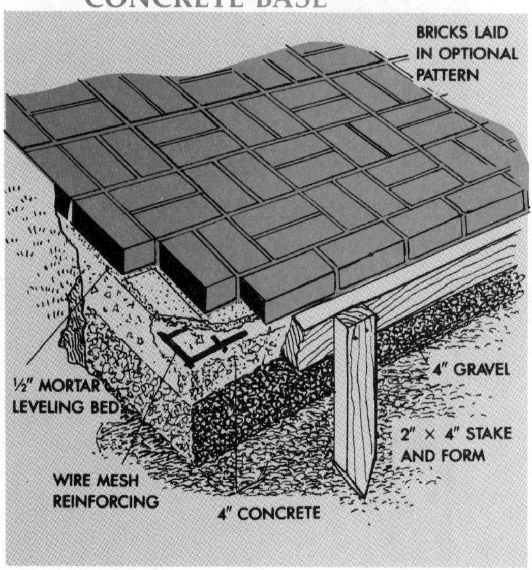

You need not wait for the concrete to cure completely before laying your paving material. As soon as the slab will support your weight and is dry enough to work on in comfort, you can start laying the paving units. Spread a mortar bed for several units just as for brick laying (see Chapter 12) and butter the paving unit so that, as it is swung into place, it butts against its previously laid neighbor and leaves a joint of mortar about ½ inch in width. The mortar bed should also be about that depth when the unit is laid. Check with the mason's level frequently to maintain the units in good relationship to each other, with no dips and no hillocks in the finished surface. Be sure that no air pockets are left under the units where frost and moisture can enter and cause havoc later on. Bed the units well and avoid this.

The joints may be tooled so that they are flush, or if you want a more interesting texture tool them lightly with a 1-inch pipe (see Chapter 13). This will emphasize the joints slightly, without raking them so deeply that they will collect dirt and debris and make the paving hard to keep clean.

I recommend that the paving units be soaked with water just as you would soak them if they were being built into a wall, so that they will not extract the moisture too rapidly from the mortar. After the paving has been laid for half a day or so, sprinkle it lightly with a hose set to a fine spray, or with a sprinkling can, to prevent its setting and curing too rapidly. Spray it again once or twice a day (more frequently if the weather or the climate is hot) for about a week, after which time it will be properly cured and you may cease.

OTHER PAVING IDEAS

Occasionally today one finds wooden paving blocks being used where wood is available and cheap. Waste blocks from sawmills, limbs or large tree trunks sawed through and used with the rounds of the wood facing upward, redwood blocks, and many other variations are possible according to the availability and the price of the wood in your region. All of these mentioned should be set on sand on top of 3 to 4 inches of crushed rock, because good drainage is mandatory if the wood is to last very long. Sand is filled into the spaces between square blocks, and smaller rounds or triangles of split wood are forced into the spaces left between the round slices of limb or trunk.

Wood paving is never so permanent as brick, stone, and others of the more impervious materials; but it has a very rustic, pleasant look which complements certain types of homes, and it will last for some years if properly laid with good drainage below it. Various hardwoods and redwood stand up better under wear than do softwoods, but all will last longer if they are well soaked with wood preservatives before being laid. (See Chapter 4.)

Wooden decks are also coming into greater use, particularly where living areas must be built out from a house on a hillside, and where it is not desirable to bulldoze into the hill to level a spot for the patio. On other hillside sites, part of the patio is on level ground and a wooden deck extends the living space out from it, wood being used in part of the leveled ground, paving to integrate it with the deck part of the patio. Old railroad ties can be use for paving; if they are sawed up and set on end with the crossgrain part

To protect a tree from mower damage and yet make close clipping easy, set bricks on edge on a sand or concrete base in an octagon. Pie-shaped cement blocks at the corners help to hold the bricks in place. A neat look and easy watering are assured by the oversize pebbles inside.

taking the wear, they will last several years, for they are well creosoted before being laid as ties for the railroad. This type of paving is well suited to tying in with a wooden deck, the sympathy of materials being evident to all observers. Garden timbers, 6″×6″ and 8″×8″, 8 feet long, are now found in lumber yards and garden supply centers. Sometimes shorter lengths are also available. These are usually treated with a preservative but should have another coat or two applied to ensure years of protection from decay. These timbers may be used for edges, divisions of paving, and for risers of steps.

On the following pages you will find a number of suggested patterns for paving which should give you a good start in choosing the design you'll feel best able to create, or the one most suited to your particular paving problem. Study them well—perhaps even lay out some of the patterns as a test to see which may suit you best, using borrowed bricks or other paving material if you are not yet ready to make the final investment. You may come up with a fresh new pattern of your own which will be more to your liking than any offered here. If so, by all means use it.

But whatever pattern you choose, don't forget to put it down *properly*. There is no substitute for care and good craftsmanship.

PAVING CURVES AND CORNERS

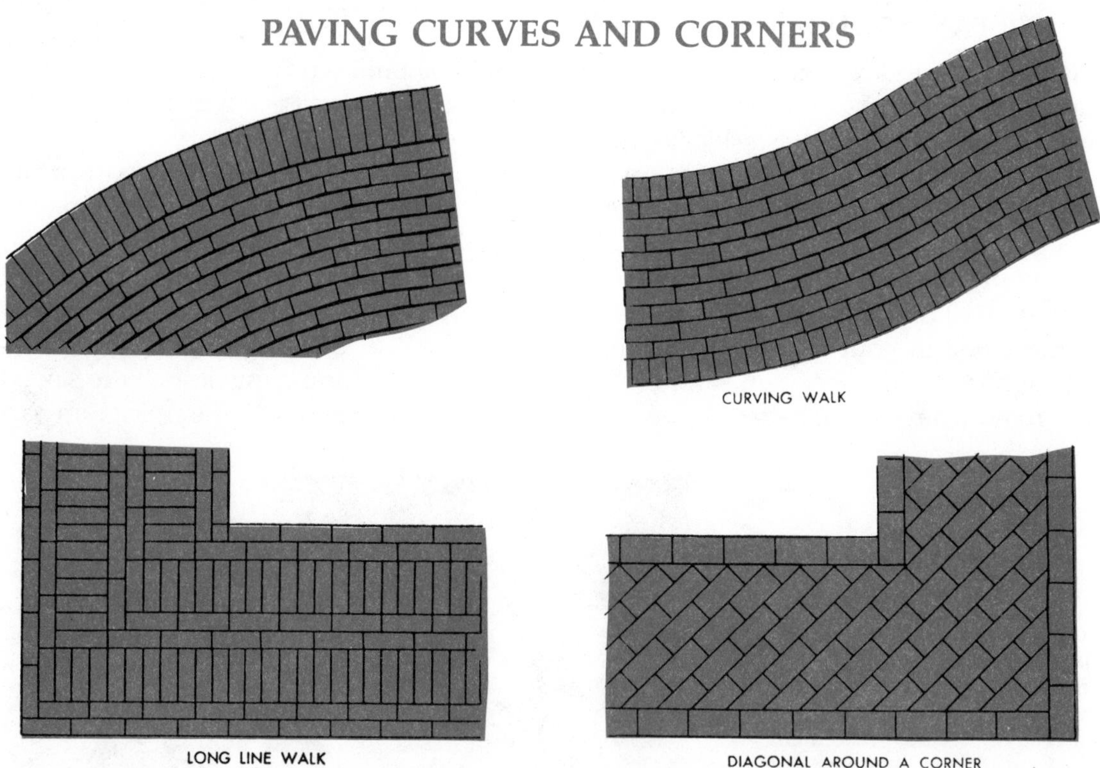

Top, if curves are kept shallow, bricks set on edge will leave only small spaces between them. And sharp corners need not be dull.

BRICK PATTERNS FOR PATHS AND WALKS

Shown here are various ways that bricks can be used in combination. (In all cases mortar joints are included in figuring the modular sizes.) Three bricks laid on end horizontally or two laid on end vertically equal the length of one brick. Two bricks laid flat or three laid on edge equal one brick length.

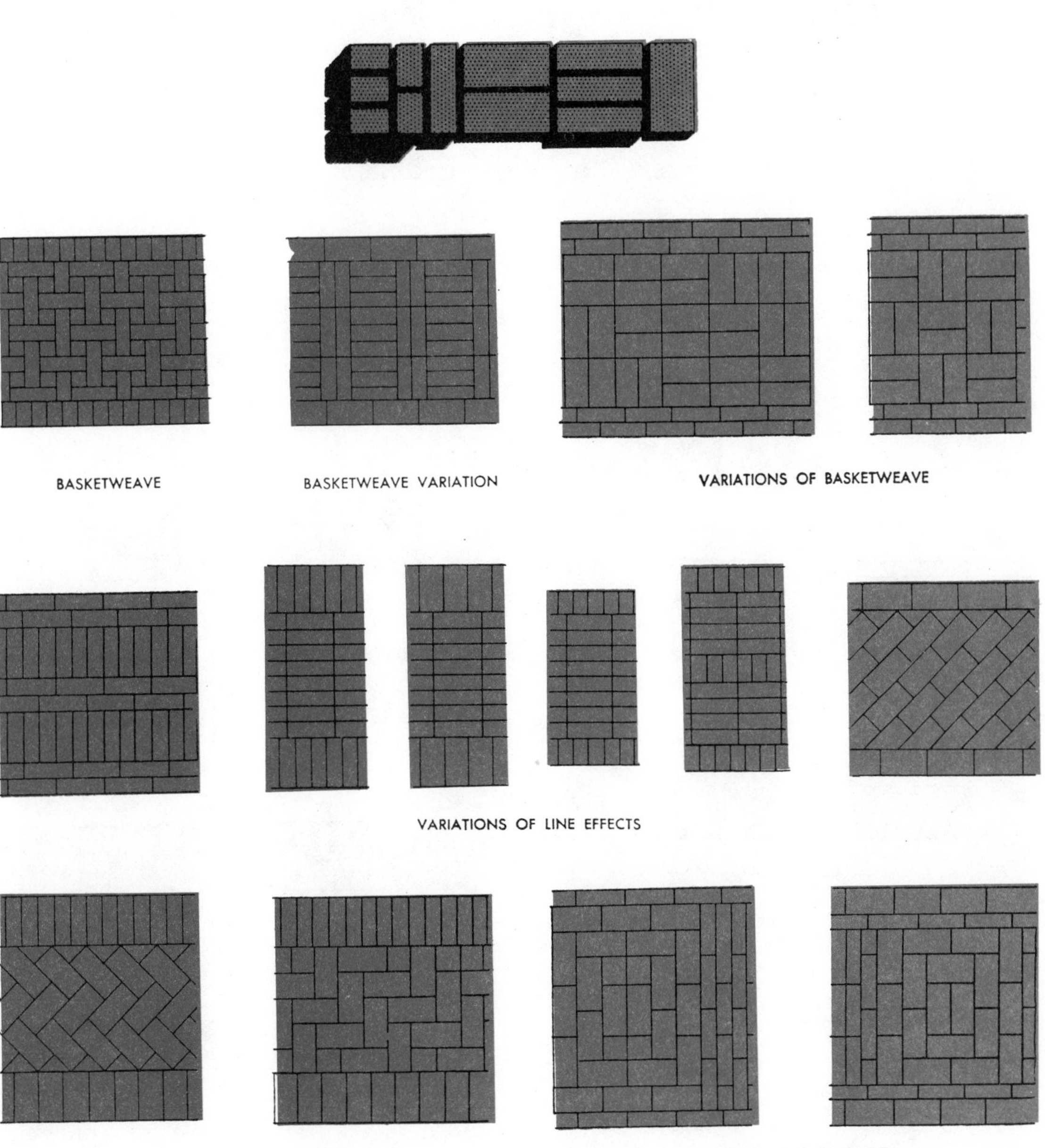

BRICK PATTERNS FOR STEPPING STONES

Where the traffic across the lawn or through plantings is heavy enough to cause wear, set in stepping stones. They may be made of bricks, taking their cue for pattern from that of the walk or patio with which they connect. Several of the designs shown on these pages utilize brickbats or broken bricks to advantage, saving money by using waste materials. Note the variety of patterns possible, particularly noting variations of bordering the paths. If you do not find a design here which you like, work out one of your own—brick combination possibilities are infinite.

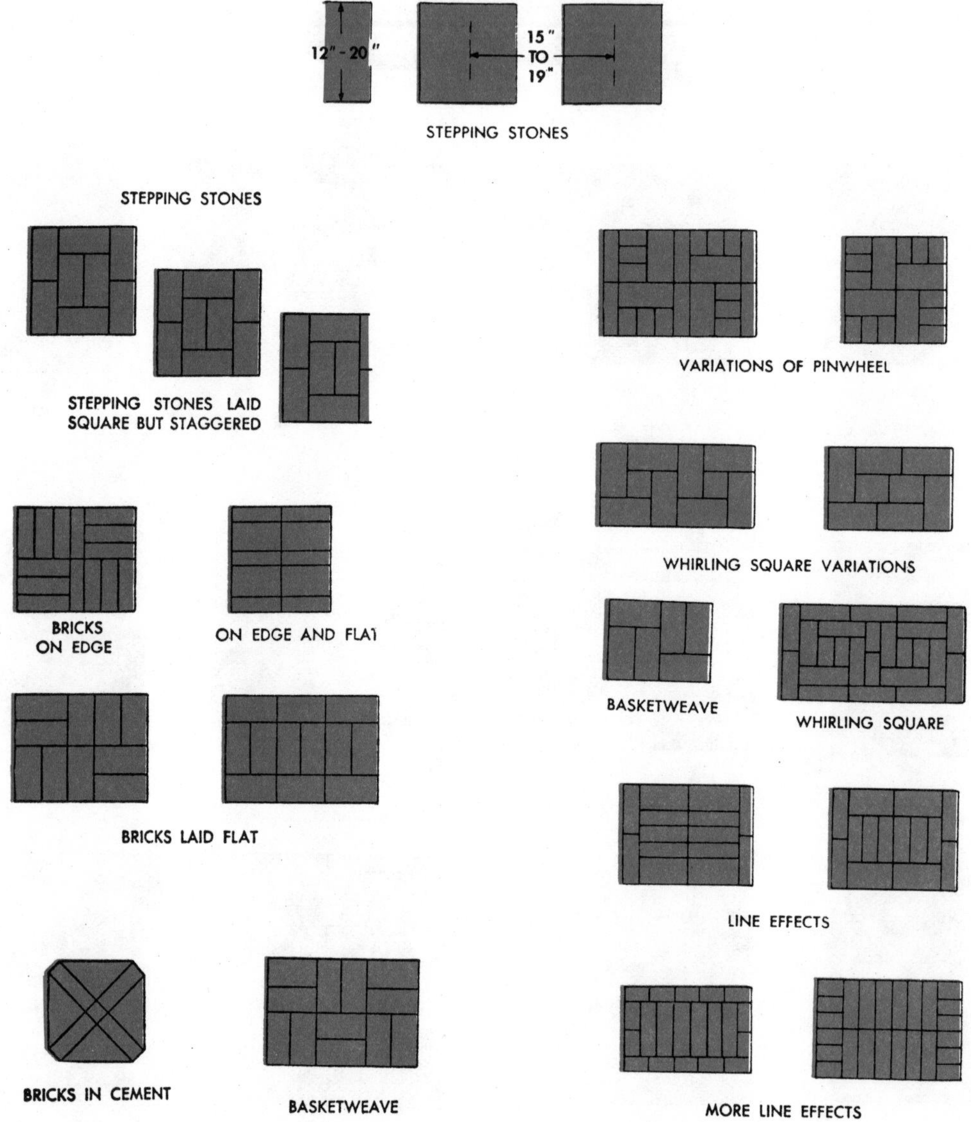

WHY NOT ENTER ON THE BIAS?

Where the entry is set between two uneven projections of the house, don't think you must square off the entry platform. Make it on the bias, leaving a triangular bed for permanent plants, dress it up with pots of flowers and houseplants through summer. Pave adjoining walks with brick, too, and if you wish, extend the walk into a sitting area.

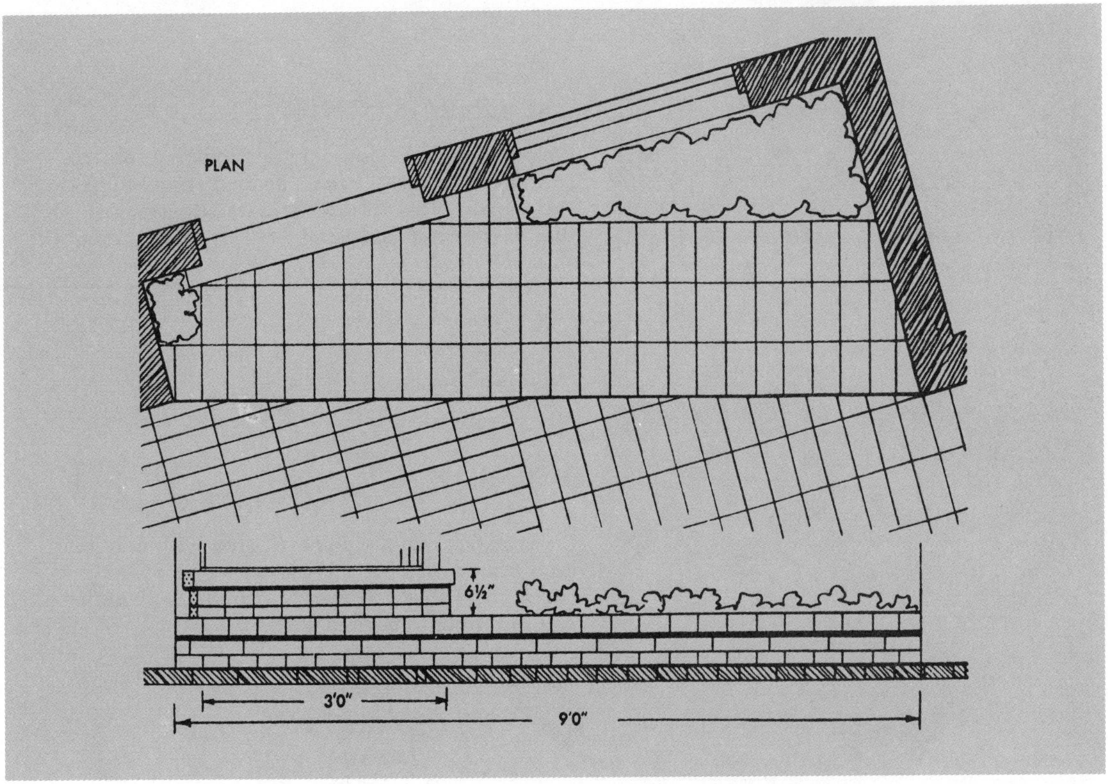

PLAN

6½"

3'0"

9'0"

PATIO BRICK PATTERNS

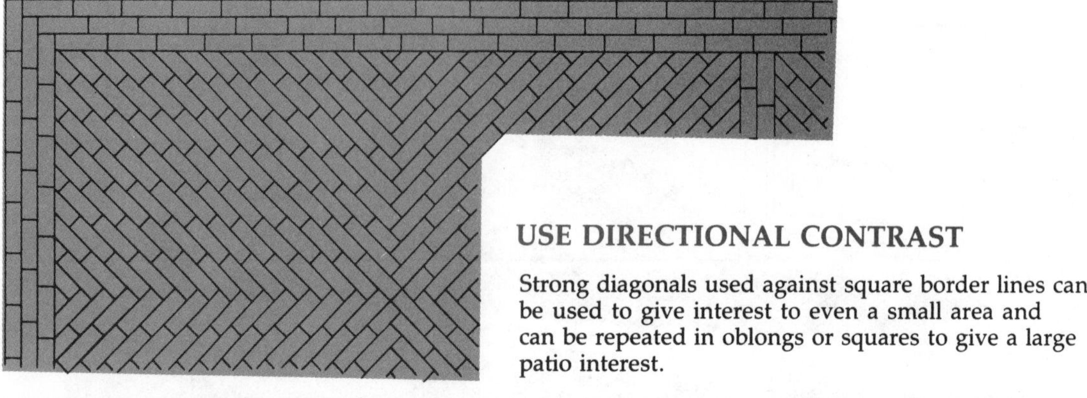

USE DIRECTIONAL CONTRAST

Strong diagonals used against square border lines can be used to give interest to even a small area and can be repeated in oblongs or squares to give a large patio interest.

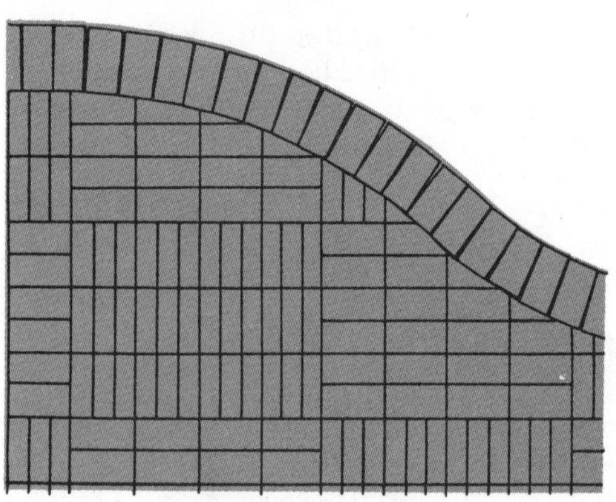

USE LINEAR CONTRAST

On small patios using only one material, obtain contrast with line—curves against straight lines; extra linear effect of brick laid on edge against that of the brick laid flat.

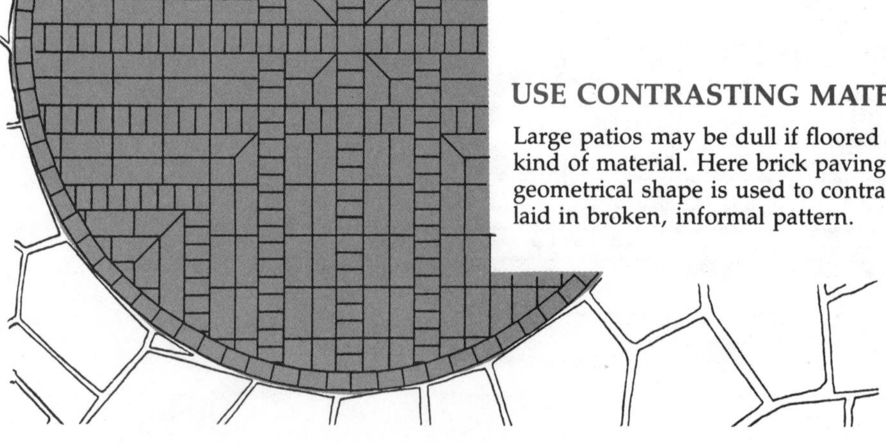

USE CONTRASTING MATERIALS

Large patios may be dull if floored with only one kind of material. Here brick paving in a geometrical shape is used to contrast with stone laid in broken, informal pattern.

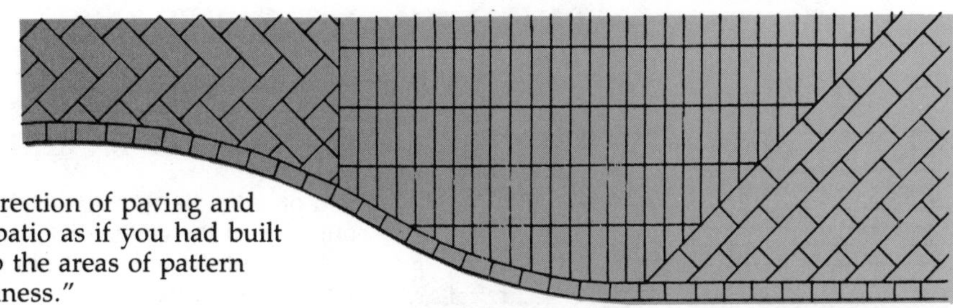

TRAFFIC GUIDES

Vary the patterns and direction of paving and guide traffic across the patio as if you had built paths to contain it. Keep the areas of pattern unequal to avoid "jumpiness."

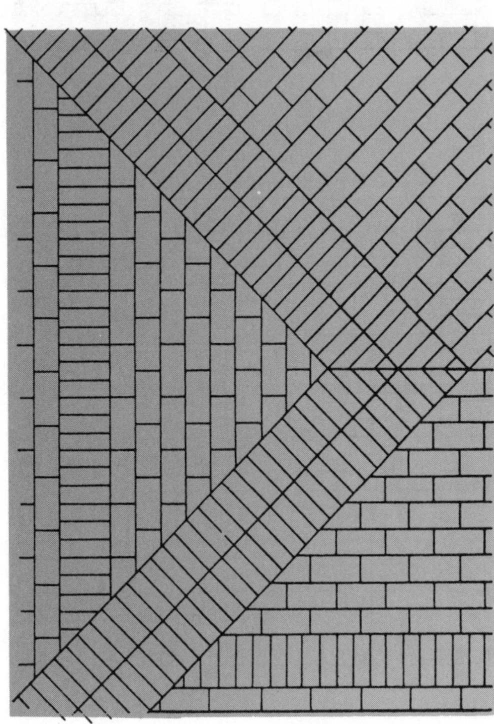

VARIETY SPICES THE PATIO

Add interest with angular patterns of brick paving, using strongly defined header courses to divide areas. Particularly good with modern, it fits well with traditional houses, too.

USE WOOD WITH BRICK

Brick paving laid flat, on edge, at an angle or herringbone style in large squares (3′ to 4′) is given unity by 2″ × 4″s of cypress, redwood, or other wood treated with a preservative.

PATIO PAVING PATTERNS

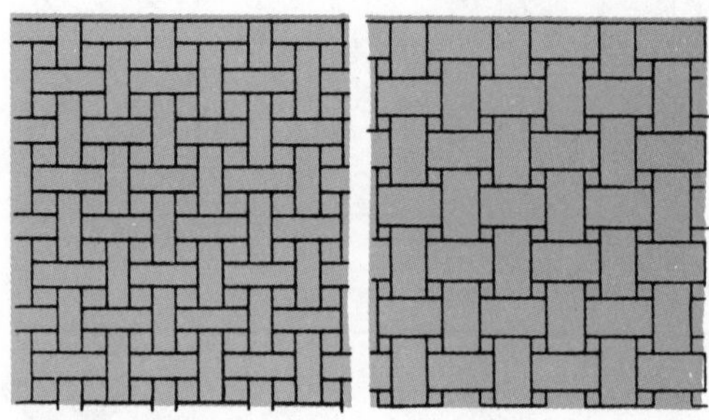

SMALL-SCALE BASKETWEAVE

Laid on edge (left) or flat (right) and centered on the long side of the cross brick, this is a most useful pattern. Fill the holes with broken brick cut to fit or with mortar cement.

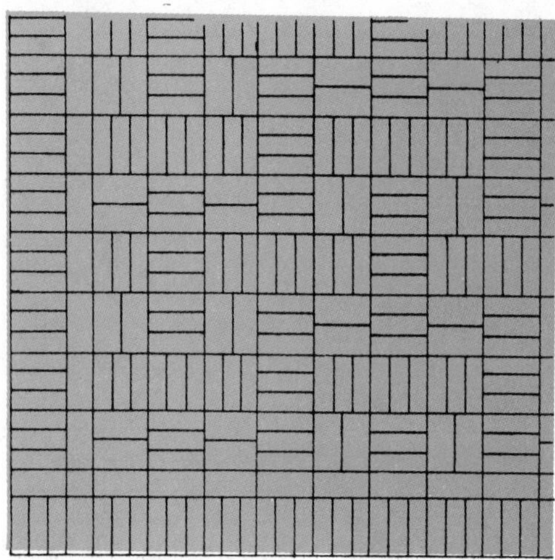

LARGE-SCALE BASKETWEAVE

Bricks laid on edge contrast with bricks laid flat in this paving design from Mexico. Further interest can be obtained by using two tones of brick or by filling some spaces with cement.

WHIRLING SQUARES

Bricks laid in this pattern give an interesting offbeat effect. Centers can be filled with broken bricks cut to fit space or with cement tinted to harmonize with color of the bricks.

CONCENTRIC SQUARES

Build rows of brick around a pair of ¾ bricks until the desired area is covered. Lay the border rows at right angles, either flat or on edge, and repeat oblongs to cover the area.

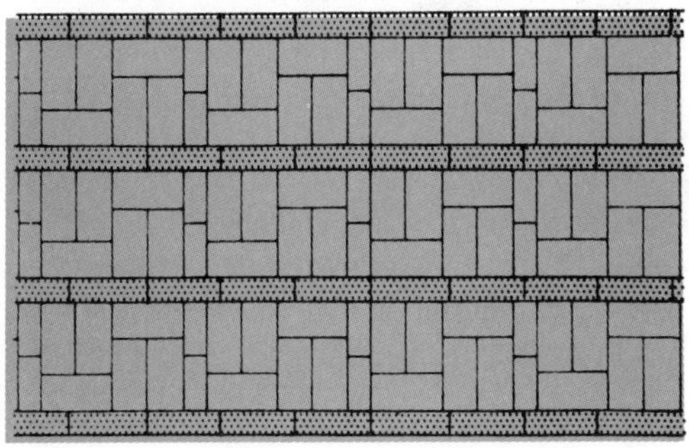

DIRECTIONAL LINES

Long lines of brick laid on edge, parallel to the house, can make a boxy square seem longer and narrower, especially if bricks are darker than those laid flat.

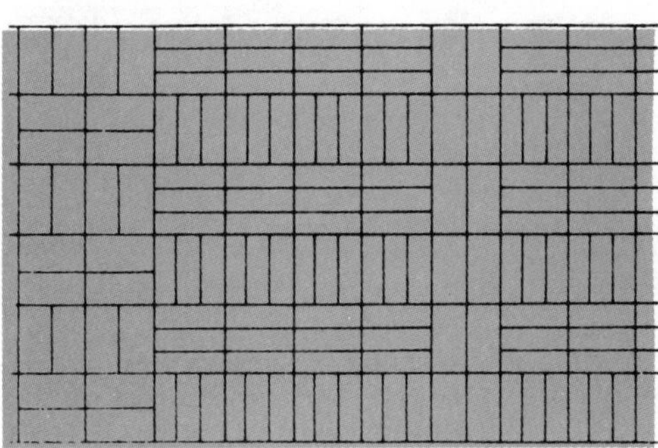

DIRECTIONAL PATTERN

Adaptable to walk or patio, long lines are interrupted occasionally with cross courses laid flat. Further emphasis for length can be achieved by alternating the colors of courses.

COMBINING VARIOUS PAVING MATERIALS

CONCRETE WITH WOOD

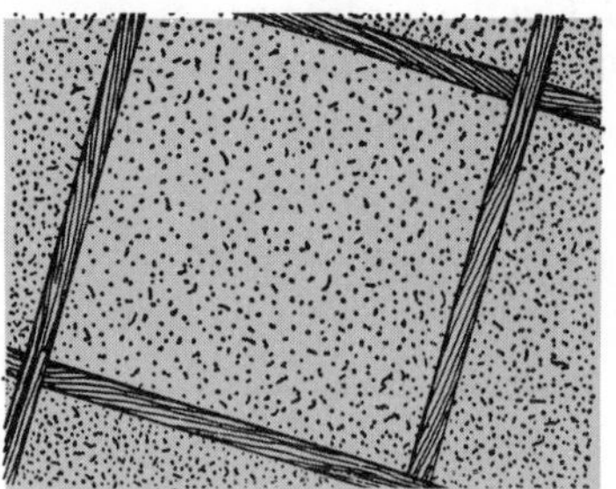

Make forms of redwood or other preservative-treated wood and fill evenly with natural or tinted concrete for variety.

COMBINATION FOR WALKS

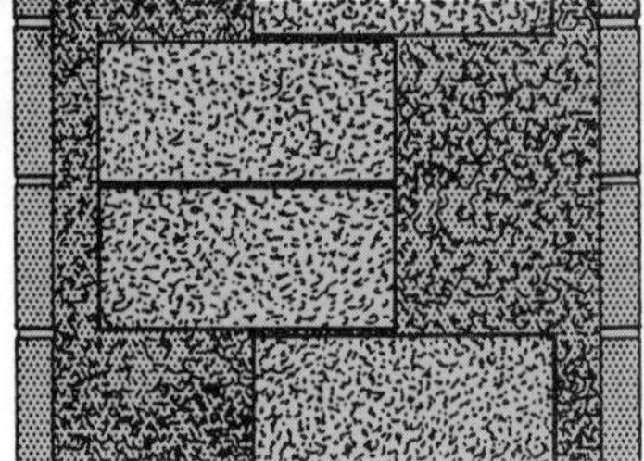

Concrete blocks paired and set in brickdust or gravel bordered with bricks laid on edge makes a good, visually attractive path.

BLOCKS OF VARIOUS KINDS

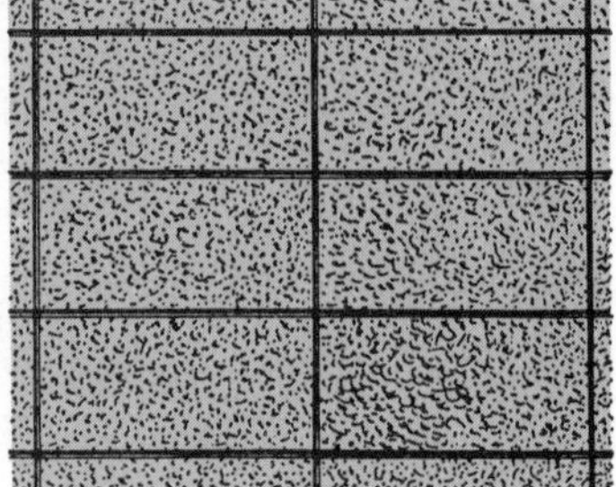

Inexpensive blocks—cement, cinders, pumice, adobe—when set in sand, are easily replaceable if broken.

TILE AND CONCRETE

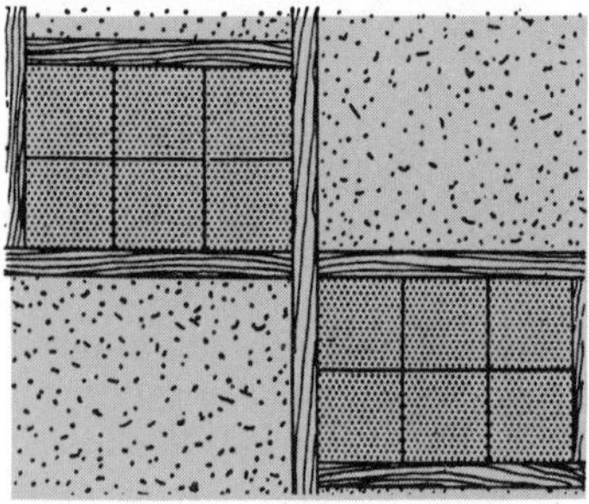

Patio tile, fairly expensive to use on big areas, may be used in selected sections with wood and concrete.

RANDOM SQUARES

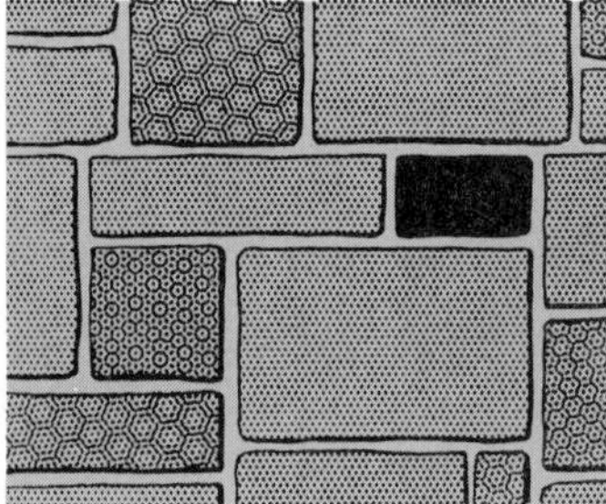

Stones of varying sizes and shapes, roughly squared off, can be fitted together to give a serene, stable effect.

CRAZY PAVING

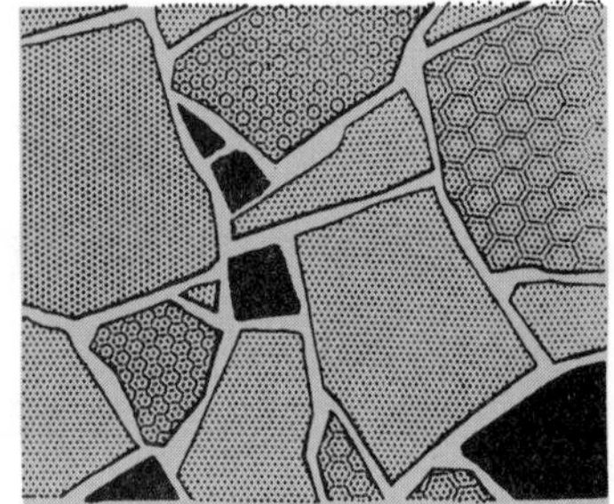

Vari-colored stones of many angular shapes can be used to advantage where paving needs informal touches.

PEBBLES OR GRAVEL

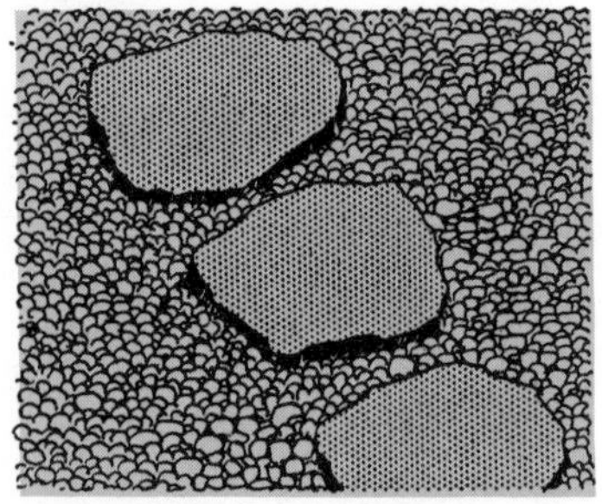

Informal patios or path areas can use gravel or larger pebbles with irregular stepping stones to make a walk.

TREE TRUNK BLOCKS

Wood blocks treated with preservative make good paving; fit rounds together, then fill holes with sand or soil.

SQUARE WOOD BLOCKS

Pave with redwood, cypress, or other hardwood blocks or use sections of railroad ties bounded by ties laid flat to form blocks.

CHAPTER 19

CASTING PAVING BLOCKS

You can make your own paving blocks, if you wish, by casting them in any size, any shape, or any color that you desire. It is not really a hard job, although it will entail making your own concrete, finishing the surface of the blocks, and making the form in which they are to be cast. If only a few are made at any one time, however, it should not be too difficult a project. If you make the forms and hold them in readiness, you may be able to save money by using left-over concrete from other projects, getting a dividend with no expenditure of money or effort. You may even want to mix a bit extra for the other projects each time and save the labor of a special mixing, which would be required for making the blocks alone.

All that you'll need is some lumber for the forms, some building paper or felt,

FORMS FOR CASTING PAVING BLOCKS

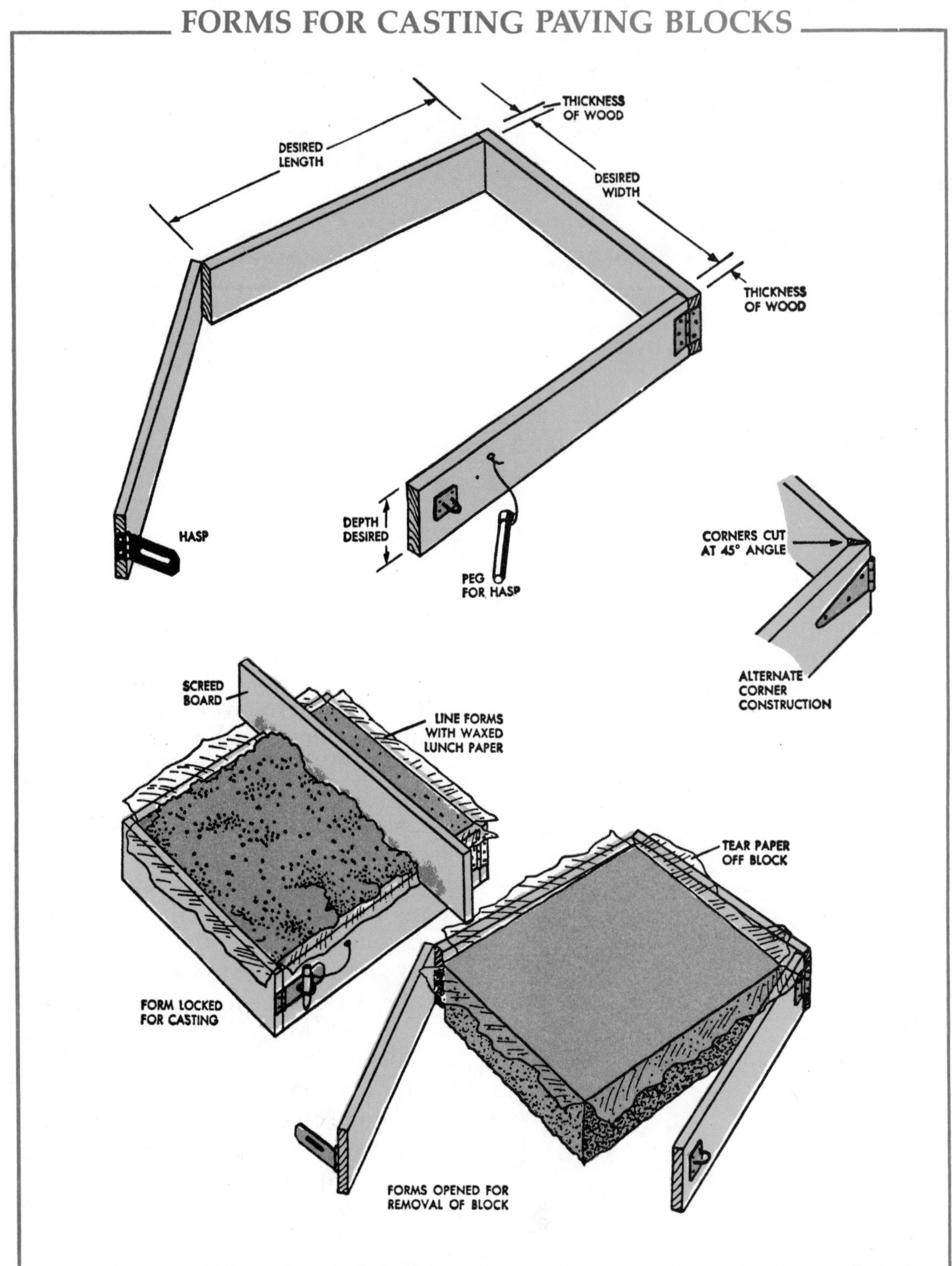

some polyethylene plastic, some sand, cement, gravel, and a place to mix the concrete. Perhaps a metal wheelbarrow is as good as anything for the purpose. You'll also need your garden hoe for mixing the concrete, a straight edged board to use as a screed, and a trowel and float to give a final surface to the blocks.

MAKING THE FORMS

The only requisite for the forms is that the wood be straight and true—not warped out of shape—and reasonably smooth so that the concrete will not stick to it. Oddments of 1-inch boards can be ripped down to an even measure, the height you have chosen for the thickness of the block, cut to the proper length, and any roughnesses smoothed down. It is a good plan to cut several sets of sides and ends simultaneously, clamping the boards together while they are being cut so as to ensure that all will be exactly the same dimensions and that all the forms will be even and squared up. Hinges are installed on the outside edges of three corners, and a hasp on the fourth with a wooden peg to keep it firmly closed. Thus, when the block is cast and has set sufficiently, the hasp is loosened and the hinged form can be peeled off easily. Make at least two forms; half a dozen or more will be none too many if you plan to make many blocks for paving. Fewer than that will make it hardly worth while to mix up a batch of concrete for the casting. By using a rather stiff concrete mixture—one made with less water—the cast blocks will

REMOVABLE FORMS FOR CASTING FLAGSTONES IN PLACE

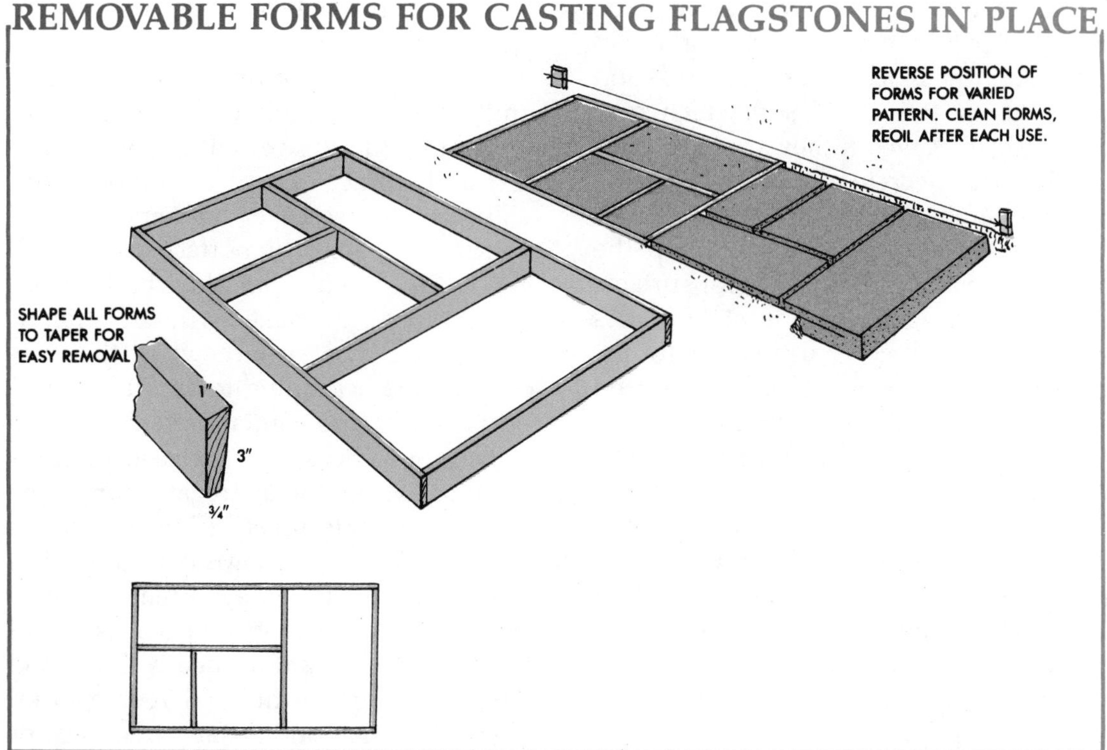

hold their shape and allow the forms to be removed soon after casting and reused.

Before casting the blocks, brush the forms with old crankcase oil saved from an oil change in your car. Any sort of oil or grease can be used, so long as the forms are thoroughly brushed with it before each casting to prevent the cement's adhering to the wood. Or, what is easier is to wrap the forms with waxed lunch paper held in place by a strip of masking tape. To remove it, cut the paper with a razor blade and lift off the form. The paper helps to hold the concrete and can be torn off or left on the sides to disintegrate when blocks are set in the soil.

PRELIMINARY OPERATIONS

On a *level* surface place a piece of building paper or felt somewhat larger than the form. On bare soil this will prevent the moisture from the concrete being lost in the soil, or the block picking up grass and stray bits of twigs and soil which may have to be removed if they are to be mortared onto a concrete base later. If you are using a garage floor, a walk, or a driveway for the casting, this will keep the blocks from adhering to the floor surface. On these surfaces use at least 18 inches extra paper all the way around the forms, so that the splashes, blobs, or screed scrapings will fall on the building paper and not on the cement or concrete floor. A piece of plywood or hardboard also makes a good casting base. Cover it with polyethylene plastic so that the concrete will not adhere to it. Such pallets can even be used on rather uneven ground, when properly underpinned to make them level.

Either a trowel or a large-sized vegetable- or fruit-juice can may be used to scoop up the mixed concrete from the wheelbarrow so that it can be poured into the forms. Be sure to fill each corner well. Use a block of wood to ram the concrete gently down into each corner and to joggle the rest of it gently to release any air bubbles and pockets. Do this when the form is half full and again when it is completely filled. When it is half full, too, is the time to insert any reinforcements of wire you may wish to use. Then fill the form to the top, pack it down well, and add a bit extra so that it bulges a little on top. Using the screed board—any good straight board a little longer than the width of the forms can be utilized—gently scrape the concrete forward with a zigzag motion, a kind of sawing motion. Let the board ride on the tops of the form boards as it removes the excess concrete, and as it scrapes off whatever water rises to the surface, too.

Finishing can be done with the float and trowel (for method see Chapter 14) for a smooth surface; but if you want a textured surface or a patterned one, you will want to use other implements once you have floated the surface smooth. A good stiff broom or an old whisk broom may be used to make swirls or straight striations in the surface when the concrete is just beginning to set. It can also be used to scrape regular patterns into the surface or to brush out the nearly set cement to expose the aggregates for an exposed aggregate finish. (This is detailed and also shown in photos in Chapter 14.) Various other implements may be used to imprint patterns in cast blocks: small tin cans either round or square, thin wood blocks or strips of tin soldered together in crosses, diamonds, stars, triangles, or other geometric or freeform shapes, or cookie cutters—all of these may be utilized to print designs at regular intervals or as your fancy dictates. Or use the pattern stamp shown on page 343 for imprinting concrete patios. The size and shapes of the paving block will be determined by the dimensions of the pattern.

CASTING BLOCKS IN OTHER WAYS

If you wish to cast patio or stepping stone blocks without the trouble of building wooden forms, you can sometimes use the soil itself for the form, casting the blocks in the exact location in which they are to remain. Be sure, however, that the soil is reasonably firm and not too sandy, so that it will hold its shape and not crumble, destroying the edge you want to maintain for the block. Water the soil well a day or two in advance of digging it out so that it will be moist and hold together.

Cut the stepping stone or patio block spaces in the lawn or the soil with a sharp, square-ended spade, then dig it out carefully with a trowel, using a putty knife to remove the corner earth and keep the corners square, if that is the effect for which you are striving. Stepping stones should be at least 2½ inches thick, with 3 to 3½ inches being preferred, and they should be cast on two or more inches of pea gravel or sand or cinders to provide drainage and prevent frost from heaving them. The concrete is poured in on top of the drainage layer and lightly rammed with a wooden block when the form is half full; then wire reinforcements are set, and the rest of the hole is filled and lightly tamped to release air bubbles. The screed board or the trowel and the float alone may be used to level off the concrete with the surface of the soil.

You may prefer to use freeform or sim-

Tiles cast face up can be colored using the easy, economical dust-on method. Dust-on coloring mix is sprinkled evenly over the surface after being struck off.

Now, float dust-on coating into surface. Follow with a second dust-on application and floating. By this time, coloring will have penetrated about ⅛", and the surface will be colored evenly.

ulated "crazy-paving" forms rather than squared forms for your stepping stone or paving. They will look more natural if you striate or lightly brush and roughen the surface of the concrete, and will be less dangerous underfoot in wet weather than if they had smooth surfaces.

If you want your stones colored, you may mix two batches of concrete. With the natural batch fill the forms to within about ¾ inch of the top. Then pour the colored concrete layer and finish it as described for ordinary concrete. See Chapter 14 for details on colored concrete.

WHAT SIZE FOR THE STONES?

If blocks are to be used for stepping stones, the size is largely a matter of individual preference, but will also be governed by the distance from center to center of the stones. As they are finally laid they should be comfortable for the average adult pace; 14 to 18 inches center to center is a good average for the casual garden stroller. If, on the other hand, the blocks are to be used in a pattern (see Chapter 18) on a patio or a walk, then they must be worked out carefully to an exact modular size so that they can be easily fitted together when they are laid. In this case the usual ratio is 2 to 1—that is, the length equals twice the width. Make the length about ¼ to ½ inch less than the exact double measurement of the width to allow for joint spaces between blocks when they are finally laid.

Blocks larger than 16″×32″ are practically impossible to transport, and are unwieldy and heavy even if they are to be moved into place nearby. The maximum size I recommend is 12″×24″ for a 3-inch thickness. These may be placed on rollers and guided into the place where they are to be permanently set, then shifted a little with a crowbar for final placing. Blocks smaller than the above sizes are easily handled.

Consider the need for half blocks, two-third, and one-third sizes, if the blocks are being laid in a staggered block pattern; and make the forms to cast them exactly as for the full-sized blocks, but use the proper dimensions. Hexagonal, triangular, and octagonal forms may also be worked out by the do-it-yourselfer; when carefully measured and well cast they will fit together exactly and with beautiful effect. Diamond patterns also may be used, being made fat or thin according to the space and the effect wanted. Long thin diamonds will make a narrow space look longer and narrower if the diamonds are used with the long measure parallel to the length of the narrow space; but if they are used the other way around, the narrow space seems less long and narrow, a more pleasantly proportioned area. Consider this principle when paving a patio which is long and narrow, or one which is too square for good proportions but about which nothing can be done because of space factors beyond your control.

MIXING THE CONCRETE

Accurate measurement of ingredients, plus thorough mixing of them, always makes good, strong, durable concrete. The following proportions will make a good basic mixture:

- 1 part portland cement
- 3 parts of sand (or sand plus gravel or other aggregates)
- ½ part of water (varied for a good workable mixture)

To get some idea of what quantities of materials will be needed, fill your locked-up form with sand, heaping it up a little. Then open the form and pour this sand into the pail or other receptacle you will be using for measuring the ingredients. Three times the quantity of this measure of sand with 1 measure of cement and ½ measure of water will make *three* paving blocks. Although a total of *five* measures have been used, the water carries the fine particles of cement between the particles of sand, so there will be no appreciable increase of quantity over the measure of sand.

A metal wheelbarrow or a wooden mixing box may be used; or you may wish to consider buying one of the small 5-gallon-pail mixers that will save a lot of hand mixing. If you are using the wheelbarrow or mixing box, put in all the dry ingredients first, then thoroughly mix them with the hoe until there are no more streaks of pure cement or pure sand, but just a mass of even gray-brown color. Then make a "saucer" or "bowl" hole in the middle of the heap and pour in a half-measure of water, mixing it in gently and thoroughly until it is absorbed; then add a little more water and mix, repeating until the full half-measure is used. Be sure to use *only enough water* so that the concrete is loose enough to be easily mixed and worked, but is not watery nor too stiff to spread easily and permit finishing. It is better to mix a little and try, mix a little and try again, than to get the mixture too watery and be forced to add more sand and cement in the attempt to bring it back to the right texture, thus probably upsetting the balance of the ingredients. If by any chance the mixture should become too wet, add your ingredients in the same ratio, 3 of sand to 1 of cement, using a cup or small tin can, and mixing the dry ingredients in a bucket or box before adding them to the wet mix.

You can tell when the mixture is right by testing it with the trowel or by pushing the hoe away from you with a backward stroke through the mixture. If it is too stiff, it will be grainy and crumbly; if it is too moist, it will look soupy or liquid with a good bit of water working to the surface. But if it is just right it will mix easily and not be grainy nor so wet that it does not hold its shape.

When you are going to be making a large number of stones or when you want a brushed aggregate finish, gravel can be added to the sand. Then use 1 part cement, 2¼ parts sand, and 2½ parts coarse aggregate. Again, use ½ part water. The gravel will merely add bulk and volume to the sand, which may be an asset when you are mixing a large quantity. You can, of course, mix any amount of concrete, from a bucketful to a bathtubful or more, provided the proportions are accurately measured and thoroughly mixed.

CURING THE BLOCKS

Basically the same methods are employed for curing concrete blocks as those used for curing any concrete. (See Chapter 14.) The exact method used here is to release the pin from the hasp of the form and remove the form from the cast block when it has been well dried for a day or two. Let the blocks cure in place for another day, sprinkling them lightly with water or covering them with straw or a 3-inch layer of vermiculite, or doing both the covering and sprinkling to prevent too-sudden drying out in hot weather. If you are casting indoors in a cool basement or garage, it will be necessary to sprinkle only once in a while, every other day or so, but if you are using a heated basement or garage, or in hot weather outdoors, sprinkle them lightly each day.

After a week or ten days of curing (you can either leave them in the place where they were cast or put them in a pile with 1-inch wood strips between blocks to permit circulation of air between them) the blocks will be ready for permanent placement. They can be laid in various ways, as detailed in Chapter 18, mortared in place or laid on beds of tamped sand, cinders, gravel, or crushed stone.

Naturally blocks which have been cast in position need not be moved, but will be already in place. Fill in around them with sifted soil and plant grass or whatever you wish between the cast blocks. A pleasant style, borrowed from the Orient but now well established for garden use, is that of placing stepping stones among large aggregates of selected color and sizes; or of setting them in beds of moss with a variety of tiny wild ferns, miniature violets, and other wildlings sprouting from alongside the stones or carpeting the areas between them. Cast blocks used in this latter way, as well as those set in selected aggregates where the scheme is informal, might better simulate natural stone both in color (subdued, stonelike hues) and in texture and form (rough, irregular surfaces and informal free-form rocklike shapes).

CASTING TERRAZZO TILES

With a little extra effort you can make striking-looking terrazzo tiles that interlock to form a patio or walkway. The tiles are cast using the inverted two-course method. That is, the bottom of the casting becomes the top of the tile. A stiff, uncolored base course mix is used so that the forms can be stripped right after casting. This gives a slight slumped effect, which merely makes them look all the more handmade.

As soon as the tiles have firmed up enough that it can be done without damage, the colorful terrazzo marble aggregate is exposed with a disc sander, making

You can make tiles with a white marble-chip terrazzo finish at home in a wood form you make yourself. It's easy to make several tiles in a short time, as shown on the next page.

MAKE YOUR OWN TERRAZZO TILE FORM

6½" R.
2"
2"
6½" R.
END FORM
1" × 2" × 28"
2" × 8" × 30"

Gently place a very stiff sand-mix base concrete over the marble-chip terrazzo topping (now hidden against the pallet base) without waiting for it to set. Be careful that you don't punch the uncolored concrete through the chip layer below where it would show dark on the eventual surface. Smooth and strike off flush with forms.

If the mixes are sufficiently stiff, forms can be lifted off right away. The tile and its pallet can be carefully moved to a safe spot. With more 2′ × 2′ plywood pallets you can continue casting. When tiles are about 12 hours old, invert them between two pallets and expose marble chips on the surface.

the texture like true ground terrazzo but without the tedious grinding. The timing of the sanding is important. The tiles need to gain some solidity so you can invert them without harm. About 12 hours setting time is needed. If the sanding is done too soon, marble chips will be flicked out of the topping course. If done too late, however, it will prove tough to get the desired exposure. To keep from cracking, the completed tiles needed to be moist-cured on pallets for several days before they can be carefully removed and the curing continued.

The terrazzo tiles in the photograph were set on a sand bedding and pea gravel was raked into the joints between. They could just as well have been set in mortar on a reinforced concrete base. This would have produced a formal appearance. Color combinations of marble chips and concrete matrix can be any that you choose. Those shown featured green and brown chips in a pale green matrix made with white portland cement and 1½ percent (by weight of cement) green coloring pigment. Other samples that look especially attractive are white chips in a brown matrix; brown on brown; black on blue; beige on pale pink; crystal on blue; black on green; brown on white; and black-and-white chips on a yellow background. There are few limits to creativity.

BUY CAST PAVING BLOCKS

Exposed aggregate paving stones in circular as well as square shapes are becoming more widely available. You may wish to spare yourself the labor of casting and finishing exposed aggregate paving blocks, by buying some of these. When they are on sale, the price may compare favorably with do-it-yourself materials' cost. They can be placed where you wish, and the spaces between them filled with conventional smooth-finished concrete which you mix and lay yourself, thus getting the best of two worlds. Care must be exercised, of course, not to slobber concrete on the surface of the bought blocks. Perhaps covering them with sheets of polyethylene plastic would be the easiest way to protect them, stripping it away when the concrete has hardened.

Whether you use stepping-stones as wear-savers for traffic areas in the lawn, or as a feature of the garden in ways such as those suggested, you will find them easy to make, most worthwhile additions to your outdoor scheme.

CHAPTER 20

MAKING PEBBLE MOSAIC PAVING

Although at first glance the patterns of pebble mosaic may look rather difficult for amateurs to achieve, they are actually quite simple. There is a long history of paving which utilizes pebbles set into cement in patterns, going back at least as far as Roman times and probably even earlier. In recent excavations abroad, villas much older than those in Pompeii have been uncovered to reveal various types of pebble mosaic. The craft reached its greatest height, perhaps, in the gardens of Spain and Italy in the 16th and 17th centuries, and since then varying degrees of excellence have been achieved in various parts of the world. The art has been revived abroad and is now finding increased favor among enthusiastic do-it-yourselfers in America.

The ingredients are of the commonest sort—pebbles, cement, and sand. While the latter two must be bought, usually, the pebbles can be had for the gathering on beaches, in the beds of brooks and rivers, or on gravelly slopes and fields. It is also possible to buy them in some places where nature has not favored the terrain with a natural occurrence; but most people will want to collect their own, because part of the fun in this creative activity is in picking up your own pebbles. Naturally, you should first obtain permission from owners of private property.

There are three major sorts of pebbles which will be useful in achieving good design results: round, ovoid or egg-shaped, and flat oval-shaped. You will also find color to be important, for it is by matching sizes, shapes, and colors that effective designs are produced. Black or dark pebbles set into light or medium backgrounds, white pebbles used as focal points or as arabesque patterns, and designs set into dark pebble backgrounds—these are the effects for which to strive, with which to make your designs unusual and effective.

Although it is perfectly possible to pave an entire patio with pebbles, you should be sure you have the time and the ambition to gather sufficient numbers of pebbles to complete the task. Most people find that pebble mosaic is best used as a garnish, providing a bit of excitement or a *pièce de résistance* which will give sparkle to some part of the outdoor picture, lifting it out of the ordinary. Edge a walk with pebbles, make a "welcome mat" at an entrance or a gateway, floor a shallow pool, or make an interesting insert in the pavement of a large patio, and you will have fun without being overwhelmed by the magnitude of the task.

TRIAL RUN

The first step in planning a pebble mosaic is to assemble a sufficient quantity of pebbles so that you can experiment with them and decide upon the nature of the design which you'll want to make. Also it will help you to determine what quantities of what colors and sizes of pebbles will be needed for the entire project. Try to select the colors and shapes which are available in fair quantities, so that you'll not have to make a lifetime project of finding the proper ones. Draft your family as assistants and have them help you pick up pebbles of the size and kind you finally decide upon. You'll be surprised how the stockpile grows each time you combine a picnic or a beach outing with the gathering of pebbles. Sort them as to size and color, storing them in large cans or small wooden boxes for future use. The economy-sized fruit-juice cans make good containers which are not too large to be handled conveniently, but which will hold a good supply of stones. When your total supply reaches about a half bushel or more, you are ready to begin a trial run or "sketch" of your design.

Knock together a rough wooden frame or better still a shallow box of the size of the project you have in mind. It should not be deeper than 2 to 3 inches and should be filled with sifted sand or loose soil. Sand is better, because it will not adhere to the pebbles, while soil may get muddy and have to be washed off pebbles before you attempt to use them in cement. Water the sand bed and let it settle a bit; then start pushing your pebbles down into it to make the designs and patterns you want to carry out. It is immediately apparent that working in sand is less irrevocable than working in cement mortar; you can make any changes of pattern you wish merely by lifting out the pebbles and replacing them, wetting down the sand again if you need to.

Some people work out their designs in such shallow boxes of sand beforehand, with a second frame or box for the permanent design. They lay cement mortar in the second box for part of the final design, and then remove the pebbles from the temporary box design one by one and insert them in the mortar for permanent placement. However, you may not want to go to all that bother, for once you have worked out in sand the way the designs are to be made you will know that you

You can cast exposed-aggregate stepping stones upside down, thus saving the step of having to expose the stones by washing and brushing. Simply push stones about one-third of their depth into a layer of sand on which the form rests. This form knocks down—made of metal strips. It adjusts to various sizes and shapes.

Then place concrete into the form over the stones. If you want the matrix to be colored, first put in a layer of colored concrete covering the stones, then plain base concrete. Strike off and let it harden upside down.

The finished casting pulled from the sand has stones tightly held by concrete and nicely exposed without much work or careful timing required.

can do it in cement, too. But this trial run will give you some idea of the quantities of pebbles needed for the entire job so that you can assemble them before you begin the final design in cement.

HOW TO SET PEBBLES FOR BEST EFFECTS

Flat, oval-shaped pebbles are usually set on edge, working them in rows or lines, each pebble being pushed down closely to the next one, as seen in the illustrations. Other flat pebbles, also set on edge, may be worked across at right angles or at contrasting angles to the first group to give background texture and direction. Round or egg-shaped pebbles might be used as a background for contrast of texture, as well as for color contrast, if you wish. Another effective pattern is obtained by using the flat patterns in a chevron or braid design, with other parts set differently. (See the illustration among the paving examples at the end of Chapter 18.) Don't neglect a change of pace and texture obtainable by using pebbles of several different sizes as well as differently shaped ones.

Your fancy will dictate what pattern and design to use—modern abstract, nonobjective designs, or copies of old arabesques, geometric, or regular patterns—whatever you may choose to relate to the style of your house and to give the effect you want to achieve where you will be making the mosaic. Beyond integrating the design with the surroundings, the sky is the limit for your inventiveness and creativity.

Try anything which occurs to you in your trial run. Put fair-sized round pebbles (2 to 2½ inches) at regular intervals and surround them with oval-shaped pebbles set on edge to follow the outlines of the circle of each round pebble. Between these regularly placed circles, fill in the background with flat oval-shaped pebbles also set on edge but running in straight lines, choosing a contrasting color. This is merely an example of how you can begin; you will find dozens of other patterns occurring to you as you

MOSAIC OF PEBBLES

Small water-smoothed pebbles of same size, color make decorative patterns set in cement.

SMALL BOULDERS

Trees or plants set into paving need water. Set similar sizes of stones around plant in soil, sand, or peat moss.

work in the trial-run sand box. Try anything you like, secure in the knowledge that it is not irrevocable; and then, when you finally make up your mind about what you are going to do, you are ready to prepare for the final steps.

Count the pebbles in the design if you find you do not have enough to complete it and then find more of the proper ones. Don't start until you have more than enough of every kind to complete the job. Then you can prepare to set them in the cement mortar. Bring your various cans or boxes of pebbles out and place them where they can be reached; count them once more to be sure that you have 5 to 10 percent more than you think will be necessary, thus taking care of any miscalculations.

LAYING THE CONCRETE BASE

Dig out the area to a depth of 8 to 9 inches, roughly leveling it, but keeping a slight pitch away from any buildings nearby to ensure good drainage. Fill the space with about 4 inches of coarse rubble or other porous material, such as cinders, gravel, or crushed rock; then roll and tamp the layer until it is firm. Set the forms for the concrete base in place, and mix enough concrete to fill the area to a depth of 3 to 4 inches (or to within 2 inches of final surface), using a formula of:

1 part portland cement
2¼ parts sand
2½ parts ¾-inch maximum-size gravel, aggregates, or crushed stone

(Consult Chapter 14 for method of mixing and making concrete and installing forms.) Be sure to use good *clean* sand and aggregates, for dirt and dust and other matter may cut down or destroy the effectiveness of the concrete. If your sand and gravel piles seem very dusty and full of dirt, they can be hosed down to wash them. Wash off the drainage section, too, using a fine spray so that when you pour your concrete on top of it there will be adherence with the drainage material; washing just before pouring concrete will also keep moisture from being drawn quickly out of the concrete by the drainage base, because the drainage material will be wet already.

After the concrete is poured and leveled, cover it with boards, building paper, or wet sacking held off it by strips of wood to prevent its drying out too rapidly. In cool weather it may be simpler merely to shade it to keep the moisture from drying out too quickly.

Remove the covering and test it each day. When it has set enough to support your weight but is not yet really dry (usually two days in summer, and two to four days or more in the cooler times of the year in most places), you will be ready to begin your mosaic work. Mix enough mortar to cover to a 2-inch depth an area of about 12 to 18 inches—a bucketful will be enough to cover a square of this size. Spread it on the concrete, trying to make the edge of the mortar coincide with the edge of the pattern or design you are using, so that the next unit can be joined without an obvious joint showing. Some people use a board or a piece of heavy metal bent into shape to contain the mortar; others merely place the mortar roughly, leaving an edge which can be cut cleanly away before it dries so that fresh mortar can be placed to abut with and bond to the finished section. Or, if the work is being finished for a day and is to be covered for the night and resumed the next day, the mortar is cut away to the edge of the finished part of the mosaic before being covered. Next day, before placing fresh mortar next to it, all the edges should be carefully wet down to ensure bonding.

MORTAR MIXTURE

A prepared mortar mix, bought by the small bagful, may be used. This allows the hard-pressed weekend do-it-yourselfer more time to spend on the creative side of the job. Or, if you prefer, you can mix your own mortar. If so, use a formula of 1 part portland cement to 2 parts sand, adding water bit by bit and mixing it in well, then adding a little more and mixing that in, until the proper consistency has been reached. This will be apparent when the mortar is still rather stiff but can be easily spread without running. Some people like to use a bit of lime putty or fire-clay in the mortar mixture to prevent its setting too quickly and also to make it more workable. Proportions suggested are 3 parts portland cement, 6 parts of sand, 1 part of fire-clay or lime putty. Check with your building materials dealer for the availability of these materials. You can also use a prepackaged mortar mix to which you simply add water sparingly to proper consistency.

Lay the mortar to a depth of 1 inch to 1½ inches, depending upon the size of the pebbles. Remember that if the mortar is too loose and wet the pebbles will sink into it and be lost. If the mortar is too stiff, the pebbles will be difficult to insert in it deeply enough to engage the mortar and make a secure bond. A little practice will enable you to work out just what stiffness and what depth to make the mortar. As your adeptness increases you will be able to increase the size of the area on which you work, but remember that most cement mortar will set within an hour or so, and by two hours will be getting really hard. It is a good plan to keep the area fairly small, thus avoiding disappointment, wasted mortar, or the risk of its not bonding properly and having to be ripped out and done over.

METHOD OF WORKING

The pebbles will bond better with the mortar if they are inserted slightly moist, but with no free water on them. In other words, do not use *wet* pebbles nor *dry* ones. Some people wash the pebbles and keep them in cans (the cans in which they have been sorted for size and color will do nicely), and thus keep dust and dirt off them so that they will be fresh and clean when they are placed in the mortar. Wet and then let them drain well. The moisture will aid in creating a strong bond. Lay out the design divisions in advance so that you can plan ahead which areas to work on in each session. In the case of steps, for instance, you can do a step at a time, unless they are very broad or very long. For an entrance "doormat" design, divide the pattern into segments, using the important lines as divisions which would look well as joints, if that is possible. Then place the mortar and do each segment separately. If the design does not permit an easy division, then compromise and do the best you can in dividing it up into easy stages.

Just as in other concrete work, large areas will need joints that will permit the concrete to expand and contract with the changes of weather without cracking or buckling. For any project of less than 10 feet square, however, no joint will be needed.

Make the mortar deep enough so that the pebbles can be inserted at least half-way—two-thirds of their depth, if possible. In regions where the weather is likely to have sharp changes of temperature and a good bit of frost, it is a good plan to sink them as deeply as possible, so that they are barely above the surface of the mortar. This will prevent the pooling of snow and ice which, by freezing, may cause the surface of the mosaic to open and crack, causing deterioration.

As you work with the mortar, try spreading it and leveling it with a long board before you begin to insert the pebbles. Keep a tap block handy. This can be made of a board with a block or metal drawer handle on the top side to enable you to grasp it easily. Wherever you have finished a section about 8″ × 12″, take the tap block and gently tap the pebbles to force them into the mortar and level them.

After the areas are finished and the mortar begins to set, use an old whisk broom to lightly brush away any loose sand or mortar and to even up the mortar between pebbles. Be sure to use it *lightly* so that the pebbles are not dislodged. An old soft cloth or an old sponge which is damp but not too wet may also be used to clean the surface of excess cement and sand. Again, use it *lightly* and do not scrub away the mortar or pebbles.

FINISHING THE JOB

Cover the section with a piece of building paper or wet sacking when you have finished it; if a heavy rain is imminent, it may be well to cover it with a tarpaulin to prevent the rain from falling on the wet mortar. Uncover it the next day and sprinkle it with a hose, the nozzle adjusted to the finest spray; then cover it again or put on a layer of 2 to 3 inches of vermiculite, sand, or some other absorbent material. Sprinkle this with the hose twice a day for a week or so. In summer or when the weather is hot, a few days may suffice to cure the cement; but moisture then is even more necessary to its proper curing, so in very hot weather sprinkle it three times daily.

When the mosaic is completely dried and cured, probably ten days to two weeks after completion, brush on a solution of muriatic acid (see "Cleaning the Wall," Chapter 12) to remove smears of cement and blobs of mortar. Be careful not to let it remain on too long, because it may injure the mortar; rinsing with a hose and light scrubbing with an old broom will do the trick. Also keep the acid from splashing on your clothes or flesh or in your eyes, for it may burn and irritate.

When the mosaic is cleaned and rinsed, the job is complete, and you can have an unveiling party to show off your handiwork to your admiring (and envious) friends before settling down to enjoy your creation in the years to come.

CHAPTER 21

DRIVEWAYS

Practically every house built these days has a garage, or at least a carport, to house the ever-present automobile. Many houses sport a two- or even a three-car garage to accommodate the several cars of the various members of the family. As many car owners have found out, not only must the garage be remodeled and modernized but the driveways, too, should be brought up to date.

Because the number of cars parked on streets is becoming a nuisance of alarming proportions, wise homeowners will do their best to provide off-street parking for guests' cars, or for their own when not in the garage. Clever homeowners are dispensing with the usual walk across the front lawn, placing it instead beside the driveway, thus making the front yard easier to look after and mow, while adding to the visual dimensions of the lot by

In a sense, the driveway is the welcome mat of the home in these days when guests arrive more often by car than on foot. Make sure that the entrance is attractive. An exposed-aggregate paving is handsome, offers traction in winter in cold areas.

the unbroken expanse of the lawn achieved by this practical plan.

To save wear and tear alongside an existing but too-narrow drive, "landing" strips may be provided, narrow walkways of blocks or cast concrete segments that allow driver and passengers to bypass parked cars and descend on paving, not lawn.

New homeowners, anxious to lay out a plot plan to achieve the utmost efficiency and beauty, should particularly study this section to become cognizant of the problems before embarking on the project of building the driveway. And those with their plots already developed may well examine these pages and reevaluate their driveways, too, with an eye to improving them. Aside from the convenience and the improved efficiency, there is a cash value in having a modernized driveway. According to realtors, it will be a distinct asset if you should decide to sell your home.

CHECK YOUR REQUIREMENTS

- Is your driveway clear of tree limbs and shrubbery so that no brush or twigs will scratch the top and sides of the car?
- Must you back your car into the street to turn around, or can you turn around on the lot and head into the dangerous street area?
- How wide is your driveway? If it is not wider than the bare minimum of 8 feet, it cannot be negotiated easily by cars and delivery and other trucks.
- Can you descend easily from the car

when it is parked in the driveway, without getting your shoes wet or muddy in inclement weather and without injuring the lawn?

- If your driveway turns at a right angle, is the minimum radius 18 feet (inside edge), and if it is a complete circle is the minimum radius of the inside 19 to 20 feet?
- If the driveway has a circular turnaround, is the width of the traffic surface 10 feet or, better still, 11 feet?
- Is the driveway approach to the garage level? If not, icy weather will make it difficult to negotiate when you try to start again after stopping to open the garage doors. There will be the added danger of skidding into the door posts. The driveway should be level or nearly level for a car's length or more out from the garage doors. If the floor is not paved, the garage can be excavated, and the driveway and floor brought into proper relationship. The doors can be lowered to conform to the new level.
- Even though your driveway may be adequate for *your* car, can garbage trucks, delivery trucks, oil trucks, or the oversized cars of your friends negotiate it without getting scratched by tree limbs or without having trouble with the turns?
- Is the surface of the driveway adequate, or does it need improvement with a permanent paving, such as concrete, or some fairly durable one, such as blacktop?

Once you have the answers to these questions you are ready to make your plans to increase the safety, as well as the usability, of your driveway. The first thing to do is to take measurements of the space to be covered, whether it is an old driveway being modernized or a new one being laid out from scratch. Measure the distance from garage to street or road, the distance from the lot line to edge of driveway from the house to lot line, and note location of any trees or shrubs. Survey plant material to see if any will have to be cut down or moved to prevent trouble in future on the driveway, or if pruning may be necessary.

CHARTING THE DRIVEWAY

Lay out the measurements on squared graph paper and put some tracing paper over the plan. Start sketching the course of the driveway as you think it should go. On small lots, of course, it is usually best to run the driveway directly to the street, the straight course taking up as little as possible of the lot space. On the other hand, it may be to your advantage to consider some other plan, such as those in accompanying illustrations. Try a number of approaches on the tracing paper. It won't cost much, and you'll probably run onto just the one for you if you persevere.

When you think you have a plan which suits your problem, plot it on the graph paper, and then measure it and stake it out on the ground. You can make doubly sure, before committing yourself to the expense or labor of executing the driveway, by waiting for dry weather; then driving your car along the staked driveway; backing up; turning around and in every way you can think of, giving it a final test. Then when you have reset the stakes (if you decide it needs revision) and tested it again, you can start to dig it out or have it bulldozed, or have the

HOW TO LAY OUT THE DRIVEWAY AND TURNAROUND

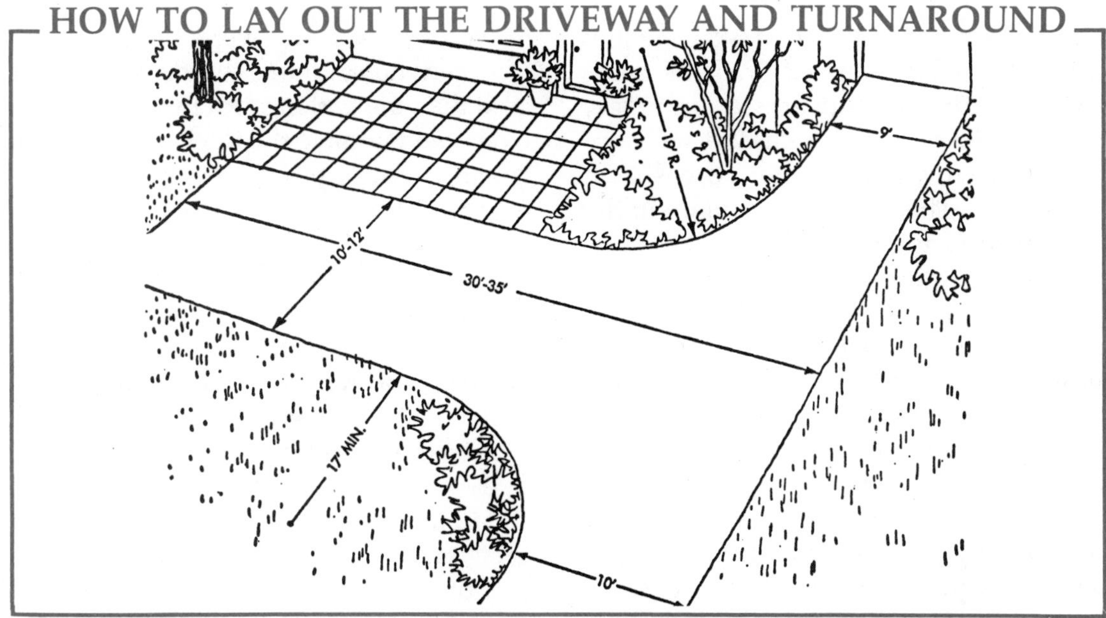

Avoid the dangers of backing straight into the street by making a back-in turnaround. This can be a means of extending the patio as shown above or it can be separate (below) to form extra guest parking space.

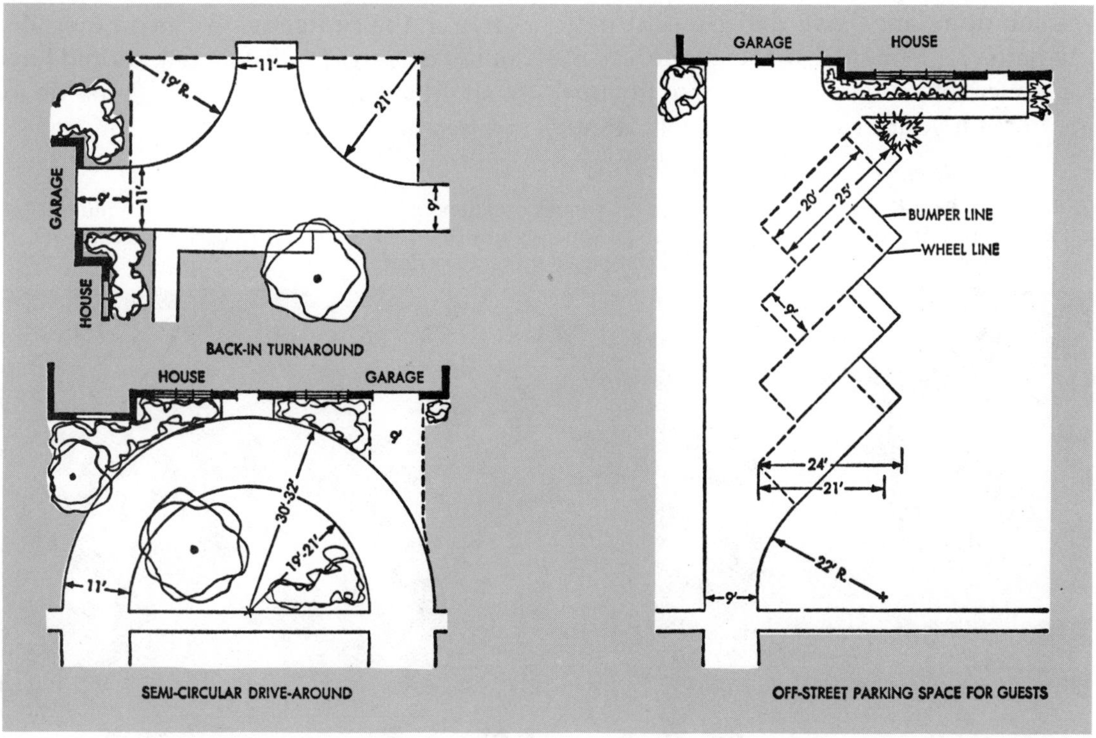

BACK-IN TURNAROUND

SEMI-CIRCULAR DRIVE-AROUND

OFF-STREET PARKING SPACE FOR GUESTS

paving contractor lay it, if you are not doing the work yourself. Provide sufficient depth for subsurface drainage, which a bed of gravel or cinders will supply, and crown the center to assist in draining it. Then whatever you do in the way of surfacing will be secure.

Consider the off-street parking shown and see if you can adapt it to your own layout. This is well worth considering now, even though it may not all be done at one time. Bulldozer time spent now will cost less than a second trip later on; and if you are having a contractor figure the job, see how much more it would cost to have the parking area surfaced now, and how much it would be for the same job done in two takes, one separately later on. The difference may be more than the cost of the interest on a loan which, if taken out now, would allow you to get the job done and have the use of it immediately. Payment can be made on a loan over several years. Of course, if you are doing it yourself, you'll probably want to spread the work over a long period of time anyhow, doing the driveway first, and then the parking area in sections. That way you will save the interest on the loan *and* the cost of the labor, too.

PERMANENT PAVING MATERIALS

Concrete. Laid on a bed of 2 to 3 inches of crushed stone, gravel, or well-tamped cinders, and reinforced (see Chapter 14), concrete is the best I can recommend. Concrete strips for wheels only may be laid, with wear and permanence provided for by use of flagstone, bricks, concrete blocks, brushed aggregate concrete, or other materials between these tracks. I do not recommend lawn between the strips because of the constant need for repairs due to oil dripping from the cars, or to wheels running off and gouging the lawn in the center as well as on the sides of the driveway. All concrete should have a slightly roughened finish to provide for wet-weather traction.

A driveway need be only one car wide, but it should broaden as it approaches a two-car garage or carport, permitting the car to enter the garage squarely (on the right here) and to back out and reach the narrow driveway with a minimum of complicated maneuvering.

Paving brick. When laid on concrete and well mortared together paving brick is very satisfactory, giving good wear and providing a certain amount of traction in wet weather. The color of paving brick is usually pleasant, but its cost is commensurate with its permanence and beauty. Lay them on 4 inches or more of reinforced concrete base.

Stone paving blocks. These may be obtained second-hand in some areas. They may be used on a gravel or sand bed, but are better when laid in concrete. Fitted tightly and set level, they make most interesting patterns, as can be seen in pictures of driveways, forecourts, and even in streets.

Brick patterns can be used to delineate curves, as in this mortarless brick driveway. Bullnosed brick curbing has been mortared and set on a reinforced concrete footing. Such a permanent edging keeps the pavers from separating.

Two types of concrete pavers are manufactured: this solid unit used for paving walks, drives, patios; and open units that allow grass to grow through them. The open blocks are used largely for soil stabilization. All are available in a variety of patterns and colors.

Note the angles from driveway to street that give vehicles opportunity to enter or leave without damage to the lawn. On a narrower driveway, a curve or quarter-circle from walk to street would be preferable and perhaps a little more graceful.

Blacktop. Although not really permanent, blacktop is definitely cheaper than any of the more permanent paving materials. It will need repair and maintenance in order to be satisfactory, particularly in frost areas, so that the cost over the years may amount to as much as permanent paving. It may heave and crack in zero weather. In summer or hot weather it may also "roll" under the weight of cars, as it softens in the heat. One other factor should be considered if the driveway is adjacent to the windows of the house. Dark colors absorb heat and, although this may be desirable in snowy weather, in summer the absorbed heat may be unpleasant for hours after sundown. Blacktop provides excellent traction with its rough texture. Should weeds or grass appear in this rough texture, control them by spraying with weed killers.

For this residence, 3,300 sq.ft. of concrete block pavers were used for the driveway, patios, and other outdoor living areas. These pavers easily support heavy vehicular traffic.

NOT PERMANENT, BUT USUALLY SATISFACTORY

Gravel. Small-size, perhaps pea-size, gravel, when well compacted by rolling and use, makes a good driveway surfacing for level or nearly level surfaces. On hillsides or on decided slopes, moderate rains will wash and roll even sizeable gravel considerable distances. On any slope, heavy downpours will strip the driveway to the soil level and beyond. But for level surfaces, gravels in any of the various colors are pleasant because they are natural materials. One drawback is that gravel may be thrown on adjacent lawns by cars and by snowplows in winter.

Crushed rock or stone. In large sizes this makes a good base for gravel, blacktop, concrete, and smaller sizes of crushed stone aggregates. Marble chips, pink granite chips, bluestone, greenstone, and various other sorts and colors of stones may be available in your area, and they make handsome surfacing. The same drawbacks noted above for gravel apply here, perhaps even more so if the grade of crushed stone used contains very small particles. Check local materials and select from them.

NOT RECOMMENDED

Do-it-yourself blacktop. This is unlikely to bear heavy loads and resist the punishment of wheel wear. Heavy tamping or rolling (such as is done by contractors) is usually required to make this suitable for heavy duty. You might save money if you arrange with the contractor to let you do the labor of digging out and leveling, leaving the laying of the surfacing to be done by his men. Be sure to work out with him *exactly* what you are to do and what he is to do, so that there will be no misunderstandings later on. Follow his specifications for the underpinnings so that they will hold up the paving under all use.

Clay or clay mixture. Clay is very slippery in wet weather and even when used in a mixture with sand will probably wash out in a short time. Also, it is very messy when tracked indoors.

Oiled soil. While this may be satisfactory for roads, it is not recommended for use on home driveways. Around the house, oil may splash on lawns and flower beds adjacent to the driveway, destroying and injuring the plants. It will also track into the house for some time after being laid, ruining rugs, staining floors, and disintegrating some of the synthetic tile which is used so much these days.

Whatever the final choice may be for surfacing, remember that a driveway is only as good as the plan on which it is built. Be sure to give it sufficient advance thought and planning so that it can be used without regret or irritation, or without expensive revisions, later on.

CHAPTER 22

DECORATIVE PLANTERS

One of the best ideas in the home garden field in recent years has been the introduction of the decorative plant bed. It may be raised above the level of the patio so that its front wall becomes a seat wall; it may be a showplace for favorite perennials or annuals; it may be ablaze with bulbs all spring; and in the autumn it may carry the glowing fire of chrysanthemums up to the very gateway of winter. All these things and many more are possible with planters.

On the practical side, too, it has much to offer. It lifts up your plants from ground-level and provides a seat from which to do your weeding, your spraying, your transplanting and maintenance work, taking away the hazards of doing your garden work while kneeling or nearly standing on your head; and it offers an exhibition place for miniature plants where they can be more easily seen, worked with, and studied in the fullest comfort. For those troubled with moles and mice, the planter offers a degree of protection from these pests, particularly from moles. In our own place we once lost all but three tulips of nine dozen planted one year, to moles who were followed by mice. Since then we built our planter alongside the house, and our tulips now enjoy security. They like the well-drained bed even better than the other place beside the patio, which we now devote to narcissus bulbs, having found that rodents leave them alone.

Masonry planters are best built rather low—seat-height alongside a patio, or even of a lesser height, so that they do not become too obtrusive. Masonry is the most permanent material for a planter, but seat walls of redwood planks or other durable, preservative-coated woods may be adapted, built with the heavy wood frame exposed or concealed on the patio side, as you wish. Using roofing paint to waterproof the inside of the wood will help to preserve it, making it resist moisture and bacteria better. Be sure to allow it plenty of time to dry and get rid of its noxious gases before filling the planter with soil and planting.

Seats on masonry planters need not be made of masonry. It is possible to embed bolts in the mortar or concrete and fasten wooden seats to them, so that you combine the permanence of masonry with the contrast of wood textures and beauty.

Masonry planters also give one a chance to use curving lines effectively in the garden—to follow the curving line of a patio or to give visual interest to a low retaining wall which would be rather dull

Concrete blocks make it easy to build an oversized planter. Set on a straight footing at an angle, 4″ solids are placed above and below 8″ hollow-core blocks. Finish off top with 1½″ or 2″ solids, with joints lightly raked to make a handsome permanent plant bed.

if kept straight, but which leads the eye about the garden because of the beauty of its curves.

There are many places where planters may be effectively placed: beside the front or back doors; beneath a picture window so that plantings are lifted up, making a foreground to the picture seen through the window; beside or incorporated into the patio; flanking steps; on the upper side of a retaining wall or on the lower side with the wall as a backdrop for the plants—I could go on detailing the possibilities endlessly, for more come to notice every year.

The possibilities for plantings to be used in the planters is very wide, too. Roses, perennials, bulbs, annuals, small blossoming shrubs, all-green shrubs, evergreens, which may be clipped into geometric shapes if that is your hobby, even trees may be placed in a planter and used with low-growing plants around them. For those who are away during the summer I recommend planters with spring bulbs planted under periwinkle, which will give them first a burst of spring blossom and then a neat and orderly green carpet through the summer. In late summer pots of chrysanthemums can be used, either set into the planter in the soil or merely placed on top of it among the periwinkle plants. This will give two bursts of bloom a year.

Others who have small planters keep them gay all summer long by putting a succession of planted pots in them, starting with bulbs forced in pots, and then following with a succession of annuals. Every time a pot of flowers begins to fade, a replacement is brought in from the back garden where a battery of pots is started and kept going for this purpose. In the autumn potted chrysanthemums are brought in as replacements. The trick here is to use pots of the same size throughout, packing peatmoss or vermiculite around them to help to keep them moist and cool and watering them each day; and then putting a replacement pot in the hole left by the one removed. It can be quite a fascinating game, not to mention the interest it will add to your garden. This same idea can be adapted to a planter placed under a picture window so that all season long you will see flowers from the house as you look out.

Modern gardeners will also find other plants and effects which will fit well in the planter. The succulent family—the best known is the "hen-and-chickens"—and the many kinds of stonecrop *(Sedums)* make good planter crops, some fascinating effects being obtainable with the varying colors and textures, the various heights, and the unusual blossoms which appear on them at times. Combining them with pebble carpets in which are set stones of various sizes or nestling them among granite or marble chips, using water-washed round stones in large sizes and interesting colors are other ways to make showpieces of your planters. Some people, taking their cue from Japanese stone gardens, use big rocks or irregular stones with only two or three plants and perhaps a piece of driftwood of unusual shape, interesting texture and color to get a very restrained but most artistic effect. A spotlight can be placed to light the planter at night, giving it a function to perform around the clock. Perhaps you will find even more unusual and original ways to fill your planter, ways which will make it a real conversation piece. You might want to make it into a miniature garden, using dwarf evergreens, tiny plants, and little deciduous shrubs. The dwarf roses which grow only a foot or so high would be good subjects, and rocks, tiny waterfalls, and picturesque trees in the Japanese bonsai fashion would be good additions.

Don't forget that the parapet or seat wall is also a good place to display pots of plants. Houseplants summering on the patio, if the sun/shade conditions are right, can stay on the wall all summer. If there is too much sun, they can rest on the wall for a few days, and potted plants prepared especially for use around the garden can be placed along the planter wall where they will lend their beauty when it is needed, and be transported to other parts of the garden when needed there.

A way to extend and widen a patio with squares, seen here at a flower show, can be adapted to the home. Square plant beds let into the herringbone brick paving make a place for flower color, and if potted plants are used, allow color changes.

PRACTICAL CONSIDERATIONS

You should be sure to make the footings and foundation for your planter deep enough and strong enough to carry the wall load, so that the planter will not sag or buckle or, if it is being placed against a building, pull away from it. If the inside of the planter is plastered with fine cement mortar it will better resist damage through moisture seepage. Or it may be tarred to prevent damage from moisture. Be sure to wait until the tar is well dried before filling the planter with soil. When the planter is joined to the front of an existing building, a membrane of waterproof material (consult your building materials dealer for what to use) should be placed in front of the existing wall to prevent moisture from soaking or seeping from the planter into the building against which it is placed. It is well to use a membrane *and* a layer of masonry—a single course of bricks, for instance—at the rear of the planter.

Wherever you place your planter, and however you plant it, you will surely find it one of the most interesting projects of any you will build in your garden.

ANGLING FOR INTEREST

If your patio is useful, but seems to lack something, an angular planter will add both visual and architectural distinction. Added seating space for outdoor parties is found on the front wall, backed up by plantings of bright flowers silhouetted against a higher brick wall which may be used to conceal some undesirable aspect or gain privacy. The seat is of 2″ planks.

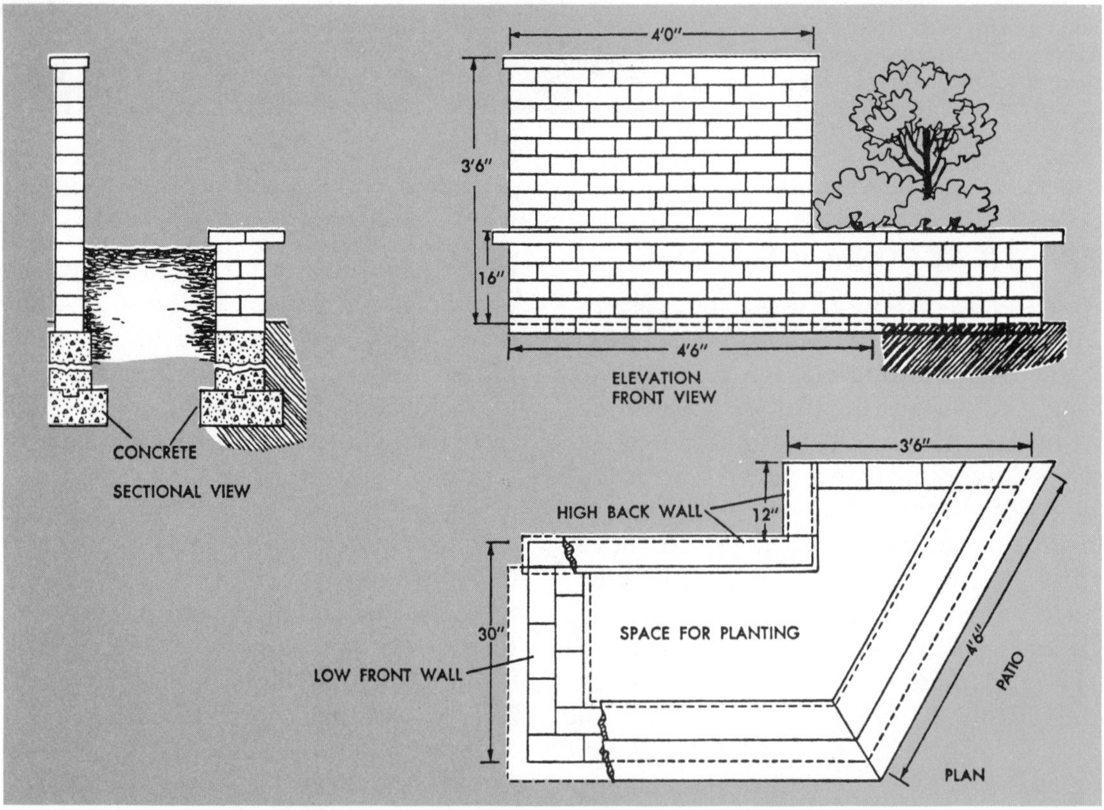

CONCRETE
SECTIONAL VIEW

4′0″
3′6″
16″
4′6″
ELEVATION
FRONT VIEW

3′6″
HIGH BACK WALL
12″
30″
SPACE FOR PLANTING
LOW FRONT WALL
4′6″
PATIO
PLAN

DRESS UP YOUR DOORWAY

The front door, usually so nondescript in a small house, can be featured if a plant box is built beside it. Incorporate it with the steps, using same materials for both—bricks, blocks, stone, or combinations—for best visual value.

Note the "membrane." It's a necessary feature with a wooden house, a good idea for a masonry one; it gives protection from moisture. Rough-plastering the inside of box with cement conserves water, helps preserve masonry.

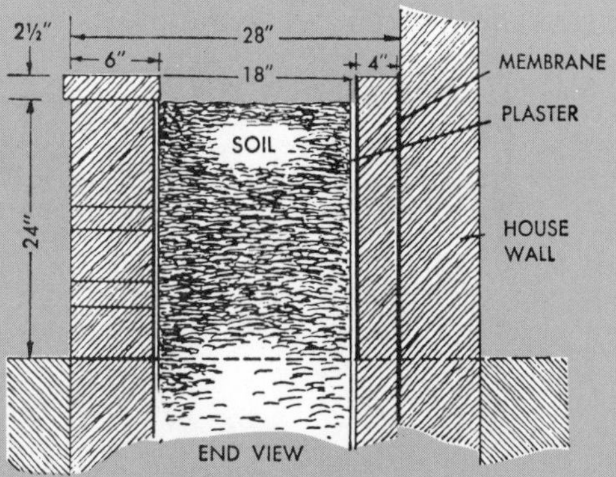

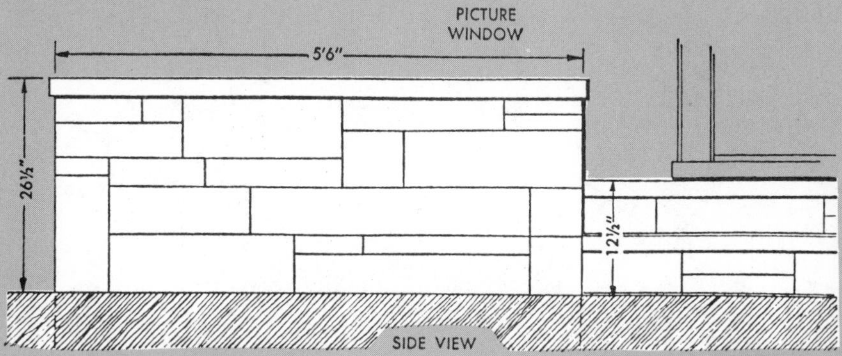

2½"
28"
6"
18"
4"
MEMBRANE
PLASTER
SOIL
HOUSE WALL
24"
END VIEW

PICTURE WINDOW
5'6"
26½"
12½"
SIDE VIEW

CURVES GIVE VERVE

Although only two steps are required between levels, a low planter backed by a low wall will add considerable variety and grace to the edge of a patio. It may also be used on the level for, being low, it does not interfere with the view or limit a feeling of space, yet traffic is restricted and defined, while the plants contribute color.

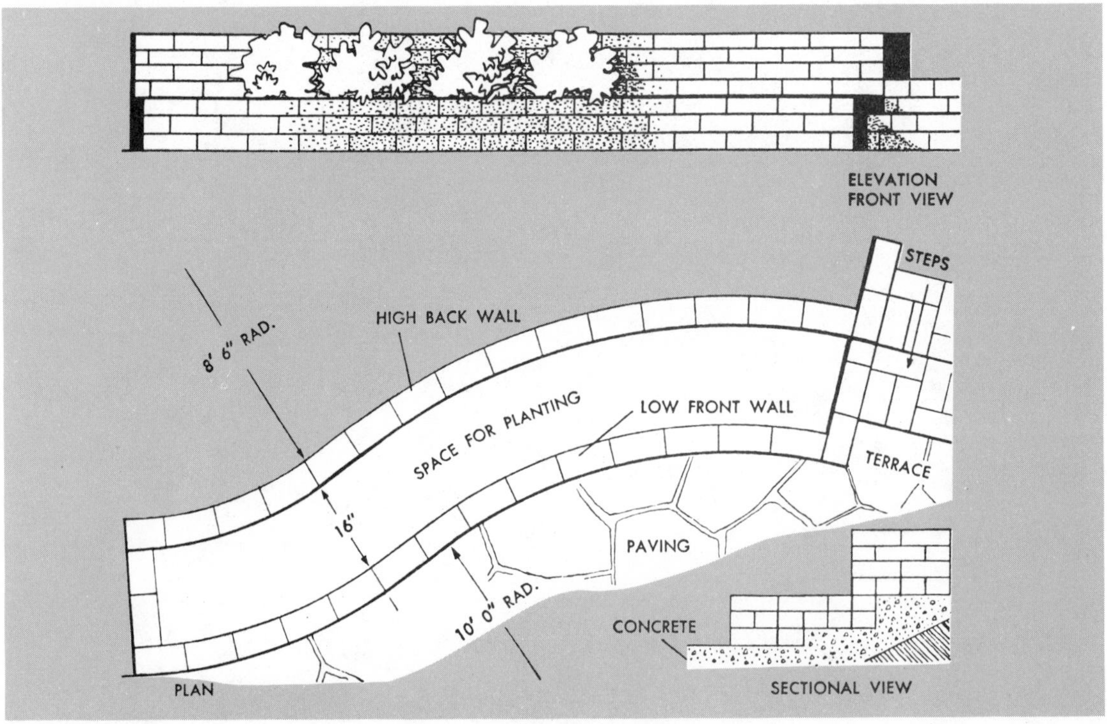

ELEVATION
FRONT VIEW

STEPS
HIGH BACK WALL
8' 6" RAD.
SPACE FOR PLANTING
LOW FRONT WALL
TERRACE
16"
PAVING
10' 0" RAD.
CONCRETE
PLAN
SECTIONAL VIEW

PLANKS AND BRICKS FOR MOVABLE PLANTS

Atop a brick parapet a one-brick-thick wall supports plank shelves, bricks laid crosswise to project. The idea adapts to other uses, of course. The drawing shows a solid brick wall, the plan shows a way to open it up by omitting bricks, which can be employed in building the parapet brick wall, too.

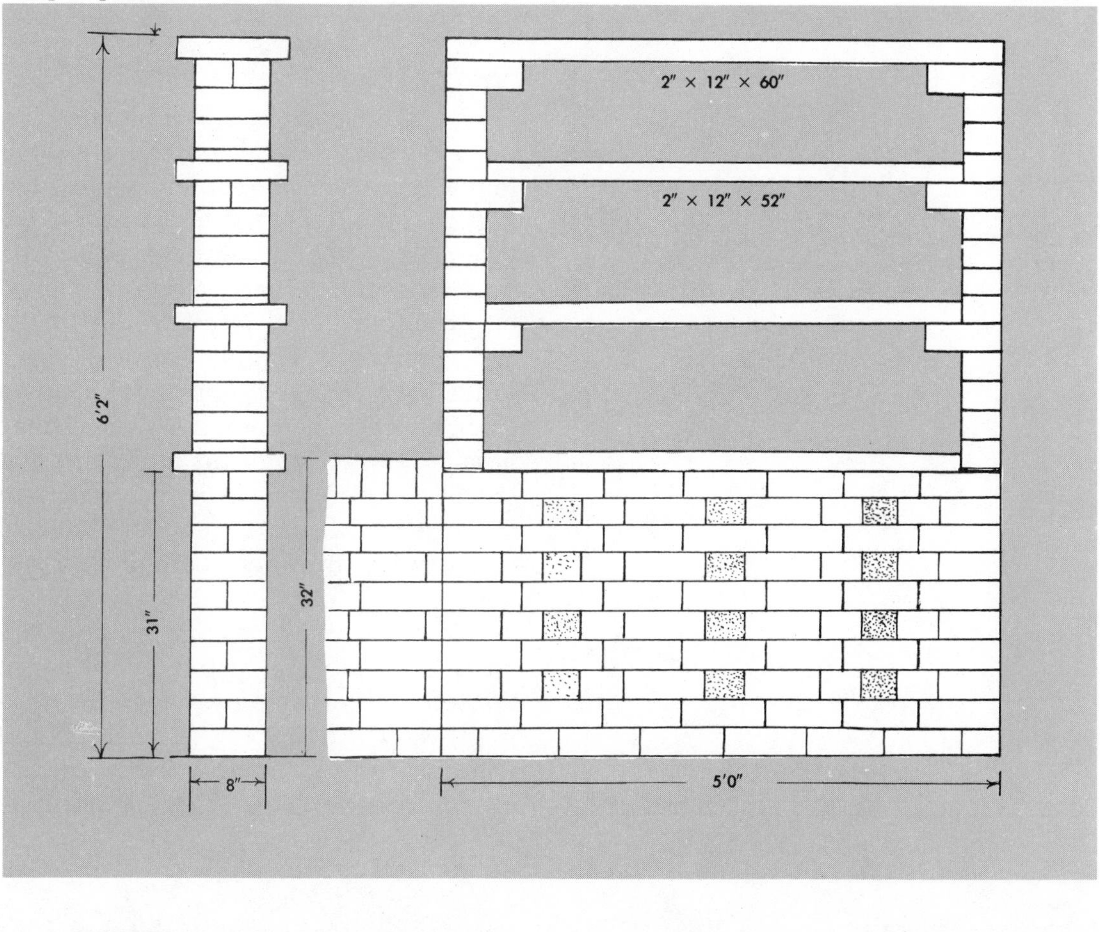

2″ × 12″ × 60″
2″ × 12″ × 52″
6′2″
31″
32″
8″
5′0″

CHAPTER 23

THE POOL

Until lately it was only the rich who could afford to have pools in their gardens. Even today, when a garden pool is mentioned, most people envision an elaborate, formal pool with fountains and statuary, requiring a good bit of money and a lot of work to build and maintain it. Happily for most of us, times have changed, and today many a small home garden possesses a charming little pool which adds much pleasure and beauty to our outdoor living. Each year more people discover the possibilities of pools and joyfully add them to their gardens.

Nowadays we take a tip from the Japanese and other Far Eastern peoples who know that, however tiny may be the trickle of water running into a small pool, it will give forth a sound which is cooling to our mental climate and conducive,

A free-form swimming pool adapts well to odd-shaped areas, making a most interesting statement in the garden scheme and adding to the family's pleasure. Poolside areas here are finished in brushed-aggregate cement, thus tying in with the large rocks on either side.

therefore, to physical coolness in the oppressive heat of summer.

No longer is it necessary to have a constant water supply running into the pool and draining out that can make one's water bills mount up in a city and in the country can wear out the electric pump. Instead we now use small recirculating pumps, which take the water that drains from the pool and force it back up through the fountain jet or other inlet. Only occasionally is it necessary to replenish the water lost through evaporation. Once in a while, of course, all pools must be drained, scrubbed out, and refilled, but the cost of this is minor. Recirculators aerate the water constantly as it falls into the pool so that it is kept from stagnating, and many of them have a strainer attachment which prevents debris from fouling the line.

We have learned, too, that pools need not be deep. Even when we want to grow water lilies and other aquatic plants in them, we need only make plant pockets deep enough to contain the roots of the plants at the proper depth and wide enough to hold sufficient soil for their growth. Pockets can be made which are just large enough to hold tubs or boxes of water lily roots. These may be sited outside the main pool in a separate pocket, with a connecting canal to provide water from the main pool. Or the pocket may be placed in the center of the pool. The remainder of the pool may be quite shallow.

Another trick is to paint shallow pools,

4 to 6 inches deep, a dark color, such as deep green, black, or navy blue. This will give just as much mystery and depth as if the pool had been made 6 feet deep. Many pools today function as mirrors to reflect and to give added dimension to some garden aspect—a picturesque tree, an architectural feature, a doorway—or to give focus to some fine view or garden vista. Being shallow, these pools will save water and at the same time present a safety factor where young children are likely to be playing around the garden.

Another development is the use of the "saucer" pool, a shallow pool which tapers outward and upward from the center. It has many advantages, particularly in regions where winter freezing and consequent damage to the sides of the pool may give pause to the prospective pool builder. In this type of pool, when the ice freezes and expands it must move upward because there are no vertical sides for it to push outward. So there is no way the pool can be damaged. These pools are easy to drain, being easily siphoned out, and what water remains in the bottom can be whisked out with a broom. They are easily scrubbed out this same way. No source of water is necessary unless you want one, your garden hose being sufficient when it is needed. Some pools are placed along the course of natural rills or tiny brooks which serve as catch basins here and there, placement under little cascades or small waterfalls being particularly good.

PREFABRICATE YOUR OWN BROOK

It is possible to build your own rill or brook into your hillside. Or build up a little hillock if your place is not naturally hilly and in this install the recirculating pump. Place rocks in a natural-looking outcropping among and over which the water will flow down in a series of little cascades, to drop into the saucer pools, flow out in a cement canal between stones, and then go over another rock to fall into the next pool.

Saucer pools need not be circular. They can be freeform, somewhat serpentine in shape, even square, so long as the corners are rounded and the pool tapers upward from the center, leaving no angular sides against which ice can press. The edges of the pool may be architectural or natural. A coping may be raised above the level of the patio 6 inches, 12 inches, or even more, or the pool may be sunk into the patio with the rim even with the paving. In a natural setting, stones may be set around the edge to overhang it a bit, with soil piled up around them on one side; on the other side the pool may be level with the grass. Ivy or other ground cover can be trained about the edge to mask the masonry or concrete if you wish, making it look as if Nature herself had placed the pool there.

On a patio it is sometimes interesting to have the pool left in its natural color or painted with a swimming-pool waterproof paint the color of the sky. Beautiful water-washed pebbles gathered from the beach or from along a stream can be arranged in the bottom in patterns to form a pleasant bit of contrast. Not all of them need be the same size, and a range of color will be agreeable, too. Wet stones show their colors to best advantage, so your showpieces are always at their best in a pool.

Or if you have many pebbles available, you might use them in making a pebble mosaic (see Chapter 20) in some interesting design in the bottom of your pool. This type of pool should have a drain and cover so that it can be kept free of water in winter. Designs can be anything you like—aquatic motits, geometric patterns, nonobjective modern patterns; or you may want to take your inspiration from Japanese gardens where the sand is raked in swirls to simulate water; you can imitate the swirls across the bottom of your pool. There are many fascinating ways in which a pool can be embellished, even formal mosaic in the manner of the old Romans being a possibility. For this, a shallow pool is ideal because it enables the design to be seen easily.

POOLS FOR WADING, SWIMMING

Another feature of the outdoor life in our country today is the backyard swimming or wading pool. Many people build small pools where their children can splash about and wade during the summer. In colder seasons the pool is drained, the drain plugged, and the pool filled with sand to become a sandbox for the youngsters, so that it is used during spring and autumn as well as in the hot seasons. Later on, when the children have grown, the pool can be adapted to growing aquatic plants and made a feature in the garden picture. Thus, for one price, one expenditure of labor, you get continuing use of this garden feature for many, many years.

It is now possible to buy prefabricated swimming pools which you can have installed or install yourself. They are not very cheap, however. You can also dig out your own pool and build a perfectly adequate one for yourself, provided that there is a cheap source of water. The number of gallons required for even a

A swimming pool of modest size with a raised curb on all four sides can be built by an ambitious amateur with some experience in concrete work—building forms, casting, reinforcing, and curing all surfaces before final finishing with a smooth coat followed by pool paint.

A swimming pool that echoes the line of the raised patio nearby, is graduated from deep at one end to shallow near the circular wading pool where children can play (foreground), and is bordered by a wide walkway, useful for sunning and for keeping debris out of the pool.

minimum-sized pool is formidable, and if you are on a water meter you may want to think twice before getting carried away. Also there should be a good place to drain the pool, either a sewer or some lower spot where it will run away quickly without violating any local laws. Unless your pool has a filter treatment apparatus, pool water should be changed periodically, once every week or ten days, even if you use chlorine or some other disinfectant recommended by health authorities to kill bacteria in the water.

PLACEMENT OF POOLS

This is a problem which deserves serious thought. Overhanging trees will drop their leaves into the water, and may in time shade the pool and make it too cool for comfort on days which are pleasant but not hot. Leaves, grass, debris of all kinds may blow into the pool, too, or be tracked in on the feet of the bathers unless you take measures to prevent it. Leaves and debris can be netted or vacuumed out of the pool before they attract algae and other organisms and begin to disintegrate and decay, and you can always place your pool away from the trees so that they won't shed leaves directly into it. You can pave the verges of the pool so that less trash is tracked in by the bathers; but if you raise the masonry edge to a foot or so above the ground level and install a footbath beside the entrance to the pool's platform for bathers to use on entering it, you will immediately gain some advantages. First and most important, there will be several cubic yards less of soil to be excavated. Then, the coping will prevent surface debris from blowing into the pool; it will serve as a seat wall around the pool; and it will also be a deterrent to people's falling into it at night if they are unfamiliar with the property.

Where the property slopes it is possible to take advantage of this fact in building a swimming pool. The floor of the pool can slope with the land and only enough excavation will be necessary to have proper footings cast and to have enough earth left to fill in as necessary around the pool on the sides.

WADING POOLS

These pools, being built for children, should never be very deep. Depending on the age of the child, they may vary from 12 to 27 inches tapering upward to 6 to 9 inches in depth. Small children should never use them without the supervision of an adult; so that it may be well to place the pool where the parent can see it from the house. A suggested size is 5′×7′, but any size which you find convenient may be used. If you plan to use the pool later on for plants, you may want to check the recommended depth for water lilies and make the deep part of the pool that depth. If it is deeper than you think is safe for your child, fill the pool only part way. A wooden cover may be made to place over the wading pool when it is not in use to prevent children from wandering into your yard and using it without supervision. Small children can have accidents very quickly and it is well to foresee them. The cover will be useful later on as a winter covering for the pool when it is drained.

POOL OVERFLOW AND DRAINAGE

To prevent the pool from overflowing (and even those with no jet or regular source of supply may catch rain water and need drainage facilities when they overflow), some provision must be made in the form of an overflow channel or a removable pipe which screws into the mouth of the regular drain. This pipe should have a strainer or screened cap to prevent the entry of leaves or other debris which would clog the drains. Overflow pipes may be made of brass, also the fittings and piping of the pool. This lasts indefinitely without corroding, and it will never rust, or course. However, today polyvinyl chloride piping is often used and has proved quite satisfactory.

The overflow pipe should be just long enough when screwed into the drain to reach the top water level. (See overflow pipes in the plans.) The recommended mushroom-shaped cover will remain above water level, the excess water flowing freely under the cover and into the pipe. Whenever the pool is to be completely drained it is a simple matter to unscrew the pipe from the drain and allow the water to flow out of the bottom of the pool. First, however, all the debris and leaves which may be in the pool should be removed, or, if this is not possible, reach down to the bottom drain as soon as the overflow pipe is unscrewed and cover the drain with a square of ¼-inch-mesh wire screen; hold it in place by weighting it with a couple of bricks. This will prevent debris from entering the drain and clogging it.

WINTER CARE

In severe climates some provision must be made for the protection of pools in winter—or at least all pools with straight sides, since saucer pools need not be protected. For straight-sided pools, some authorities recommend a yearly draining, in autumn, then a scrubbing out with a coarse scrubbing brush or an old broom, using hot water with a detergent and disinfectant added to it. Then the pool should be covered. For swimming pools and also for straight-sided garden pools, other authorities recommend that they be left filled to assist in resisting inward pressures from the soil as it freezes. Floating a small log or two on the surface of the water will keep ice from becoming too solid on the surface as it freezes. In spring, the pool should be drained, scrubbed out with water with detergent and disinfectant in it, and then refinished with a good waterproofing paint. When it is thoroughly dry, refill and it is ready for the summer season.

For covering small or narrow pools, some people use boards covered with a tarpaulin and weight this with more boards to prevent winter winds from whipping it. This is never decorative and not always effective. I advocate making a winter cover of exterior plywood of a size which will cover the pool completely. A frame of 1″×4″s or 2″×4″s, braced as needed across the center if it is a large pool, will make a strong cover and, as it stands up only 4 inches, an unobtrusive one. Plywood can be either nailed or screwed to it. Any water which might seep into the pool will leave through the drain—this should be left open all winter with the wire screen over it—and there should never be enough water gathering at any time to become a problem by freezing. In spring, wash out the pool again as recommended above; remove all leaves and other debris from inside and near it so that spring winds do not blow them into it; install the overflow pipe; and it is ready to be filled so you can enjoy the pleasures of a garden pool again during the green months.

There are also coverings of plastic or other fabric which can be bought. Most are made to fit commercial or prefabricated pools so it might be wise to see what sizes are available, what means of securing them are required, and build your pool accordingly.

A large L-shaped free-form pool with a slide for the kids, a diving board, and a handsome retaining wall of split concrete blocks shaped to complement the pool pattern is elaborate and may be beyond all but experienced do-it-yourselfers.

Perhaps you will want to make your winter pool cover into a feature, something which is good to look at and not just a necessary appurtenance. In that case, look over the patterns shown among the fences and trellises in those chapters of the book and choose one to adapt as an appliqué design on the plywood top, using trellis strips or other light wood. Possibly you will want to make a little railing around the edge of the cover, using one of the designs which are shown in other sections of this book for your inspiration.

CASTING POOLS WITHOUT FORMS

The least expensive and in some ways the easiest way to make your pool is to cast it in concrete without forms and preferably with no drain. You merely excavate the soil to the depth of the water you want plus the 6 to 8 inches for the concrete itself, leaving the sides sloping no more steeply than 45° and preferably 30° or less, so as to prevent ice damage in winter. The water line should be accurately determined in advance to make it possible to carry the concrete to a uniform distance above the water line. First decide what the level of the water should be, then outside the concrete area drive a stake and adjust its top 1 or 2 inches above the desired water line. Drive stakes around the pool outside the concrete area at intervals, using a spirit level—or a mason's level—to insure that they are all at the same height. As you cast the pool, carry the concrete to this point, and then level it to the height established by the stakes. Be careful not to disturb placement of the stakes as you are working about the pool, pouring concrete.

Another way of finding this line will be to fill the pit with water, first binding tightly an old sock or glove over the end of the hose so that it does not squirt on the sides and cause them to fall in. When the pit is filled to within a couple of inches of the water line you wish, stop the flow and let the water soak into the soil. A heavy mason's cord can be secured 3 inches above this line by wrapping it around large nails or using large "hairpins" made from wire coathangers. It is to this point (3 inches above water soak line) that you will carry the concrete.

When the water has soaked away, dig out the bottom again to remove any silt which has slid down; and then you are ready to cast the concrete. Use a formula which will make a good stiff mix so it won't run when placed on the sloping side of the pit. One such is:

1 part portland cement
2¼ parts sharp sand
2 parts ¾″ maximum-size gravel or crushed stone
Water enough for stiff mix (about ½ part)

The pool must be cast all at once, so be sure to have enough material on hand to complete the job. Start in the early morning so that you will have all day for the job and be able to finish it. Lightweight welded-wire fabric can be used for crack-containment reinforcing, or you may use ½-inch reinforcing rods bent to shape, criss-crossed and wired together, making 6- to 8-inch squares. This configuration of bars makes truly reinforced concrete. These reinforcements may be laid on brickbats placed every 18 inches or so to keep them off the ground. The concrete is shoveled carefully over this so that it falls through the mesh until it reaches a depth of 6 inches. Tamp it occasionally to be sure that no air pockets are left in the concrete. Finish the concrete with the trowel and float (see Chapter 14), working from planks laid across the pool if you cannot reach the center from the sides. Level off the concrete at the top even with the line established with the cord, and finish it smoothly. If you wish, you may set stones in the edge of the concrete while it is still wet, or you may mortar them in place afterward. Do not let them overhang *below* the water level, however, or ice may dislodge them and make the pool leak.

Carefully built, a pool of this sort will fit in any natural landscape and should last for many years, even in climates which are fairly severe. If you want to plant very close to the pool, finish the top edge to about a 3-inch thickness, making a form of plywood or hardboard if necessary to maintain this width. Then the plants can come very close and overhang to obscure the hard edge and make it blend into the landscape. Painting the pool a dark color or using a finish coat of dark-colored concrete will also keep it in its place and obscure the hard edges.

PLANTING THE POOL

Water lilies can be made to grow even in a washtub set into the lawn, given proper care and consideration. Therefore, you have every reason to expect them to grow well in a small plant pocket especially constructed for them in a pool, even if it is a shallow one. There are many other plants especially adapted to pool-side or in-pool growing conditions, which will dress up your pool and make it a feature. Once planted, they will need no weeding, no constant cultivation, no watering, but only planting and occasional feeding to make sure that all is well with the plants. In cold climates the lilies and other tender plants must be taken up and stored indoors. In this case the best solution is to plant them in tubs or boxes which can be lifted from the pool when it is drained for the winter to take them indoors.

Water lilies need at least a cubic foot of soil for each root. You can use a butter tub or buy a specially made lily tub which will hold this amount of soil, using good rich leafmold or rich garden soil with peatmoss added. By making a box with ½-inch openings between boards and lining it with a burlap bag before filling it, you allow lily roots to emerge to the water if they wish, but the soil is retained in the box. Good roots will enable the lilies to grow large with many leaves spreading in the pool and many flowers. By restricting root area even the larger-growing lilies can be kept to small space and reduced in scale to be appropriate to smaller pools. Cypress or hard pine may be used for the box.

Placing an inch of gravel or sand on top will prevent the soil from washing out of the box and fouling the pool. Check with your plant dealer to see what conditions lilies need, to determine which will be best for your pool. Some need shallower water than others, in which case you can set the box or tub on bricks or blocks to bring it to the proper level for the length of stem the lily will grow.

It is not necessary to change the soil every year. Merely dig out a little hole or two and put a bag of plant food in the soil pockets, covering them with soil and the sand or gravel. Dehydrated cow manure is a good food to use when inserted this way. Don't neglect these yearly feedings, because even though lilies grow in limited amounts of soil they relish rich feedings. Lily tubers may be left in the tub for storage, but you may dig them up if you wish and, after washing them carefully, store them in coarse sand or vermiculite in a box covered with wire screen to keep mice from eating them. Keep them in a dark but airy place, where the temperature is about 50° and the atmosphere is not too dry. In some areas of temperate climate it is possible to keep the lilies in the pool once it is drained. (Check with your plant dealer when you buy your lilies on this possibility.) Drain the pool and fill it with leaves to cover the tubs to a foot or more, first covering the tubs with wire or plastic screening to prevent mice from entering and eating the tubers. The pool should be covered with either the kind of cover advocated earlier or, for small pools, two or three layers of tar paper weighted with boards to prevent their blowing off. A tarpaulin over the top of the paper will prevent water from soaking into the pool through openings between sheets of the paper.

OTHER AQUATIC PLANTS

Either actually in the pool or alongside it where they get plenty of moisture, other aquatic plants may also be used. Some prefer shallow water, some need greater depth to grow well, and some need only moist soil and a humid atmosphere to thrive. Siberian and Japanese iris are in this latter category, liking their roots moist but not standing in water; while the yellow iris, *Iris pseudacorus,* will grow either alongside a pool or in the water. There are many other plants with which to dress the edges of pools in natural or formal ways to make them a delightful feature of the home garden. Ferns like moist soil and shade, and so do primroses, Virginia cowslip, forget-me-nots, and many other plants. Most of them are hardy perennials; and they may be supplemented by tender plants, such as caladiums, which have exciting and wonderfully colored leaves; or, if the size of your pool will permit the use of their large relative, elephant's ears, you can plant a bulb in the spring and take it up for winter storage.

If you have a very small pool sunk into your patio you may want to forget about permanent plantings and enjoy it for itself, or just place a pot or two of houseplants or flowering annuals alongside it to give it interest. Trailing ivy, grape-leaf-ivy, succulents, miniature or bonsai trees, fuchsia, impatiens, flowering begonias of the tuberous- or fibrous-rooted types, coleus, and many other pot plants may be used to give a touch of living green or a flash of color to the pool's edge. Use weathered wood blocks or stack a couple of cinder or cement blocks in an interesting way and set your pots on them. Perhaps a piece of driftwood can be incorporated so that it and the plants are reflected in the pool.

Whatever the size of pool you build, whether it is just a saucer set in the ground or a large reflecting basin with lilies and other plants in it, you will find that adding water to your garden is a most worthwhile idea and you'll enjoy your garden all the more because of it.

MINIMUM-SIZED SWIMMING POOL

In regions with a cheap water supply, swimming pools are not a luxury. Built partly above ground, this one minimizes excavations, cuts down danger of children's stumbling into pool. In warm regions drain may be omitted if siphon or submersible sump pump is used for weekly refilling. Concrete is finished smoothly, painted white or in color each year with a good waterproof paint made for swimming pool use.

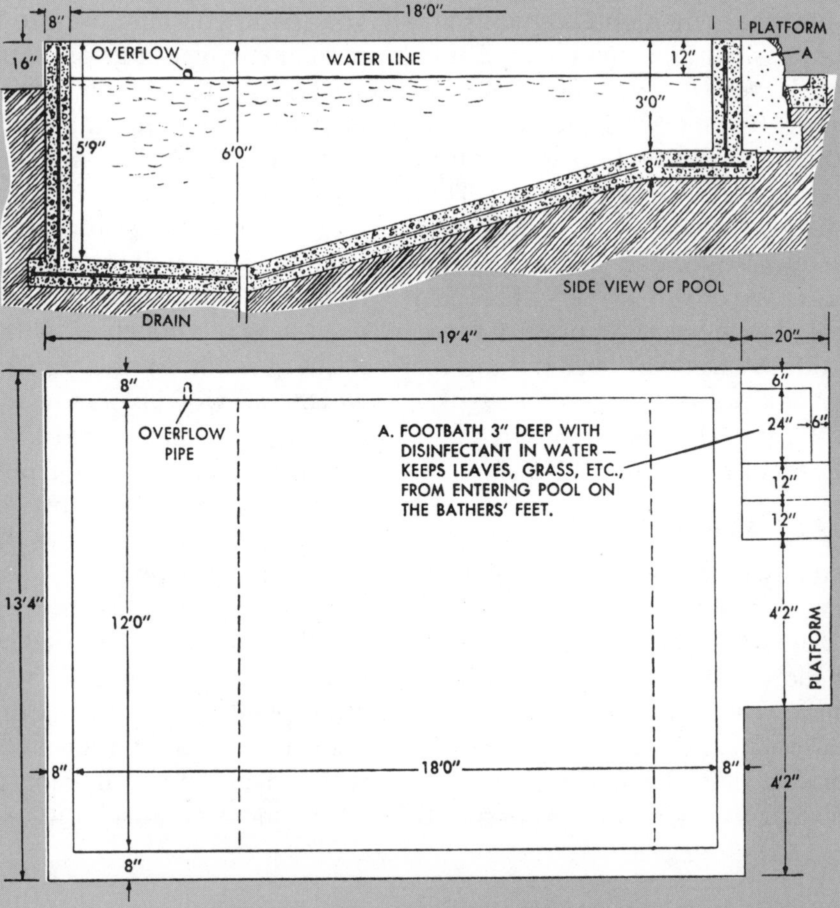

8″ 18′0″ PLATFORM
16″ OVERFLOW WATER LINE 12″ A
3′0″
5′9″ 6′0″
8″
DRAIN

SIDE VIEW OF POOL

19′4″ 20″
8″ 6″
OVERFLOW PIPE
A. FOOTBATH 3″ DEEP WITH DISINFECTANT IN WATER — KEEPS LEAVES, GRASS, ETC., FROM ENTERING POOL ON THE BATHERS' FEET.
24″ 6″
12″
12″
13′4″ 12′0″ 4′2″ PLATFORM
8″ 18′0″ 8″ 4′2″
8″

SWIMMING POOL PLAN — DIMENSIONS ADAPTABLE

SQUARE POOL SET INTO PATIO PAVEMENT

A pool need not be deep or large to increase the enjoyment of all who behold it. This tiny square pool is adaptable to many locations; as shown here, it is set into a brushed-aggregate concrete patio, a small jet supplying the tinkle of falling water. A recirculating pump permits use of the same water again and again. Square the pool's edge, or curve it (see detail, below), put loose, water-washed stones in several colors on the floor as indicated in the drawing above. Potted plants set on weathered wood planks or low cinder blocks embellish, as well as protect, the inlet jet from hurrying feet. Dispense with jet—and cut plumbing expenses. Use a hose to fill, siphon pool.

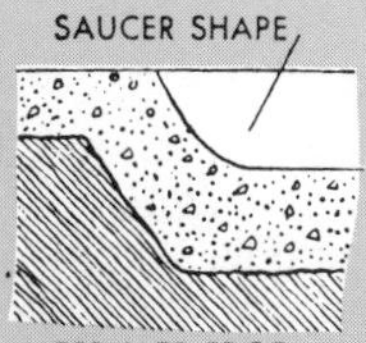

SAUCER SHAPE
ALTERNATE EDGE

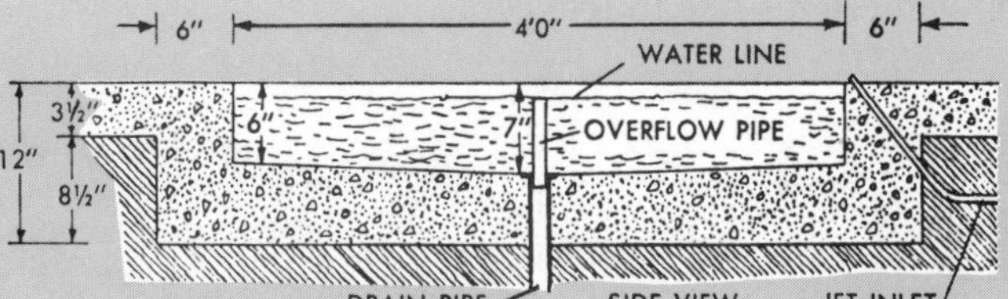

6" 4'0" 6"
WATER LINE
12" 3½" 8½" 6" 7"
OVERFLOW PIPE
DRAIN PIPE
SIDE VIEW 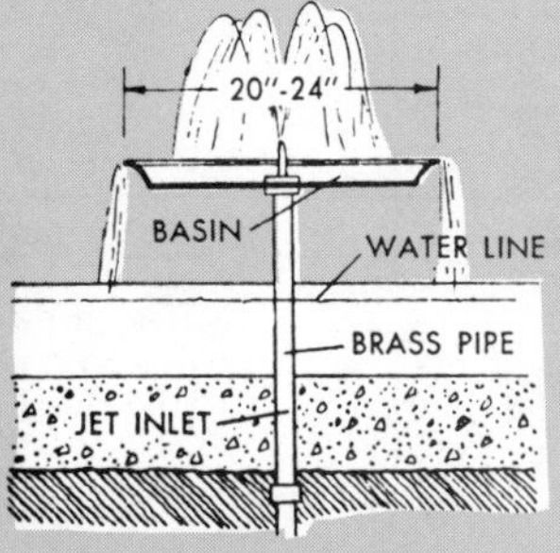
JET INLET

20"-24"
BASIN
WATER LINE
BRASS PIPE
JET INLET

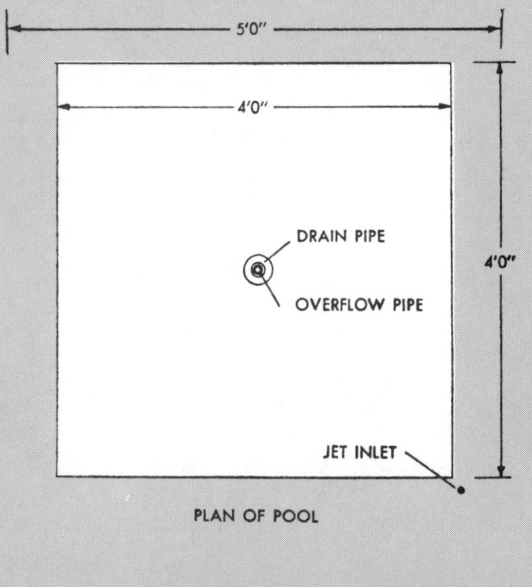

5'0"
4'0"
DRAIN PIPE
OVERFLOW PIPE
4'0"
JET INLET
PLAN OF POOL

ALTERNATE IDEA FOR JET

You could place the inlet in the center of the pool, the drain in a corner. Shown here is this alternate idea, utilizing a brass or aluminum tray with high edge, or a low bowl, for the basin. Drill a hole in the bottom, and secure basin with nuts and washers to the jet pipe. Jet spray falls into the basin, overflows, and falls into the pool.

TRIPLE POOL FOR A PATIO

Any patio profits from the sound of running water, for even when it is torrid the sound of splashing water helps one to feel cool.

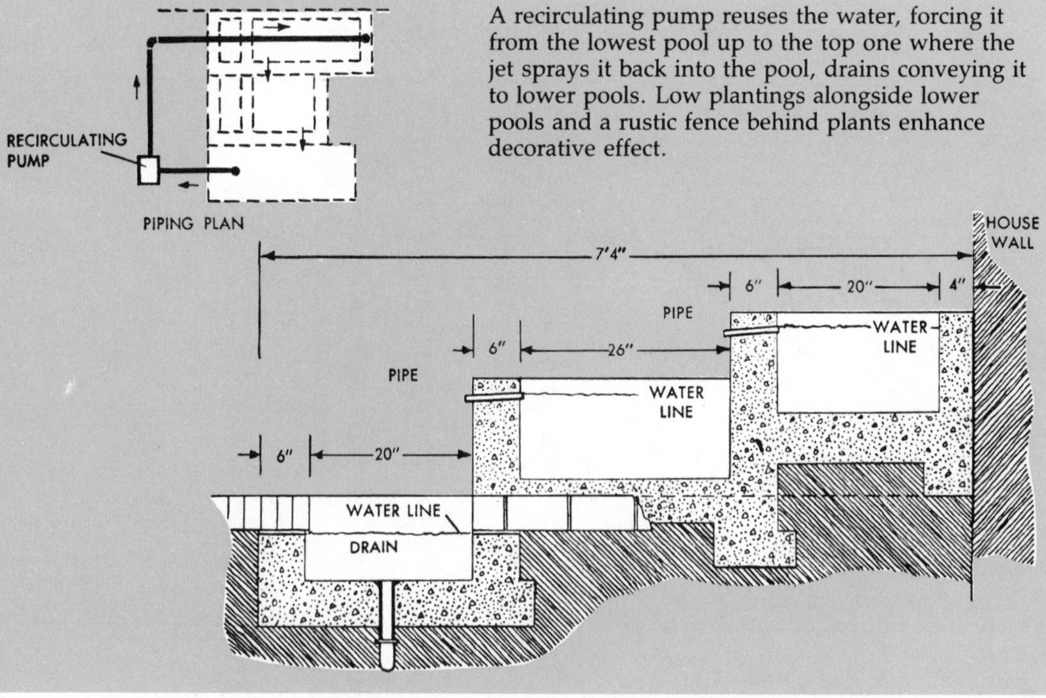

A recirculating pump reuses the water, forcing it from the lowest pool up to the top one where the jet sprays it back into the pool, drains conveying it to lower pools. Low plantings alongside lower pools and a rustic fence behind plants enhance decorative effect.

RECIRCULATING PUMP

PIPING PLAN

HOUSE WALL

7'4"

6" 20" 4"

PIPE

WATER LINE

6" 26"

PIPE

WATER LINE

6" 20"

WATER LINE

DRAIN

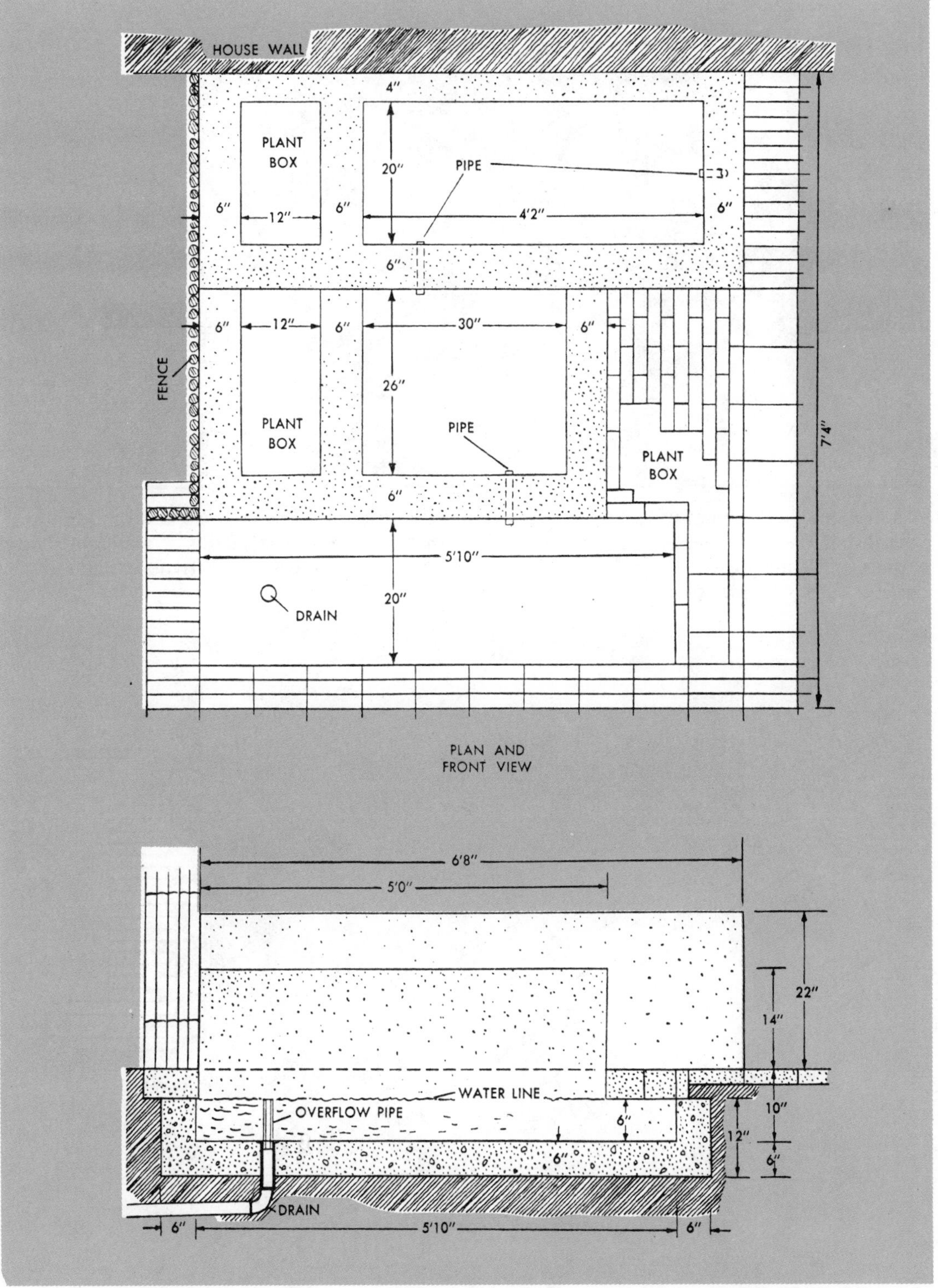
HOUSE WALL
PLANT
BOX
4"
20"
PIPE
6"
12"
6"
4'2"
6"
6"
6"
12"
6"
30"
6"
FENCE
26"
PLANT
BOX
PIPE
PLANT
BOX
6"
5'10"
DRAIN
20"
7'4"
PLAN AND
FRONT VIEW
6'8"
5'0"
22"
14"
WATER LINE
OVERFLOW PIPE
6"
10"
12"
6"
6"
DRAIN
6"
5'10"
6"

WATER WALL FOR A PATIO

PAVING
GRAVEL
SOIL
CONCRETE FOOTING FOR STEPS

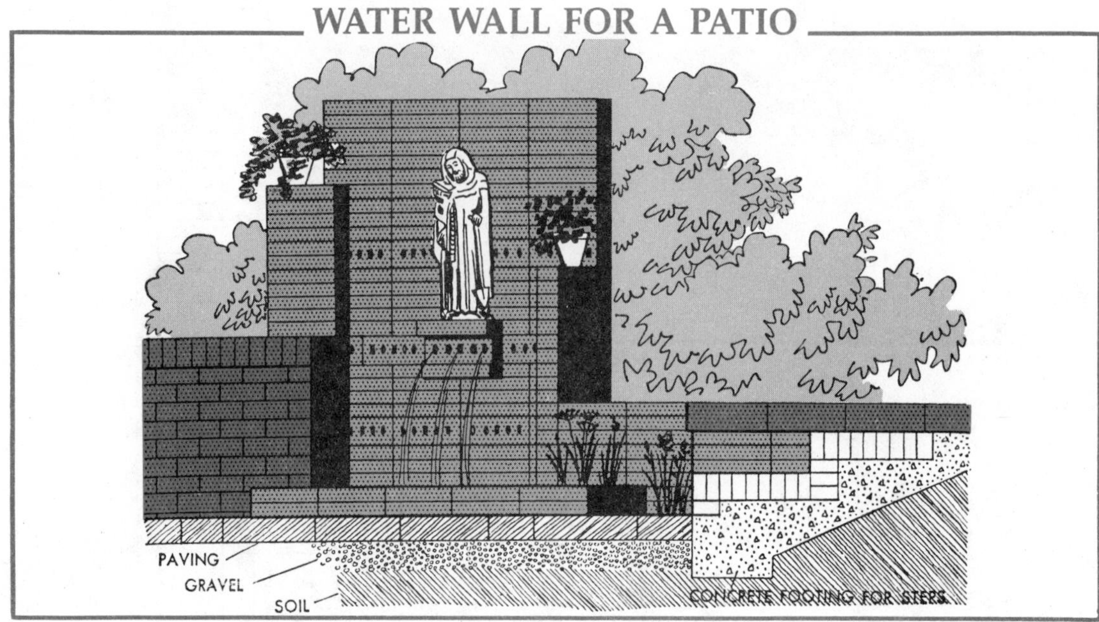

A simple wall of Roman brick laid flat in stacked bond, with a few courses laid on edge to reveal their mortar holes and provide openings for simple copper pipe jets of water. Although a piece of sculpture is shown here to reflect in the pool, a piece of driftwood, painted ceramic tiles, or some other feature might be used as focal point.

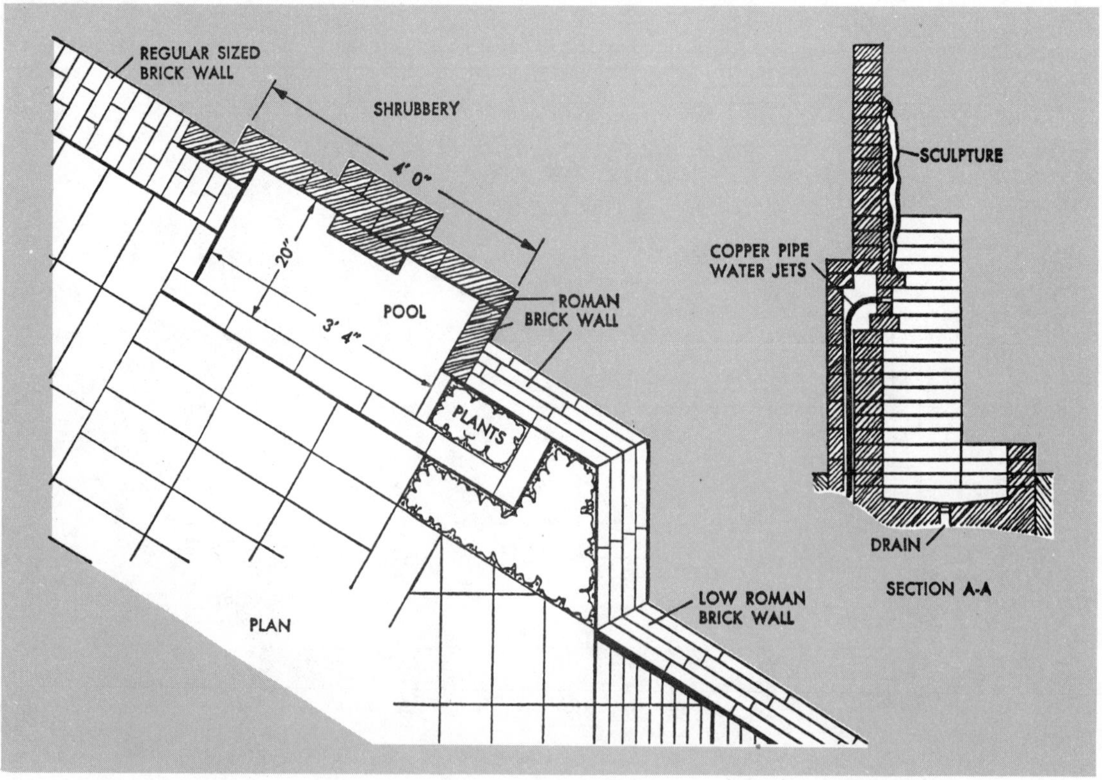

REGULAR SIZED BRICK WALL
SHRUBBERY
4' 0"
20"
3' 4"
POOL
ROMAN BRICK WALL
PLANTS
LOW ROMAN BRICK WALL
PLAN
SCULPTURE
COPPER PIPE WATER JETS
DRAIN
SECTION A-A

SPLIT-LEVEL POOL FOR THE PATIO

Does this look familiar to you? It is adapted from a design for a planter in the preceding chapter. Main differences are these: The back wall has the pipe for the inlet inside the block of masonry (a recirculating pump may be housed in it, too, if desired) and the wall of part of the triangular section has been raised to form a pool higher than the seat wall. Also, stone has been used for coping instead of wood, as used for seat in planter design.

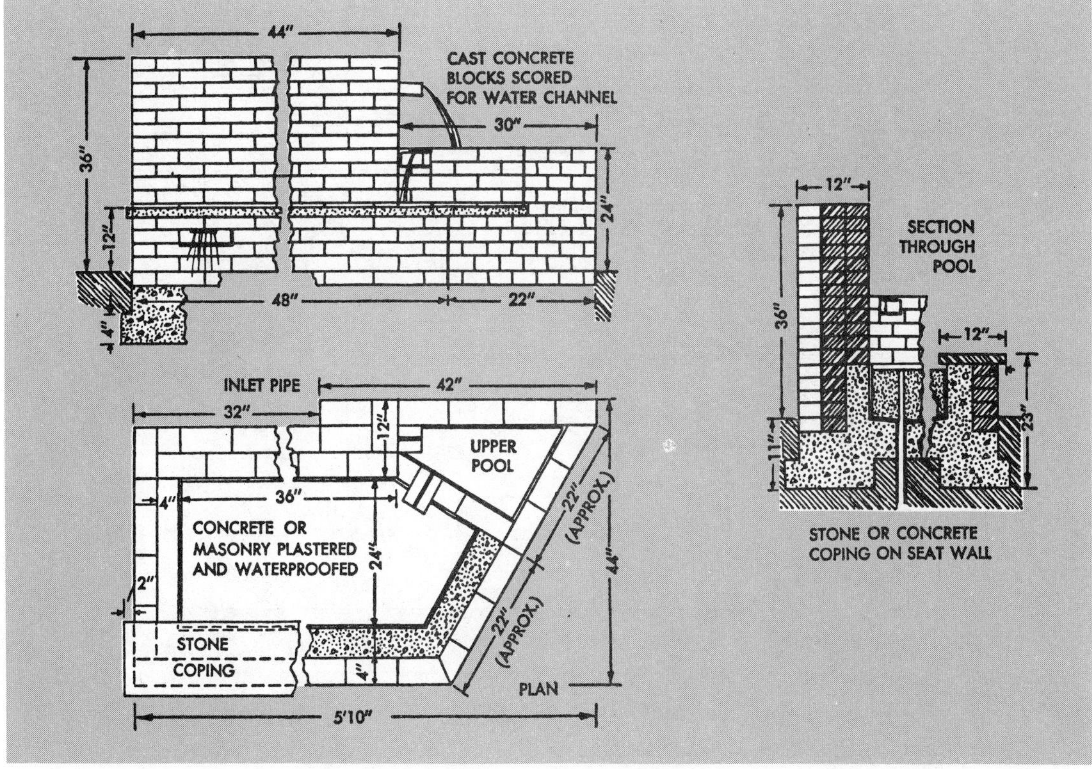

A REFLECTING POOL BESIDE THE HOUSE

A REFLECTING POOL BESIDE THE HOUSE

To provide reflections, a pool need not be deep, and this one is only 8″ in depth with deeper planting pockets provided for the water lilies. Lilies, planted in tubs, may be set on bricks to raise them if they are short-stemmed kinds. Note that drainpipe services both planting pockets, has overflow pipe to draw off excess rainwater, although pool is filled with a hose. If a shallow pool is painted a dark color—deep blue, green, or black—nobody can tell exactly how deep it is. Also, the reflecting qualities are improved by using a dark color, and where plants are used, soil pockets don't show.

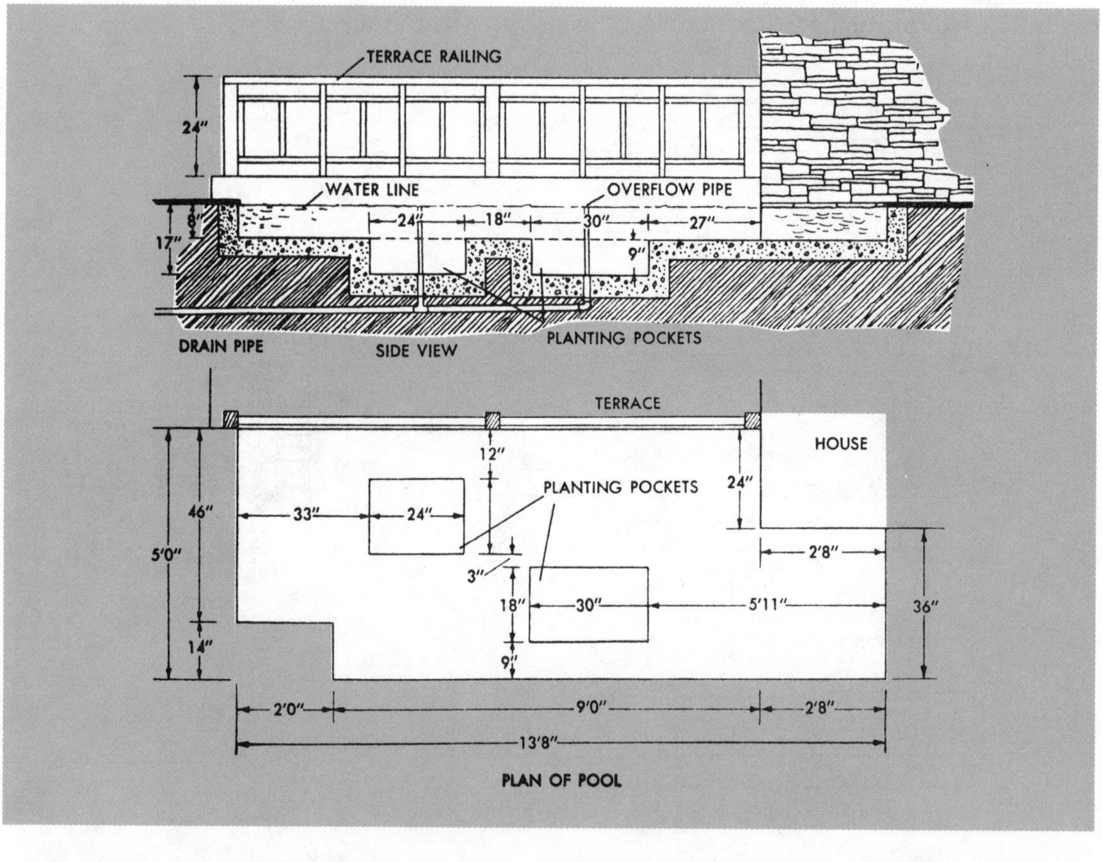

TERRACE RAILING
24″
WATER LINE
OVERFLOW PIPE
8″
17″
24″
18″
30″
27″
9″
DRAIN PIPE
PLANTING POCKETS

SIDE VIEW

TERRACE
HOUSE
12″
PLANTING POCKETS
24″
46″
33″
24″
5′0″
2′8″
3″
18″
30″
5′11″
36″
14″
9″
2′0″
9′0″
2′8″
13′8″

PLAN OF POOL

NO-DRAIN SAUCER POOL

Easiest and cheapest to build is the "saucer" pool, since a hose suffices for water supply and when it needs draining for cleaning, water is swished out with an old broom and it is scrubbed as it is drained. In winter, in frosty regions, saucer shape prevents any damage from freezing, for there are no sides to break as ice expands. Set rocks into wet edge of cement or place them later and plant between them. The overflow channel takes care of excess water from rains and can be masked by planting or use of rocks.

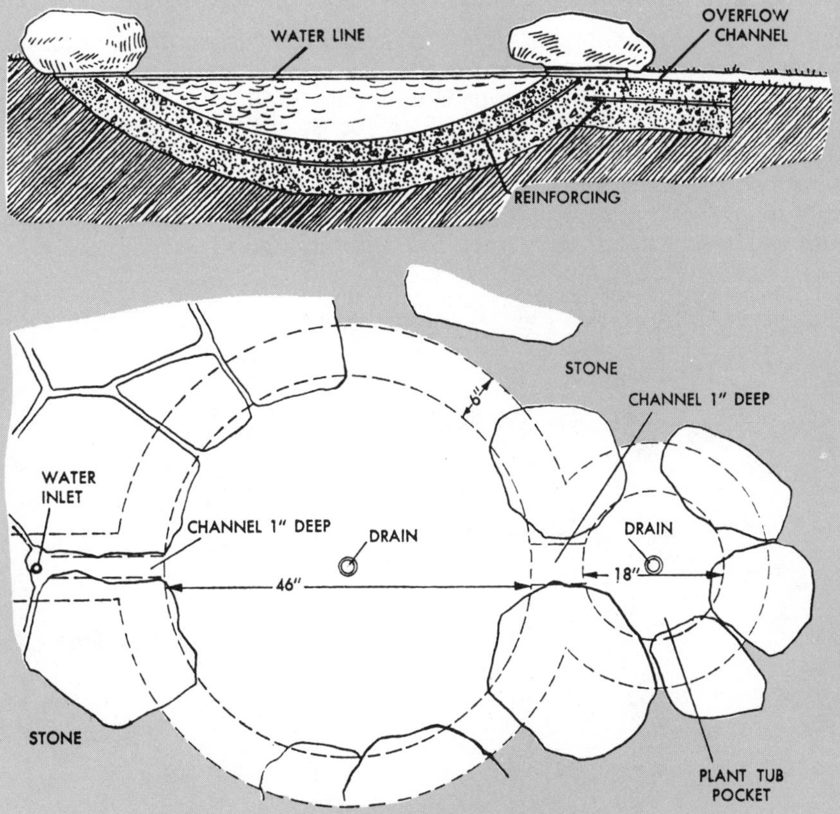

WATER LINE
OVERFLOW CHANNEL
REINFORCING

STONE
6"
CHANNEL 1" DEEP
WATER INLET
CHANNEL 1" DEEP
DRAIN
46"
DRAIN
18"
STONE
PLANT TUB POCKET
PLAN OF POOL AND PLANT POCKET

TWO WAYS TO USE SAUCER POOLS

The various ways in which simple round pools can be used seem to be endless. Raise them up a few inches above soil or pavement of the patio; put them in a lawn and sink them to ground level, install a jet with a removable overflow drainpipe or merely depress a portion of the rim to allow for overflow of rainwater. (A concrete ditch 2′ long will lead overflow water away and keep it from seeping into soil, causing frost trouble beneath the pool.) Saucer pools can be made of concrete smoothly finished, or in brushed aggregate with stones showing in a rough texture, finished with mosaic patterns of your own devising or merely painted with waterproof paints developed for swimming pools.

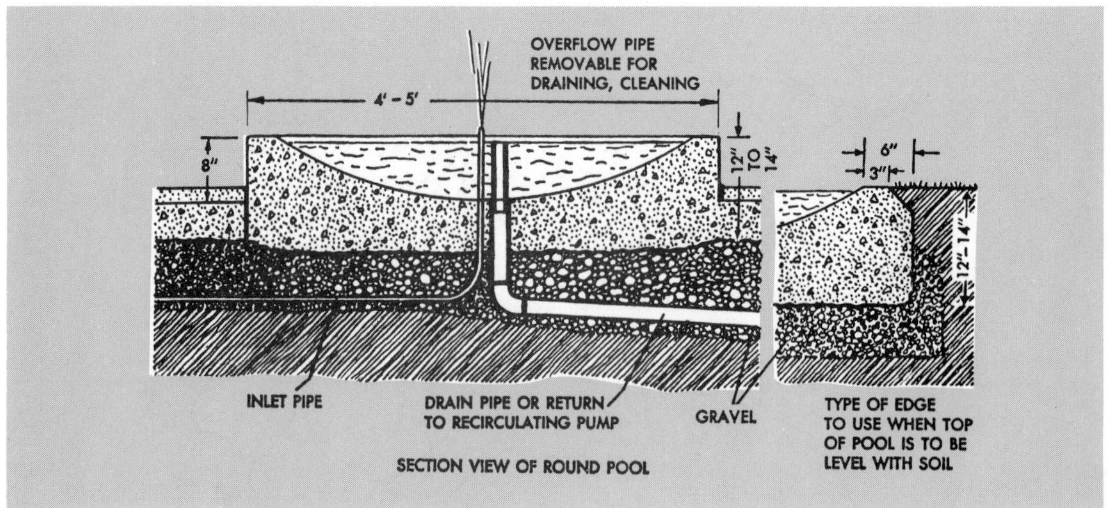

SECTION VIEW OF ROUND POOL

POOL FOR NATURAL PLANTINGS

An easy-to-make concrete pool can conform with its natural surroundings if stones are set into the edge of the pool while concrete is still wet. Paint pool a dark color and use plants around it to mask even more the fact that it is man-made and it will fit into its environment. Cattails and other water plants can be grown in an adjacent pool partly filled with soil. Note that both pools are frostproof saucer shape.

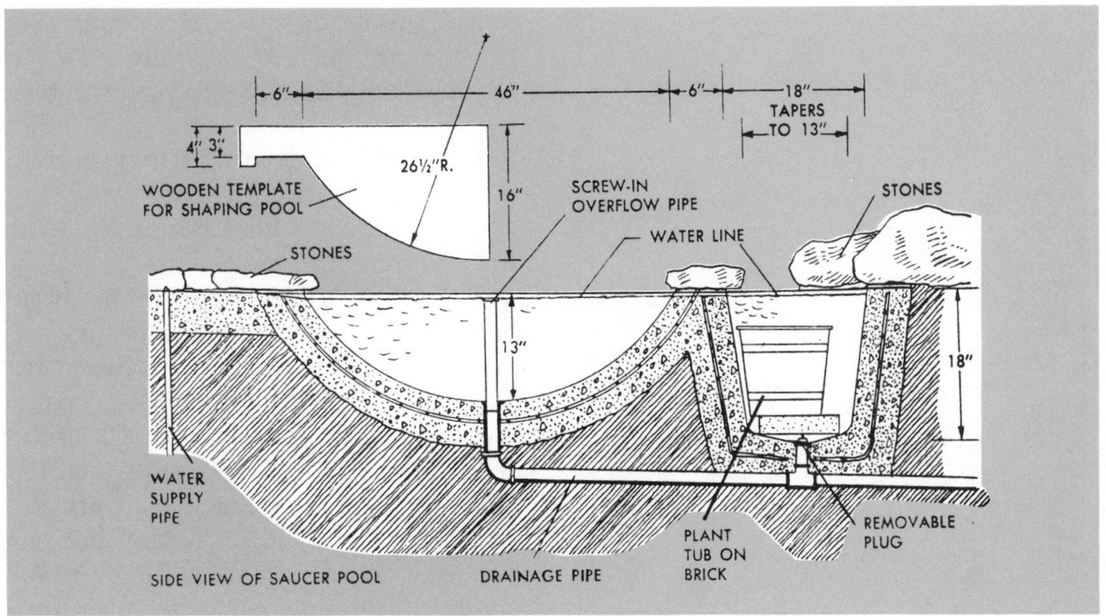

CHAPTER 24

VERSATILE WALLS

When a man's home was his castle—literally—walls had a very definite function. They had to surround the castle, be high, strong, and permanent, able to take the shock of whatever assaults might be made on them from outside. Today, however, their function is less grim and they perform their duties with grace and beauty in a variety of architectural forms. Walls are truly coming into their own.

Today walls may form the boundary line between two properties, or they may be the line of demarcation between two parts of the garden. The wall can separate the beauty of the living portions of a property from the useful and functional, but unlovely, service areas. It can act as a sound barrier or noise-cushion between a house and a busy street. It may be low enough to become useful as furniture—

The versatility of concrete is here demonstrated by the curving concrete edge of the flower beds which helps to cut maintenance labor. The split concrete-block retaining wall above the bed echoes curves, and high wall with grilles borders the lot.

the seat wall is now an accepted fixture in outdoor planning—or it may rise high enough to screen out the prying eyes of nosy neighbors or curious passersby, or to break the force of winds which might sweep the patio. Walls may be solid or pierced; smooth or very much textured; may sport any color of the rainbow, be unobtrusively painted to match the house, or be left in the sober and subtle natural hues of the material of which they are built.

A wall may be used to retain and hold back a hillside where it has been necessary to bulldoze out a driveway, walk, or patio on a sloping site. It may be used to retain the roots of a tree around which the land has to be sliced down and evened as living-space and for which the shade of the tree will be needed. In every case the wall becomes a distinct asset to the property and by its permanence will continue to give satisfaction for many years to come. It has a useful function, but it can also contribute great beauty.

The wall is a year-round joy. In the growing season it will be a good foil for showing off your plants, your trees, and your shrubs. In winter it will give architectural form to the winter landscape, even under the snow, and is a background for bare branches so that their beauty can be appreciated. A garden with walls need never look so forlorn in winter as one which depends entirely on plant material for its effect. The walls are the "bones" of the garden on which the "flesh" of plant material is hung, and, as with humans, good bone structure will make the flesh more charming and beautiful. The wall can be the focal point of the garden, pairing well with steps and pools, with pergolas and shelters, concealing or revealing as the builder chooses, and tying in with the paving material of walks and patios.

Because of its character, the wall can do wonderful things for the design of your garden. It need not be built always on straight lines, although this may be the easiest and safest course for the do-it-yourselfer to follow. It may flow in sweeping curves, be built in geometric arcs or semi-circles, angle off the straight line to make a compelling pointer to the focus of interest of the garden. High walls or low ones that are merely raised edges to define flower beds or terraces—all have their places in the outdoor picture today.

PRACTICAL WALLS

The easiest walls to build, quite naturally, are low ones. Blocks or bricks are the best materials to use because they are of even size and thus are easy to fit together into a trim structure. But because of their smaller size and lesser weight, bricks are easier to manage than blocks, a factor to remember if you plan to build a high wall. Hoisting heavy blocks to shoulder height consumes energy and is tiring to the muscles. On the other hand, a block wall goes much faster because of the size of the units.

Bricks have many tones and textures, mostly warm, and my preference is for the smooth finishes rather than the wire-cut ones. The former, when laid with a raked joint, make a most beautiful texture in sunlight. Blocks are larger and clumsier looking, and not always so pleasant in color, although both bricks and blocks may be painted. (See Chapter 12.) Where a long, low line is wanted, a wall built of 2- or 3-inch solid concrete or cinder blocks will achieve this effect. Where a fairly

Six-foot-high privacy walls built of diamond-patterned concrete grille blocks set between heavy piers of concrete blocks give distinct character to a yard, help to lift a somewhat usual kind of house into a class of its own, making it more original.

Enclosed by high dark-colored concrete-block privacy walls, a circle of lawn is bordered by a brushed-aggregate walk and paving that extends indoors. The fire-pit seat and wall are built of light-colored concrete blocks, softened by the plantings set behind them.

smooth texture is desired, the wall of blocks with no emphasis on the joints will be a good answer, the texture of the blocks being rather pleasant, especially when painted. Such a wall will be cheaper to build than a brick one, too.

Where walls must be built on a hillside, step them down gracefully from level to level, with posts or piers forming logical points at which to make a break and start a stretch lower down according to the amount of drop in the grade. Similarly, a wall may start out high on level plots where concealment is needed, drop by degrees to a seat wall, and dip to form a 6-inch parapet around a pool. It may rise again to make a seat or a privacy wall, to frame a good view, or to blot out an undesirable one.

WALLS CAN BE FRIENDLY

Not all walls are built for the purposes of concealment or protection of privacy, nor must they be solid and therefore somewhat unfriendly. The pierced wall, of which are shown many examples in upcoming pages, is a favorite of gardeners today because it encloses an area, yet gives it ventilation (important for humans as well as plants) while maintaining privacy.

Brick walls make beautiful fences. Laid on a curving concrete footing reaching below the frost line, the single tier of bricks gains bracing from its curving shape. Double courses at the top are both for strength and appearance. Pilasters every 10′ add strength.

A brick wall with openings lets through light, air, and a partial view in both directions, though it gives less privacy than a solid wall. Such a wall is harder to lay than a solid one, because you have to remember to incorporate the pattern as you go.

Compelling strong curves give skeletal design and direction to the outdoor scheme. Making a wall of the sort shown here adds dimension as well as form. Stacked-bond concrete blocks with well-fitted joints provide a certain pattern and texture.

It will break the force of hot or cold blasts of winds which sweep your land, taming them so that outdoor living can be made not only possible but even pleasant during normally severe weather. The decorative effect of bricks and blocks can hardly be praised enough, for they may be assembled in myriad ways to give practically any textural effect desired. No wall need be a blank enclosure when texture and shadow effects are present, even if no plantings are used with the wall.

Speaking of blank walls brings to mind the case of the high retaining wall. Often it may be a thing of necessity rather than one of beauty, yet this need not be the case. For the do-it-yourselfer any wall of more than 3 or 4 feet in height is a considerable undertaking, particularly if the wall is to be made of concrete. I advise

Concrete-block grilles give light while maintaining privacy by day and contribute pattern to lighted windows at night. Such grilles keep hot sun from windows, too-bright light from rooms. Single-core units set vertically overlap horizontal solid blocks.

Open-block walls not only allow air to flow freely through, ventilating outdoor living spaces such as patios, but also make handsome and effective architectural points. The two versions shown here make ever-interesting patterns of light and shade for visual enjoyment.

that, if the wall must be of more than 4 feet in height to retain the soil of a hillside, you hire a contractor to build it for you. In any case, it may call for a building permit and resultant inspections at various stages. If you wish to veneer the concrete later on with bricks or blocks, you will be able to do so if you arrange to have the foundation project enough to hold the veneer.

I'd like to raise the question of whether or not retaining walls need to be so high. There is a bleakness which is very grim about the large stretches of unrelieved masonry. They also have problems of bracing and of making heavy footings to hold their weight. It would be less troublesome to make a few terraces down the hillside, with retaining walls spaced 3 to 8 feet apart. You could build these yourself without a permit in many places. Footings would be less expensive and the weight of each wall less, the strain being divided between the two or more walls rather than concentrated on one. Besides all this, the esthetic effect would be more pleasant. Planting beds in front of each wall would give a chance for shrubs, evergreens, or flowers; and the long lines of the walls would make the hillside seem less dominant, because they would expand the visual width of the property and minimize the apparent vertical measure. Vines could be trained to hang over the edge and soften the lines of the walls, and tall-growing shrubs would also break the lines interestingly.

THINGS TO CHECK ON

The first thing that must be determined is your property line, if the wall is to be built on or near it. You must be sure not to encroach on the neighboring property, or you may face a lawsuit or other unpleasantness and expense. It might be well worth the money to have the property re-surveyed and permanent markers inserted at the corners if there is any question about the exact location of your property lines.

You should also check with the local building inspector's office to see if there are any ordinances which limit the size, height, material, or character of the wall you plan to build; whether or not a building permit will be necessary for the construction of the wall. A permit may be required in some cities and towns. The inspector also can give you any restrictions regarding setbacks and finish, and any other information contained in local codes which you will need to know. Codes

A grille-block wall encloses a patio to the right. Grille blocks are available in a great number of patterns and degrees of openings vs. solidity.

Two more open-block walls demonstrate possibilities offered for texture and pattern. Left, alternate rows laid in half-overlap make an informal pattern. Right, open cube blocks are combined with solid cube blocks to relieve and open up an uninteresting wall.

Light and shade always enhance block textures, but, when laid with alternate blocks recessed, a strong diagonal pattern is achieved by shadows. The wall and circular planter are built with slump blocks, which are similar in texture to adobe bricks.

Patterned blocks can be laid in numerous ways to create different wall designs. While each block here simply has a small triangular recess in each end, the way they are laid in the wall builds the design.

in most places are mainly concerned with strength and stability of the construction so that no public hazard will result from its being built. They're also concerned with setbacks and sight distances. In cold areas there may be some requirement for footings or foundations, because frost might heave the wall, crack it, and make it a potential danger. Where retaining walls must be built, even though they may be within the boundaries of your property and not on the edge, there may also be some restrictions locally, so you should check on them, too.

These things sound more important and complex, probably, than they actually are. The important thing is to check on them before you build, before you commit yourself to an order for building materials or even excavate, so that you will know the restrictions within which you must work. Then you can go ahead with an unclouded mind to the planning and building, secure in the knowledge that you're doing the right thing and that your wall won't have to be pulled down and rebuilt to meet some regulation you didn't know about at the beginning.

THICKNESS OF WALLS

Walls up to a foot high and freestanding need not be more than one brick course in thickness—approximately 4 inches—and unless they must withstand weight or pressures from soil, as in a retaining wall, this may even go a few inches higher. Retaining walls and those higher than a foot or so are better made two bricks

Another patterned wall utilizes shaped blocks for its basic pattern, with single-core blocks set one above the other in staggered formation to give three-dimensional texture by their projection. Or, use solid blocks with open-single-core for wall according to taste.

Decorative effects may be achieved with little effort by using shaped blocks such as the diamond pattern here. Other blocks of many kinds are available in some areas, obtainable readily or on special order. Consult local dealers to see what choices are offered.

in thickness—about 8 inches—while those used for seat walls, 16 to 18 inches high, may be two or three bricks wide, the three-brick width of 12 inches being preferred where the seat is all masonry with no wooden seat atop it. Walls may also be made of blocks, as detailed elsewhere, 4-inch-wide blocks being the narrowest width recommended, 6-, 8-, 10-, and 12-inch-wide blocks being adaptable to various walls for various purposes. Concrete may be cast as a wall, too, 4 to 6 inches being the narrowest it is practical to cast for low walls. Above that, use any width that is practical for your purpose. Remember that all walls should be built on a proper footing. The general rule is to make the footing as deep as the width of the wall. That is, an 8-inch wall would have a footing 8 inches deep. In heavy frost areas deeper footings may be advisable. The width of the footing should be double that of the width of the wall—16 inches in the case of an 8-inch wall—with the wall centered on the footing.

Block and concrete walls may be topped with a soldier course of bricks (see Chapter 12), finished with coping blocks, cut stone, or cast concrete to provide an overhang so that moisture does not drip or run down the face of the wall. Bolts may be embedded in the mortar or concrete so that wooden planks or other wooden seats may be fastened to the top of the masonry wall. Providing the proper finish on the top of the wall is important not only to the looks of the wall but also to ensure its durability. Walls of blocks or concrete may be veneered on the face with bricks where they are used for low retaining walls.

Walls of waist height or higher which are of more than moderate length may require the insertion of pilasters or piers every 10 feet. Intervals of 6 to 8 feet would be safer with higher walls. The exception to this rule is the serpentine wall, whose double curve, if based on a proper footing and foundation, will withstand a great deal of stress and strain merely by exerting opposing pressures of its own. A

Concrete-block wall columns combined with precast-concrete-slab patterns are all laid on a cast-in-place concrete footing to enclose a yard. Use of flush joints and coats of paint minimize the concrete-block appearance of the wall.

curved template or form built of hardboard or thin plywood, bent to the proper radius, and fastened to a wooden frame will be of assistance in building a serpentine wall quickly and easily. Lay out the basic curves for the first course on the foundation by using a stake, with a cord for a radius to mark an arc. Where this arc joins the arc made from the opposing radial center, the bricks or blocks are laid to join and then go in the opposite curve. For taller serpentine walls deeper curves are needed than for low ones, but for even shoulder-height walls a single-thick course of bricks is all that will be necessary. If you have ever seen the beautiful serpentine walls at the University of Virginia at Charlottesville, Virginia, that were designed by Thomas Jefferson, you know the truth of this statement.

If you wish to make wider serpentines, it is a good plan to run headers to tie together the double or triple courses every four to five courses.

BALUSTRADES

Rather than making solid walls to edge patios and thus preventing the unwary guest from falling into flower beds below, use a balustrade to give the proper finish and designation to the edge and to signify the change in level. The flowers or shrubs beyond can be seen through the openwork and it will also allow ventilation and air circulation. As shown in the drawings, bricks may be used to build balusters. The details show some of the ways in which bricks can be laid, some high and some low balusters made this way, but all of them practical and tying in well with brick-paved patios and brick-faced walls.

Balusters are not the easiest of projects for the do-it-yourselfer to attempt for they require a precision and skill in handling if they are to look right and stand up to the weather; but if you take your time in building them, use care and take the trouble to fit them as perfectly as you can, you will be rewarded with an unusual balustrade, one that you can be proud of and one that will be much admired by your guests.

STONE WALLS

Stone is a beautiful medium. It is rather more difficult to manage than blocks or bricks, but the final result will more than justify all the fuss and fuming you may have to go through. Stones are probably heavier than most other materials and, being irregular in shape, they are harder to fit together. Stone mortaring is more difficult than mortaring other materials, too, because the stones may squeeze the mortar out with their weight. In cases of this sort you can insert chips of stone between courses to hold up the weight until the mortar hardens. Chips may be set permanently in mortar.

If stone is abundant on your property it may be the cheapest material to use, because it can be had for the mere labor of picking it up and taking it to the site of the wall. Use a rich mortar to be assured of a good strong joint, increasing the cement formula by ¼ to ½ part for each other part, making the mortar a bit stiffer than for use with bricks or blocks. It may be pointed out that more mortar may be required for stone walls than for brick or block ones due to the unevenness of the materials and the need for filling holes with mortar.

Whether laid in mortar or laid dry, the

stone wall should be "battered"—sloped back—toward the top in the ratio of 1 to 2 inches for every 2 feet of wall height. Where the wall is to be laid dry and also used for a retaining wall, the batter should be 8 to 12 inches for every 5 feet of height. This will enable it to withstand the soil pressures.

DRY STONE WALLS

This is one of the most beautiful of stone walls and, once the trick is mastered, one of the easiest to construct in many ways. The most suitable stones for it are those which are naturally rather flat, those which come from stratified outcroppings or which occur naturally as flattish blocks. Boulders and other rounded rocks are not so suitable and may cause failure of the wall due to their shape. Large boulders can be cracked and broken to secure flat edges, but the smaller ones are definitely to be discarded.

The dry stone wall need not be built on a foundation, the lower stones merely being set in a trench dug 6 to 18 inches below soil level on a base layer of crushed rock or rubble stone which has been well compacted by tamping. This will assure good drainage (it may be omitted in dry and mild climates) and will prevent frost-heaving which might dislodge or unsettle stones and necessitate repairs. A well-built dry stone wall will fit the stones together so carefully that they will hold themselves in place by their own weight and the pull of gravity. (See the illustrations on page 478 for the details on laying it.)

Dry stone walls can be planted with a variety of rock plants, which will enhance their beauty and attractiveness.

A FEW FINAL CAUTIONS

When you are building retaining walls be sure to provide for drainage behind them, either by laying drain tiles to carry away seepage or by leaving weep holes in the face of the wall to allow it to drain away. Footings and foundations are important to all walls. The stability and permanence of your wall will depend as much on the time and care you expend on what *doesn't* show below ground as it will upon the superstructure and the care with which that is built. Don't neglect the underpinnings! (See Chapter 14 for methods of making footings.)

After you have built your wall be sure to plant its surroundings well to give it the setting it deserves. Softening the sharp architectural lines by beautiful plants in front of or behind the wall, training a tendril of vine over the edge or on the face of a wall to contrast its soft lines with the crisp ones of the masonry will help to knit the wall into the fabric of the garden's design, quickly, beautifully, and permanently.

Never allow any walls to become so overgrown with ivy or any vine or shrubbery that they can't be seen, or that they lose their character. Remember that walls are the "bones" of your garden which must never be completely obscured by the fat "flesh" of growing things, or the garden design will become a bit flabby and unable to exhibit its true character. A little careful, judicious pruning will quickly bring it back to its youthful loveliness and visibility.

A wall, to repeat, can be the focal point of the garden, a year-round joy. I am sure you will agree as soon as you build one.

ADDING STRENGTH AND STABILITY

Tall walls that need piers for added strength may project in front the thickness of one brick and may also project on the back of the wall. Headers in alternating courses tie pier into wall (see plan view). Retaining walls (below) may be backed up with blocks, faced and capped with bricks. Note walls are centered on footings for stability.

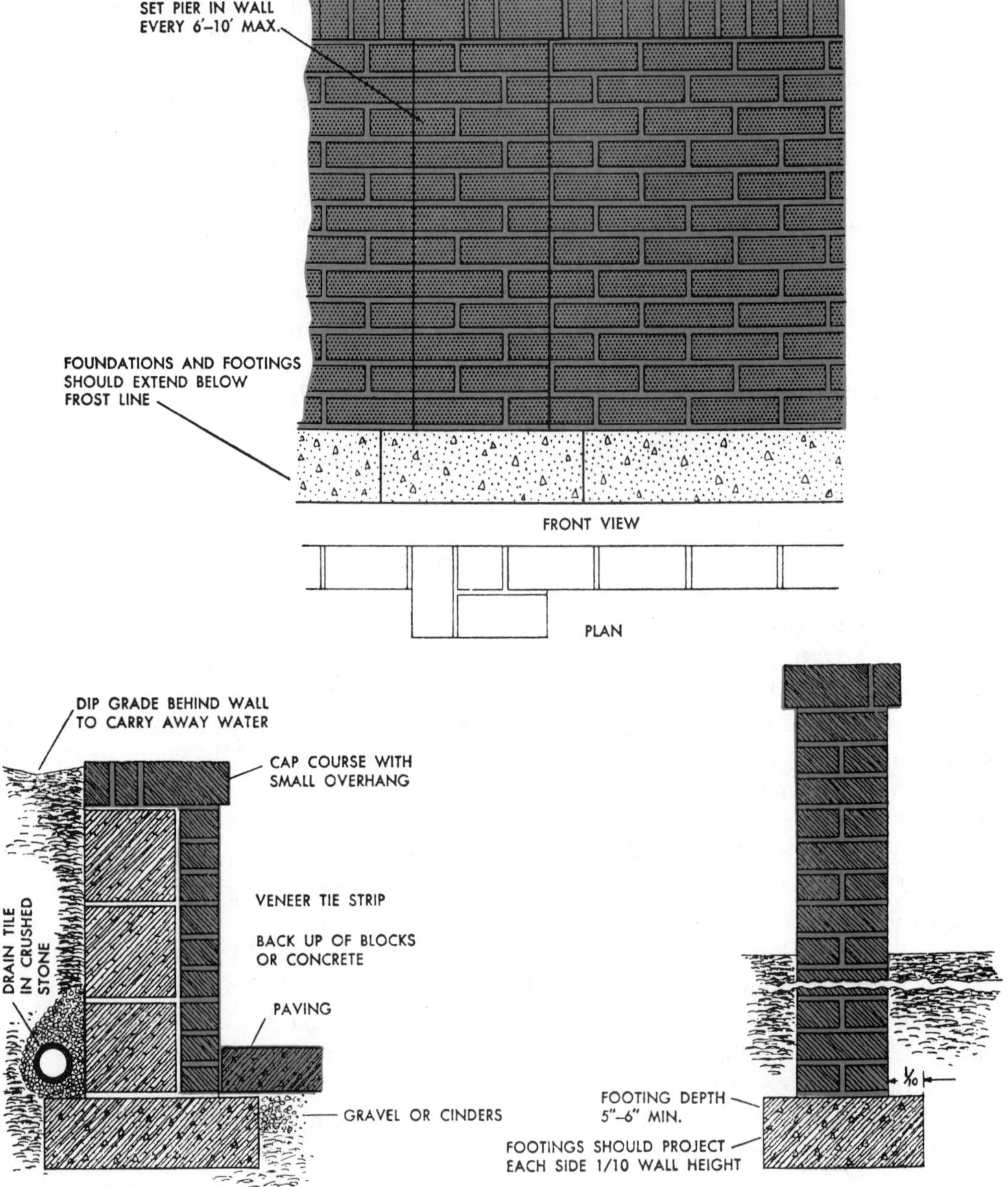

OPEN WALLS AND VENTILATION

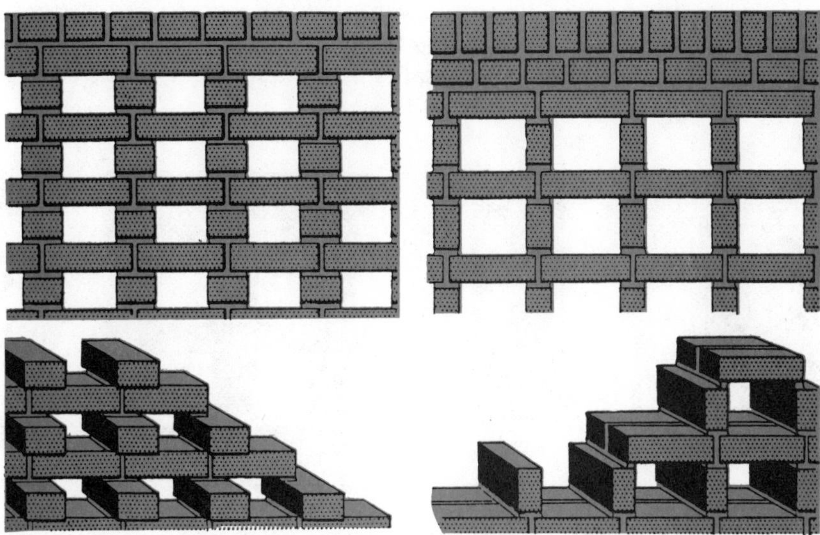

All courses are laid flat, every other brick in header courses being omitted and stretcher joints centering on header bricks. The resulting shadows lend great textural interest. In this variation of the Rolok wall, a double stretcher course is laid with the joints centering on the upright headers, spaces between headers being left open for passage of air.

A SOLID WALL WITH TEXTURAL INTEREST

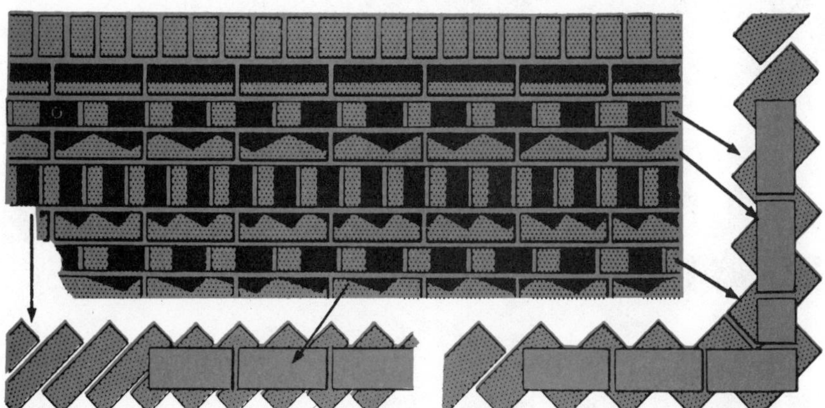

For a wall beside a driveway, a walk, or some other place with no room for plantings, get interest by texture and shadows. Lay a flat stretcher course centered on alternate header courses, one laid flat, the other on edge, both at a 45° angle to wall axis. Shadow effects resulting from this decided texture will make wall notably interesting architecturally.

BALUSTRADE DESIGNS

Brick balustrades lend a decorative touch, offer plenty of scope for ingenuity in creative designs. Openwork brick balusters give strength and support while allowing for ventilation and providing pleasing patterns in the landscape. Balustrades built on the edge of a patio give extra seating space for outdoor parties.

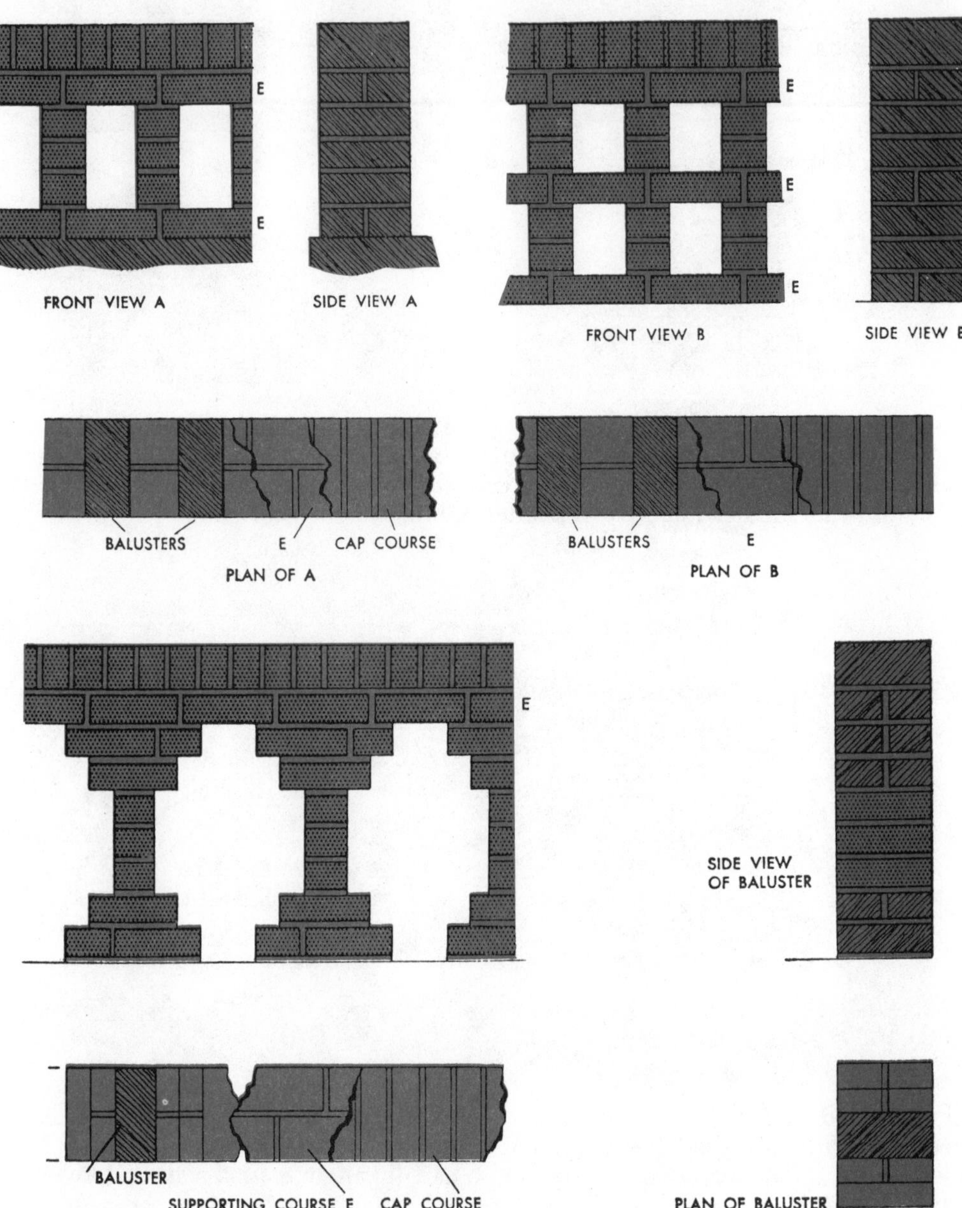

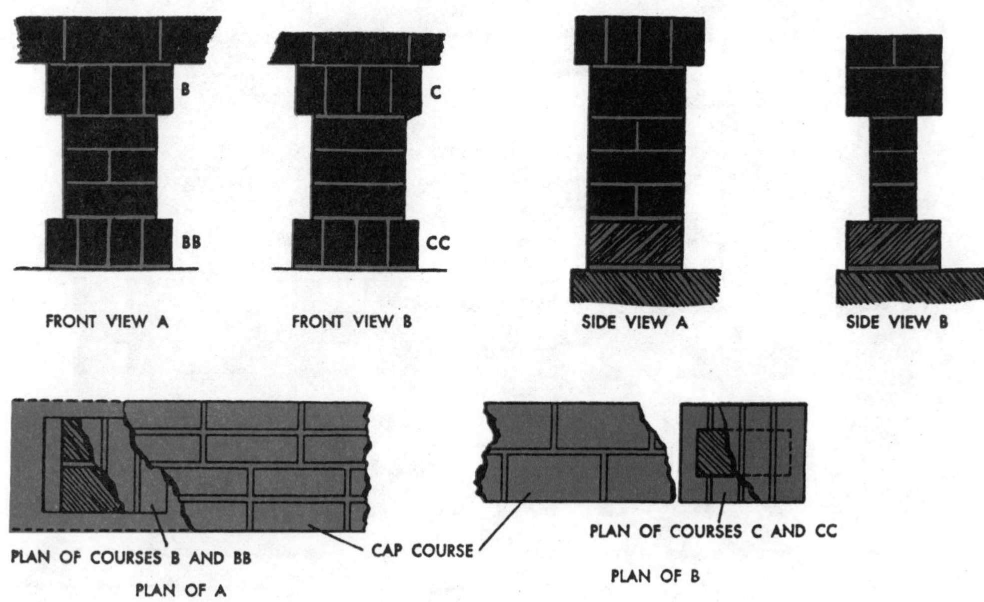
B
BB
FRONT VIEW A
C
CC
FRONT VIEW B
SIDE VIEW A
SIDE VIEW B
PLAN OF COURSES B AND BB
PLAN OF A
CAP COURSE
PLAN OF COURSES C AND CC
PLAN OF B

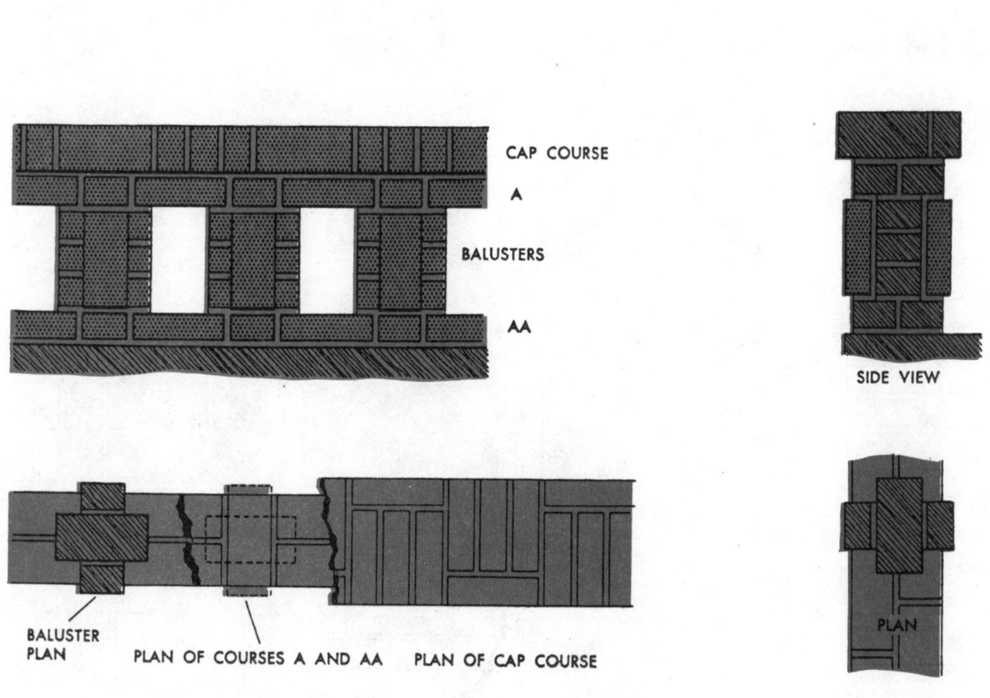
CAP COURSE
A
BALUSTERS
AA
SIDE VIEW
BALUSTER PLAN
PLAN OF COURSES A AND AA
PLAN OF CAP COURSE
PLAN

CROSS AND SQUARE PATTERN

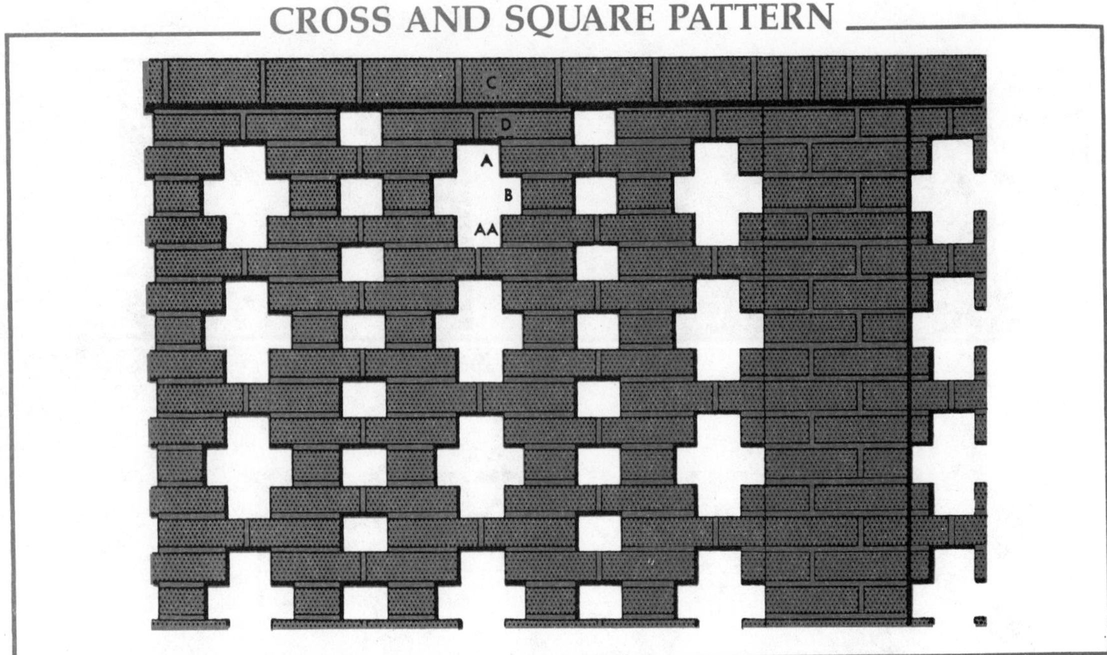

Built two bricks thick with three-brick piers inserted every 6′ to 9′, this open-work pattern is decorative yet strong. Of interest to amateurs is the fact that no bricks need be cut except where it may be necessary for fitting into piers. It may also be adapted to single-brick thickness with two-brick piers at intervals for strengthening.

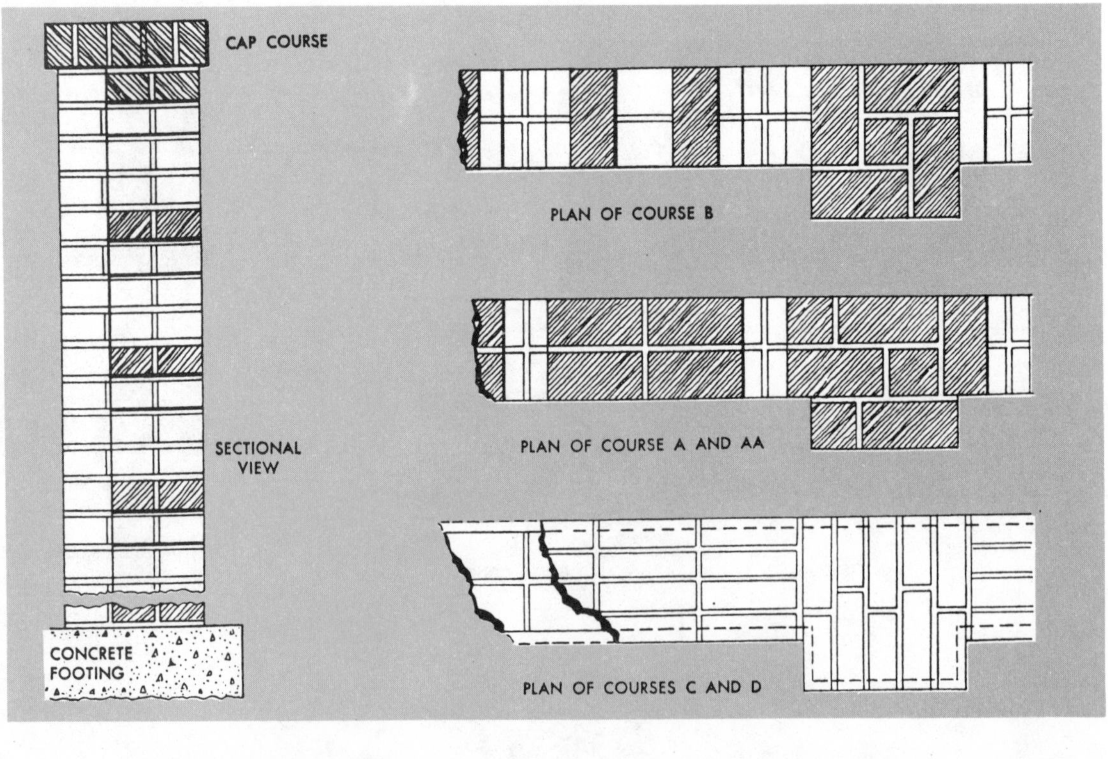

CAP COURSE

PLAN OF COURSE B

SECTIONAL VIEW

PLAN OF COURSE A AND AA

CONCRETE FOOTING

PLAN OF COURSES C AND D

STAGGERED-CROSS PATTERN

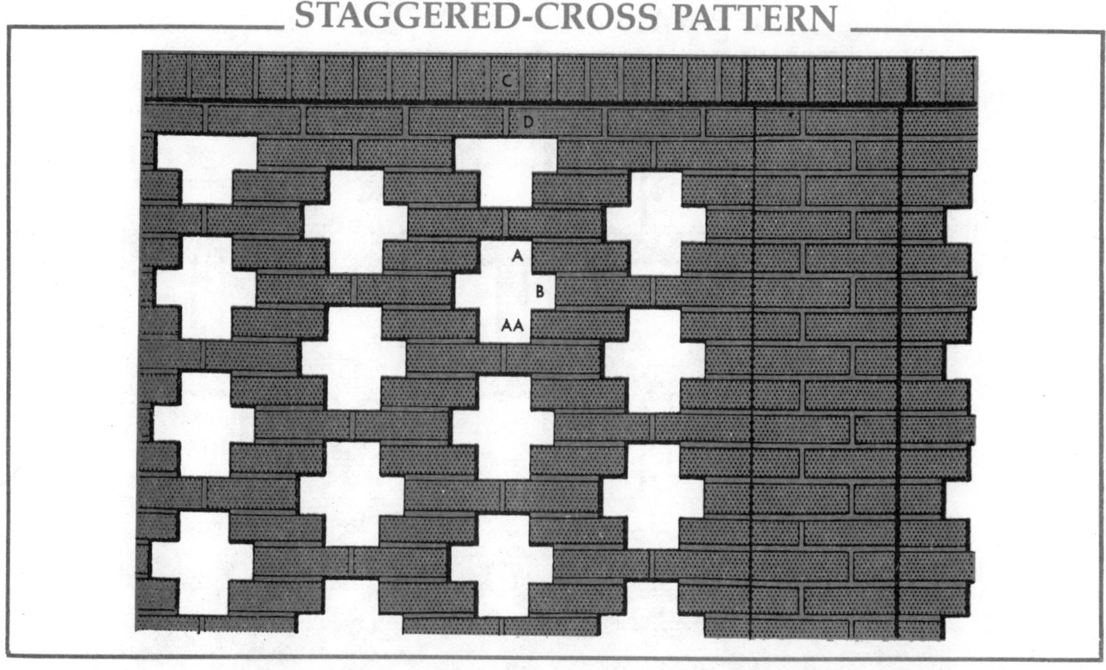

Another wall design which may be built with a minimum of brick cutting is this single-brick wall, three brick piers set at intervals of 6′, the pleasant cross design set alternately, vertically. Note how the solid top courses provide support for the cap course without materially affecting the regularity of the design or adding undue weight.

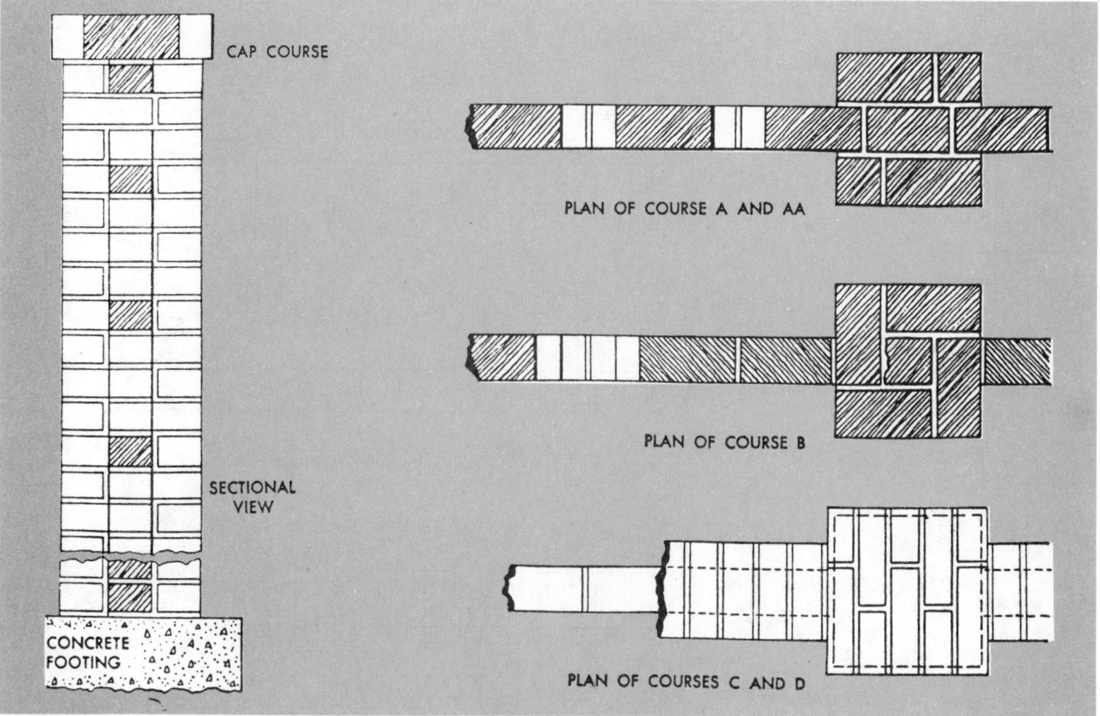

GRAND OPENING

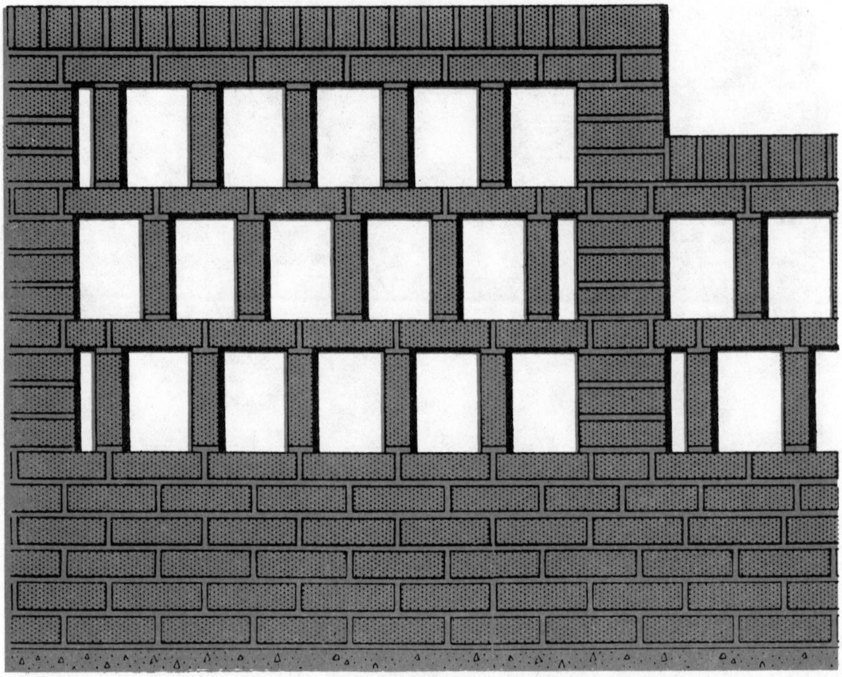

Clean lines and pleasing regularity make a wall compatible with either traditional or modern houses. Two-brick thickness is used throughout, including the piers which are set no more than 6′ apart. Build as shown, above a solid low wall, or keep wall open.

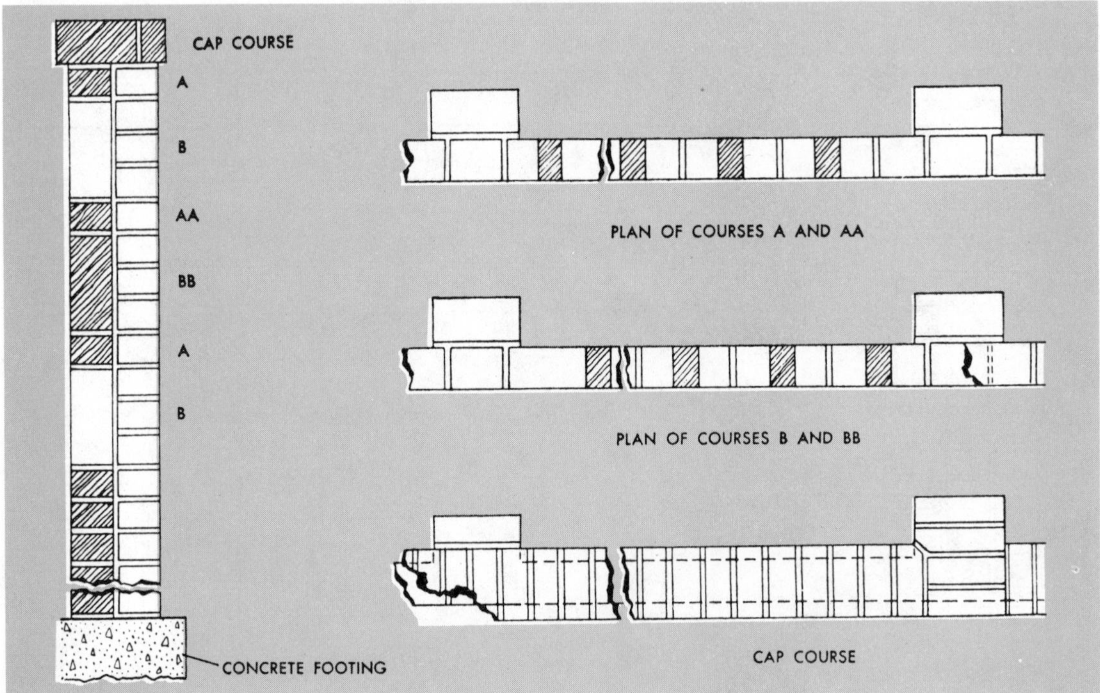

CHECKERBOARD AND CURVES

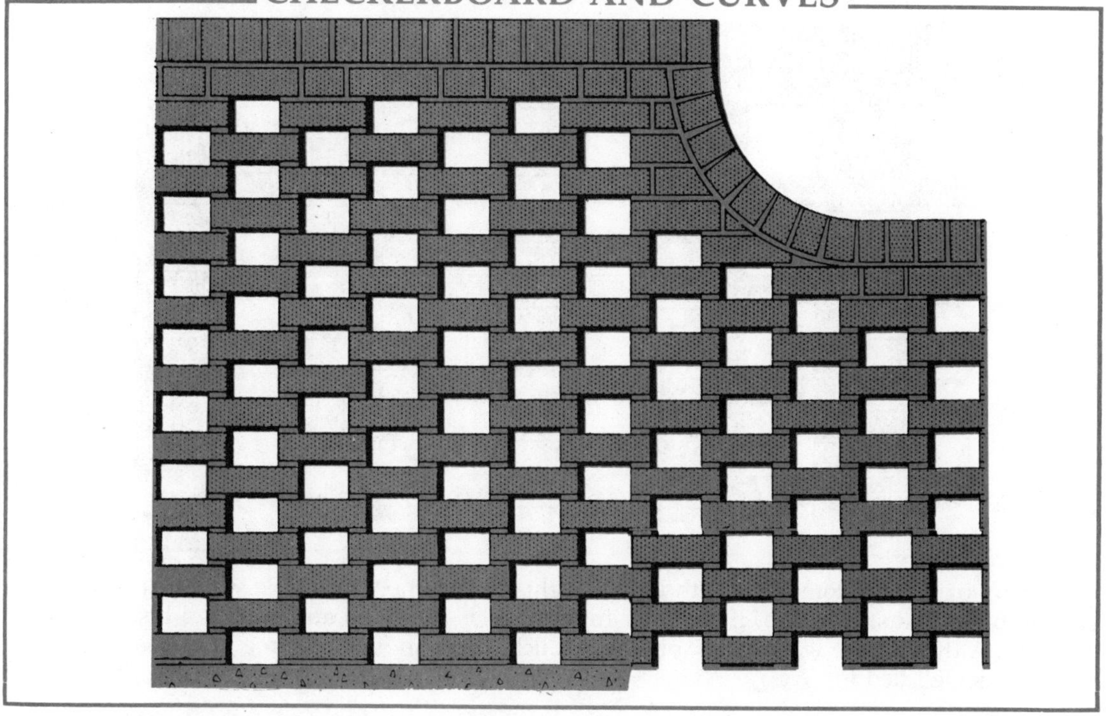

A single-brick thickness makes a lighter-weight wall, especially when openings are left between bricks equal to one brick-end plus mortar joint. Place piers every 6′ or 8′; between piers step wall down with a curve as shown, to follow slope.

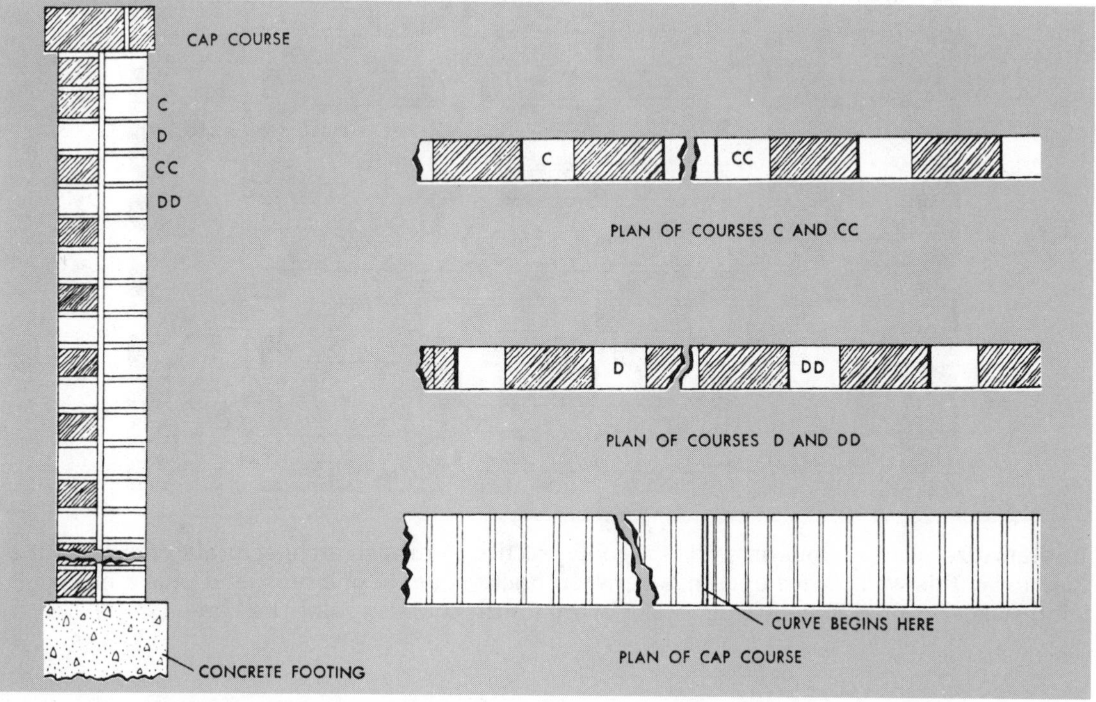

FOURSQUARE AND ON THE LEVEL

Regularity of pattern combined with light weight make a most desirable wall. This one is easy to build and sturdy, too, if a proper foundation is provided and piers are inserted every 6′ to 10′. Although the wall is only one brick thick, piers should be three bricks square and wall bricks well tied in.

ZIG AND ZAG FOR EXCITEMENT

To dramatize plain surroundings it is a good practice to furnish architectural excitement. It is easy to lay this wall. Leave openings between bricks equal to one brick-end plus a mortar joint; stagger courses one-quarter. Make every fourth course a solid "tie" one.

COURSED PATTERNED ASHLAR—TWO VERSIONS

Something of the charm of the ashlar pattern so frequently used in stone masonry may be obtained by grouping various stock sizes of blocks together into a "module" which repeats over and over. At corners and around openings for gates it will be necessary to improvise to fill out the blocks evenly. Don't let too many vertical joints align.

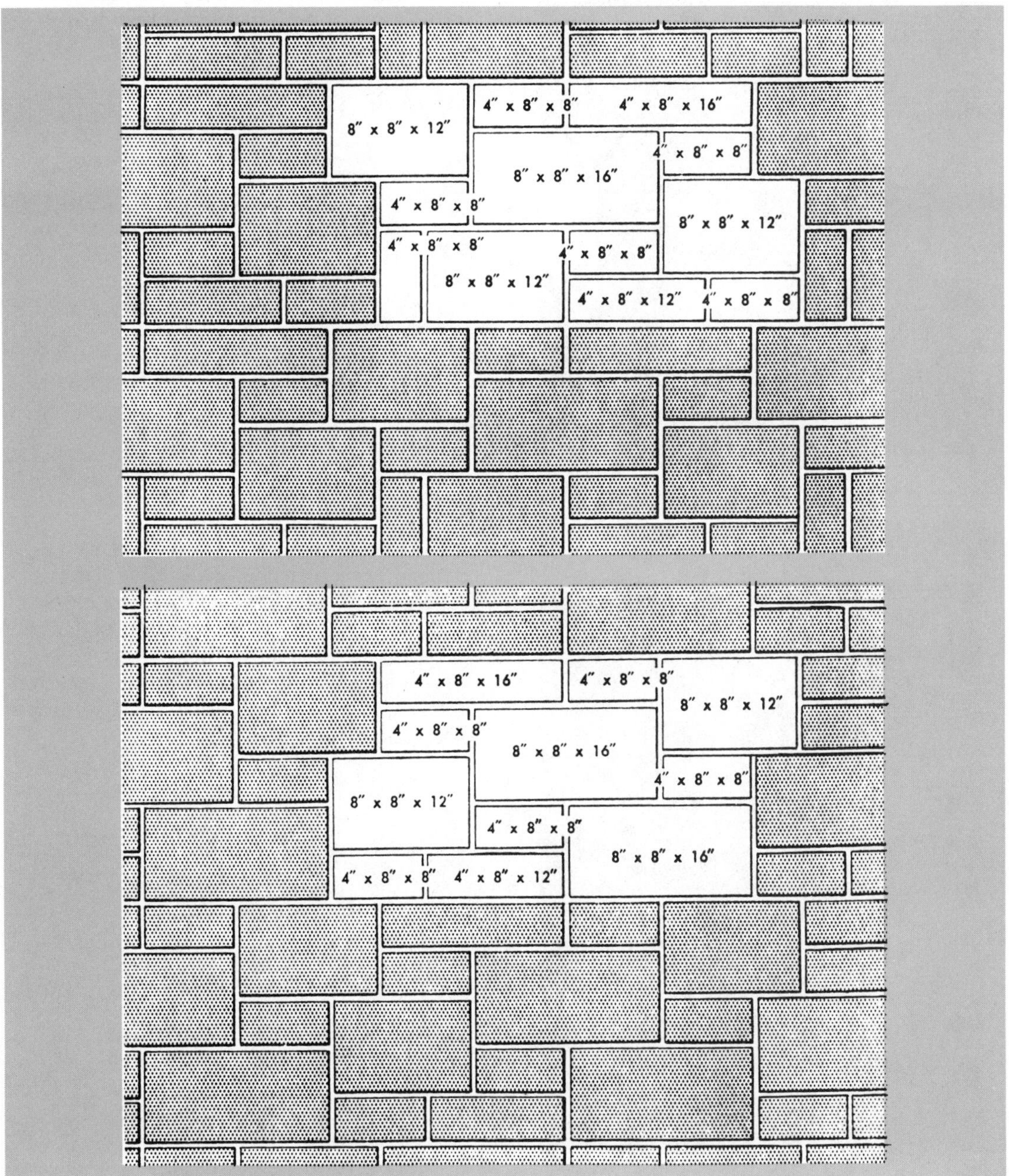

WHIRLING SQUARE PATTERN

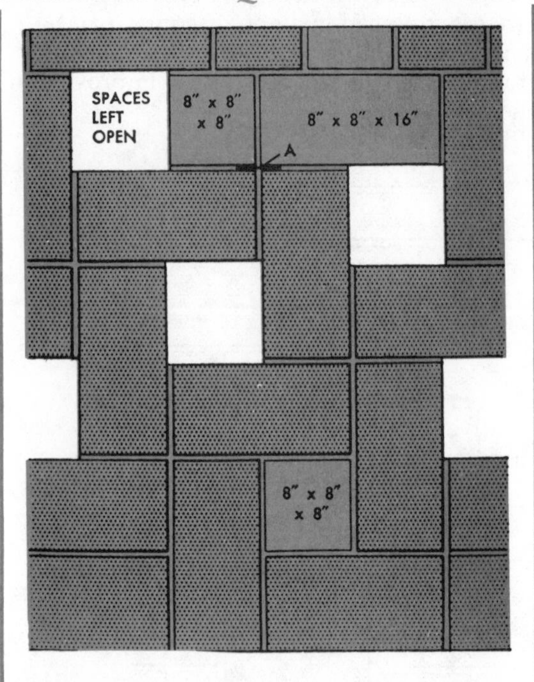

By laying every other block vertically as indicated, squares will occur which may be left open as seen in the upper part of the drawing or filled with square blocks as shown below. Scrap iron rods inserted in the mortar (A) will tie the wall together, making it strong and secure however it is constructed.

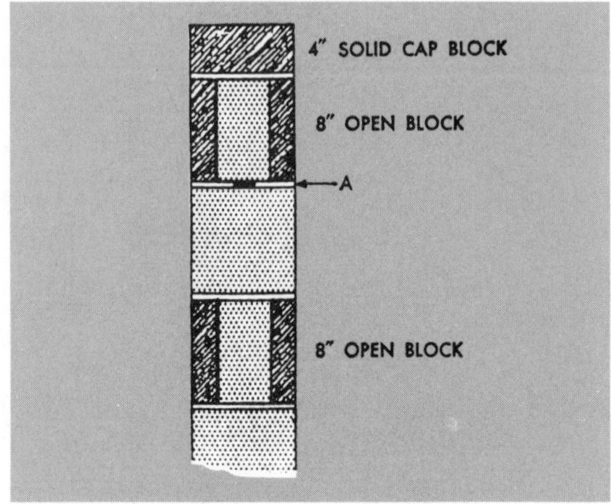

DOUBLE BASKETWEAVE

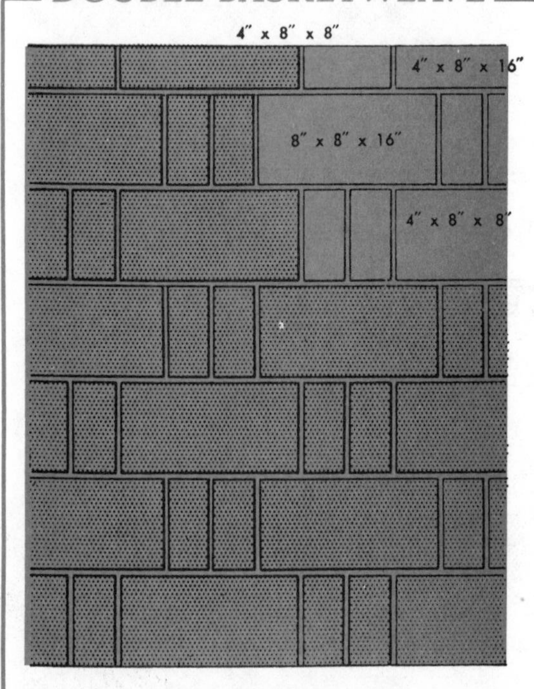

An interesting variation of basketweave pattern is seen in this wall. Note the 4″ × 8″ × 8″ blocks which are the basis of the linear pattern; or they might be laid horizontally instead, which would give a long-line horizontal effect. If less pattern is desired, 8″ × 8″ blocks may be substituted; also easier to build.

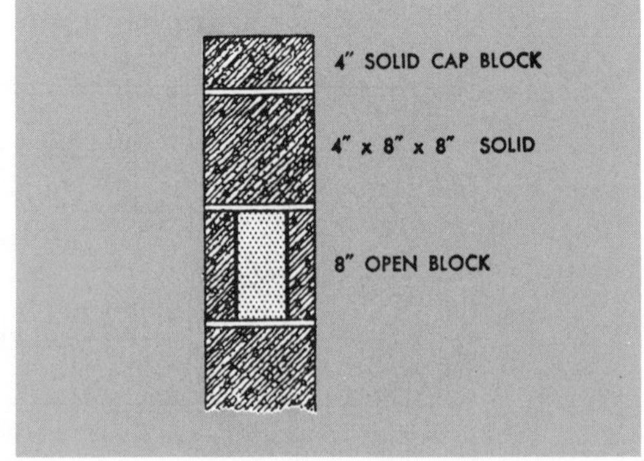

REGULAR COURSED ASHLAR

Two 4" blocks laid together space out to be equal, vertically, to an 8" block. Regular designs result from alternating; irregular patterns from laying every second block, as shown here, staggered to give motion to the pattern. Or they may be scattered here and there, to break up the monotony of a plain wall. Raked joints increase effectiveness.

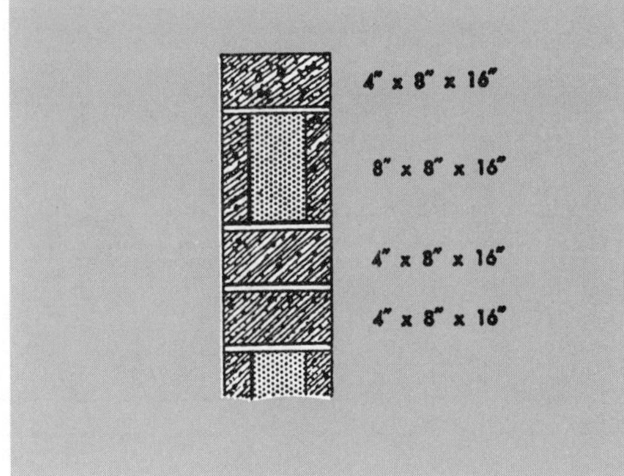

SPACED-COURSE ASHLAR

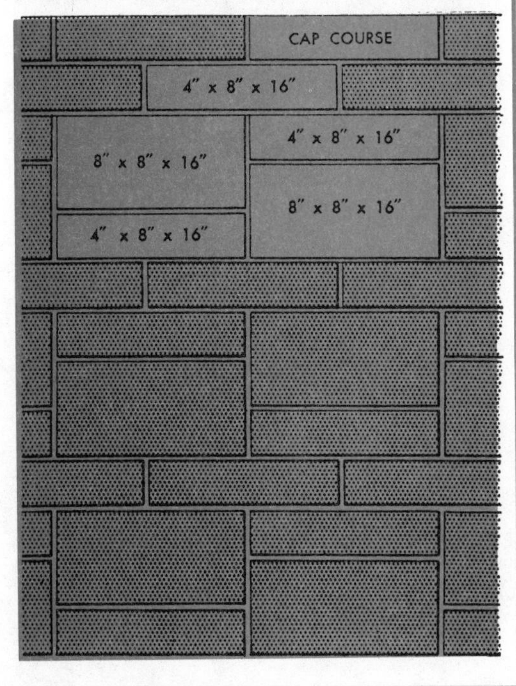

By laying a 4" block on top of an 8" block and next to it a 4" block under an 8" one, a pleasing variety of pattern is obtained. A 4" block "spacer course" between courses will tie the wall together successfully and give a coherence and unity to the design. Concrete blocks may be used for the main courses, cinder blocks used for "spacers."

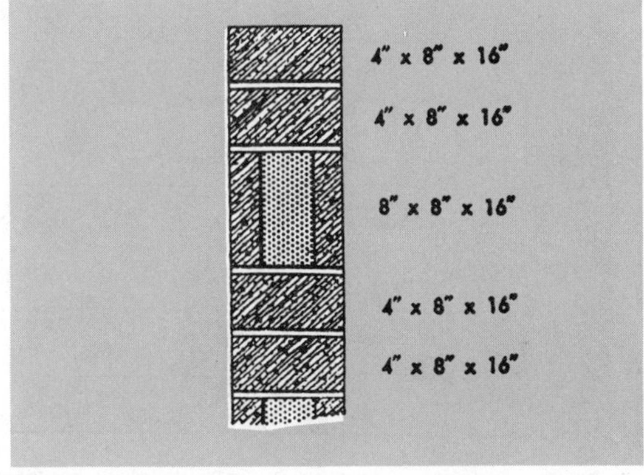

TO LENGTHEN, USE LINES

Narrow blocks set with the holes exposed give a strong horizontal line. 4″ blocks are used here but 6″ or 8″ blocks would serve equally well and give greater ventilation.

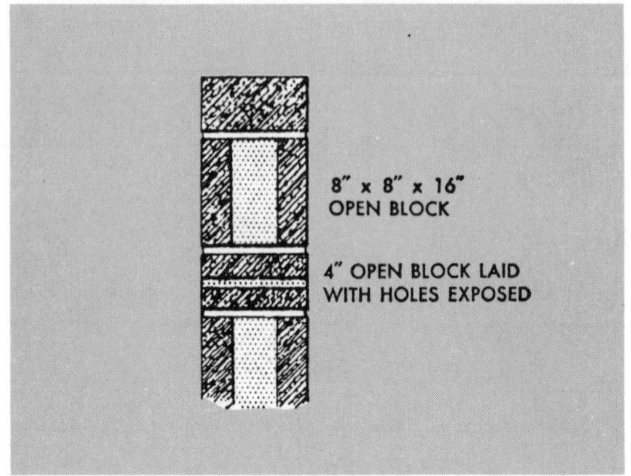

PEEKABOO WALL

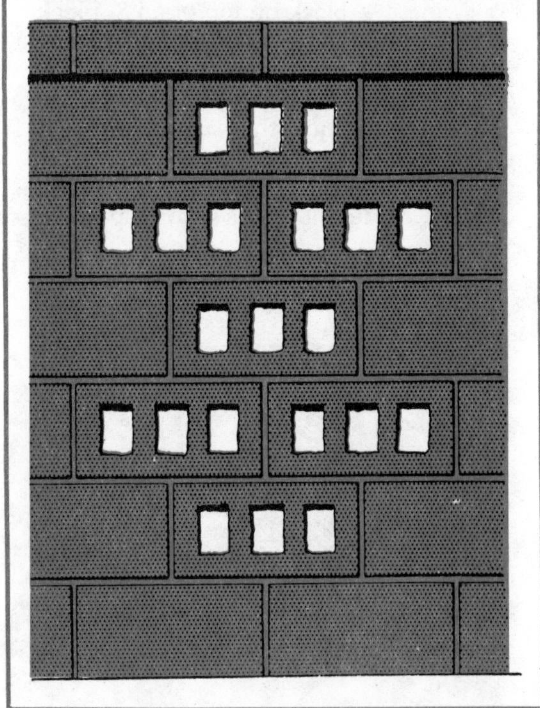

Ornamental effects are possible when a few blocks are laid to expose their holes in walls otherwise solid. 8″ blocks must be used for all units.

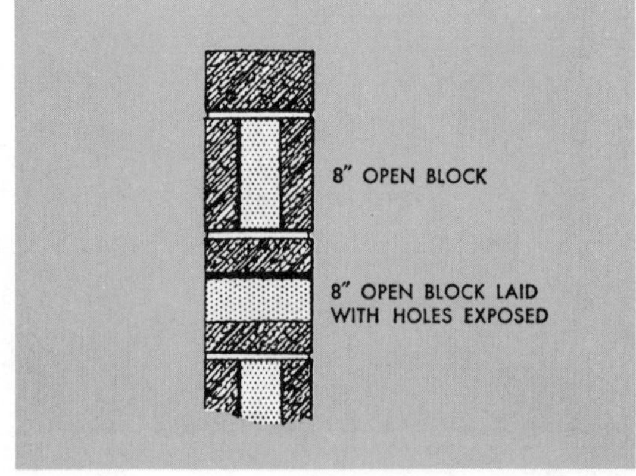

OPEN AND SHUT CASE

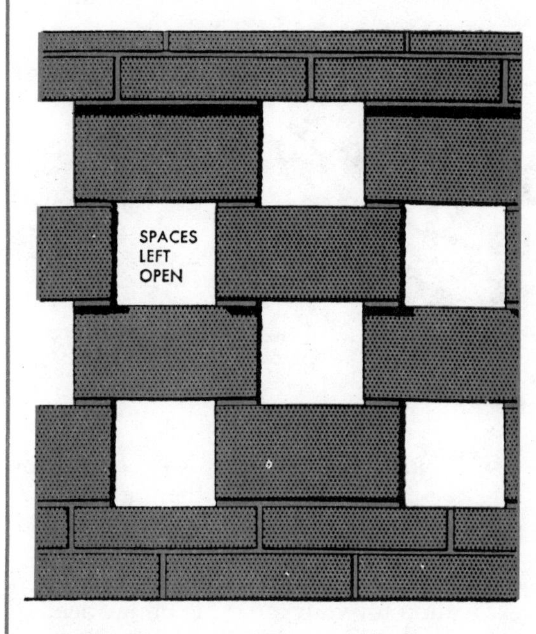

An interesting checkerboard effect results from overlapping blocks ¼ and leaving openings between. Obtain extra shadows by alternating narrow and broad courses.

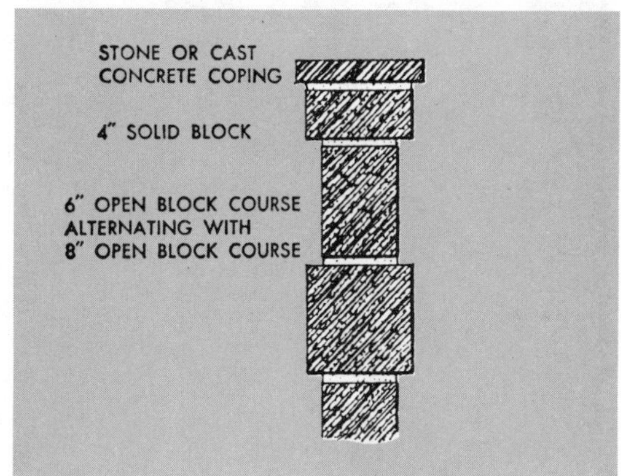

BRICKS AND BLOCKS

Another interpretation of the long line. To give wall unity, paint it all one color, or paint either bricks or blocks a color that will harmonize with the natural color of the other.

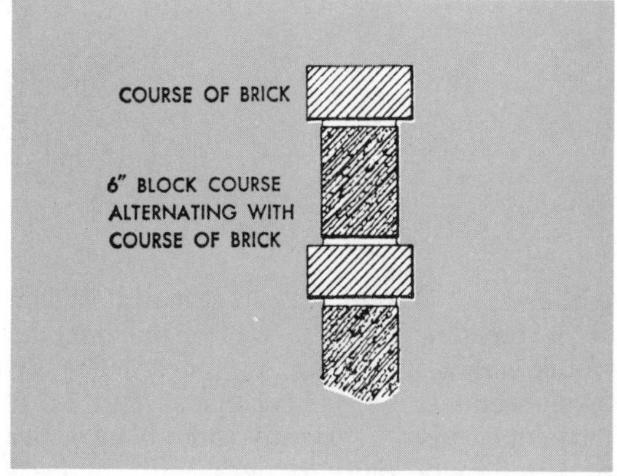

CURVING SUGARLOAF WALL

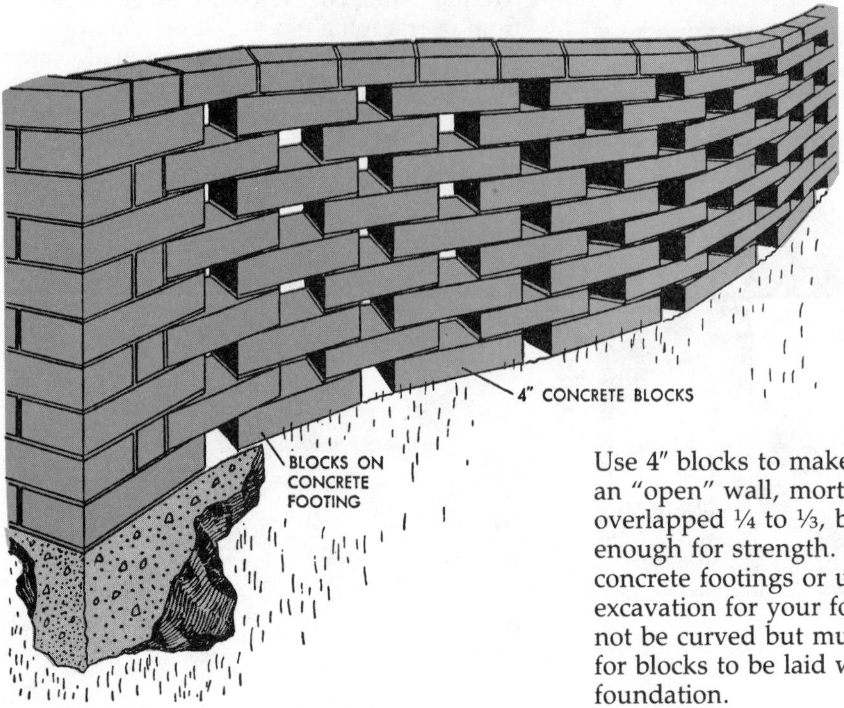

4" CONCRETE BLOCKS

BLOCKS ON CONCRETE FOOTING

Use 4" blocks to make slow, easy curves, on an "open" wall, mortaring them in place overlapped ¼ to ⅓, but make corners solid enough for strength. Build forms for the concrete footings or use sides of the excavation for your forms. Footings need not be curved but must allow enough space for blocks to be laid without overhanging foundation.

MAINLINER WALL

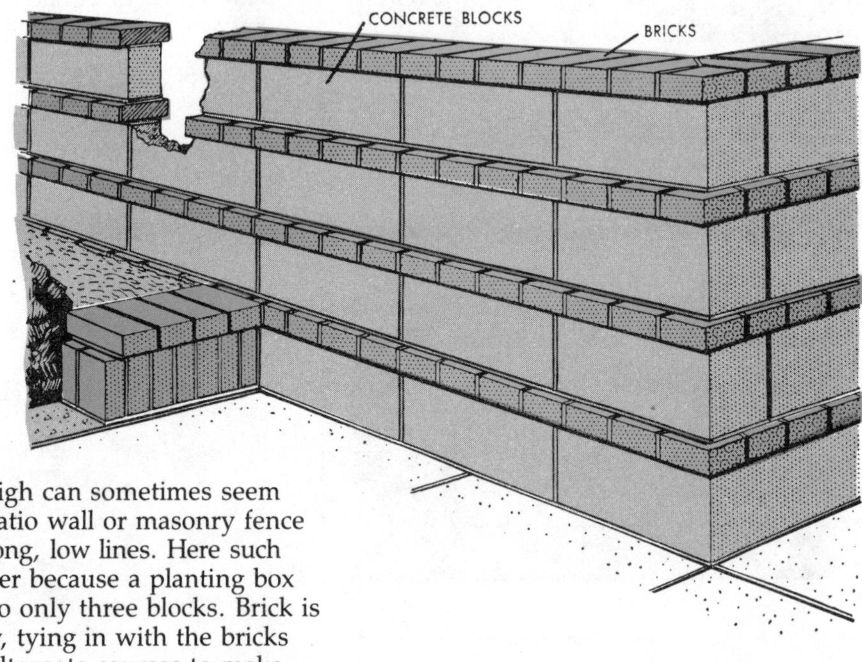

A house that is too high can sometimes seem lower, broader, if a patio wall or masonry fence is built emphasizing long, low lines. Here such a wall seems still lower because a planting box (left) cuts it visually to only three blocks. Brick is used to provide unity, tying in with the bricks used in the wall for alternate courses to make shadow line.

STRAIGHT AND NARROW SUGARLOAF WALL

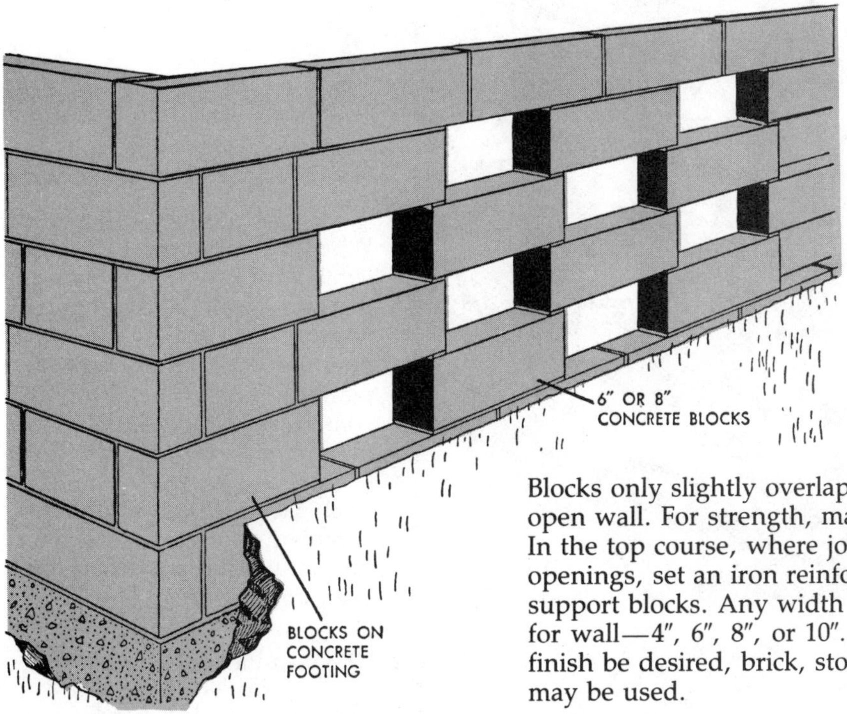

6" OR 8" CONCRETE BLOCKS

BLOCKS ON CONCRETE FOOTING

Blocks only slightly overlapped make an airy open wall. For strength, make the corners solid. In the top course, where joints occur above openings, set an iron reinforcing rod in mortar to support blocks. Any width of block may be used for wall—4", 6", 8", or 10". Should a coping finish be desired, brick, stone, or cast concrete may be used.

UP AND DOWN COMBINATION

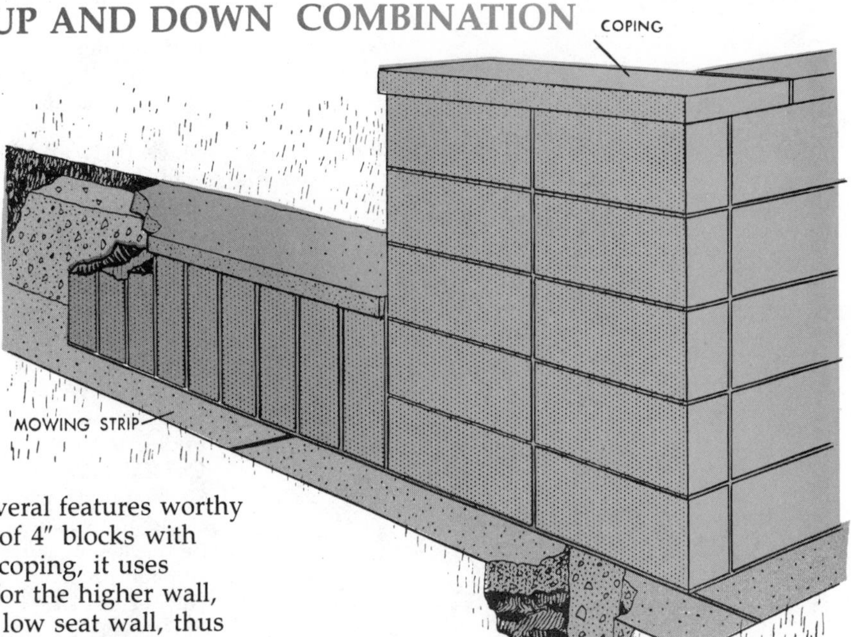

COPING

MOWING STRIP

This wall combines several features worthy of note: Built entirely of 4" blocks with stone or cast-concrete coping, it uses horizontal placement for the higher wall, vertical setting for the low seat wall, thus contrasting visual lines interestingly. Note that mowing strip is cast separately from the footings, with expansion joints to prevent cracking.

PLANTS IN DRY STONE WALLS

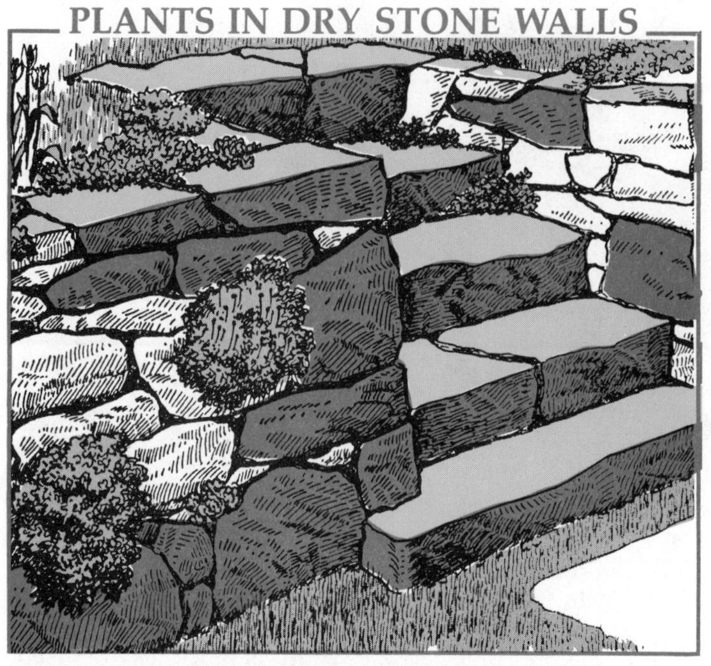

When a sloping plot is being leveled for use as a terrace, a dry stone wall (laid without mortar) often makes a good retaining wall, and offers planting possibilities. Properly constructed, it will last indefinitely, resisting the thrust of frost and gravity's pull. Rock garden plants and succulents are good subjects for planting because they add color and texture.

CONSTRUCTION

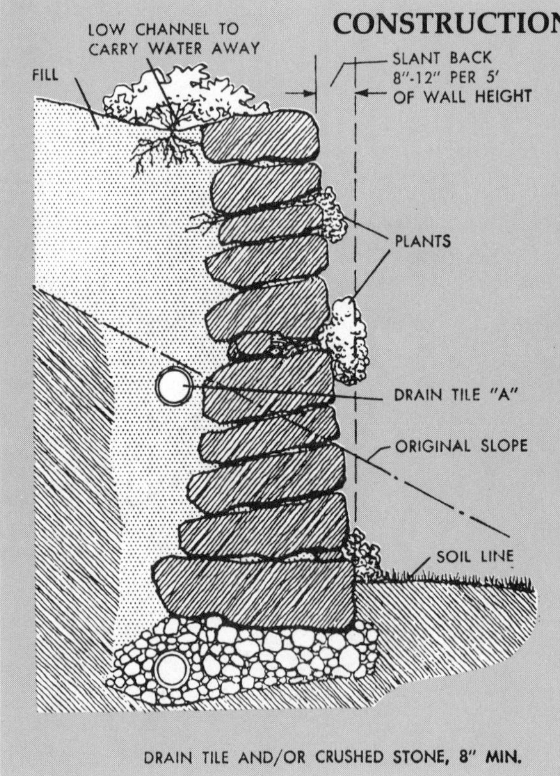

DRAINAGE under the wall is mandatory. Use 8″ to 12″ of coarse rubble or crushed rock for a base, excavating so that the base of bottom course is set 6″ below soil level, 12″ or more in regions of deep frost. In wet climates use a line of drain tile in rubble, with a second line just below the original slope line which will carry away excess water.

SLANT THE WALL back 8″ to 12″ per 5′ of wall height (in wet climates use 12″). Tilt up all stones to catch rain, convey it back and downward, thus preventing soil washouts.

MAKE CREVICES for plants as courses are laid. Keep joints narrow at front, broaden toward rear for root space. Plant before laying next course, packing soil firmly and watering well. Mix leaf mold or peat moss together with soil to prevent undue erosion.

OTHER TIPS: A low ditch behind wall keeps mud from washing over wall face; plants in beds along the top soften wall's hard lines. Be sure to chink with stone chips to prop up stones, keep wall firm and secure. Don't space plants too evenly; don't overplant or you'll have a frowzy wall that is never neat.

HOW TO HOLD UP A BANK

Chimney blocks set on gravel make a very successful bank-holder. Set them so that the blocks overlap the width of the thickness of the block. Fill in behind with 2" blocks and when all blocks are in place fill in with good soil, plant roses, flowers, or what you wish. Pave with 2" concrete blocks laid on tamped gravel or sand for best results.

GENTLE SLOPE HOLDER

A few rows of chimney blocks overlapped as shown and filled with good rich soil will not only hold the bank but when perennials, annuals, herbs, or roses are in flower, this bank will be a tremendous garden asset. Wood plank holds back soil while a mowing strip of blocks finishes off the bottom of slope.

TREE UNDER A PATIO

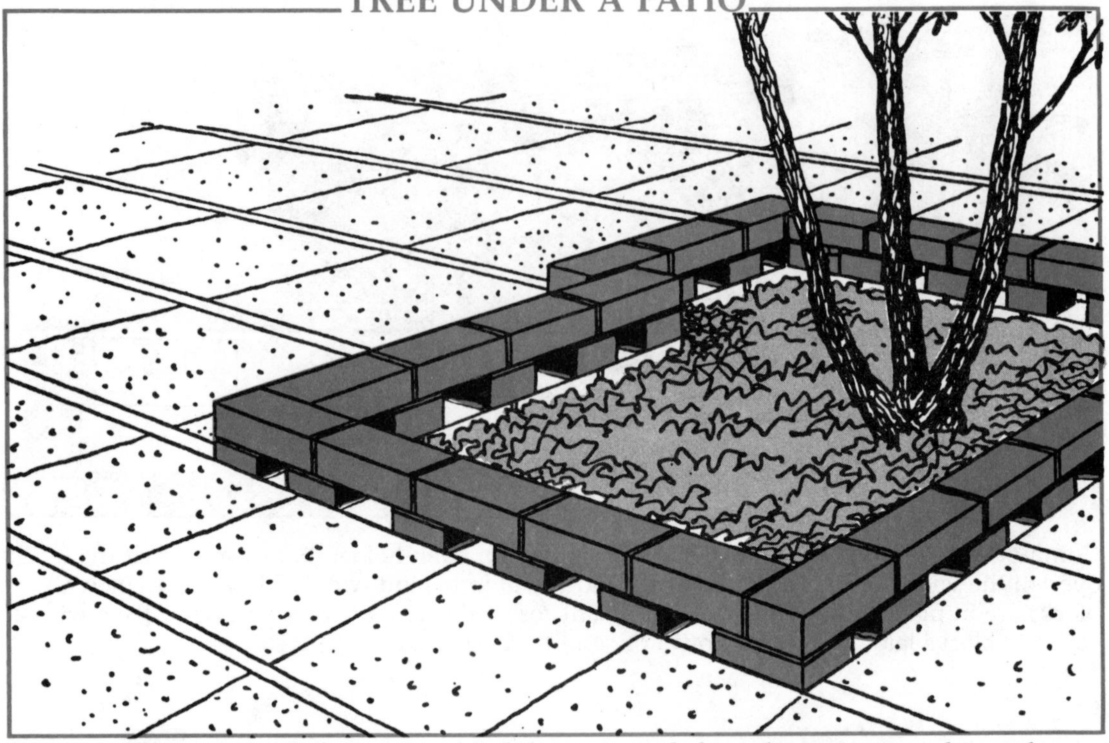

When an existing tree is below paving level, box it in and slope the patio toward it so that moisture will drain through openings in the bottom course of a low brick wall surrounding it. The deeper the tree hole the higher the wall should be. You may want to make it high and wide enough to use as a seat, employing either wood or masonry.

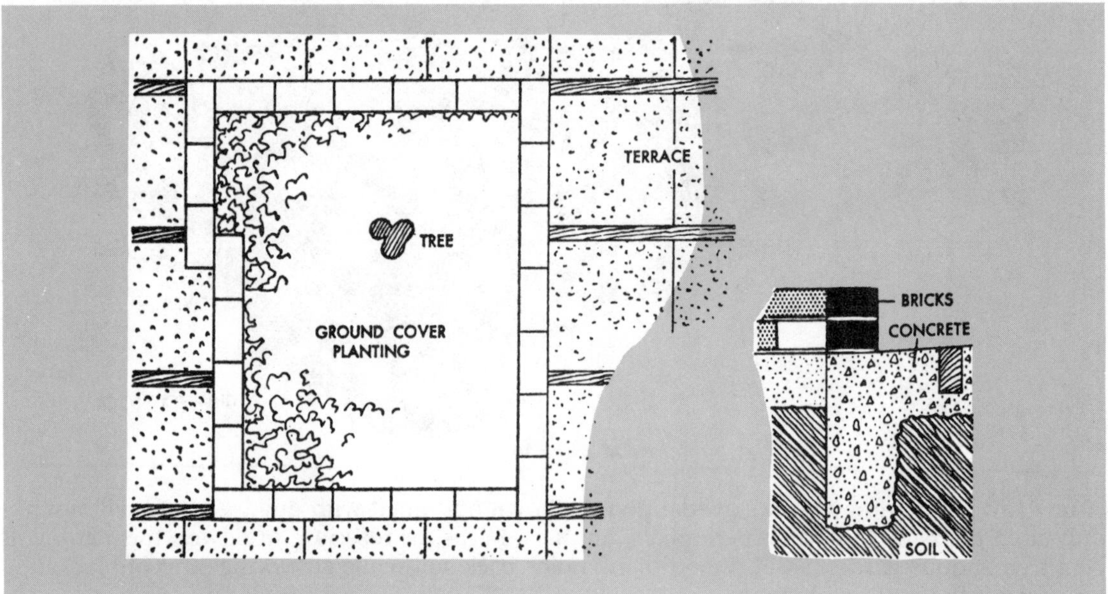

"ROUND THE MULBERRY BUSH"

Sometimes a circular wall is the best answer, especially ending a patio wall. Here a low retaining wall circles the tree, pie-shaped steps rising to winding path. Broken bits of an old cement sidewalk are salvaged for use; their rough sides with gravel showing will give the wall an agreeable ruggedness. Or use split block, rough side facing out. Lay with raked mortar joints or lay it dry.

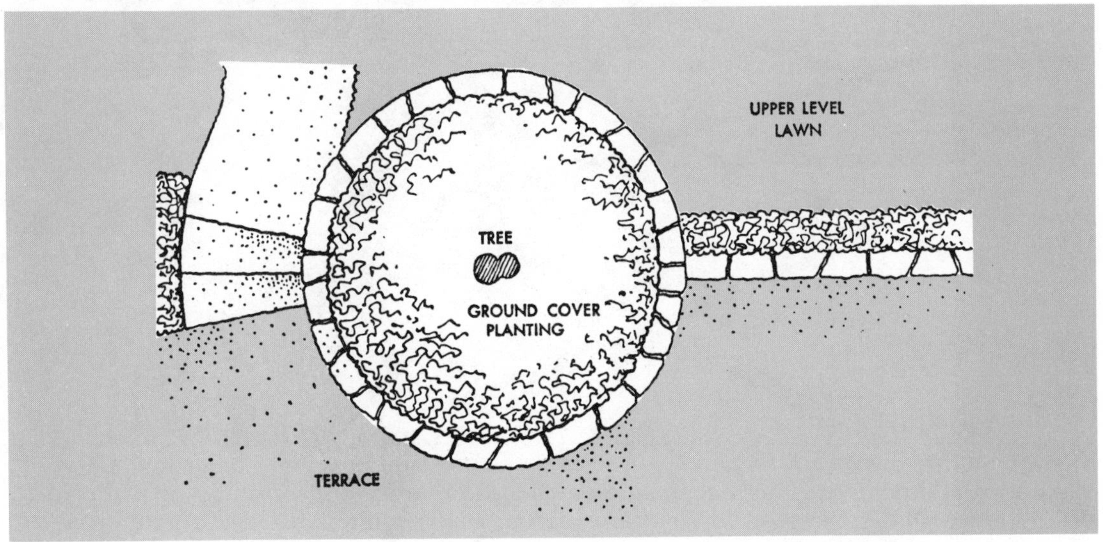

SPARE THAT TREE—YOU'LL NEED IT

Don't cut down a tree because it interferes with your plans for a patio. By carefully excavating and providing a masonry box around it, you'll keep it to shade your patio. Roots extend outward to tips of branches; most trees need about ⅔ of these roots to maintain good health. Don't cut root area drastically or tree may die.

RETAINING WALL RETAINS A TREE

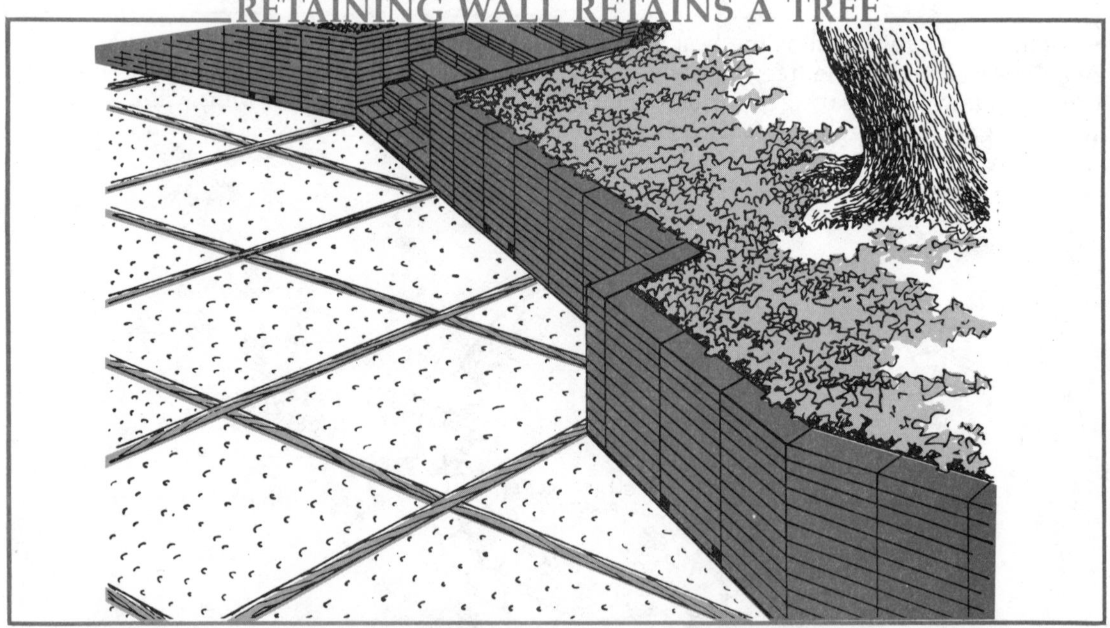

If a slope must be cut back to gain space for a patio, a retaining wall becomes necessary. Make a jog around an existing tree, gaining architectural interest by slanting the wall. Note that masonry units set in stacked bond in retaining walls require a backing of reinforced concrete or masonry to give walls strength needed to withstand soil pressures.

APPENDIX

SCREWS AND NAILS

WOOD SCREWS

Screws are the best choice for joining two or more pieces of wood, either permanently or so that the wood members can later be disassembled. A plastic wood filler deep in the screw hole itself will assure a strong bond between screw threads and the wood.

Screw sizes. Screws come in a variety of lengths; screws between ¼″ to 1″ have length increments of ⅛″. Between 1 and 3 inches, the length increments are ¼″. Between 3″ to 5½″, the increments are ½″.

Screw gauges (diameter) run from 1 to 12 sequentially (1, 2, 3, etc.) but from 12 to 24 by twos (12, 14, 16, etc.). Not all gauges are made in all sizes or all kinds of screws, so you may need to compromise in your selections.

WOOD SCREWS

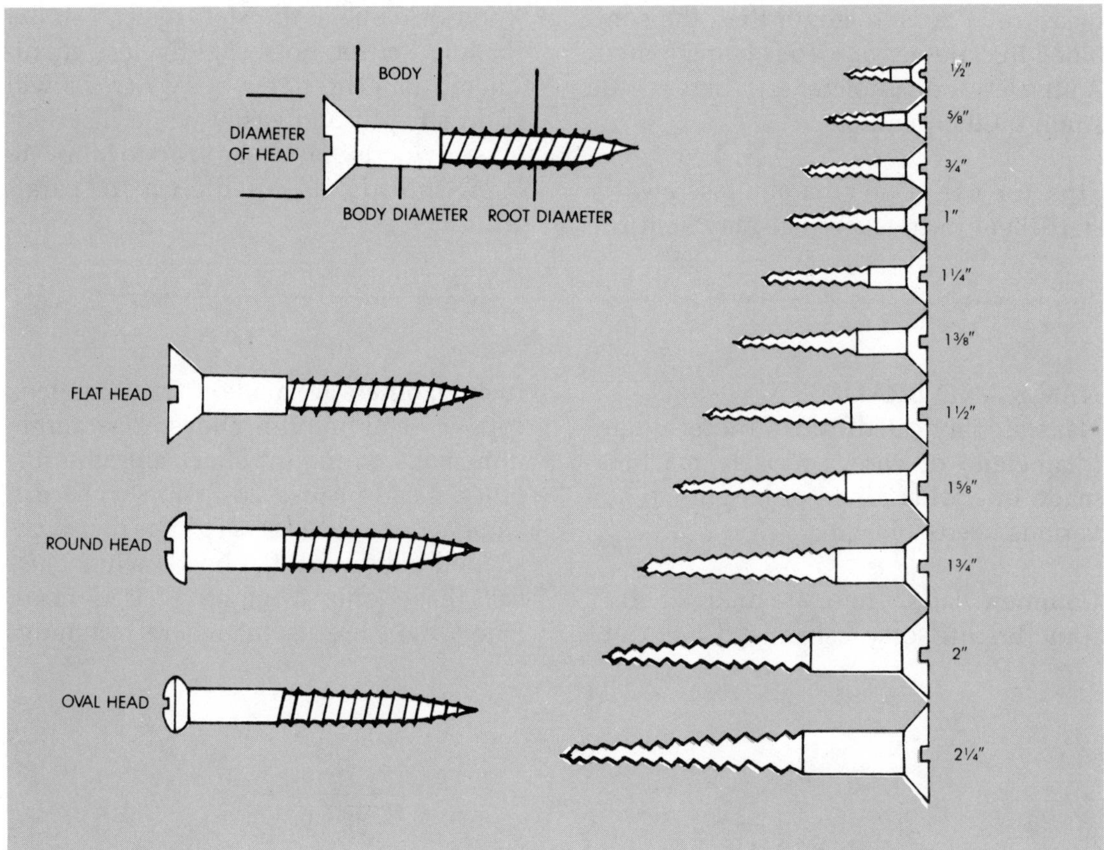

Screw heads. There are four major types of heads: *flat, round, oval* and *phillips* (see drawings) and a further kind called *lag screws,* which are hex- or square-headed and must be turned with a wrench, not a screwdriver because they are not slotted. The phillips head is double slotted and requires a special screwdriver. Lag screws are heavy and are best used to join heavy beams or timbers.

Buying screws. Screws usually come in boxes of a gross but are sold in smaller quantities by shops or are packed in varying quantities at a higher price than the large lots. Some shops sell them in single or dozen lots. The choices may include several materials or finishes. They may be steel—either unfinished or blued, cadmium- or zinc-plated. Or they may be rustproof brass or aluminum. Bear in mind that because of the dozens of sizes and kinds, not all are widely stocked; off-sizes or special kinds or varied gauges may not always be available.

Steel screws are cheapest. But for outdoor work, consider that they may rust and stain the wood or paint, even disintegrate in time if not kept covered. Aluminum should be joined with aluminum screws, for other materials cause corrosion from galvanic action. Screws should measure ⅛″ less in length than the combined thicknesses of woods being joined. A little less long is tolerable if there is little strain on the joint.

Tips for use. Don't hammer screws to start them in because that may split the wood or damage the slot. Instead drill a shallow starter hole slightly less in diameter than the screw body. Screws will go in straight and easily when inserted. In hardwoods, *do not* use soap to lubricate screw threads; use candle wax or paraffin.

NAILS AND BRADS

Nails are fabricated from various gauges (diameters) of wire, precisely machine-made in a wide range of lengths to suit various needs.

Common Nails. These are made of steel, some bright, some galvanized, to retard rusting; others are made of stainless steel, copper or aluminum alloys. Use aluminum nails to mount sheet aluminum—other metals cause corrosion from galvanic action. *Common nails* have diamond-shaped points and flat heads while *finish nails* have only a slightly flared head. Finish nails are useful where fastenings

COMMON NAILS

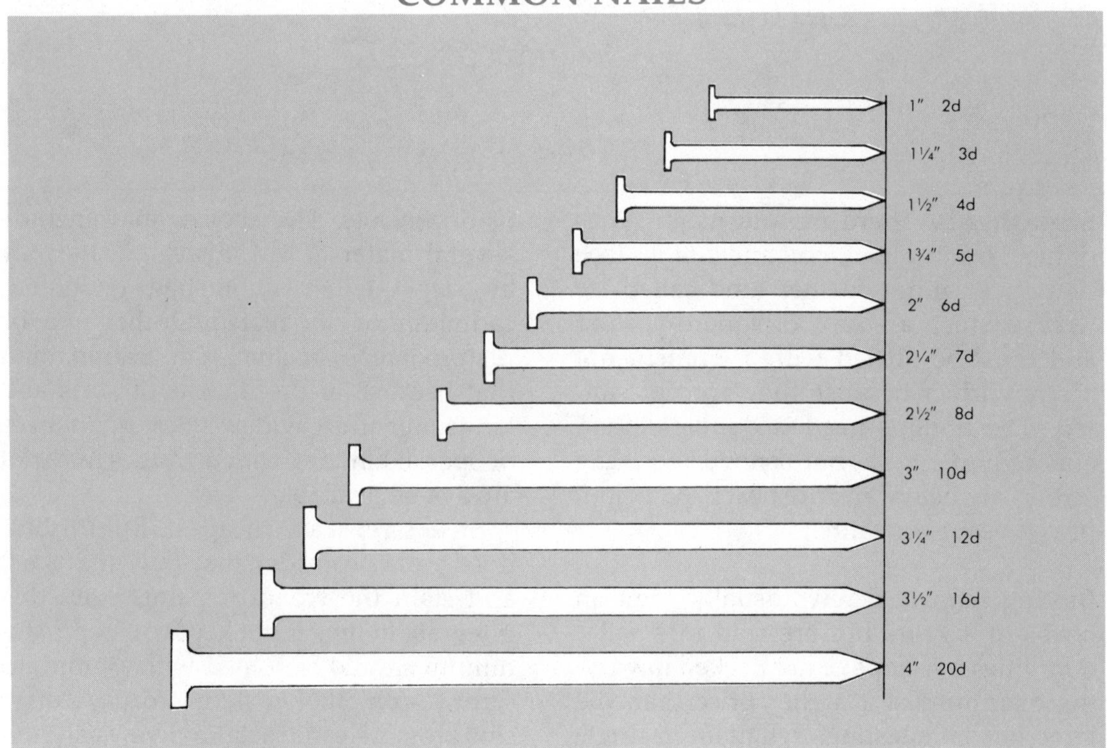

should be countersunk with a nail set, the holes filled for a smooth look. Because finish nails have such a small head they are less able than common nails to hold wood stressed directly toward the head.

Nails are sold by "penny" length (d). On boxes you will find 4d, 8d designations, or whatever. The name "penny" derives from the old days when nails were sold by the pound. A thousand 10-penny nails, for instance, weighed 10 pounds, hence 10-penny and written 10d (the English abbreviation for penny) for convenience. See the accompanying chart for various "penny" lengths. Common nails come in 2d to 60d (1-inch to 6-inch) lengths. The most useful for projects in this book are 4d to 20d.

Brads. These are small, thin, finishing nails from ½ to 1½ inches long. There are two or three gauges (diameters) in each length. Brads are, however, graded by length, not by the penny system.

Masonry Nails. These are zinc-coated to resist rust and are made of hardened steel so they can be hammered into bricks, concrete, and cinder or concrete blocks. Lengths vary from ½ to 2½ inches.

Shingle Nails. These have large flat heads and sharp diamond points, usually 1¼ or 1⅜ inches long. They have many uses other than for holding down shingles.

Buying nails. Nails are sold by the pound as well as in boxed lots and in mixed sizes of assorted lengths for people who may need only a small quantity of nails in given sizes. The cheapest way to purchase is in quantity by the pound or by watching for sales of boxed nails at lumber supermarkets. Brads are sold by the box or in small quantities in plastic "bubbles" attached to display cards.

Storage. Keep nails in a dry place to avoid rust. In using nails in various woods, drive them part way into the first piece (supported) before adding the first piece to the second, to assure straight driving. If the wood is hard or likely to split, drill pilot holes before driving the nails.

INDEX